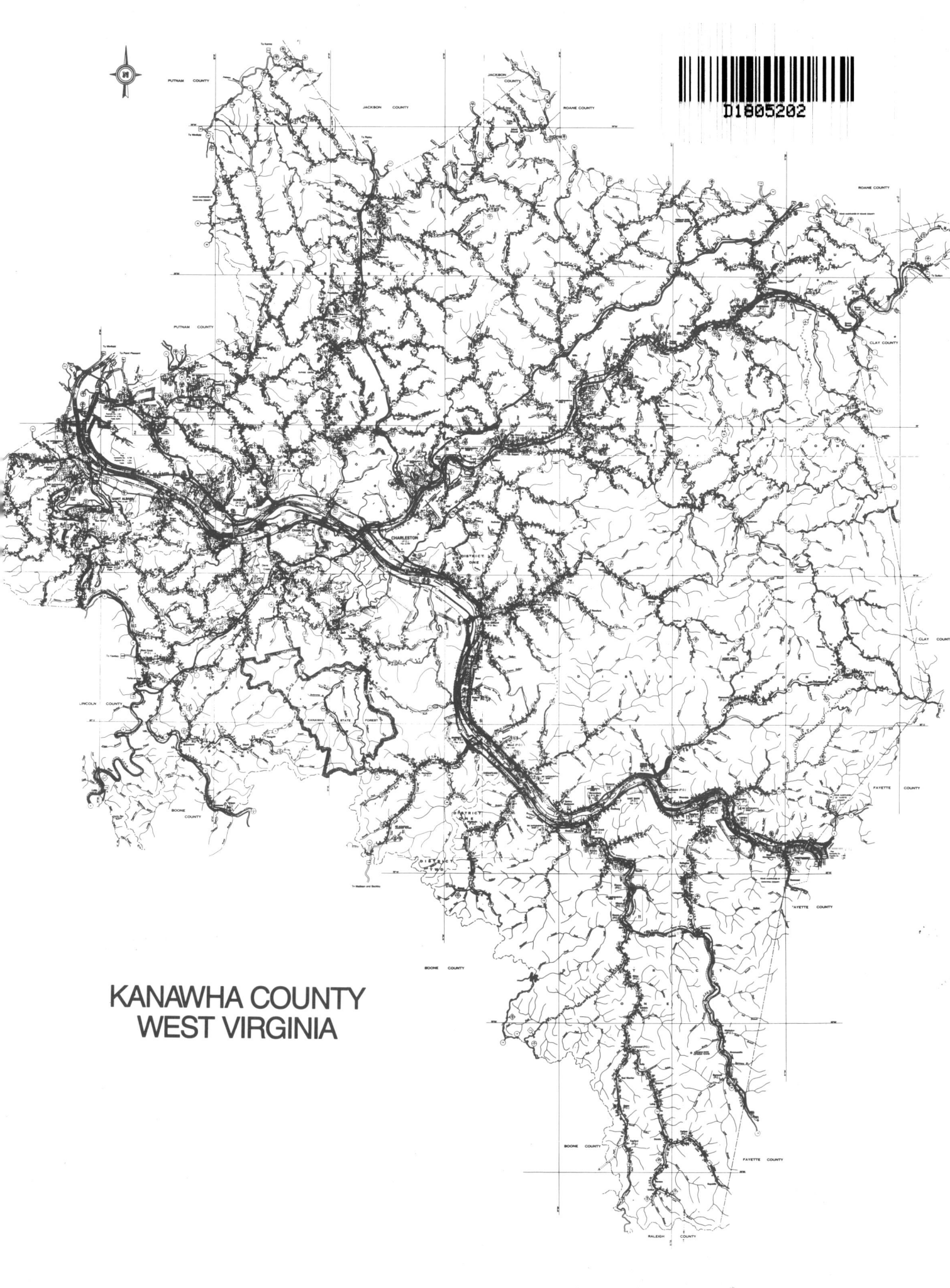

Kanawha County Images
A · BICENTENNIAL · HISTORY · 1788-1988

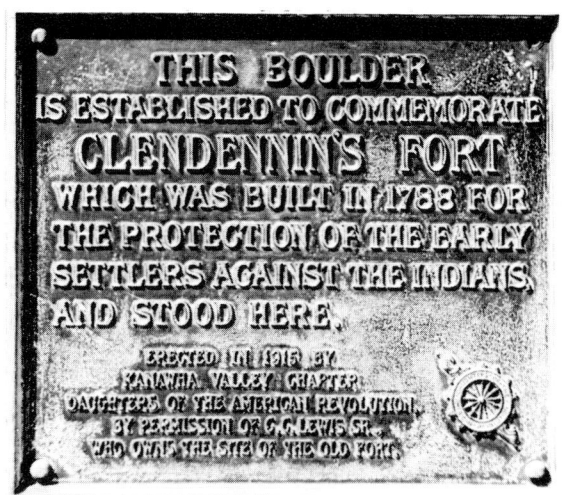

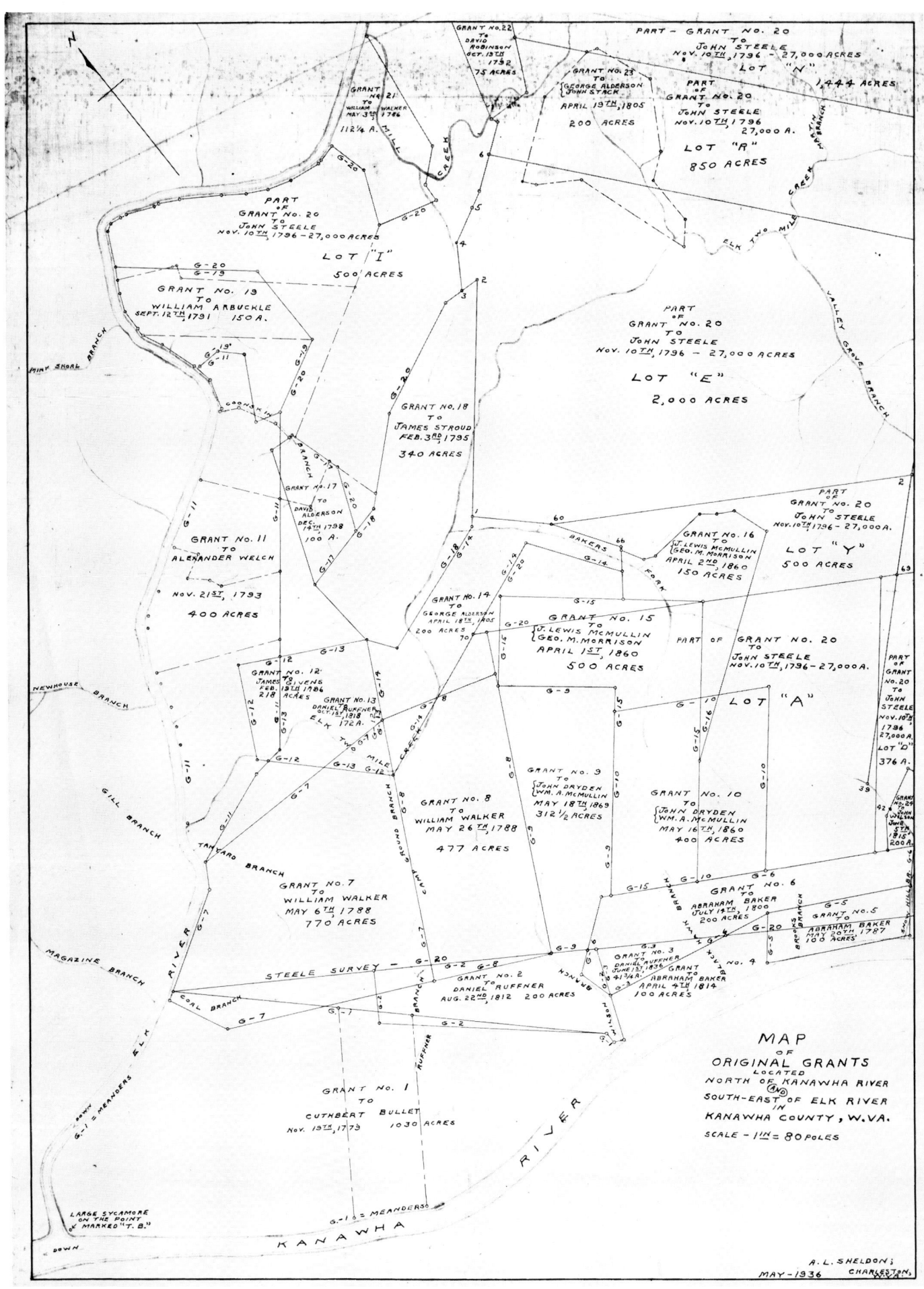

Kanawha County Images
A · BICENTENNIAL · HISTORY · 1788-1988

by STAN COHEN
with Richard Andre, Research Associate

Copyright © 1987 STAN B. COHEN

All rights reserved. No part of this book
may be used or reproduced without written
permission of the publisher.

LIBRARY OF CONGRESS
CATALOG CARD NO. 87-90434

ISBN 0-933126-69-7

First Printing: November 1987

Typography: Arrow Graphics & Typography
Layout: Stan Cohen

PUBLISHED JOINTLY BY
PICTORIAL HISTORIES PUBLISHING COMPANY
4103 Virginia Avenue SE
Charleston, West Virginia 25304
AND
KANAWHA COUNTY BICENTENNIAL, INC.
Charleston, West Virginia

Preface

Kanawha Countians are justifiably proud of their rich heritage and tradition. Ours is a history encompassing ancient Indian settlements, the ravages of war, and the development of the state's most modern and progressive county.

We, at the Kanawha County Commission, are pleased to have played a part in the publication of this pictorial history. Stan B. Cohen, Richard Andre and the Kanawha County Bicentennial Commission are to be complimented for a job well done. Certainly, as the reader will soon determine, the adage, "a picture is worth a thousand words" is proven by this outstanding work.

We ask the reader to travel through the county's history in the following pages. Then, join us in looking forward to a future as bright and glorious as our past.

COUNTY COMMISSION OF KANAWHA COUNTY

Louis H. Bloom, President

F. Douglas Stump, Commissioner

Don Joe Hunt, Commissioner

For many of us, history means a now-quiet battleground or an adventurous romp through a musty attic, both activities aimed at securing a glimmer of knowledge or souvenir of events long past our frame of reference. History is more than that; it is the very air we breathe and ground we trod in the course of everyday life. Our routine today will mark the interest and study of people in the future generations, as they contemplate the progress made by city and citizens during the "good old days."

Charleston's history is rich and entertaining, reflecting the building of our state's urban hub and the transformation of a wilderness outpost into a modern and progressive community. We did not emerge as a jewel among the green hills overlooking the Kanawha and Elk Rivers overnight, and the story of our growth paints a fascinating picture of the events made possible by dedicated men and women with great vision. Charleston and the Kanawha Valley are in a state of becoming one of America's great metropolitan areas, while still enjoying our unique mountain heritage which sets us apart.

From the past, we have carved out our own special niche; for the future, we will remain strong and true to our cultural identity and the influences left behind by those who have built our "Renaissance City."

James E. "Mike" Roark
Mayor, City of Charleston

Introduction

I cannot remember a time when I was not interested in history. Growing up in Kanawha County on Charleston's East End, I played in the rubble pile of what was formerly John Q. Dickinson's elegant home on the Kanawha Boulevard. I found ledger books that dated back to the 1830s and many old pamphlets about the history of the area, some of which are featured in this book. I was fascinated with stories of Daniel Boone, Fort Lee, and the early salt industry. This book is the result of many years of study of the history and collecting artifacts from Kanawha County's colorful past.

Every area in our great country has its own unique history. And although Charleston and Kanawha County's history may not be unusually unique when compared to other parts of the state or nation, a native or long-time resident will certainly be fascinated with the changes that have taken place throughout the years.

The county's industrial development, in particular, is unique for the eras it spanned and the number of developments that were initiated here. I have charted this industrial history with a brief narrative and accompanying photographs.

Industrial development, however, is only one facet of the county's history that covers over 200 years of recorded events and thousands of years of ancient Indian history. Although two hundred years is but an instant in the earth's history, it is a great span of time to condense into one volume, giving each segment its due space.

This book is a tribute to the 1988 bicentennial of Kanawha County and the city of Charleston. For this reason, I have chosen to concentrate on the events of the past 200 years.

The first seven decades of the city/county history are portrayed in approximate chronological order. However, because photographs were more common after the end of the Civil War, I switched to a subject category in the later part of the book to take advantage of the many photographs available.

This book is not meant to be a definitive history of Kanawha County nor the city of Charleston. I will leave that to other historians. For more detailed narrative histories one should consult the bibliography at the end of this book. This is meant to be the definitive photographic history of the city and the county, and where possible, I tried to use photographs that have never been published before. I have also tried to correct as many discrepancies as possible. Any errors in this book are my responsibility.

Finding these photos and memorabilia was not an easy task. Although there have been some long-time photographers in the area, such as Gravely and Moore, and Bollinger, finding their complete collections was impossible. Fortunately, a large portion of these early photographs have been given to the state archives and Kanawha County Public Library. I contacted many other archives in the state, Virginia, and Washington, D.C., along with dozens of individuals, businesses, industries, and government and private organizations.

Although I made a reasonably thorough search for pictures, I am sure that once this book is published, photographs will literally "come out of the woodwork." If this book serves no other purpose, perhaps it will be a focal point for a future photographic record of the area's history.

It is a shame that today there is no individual photographer who is recording the everyday street scenes to include in a tricentennial history. We must rely on newspapers for the only pictures of day-to-day life.

For the past three years, I have been immersed in the history of the county, which has made me appreciate the people who have lived or live in our area and the sites that have been preserved throughout the country as "our little bit of history." I hope my efforts, and the efforts of all those who have a part in this project, will instill a sense of pride in the accomplishments of the people who developed Charleston and Kanawha County.

History is made by people: some good, some bad. We cannot change what has happened, but we can appreciate what we have today. History is also a fascinating subject that one lives everyday. For that reason, I have taken particular care in the photo captions to try and relate the photos to the present, whenever possible. I hope that people will appreciate this and find it interesting.

Now sit back and enjoy the past 200 years.

STAN COHEN
November 1987

Acknowledgments

A book of this magnitude could not have been completed without the help of many people. I spent three years doing extensive research and gathering photos to add to some photos that I have had in my collection for decades.

A great deal of credit for the completion of this book goes to my research associate, Richard Andre of Charleston. Richard spent many long hours searching for photos, following leads, interviewing people and digging up information. This book could not have been done without him. And both Richard and I are indebted to his father, Bernard E. Andre, who left a remarkable collection of both written and photographic county history. Mr. Andre was perhaps the most meticulous of the present-day amateur historians.

A special thanks must be given to members of Kanawha County Bicentennial Inc., my partners in this book. Mimi Tann, former treasurer of the commission, initially introduced me to the commission in 1984. Joseph C. Jefferds, Jr., the chairman, was the guiding force behind this book project. My mentor and advisor, Dr. Otis K. Rice, a very well-known and respected author and historian from West Virginia Institute of Technology, was a great help with providing photos and information, and checking for historical accuracy. Many other members of the commission provided help and encouragement.

A special thanks goes to the following people. Paul Marshall, of Paul Marshall and Associates of Charleston, has contributed much to the preservation of local history and provided me with many photos and a great deal of information. Todd Hanson of Tad, whose enthusiasm for Campbells Creek and county history was an inspiration to me, provided most of the photos and history of that area. My good friend, and a premier Civil War historian, Terry Lowry, made the Civil War chapter possible. Dave Moore of S. Spencer Moore Company processed many of the photos in this book and provided insight into his company's history. Fred Armstrong, Dick Fauss, Debra Basham, Mike Keller and the entire staff of the Department of Culture and History were a tremendous help in obtaining photos and memorabilia from their extensive collection. Mrs. Susan Harper, Ms. June Martin, and former head librarian Nick Winowich of the Kanawha County Public Library let me use their extensive photo collection and provided long hours of consultation. The staffs of the Virginia State Library and Virginia Historical Society were extremely helpful. Dr. George Parkinson and his staff at West Virginia University helped research their photo collection. Gerald Sutphin, a longtime steamboat researcher from Huntington, gave me access to his vast photo collection and provided much of the information for the River System chapter. My friend and neighbor, Phyllis Sherman, gathered much of the information and photos on the cultural heritage and Jewish history of the area. William Wintz, author of several area history books, provided photos of Nitro, St. Albans and Cross Lanes. James Randall provided photos on black history. Rick Hamilton provided the postal history items. Rodney Collins of the Historic Preservation Unit, Cultural Center allowed me to use his extensive files on historic places. Caroline Haefele edited the book.

Many other people provided photographs or information for this book, and my sincere apologies if I inadvertently left anyone out. Laura Watkins, Black Diamond Girl Scout Council; Patricia Moyers, Executive Director, YWCA; Gary Chernenko, Public Affairs, CAMC; Linda Fittro, Kanawha County Parks and Recreation Commission; Jim Buckalew, Athletic Director at the University of Charleston; Doug Bumgartner, Kanawha Coin Shop; Reverend Calvin Martin, Glasgow; Melody Finley; Mrs. Jacqueline Davis; Tom Dixon, C & O Historical Society; Mrs. Sarah Bing; Mrs. Forest Barker, South Charleston; Mrs. Margaret Stryker, New Smyrna, Florida; H. Jarrett Walker, Jarrett Printing Company; John Chapman, Charleston Area Chamber of Commerce; Shorty Hardman and Dick Hudson, formerly of the *Charleston Gazette* and *Charleston Daily Mail;* Anne Carroll and John Frail, Kanawha County Clerk and Recorder's Office; Charleston Police Department; Frank Badger, Head Librarian, University of Charleston; Larry Allen, Allen Blueprint; Mr. and Mrs. A. Raymond Buckley, Georges Creek; Mr. and Mrs. Adrian Edwards, Belle; J.D. Waggoner, Malden; Ms. Roxana O'Conner, St. Francis Hospital; Tim Barber; Dr. A.C. Dixon, D.D.S.; Kelly Bratton, Malden; Mary Hill, West Virginia Water Company; Jack Shaner, Appalachian Power Company; J.B. Thompson, Telephone Pioneers of America Museum, Charleston; Bill Wyatt, Buckskin Council, Boy Scouts of America; Leo Gardner; Mike Bell, Kanawha County Board of Education; Paul Wilkerson, West Virginia Department of Highways; Chuck Gardner, Charleston City Manager; Mayor James Roark's office; Tom Cook, Pfaff and Smith Company; Carol Throckmorton, Kanawha Valley Bank; Rev. James B. Moellendick, Union Mission; Judy Romano, Eagle Aviation; Charles Carlson, Loudendale; Mrs. Turner Ratrie, Malden; J. Kemp McLaughlin, West Virginia Air National Guard; Jack Smith; E.S. Goodson, Smithers; Henry Young, Clendenin; Clendenin Women's Club; Milton Back, Kanawha Valley Regional Transportation Authority; the staff of Sunrise Museums; William Sparkmon, Pratt; Dr. Charles Quarles, Spindale, North Carolina; Benjamin Polis, Columbia Gas Transmission; Calvin White, Charleston; Florence Seaton, Women's Club of Charleston; Mrs. Robert W. Lawson, Jr.; John Ingrahm; Amherst Industries; Carl Wolfe; Patty Holt Nugent, Pratt; Daniel Davidson; Miss Ann Lewis, Emich; Jack Liming, Clendenin; Gary Bays; and Janet Breshler, Elkins.

The Greater Kanawha Valley Foundation is especially thanked for financial support that has ensured publication of this work.

Photo Credits

SWV—West Virginia State Archives and Museum, Charleston
KCL—Kanawha County Library
WVU—West Virginia University Archives, Morgantown
RA—Richard Andre (via B.E. Andre) Collection, Charleston
NA—National Archives, Washington, D.C.
LC—Library of Congress, Washington, D.C.
PM—Paul Marshall Collection, Charleston
CN—Charleston Newspapers
EG—E.S. Goodson Collection, Smithers
APC—Appalachian Power Company
COHS—Chesapeake & Ohio Historical Society
GS—Gerald Sutphin Collection, Huntington
WW—William Wintz Collection, St. Albans
TH—Todd Hanson Collection, Campbells Creek
DH—Dick Hudson Collection, Charleston
USAMHI—U.S. Army Military History Institute, Carlisle, Penn.
KRTA—Kanawha Valley Regional Transportation Authority
CAMC—Charleston Area Medical Center
CPL—Clendenin Public Library
JR—James Randall Collection

Note: All modern photos were taken by the authors, unless otherwise noted.

*Denotes sites on the National Register of Historic Places.

Contents

Preface	v
Introduction	vi
Acknowledgments	vii
The Setting	1
CHAPTER ONE: The Ancients	2
CHAPTER TWO: The Making of a County	8
CHAPTER THREE: Life in the County: 1800-1860	24
CHAPTER FOUR: Red Salt from Kanawha	34
CHAPTER FIVE: The River System	50
CHAPTER SIX: The Terrible Conflict—Civil War 1861-1865	82
CHAPTER SEVEN: The Railroads	108
CHAPTER EIGHT: King Coal	128
CHAPTER NINE: Industry	154
CHAPTER TEN: From Streetcars to Airplanes: Other Forms of Transportation	180
CHAPTER ELEVEN: Life in the County: 1865-1918	202
CHAPTER TWELVE: The Moving Capitol	228
CHAPTER THIRTEEN: Streetscapes	252
CHAPTER FOURTEEN: Flood and Fire	274
CHAPTER FIFTEEN: Life in the County: 1919-1941	286
CHAPTER SIXTEEN: Teaching the Mind	304
CHAPTER SEVENTEEN: Healing the Body and Soul	318
CHAPTER EIGHTEEN: For the Good of the People	338
CHAPTER NINETEEN: Organizations	348
CHAPTER TWENTY: Enjoying the Good Life	360
CHAPTER TWENTY-ONE: Utilities	396
CHAPTER TWENTY-TWO: Life in the County: 1942-Present	408
CHAPTER TWENTY-THREE: Towns in the County	414
CHAPTER TWENTY-FOUR: A View of the Present from the Past	452
The Historians	458
Appendix	460
Index	462
Bibliography	466

This book is dedicated to the memory of the original Kanawha County historians—Dr. John P. Hale, William S. Laidley, George W. Atkinson and Virgil A. Lewis—and to the modern historians, both amateur and professional—Julius A. deGruyter, Ruth Woods Dayton, Roy Bird Cook, George W. Summers, Forrest Hull, Boyd Stutler, Harry Brawley, B.E. Andre, William Wintz, and Dr. Otis K. Rice—and to my mother, who nurtured my interest in history.

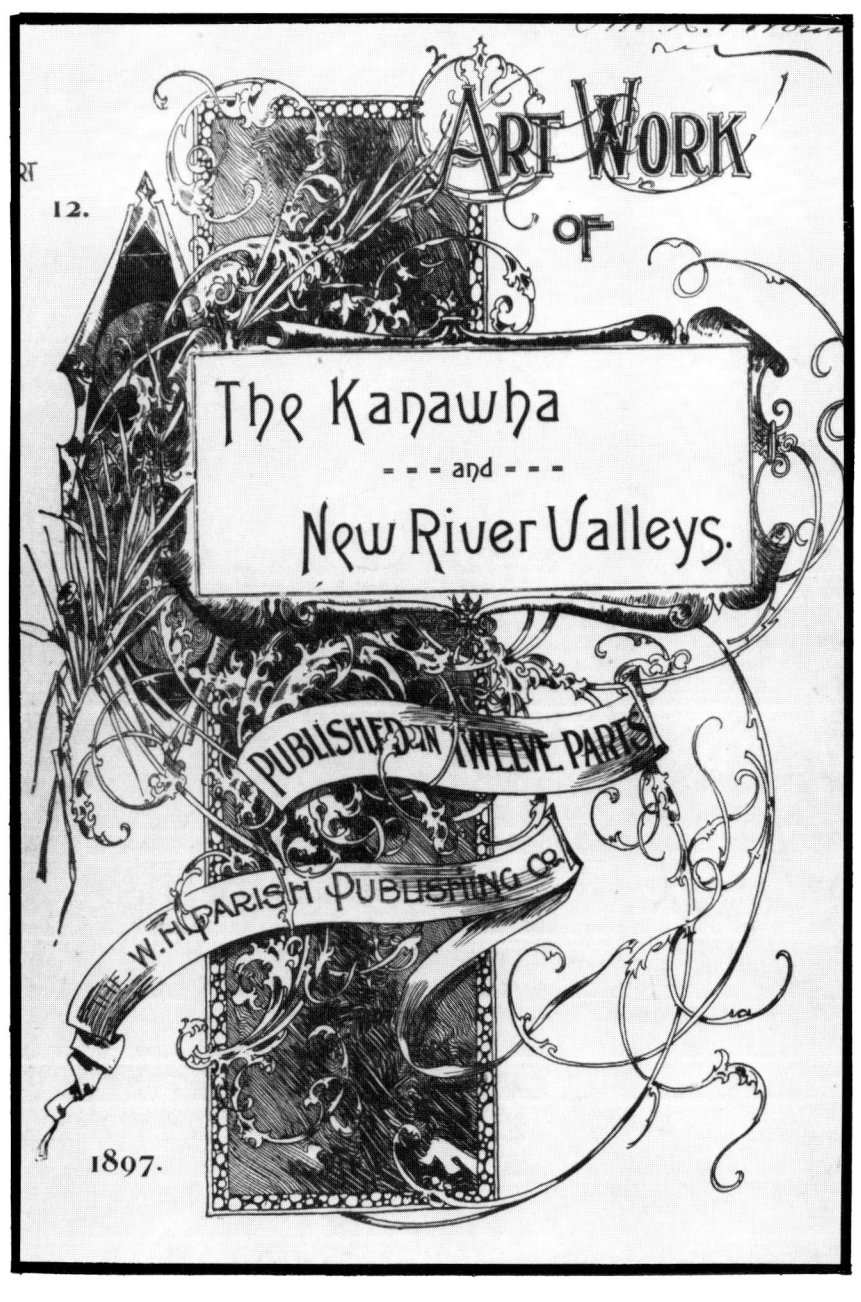

The Setting

With a total area of 913.38 square miles, Kanawha County is the fourth largest in the state of West Virginia, smaller in area than Randolph (1,046 square miles), Greenbrier (1,022), and Pocanhontas (942). The county lies between parallels 35° 50' and 38° 40' north latitude and meridians 81° 10' and 81° 55' west longitude. It is bounded by Jackson and Roane counties to the north; and Clay, Nicholas, and Fayette counties to the east; Raleigh and Boone counties to the south; and Lincoln and Putnam counties to the west.

Within the county, elevations range from 542 feet, the river level at the border of Kanawha and Putnam counties, to 2,650 feet, a knob on the Kanawha-Raleigh county line. The difference in elevation is 2,108 feet.

The name Kanawha may have evolved from the Indian name of a branch of the Nanticokes, who lived in the area bounded by the Potomac River on the north and the New River on the south. The tribe was alternately called the Conoys, Conoise, Canawese, Cohnawas, Canaways, and Kanawhas. On Wyman's 1770 map of the British Empire, the river is shown as the "Great Conoway" or "Wood's River," and in a 1789 survey, the name was spelled Kenhawa. Daniel Boone, in one of his surveys, spelled it Conhawway. The river, at times, was also designated as the New, clear to its mouth at the Ohio River.

The Kanawha River bisects the county, running roughly from the southeast to the northwest. The largest inland waterway in the state and one of the larger tributaries, along with the New River, of the Ohio River, the Kanawha is 99.5 miles long, 43 miles of which are in Kanawha County.

When Kanawha County was created on November 14, 1788 from the western portions of Greenbrier and Montgomery counties, its borders stretched from the Ohio River to the west, to the summit of Sewell Mountain to the east, the Big Sandy River to the south, and the headwaters of the Little Kanawha River to the north.

Before the Civil War, sixteen other counties were created with land partially or wholly carved from the original Kanawha County. Wood County was created in 1798; Mason, 1804; Cabell, 1809; Nicholas, 1818; Logan, 1824; Jackson and Fayette, 1831; Braxton, 1836; Wayne, 1842; Gilmer, 1845; Boone, 1847; Putnam, 1848; Raleigh and Wyoming, 1850; Calhoun, 1855; and Clay and Roane, 1856. No other divisions were made after West Virginia became a state in 1863.

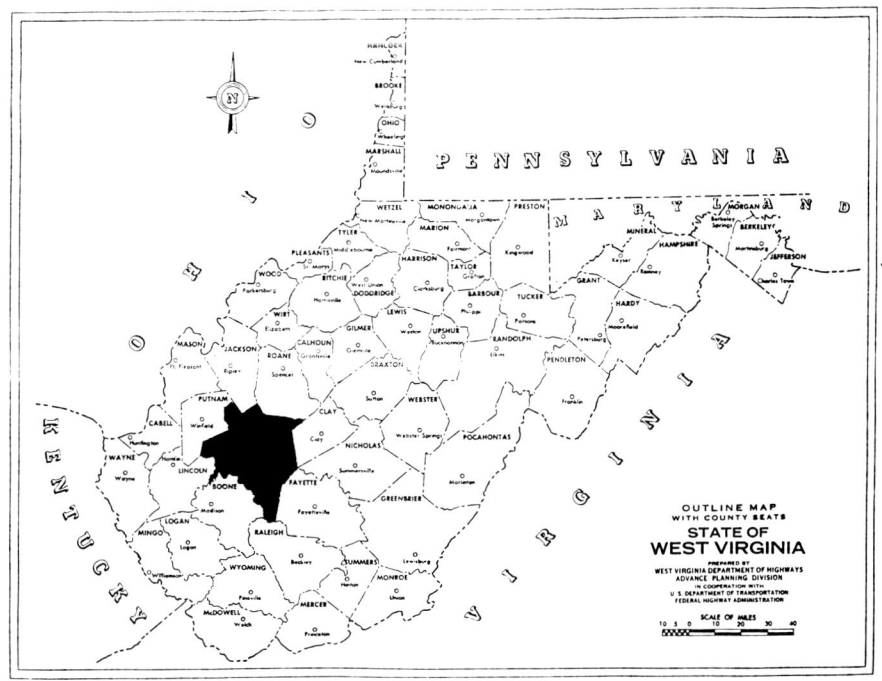

The Ancients

Pipe from Mound, Kanawha County.

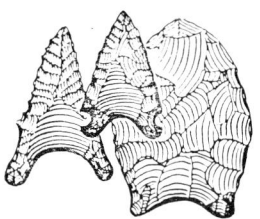

An ancient Indian burial mound in Kanawha City on the site of the City National Bank. This scene is looking east—the Village Apartments are in the background.
COURTESY TERRY LOWRY

The Kanawha Valley was once well-known for the number of burial mounds and other mementos left by the prehistoric peoples who lived in the area. Today, only two mounds and some petroglyphs are still intact, although campsites and other artifacts are unearthed from time to time.

Early Paleo-Indian hunters came into this area 10,500 years ago from the west to look for game. When most of their prey became extinct—the buffalo was the exception—these hunters turned to small game and fishing. (It's hard to believe that in the narrow valleys and dense forests of Kanawha County, the buffalo was still roaming as late as the 1800s. The last of these beasts was killed in 1815.)

No one really knows for sure where the earliest hunters came from. According to Dr. John P. Hale, in his 1891 book, *History of the Great Kanawha Valley*, "some of the ancient Aztecs, or Toltecs, or Pueblos might have occupied the Mississippi Valley for several generations or centuries before being, perhaps, conquered and driven out, or nearly exterminated, and the remnants absorbed into the local tribes following them, forgetting, after a time, the history of the works their ancestors had built."

Contemporary archaeologists suggest, however, that the Kanawha people emerged from the same roots as the other natives who occupied the Eastern United States. They cite the fact that the spears, arrowheads, pipes and ornaments found elsewhere in the region closely resemble those of the early Kanawha peoples.

The first of these eastern cultures was called Archaic, which persevered until 1,000 B.C. Particularly important evidence comes from the deeply stratified (layered) St. Albans site with artifacts dating between approximately 7,000 and 2,000 B.C. This site is one of the most important Archaic sites in the Eastern United States. Then the Adena culture rose up, apparently a spontaneous development of Late Archaic people influenced by funerary ideas from the south. The Kanawha Adena people were related to the Adena in Ohio, where mound-building was also prevalent. The Culture can be divided into three phases: Early (1,000 to 500 B.C.), Adena (500 to 200 B.C.) and Murad Climax (200 B.C. to 100 A.D.) Another mound-building group, the Armstrong Middle Woodland, related to Ohio Hopewell followed the Adena in the Kanawha Valley between 100 A.D. and 700 A.D. No longer nomads, these people lived in huts made of poles and woven straw laid out in circular-shaped villages. Burial practices differed during each phase, but it was the Adena period that produced the largest mounds.

From 1883 to 1885 the Smithsonian Institution made a detailed study of the Kanawha Valley mounds under the direction of Professor Cyrus Thomas and Colonel P.W. Norris. The Smith Mound, on the Colonel Benjamin H. Smith farm in what is now Dunbar, measured 175 feet in diameter and stood 35 feet high. It no longer exists. The Criel Mound on the Criel farm in what is now South Charleston was 33 feet high, but the top had been flattened some years before so it could be used as a stand for judges to observe the horse races

that coursed around the base of the mound. Norris sank a shaft through the mound and found a large log tomb containing 11 skeletons, one 7 and a half feet long, laying in the prone position. There were shell beads, and three-inch lance points buried with the dead, and one skeleton had a thin sheet of hammered copper folded about its head. Today, The Criel Mound is a dominant attraction of South Charleston, which has altered the mound somewhat and surrounded it with a small city park.

While it seems clear who's responsible for the burial mounds of Kanawha County, the massive stone wall built on a ridge east of Paint Creek, and similar structures all along the Kanawha River, are less well understood. Following the Adena and the Armstrong, were the late Woodland mound-builders (700-1,200 A.D.), who began to experiment with growing corn and other crops.

The period of Indian settlement in the valley from 1,000 A.D. to 1,690 A.D. is known as the Fort Ancient Period. Mound-building continued but mounds were located in large villages which were occupied by people who developed an extensive agricultural economy and buried their dead below their living quarters and in mounds. Much physical evidence, including petroglyphs, remains from this time.

The era from 1,450 to 1,690 A.D. is known as the Protohistoric or Clover Phase. A tribe called the Moneton lived in the lower Kanawha Valley around St. Albans and near Buffalo in Putnam County. The first white man to see these Indians was probably Gabriel Arthur, who was brought to the valley in 1673 as a captive of the Tomahitten (Cherokee) Indians. By 1755 the last of the Monetons had left the Valley.

In the late 1600s the Five Nations of the New York Iroquois sent their Mohawk and Seneca warriors into what is now West Virginia and drove out all the other tribes in the area. The Cherokees retreated a short distance south, but refused to be pushed further, and a buffer zone, which included the Kanawha Valley, was created between the two tribes. For years, the only Indians brave enough to venture into this no-man's-land were Shawnee hunting parties ranging out of Ohio. It wasn't until 1768 by the Treaty of Fort Stanwix that the Virginia colonial government gained control—at least on paper—of the Kanawha Valley region. But the powerful Shawnees—who insisted that the hunting rights to the zone belonged to them—would continue to be the biggest problem settlers had to contend with in the early days of Kanawha County.

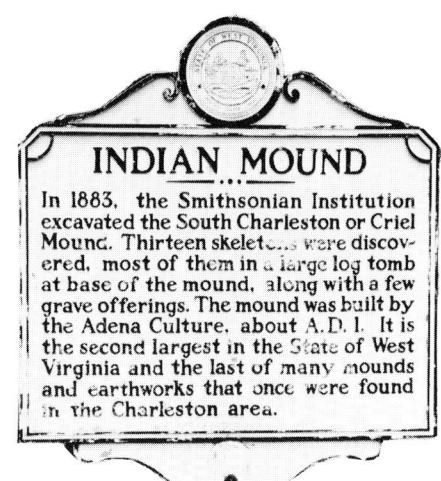

The Criel Mound at South Charleston shown as it was in the 1920s. This is the largest and one of the only remaining mounds in the Kanawha Valley. Originally the mound was 520 feet in circumference and 33 feet high but it has been altered through the years to make it suitable as a park and recreational area for the City of South Charleston.
KCL

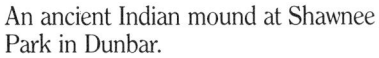

An ancient Indian mound at Shawnee Park in Dunbar.

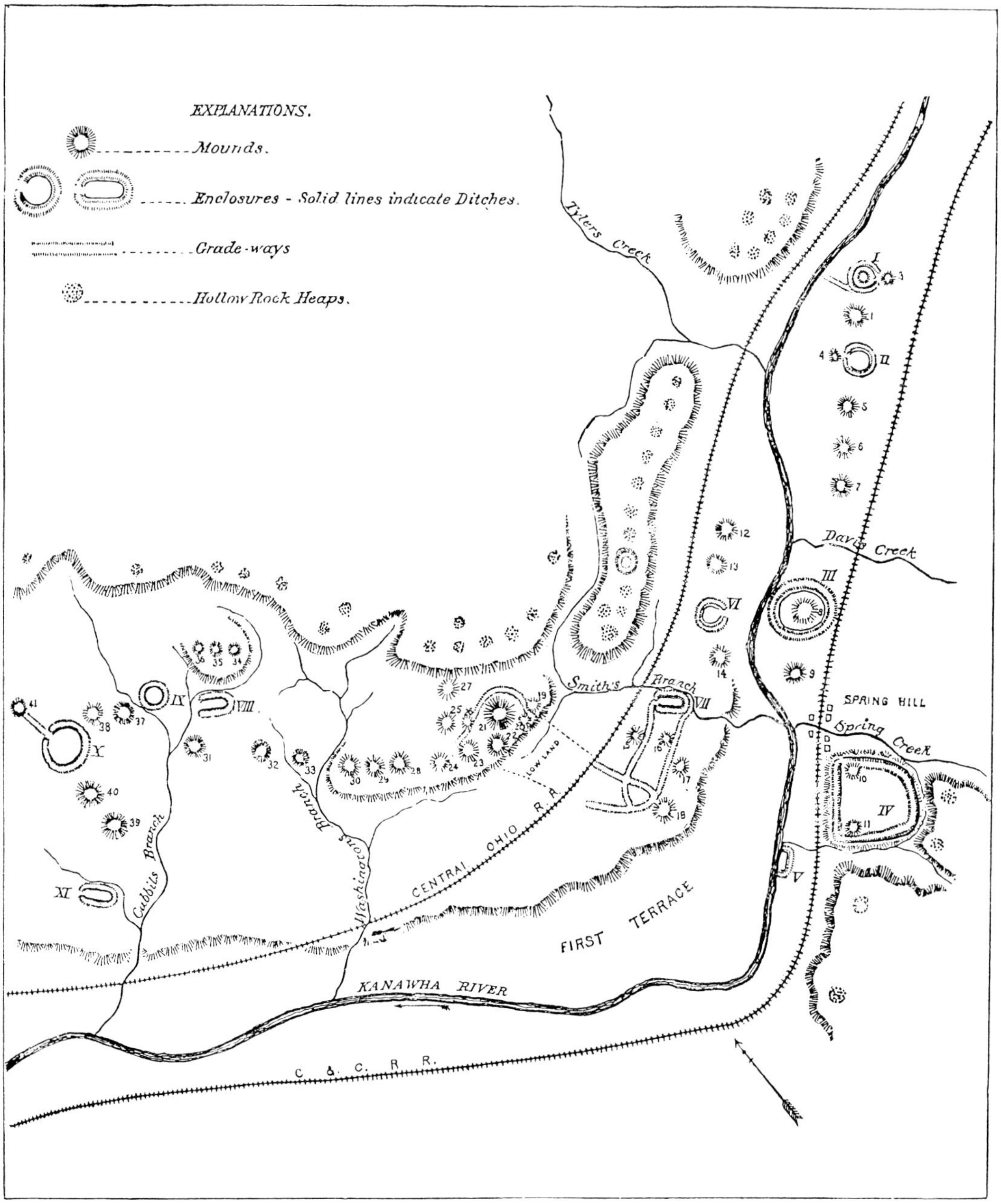

An 1887 map of ancient Indian works in the Spring Hill, Dunbar area.
COURTESY SMITHSONIAN INSTITUTION

Cross-section of the Criel Mound. COURTESY SMITHSONIAN INSTITUTION

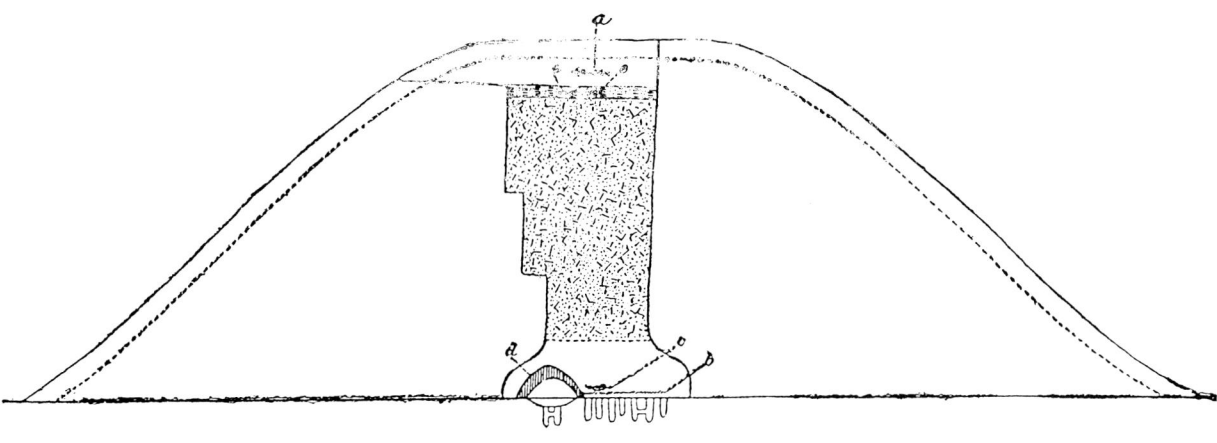

MOUND
With so-called
"ALTAR"
KANAWHA COUNTY
WEST VIRGINIA
FROM THE FIFTH ANNUAL REPORT OF THE
SMITHSONIAN INSTITUTE
C. E. KREBS, ASSISTANT GEOLOGIST, MARCH 7TH 1913.

SKETCH
SHOWING LOCATION OF
MOUNDS
IN THE KANAWHA VALLEY
WEST OF
Charleston, W. Va.
Scale:- 1" = 1 Mile
EXPLANATION
Mounds
Enclosures,
(Solid lines indicate ditches)
Grade-ways
Hollow Rock Heaps
DATA COLLECTED FROM
THE FIELD AND FROM PLATE 5
OF THE FIFTH ANNUAL REPORT
OF THE
SMITHSONIAN INSTITUTE
C. E. KREBS, ASSIST'T GEOLOGIST
MARCH 7TH 1913.
CITY LIMITS
Sattes
Institute
Branch
Hollow
Dutch
Landers Br.
Tyler
Creek
Falls
Br.
N
Mound
RAILROAD
CHESAPEAKE AND OHIO
KANAWHA
RIVER
Farm
Finney
Aarons
Creek
MICHIGAN
Blaine I.
South Charleston
KANAWHA AND
RAILROAD
Ward
Hollow
Spring Hill
Upton Cr.
Davis
Creek
Sugarcamp Br.

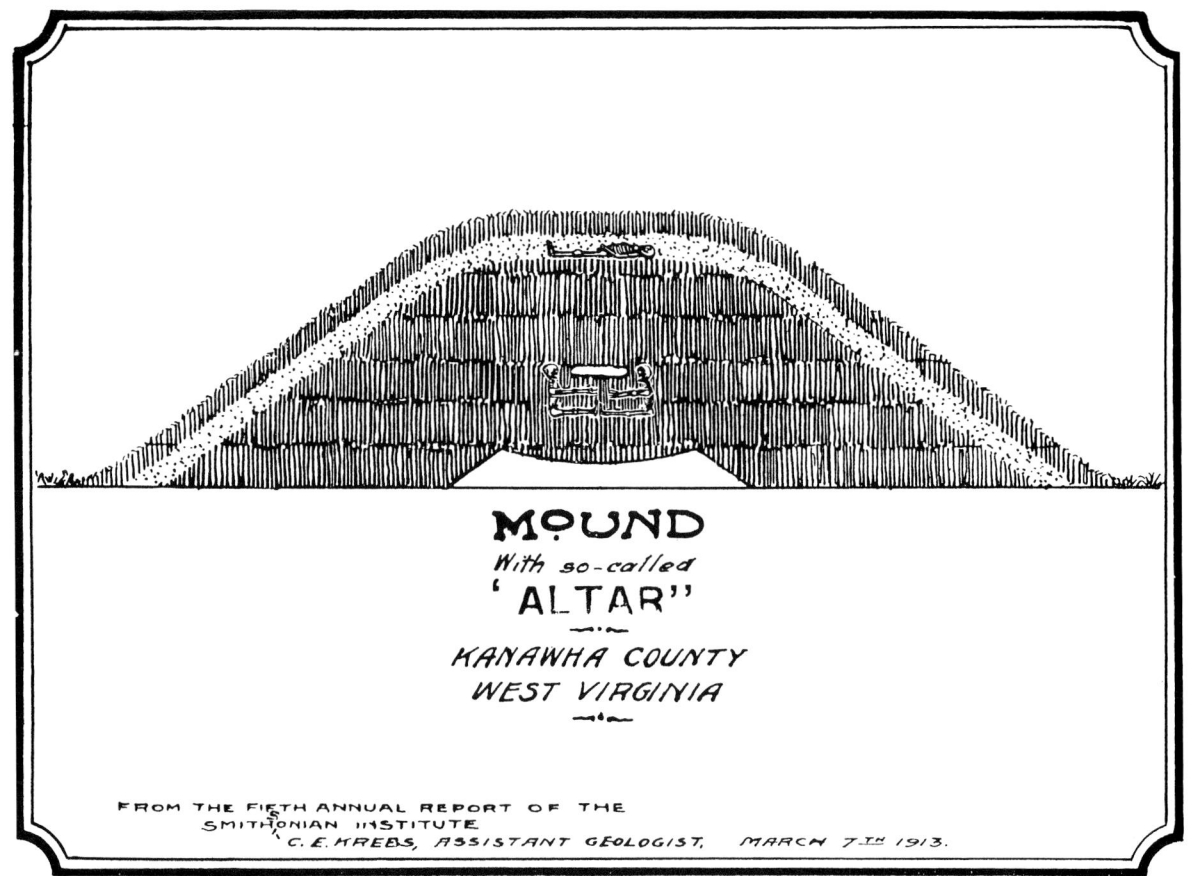

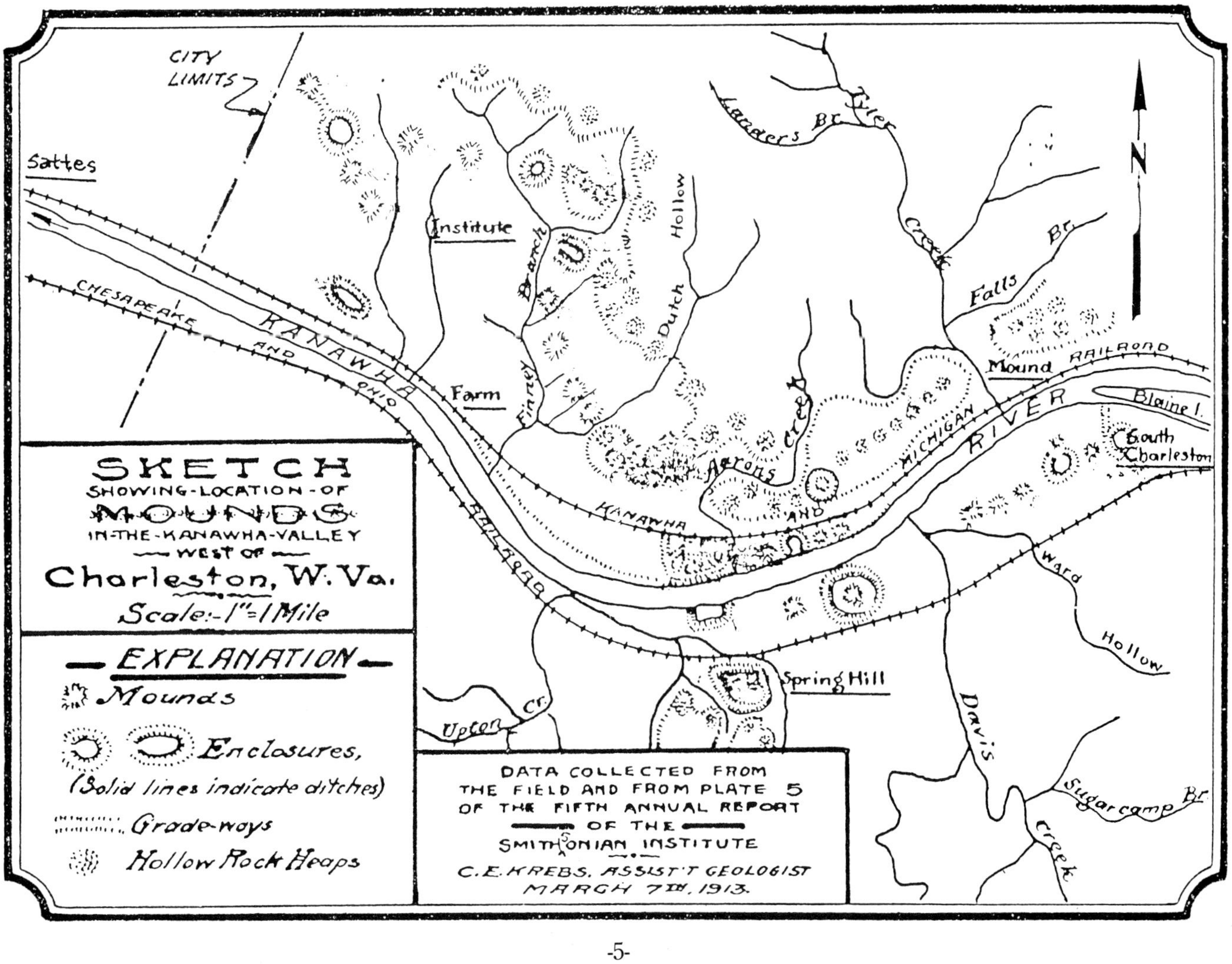

This artist's rendering of Fort Lee shows the stockade, George Clendenin's two-story house, and other settlers' cabins. The house was about 36′ long, 18′ wide and 18′ high. The stockade was constructed of logs placed upright and set side by side in ditches, which formed a 250′ × 175′ structure. DRAWN BY RICHARD ANDRE

Chapter Two

The Making of a County

FORT LEE

A western frontier outpost, guarding settlers against the Indians. Built here in 1788 and named for Gen. Henry "Light Horse Harry" Lee, one of Washington's most trusted officers. Later Lee was governor of Virginia.

Wm. Clendenin, Captain of Rangers,
to the Governor.
October 9th
1793
Kanhawa

Sir:

On the Twenty-Eighth day last month, about Four Indians were discovered within about four miles of Fort Lee. It was late in the evening when discovered, and consequently no pursute could take place after them that night. At the same time I had made every arrangement that my Judgement dictated to detect them the next day. The Indians however finding themselves discovered, stole Mr. Beaker's canoe that night and went down the River Kanawha. A few days before my Brother Geo. Clendenin, with some of the neighbours had gone down the River as far as Point Pleasant, with whom I had sent a soldier in order to Assist in bringing up some powder, as I found the Company entirely destitute when I took command of them, and expecting that they would meet with the Indians on their return, I thought it prudent to give them notice if possible. Mr. Andrew Lewis and Joseph Burwell voluntarily offered their service for that purpose, and accordingly took a light Canoe and set out. The Indians had put out at the mouth of Coal River, about twelve miles below Fort Lee and hid their canoe, at which time said Lewis and Burwell past them. That night my Brother, with his party, say about half way between Fort Lee and the point, and in the night Lewis and Burwell passed them. After they passed them about a mile and a quarter, they hid their canoe and went to shore, during which time the Indians passed Brother and Lewis, & Burwell also. The Indians went on untill they went in Sixteen miles of the point, where they drew up their canoe in the mouth of a creek, and sat down in order to watch her. About ten o'cl'k in the day following, Burwell and Lewis came by and accidentally discovered the canoe or part thereof, and not knowing what canoe it was, went to see her. They could not be certain of her untill they were quite close, when on a sudden they heard the Indian's Guns cracking, and Mr. Lewis being steering the canoe whilst Mr. Burwell stood up with his gun in his hand, Lewis suddenly wheeled the canoe Round in order to make his Escape. The Indians fired from their ambuscade struck Lewis on the Right arm and knocked him out of the canoe. Burwell, Hero-like, laid down his gun, took hold of Lewis and dragged him into the canoe; Then took hold of both guns and proceeded to steer off the canoe, when the Indians Shot him in at the point of one of his hips, and out at the Grine contrary to the Hip. He however never failed to carry away the canoe with Lewis whilst the Indians Repeated their fire at him. Lewis dared the Indians to come on, but they Still concealed themselves under their ambuscade. I presume the Indians had discovered my Brother's party the evening before, and expected them at hand, wherefore seeing Burwell out of their reach, Run immediately away and did not pursue. Burwell carried the canoe to the point about the middle of Evening. My Brother, Mr. George Clendenin, has since visited them and informs that Mr. Lewis's Right arm is cut off and that there is no doubt but he will recover. Burwell he brought home with him, who is almost well.

The Indians are daily among us, But in very small parties, and act with so much caution that I have never as yet been able to fall in with them, tho' daily laying and forming plans to decoy them.

On the seventh of the present Instant, I rec'd your late favor, with an extract of the Secretary of War's letter to your Excellency, and assure you that you may rest satisfied that nothing on my part shall be wanting to complete your most Sanguine wishes.

I have the honor to be with great Respect,

Your Excellency's Ob't Servant.

P.S. Serg't Johnston, who forwards this, bears an express to the Speaker of the House of Delegates, Requesting a wait for an election. I acted as sheriff and could not hold one at the time appointed by law, from invasion and infectious disease. I presume he will be paid his Express from the Legislature or by their order; he is in service-the hire of the Horse and his own necessary expences is all that is necessary.

WM. CLENDENIN, Sh'ff.
From *Calendar of Virginia State Papers and Other Manuscripts,* 1886.

The Making of a County
Early Visitors and Settlers

History gives credit to young Gabriel Arthur for being, in 1673, the first white to view what is now Kanawha County. John Peter Salley and John Howard, who first discovered coal in Boone County, also viewed the Coal and Kanawha rivers and the site of Nitro in 1742.

The first whites to view what is now Charleston were Mary Ingles, her three children and her sister-in-law, Betty Draper. But that opportunity was entirely against their will. On July 8, 1755, they were snatched by raiding Shawnee Indians from their settlement at Drapers Meadows near present Blacksburg, Virginia (the first permanent settlement west of the Allegheny Mountains), then force-marched down New River, across Flat Top Mountain, and down Paint Creek where they crossed the Kanawha River. Three days after her capture, Mary Ingles gave birth to a girl. The war party stopped at the mouth of Campbells Creek long enough to process some brine into salt before continuing their journey down the Kanawha to the Shawnee homeland on the Sicoto River in Ohio, and finally to Big Bone Lick in Kentucky—about 50 miles below present-day Cincinnati, Ohio.

Here the captives were traded to new owners. Mary Ingles' two sons were taken from her, but she was allowed to keep her baby. Ingles was well treated because of her abilities as a cook, nurse and seamstress, but seeing a chance to escape, she fled with an old Dutch woman captured by the Shawnees earlier in Pennsylvania, on a harrowing 40-day trip back to Drapers Meadows. It took six years of negotiations with the Indians, however, before Betty Draper was returned to her family. (This story was related in great detail in *Trans-Allegheny Pioneers*, written by Mary Ingles' grandson, Dr. John P. Hale.)

Mention has been made in several early histories of another early visitor to the county, a Algerian named Selim. He was captured by pirates in North Africa and brought to Louisiana as a slave. After escaping in 1759 from the plantation he was working on, he started on a long journey up the Mississippi to the Ohio, up the Kanawha to the Greenbrier River and finally to a spot near Warm Springs, Virginia, where he was found near death by settlers. Selim survived and eventually returned to Algeria.

Western Virginia, including present-day Kanawha County, had been closed to settlement at the end of the French and Indian War in 1763 by the British Government. In the meantime, the Shawnees had chased most of the settlers in the Greenbrier area back across the mountains into the Shenandoah Valley. But Matthew Arbuckle, a hunter and trapper on the Greenbrier River, ignored the law and passed through the Kanawha Valley in 1764 on his way to sell furs at Point Pleasant.

No one else ventured into this forbidden zone until after 1768 when treaties with the Indians opened up the area once again. In 1771, two young backwoodsmen, Simon Kenton and George Strader, along with an elderly John Yeager, established a hunting and trapping camp at the mouth of the Elk. Two years later, a band of Indians attacked their cabin, killing Yeager. Kenton and Strader escaped to the Ohio River.

By 1773, several land surveys had been made in the Kanawha Valley. Colonel Thomas Bullitt surveyed what is now the city of Charleston and William Crawford surveyed what is now Nitro and other areas of the valley for George Washington, who was awarded this acreage for his service in the Indian wars.

The Fry Military Grant of 1773 was surveyed in what is now Nitro, Cross Lanes and the Poca area. It was given by the King of England to various soldiers for their service in the French and Indian War.

In 1773, Walter Kelly founded the first settlement in Kanawha County at the mouth of Kelly's Creek in Cedar Grove. The next year, unfortunately, Kelly was killed by an Indian party. Several others tried to settle in the Kanawha Valley in 1773 but were driven out by Indians.

There is some dispute about the year the Morris clan began living in the valley. Some say Leonard Morris settled on Slaughter's Creek as early as 1771; some say that date is years early and that the first Morris settlement was William Morris' at Cedar Grove in 1774. At any rate, Leonard later settled at the mouth of Len's Creek where Marmet is now located. Robert Hughes settled at present-day Hugheston, Joseph Carroll at present-day Shrewsbury and John Jones at present-day Pratt.

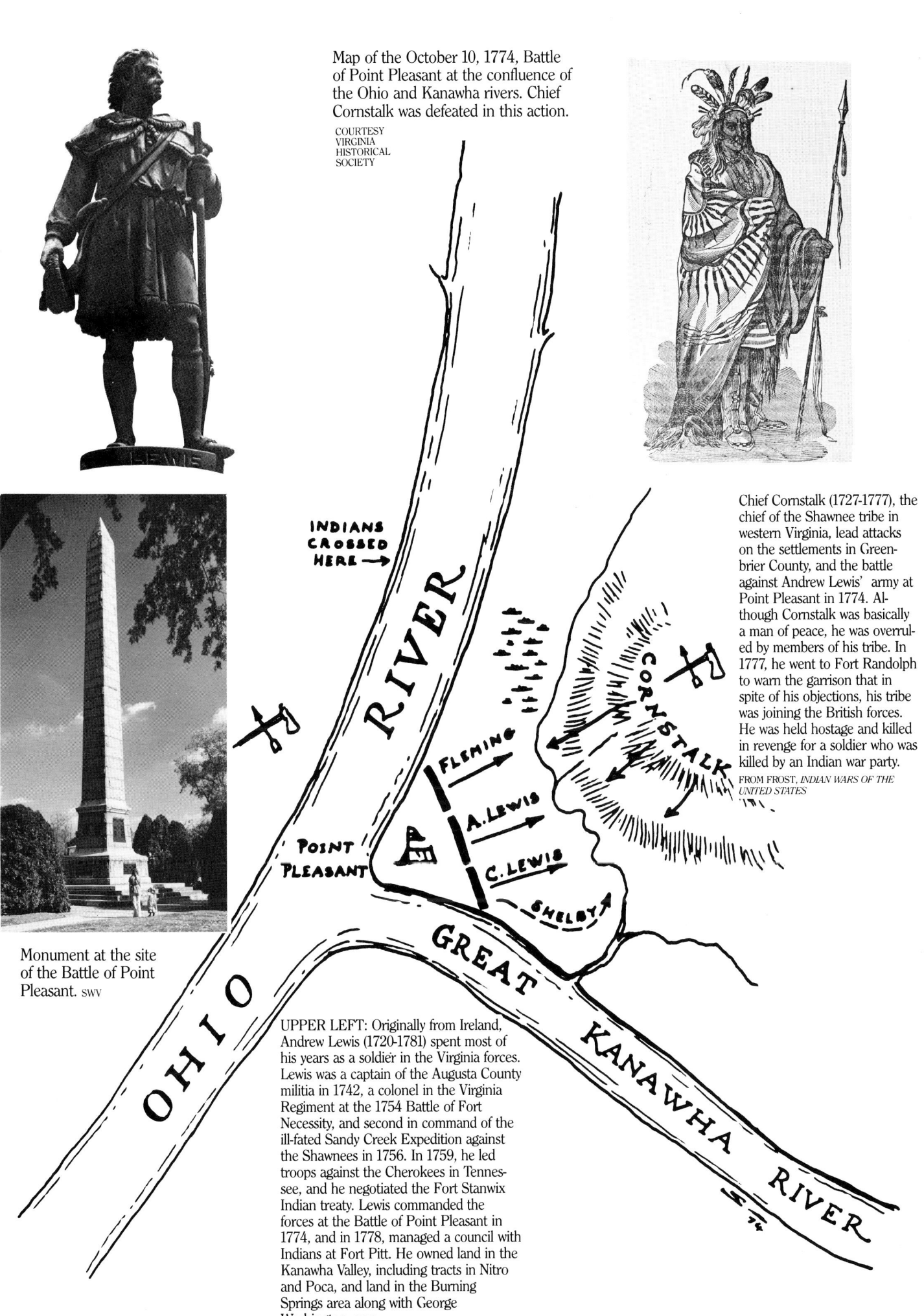

Map of the October 10, 1774, Battle of Point Pleasant at the confluence of the Ohio and Kanawha rivers. Chief Cornstalk was defeated in this action. COURTESY VIRGINIA HISTORICAL SOCIETY

Monument at the site of the Battle of Point Pleasant. SWV

Chief Cornstalk (1727-1777), the chief of the Shawnee tribe in western Virginia, lead attacks on the settlements in Greenbrier County, and the battle against Andrew Lewis' army at Point Pleasant in 1774. Although Cornstalk was basically a man of peace, he was overruled by members of his tribe. In 1777, he went to Fort Randolph to warn the garrison that in spite of his objections, his tribe was joining the British forces. He was held hostage and killed in revenge for a soldier who was killed by an Indian war party. FROM FROST, *INDIAN WARS OF THE UNITED STATES*

UPPER LEFT: Originally from Ireland, Andrew Lewis (1720-1781) spent most of his years as a soldier in the Virginia forces. Lewis was a captain of the Augusta County militia in 1742, a colonel in the Virginia Regiment at the 1754 Battle of Fort Necessity, and second in command of the ill-fated Sandy Creek Expedition against the Shawnees in 1756. In 1759, he led troops against the Cherokees in Tennessee, and he negotiated the Fort Stanwix Indian treaty. Lewis commanded the forces at the Battle of Point Pleasant in 1774, and in 1778, managed a council with Indians at Fort Pitt. He owned land in the Kanawha Valley, including tracts in Nitro and Poca, and land in the Burning Springs area along with George Washington. SWV

The gravestone of Fleming Cobb(s) (1767-1846) in the family cemetery next to Kanawha County Club grounds. Cobb came to Fort Lee in 1789, and served as a ranger. In 1790, Cobb was pursued by Indians as he travelled by canoe carrying ammunition from Fort Randolph at Point Pleasant to Fort Lee, under the cover of darkness. In the early 1790s, he killed the last Indian in the valley on Wilson's Island, a short distance below Blaine's Island. As the Indian landed his canoe on the island, Cobb, standing on the south side of the river, fired a shot, and killed him instantly. Cobb's uncle, Thomas Upton, left him the homestead farm at the mouth of Davis Creek, where Cobb's descendents lived until 1945. ww

Other survey parties came through the valley in 1774 including that of John Floyd, who was on his way to the Ohio River. He surveyed the present site of St. Albans for George Washington. That year more important events were shaping up to the west which would have a direct effect on the settlement and formation of Kanawha County.

Lord Dunmore's War, and the ensuing Battle of Point Pleasant on October 10, 1774, was by some accounts the opening volley of the Revolutionary War. Dunmore, the Governor of Virginia, was determined to stop Shawnee Indian attacks on settlements along the western frontier. He led a 1,200-man army from Fort Dunmore, at present-day Pittsburgh, down the Ohio River. Andrew Lewis, a prominent Virginian, would lead another 1,000-man army from Camp Union, at Lewisburg, down the Kanawha River to the Ohio. The plan was for these two armies to meet and trap the Indians. Lewis' army arrived first, at the confluence of the Ohio and Kanawha rivers at present-day Point Pleasant on October 8. Chief Cornstalk, the Shawnee leader attacked Lewis two days later with a force of 1,000 but was defeated. Dunmore's force didn't arrive in time to take part in the fighting. This battle led to the Treaty of Camp Charlotte, which guaranteed the neutrality of the Shawnee tribe during the first two years of the Revolutionary War. Fort Blair was established at Point Pleasant after Cornstalk's defeat. In 1776, Matthew Arbuckle built the stronger Fort Randolph to take its place.

Fort Randolph was abandoned in 1779 and whatever settlers were left in western Virginia were forced to seek refuge in the Greenbrier area. "We have been away from our plantations for three years past, and now desire to return," despaired one petitioner addressing Governor Harrison at Richmond in the winter of 1781-82. "We implore Your Excellency for a fort, and garrison of County Militia to be established at the mouth of Elk River."

The Virginia government, hardpressed for money and men, could do little to provide protection for its "western" settlements. Five years later, a new fort was built at Point Pleasant and there were small settlements founded at Cedar Grove and Len's Creek (Marmet). In 1786, Lewis, Christopher and Samuel Tackett, along with R. John Young and their families, built a compound, log houses and a stockade at the mouth of Coal River. This complex would be called Tackett's Fort. A year and a half later, 31 people lived there. In March 1790, several of the settlers at the fort were kidnapped by Indians and taken to Michigan. These hapless captives were used for barter, released, and sent home. Six months later, the Indians attacked the fort again. They killed Christopher Tackett and several children, and burned down everything in sight. Other members of the Tackett and Young families managed to escape.

The Fry Military Grant, made by the King of England, included the present sites of Nitro, Cross Lanes and the Poca area. Grantees were: 1 - Colonel Thomas Bullitt; 2 & 10 - General Adam Stephen; 3 - Lieutenant William Wright; 4 - Colonel Joshua Fry; 5 & 9 - Colonel Andrew Lewis; 6 & 8 - Major Peter Hogg; 7 - Captain Thomas Savage; 11 - Captain John Welper. ww

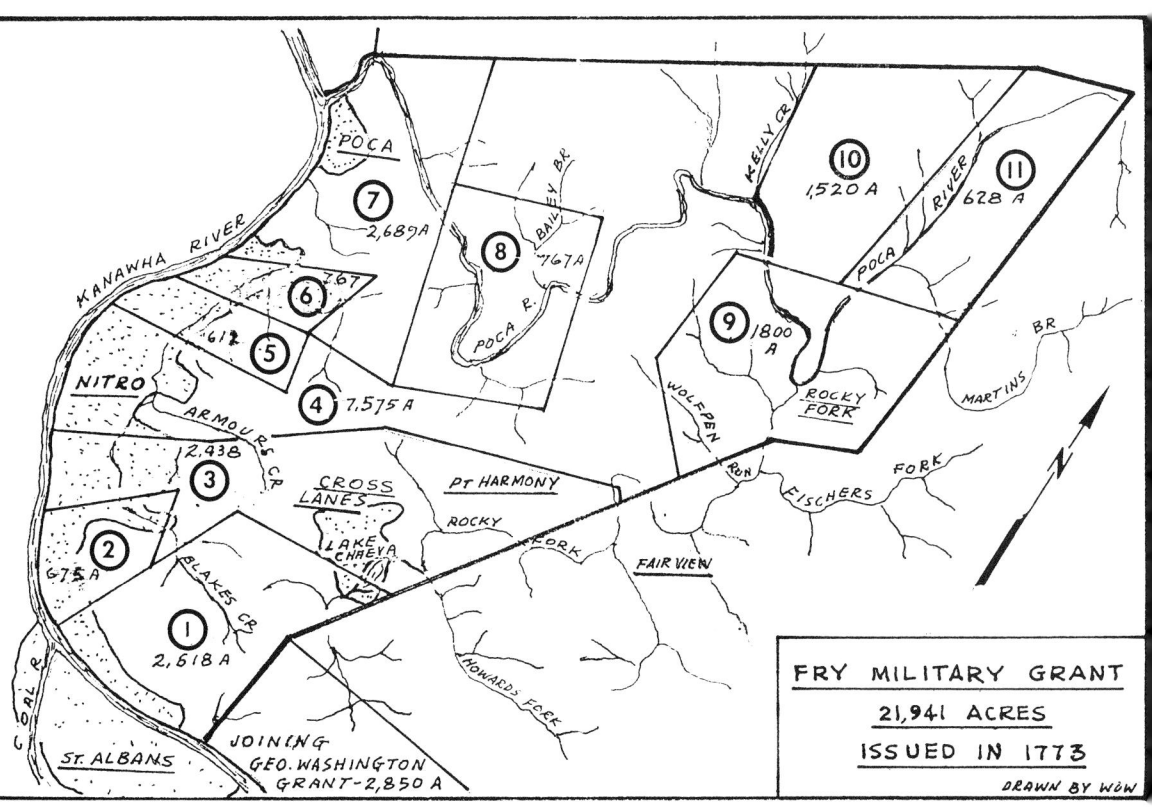

Tackett's Fort at the mouth of Coal River, which is present-day St. Albans. This fort was burned down by the Shawnee Indians in 1790. PM

Finally, in April 1788, George Clendenin and a band of 30 rangers arrived near the mouth of the Elk and established the first permanent settlement within the present boundary of Charleston. This happened to be on land that George had purchased in 1787. Accompanying George were his brothers William, captain of the rangers, and Alexander. They built a stockade, a two-story house and cabins on a site at the present corner of Brooks Street and Kanawha Boulevard. This site offered a good spot for a canoe landing and a vantage point above the river. William Clendenin built a smaller blockhouse a half mile above the fort near the present Executive Mansion. The establishment of Clendenin's Fort gave some protection to the settlers but the Indian menace remained very real until General Anthony Wayne's victory over the Indians at the Battle of Fallen Timbers in Ohio in August 1794. This action effectively removed the Indian population of western Virginia. The last person to be killed by an Indian was Shadrack Harriman in 1791 at his home at the mouth of Venables Branch in South Ruffner.

During the summer of 1788, Clendenin was in Richmond as a delegate to the convention to ratify the new Constitution of the United States. He pushed hard for the formation of a new county in the western section of Virginia, where he had recently established a fort. The state legislature authorized this new county on November 14, 1788; on October 1, 1789, it was official. Kanawha County was formed from parts of Greenbrier and Montgomery counties and was ten times its present size. The boundaries of neighboring counties had been changing for years. From 1734 to 1738, when Augusta County was formed in the southern part of the state, Orange County comprised all the land in Virginia west of the Alleghenies. In 1769, a portion of Kanawha County was part of Botetourt County. In 1777 it was part of Greenbrier and Montgomery counties. And parts of Kanawha County are now parts of 16 other counties.

The county's first court of law was convened in 1789 at Clendenin's house at Fort Lee with Thomas Lewis as sheriff, William H. Cavendish as clerk, Reuben Slaughter as surveyor, George Clendenin as county lieutenant of Militia and Daniel Boone as lieutenant colonel.

Clendenin, along with Andrew Donnally, Sr., were the first representatives of Kanawha County in the 1790 Virginia House of Delegates. In 1791, Daniel Boone took Donnally's place.

The first county building erected was a two-story log jail. Its bottom floor was dug into the bank of the Kanawha River. The first courthouse building was erected in 1796 on the present courthouse site. It would stand until 1817, when the second one was built. County court records show that the structure measured 30 feet by 40 feet with "two good floors, two doors, four windows, one pair of stairs and stair door, a fashionable seat for the Magistrates and Clerk, attorney's table, bench and bar." For unknown reasons a county clerk's office was built, in 1802, several hundred yards to the east on the site of the future Ruffner Hotel.

Officers and Rangers Who Built and Garrisoned Fort Lee, April 1788

Colonel George Clendenin
Captain William Clendenin
Lieutenant George Shaw
Ensign Francis Watkins
Sergeant Shadrack Harriman
Sergeant Reuben Slaughter

Privates

John Tollypurt	Michael Newhouse
Samuel Dunbar	Robert Aaron
John Burns	William Carroll
Isaac Snedicer	Thomas Shirkey
William Miller	Nicholas Null
John Buckle	Archer Price
James Edgar	Benjamin Morris
Levi Morris	William Morris
Joseph Burwell	William Turrell
William Boggs	John Cavinder
William Hyllard	Henry Morris
Charles Young	William George
Alexander Clendenin	John Moore

FROM *PIONEERS AND THEIR HOMES ON UPPER KANAWHA*, RUTH WOODS DAYTON.

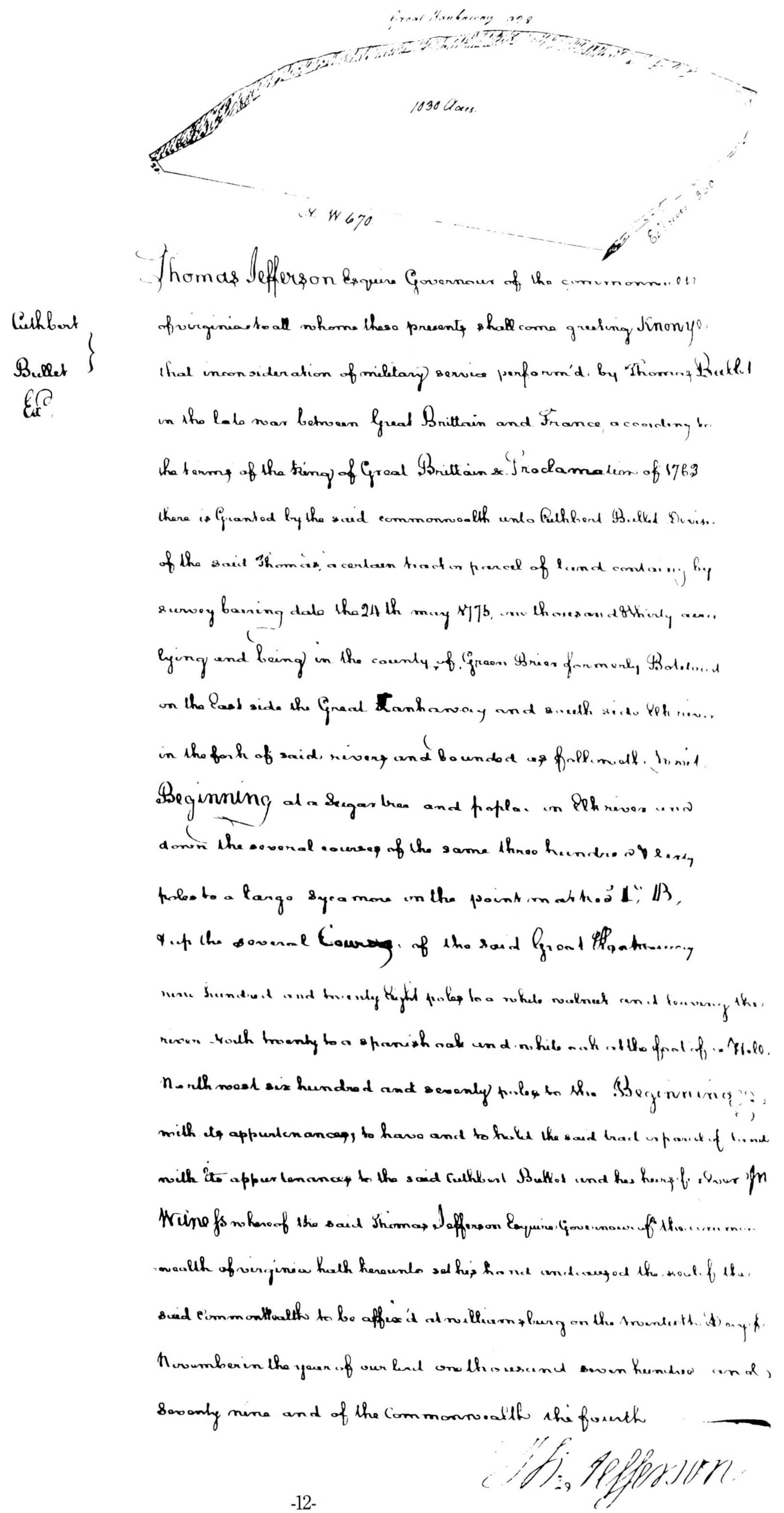

Copy of Cuthbert Bullitt's deed to 1,030 acres at the site of Charleston, signed in 1779 by Governor Thomas Jefferson. CN

Cuthbert
Bullet
&c.

Thomas Jefferson Esquire Governour of the commonwealth of Virginia to all whome these presents shall come greeting Know ye that in consideration of military service perform'd by Thomas Bullet in the late war between Great Brittain and France, according to the terms of the King of Great Brittain's Proclamation of 1763 there is Granted by the said commonwealth unto Cuthbert Bullet Devisee of the said Thomas, a certain tract or parcel of land containing by survey bearing date the 24th may 1775, one thousand thirty acres lying and being in the county of Green Brier formerly Botetourt on the East side the Great Kanhaway and South side Elk river in the fork of said rivers and bounded as followeth. to wit. Beginning at a Sugar tree and poplar on Elk river and down the several courses of the same three hundred & forty poles to a large Sycamore on the point marked C. B, & up the several Courses of the said Great Kanhaway nine hundred and twenty eight poles to a white walnut and honey locust, leaving the river South twenty to a spanish oak and white oak at the foot of a Hill. North west six hundred and seventy poles to the Beginning, with its appurtenances; to have and to hold the said tract or parcel of land with its appurtenances to the said Cuthbert Bullet and his heirs forever In Witness whereof the said Thomas Jefferson Esquire Governour of the commonwealth of Virginia hath hereunto set his hand and caused the seal of the said commonwealth to be affix'd at Williamsburg on the twentieth day of November in the year of our lord one thousand seven hundred and seventy nine and of the Commonwealth the fourth

Th: Jefferson

Daniel Boone

One of America's best-known pioneers, Daniel Boone, lived for a time in Kanawha County. Born in Berks County, Pennsylvania, on November 2, 1734, Boone was the sixth of Squire and Sarah Boone's eleven children. In 1752, the family moved to the Yadkin River Valley of North Carolina, where Boone grew up.

In 1755, he participated, along with George Washington, in Braddock's Expedition against the French at Fort Duquesne at Pittsburgh. He was married to Rebecca Bryan for 56 years and fathered 10 children.

Boone moved his family to the newly colonized Kanawha Valley in early 1787 or 1788 (records are not clear about the date). He lived in a double log cabin (two rooms connected by a roofed passageway, with a porch in front) on what is now Kanawha Avenue in Kanawha City, opposite and a little below the mouth of Campbells Creek. He hunted with his friend Paddy Huddleston at Kanawha Falls and Gauley River, and practiced surveying whenever he could.

Boone and his wife had lost two sons in Indians attacks, so in the 1780s the Boones adopted a young girl named Chloe Flinn, whose parents had been killed by Indians at the mouth of Cabin Creek. A lieutenant colonel with the Kanawha Militia, Boone helped organize the county. After he was elected in 1791 as a delegate to the Virginia Assembly, he walked the entire way to Richmond to take his seat.

When the area became "too crowded," Boone packed his family on a flatboat in the summer of 1791 and floated down to his beloved Kentucky. Even the short stay at Richmond was too much for this wilderness pioneer. Although Daniel Boone was most famous for his pioneering efforts in Kentucky, his later years were spent in the midwest and Missouri, where he died in 1820.

Monument erected in 1928 by the Kanawha Valley Chapter of the DAR to honor pioneer Daniel Boone. The monument now sits just east of the Boy Scout office in the Daniel Boone Roadside Park on US Route 60 East.

Copy of Daniel Boone's original 1791 survey near the site of Point Pleasant. SWV

Daniel Boone (1734-1820).
AUTHOR'S COLLECTION

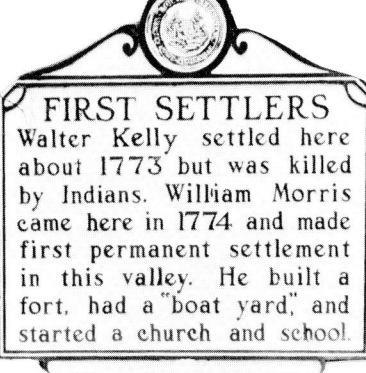

FIRST SETTLERS
Walter Kelly settled here about 1773 but was killed by Indians. William Morris came here in 1774 and made first permanent settlement in this valley. He built a fort, had a "boat yard", and started a church and school.

With Fort Lee firmly established, a plat for a new town was laid out at the mouth of the Elk sometime before 1794 on land owned by Clendenin. Two streets were named—Front, along the river, and Main, later to become Virginia Street.

Most people believe that George Clendenin named Charleston after his father Charles. Whatever the name's origin, a new town, to be called Charlestown, was authorized by the Virginia legislature on December 19, 1794. The first trustees were Reuben Slaughter, Andrew Donnally, Sr., William Clendenin, John Morris, Abraham Baker, John Young and William Morris. It would take several years before the name was shortened to Charleston and not officially adopted until 1818.

The Clendenin Family

The Clendenin clan (originally spelled Clendinen) was a prominent family that settled in Greenbrier County in 1761. The Clendenins were forced to flee during Pontiac's Uprising but returned in 1769 after Indian treaties opened up the trans-Allegheny frontier. Charles was the family patriarch and George, born in Scotland in 1746, was the founder of Charleston and the principal organizer of Kanawha County. George accompanied Andrew Lewis on his march to Point Pleasant in 1774, where he saw the Kanawha Valley for the first time. He returned in 1785 to observe construction of the "old State Road" from Lewisburg to Cedar Grove.

George became a prominent landowner in Greenbrier County, the formation of which he helped sponsor along with his father. He represented the county in the Virginia House of Delegates. While attending a session in Richmond in December 1787, he bought a 1,030-acre tract of land on the north side of the Kanawha River from Judge Cuthbert Bullitt. Bullitt had inherited this land from his brother, Colonel Thomas Bullitt, who was awarded this "western" tract at the mouth of the Elk for distinguished service in the Braddock war in 1753, and in the expedition against Fort Duquesne under General Forbes in 1758.

After Thomas Bullitt surveyed his land in 1775 he ascertained that it included 1,240 acres on the west side of Elk River and 2,618 acres opposite St. Albans.

Clendenin built a fort on his new holdings in April 1788. It was called Clendenin's Fort, then Fort Clendenin and finally, about 1792, Fort Lee after Virginia's Governor, Richard Henry Lee, a Revolutionary War hero and father of Confederate General Robert E. Lee.

Following the signing of the peace treaty with the Indians in 1794, effectively ending the Indian menace on the frontier, Fort Lee was closed as a military post and Clendenin's command was transferred to Point Pleasant. George's father died at the fort in 1790 and was buried on the grounds. George became embittered: first, by the failure of state officials to reimburse him for the money he had spent to maintain the garrison; secondly, by his rather abrupt dismissal and, thirdly, by the lack of recognition given him for his efforts to settle the frontier. He sold the remainder of his land to Joseph Ruffner in 1796 and moved to Ohio, where he died the next year.

William Clendenin also sold his land to Joseph Ruffner and moved to Point Pleasant in 1797 and later to Gallipolis Ferry in Mason County, where he died in 1828.

William Clendenin (1753-1828) was one of the founders of Charleston and Kanawha County, and a major in the militia.
FROM LAIDLEY, *HISTORY OF CHARLESTON AND KANAWHA COUNTY*, 1911

Thomas Bullitt's surveys, one above and one below the mouth of the Elk, May 1775. The 1,240 acres were left to Cuthbert Bullitt's daughters. Part of this area was eventually purchased in the early 1870s by J. Brisben Walker for his new "Elk City," now Charleston's West Side.
FROM LAIDLEY *HISTORY OF CHARLESTON AND KANAWHA COUNTY*

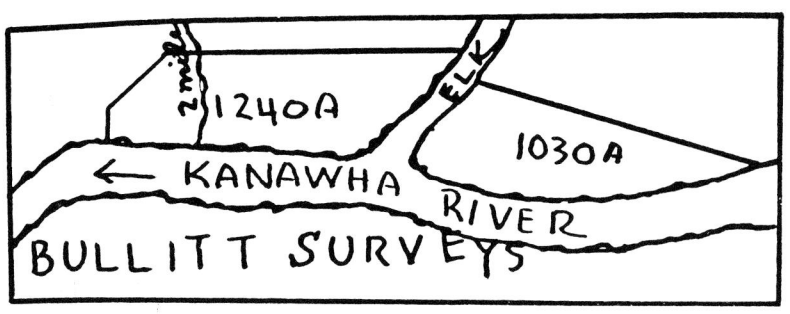

Clendenin's Fort or Fort Lee

The historic blockhouse at Fort Lee has stories to tell. After the Indian menace had passed in the early 1790s and the Clendenins had sold the fort to Joseph Ruffner in 1796, it fell into disrepair. The stockade lasted until 1815, and the blockhouse was used as a dwelling for many years. Several owners followed, including Joseph and David Ruffner, James Wilson, John Truslow, Dr. John P. Hale, Mordecai Levi and finally Thomas Jeffries.

Hale purchased the original lot and blockhouse in 1872 and moved the building to 1209 Virginia Street. In 1882 Jeffries purchased the structure, which by this time had been considerably altered. Here, Jeffries describes the final day of the historic structure: "Our family occupied this house until April 1, 1891, when it was destroyed by fire. The destruction was almost complete, but as the building fell in some of the logs rolled free and we succeeded in saving parts of two or three. From one Dr. Hale had a table manufactured as a relic of the old fort, which now stands in the collection of the State Department of Archives and History. From another section Mr. Cam Savage made two gavels one of which I presented to Kanawha Lodge No. 20 A.F. & A.M., and the other one to Odell S. Long Lodge of Scottish Rite. A small section was cut into bits of board and were retained in the family."

The fort stood for almost 103 years. The first white child born in Charleston, General Lewis Ruffner, entered the world there on October 1, 1797. The last child born there was Thomas Jeffries' nephew, Stephen Riggs, who arrived October 3, 1888.

This sundial was erected on Kanawha Boulevard in 1917 by the Colonial Dames of West Virginia in memory of Charles Clendenin. It has been relocated to the Lee Street Triangle. KCL

A small table made from logs salvaged from Fort Lee's blockhouse (Clendenin's mansion house), at the W.Va. State Museum, Cultural Center, Charleston. SWV

Monument erected in 1915 at the site of Fort Lee by the Kanawha Valley Chapter of the DAR. The plaque in this photo was placed on the boulder in 1930, and it perpetuates the myth of Anne Bailey. SWV

The home of prominent Charleston businessman, C.C. Lewis of Lewis, Hubbard & Co. at 1202 Kanawha Street, was built on the site of Fort Lee in the late 1800s.
1907 CHARLESTON DIRECTORY

The Myth of Anne Bailey

One of the most widely told stories of the Fort Lee era is the ride of "Mad Anne" Bailey to bring ammunition to the embattled garrison from Lewisburg. Bailey, born Anne Hennis in England about 1742, made her way to Staunton, Virginia, laboring as an indentured servant. She married Richard Trotter, who had served in Braddock's campaign. Trotter was killed at the Battle of Point Pleasant. Vowing to avenge his death, Anne dressed in men's clothes and became a courier and scout along the frontier, where she got her nickname.

Between 1789 and 1791, the story goes, Fort Lee was besieged by Indians. When the defenders inside ran low on ammunition "Mad Anne" volunteered to make a dangerous ride to Lewisburg to replenish stocks, which she did with great dispatch. Roy Bird Cook, however, doing research for his book *The Annals of Fort Lee*, could find no basis in fact whatsoever that there had ever been a "siege" of Fort Lee or a ride to Lewisburg to secure munitions. Nonetheless, Bird's book doesn't seem to have dampened enthusiasm for the legend at all.

In 1785, "Mad Anne" married John Bailey in Lewisburg and the couple supposedly moved to the Kanawha Valley (but not, as some have stated, to Fort Lee). John Bailey died in October 1794. Anne lived the last of her days with her son, William Trotter, near Point Pleasant. She died in 1825 near Gallipolis, Ohio.

Anne Bailey.
COURTESY OTIS K. RICE

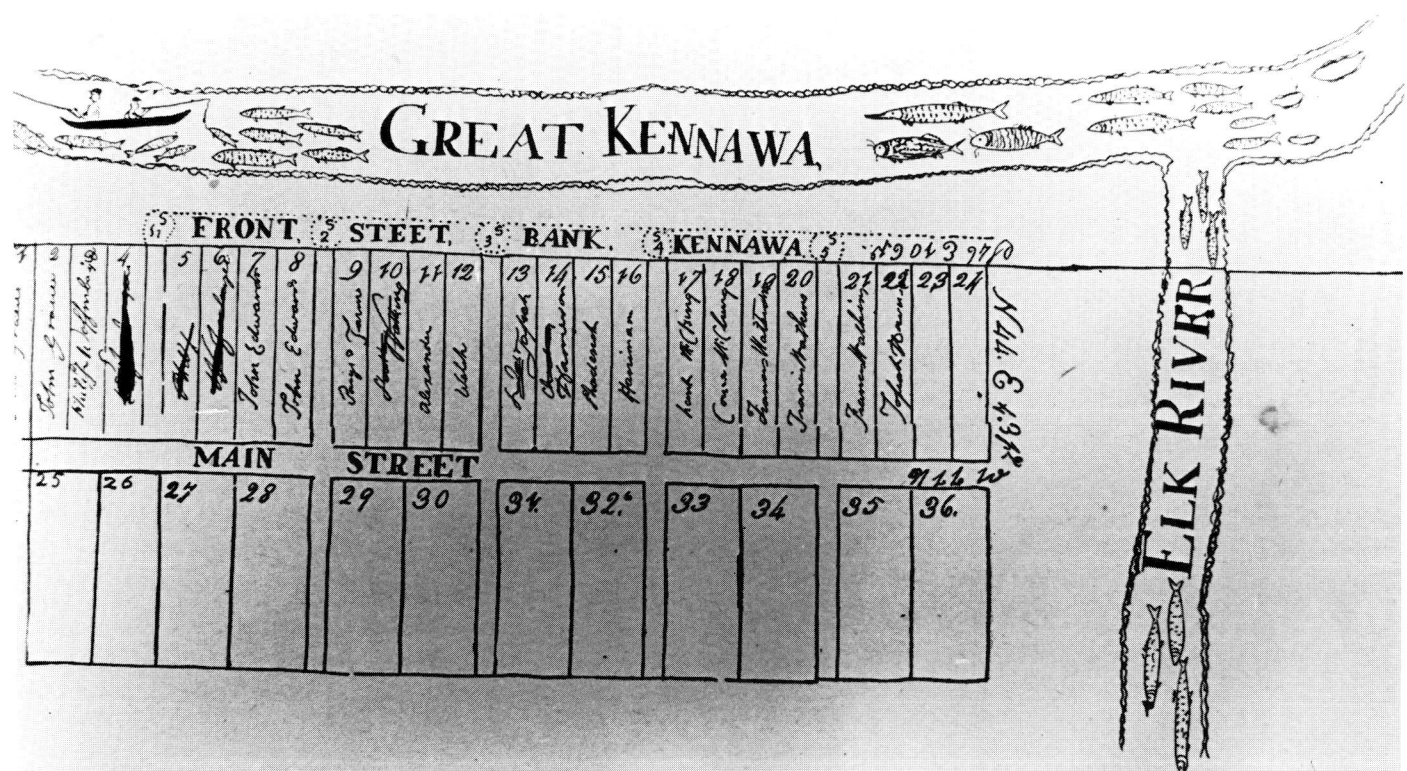

Alexander Welch's plat for a town he simply called "town at the mouth of Elk." The surveyor of Greenbrier County, Welch was hired by the land's owner, George Clendenin, to survey the area before Charleston was established in 1794. The plat contained 36 lots, and it was later extended to Dunbar Street by Kanawha County's first surveyor, Reuben Staughter.
FROM LAIDLEY, *HISTORY OF CHARLESTON AND KANAWHA COUNTY,* 1911

Kanawha County's Early Pioneers

You can't spend a day in Kanawha County without brushing up against reminders of the pioneers. Their names are everywhere: on street signs, on maps, on the buildings. The parks and creeks and forests are named after them and their descendants pass you on the street. It's not surprising, considering the economic history of the county, that the most prominent of the county's first settlers were involved in the salt business.

Young Family. John and Keziah Young. Keziah was the daughter of Lewis Tackett who built Tackett's Fort at St. Albans. The Youngs survived an Indian attack on the fort and escaped at nightfall by canoe to the safety of Fort Lee. John Young came to the Kanawha Valley in the 1780s. The Youngs raised 11 children.

Laidley Family. The Laidley family was one of the county's most prominent. James Grant Laidley, from Wood County, married Harriet Quarrier of Richmond. Their son, James Madison Laidley, moved to Kanawha County in 1840 with his wife Annie and built "Glenwood" in 1852. Their son, George S., served as Superintendent of Charleston schools from 1878 to 1922. John Osborn Laidley was a prominent Cabell County lawyer. His son, William Sydney Laidley, was also a lawyer. William was active in Kanawha County government and wrote an important book on county history in 1911. Descendants of the Laidley-Quarrier family have been influential in community affairs for many years.

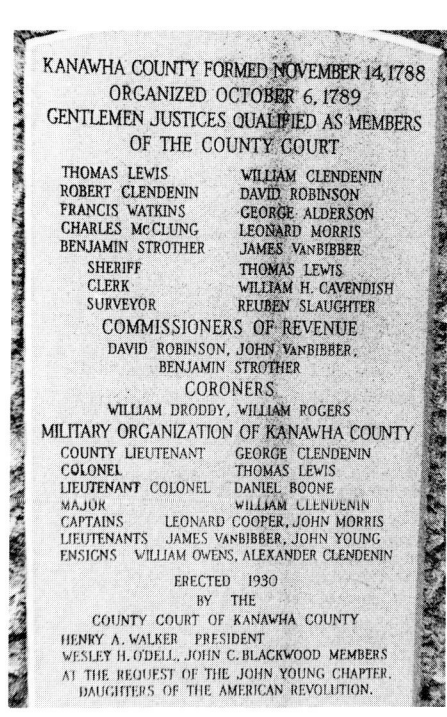

Whitteker Brothers. William Whitteker arrived in the valley about 1800 and spent his life as a fur trader, salt maker and merchant. Aaron Whitteker arrived in 1810 and was one of Charleston's first merchants. He was also a prolific builder of early homes and commercial structures. The McFarland home, built in 1835 by William's son Norris, still stands at 1310 Kanawha Boulevard.

James C. McFarland. He moved to Charleston in 1813 and became one of the town's first merchants on Front Street. He served in the Virginia legislature in the 1820s and had considerable land holdings in the area. In 1832 he became president of the county's first bank, the Bank of Virginia.

George Alderson. He was one of the original members of the Kanawha County Court and one of the first sheriffs. His father, John Alderson, Jr., was a minister and is thought to have discovered Burning Springs. The present courthouse stands on the lot first owned by George Alderson.

Noyes Family. Noyes has been a prominent name in county history since Issac Noyes, one of four brothers, first came to the valley in 1804. Brothers Bradford, Charles and Franklin followed. The brothers got involved in the salt and retail business and became prominent in civic affairs.

Joseph Lovell. Colonel Lovell was a lawyer, salt maker and merchant who came to Charleston about 1815. His step-father, Major James Bream, joined him in 1816 and they became large landowners in Charleston. At one time Bream owned all of the land from Elk River west to Elk Two Mile. In 1818, Joseph married Bettie Washington Lewis, a descendent of George Washington's sister.

Quarrier Family. One of the best-known families in the Kanawha Valley. Alexander Quarrier emigrated from Scotland to America in 1774, served in the Revolutionary War, moved to Richmond, Virginia in 1786 and to the Kanawha Valley in 1811. He was a member of the Kanawha County Court. His son, Alexander W., was clerk of the county court and the Circuit Superior Court of Law and Chancery. William A., son of Alexander W., was a lawyer, member of the Kanawha Riflemen and a state legislator. The family was instrumental in the development of Charleston and the Kanawha Valley.

Dickinson Family. Another very prominent family in the early development of the county, especially in the Malden area. Joseph Dickinson was the patriarch. His son, William, and William's partner, Joel Shrewsbury, established the Dickinson and Shrewsbury Company around 1810 and went into the salt business. Prior to the Civil War, they were the largest salt producers in the area. The Dickinson family continued in the business until 1945. William's son, John Quincy Dickinson, was one of the founders of the Kanawha Valley Bank in 1867 and later became bank president.

Shrewsbury Family. Well-known early salt producers, Samuel, Jr. and John Shrewsbury, married the daughters of Colonel John Dickinson, who had received a land grant at Campbells Creek which was the start of the county's giant salt industry. Joel Shrewsbury was associated with William Dickinson in the salt business in Malden.

Dr. Spicer Patrick. One of the valley's early civic leaders, Patrick came to Charleston in 1816 after earning a medical degree. He was one of the earliest, and largest, land owners on the west side of Elk River. Not only was he a delegate from Kanawha County to the Virginia legislature and a member of the Virginia Secession Convention of 1861, where he voted against the Ordinance of Secession, he was also a member of the Kanawha County Court and the first Speaker of the House of Delegates of the new state of West Virginia.

Colonel John Reynolds. One of the early officers of the Kanawha County Court. He became county clerk in 1793 and served as a delegate to the Virginia legislature in the early 1800s. He was a major land owner in Charleston, and a founding member of the Kanawha Salt Company.

The Goshorn Family. George Goshorn moved to Charleston in 1822 and became a well-known businessman, hotel owner, and ferry operator on the Kanawha River. Two of his sons, John H. and William F., opened a dry goods store in 1839. It later offered groceries and hardware and changed its name to the Goshorn Hardware Company.

James H. Fry. Fry came to Charleston in 1818, became a lawyer and later a salt maker. He was a deputy sheriff, sheriff for four terms and served three terms in the Virginia legislature.

The Morris Family. One of the oldest and largest families in the county. William Morris, Sr. settled at Cedar Grove in 1774. His sons settled other areas of the county. Leonard moved to the mouth of Lens Creek, now Marmet, and John to the south side of the Kanawha River opposite Campbells Creek. William, Jr., fought in the Battle of Point Pleasant, was one of the first trustees of Charleston and served as a delegate to the Virginia legislature. He lived at Kelly's Creek and was buried at Virginia's Chapel at Cedar Grove. His son, William Morris III, invented certain salt drilling tools, which were later adapted for use in the oil business. Leonard Morris was also a veteran of the Point Pleasant battle, one of the first justices of the new Kanawha County Court, and, in 1798, became sheriff. Levi Morris, another son of William, Sr., was considered the founding father of the town of Montgomery. Another son, Benjamin Morris, was also an early settler in Montgomery. John Morris fought in the Battle of Point Pleasant and was along on George Rogers Clark's expedition to open up the Northwest Territory in 1778 and 1779. Morris was a Kanawha County militia captain and one of the first trustees of Charleston. The descendants of William Morris, Sr. have been prominent in county affairs for generations. One of the best known is Morris Harvey, benefactor of the college which bears his name.

Aaron Stockton. Came to the Kanawha Valley with his brother-in-law, William Tompkins, after the War of 1812. Stockton became a salt maker, then moved to Kanawha Falls where he established a ferry and sawmill.

Colonel Andrew Donnally, Sr. emigrated from Ireland to the Valley of Virginia in 1750. Donnally constructed Donnally's Fort at Lewisburg in 1771, and was appointed Sheriff and County Lieutenant of Botetourt County, and County Lieutenant of Greenbrier County. He was a trustee of Lewisburg when it was incorporated in 1782. Donnally moved to Point Pleasant, and then to Charleston, where he was one of the first two delegates to the House of Delegates in Richmond in 1790, and again in 1803. One of the first trustees of Charleston, Donnally owned a lot of land, especially in the Kanawha City area. He was one of the early and largest salt makers, and in 1820, he brought the first steamboat up the Kanawha River to Charleston. When Donnally died about 1825, his son Andrew Donnally, Jr. inherited his father's civic and business interests and became a prominent figure in early county government. swv

Kanawha County from 1738 to 1851
Maps from Edgar B. Sims, *Making A State*

AS OF 1738

AS OF 1780

AS OF 1790

AS OF 1800

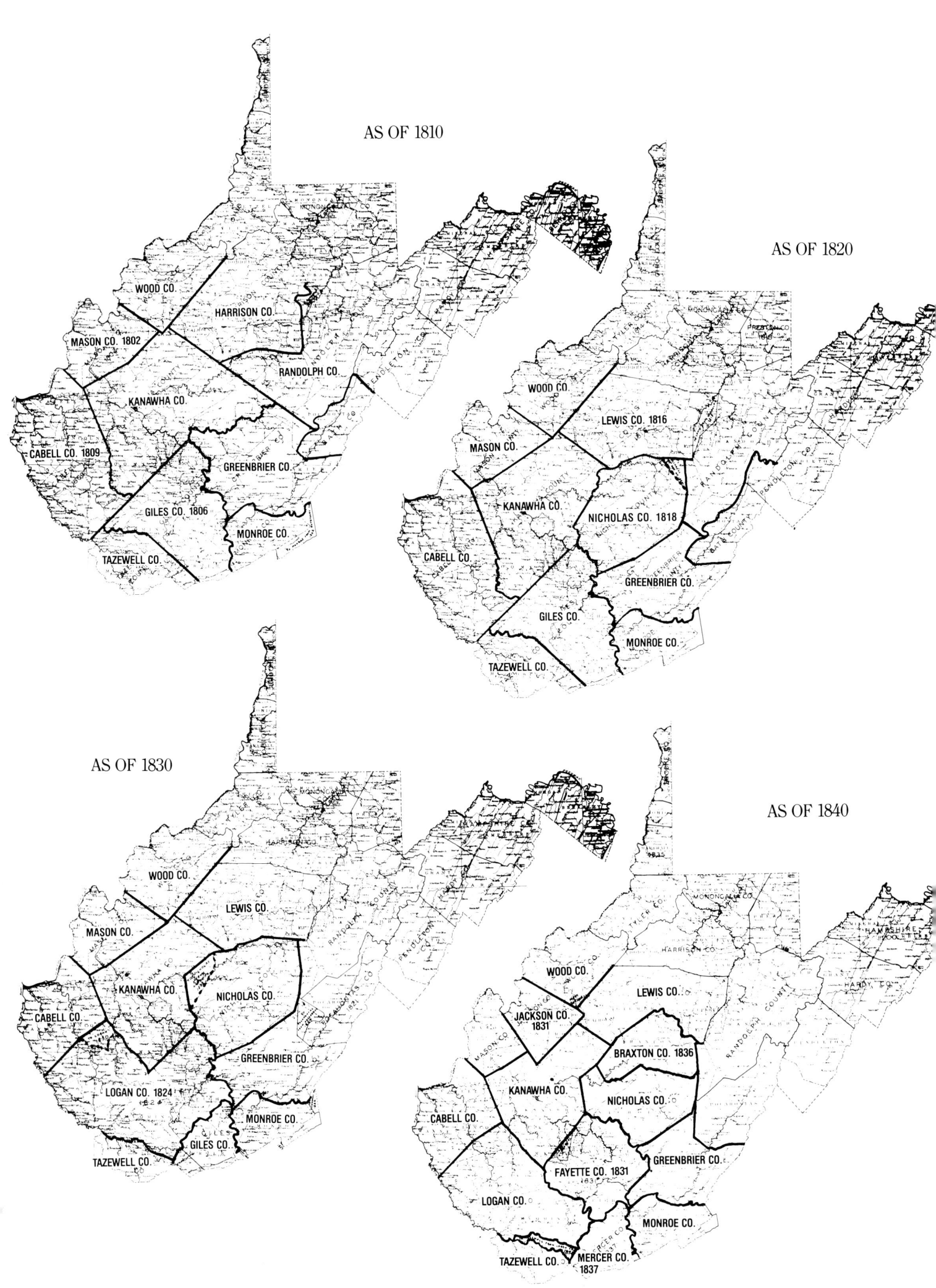

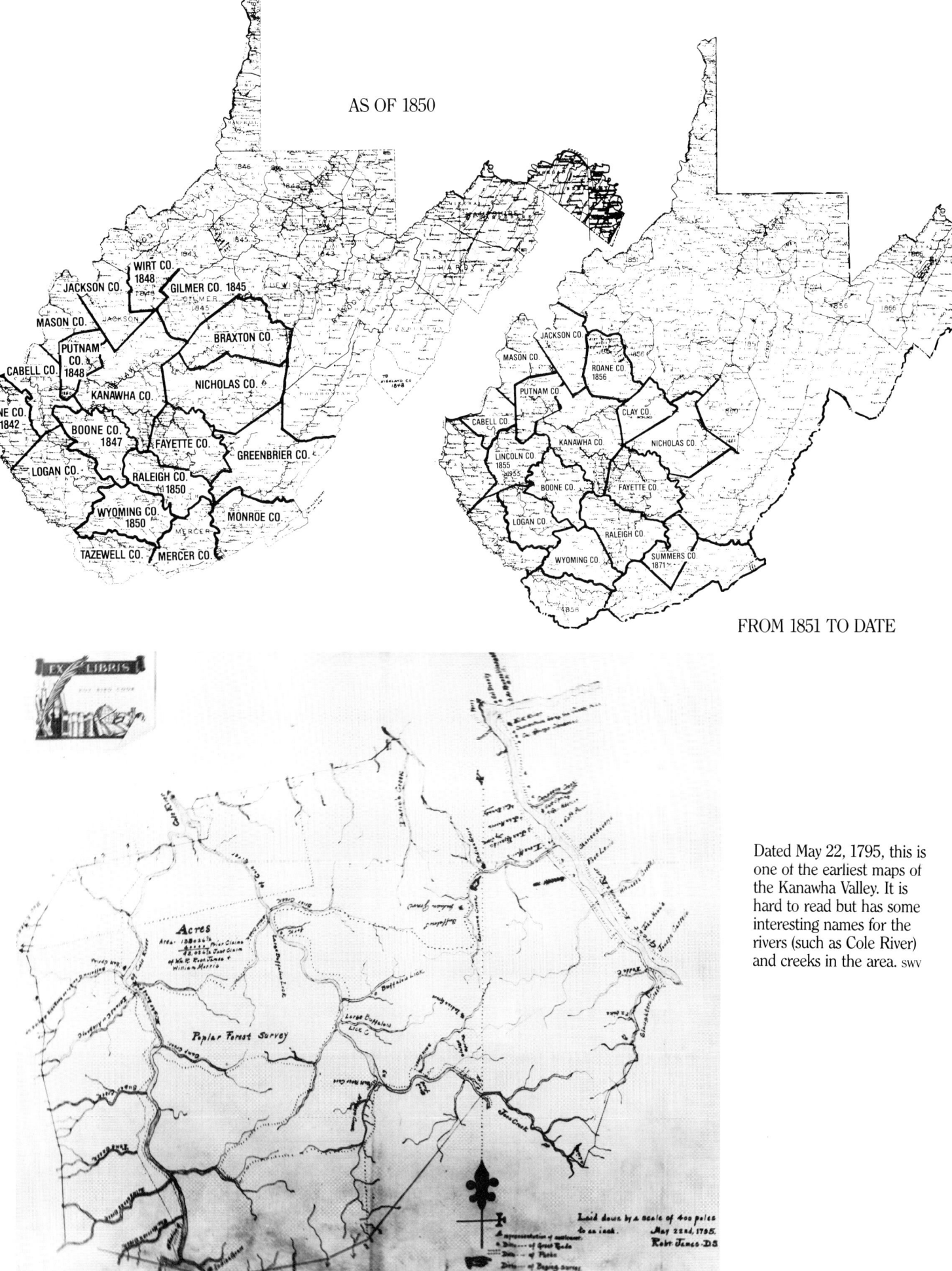

AS OF 1850

FROM 1851 TO DATE

Dated May 22, 1795, this is one of the earliest maps of the Kanawha Valley. It is hard to read but has some interesting names for the rivers (such as Cole River) and creeks in the area. swv

This painting of the Charleston riverfront was done in 1854 and appeared in Parish, *Art Work of the Kanawha and New River Valleys,* 1897. The town had a little over 1,000 people and a number of buildings, churches and dwellings clustered in the present-day downtown area. The center of the painting is the present-day levee.

Chapter Three
Life in the County: 1800-1860

Life in the County: 1800-1860

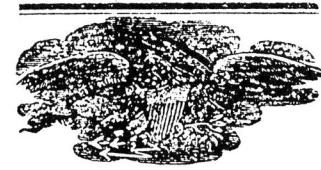

THE BANNER.

FRY & LEWIS,
WILL give Fifty cents a Bushel for good merchantable wheat, delivered in their Mill, or Forty-five cents a bushel for such wheat, at the water's edge or landings of the Farmers, on the Kanawha river; provided it is put in good salt-barrels. They will pay the neighborhood market price for the barrels in *goods*.

In all cases the wheat to be paid for on the miller's receipt and certificate of quality.

So far as persons, letting them have their crops, may want flour for their own family use, they will give a barrel of flour for six and a half bushels of wheat, the farmer furnishing the barrel.

They have on hand a general assortment of Summer and Fall Goods, Groceries, Provisions, &c. which they will sell low for cash or country produce.

Coal's Mouth, Aug. 1831.   48

NEGROES FOR SALE.
THE SUBSCRIBER wishes to sell 8 or 10 likely Negroes, consisting of 1 man, 4 women and several children from 1 to 10 years old. Persons wishing to purchase will apply to
FRANCIS THOMPSON.
Coal's Mouth, Aug. 1831.

"Charleston was beautifully situated and finely ornamented with shade trees. There are a greater number of comfortable dwellings than are usually met with in western towns of the same population. The external appearance of the village is enough to satisfy anyone that it contains much respectable and cultivated society, where true Virginia hospitality may surely be found."

—Editor of *The Cincinnati Chronicle, 1831*

At the beginning of the nineteenth century, several hundred people were scattered up and down the Kanawha Valley, but the population was concentrated around the new town of Charleston, where there were about 65 residents, 12 houses, a jail and courthouse. The threat of Indian violence had passed, and people were now occupied with establishing the local commerce and industry. A post office, named the Kanawha Court House, was established at Front and Hale streets in 1801. The salt works were just getting started in the Campbells Creek area that later became the center of business and population in the county.

Joseph Ruffner owned most of the area between the Elk River and the present capitol, which he bought in the late 1700s from the Clendenin brothers. Ruffner had extensive land holdings in other parts of the county, which increased when he purchased the Dickinson Tract around the Campbells Creek area.

James Wilson and Andrew Donnally were also large landholders in the early 1800s. As these large landowners ventured into the salt business, wealth in the county began to accumulate amongst a few families.

For several decades, Charleston grew slowly while its neighbor to the east, Kanawha Salines, became the center of activity. At the western edge of the present county Thomas Teays inherited the "Teays Grant" in the Coalsmouth area. In 1800, Teays built a log cabin on the west side of the mouth of Coal River, and he obtained a franchise to establish a ferry. Teays also built an inn to serve travellers on the "Old State Road" that passed his property.

Since 1794 George Clendenin had operated a ferry across the Kanawha River, and when Joseph Ruffner bought Clendenin's land, he took over the ferry operation. George Goshorn later ran a ferry service across the river for many years.

By 1810 there were 3,866 residents in the county, including 352 slaves. Charleston had 100 residents, and the bulk of population was concentrated in the salt-producing area east of town. Slaves, brought in by settlers from eastern Virginia, had been in the county almost since its formation, and they were mainly domestic servants. The early saltmakers did not employ slaves, they relied instead on the white workers who migrated to the valley from the east. The War of 1812 depleted this work force, however, and slaves were brought in to do heavy manual labor. The big salt concerns such as Shrewsbury and Dickinson, Andrew Donnally, the Ruffners, William Tompkins and Franklin Noyes employed as few as 20 to as many as 100 slaves.

Originally a game trail that was also used by various Indian tribes, the "Old State Road" was improved from the east to the Ohio River. A few years later, this became the James River and Kanawha Turnpike. After the road was improved mail arrived every two weeks from the east, and taverns and hotels, such as Buster's Tavern at the corner of Court and Front streeets, sprang up to house the weary travellers.

Much of the county was still a frontier, except for the more settled areas along the Kanawha Valley. The rest of the county was largely unsettled until after the Civil War, when improved transportation allowed men and machinery to penetrate the rugged, heavily forested drainages.

Dr. John Eoff was the first resident doctor in the area in 1811, and the first court was held in 1809. The first established merchant in Charleston—Henning and McFarland General Mercantile—opened in 1813. In 1815 the first commercial sawmill was established on Elk Two-Mile to supply lumber for the growing salt industry. Mercer Academy, the county's first school of higher education, opened in 1818. That same year, the first newspaper, *The Kanawha Spectator* was published, which was soon followed by *The Kanawha Patriot, The Western Courier* and *The Western Register*, all of which were short-lived. The first library was formed in 1823. In 1825 the first drugstore west of the Alleghenies, the well-known Rogers Drugstore, was started on Front Street by Henry Rogers. The drugstore stayed in the family until 1909, when it was purchased by Dr. T.B. Stalnaker. The drugstore did business well into the 1950s. The Bank of Virginia opened a branch office in 1832, which was housed in a dignified, columned building on Front Street. James C. McFarland was the bank's founder and its first president. When James Wilson was drilling for salt near present-day Brooks Streeet in 1815, he struck natural gas—the first gas well drilled in the U.S.—which later became a major industry in Kanawha County.

The old log courthouse was replaced in 1817 by a brick building which was the seat of county government for the next 75 years. In 1818 an act passed by the Virginia General

WB A p 31

Amount brought forward —
19 Stacks of hay at $6 per ton — stacks supposed in the aggregate to contain 38 tons — — 228 00

Blackwell Chilton
Dr. J. N. Clarkson
John Hansford Jr.

A List of Slaves of the Estate of David Hudson Decd

One negro man named	Jesse	20 00
One " " "	Sam	300 00
One " " "	Andy	400 00
One " Woman "	Delphy	150 00
One " " "	Hannah	300 00
One " " "	Maria	300 00
One " Boy "	Lewis	400 00
One " " "	Warren	400 00
One " " "	Armstead	360 00
One " " "	Fountain	250 00
One " " "	Simon	300 00
One " " "	Alexander	150 00
One " " "	Shadarack	100 00
One " " "	Stephen	100 00
One " Girl "	Lizzy	150 00
One " " "	Mary	300 00 $3970 00

Blackwell Chilton
Dr. J. N. Clarkson
John Hansford Jr.

At a Circuit Superior Court of Law and Chancery for Kanawha County held at the Court House thereof on the 21st day of June 1845 — The foregoing Inventory and appraisement bill of the Estate of David Hudson decd was presented in Court and ordered to be recorded.
Teste A. W. Quarrier clk

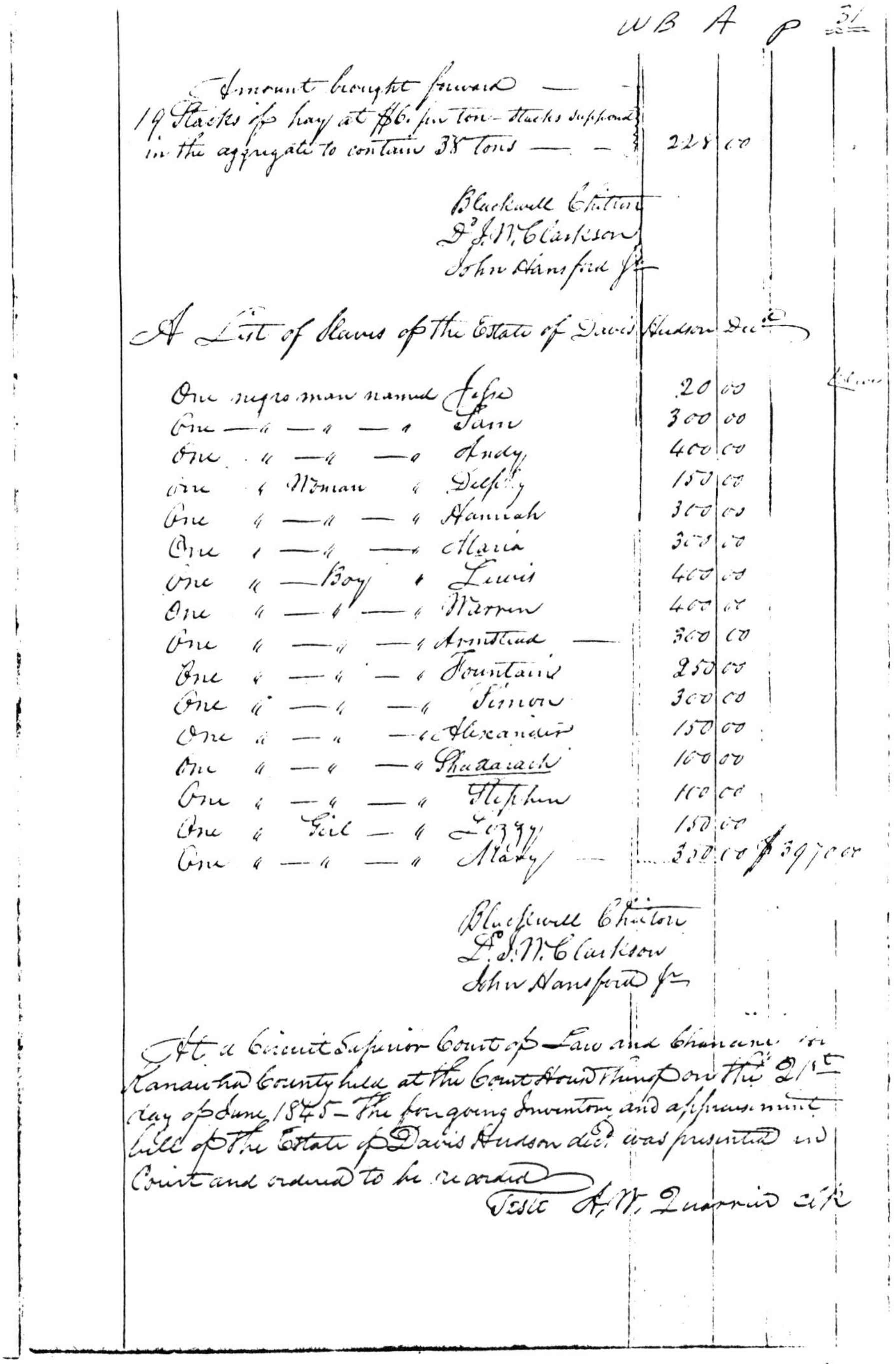

List of slaves from the estate of David Hudson, dated June 21, 1845, on file in the records of the Kanawha County Clerk and Recorder. Hudson owned 16 slaves at the time of his death worth $3,970. The document was signed by A. W. Quarrier, clerk at the time.

Assembly formally established Charleston as a corporate entity, and the name Charlestown was officially changed to Charleston. The law established the procedures for electing seven people to serve as the town's officers. One of the first city ordinances severely restricted the movement of slaves within the town. By 1820 Charleston had a population of 500, which was small in comparison to Kanawha Salines.

As early as 1829, the people of Kanawha County and other western Virginia counties felt neglected by the Richmond government, and a state constitutional convention was held in October 1829 to address these issues. Kanawha County's delegate to the convention was Judge Lewis Summers. Some reforms were made, but they did not satisfy the westerners' demands.

The Kanawha Valley suffered some severe floods in the 1800s: the first in 1822, another large one in 1840, and the worst in 1861. In 1844, an unusual hurricane-like wind travelled in a narrow path down Ferry Branch and across the Kanawha River to knock the top story off a brick building on Kanawha Street. A cholera epidemic swept through the valley in 1849 that killed whites and slaves alike.

Dismal looking places with bare, unhospitable-looking mountains, from which all the timber has been cut.

—Author Anne Royall

Charleston's first mayor, Jacob Goshorn, was elected only four months before Federal troops moved into Charleston following the Battle of Scary Creek in July 1861. Goshorn surrendered the town to the Federal troops, then fled south for the remainder of the war. He returned after the war to resume his business career.
OFFICE OF THE MAYOR, CHARLESTON

By 1840 Charleston had more than 1,000 residents. The salt industry boomed, and fine homes were built on the banks of the Kanawha River, and more and more businesses opened up. In 1850 the county's population had increased to 15,353, which included 3,140 slaves and 212 free blacks. The bulk of the population was still concentrated in the areas around the salt works.

A second constitutional convention took place in Richmond in October 1850, and George W. Summers and Benjamin H. Smith were Kanawha County's delegates. Additional reforms were passed for the benefit of the western residents. The east-west problems persisted, however, until 1863, when the state of West Virginia was created. In the 1830s, Stephen Teays and Philip Thompson constructed a covered, toll bridge that crossed Coal River at Coalsmouth on the James River and Kanawha Turnpike. The first bridge over the Elk River was built in 1852.

According to the 1860 census, there were 1,500 people in Charleston. The industries in the county thrived. Salt was shipped downriver to western cities. And in 1856, coal was shipped downriver from the mines along the Kanawha River's tributaries in the eastern part of the county, and from mines along Coal River in the west. Cannel coal from the Coal River area and the Elk River area near present-day Clendenin and Paint Creek was a growing business. Navigational improvements on the Kanawha and Coal rivers made it easier and more efficient to transport commodities downriver to western markets.

A new Virginia law passed in early 1861 enabled the citizens of Charleston to elect a mayor, a recorder and councilmen, to levy taxes and to extend the city's boundaries. For the first time, Charleston's citizens reaped the benefits of self-rule. By this time, the town's boundaries had been extended east to present-day Bradford Street and north to the Piedmont Road area. From Bradford Street to the present state capitol, and west of Elk River there were a few houses and farms.

The Civil War completely changed the character of Kanawha County. The rather complacent, "old South" atmosphere in Charleston, and the county as a whole, came to an end when the nation became divided during the terrible conflict between the North and South.

This is possibly the earliest known impression of Charleston (1836). It was published in Howe *Historical Collections of Virginia*, 1845. It shows Kanawha Street looking west from present-day Capitol Street. Buildings on the right include the Branch Bank of Virginia (columned portico), McFarland's Kanawha House tavern (with the four chimneys) and the Summers Building. On the left include Captain James Wilson's Ferry, James A. Lewis' store and post office and Aaron Whitteker's store (where present levee is now). WVU

WESTERN VIRGINIAN.

THE PROSPERITY OF OUR COUNTRY.

BY MASON CAMPBELL. CHARLESTON, (KANAWHA COUNTY,) WEDNESDAY, DECEMBER 20, 1826. VOL. I.—NO XXIV

ESSAYS UPON FRENCH SPOLIATIONS.

WITH

Some Observations upon the importance of Commerce.

By Fitzsimmons, a Native of Pennsylvania.

No. XVII.

During the invasion of Egypt by Bonaparte, in the year 1799, he entered into a contract with a commercial house at Algiers, to supply the French army with grain.

These supplies it appears were regularly furnished to a very great amount; but difficulties having arisen with respect to a settlement of their accounts, a large sum remained due to them, at the time Bonaparte left Egypt.

Finding no prospect of obtaining their lawful demand, the House at Algiers at length applied to their own government to interpose its authority in support of their claims.

It is understood that Napoleon offered to indemnify them, provided the Algerine government would adopt some hostile measures against England.

Be this however as it may, under various pretexts, payment was never made during Napoleon's reign.

After the restoration of the Bourbons, This claim was renewed by the Algerine government, and was eventually admitted, and provision made for it between France and Algiers.—The French Minister of Finance, in his annual budget for the year 1820, asked and obtained of the two Chambers, a grant of six million of Francs, to carry into effect this treaty, or in other terms, to provide for *this claim, which was actually paid.*

Thus we see, that not only the subjects of all European Monarchs have been indemnified by France, but the piratical government of Algiers, has obtained indemnity for its subjects, whilst the citizens of the United States, who have been robbed of millions, of the fruits of their industry, are alone left without redress.

Spirit of '76, whither hast thou fled.

No. XVIII.

At the commencement of these essays, several important parts of the Convention of 1800, were quoted as a foundation, upon which we build our rights to indemnity from France.

Through oversight, the 9th article of that Convention, which is *permanent* in its nature, was omitted

That Article is in these words—"Neither the debts due from individuals of one nation to individuals of the other, nor shares or monies which they may have in the public funds, or private Banks, *shall ever in any event of war, or National difference, be sequestered and confiscated*

If, in the event of war, private property, which had arrived in France previously thereto, could not be sequestered or confiscated, how much greater right have we to restitution of that which came in, under the protection of a treaty, during profound peace—a peace which has never since been interrupted?

But without a treaty, the established usage of Nations is, to respect private property, found on land when war is declared. At the commencement of hostilities between Great Britain and France, in the year 1793, the French Government seized all British property, found in France. Convinced of that injustice, the present French Government stipulated to make restitution, by the treaty concluded at Paris, in May, 1814. This stipulation which formed an additional article to the Treaty of peace, may be found in Niles' Register, for August, 1814, and is in the following words:

"There shall be granted by both the Powers, immediately after the ratification of this Treaty of peace, a release of all sequestrations which may have been put since the year 1792, upon all the funds, revenues, credits, or other effects, whatsoever, of the high contracting parties of their subjects."

Although this article had the *appearance* of being mutual, it operated altogether in *favor* of Great Britain.

By virtue of this article of the Treaty, a gross sum was paid by France to Great Britain, who appointed Commissioners to divide it amongst the claimants Thus we see that France has done an act of justice to her old enemy, which she denies to a nation, who always treated her as a friend.

No. XIX.

The *right* of the citizens of the United States to indemnity from France, it is presumed has been fully established. The next subject to consider, is her *ability* to make restitution.

A most mistaken idea exists in the minds of many of our countrymen that France is so exhausted by wars, that she is unable to indemnify us.

It is true, the allied powers imposed upon her heavy contributions, but the greater part of the money paid to them, was expended within her own territory.

France, possessed of thirty-five millions of inhabitants—with the finest climate and the most fertile soil in Europe—with a population as ingenious as industrious—as distinguished in arts as in arms: though she may have been momentarily depressed, *can never be poor.*

Twelve years of peace and prosperity have enabled France to regain her wealth and recover her strength. She has risen like a giant, refreshed by his slumbers.

No greater proof can be required of her resources, than a knowledge of the fact, that her annual revenue amounts to, from eight hundred and fifty to nine hundred millions of francs—equal from one and sixty, to one hundred and seventy millions of dollars, which is collected without difficulty.

This immense and annual revenue is not liable to fluctuate, as it is principally derived from internal taxation, the duties accruing from foreign commerce, not furnishing more than eight per cent of this sum.

Admitting therefore the amount of their claims upon France, since the Louisiana Convention, to be fifteen millions of dollars—it would not require the tenth part of one year's revenue to discharge the whole of them.

The French Ministry could obtain a loan any day they pleased, sufficient to pay our whole demands.

Nothing therefore is wanting on their part, but a sense of justice.

At present, there is but little prospect of their being influenced by such consideration.

Appeal after appeal has been made to their justice, but without effect.

Mr Gallatin's labours in behalf of the claimants are before the public, who are competent to judge of the zeal and ability with which he maintained their rights.

Mr. Brown, his able and efficient successor, also takes a deep interest in vindicating the rights of his injured fellow citizens.

But without some coercive measure on the part of Congress, the claimants have but little to expect.

My next number will close these essays, in the form of an address to our National Legislature.

No XX.

To the Honorable the Senate and House of Representatives of the United States of America, when in Congress assembled.

May it please your Honorable Body—

Since the introduction of Christianity, the most important event which has occurred in the world grew out of a spirit of *commercial enterprize.*

The Republic of Genoa derived her wealth and consequence from her commerce; and, although she was not in a situation to furnish Columbus with the means of giving immortality to his name, she gave him a nautical education, and an undaunted spirit of commercial enterprize, to which we owe the discovery of America.

To a like commercial spirit, we are in a great measure indebted for the unexampled prosperity of this great and growing Empire. Commerce has caused our wilderness to blossom like a rose.

A foreign market for the surplus produce of our soil has converted millions of uncultivated acres into fertile plains

Our commerce visits every clime, & whitens every sea. The annual exports of the United States fall but little short of One Hundred Millions of dollars!

Nearly one fourth in value, of the returns of this immense commerce, is paid in duties, into the public treasury, and employed in defraying the expenses of our National Government, thus exempting our *soil* from taxation. Commerce is the parent of Liberty. To prove this, we need not refer to Carthage or other ancient Republics. We need only cast our eyes towards the late Spanish possessions in our Southern Hemisphere. For ages, the ports of these colonies had been sealed against foreign commerce, during which time their inhabitants groaned under the yoke of an iron despotism. The invasion of Spain, however, left them free to throw open their ports to the trade of all nations. Commerce, freighted with Freedom, no sooner unfurled her banners, than man recovered his lost dignity. A group of degraded colonies became a confederation of Sovereign and Independent States. So intimately is a spirit of Freedom identified with a spirit of commercial enterprize, that liberty can never die whilst commerce survives.

It is needless to mention the influence of Commerce in civilizing, refining, and in multiplying the social relations of men. A distinguished author observes that "*Commerce is the golden girdle of the Globe.*"

These observations on the importance of Commerce, are made, with a view of showing its claims to National protection. But, whilst Commerce enriches the public treasury and invigorates public liberty—while it enhances the value of our soil, and rewards the hand which cultivates it—whilst it affords employment and competence to the artizan and mechanic—whilst, by giving extended circulation to wealth, it creates occupation for the arm of industry, in a thousand various forms—in fine, whilst commerce promotes the general prosperity of the nation, it is a melancholy reflection, that the great majority of those who pursue it as a profession, enjoy the least of its benefits, Where one Merchant acquires an independence by commerce, alas! how many are engulphed in the vortex of Bankruptcy!!!

These misfortunes are sometimes occasioned by sudden changes in foreign markets—sometimes by fluctuation in the value of the circulating medium at home. Often by misplaced confidence, and frequently by the injustice of foreign powers. Losses of the latter description have given birth to the present address.

During the late wars in Europe, numbers of our fellow citizens, confiding in the relations of peace and amity subsisting between the United States and France, and relying upon the faith of the law of Nations, as well as the solemn obligations of a public treaty, embarked largely in foreign Commerce, particularly to the continent of Europe.—It is not intended here, to go into *details* of the various depredations committed upon our lawful Commerce, by the Government of France.—At present it is only necessary to state.—That between the years 1807 and 1810, property belonging to the citizens of the United States, to the amount of Three Millions of Dollars, was sequestered by the French Government at Antwerp, at St Sebastian, and in Holland, which was afterwards disposed of, *without even the form of a trial,* and the proceeds thereof, employed to defray the public expenses of France.

That in various instances, the ships & cargoes of our fellow citizens were burnt upon the high seas, without even the form of a trial.

That a large amount of American property, was condemned by the Emperor *himself,* in direct violation of the existing treaty, as well as of the universal principle of the law of nations, which prohibits a Sovereign from becoming the judicial interpreter of his own edicts.

That where condemnations took place by the regular tribunals, in most instances, the forms of law were totally disregarded, and the proceedings of the French Courts, become a mere judicial mockery.

That notwithstanding these flagrant violations of our rights as an independent nation, no redress has been obtained from France.

What aggravates this injustice is, that not only the subjects of all the Monarchs of Europe, who had demands against France, have been indemnified; but the subjects of the piratical government of Algiers, have also received indemnity for their claims.

This appeal to your Honorable Body, does not proceed from any want of confidence in our present Chief Magistrate. His illustrious talents, and past zeal in the cause of the claimants are sufficient pledges that nothing on his part will be wanting to obtain them justice. But without the authority of Congress, the moral power of the Nation, is all that the Executive can wield. Its physical powers, the Constitution has wisely confided to the National Legislature.

Therefore to the wisdom of Congress alone, can the claimants appeal, for a vindication of their violated rights.

A free Government is a mutual compact, wherein allegiance is exchanged for protection.

Your injured fellow citizens have fulfilled, and continue to fulfil, their allegiance to their government, and in return, they ask of your Honorable Body, that protection, which they consider that their allegiance entitles them to claim.

FITZSIMMONS.

Instinct.—The following fact goes far towards proving that instinct differs chiefly in degree from reason:—A few years since, a pair of sparrows, which had built in the thatch roof of a house at Poole, were observed to continue their regular visits to the nest long after the time when the young birds take flight. This unusual circumstance continued throughout the year; and in the winter, a gentleman who had all along observed them, determined on investigating its cause. He therefore mounted a ladder, and found one of the young ones detained a prisoner, by means of a piece of string or worsted, which formed part of the nest, having become accidently twisted round its leg.—Being thus incapacitated from procuring its own sustenance, had it been fed by the continued exertions of its parents.

WOMAN.

"*Daughter of God and Man.*"—MILTON.

There is a language of the heart
That mocks all learning's studied art,
There is an utterance of the soul
That laughs at scholarship's controul,
Breathes forth in verse a living thought,
With feeling, love, and nature fraught:
Woman's the theme, and who would e'er require
One borrowed string to animate his lyre?

There is a witchery that lies
Within the sunshine of her eyes,
More potent than the magic spell
Of talisman, or fairy dell.
Who has not felt her very name
Inspire his heart and thrill his frame?
Idolatry! the frowning world may cry,
But who has loved nor felt the ecstacy?

O who has ever in that hour,
When Woman's love and Woman's power
Have twined their influence round his heart
Felt not that Woman can impart
By smile—or glance—or smothered sigh,
A world of bliss and constancy?
Priestess of love! how oft thou'rt left to mourn
Man's perfidy—forsaken and forlorn.

There is a vigil in the sky
That marks the villain's perjury;
How can he hope to be forgiven
Who breaks on earth his vow to Heaven?
He wedded in this world may be,
But Hell, like his inconstancy,
Will echoing yell the oath that fires his breath,
And brand it in the registry of death.

Pleasure's poor and gaudy toy,
A forgery on solid joy,
A gilded chain that drags the slave
Helpless and childless to the grave,
The haunted Libertine, who lies,
Without one hand to close his eyes,
Sighs to the passing breeze his dying groan,
Compassionless—unwedded and alone.

Man has a wandering heart—his soul
Spurns fetters, slavery and controul—
To-day he climbs the snow-clad steep,
To-morrow ploughs the foamy deep—
And now he roams the mountain side,
Without a friend—without a guide,
Till Woman bids his way-ward steps to cease
And turns his Arab thoughts to home & peace.

Woman! companion of my life,
Less lov'd when maiden than when wife;
How fondly do I sing to thee,
Of wedded love and constancy.
Dear mother of my child, I trace
Thy emblem in her artless face—
I clasp the lisping babe, receive a kiss,
And feel a father's love—a father's bliss.

'Tis Woman's voice in accents low,
That hushes first the infant's wo;
'Tis woman's fond maternal arms
That shield her boy from vain alarms;
Uprear him in a world of cares,
And save him from its countless snares.
Nurse of mankind! I fondly view in thee
The watchful guardian of our infancy.

Now would I Woman's Friendship sing—
Oh! 'tis a pure undying thing!
The dew that gems the blossom'd thorn
Shines brightest in the sunny morn;
But faithful Woman can bestow
A light to gild the night of wo!
Her love, like moon beam on a stormy sea,
Sheds o'er cares its own serenity.

I've found the world a faithless thing;
Man's friendship weak and perishing,
Man's friendship?—'Tis the ocean's spray;
The froth that rude winds sweep away!
You ask where constancy can rest;
Go find it in a Woman's breast!
I would not give one fair, lov'd friend I boast
For all the Wealth of India's golden coast!

When pale disease, with all her train,
Fevers the blood and fires the brain,
'Tis Woman's sympathetic art
Quells the wild throbbing of the heart;
The mortal pang, the burning sigh,
In nature's latest agony!
O fair physician! thou art ever near,
With oil and wine the drooping frame to cheer

I ask not, on the bed of death,
Proud MAN to watch my fleeting breath;
Let WOMAN'S prayer embalm the hour!
For oh, it has a soothing power,
To calm the awful struggle here,
To brighten hope and banish fear;
To raise new prospects of a land on high,
Where death is swallowed up in Victory!

Strength of Sword Fish.—During the passage of the Sarah, West Indiaman, from Jamaica, her crew felt a smart shock, as if the ship had struck on a rock, and it was expected that she would leak. No leak, however, occurred: and on her arrival in the West India Docks, a short time back, when her cargoe was taken out, it was found that she had been struck by a sword fish near the keel. Such was the extraordinary force of the animal, that its spike had penetrated through the copper, through the plank, and had gone through three inches into a hogshead of sugar laying at the bottom of the vessel. The Sarah Wad has been obliged, in consequence, to go into a dry dock for repair.

The last number of the London Westminster Review contains an elaborate, extensive, and severe article on the conduct of the *Greek Committee* formed in London in 1823 It refers, in the following terms, to the New York agency in the equipment of vessels for Greece:

Among the largest items by which the expenditure of the received loan is accounted for, is the sum of £155,000, employed in America for the building of frigates. Nothing but infatuation, gross ignorance, or dishonesty, will serve to account for this strange misappropriation of the Greek money. At a moment when instant assistance to Greece is all important—at a moment, too, when it is within our knowledge that many ships of war, cheap, and ready for sea, were to be found in European ports, a *cavalry officer* is engaged, at an enormous salary, and despatched to the United States, with vague instructions—inconsistent, too, with the orders of the Greek Government; and, after spending £155,000 in the erection of two frigates, it is discovered that a very large sum, not less than £50,000 more, is waiting to complete them; and the result is, that both of them, got confiscated as security for the debt for which they are said to be responsible. The most favorable result that can now be anticipated is, that one should be sacrificed to save the other; and the Greeks will possess a frigate at a price for which all the annals of official jobbing present to parallel."

MASONIC NOTICE.

THE BRETHREN of Kanawha Lodge No. 104. are hereby notified to assemble at the Masonic Hall, in Charleston, on Wednesday the 27th instant, at 9 o'clock, A M for the purpose of celebrating the anniversary of St John the Evangelist Transient Brethren are invited to attend.

By order of the W. M.

MASON CAMPBELL, Sec.

Dec. 13. [23.

FEMALE EDUCATION.

THE SUBSCRIBER informs the public that her School for the instruction of YOUNG LADIES, will again be opened, after a short recess, on the 1st day of January next, at her residence near the Mouth of Coal. Her course of instruction embraces Orthography, Reading, Writing, English Grammar Geography, History, and plain and ornamental needle work.

Possessed of some experience in teaching, and anxious to make the instruction of Youth her permanent business, she assures Parents and Guardians, that every means within her power, will be used, to promote the moral and intellectual improvement of her Pupils; at the same time, that the strictest attention will be paid to their deportment and manners.

Her terms for a Session of 5 months, are, 10 dollars for Tuition, and 40 dollars for Board, including Washing and every expense, except Bedding, which each young Lady is expected to furnish for herself.

ELIZA R. FRY.

Rose-Mount, Dec. 10, 1826.

Take Notice.

I FOREWARN all persons from trading for a note or bond of seven hundred dollars, given by me to Mrs. Mary Forqueran, administratrix of the estate of John Forqueran, and now in the hands of Peter L. Forqueran

ARTHUR FORQUERAN.

Oct 14, 1826.

New Store in Charleston.

ROGERS & SHREWSBURYS

ARE now opening in Judge Summers' Brick Store, an extensive and well assorted stock of Fall and Winter DRY GOODS, (entirely fresh); which, together with a general assortment of

Groceries,
Hardware &
Queensware,

they will sell low for Cash, or in exchange for such articles as may suit.

N. B.—WANTED TO PURCHASE, 4 or 5 Flat Boats, and 1000 empty Salt Barrels. October 16, 1826.

Take Notice.

THE Firm of BRIGHAM & NOYES is now dissolved by mutual consent of the members of the firm. They are anxious to realize all debts which may be due to it, and for this purpose have placed their claims in the hands of Benj. H. Smith Atty. for collection, who, unless they are speedily settled, is directed to commence suit upon them.

ISAAC NOYES.
BRADFORD NOYES,
FRANKLIN NOYES.
WILLIAM BRIGHAM.

Nov. 30, 1826. [22

COURTESY CARL WOLFE

KANAWHA REPUBLICAN.

E. W. NEWTON, Editor and Proprietor. CHARLESTON, KANAWHA COUNTY, VIRGINIA, DECEMBER 7, 1858. VOLUME XVII---NUMBER 49

BUSINESS CARDS.

Dentistry. DR. B. P. BELKNAP; RESIDENT DENTIST.

MILLER & NEWMAN. ATTORNEYS AT LAW,

N. & H. FITZHUGH, ATTORNEYS AT LAW.

AMISS & LOOMIS, Attorneys at Law, PARKERSBURG VA.

CARR & READ, ATTORNEYS AT LAW,

PARKS & MOSELEY.

JOHN S. SWANN, Attorney at Law,

FITZHUGH & MOORE, ATTORNEYS AT LAW,

V. HENDRICK,

MOORE & GALLUP, ATTORNEYS AT LAW.

M. J. FURGUSON, ATTORNEY AT LAW,

DR. WATKINS & SON.

ALEX. T. LAIDLEY

J. M. & Rich'd Laidley. Attorneys at Law.

BARKSDALE & READ, Tobacco Commission Merchants, RICHMOND, VA.

FORREST HOUSE, FRONT ST. NEAR S. B. LANDING. Guyandotte, Va.

MALDEN HOUSE.

AMERICAN HOUSE, Steamboat Landing, GALLIPOLIS, O.

LAW FIRM.

SOMETHING FRESH.

R. W. POINDEXTER, GENERAL COMMISSION AND FORWARDING MERCHANT,

W. F. & J. H. GOSHORN,

SPRING & SUMMER GOODS,

The Hardware Department

Dr. George Van de Linde

LEMUEL H. SARGENT, Commission Merchant, AND PRODUCE DEALER,

GREASE YOUR MACHINERY.

MALDEN SCHOOL.

PICKETT Tobacco Warehouse, LOUISVILLE, KY.

PAPER HANGINGS.

SHINGLES.

JUST RECEIVED.

Poetry.

HE'S COMING.

Select Story.

The Hunter's Reward.

THE BOONE WAGONER.

Temperance Facts.

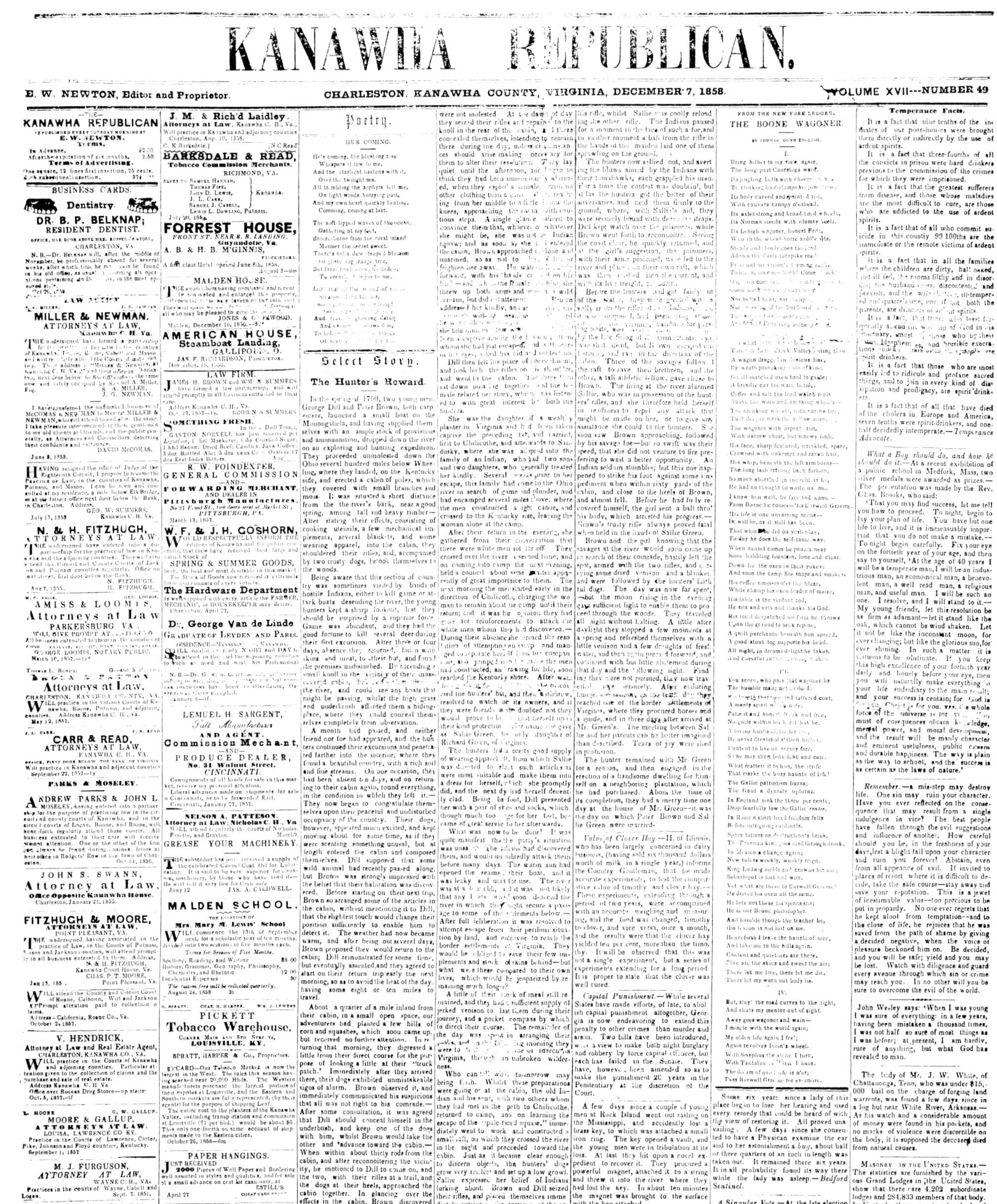

This December 7, 1858 issue of the *Kanawha Republican* is interesting reading, especially the ads where a number of well-known names appear, some of which are still with us. COURTESY CARL WOLFE

VIRGINIAN -- Extra.

CHARLESTON, Va., November 5, 1852.

GLORIOUS NEWS!
UNPRECEDENTED TRIUMPH!
The Whig Party Anihilated!!!
NOT A "SLIDE," BUT AN AVALANCHE!!
PIERCE & KING SWEEP THE UNION!!!!

The following telegrapeic dispatch was received late last night:

State	Majority	For
INDIANA,	20,000 majority for	Pierce!!
OHIO,	15,000	do do
MAINE,	12,000	do do
CONNECTICUT,	3,000	do do
MARYLAND,	5,000	do do
N. YORK CITY,	10,762,	do do
NEW ORLEANS,	100,	do do

SECOND DISPATCH.

We received this morning at 10 o'clock the following additional returns showing that New York, Pennsylvania, Massachusetts, Michigan, Delaware &c. have probably all gone for Pierce and King; most of them by unprecedented majorities. Thus far Scott has not received a single State.

The following are from regular reporters for the city Press in Baltimore.

VIRGINIA—Richmond, Scott's majority 840, whig gain; Henrico, Scott's maj. 150; Lynchburg, Scott's maj. 45; Petersburg, Pierce's maj. 121, whig loss 245; Norfolk, Pierce's maj. 400; Portsmouth, Pierce's maj. 160; Chesterfield, Pierce's maj. 350; Alexandria, Scotts maj. 64, whig loss 150, Fredericksburg, Scott's maj. 42 whig loss.

KENTUCKY—One report says doubtful, another says returns show a steady whig gain—over last governor's election. Louisville, Pierce 2,795, Scott 2,722, Pierce's maj. 73; Fayette co., Scott's maj. 500, Nelson co., Pierce's maj. 500.

MARYLAND—Baltimore, Pierce's maj. 4,477; returns from the country show State gone for Pierce by 3 to 4 thousand majority.

PENNSYLVANIA—Philadelphia city and county, Pierce's maj. 1,000, whig loss 11,000; Allegheny co., Scott's majority 2,000, whig loss 1500 York co, returns, democratic maj. 6, gain several hundred; Washington, Pa., democratic gain in district 3 ···; Fayette co., democratic gain of 400. Returns show that Pennsylvania has gone for Pierce by unreasonably large majorities. Reporter says New York city gives Pierce about 10,000 maj., Pierce has carried the State by about 20,000 maj.

DELAWARE—Wilmington, Pierce's maj. 200; Newcastle co., 82 gain for Pierce, State doubless gone for Pierce.

MASSACHUSETTS—In Boston, Pierce gains 6,136 over Taylor's vote, and State has probably gone for Pierce.

MICHIGAN—Gone for Pierce largely.

OHIO—Lucas county gives Scott State for Pierce.

MAINE—Gone for Pierce.

NEW HAMPSHIRE,—Gone for Pierce.

MISSOURI—St. Louis, Pierce 1,000 majority; Jefferson city, Pierce 67 majority; Weston, Scott 11 maj.; St. Joseph's, Pierce 62 maj.

TENNESSEE—Nashville, Scott 500 maj.; Memphis, Scott gains 254 over Taylor.

NEW ORLEANS—Unexpected democratic gains; Baton Rouge, Scott 81 maj., whig gain.

Great ☞Whig☜ Land Slide in Kanawha!

Democratic vote more than doubled!!

Democratic gain on Governor's vote last Fall 754!

The following is the full vote of Kanawha county:

	Scott.	Pierce.
Kanawha C. H.	405	194
Kan. Salines	206	76
Brookes' Store	96	26
Fandy	73	54
Given's	48	65
Slat Woods	15	54
Aultz's	33	58
Atkinson's	17	19
Forks of Coal	68	70
Coal Bridge	48	53
Richard's	59	22
Gatewood's	57	23
Harper's	33	05
Lowes'	40	26
Dog Creek	30	25
	1228	773
	773	
Scott's majority	455	

Democratic gain in the county over the vote for governor last Fall 754

MASON COUNTY—Scott's majority 64.

PUTNAM—Pierce's majority 25.

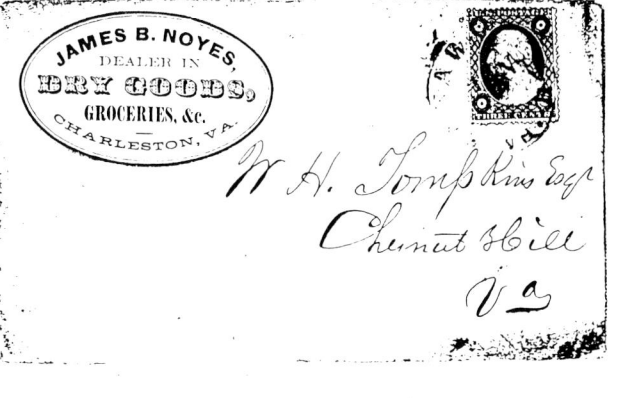

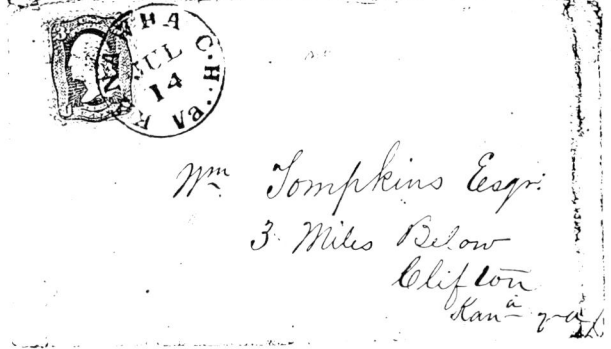

COURTESY RICK HAMILTON

Kanawha County's First Legal Execution

On January 23, 1858, Susan Turley, the wife of former Baptist preacher, Preston Turley, was reported missing. The authorities first thought that she had drowned in a nearby river. But further investigation revealed that Mrs. Turley, the mother of three children, had had trouble with her husband. Although Turley told an incoherent story about discovering that his wife was missing, the neighbors who were familiar with the family's troubles, suspected that she was murdered.

A search party dragged the river and found her body attached to a heavy stone. Her neck had been broken, and her forehead was severely wounded. The husband had several explanations for his wife's murder but finally it became obvious that he had committed the crime. Preston Turley was arrested and brought to trial in June 1858. The court handed down a guilty verdict and sentenced Turley to hang. Turley escaped from the rather crude jail, but he was soon captured, and his execution was set for September 17, 1858, at Ferry Branch across the Kanawha River from the courthouse.

Excitement grew as the time for the county's first execution drew near, and all the town seemed determined to witness this gruesome event. Some enterprising citizen, who realized that the Goshorn Street ferry would be inadequate to transport the public, decided to build a bridge across the river and charge the public for crossing. This first man-made bridge across the river was made up of a number of salt barges roped together with boards laid on top as a roadway.

Sheriff Slack rode with the prisoner in a wagon and local citizens walked along as guards. Turley sat on his coffin and waved to people he knew in the crowd. His mother, father, and his two oldest children stood on the gallows as he was hanged.

Lewis Summers (1778-1843) was a native of Fairfax, Virginia, and an older brother of George W. Summers. Summers made his first trip through the Kanawha Valley in 1808, and in 1813 he purchased a home site in Putnam County, which he called Walnut Grove. In 1819, he became a judge of Kanawha Circuit Court, where he presided until his death. Summers also served in the 1817 Virginia Assembly, and in the 1829-30 Virginia Constitutional Convention. He was instrumental in building the first Episcopal Church in Charleston in 1834. SWV

A stock certificate probably issued for a new coal company, circa 1850s. SWV

George W. Summers (1807-1868) was a prominent politician in Kanawha who served in the Virginia House of Delegates, U.S. House of Representatives and the Virginia State Reform Convention of 1850-51. He was also the Wig candidate for governor of Virginia in 1851, but lost the election. In 1861 he was a Virginia commissioner to the Washington Peace Conference and represented Kanawha County in the 1861 Virginia Succession Convention where he voted against succession. He remained neutral during the Civil War. SWV

Benjamin H. Smith (1797-1887) was a prominent lawyer in Charleston before and after the Civil War. Smith served in both houses of the Virginia legislature, the 1850-51 Virginia Constitutional Convention, and the West Virginia House of Delegates. He was defeated by the incumbent governor of West Virginia, in the 1866 gubernatorial election. From 1869-70, Smith was also president of the Statehouse Company, which built the first capitol building in Charleston.
COURTESY OTIS K. RICE

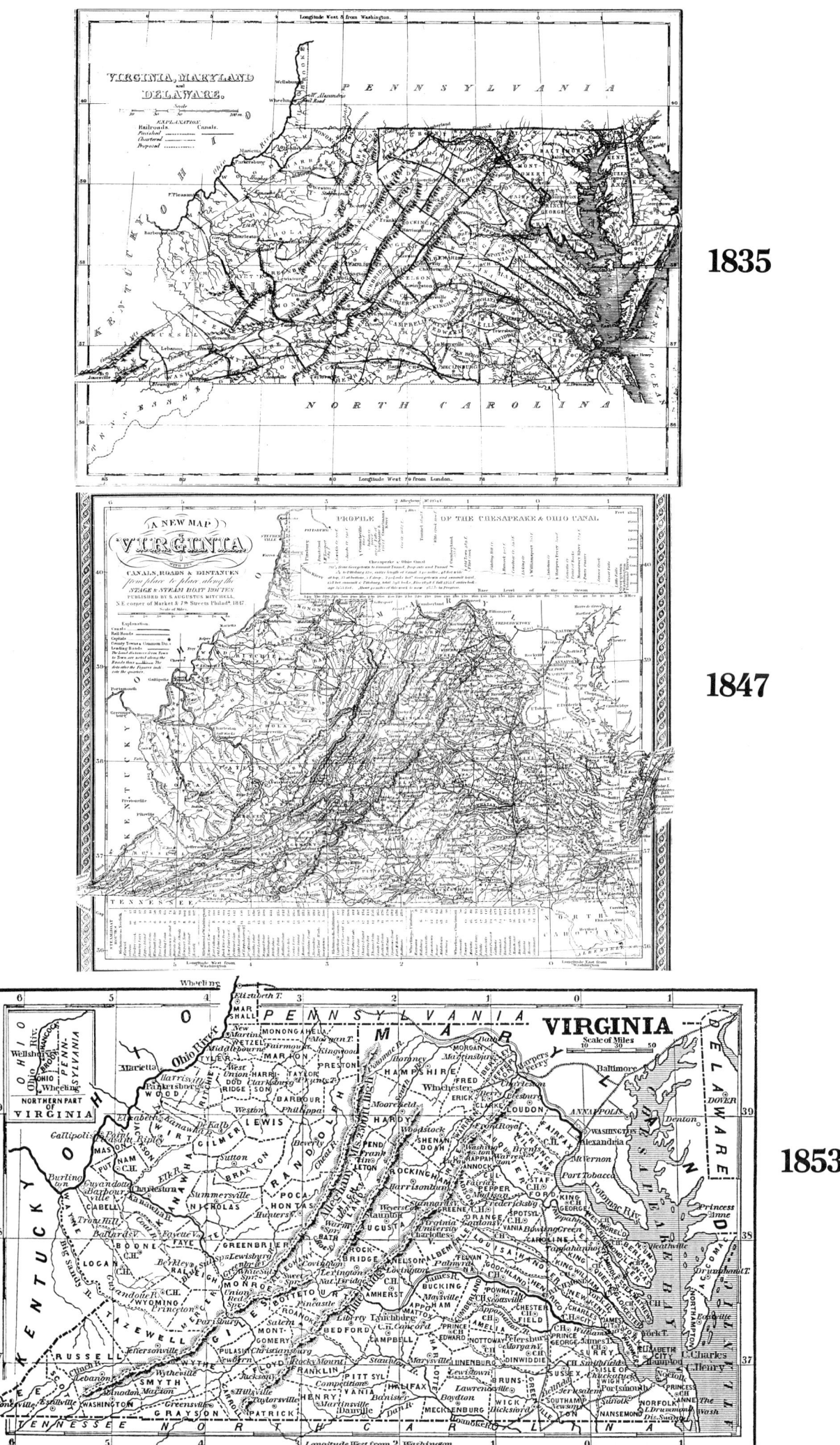

Malden, the center of the salt industry, was first known as Terra Salis, later as Kanawha Salines, and still later as Malden—the present name. In its most prosperous days salt furnaces were in operation on both sides of the river, extending about fifteen miles above the town, and furnished employment, directly and indirectly, to about 3,000 persons.

AMERICAN JOURNAL OF SCIENCE, 1836

View of the "

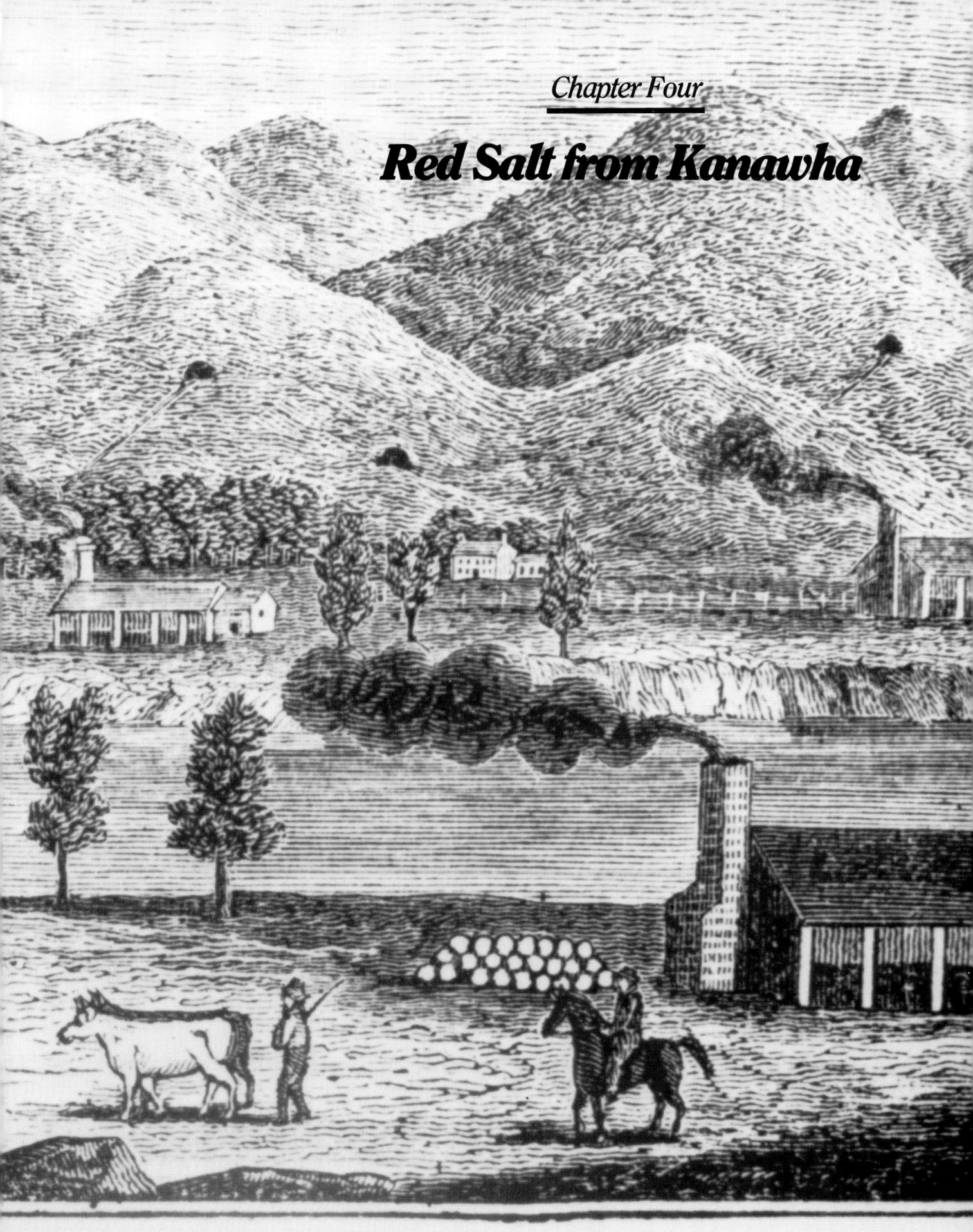

Chapter Four
Red Salt from Kanawha

"...nawha Salines."

Location of Salt Furnaces in the Kanawha Valley
{1797—1868}

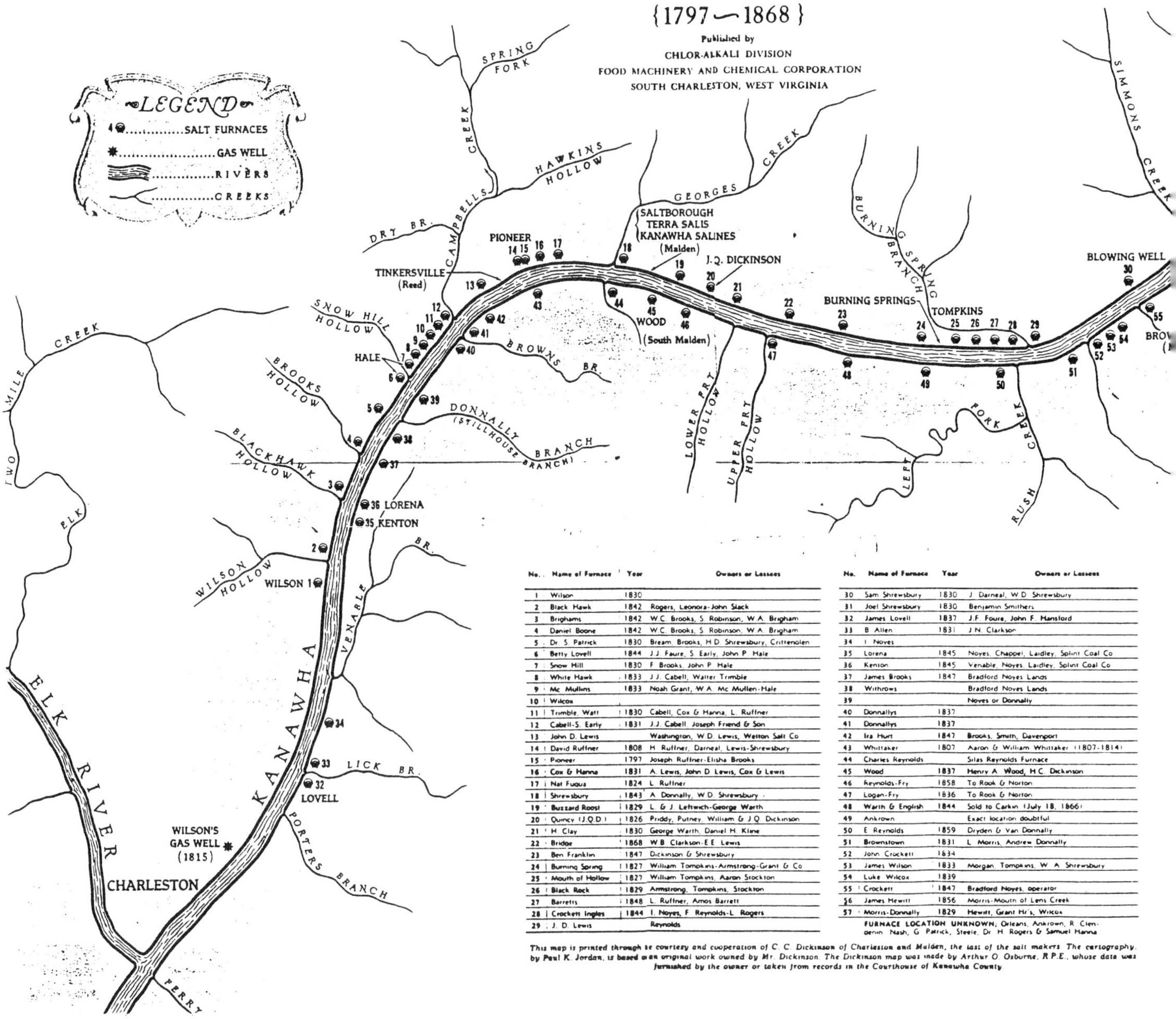

Published by
CHLOR-ALKALI DIVISION
FOOD MACHINERY AND CHEMICAL CORPORATION
SOUTH CHARLESTON, WEST VIRGINIA

No.	Name of Furnace	Year	Owners or Lessees
1	Wilson	1830	
2	Black Hawk	1842	Rogers, Leonora-John Slack
3	Brighams	1842	W.C. Brooks, S. Robinson, W.A. Brigham
4	Daniel Boone	1842	W.C. Brooks, S. Robinson, W.A. Brigham
5	Dr. S. Patrick	1830	Bream, Brooks, H.D. Shrewsbury, Crittenden
6	Betty Lovell	1844	J.J. Faure, S. Early, John P. Hale
7	Snow Hill	1830	F. Brooks, John P. Hale
8	White Hawk	1833	J.J. Cabell, Walter Trimble
9	Mc Mullins	1833	Noah Grant, W.A. Mc Mullen-Hale
10	Wilcox		
11	Trimble, Watt	1830	Cabell, Cox & Hanna, L. Ruffner
12	Cabell-S. Early	1831	J.J. Cabell, Joseph Friend & Son
13	John D. Lewis		Washington, W.D. Lewis, Welton Salt Co
14	David Ruffner	1808	H. Ruffner, Darneal, Lewis-Shrewsbury
15	Pioneer	1797	Joseph Ruffner-Elisha Brooks
16	Cox & Hanna	1831	A. Lewis, John D. Lewis, Cox & Lewis
17	Nat Fuqua	1824	L. Ruffner
18	Shrewsbury	1843	A. Donnally, W.D. Shrewsbury
19	Buzzard Roost	1829	L & J. Leftwich-George Warth
20	Quincy (J.Q.D.)	1826	Priddy, Putney, William & J.Q. Dickinson
21	H. Clay	1830	George Warth, Daniel H. Kline
22	Bridge	1868	W B Clarkson-E.E. Lewis
23	Ben Franklin	1847	Dickinson & Shrewsbury
24	Burning Spring	1827	William Tompkins-Armstrong-Grant & Co
25	Mouth of Hollow	1827	William Tompkins, Aaron Stockton
26	Black Rock	1829	Armstrong, Tompkins, Stockton
27	Barretts	1848	L. Ruffner, Amos Barrett
28	Crockett Ingles	1844	I. Noyes, F. Reynolds-L. Rogers
29	J. D. Lewis		Reynolds
30	Sam Shrewsbury	1830	J. Darneal, W.D. Shrewsbury
31	Joel Shrewsbury	1830	Benjamin Smithers
32	James Lovell	1837	J.F. Foure, John F. Hansford
33	B Allen	1831	J.N. Clarkson
34	I Noyes		
35	Lorena	1845	Noyes, Chappel, Laidley, Splint Coal Co
36	Kenton	1845	Venable, Noyes, Laidley, Splint Coal Co
37	James Brooks	1847	Bradford Noyes Lands
38	Withrows		Bradford Noyes Lands
39			Noyes or Donnally
40	Donnallys	1837	
41	Donnallys	1837	
42	Ira Hurt	1847	Brooks, Smith, Davenport
43	Whittaker	1807	Aaron & William Whittaker (1807-1814)
44	Charles Reynolds		Silas Reynolds Furnace
45	Wood	1837	Henry A. Wood, H.C. Dickinson
46	Reynolds-Fry	1858	To Rook & Norton
47	Logan-Fry	1836	To Rook & Norton
48	Warth & English	1844	Sold to Carbin (July 18, 1866)
49	Ankrown		Exact location doubtful
50	E Reynolds	1859	Dryden & Van Donnally
51	Brownstown	1831	L. Morris, Andrew Donnally
52	John Crockett	1834	
53	James Wilson	1833	Morgan, Tompkins, W.A. Shrewsbury
54	Luke Wilcox	1839	
55	Crockett	1847	Bradford Noyes, operator
56	James Hewitt	1856	Morris-Mouth of Lens Creek
57	Morris-Donnally	1829	Hewitt, Grant Hr's, Wilcox

FURNACE LOCATION UNKNOWN: Orleans, Ankrown, R. Clemenin Nash, G. Patrick, Steele, Dr H. Rogers & Samuel Hanna

This map is printed through se courtesy and cooperation of C. C. Dickinson of Charleston and Malden, the last of the salt makers. The cartography by Paul K. Jordan, is based on an original work owned by Mr. Dickinson. The Dickinson map was made by Arthur O. Osburne, R.P.E., whose data was furnished by the owner or taken from records in the Courthouse of Kanawha County.

A typical flatbottom boat, similar to those used on the Kanawha River for transporting salt from Kanawha Salines downriver to western markets. Some of these were floated all the way to New Orleans, where they were sold for their lumber. Hundreds of these boats were built on the Kanawha and Coal rivers before the Civil War to transport thousands of barrels of salt. These boats were 50 to 75 feet long and 10 to 18 feet wide. Later models were built twice as large.

COLLOT, A JOURNEY IN NORTH AMERICA, ATLAS, 1826

Red Salt from Kanawha

Long before the large salt makers took hold in the Kanawha Valley, the early settlers discovered they could distill salt in kettles from brine taken from the surface pools in the area. Hunters also took notice of the salt brine because game collected around pools, attracted to the salt. By 1780 Thomas Jefferson, Virginia's governor, issued a patent to George Washington and Andrew Lewis for 250 acres of land around the Burning Springs area, just above present-day Malden. After a rain, water collected in holes in the ground, and when natural gas bubbled up into these holes, it would be ignited. Washington willed the land to his nephew, Lawrence Augustine Washington, and in 1839 it was sold to the Dickinson and Shrewsbury Company.

The commercial manufacture of salt began in the Kanawha Valley in 1797 when Elisha Brooks devised a crude but effective method of producing salt in bulk. On the land adjoining the salt spring that he leased from Joseph Ruffner, Brooks produced up to 150 pounds of salt per day by sinking several gums, or hollowed-out logs, into the ground and dipping out the brine with a bucket attached to a long pole on a pivot. Brooks did no settling or purifying, so the salt contained many impurities. This was the beginning, however, of a vast industry that spurred the economy, settlement, and development of the Kanawha Valley.

This local salt became known as the "red salt from Kanawha" because of its iron impurities, and earned a reputation for its strong, pungent taste and superior qualities for making butter and curing meat.

Large scale salt production began in 1807 when David and Joseph Ruffner, Jr. used an iron drill with a chisel bit to drill a well 40 feet deep through bedrock. The resulting brine was two and one-half times as strong as the brine that Brooks first produced; from 200 gallons of brine, they could produce a bushel of salt at a cost of four cents a pound. As time went on, they drilled even deeper wells, which produced a more concentrated brine.

By 1815 there were 52 furnaces and 15 to 20 wells that produced thousands of bushels of salt on both sides of the Kanawha River. Using wood as fuel, the salt was cooked in huge iron kettles, then shipped downriver on rafts and later on large flatboats to markets in the west.

Many of the innovations and inventions that were made in the salt industry along the Kanawha had long-range implications for the future. But more immediately, they decreased production costs, and tremendously increased the production of salt. In 1817 David Ruffner was the first salt producer to use coal, which was a more efficient fuel than wood, as a fuel for boiling from brine. William H. Tompkins, in 1841, struck a large flow of natural gas while drilling for salt, and was the first producer to use gas as a fuel. This new fuel even lighted the salt works at night.

In 1827 Lewis Ruffner and Frederick Brooks were the first producers to use a steam engine for drilling and pumping wells. Four years later, Billy Morris, an ingenious well-driller in the area, invented "slips"—a long, double-link of metal placed just above the drill bit to give the bit a sharp, rapid cutting fall. These "slips" or "jars," as they later became known in oil and gas drilling, made deep drilling possible. When Edwin Drake was about to drill his first oil well in Titusville, Pennsylvania, in 1859, he employed both the well-drillers and the know-how from the Kanawha Valley.

Salt makers in the valley were producing over a million bushels a year by 1835, when George H. Patrick from Onondaga, New York, came south to introduce a new kind of steam furnace for evaporating salt. Andrew Donnally and Issac Noyes were the first salt makers in the area to adopt Patrick's new method of evaporating salt, but after some improvements, the Patrick furnace was adopted by all the Kanawha salt makers. Patrick's Patented Steam Furnaces replaced the old kettle furnaces that were used for years. The furnace required less labor and fuel and produced a purer, finer salt in larger quantities, and the old "red salt from Kanawha" was replaced by a better, white salt.

John P. Hale built the largest steam furnace (called the multiple-effect furnace) at Snow Hill, a small village between Malden and Charleston. In one year it produced 140,000 bushels of salt, burning 1,200 bushels of coal per day.

In the early days, several modes of transportation were used to get the salt to markets. Before roads were improved, limited quantities of salt were transported by pack horse.

1842 postal stamp, Kanawha Salines, Virginia.

"Kanawha Salines, or Malden, a post town in Kanawha County, Virginia, on the Great Kanawha River, 260 miles W.N.W. from Richmond. Has a bank and numerous stores, 4 churches, 2 seminaries. Population about 1000.

—1855 Virginia Gazetteer

By 1897 when these drawings were made only one salt works remained in the Malden area. The years of the Civil War had destroyed many of the facilities and demand for Kanawha salt declined after 1870 when Chicago replaced Cinicinnati as the meat-packing center of the country. Because of the transportation costs, Michigan salt was cheaper in Chicago than Kanawha salt. WVU

When the James River and Kanawha Turnpike was improved, between 1818 and 1823, wagons were used to haul salt to the east. Flatboats and later steamboats hauled or towed barges down the Kanawha and Ohio to the Mississippi River, and by 1824 there were daily and weekly boat schedules.

Early in the century, better production methods and increased competition, however, began to drive salt prices so low that business was becoming unprofitable. The Kanawha salt makers then decided to band together, and in 1817 they formed the Kanawha Salt Company, probably the first industrial trust in America. At its first organizational meeting, the salt makers formed a cooperative sales organization, limited production, and fixed prices. The company controlled the industry for the next 16 years, and intermittently for 60 years. The salt business boomed; during its peak year of 1846, over three million bushels were produced. This flurry of activity attracted other industries such as lumber, shipping, barrel-making, and boat-building, and for a time Malden was one of the wealthiest communities in the state.

As the industrial furnaces polluted the air, and hundreds of workers crowded into the Salines, many of the wealthy salt producers started to move downriver to the smaller town of Charleston. They built many fine homes along Front Street (Kanawha Boulevard) and other areas of the quiet little town. Charleston was literally built by the production of salt at the Salines and other areas, and many of the present-day street names are reminiscent of these early salt barons.

The Civil War brought down the curtain on the salt industry. During the war, Union forces destroyed some of the furnaces to keep them out of the hands of the Confederacy. Then, during the Confederate occupation in the fall of 1862, thousands of bushels were produced and hauled over the mountains to the salt-starved southern troops. Finally, without men to run the salt works, slaves to work the furnaces, and markets, the various salt works fell into disrepair.

> "Kanawha Salines is a flourishing village 6 miles above Charleston. The salt works on the Kanawha are very extensive, employing near 3000 persons in their operations. Near three million bushels of salt is here manufactured annually, which find a ready market in the States of Ohio, Indiana, Illinois, Missouri, Tennessee and Kentucky."
> —Elliott & Nye's Virginia Directory, 1852

In 1864 the president of Kanawha Salt Company, John P. Hale, and several other pre-war salt makers attempted to reorganize the salt cartel to control the price and distribution of local salt. By this time, however, the salt industry was devastated by competition of western salt producers and the ravages of Civil War. The new Kanawha Salt Company was formed during the Union Army occupation of the Kanawha Valley, although its president, John P. Hale, had joined the Confederate Army in 1861. It has not been determined how Hale managed to put this company together or to whom salt was sold during the war, but by the time the company was organized the heyday for the salt industry was over in Kanawha County.

> Kanawha Salines, January 23, 1864.
> At a full meeting of the members of the Kanawha Salt Company on the 21st inst., it was
> Resolved, That Dr. John P. Hale, President of the Kanawha Salt Company, be authorized to sign the name of said Company in its legitimate transactions, in accordance with the provisions of their constitution.
> J. P. HALE, President.
> N. B. COLEMAN, Secretary.

PARTIAL LIST OF PRE-CIVIL WAR SALT-MAKERS

1797—Elisha Brooks
1806—David Ruffner & Co.
1806—Tobias Ruffner
1815—Aaron Stockton
1818—William Tompkins
1820—William Dickinson
1820—Joel Shrewsbury

Peter Grant
Lewis Ruffner
John Reynolds
Luke Wilcox
Lewis Summers
Dr. John Cabell
John & Samuel Shrewsbury
Andrew Donnally
A. Donnally & William Steele & Co.
Donnally & Steele & P. Alexander
A. Donnally & L. Morris
A. Donnally & L. Welch
A. Donnally & Charles Brown
Joseph Lovell
James Bream
Isaac & Bradford Noyes
Charles Venable
Daniel Ruffner
Andrew Parks
John Warth
L. & C. Morris
William Whitteker
Charles Reynolds
Armstrong
James C. McFarland
William R. Cox
John Anderson
James Hewitt
C. G. & C. Reynolds
Van B. Reynolds
Henry H. Wood
J. D. Lewis
John Welch
W. D. Shrewsbury
Moses Fuqua
Dr. R. E. Putney
George Warth
John Rogers
Stuart Robinson
R. C. M. Lovell
Dr. Spicer Patrick
J. H. Fry
Dr. Henry Rogers
Silas Ruffner
Jacob Darneal
W. C. Brooks
William Graham
John Clarkson
Dr. J. P. Hale
H. W. Goodwin
Charles Cox
David Clarkson
Gus Quarrier
Jesse Hudson
John Slack & James Ogborn
Dr. F. A. A. Cobbs
J. M. Laidley
Lewis Ruffner, Jr.
J. W. Oakes
William Dickinson, Jr.

FROM *PIONEERS AND THEIR HOMES ON UPPER KANAWHA* BY RUTH WOODS DAYTON.

Although the industry experienced a brief and moderate revival after the war, the decline in production increased during the panic of the 1870s. In 1882 the Kanawha Salt Company was swindled by a group of Eastern Businessmen, and this was practically the end of the industry.

Only the J. Q. Dickinson works at Malden remained in business after 1890, and it ceased production of salt in 1945. Most of the brine used now in the local chemical plants comes from sources outside the Kanawha Valley.

Dr. John P. Hale wrote this letter to Professor M. F. Maury, Jr., an English geologist who prepared a report on the resources of the Upper Kanawha region in 1873:

CHARLESTON, W. VA., 1st April, 1873.
To Prof. M.F. Maury, Jr.

DEAR SIR:—In reply to your inquiries as to the manufacture of salt, soda-ash, bromine and glass in the Kanawha Valley, I claim that it possesses advantages superior to any other locality in the United States. The consumption of salt in this country is approximately one bushel per annum to each inhabitant; aggregating, therefore, about 40,000,000 bushels per annum. About one half of this amount is made in the United States chiefly at Syracuse, Saginaw, Pomeroy and Kanawha, besides half a dozen smaller producing localities in as many different States, and the remainder is imported chiefly from England, with all the additions of duty, freight, commissions, exchange, risks and profits. These disadvantages limit the foreign salt chiefly to the sea-board States, while we, from Kanawha, have easy access with cheap freights to the great interior markets of the Ohio and Mississippi Valleys.

There is no other place within the United States where salt water of equal quality and abundance, coal for fuel as good, cheap and abundant, and timber for packages as good, abundant and cheap, can be found together as in Kanawha. It follows, therefore, that salt can be made, barreled, shipped and delivered in the Western markets cheaper from this region than from any other source, and this is exactly what I claim to be true.

Another most important consideration is the superior quality of Kanawha salt. Most other, domestic and foreign, has a greater or less admixture of sulphate of lime, which renders it less penetrating, and more apt to dry, cake and crust on the surface of the meat under unfavorable circumstances of climate or weather, allowing the centre to spoil. Kanawha salt is entirely *free* from sulphate of lime; penetrates and cures meat to the bone in any weather and in any climate, besides having a more lively, pungent and pleasant taste as a table salt than any other known. The packers of the West fully understand its superior antiseptic and curative qualities; and, after more than half a century's experience, prefer it to any other.

About $75,000 will erect a new furnace of a capacity of 500,000 bushels per annum. Salt can be made on such a furnace for about 10 cents per bushel in bulk, or 16 cents in barrels ready for shipment; it can be freighted to Cincinnati by tow-boats and barges for about 3 cents per bushel. The average price in that market for 10 years past has been not less than 38 cents per bushel. Allow 9 cents per bushel for commissions and contingencies (a large estimate) and it leaves a net profit of 10 cents, which gives $50,000 per year on one furnace.

Dickinson Salt Works

Just east of the town of Malden is one of the most important historic industrial sites in the county, the Dickinson salt works, which was established in 1832 by John Q. Dickinson along with his brother-in-law, Joel Shrewsbury. They dissolved their partnership just prior to the Civil War.

After serving with the Confederate army, J.Q. Dickinson returned to Malden to rebuild the business. He was active in the company until his death in 1925 at the age of 94. His son, C.C. Dickinson took over the business, and produced salt until 1945, when high coal prices and other factors forced him to shut down production.

Inorganic bromides were then produced here, which provided products for the photographic and pharmaceutical industries until 1985, when the plant's closure ended 153 years of production at this historic site.

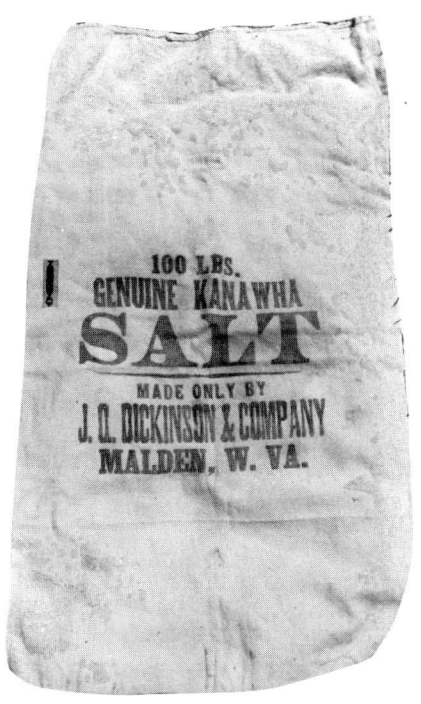

AUTHOR'S COLLECTION

An 1931 aerial view of the salt works with the town of Malden in the upper left. Route 60, which followed the route of the old James River and Kanawha Turnpike, used to go through the town center. Most of the old buildings at the salt works were consumed by flames in May 1957, although bromine products continued to be produced until 1985. GS

Long-range view of the salt works in 1897. COURTESY MRS. ROBERT W. LAWSON, JR.

The crew at the Dickinson Salt Works, circa 1930s. COURTESY MR. & MRS. A. RAYMOND BUCKLEY

Present-day views of the old Dickinson Salt Works

The office, left, and barn, right.

Tool shed.

One of the remaining old workers' quarters, still on the property.

Base for an old water tank.

Bromide works.

The Ruffner Family

A hotel, church, avenue, and hollow were named after one of the most prominent early families in the Kanawha Valley. The patriarch of the family was Joseph Ruffner (1740-1802) of Massenutten, Virginia in the Shenandoah Valley. In 1794 he purchased 1,030 acres of George Clendenin's valley land. In 1795 he bought a 502-acre tract at the mouth of Campbells Creek from John Dickinson. This marked the beginning of the salt industry in the area.

After Joseph's death, his sons, David (1767-1843) and Joseph (1769-1837) expanded the drilling on Elisha Brooks' primitive salt brine and built up the first industry in the county. They became one of the largest salt producers in the Kanawha Valley. In 1817 David substituted coal for wood fuel, which created the vast new industry in the valley—coal mining.

David's son, Henry (1790-1861), organized the first Presbyterian Church in Charleston and was the first teacher at Mercer Academy. He served as president of Washington College (now Washington and Lee University) in Lexington, Virginia, from 1836 to 1848. When he returned to Charleston, Henry built a private school named Mt. Ovis Academy in the hills behind the Salines. It was a school for young men, with students such as W. S. Laidley and Nicholas Fitzhugh, and members of the Donnally, Noyes, and other prominent valley families. It closed in 1861. In his *Ruffner Pamphlet*, published in 1847, Henry advocated an end to slavery, which he did not live to see. He died in 1861.

One of the wealthiest families in the valley, the Ruffners built several fine homes on Kanawha Street (Kanawha Boulevard), Holly Grove, a well-known inn that still stands, Rosedale (at Daniel Boone Roadside Park) and Cedar Grove.

The family was also very influential in county politics. David and Joseph served on the county court at the end of the 18th century. David's son Lewis (1797-1883), the first white child born at Fort Lee, represented the county at the Second Wheeling Convention in June 1861 and helped establish the Reorganized Government of Virginia. He was also a prominent salt maker. His son, Joel, and his wife, Viola, taught Booker T. Washington.

General Lewis Ruffner (1797-1883), second son of David Ruffner, was said to have been the first white child born at Fort Lee in what is now Charleston. After teaching for a year Ruffner went into the family's salt business. In 1823 he took control of the vast Ruffner salt holdings and became one of the largest salt makers in the valley. A leader in the formation of the new state of West Virginia, Ruffner served as a delegate from Kanawha County to the second Wheeling Constitutional Convention in 1861. AUTHOR'S COLLECTION

Ruffner Log Cabin, also known as "Rosedale," is possibly the oldest extant house in the county. Although it is not known when the house was built, it may have been before 1803 during the life of Joseph Ruffner. It was converted into a suitable dwelling by Joel Ruffner, son of Lewis, shortly after his marriage in 1827. During the Civil War a barricade was set up in front of the house by Union troops, but the only damage was a shell that lodged in one of the log walls. The house was occupied by descendants of the Ruffner family in the 1500 block of Kanawha Boulevard until 1969 when it was dismantled and the logs put in storage. In 1970, through the courtesy of the U.S. Naval Reserve, the house was moved to Daniel Boone Roadside Park and dedicated in 1976. Funds were provided by the Colonial Dames of America in West Virginia.

-42-

Cedar Grove was built in 1834 by Augustus Ruffner, fourth son of Daniel Ruffner. This substantial brick house at 1506 Kanawha Boulevard remained in the Ruffner family for more than a century.

In 1831 Daniel Ruffner conveyed to the town of Charleston a plot of ground on Kanawha Street for a cemetery. It was used as such until about 1870 when Spring Hill Cemetery was established. Many burials were later moved to other cemeteries and today the area is a small park with a U.D.C. memorial to the Kanawha Riflemen.

The Holly Grove Mansion at 1710 Kanawha Boulevard is one of the earliest and most important houses in Charleston. It was built in 1815 by Daniel Ruffner, son of Joseph Ruffner. Because of its size and location along the James River and Kanawha Turnpike, the mansion was used as an inn for many years before the Civil War. Some notable visitors included Henry Clay, Sam Houston, John J. Audubon, and in 1832, President Andrew Jackson. The house was originally built as a two-story structure, but in the early 1900s James Nash purchased the home from a Ruffner heir and made extensive interior and exterior modifications—including the addition of the circular entrance and the massive white columns. Today the home is part of the Capitol Complex which is owned by the state of West Virginia, and it has been placed on the National Register of Historic Places. COURTESY HISTORIC PRESERVATION UNIT

Henry Ruffner (1790-1861). SWV

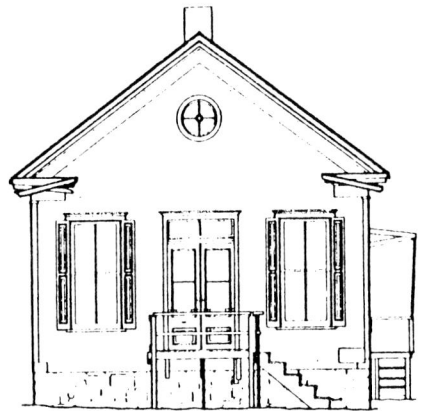

Saltborough, Terra Salis, Kanawha Salines, Malden

Since the 1790s there have been settlements near the mouth of Georges Creek, and at the Great Buffalo Lick near the mouth of Campbells Creek. And although the Morris family settled upriver at the site of Cedar Grove in 1774 and explored, hunted and scouted in the area, the Malden District was not settled until 1790, when Abraham Baker built the first cabin in the area. John Dickinson later received one of the earliest land grants in the district, a total of 502 acres that included the mouth of Campbells Creek and the salt lick. It was Joseph Ruffner, however, who became the largest land owner in the area, when he purchased large tracts of land, including Dickinson's tract, in 1795.

After the salt industry began in earnest in 1807 the town of Malden, which was also called Saltborough, Terra Salis, the Salines and Kanawha Salines, grew much larger than her western neighbor, Charleston. The Ruffner brothers built the first grist mill in 1803, and as the salt works flourished, other businesses were attracted to the area.

As the town grew, so did the need for many different kinds of services. Ezra Walker, the first teacher, was brought from Athens, Ohio to establish a school in 1820 that was supported by subscriptions paid by parents. One of the first post offices in the valley was opened just after 1800. In 1827 The Grand Lodge of Virginia chartered the Masonic Lodge, Salina No. 27, one of the oldest Masonic Lodges in the state. Three years later, the Kanawha Salines Presbyterian Church was established, one of the earliest Presbyterian churches in the valley.

In the years before the Civil War, the Salines thrived, with over 3,000 people employed at the various salt works in the vicinity, including many slaves. Yet as the town grew, so did its problems. Many of the salt works owners, who were becoming wealthy, decided to move their homes and families to the quieter village of Charleston to escape the pollution and crowded conditions that plagued the Salines.

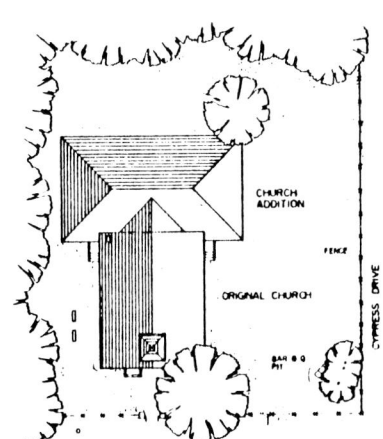

MALDEN, W.V.

1. CARTER GENERAL STORE
2. KANAWHA SALINES PRESBYTERIAN CHURCH
3. RICHARD E. PUTNEY HOUSE
4. MASONIC LODGE, SALINA NO. 27
5. METHODIST CHURCH
6. 4208 MALDEN DRIVE
7. BOOKER T. WASHINGTON PARK
8. 4105 MALDEN DRIVE
9. AFRICAN ZION BAPTIST CHURCH
10. 4001 MALDEN DRIVE
11. RUFFNER CEMETERY
12. 4212 FALLAM DRIVE
13. FERRY LANDING
14. MALDEN BAPTIST CHURCH

COURTESY KANAWHA SALINES SALT FESTIVAL, INC.

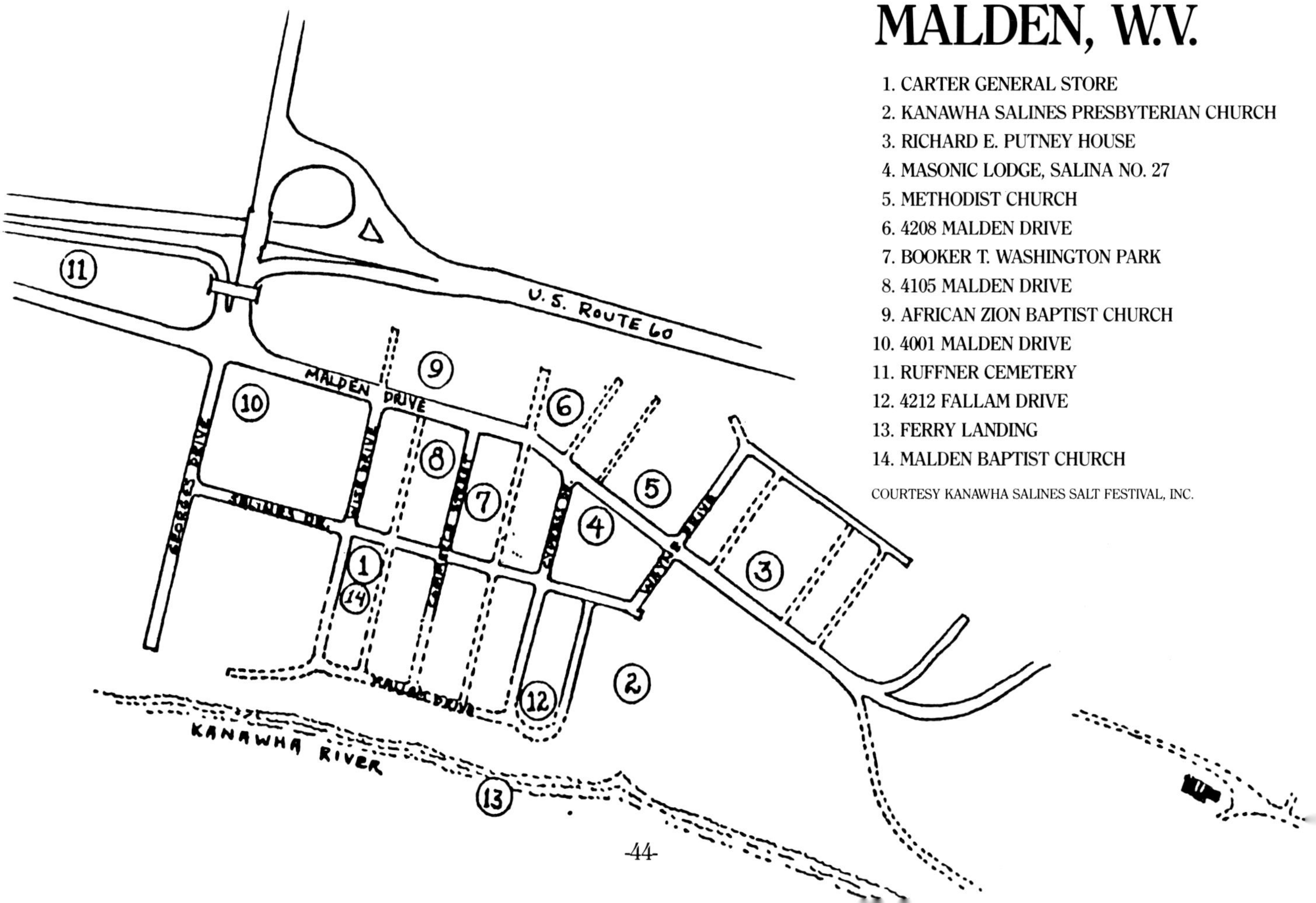

Hall of Sultanna Lodge No. 87, K of P in Malden, 1910.
COURTESY MR. & MRS. A. RAYMOND BUCKLEY

The Malden Confectionery and bus station, 1940s. COURTESY KELLY BRATTON

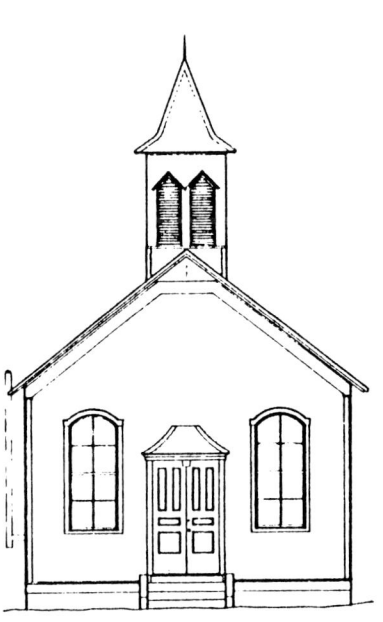

When the James River and Kanawha Turnpike (the Midland Trail) passed through town, avenues of commerce both east and west were opened. After 1824, steamboats made regular stops in the town, which provided additional access to the western markets. The Kanawha Telegraph Company organized and constructed a telegraph wire from Kanawha Salines via Charleston to Point Pleasant in 1846, which was extended in 1852 to Gallipolis, Ohio.

In 1831 David Ruffner, one of the major salt manufacturers in the area, organized a joint stock company that laid out a town on the upper end of a tract he and his brother had purchased from George Alderson and which adjoined the old Dickinson tract. The town was named Malden.

After the destruction caused by the Civil War, floods, and the decline of the salt industry, however, the town's growth stopped and Charleston became the population and business center in the valley. The turnpike (Route 60) was moved north of town, and by 1890 only the Dickinson Salt Works was still in operation. Malden had been incorporated in 1883, but two years later the charter was allowed to lapse after the town marshal was shot. On October 2, 1922, a disastrous fire further contributed to the town's decline, destroying ten homes and four businesses.

Several prominent Americans made their home in Malden at one time or another. The town's best-known citizen was the American black educator, Booker T. Washington, who lived here from 1865 to 1872 and returned later to teach school. Several of the Ruffner clan, including Dr. Henry Ruffner and General Lewis Ruffner, lived or worked in the area. General Mason Patrick, the first head of the fledgling U.S. Air Corps in the early 1900s, spent part of his childhood in Malden, as did James Leftwick, former chairman of the board of the F.W. Woolworth Company.

Maldèn is one of the most historic sites in Kanawha County, and in honor of this, the town was placed on the National Register of Historic Places in 1980.

Present-day Malden

This two-story home at 4208 Malden Drive dates from 1838, one of the three oldest buildings in town.

Carter General Store on Salines Drive, constructed in 1889, is the oldest commercial structure that remains in Malden. The exterior of the building has remained relatively unaltered.

Above: The Kanawha Salines Presbyterian Church is the oldest church in Malden, and one of the earliest Presbyterian churches in the county. The congregation was formed in Charleston in 1819, and this structure was completed in 1840. In 1933 a Sunday school building was added at the rear of the church. Henry Ruffner was one of the preachers at the church. The church was integrated and a gallery was provided for the slaves of the salt producers.

Opposite: The African Zion Baptist Church is regarded as the mother church for black Baptists in West Virginia. The congregation formally organized in 1852. In 1872 this building was erected and it remains largely unaltered. Booker T. Washington served as the church clerk and a Sunday school teacher in the late 1870s.

Middle right: The Richard E. Putney house is one of the most imposing and least-altered homes in Malden. The principal two-story brick structure was built about 1836. The one-story addition was erected in at least two stages and the wooden front porch is also a later addition. The first owner, Dr. Richard E. Putney, married the daughter of David Ruffner. In 1868 the Kanawha Salines Presbyterian Church bought the house for use as a manse. It was a private home from 1952 until 1973—when it was converted into a law office.

Booker Taliaferro Washington

Malden's best-known resident was black educator Booker T. Washington, who was born a slave on April 5, 1856, at Hales Ford, Virginia. Washington's stepfather had gone to the Salines during the war to work at the salt furnaces. At the end of the Civil War in 1865, he sent for his family in Virginia, and they joined him in the Salines, journeying 200 miles over several rugged mountain ranges, mostly on foot.

When he arrived in the Salines, Booker, at nine years of age, worked as a salt packer, an unskilled, back-breaking job. He first learned to read the number 18, which was the number assigned to his stepfather as a salt packer. Although he had an early passion for learning, he was mainly self-educated. He was also a regular member of the African Zion Baptist Church in Malden.

Booker actually took the last name Washington by accident. As a small boy, just out of slavery, he may not have known his last name, but his stepfather's name was Washington Furgenson (or Ferguson). When Booker was asked his last name at school one day, he blurted out the name Washington.

Booker was later taken in as a houseboy by General Lewis Ruffner and his second wife Viola, who took the young boy under her wing. This relationship with the Ruffners had a profound effect on the young boy, eager to learn as much as possible.

After working in the mines in the Campbells Creek area awhile, young Washington entered Hampton Institute in Virginia in 1872. He received a formal education and learned a trade as a brick mason. When he finished at the institute, he moved back to Malden to become a school teacher. He later returned to Hampton to teach.

His teaching career was so successful that he was selected to organize and head a new black school at Tuskegee, Alabama, the Tuskegee Institute, where he served as its president from 1881 until his death in 1915.

Booker T. Washington is considered one of the greatest black educators in American history. His autobiography, *Up From Slavery*, was published in 1901 and covers his years in his adopted state of West Virginia.

Booker T. Washington, possibly in Charleston. He last visited the Malden area in May 1915. The Booker T. Washington Park is located on the site of the home of Washington's half-sister, Amanda Johnson in Malden. SWV

The house where Booker T. Washington lived in Malden stood for many years within the town limits. Left: front of house, below: back of house.
SWV and WVU

There was nothing peculiar in his habits, except that he was always in his place and never known to do anything out of the way, which I think has been his course all thru life. His conduct has always been without fault, and what more can you wish? He seemed peculiarly determined to emerge from his obscurity. He was ever restless, uneasy, as if knowing that contentment would mean inaction. "Am I getting on?"—that was his principal question.

—*Mrs. Lewis Ruffner, remembering Booker as a youth*

The *Keystone* pushing empty barges along the Kanawha River, May 1943.
OFFICE OF WAR INFORMATION PHOTO BY ARTHUR SIEGEL.

Chapter Five
The River System

The River System

"Upon the whole ... of vast commercial and political importance."

—George Washington writing about the Kanawha River in 1784

West Virginia's largest inland waterway, the Kanawha River, and several of its tributaries bisects Kanawha County. The Great Kanawha flows for 43 miles in the county in an approximate southeast to northwest direction, and enters the Ohio River at Point Pleasant in Mason County, 99.5 miles west of the confluence of the New River, which rises in North Carolina, and the Gauley River flowing from the state's east central mountains. The river system's drainage area covers a wide portion of central and southern West Virginia. The Kanawha waterway has been of critical importance to the early settlement and commerce of Kanawha County, as well as portions of Fayette, Putnam, and Mason counties.

The Elk River is the main tributary of the Kanawha, and it flows for 180 miles from its headwaters in Pocahontas County to its mouth in Charleston. Originally given the Indian name that means "the river of fat doe"), Campbells Creek, Kelly's Creek, Paint Creek the Miami Indians and the "Toquemincepe" or Walnut River by the Delaware Indians. The Elk River was an important means of transportation for the timber industry, and for many years timber products were sent downriver from the north to the mills in Charleston.

The other large tributary of the Kanawha, the Coal River, flows north from its headwaters in Boone County to its mouth at St. Albans, a distance of 59 miles, 28 of which are in Kanawha County.

The other main tributaries of the Kanawha River are the Pocatilico River (an Indian name that means "the river of fat doe") Campbells Creek, Kelly's Creek, Paint Creek (originally called Moscooscepe), Ottowecepe or Deer Creek, Kanawha Two Mile, Cabin Creek, Hughes Creek and Smithers Creek.

The rivers of the county broadened the fledgling salt industry by opening up new markets to the west. And after the start of the nineteenth century, the rivers, in particular the Kanawha and Coal, played an increasingly important role in the economic life of the county.

The Kanawha was somewhat navigable from its mouth at Point Pleasant to the Falls in Fayette County, a distance of approximately 88 miles. However, because no improvements

The Falls of the Kanawha near the confluence of the New and Gauley River at present-day Glen Ferris. This painting was reproduced in color in Edward Beyer's *Album of Virginia*, 1857. COURTESY VIRGINIA STATE LIBRARY

had been made on the river by the early 1800s, rivermen were still at the mercy of fluctuating water levels and many obstacles in the river at low water.

In early 1819, the *Robert Thompson*, a crude, barge-like sidewheel steamboat, made the first attempt to journey upriver to the Kanawha Salines. She could not, however, ascend the Red House shoals, 25 miles below Charleston in Putnam County, and turned back after a two-day effort.

The next year, Andrew Donnally, a local salt producer, succeeded in bringing his steamboat, the *Andrew Donnally*, upriver to the Salines, and in 1823 his steamer *Eliza* made the trip.

With the removal of some boulders and snags in the river, more and more powerful steamboats soon followed and boat traffic became a regular operation back and forth from the Salines to the Ohio. As traffic increased, boat schedules became more regular, and the salt industry boomed. By 1840, when Alva Hansford shipped the first flatboat of coal to Cincinnati, both salt and coal barges were a common sight on the Kanawha River.

However, the cycles of high and low water and the many obstructions in the river still prevented safe passage during the first few decades of the nineteenth century. For this reason, people envisioned, as early as pre-Revolutionary War days, an all-water route that connected tidewater Virginia with the Ohio River by way of the James and Kanawha rivers. Even George Washington, who owned land on the new frontier of western Virginia, supported the idea. In 1785 the James River Company was chartered by the state to carry out this somewhat grandiose idea of connecting the two bodies of water, a plan that entailed crossing several formidable mountain ranges. The new company was empowered to improve navigation on the James and Kanawha rivers, and to build a road to the Kanawha area and possibly all the way to the Ohio River.

Unfortunately, the only river-work done was on the James River above Richmond. In 1812 the Virginia General Assembly appointed John Marshall, Chief Justice of the U.S. Supreme Court, to head a commission to study the feasibility of promoting this route as a major transportation system.

Charleston Middle Ferry,
AND
MAIL STAGE CROSSING.

THE SUBSCRIBER having lately purchased the Middle Ferry, (formerly kept by Mr Quarrier) respectfully announces to the public, that he has just completed at great expense, a large, commodious, and secure

☞ **Horse Boat,**

intended to run constantly at this Ferry. This boat is sufficiently large to transport two waggons, with their entire teams, at one time, and will ply from shore to shore in two minutes. As it is always worked by two horses, and constantly attended by hands on board, travellers going East or West will experience no delay or interruption in crossing the Kanawha at this Ferry. The landings on both sides the river will be immediately graduated and improved, so that heavily loaded wagons will find no difficulty in descending or ascending the banks. Prices same as at the other Ferries on the Kanawha River.

GEORGE GOSHORN.
Feb. 5th, 1830.

An 1860 freight bill on the *Julia Maffitt*, a steamer that plied the Kanawha River until the Civil War. COURTESY TERRY LOWRY

Marshall's commission, after a rather arduous trip on the James, Greenbrier, New, and Kanawha rivers, judged the project as commercially feasible. Other studies were made that recommended the construction of a canal around Kanawha Falls, a dam to submerge Red House shoals, and the improvement and deepening of sections of the Kanawha River.

It wasn't until 1820 that the state authorized these improvements and provided monies for implementing these studies. Ten years later, after spending over $91,000, the Kanawha had been partially dredged, its channels were cleared, some crude wing dams were built to submerge the dangerous shoals, and the James River and Kanawha Turnpike was constructed to the Ohio River.

After 1825 steamboats made regular runs to Charleston and the Salines from western cities such as Gallipolis, Cincinnati, and Parkersburg, Wheeling, and Pittsburgh to the north. Charleston truly became a river town connected via the Ohio and Mississippi rivers to waters as far away as the Gulf of Mexico. Coal, salt, and timber were hauled downriver on flatboats that were towed to the side or at the rear of the steamboats. Manufactured goods and foodstuffs were also hauled upstream to the booming salt industry towns of the Kanawha Valley.

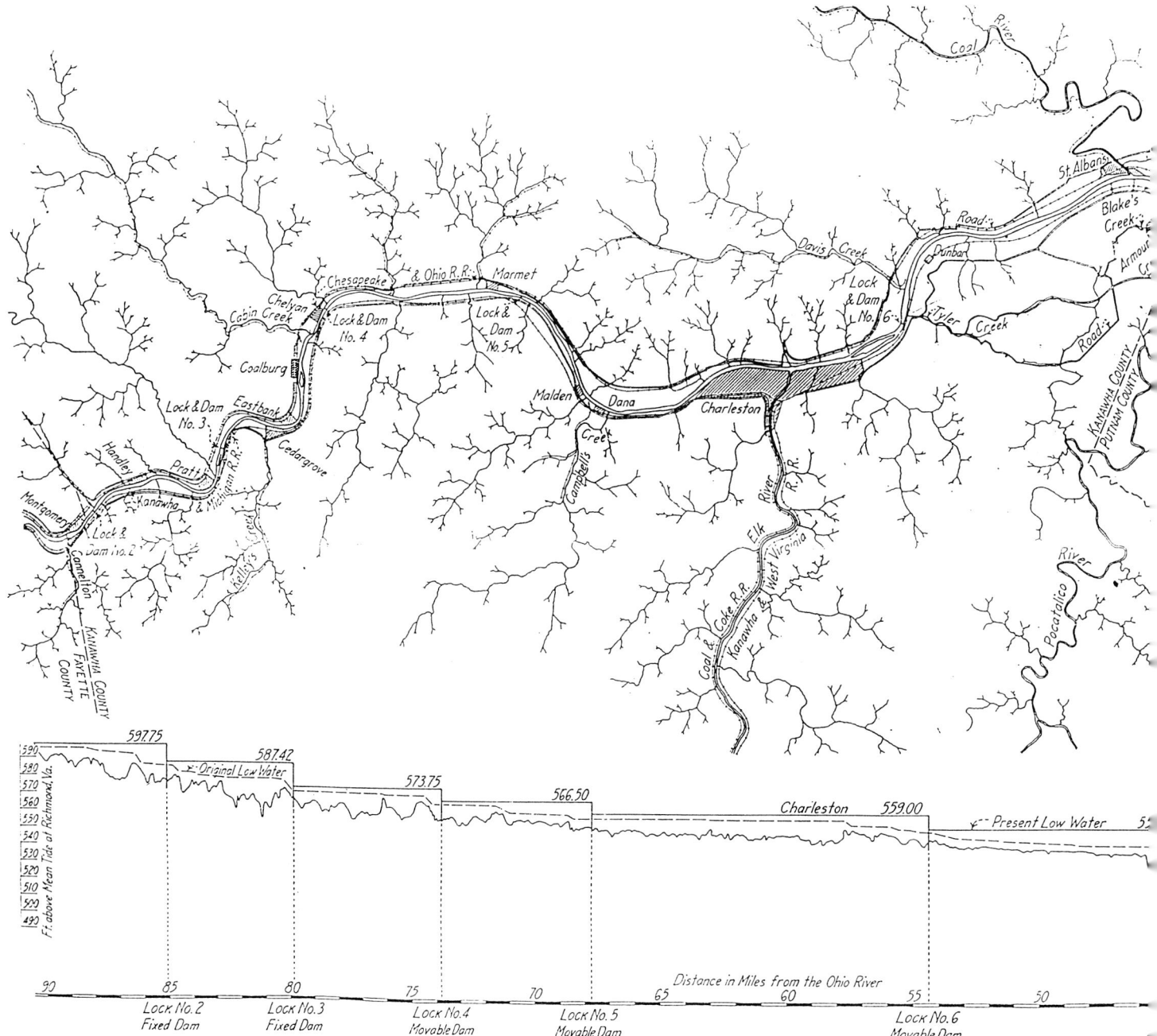

PROFILE OF

Work was constantly done on the Kanawha River to keep it free of obstacles and deep enough. But like other projects in western Virginia whose purse strings were controlled by the politicians in Richmond, there was never enough money to do an adequate job. Finally, the James River and Kanawha Company was established in 1835 to improve conditions on the river. Benjamin Wright, the chief engineer for the construction of the Erie Canal, was hired, along with a young engineer named Charles Ellet, Jr. The next year, Ellet became the chief engineer and he embarked on an ambitious program to reach the Ohio River with a water route, as Washington and many others had envisioned. By 1851 the James River and Kanawha Canal was opened from tidewater to Buchanan, a distance of 197 miles, and a railroad was planned from Richmond to Covington, which would cross the mountains to the Kanawha Valley. Some sophisticated locks and dams were also planned for the Kanawha. Unfortunately, Ellet had been dismissed for political reasons in 1839 and by the year preceding the Civil War in 1861, none of these projects were completed.

However, as coal mining became more important in the Kanawha Valley, the local coal operators frequently found that the Kanawha River wasn't deep enough to float the coal-laden flatboats downriver, which created considerable economic hardship. In 1855 the

Map from 1918.

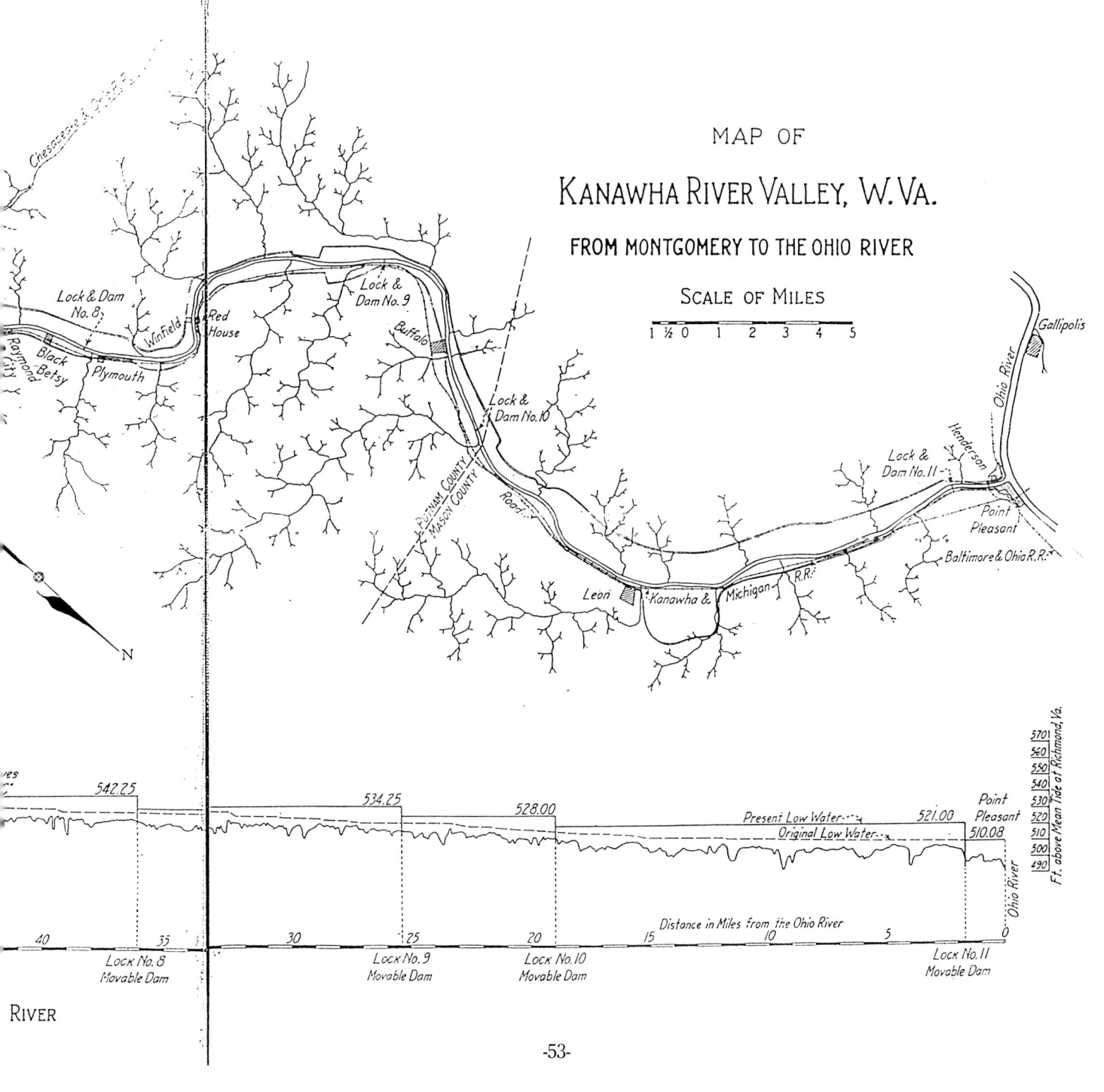

coalmen held a meeting in Charleston and petitioned the General Assembly in Richmond to help keep the river navigable year-round. The assembly established the Kanawha Board in 1858 to implement improvements on the river.

Charles Ellet, Jr., was again hired to study methods of improving the river. By this time, he had won world-wide recognition for his engineering skills in building bridges and improving waterways. He built the still-standing Wheeling suspension bridge in 1851, the world's longest at the time. He proposed building huge, stone dams on several tributaries of the Kanawha to even out the water flow and control flooding. He also proposed dredging out chutes in the worst shoals to a width of 80 feet, which would enhance navigation. Once again, however, because of the lack of funds and the continual threat of Civil War, Ellet's plans were never carried out.

The Civil War years were disastrous for the navigational improvements on both the Kanawha and Coal rivers. No work was done on the rivers during the war and the September 1861 flood, the worst in recorded history, added the final touches to the destruction. In 1861 and 1862 both sides used steamboats on the Kanawha to transfer troops and supplies, and several boats were sunk or set on fire. Both the salt industry and coal mining were disrupted by the war, and very few if any shipments were made to the west. The Confederates did ship salt overland to the east during their brief occupation of the Kanawha Valley in September 1862.

The *Liberty No.4*, *Lookout* and *Telephone*, packet boats stuck in the ice at the mouth of the Elk River near the Kanawha River at Charleston, January 1879. This is one of the earliest dated photos in the book. COURTESY C&P TELEPHONE MUSEUM

Five steamboats on the wintry Kanawha River, early 1900s. The Courthouse is the steepled building in the background. KCL

Steamers *Greenwood*, *Evergreen*, and *Cricket* at the Charleston landing in 1902. Several of the city's prominent riverfront buildings can be seen, including the St. Albert Hotel, Joseph Popp Hardware, and Rogers Drugs. GS, CAPT. JESSE HUGHES PHOTO

The *Kanawha Belle* was built in 1887 at Harmar, Ohio, and was originally named *Bellaire*. The Calvert family then bought, remodeled and renamed it the *Kanawha Belle*. The boat was used on the Charleston-Montgomery run until the night of December 19, 1901, when she plunged over the fixed dam at Lock No. 3 at Riverside. Of the seventeen aboard, only eight were saved. The official report stated that when the accident happened "the pilot thought he was going upstream." The boat originally was headed to Montgomery, but plans were changed and she was turned back toward Charleston. Musty Snyder, the pilot, was not notified of the change when he came on watch and in the darkness, thought he was going upstream. When he saw the white light on the lock wall, he thought it was on a moored coal fleet so he steered out in mid-river to miss it and the boat plunged over the dam. The machinery was salvaged and used on the *J.Q. Dickinson*. GS

An unusual river photo taken in 1903 just west of the present C&O Station, with Bridge Road on the left. This event was a shoving match between the sternwheel towboat, *D.T. Lane*, and the twin-prop steam towboat, *James Ramsey*. The Charles Ward Engineering Company built the *Ramsey* in Charleston for the U.S. Corps of Engineers. She was a newfangled propeller boat that used one-half the coal and one-third the crew that the *Lane* required. The *Lane* was built in 1871, using Civil War period engines. The *Ramsey* won the contest and eventually became a novelty on the river. GS

> "When the river is low, commerce is greatly interrupted, and the persons engaged in it suffer great loss and inconvenience; which would be completely removed, by the proposed improvement. With a good navigation on the river, it is hardly possible to anticipate the extent to which the commerce on it would be carried."
>
> —An 1819 study by state engineers Thomas Moore and Isaac Briggs

The James River and Kanawha Canal

The Great Kanawha River figured prominently in George Washington's plans for the Great Central American Waterway, which would connect the Ohio River and the Atlantic coast. Soon after the end of the Revolutionary War, Washington urged his native state of Virginia to develop the James River, which would be connected by canal to the Kanawha and Ohio rivers. He solicited the support of Benjamin Harrison, Governor of Virginia. After much lobbying, the Virginia Assembly voted in January 1785 to incorporate the James River Company, and authorized it to improve the navigation of the James River. Over the next twenty-five years, the river was cleared, and canals and locks were built that connected Richmond with the tidewaters of the Atlantic.

From 1820 to 1835 a canal was built toward the west, around Balcony Falls, where the James River flows down through the Blue Ridge Mountains, and the Kanawha River was improved. During this time, a turnpike was constructed from Covington, Virginia, to Guyandotte in Cabell County, which opened up trade and communications with the west. The canal extended west to Lexington by 1840, and in 1851 it reached Buchanan, a total distance from tidewater to western Virginia of 197.5 miles.

Because of the immense cost of building the canal over the Alleghenies to connect with the Kanawha, and the railroads' westward expansion, the project ended at Buchanan. The completed portion, however, plus the improvements to the Kanawha River and road facilities, boosted the prewar economies of Charleston and the Kanawha Valley.

A bill of lading for goods shipped by steamboat from Point Pleasant by James Capehart to Daniel Ruffner at Kanawha Salines in May 1843. It stated that the goods were to be shipped in good order excepting for the "unavoidable dangers of the river navigation and fire."

COURTESY VIRGINIA STATE LIBRARY

The Central Water Route

Before the Civil War, political leaders in Virginia joined forces with some French businessmen to propose a central route that connected the Atlantic coast to the Ohio River and the midwestern states, by way of the James, Kanawha, and Ohio rivers. Inadequate funding and the Civil War temporarily put an end to this dream until 1870, when the War Department made a study that found the plan feasible.

As part of the James River and Kanawha Canal project, they planned to dig a tunnel through Howard's Creek Valley in Greenbrier County and build locks and dams on the Greenbrier, New, and Kanawha rivers. They also proposed to deepen the Kanawha and Ohio rivers to six feet. The biggest obstacle on the Kanawha River was the 20-foot falls at Glen Ferris, which they planned to overcome by building a canal around the falls.

Total cost for this grandiose project was estimated at $47 million, a tremendous amount of money at the time. The Kanawha and Ohio rivers were eventually deepened to nine feet, and modern locks and dams were built. The idea of a central water route, however, was eventually abandoned because of sectionalism, postwar politics, lack of money and engineering expertise, and the rapid development of railroads.

Elk River Scenes

A peaceful scene on Elk, early 1900s. KCL

Below: 1916 winter scene near the mouth of the Elk River. The Virginia Street bridge is in the background. KCL

Bottom: The present site of the Kanawha Boat Club just below the Kanawha City bridge. The governor's mansion can be seen through the trees on the opposite bank. Circa 1939. KCL

This ingenious hoist was built right into the Elk River, about one mile above its junction with the Kanawha, by the Kanawha & Michigan Railway. It was used to haul railroad ties from the barges to shore. GS

-57-

Excursion & Showboats on the River

The steamer *Virginia* was originally built in 1898 as the *I.C. Woodward*, which plied the Pittsburgh to Morgantown trade route. In 1914 it was converted, at great expense, into an excursion boat and renamed the *Virginia*. During the construction of the Nitro munition plant, it operated as a ferry to and from Charleston. In 1919 the steamer was sold at a U.S. Marshall's sale and the name was changed again to the *City of Charleston*. On May 8, 1921, it burned at Gallipolis, Ohio. GS

A more recent excursion boat, the *Avalon* is shown docked at Charleston in the early 1950s. Ernest Wagner was the captain at the time. Built in 1915, it traversed the Mississippi River system until the early 1960s. The *Avalon*, which has been renamed *Belle of Louisville*, is now owned by the city of Louisville and Jefferson County, Kentucky. GS

Paden's *New Crystal Palace*, shown docked at Malden in 1889, was probably one of the earliest showboats on the river. The Paden family is seated on the right lower deck. GS

Several barges, used as showboats, traveled up and down the Kanawha River in the early part of the 20th century. Price's *Floating Opera* is shown docked at Pratt. *Edwards Moonlight* is probably docked at Charleston.

In the 1940s one of the most celebrated steamboats on the Ohio River system was the Greene Line's *Gordon C. Greene*, sister boat to the present *Delta Queen*. It was built in 1923 and cruised the river system until 1952, when it was sold and converted to a restaurant in St. Louis, Missouri. It sank during a flood in 1970.

GS

Steamers *Greendale* and *Valley Belle* on the Kanawha River, just east of the mouth of the Elk River. The Charleston Utility Company sits about where the Blue Cross building is now. GS

The *D.T. Lane* passing by one of the popular swimming areas on the Kanawha River. Riding the waves was a dangerous pastime. GS

The *Joe Cook*, owned by Pfaff & Smith Builders Supply Company of Charleston, was the first steel-hull towboat to operate on the Kanawha River. She was built in 1930 and retired in 1952. In 1947 one of the towboat's boilers exploded at Ravenswood, West Virginia, killing three people. GS

An early 1940s view of the city boat ramp and Glenn Clark's seaplane base. Clark operated seaplanes at this site from 1937 until after World War II. Note the early hydroplane racing boat in the foreground. GS

Foot of Capitol Street at the City Levee, 1920s. KCL

The Charleston City levee prior to 1918. The Charleston Wharfage Company, which owned the steamboat *Greendale* and wharfboat shown, leased the levee from the city. The wharfboat was used as a warehouse for commercial purposes. GS

> "At some of the rapids, and elsewhere, the new channels or 'dog shutes'... through and across a succession of short lengths of deep water and shoals, pursue a zigzag course which it is difficult for boats to follow.... The shutes and channels made by the state are generally too narrow.... In consequence of these defects in the existing improvements, steamboats ... have difficulty in passing through some four or five of the 'dog shutes' below Charleston, and there are some at which, in certain stages of the river, steamboats are compelled to follow the old or natural channels, which from the diversion of a part of the water through the new or excavated channels, have not as much depth of water as they would have if the river had been left in its natural state."
>
> —*Charles B. Fisk, 1855 survey of the Kanawha River*

After the war, economic conditions had changed in the county. The navigational work on the rivers was, for all practical purposes, destroyed, as was the large salt industry. Railroads were pushing their way west, and by 1873 tracks crossed the county. But there was still a need for riverboats. The coal industry was now expanding, and river transportation provided a cheap and easy means of transportation downriver to the large, western markets.

The newly created state of West Virginia re-established the old Kanawha Board, which was authorized to issue bonds and collect tolls for river improvements. Federal funds were appropriated to make some improvements, but by 1883 the board ceased operations and turned over its job to the U.S. Army Corps of Engineers.

Colonel William E. Merrill, then General William P. Craighill, and finally Addison Scott of the Corps were put in charge of improving the Kanawha. The Central Water Line project was still alive in the 1880s with the vision, now a century old, of opening a waterway that connected tidewater Virginia to the Ohio River. In 1875 the Corps' first major improvement provided for a constant depth of water in the Kanawha River. The Kanawha River Slackwater Project called for 12 locks and dams to be built from Kanawha Falls to Point Pleasant. The upper Kanawha would have fixed dams, and the nine downriver dams would have movable Chanoine wickets to facilitate the passage of the coal barges. Lock and Dam No. 4 at Cabin Creek and No. 5 at Brownstown (Marmet) were finally opened in 1880 after repeated mishaps, strikes, and contracted construction company bankruptcies. Then the Chanoine wickets, which were raised and lowered on the dam to control the water level, were found to be inadequate, and replaced by Pasquean hurters, a new French design. The hurters greatly helped the operators of the dams to control the flow of water. Addison Scott later improved on the French design with one of his own.

It took 23 years to finish ten dams (the two others were unnecessary), and in 1898 the last dam, Lock and Dam No. 11 near Henderson in Mason County, was completed. The Kanawha River became the first in the nation to be completely channelled with wicket dams, which returned benefits that far exceeded the initial construction costs and the operating expenses. For when the locks and dams were completed, the coal industry greatly expanded, shipping an average of over a million tons of coal a year at the nation's lowest freight rates.

River traffic increased for the next few decades until late 1929, when local commerce began to change. In that year, the Ohio River, from Pittsburgh to Cairo, Illinois, was converted to a nine-foot depth by the completion of 46 locks and dams. The Kanawha and other tributaries were still six feet deep, and by the 1920s the old locks were inadequate for the increased size of the coal barges. Rail shipments of coal to Huntington also increased sharply, which further eroded the river business. Nationally, the steamboat packet era was coming to a close, and in 1936 the last commercially-operated steamboat on the Kanawha River, the *Liberty*, made its final run.

Timber and forest products, which had been transported downriver for years, decreased shipments significantly in the twenties, but after 1922 there was an increase in the barge transportation of petroleum products from refineries and terminals at Cabin Creek and Pratt. Also, rapidly expanding chemical industries used the river to transport raw materials and finished products. Many of these industrial plants had located along the Kanawha River precisely because of the potential of good, cheap river transportation. By this time, the old 1890s lock and dam system had to be replaced. The Corps of Engineers conducted studies of the river, and in 1926 the Kanawha Valley Improvements Association was formed to lobby Congress for improvements, namely, a nine-foot water depth to match the Ohio's.

A wooden barge built on the banks of Kanawha River at the mouth of Campbells Creek. In the background is the Libby Owens Ford glass plant.
COURTESY AMHERST INDUSTRIES

The Gates and Hogeman dredge on Elk River, between Virginia and Lovell (now Washington) streets about 1905. The dredge is moored at Bibby's Mill landing on the river's east bank.
RA

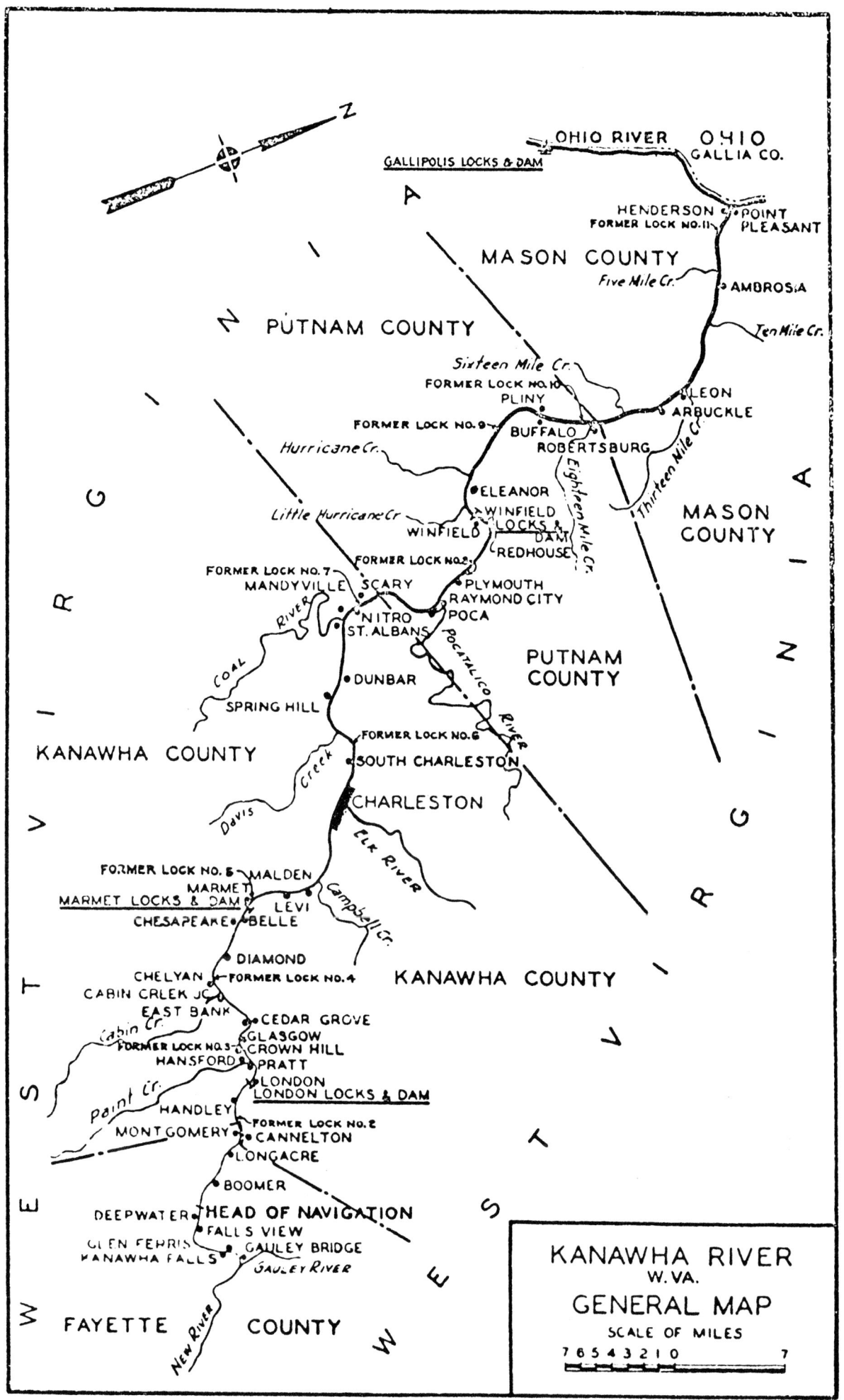

In 1930 two high dams with movable crests and twin locks, one at Marmet and one at London, were authorized. A new design from Germany that incorporated a rollergate technique was recommended for the dams, and construction began in the spring of 1931. A third locks and dam was approved in 1933 at Winfield in Putnam County to bring the entire navigable part of the river to a nine-foot depth.

The Marmet locks and dam was completed in late 1933, after delays caused by flooding and a tragic accident that killed six workers. The dam was dedicated with a steamboat parade from Charleston to Marmet, in honor of the presence of Vice President Charles Curtis. The London locks and dam was completed in June 1935. The Winfield project was started in late 1933 and finished in 1937, and was funded by the Public Works Administration (PWA).

With these locks and dams in place, the volume of river traffic grew tremendously, and new, expanded plants were built adjacent to the river. The old series of locks and dams, which were once vitally needed to improve the river, had served their purpose and were now just part of the river's history.

Addison Scott, born in New York, was a civil engineer who came to Charleston in 1873 as resident engineer for the Corps of Engineers. He was responsible for the design and improvement of Kanawha River navigation and remained in that position until 1901. After his resignation from the Corps in 1901, he remained in Charleston and spent the remainder of his life involved in civic affairs and the management of his many city investments. He died in 1927.
COURTESY OF CORPS OF ENGINEERS

"A potent factor in the dethronement of hard-hearted coal barons of other sister states who reigned supreme, had gladdened the hearts of millions of people below its mouth who have been blessed by its cheap coal and cheaper transportation, the prime and potent factor in the development of Kanawha County and the Capital City."

—*1898 Charleston newspaper reporting on the Kanawha Slackwater Project*

A 1931 aerial view of Lock and Dam No. 2 at Montgomery, just inside the Kanawha County line. GS

Lock and Dam No. 7 at Nitro in 1931. GS

An aerial view of old Lock and Dam No. 6 at South Charleston, November 1931. GS

Construction of Lock and Dam No. 6 at South Charleston on July 24, 1885. When Lock and Dam No. 6 was completed in 1886, at a total cost of $337,000, it formed a slackwater pool 14 miles long and six feet deep up to Dam No. 5. In the late 1800s, this pool became one of the largest coal harbors in the world. GS

The steamer *Winifrede*, with empty coal barges, entering Lock No. 6 on September 26, 1892. GS

Lock & Dam No. 7 on the Kanawha River, June 11, 1890. View showing cofferdam and excavation for river wall. GS

A good view of the lock of Lock and Dam No. 4 in 1890. The massive amount of stone for the lock was quarried from the surrounding hills and hauled to the site by barge. The *Wild Goose*, owned by Dr. John P. Hale, is in the lock. GS

Lock and Dam No. 4, the first lock and dam to be completed, was opened just below the present site of the Chelyan Bridge on July 3, 1880. GS

Lock and Dam No. 4 at Chelyan looking south in 1931. GS

Movable or adjustable dams. View inside one of the cofferdams during construction after parts of the wickets that form the dam and the operating bridge have been put in place. The wickets are shown as they were kept at all of the dams during the low water season to create a 6½-foot depth throughout the river to aid coal barge navigation, 1897. KCL

View inside one of the cofferdams during construction after all the movable irons and part of the wickets were in place. This shows wickets lying flat, near the bottom of the river, as they were kept during high water. The irons in the foreground were ready to receive the wickets. The wickets when raised or standing formed the dam, 1897. KCL

Construction of Lock and Dam No. 8. GS

Stone yard at the site of Lock and Dam No. 7. GS

Raising one of the lock gates into place at Lock and Dam No. 11, July 16, 1898. GS

This 1931 photo shows Lock and Dam No. 5 at Marmet and the present Marmet Lock under construction. GS

Construction of the Lock and Dam at London in October 1931. GS

Official opening of Lock A at Marmet, September 27, 1932. This is a view of *Edwards Moonlight* and *F.M. Staunton* with the dedication party being locked through Lock A. GS

Coal River History

In 1742, John Peter Salley made two important discoveries as he floated down the Coal River in his buffalo skin boat. Not only was he the first white man to see the river, he was the first to find coal in the state, for which the river was named. On some early maps it was referred to as the Louisa River. But years later, the river's name was changed back to the original because of the vast outcroppings of coal along its banks that were so fundamental to the development of the area.

Lewis Tackett built a fort at the river's mouth, at what is presently St. Albans, about 1786. During the heyday of the salt industry, before the Civil War, nearly 4,000 flatboats were built along the river and sold to the Kanawha salt producers for shipping salt to the western markets.

Coal was first shipped downstream in 1850. This cannel coal, a bituminous coal that burns brightly, was refined into paraffin and oil for illumination and lubrication. William Madison Peyton founded companies in Boone County to mine and transport this greasy substance, and in 1849 he chartered the Coal River Navigation Company that improved navigation by manually removing snags and boulders from the river channel.

Clearing the channel, however, did not significantly improve the flatboat's float downriver, and the cost of shipping was more than double the cost of mining. Peyton and other cannel coal operators then pooled their resources, and with some financial aid from the state, they proposed a slackwater project for the river that would allow steamboats and barges to be used to ship coal downriver to the Kanawha.

They hired Captain William S. Rosecrans, a former officer in the U.S. Army Corps of Engineers, to plan the project. He proposed a system of eight locks and dams to provide 35 miles of slackwater up the Big Coal River to Peytona in Boone County. In 1855 Lock and Dam A was constructed to reach mines along the Little Coal River, and Rosecrans completed the entire project in 1859 for the sum of a little over $20,000. He then resigned to pursue other projects. Ironically, he reappeared in West Virginia in 1861, as head of Union forces in the northern part of the state.

The dams were stone-filled timbercribs that rested on wooden piles, with thick boards driven across the upstream sides. The locks were timbercribs 124 feet by 23 feet, with oak planks driven around their foundations to prevent undermining.

In March 1859 the steamboat *Clifton* inaugurated steamboat commerce on the river when it made its way up the Coal River to Peytona. The high-priced cannel coal was shipped down the river for the next two years, at a rate of over 800,000 bushels by 1860. This commerce, however, was to last only a little over two years, even though a ninth lock and dam was planned to improve navigation.

In the spring of 1861 the pool behind Lock One was crowded with loaded coal barges, when a Union flotilla advanced up the Kanawha. When Confederate General Henry Wise retreated from the Kanawha Valley, he had the barges scuttled, which blocked navigation all the way up the river. The old covered bridge across the Coal was also burned down.

In September 1861 the record flood on the Kanawha and Coal rivers severely damaged the crude lock and dam structures, and the rivers were not used for commercial purposes until the close of the war in 1865.

After the war, the mines were reopened, and the lock and dam structures were repaired. Cannel coal was once again shipped to western markets, during the wetter winter and spring periods when water levels were high. In addition, timber became a big business in the Coal River drainage during the 1880s, but the logs could be floated downriver without use of the locks. Gradually, river traffic began to taper off, as the cannel coal seams played out and kerosene rapidly replaced it as lamp fuel, and as railroads inched their way up the river valleys.

All traces of the eight locks and dams are gone now, except for Lock Three's dam at Upper Falls, where in 1802 a grist mill was built that operated for many decades. Another mill was built at Lower Falls, site of Lock Two. Several lumber mills were built at St. Albans to mill the timber from the river drainage all the way into Boone County.

St. Albans has developed as the biggest town along the Coal River, and Madison, the county seat of Boone County, is located at its headwaters. The river now provides recreation, homesites, and some mining activity for the local inhabitants.

"Kanawha Valley Star."
CHARLESTON, TUESDAY, AUG. 9, 1859.

500 Men Wanted! On Coal River,
At the different points from Coal's Mouth, on the Kanawha River, to Peytona, for the Improvement of the same. A healthy location. Constant employment, and Good Wages.— Also a

NUMBER OF CARPENTERS
will be employed, by calling early. Steam boats run regularly to and from this place to Cincinnati, Pittsburg, Wheeling, and the different points on the Ohio River.
    HENRY S. KUPP, Contractor.
    Address, KANAWHA C. H., Va.
August 7th 1858.
☞ New York Herald, Philadelphia Ledger, Pittsburg Post, Daily Wheeling Argus, Cincinnati Enquirer each copy 6 times and send account to Contractor.   16

Coal River Navigation.

Major HENRY S. KUPP, with one hundred and fourteen men from Pennsylvania, reached Coal river last week, and they are now busily engaged in repairing the Locks and Dams of that river.

Major Kupp has employed many other hands, and intends, to repair the Locks and Dams and to make Coal river navigable from Peytona to Coal's Mouth, by the 15th November next. His operations have commenced on *all parts of the river*, and the improvement of the entire river will be carried on simultaneously until completed.

We are highly gratified to know that this improvement is going ahead. Its completion by next December, will be of incalculable benefit to the varied interests of the Coal river region. It will open to market a section of Virginia, unsurpassed for its superior *Cannel*, Splint and bituminous Coals.

Steamboat on Coal River.

The steam-boat "Clifton" made a trip last week, up Coal river. It passed through eight locks, and went to Peytona, the head of navigation on Coal river, a distance of thirty-five miles from Coalsmouth. The Clifton was employed by Coal Companies to tow ten empty flatboats from the Kanawha river to Peytona. Quite a sensation was created amongst the natives by the arrival of the Clifton, as it was the first steam-boat that ever was seen so far up Coal river.

From the January 30, 1860, issue of the *Kanawha Valley Star*.

General William Starke Rosecrans, a well-known Civil War officer in western Virginia and the western theater of operations, had business ties to Kanawha County prior to the war. A native of Ohio, he graduated from West Point and served in the U.S. Army from 1842-54. After resigning from the army in 1854, he went into the cannel coal business in the Coal River area. He also worked with other coal operations to improve navigation on the Kanawha River. In April 1861, Rosecrans rejoined the Union army and served as an aide-de-camp to General George McClellan during the campaign in western Virginia. When McClellan was called to Washington to take over the Union command, Rosecrans was made a brigadier-general and took over command in western Virginia. After April 1862, he commanded troops in the western theater with mixed results. Resigning from the army in 1867, he served as Minister to Mexico from 1868-69, then settled in California where he was elected to two terms in Congress from 1881-85, and then served as Register of the Treasury, 1885-93. He died in 1898.
COURTESY TERRY LOWRY

In the old days, the Kanawha River froze so solid that horses and wagons were driven on it. Mike Kelleher is standing on the ice opposite the city levee, near Capitol Street, circa 1920. The wooden Red Cross building can be seen on the city levee in the background. RA

A log jam on the Coal River in the early 1900s. Logs were cut in the upper reaches of the river and floated down to sawmills near St. Albans. RA

Brochures courtesy Gerald Sutphin

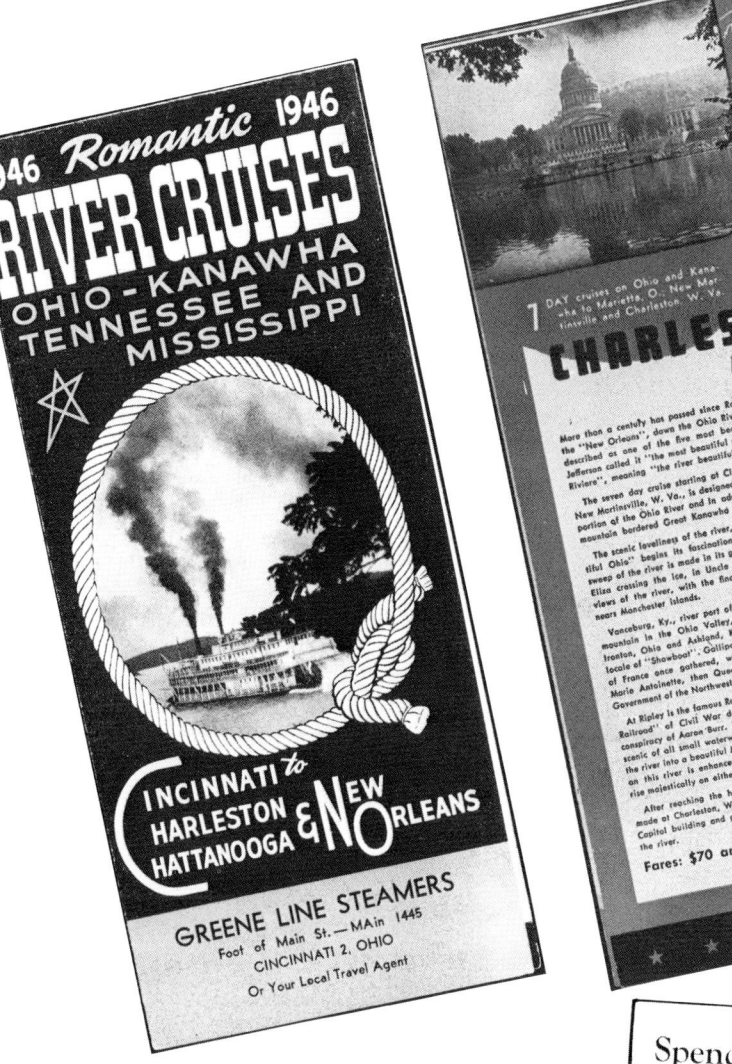
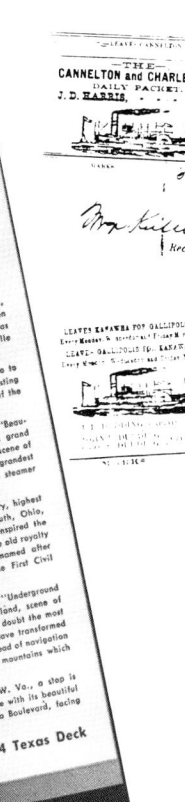
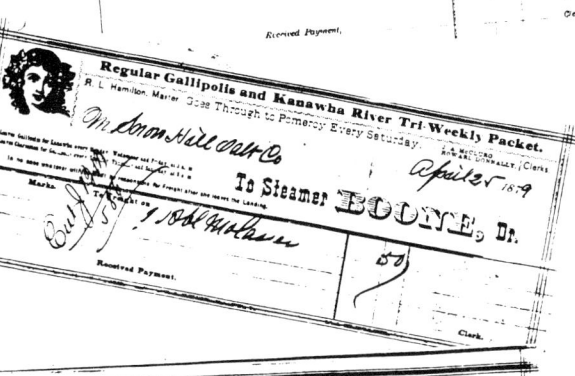

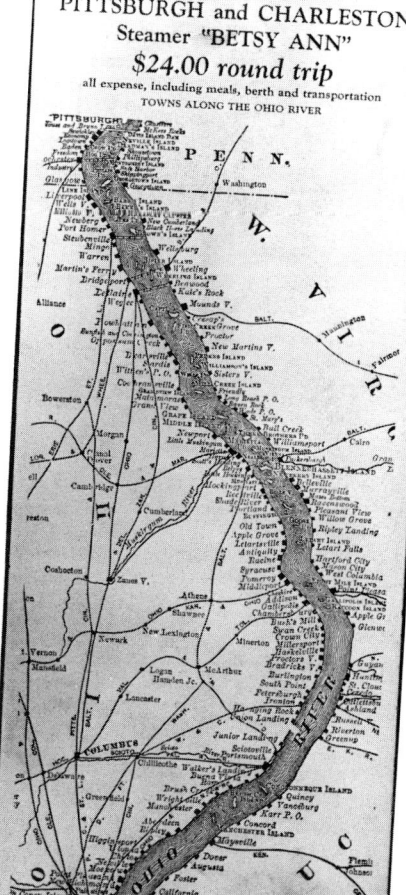

For many years one could take a steamer from Charleston to Cincinnati and on down the Ohio and Mississippi rivers to New Orleans. The Greene line was one of the larger companies on the river.
COURTESY CABELL COUNTY PUBLIC LIBRARY

The personal pleasure craft of Charles Ward, founder and owner of Ward Engineering Company, 1899. This craft was steam-powered and propeller driven. Note the temperature—100° F. COURTESY BERT PAYNE

The towboat, *Geo. T. Price*, was built by the Charles Ward Engineering Company of Charleston in the mid-1920s. SWV

River transportation on the Kanawha across from the C&O Railroad Station in 1905. Lowenstein & Sons Wholesale Hardware occupied the large building on the right. The steamboat is pushing wooden coal barges. KCL

For many years people lived on houseboats on the Elk River, circa 1938. LC

Bridges

The first railroad bridge in the county still spans the Elk River. It was built in 1883 by the Ohio Central Railroad, which evolved into the Kanawha and Michigan Railroad. The railroad built a new bridge next to the original in 1906, and this Whipple-type bridge was sold to the Kanawha Valley Traction Company for streetcar use. The sidewalk on the bridge was built in 1893 and sold to the city. With the demise of streetcars, the bridge was abandoned.

One of the older bridges across Elk River carries Virginia Street traffic.

The old Elkview bridge has now been replaced by a new bridge adjacent to it.

Engineer's drawing of the Keystone Bridge. RA

The Keystone Bridge was built in 1872-73 by J. Brisben Walker to provide access to his new development in West Charleston. It carried Virginia Street traffic across Elk River and was built of light steel with a wooden roadway. On January 13, 1879, a mass of ice from the Kanawha River backed up into the Elk, and three steamboats lifted up against the bridge and pushed it off its foundations. It was rebuilt in 1886. The present bridge was built in 1908 by the Kanawha Valley Traction Company for streetcars. Later the Keystone Bridge was moved upriver near Spring Street where it remained until the present bridge was constructed. RA

This wire suspension bridge, the first over the Elk River, was built in 1852 to connect east and west Charleston. Union troops cut the cables in 1862 to slow the advance of Confederate troops that were invading the Kanawha Valley from the east. (See page 98 for Civil War appearance). After the war, the cables were spliced together, and new planking was placed on the deck. Disaster struck again on the morning of December 15, 1904, when one of the cables snapped and the deck turned over and fell into the icy river. Two children on their way to Union School were killed, several others injured, and 11 horses were drowned. A team driver was also seriously injured. RA & WVU

This bridge was built at Lovell Street (now Washington Street).

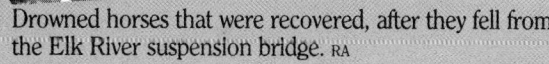

Drowned horses that were recovered, after they fell from the Elk River suspension bridge. RA

The South Side Bridge

One of very few photos of the first C&O Railroad station, at the south end of the old South Side Bridge. The present station was built in 1905. WVU

Cartoon in the *Charleston Gazette* by popular cartoonist Vintroux. Controversy surrounded the location of the bridge in the 1930s just as it does in the 1980s.

The original South Side Bridge was constructed in 1891 and served as a toll bridge until 1914. It provided easy access between the north and south parts of Charleston and lasted for 46 years, until it was condemned in 1936.
COURTESY ANDREW BROWN

In the fall of 1936, a celebration was held at the city levee when the old South Side Bridge was dropped into the river. The buildings on the riverfront were all removed when construction began on the boulevard. GS

The old bridge was destroyed in 1936 to make way for new construction. KCL COURTESY RICK HAMILTON

Laying steel girders on the south approach to the new bridge. SWV

The construction of the South Side Bridge in 1937. The bridge was opened to traffic that year. WW

Works Progress Administration funds were used to construct the new South Side Bridge in 1937. The city had to contribute $400,000 or 60 percent of the actual cost. At the time, this was the largest WPA project in the nation. NA

The north approach ramp to the new South Side Bridge as it appeared in the late 1930s. Note the massive stone blocks that were originally on the 1891 bridge. The extension of Dickinson Street to Quarrier Street was opened in 1957. SWV

Former governor MacCorkle and his associates built the Kanawha City Bridge in 1915 to provide streetcar access to Kanawha City and as far as Cabin Creek. It was a toll bridge from 1915 to 1928. On June 19, 1975, the structure was dropped into the river by a massive intentional explosion. Two new bridges, one for each lane of traffic, replaced the old bridge. CN

The approach from Charleston to the Kanawha City Bridge, May 1916. The overhead wires are for the streetcars. The rest of the bridge provided access for cars and trucks. C & P TELEPHONE MUSEUM

The C&O Railroad bridge, from Charleston's west side to South Charleston, was constructed in 1907. For a time the bridge was also used by the streetcar line to South Charleston. This photo was taken in 1931. For many years the bridge had a wooden side structure that allowed light automobiles to cross the river. It was removed in 1932 when the Patrick Street Bridge opened. GS

The Patrick Street bridge, shown here in the early 1940s, was constructed in 1932 for $850,000. It provided much-needed access between west and south Charleston. The small community at the south end of the bridge was called Bonamont. It has now been absorbed into South Charleston. KCL

This 1931 aerial view of the Patrick Street Bridge shows the entire Kelley Axe factory on the north end of the bridge. GS

Before the St. Albans Bridge was constructed, Lee's ferry operated from Sattes to St. Albans. This photo was taken in 1930. WW

The first automobile to pay a toll on the Chelyan Bridge in 1929. The toll taker is L.R. "Coxie" Eskins; the driver, Quince Dunlap; the passenger, Percy Creasy. C.H. Surface and W.H. Surface are seated in the back. EG

This is thought to be the earliest known photograph taken in the Charleston area. Several historians have placed this in 1863 or 1864. The men are lined up along Front Street (Kanawha Boulevard) outfitted in some type of fraternal regalia. A few Union soldiers can be picked out in the crowd. It is not known what the occasion was. The three story building is the Bank of the West at the corner of Front and Summers streets. E. T. Moore, who moved to Charleston from Gallipolis, Ohio, sometime during the Civil War, has his printing business sign displayed and apparently is painting a large sign with his name on it (The E has already been done). By June 1864, Moore was joined by his brother S. Spencer Moore. The business was known as Moore & Brother, Publishers. The building on the extreme right is the Laidley Drug Store with a statue of the Goddess of Health, *Hygeia*, and the word OIL on the column.

COURTESY DAVE MOORE

Chapter Six
The Terrible Conflict
Civil War 1861-1865

Civil War 1861-65

The terrible conflict of 1861-65 was a traumatic time in the history of Charleston and Kanawha County. Virginia, along with the other border states of Maryland, Kentucky, and Missouri, suffered more initially than other southern states because of the sectionalism within her borders. Eventually the western, mostly non-slave holding counties of Virginia broke away from eastern Virginia to form the new state of West Virginia.

Kanawha County, which lies in the southern portion of the state, was chaotic in the spring of 1861. Several military units, formed before the war, sided with Virginia when it seceded from the Union on April 17, 1861. Many citizens of the area were neutral or undecided about their allegiances, and by the end of the war, the county had furnished five companies of soldiers to both the northern and southern armies.

Two prominent Charleston residents, Dr. Spicer Patrick and George W. Summers, were sent to Richmond, where the eastern Virginians were clamoring for secession. Both men, along with 30 other delegates from the western counties, voted against the state's withdrawal from the Union, but they were voted down.

In the northern counties an overwhelming majority of people were for the Union and in time, they established a restored government of Virginia, loyal to the Union. After the Wheeling Convention of 1861 and approval by the United States Congress and the President, West Virginia entered the Union on June 20, 1863.

Before going on to larger commands in the east, Colonel John McCausland, a native of Mason County, played an important part in the Kanawha Valley during the early days of the Civil War. He returned home several years after the war and lived on his farm until his death in 1927. He was the last general officer of the Confederate armies to die.
COURTESY TERRY LOWRY

At the start of the Civil War broadsides were posted throughout southwestern (West) Virginia to recruit troops for Confederate service. Although this area was still part of Virginia, and sided with the Confederacy, many men remained neutral or joined the Federal forces.
SWV

Colonel George S. Patton and the Kanawha Riflemen

Colonel George S. Patton, a resident of Charleston before the outbreak of the Civil War, was one of the most colorful figures in that war. His grandson, General George S. Patton, carried on the military tradition of the Patton family in World War II.

Colonel Patton sided with his native Virginia at the outbreak of the conflict. He participated in numerous battles in Virginia and West Virginia and was mortally wounded in September 1864 while leading his troops at the Battle of Winchester. Patton was highly respected by his commanders in the field for his leadership and character.

Patton came from Richmond to Charleston in 1856 to practice law, where he was associated part of the time with Thomas Broun. Patton was a man of ability, good looks, and social attainment, as well as a man of honor and tremendous courage. He was a graduate of the Virginia Military Institute in 1852. When he came to Charleston, he formed a military company similar to the well-known Richmond Light Infantry Blues. The company was first called the Kanawha Minutemen, but in 1859 the name was changed to the Kanawha Riflemen. Young aristocrats and men of high standing flocked to join the company. Its bright uniforms and sharp drill were well-known throughout the area. The Kanawha Riflemen were said to be the best-drilled company in the entire Confederate Army, the result of Patton's superb military training.

The company was organized in 1856 and subsequently reorganized in 1858 and 1861. On May 8, a month after Virginia joined the Confederacy in April 1861, the Riflemen formed Company H of the 22nd Virginia Infantry Regiment. Patton later rose to commander of the regiment.

When the war broke out, the Riflemen issued the following statement:

Meeting of the Kanawha Riflemen

At a meeting of the Kanawha Riflemen held in the town of Charleston on the 19th day of April 1861, Captain George S. Patton, presiding, Lieutenant Fitzhugh offered the following preamble and resolution:

Whereas an unjust and unnecessary war has been forced on the country by the administration at Washington, in which our state may be required to take part; we the Kanawha Riflemen, hereby declare it to be our fixed purpose never to use our arms against the State of Virginia, or any other Southern State, in any attempt by said administration to coerce or subjugate them; and we hold ourselves ready to respond to every call that may be made on us to defend our State and section from hostile invasion: therefore, be it unanimously resolved,

That we hereby tender the services of this Company, to the authorities of the State, to be used in the emergency comtemplated in the foregoing preamble.

Which preamble and resolution were unanimously adopted.

On motion, resolved, that these proceedings be published in the Kanawha papers, and that a copy thereof be sent to the Adjutant General of the State.

George S. Patton, Pres't.
John Dryden, Sec'y.

Colonel George S. Patton

Thomas Lee Broun

John Rundle

Thomas Lee Broun was a member of the Kanawha Riflemen, an 1848 graduate of the University of Virginia, a school teacher, and a law partner of George S. Patton. He succeeded William S. Rosecrans as president of the Coal River Navigation Company in 1858.

COURTESY TERRY LOWRY

John Rundle, a Kanawha Rifleman, published the *Kanawha Valley Star*, an early Charleston newspaper. First published in Buffalo as the *Star of the Kanawha Valley* in 1855, the paper moved to Charleston in 1857 where it took a strong Democratic and pro-Southern stand. Union troops confiscated Rundle's paper in 1861.

COURTESY TERRY LOWRY

Company Orders #1 for the Kanawha Riflemen

KANAWHA VALLEY STAR
April 30, 1861

Kanawha Riflemen

Company Orders #1
April 26, 1861

1. In compliance with the requisition of a Proclamation of the Governor of Virginia dated at Richmond the 19th of April 1861, this command will hold itself in readiness for marching orders.

2. In case such orders shall arrive, each one must provide himself with the following articles at least in addition to dress and fatique uniforms, to wit: two shirts, four collars, two pair of socks, two pair of drawers, one blacking brush and box (to any two files), two pair white Berlin gloves, one quart tin cup, one white cotton haversack, one case knife, fork and spoon, two towels, two hankerchiefs, comb and brush, and toothbrush. Some stout linen thread, a few buttons, paper of pins and a thimble, in a small buckskin or cloth bag.

3. There being no knapsacks in the possession of the company one ordinary sized carpetsack will be allowed to every two men, for the purpose of holding such of the above articles as are not in constant use. The knife, fork, spoon, haversack and tin cup, must be worn about the person, the first three and the last articles to the waist belt. Immediately after the receipt and promulgation of marching orders, the carpetsacks, duly packed, must be delivered to the Quartermaster Sergeant, neatly marked with the names of the two owners. Each file will procure a comfortable blanket and upon the receipt of orders, send the same in to the Quartermaster Sergeant, shaped into a neat and compact bundle conspicuously marked with his name.

4. It is earnestly recommended that all under clothes should be woolen, especially the socks, as cotton socks are utterly unfit for marching in, and all files should wear woolen undershirts. Shoes, sewed soles, and fitting easily, but not too loosely to the foot, coming up over the ankle, are infinitely preferable to boots, and should be made strong and servicable.

5. By the liberality and patriotism of the residents of Charleston (one of them a lady) flannel cloth (grey) has been furnished for fatigue Jackets, and provision made for cutting them, all members of the company are hereby required at once to have their measures taken and Jackets cut by Mr. James B. Noyes, tailor. Many ladies have kindly undertaken to make them up. All members of the company are required to have their Jackets finished by Wednesday afternoon next at the latest. By like liberality of another resident, cloth for haversacks has been procured, and they have been cut out by another lady. They will be delivered by the Quartermaster Sergeant, and they must be finished by the same evening.

6. Assistant Surgeon Joseph Watkins will immediately, upon the receipt of marching orders, prepare and put in portable form an ample supply of medicines, and be prepared to hire medical aid whenever required on the march or in transit or in camp. He will also provide himself with appropriate instruments, & c. In this connection the undersigned gratefully acknowledges on behalf of the company the liberal offer of a citizen of this town, to furnish free of charge all medicines required.

Henry D. McFarland, whose brother was president of the Bank of Virginia, was another Kanawha Riflemen from Charleston.
COURTESY TERRY LOWRY

The overcoat of Kanawha Rifleman Levi Welch on display at the West Virginia State Museum. The Riflemen's uniforms were apparently designed by Colonel Patton, who modeled them after those worn by the Richmond Light Infantry Blues. SWV

7. Quartermaster Sergeant John Dryden will immediately, on the receipt of marching orders, procure the necessary transportation for the baggage of the command and necessary camp utensils and fixtures, and in case the order shall require a march overland, will lay in at least six hundred rations, and provide for their transportation; the ration being one pound and a half of pork or beef (as much of the latter as can be purchased fresh), eighteen ounces of meat and one-fourth pound of corn meal, and to each one hundred rations the following articles, ten pounds of rice, six pounds of coffee, twelve pounds of sugar, one gallon of vinegar, one pound of star candles, four pounds of soap and two quarts of salt. Private Joseph M. Brown is hereby detailed as an assistant to the Quartermaster and will report to him accordingly.

8. The band will go as a band, and are as such until further orders, will carry their instruments with them, but in every other respect will govern themselves by the preceeding directions.

9. The undersigned, in issuing these preparatory orders has but little doubt that the services of this command will be required to aid in driving the invader from the soil of Virginia, but has none that every Rifleman will respond cheerfully and with alacrity to the call of his State, and be prepared to do his duty bravely under the grand old flag of Virginia.

GEO. S. PATTON
Captain

"In our town there was strife, neighbor against neighbor, and in some instances the son against the father. The times were awful, and soldiers would shoot at citizens for fun."
—A resident of Saint Albans

This is the only known photo of the Kanawha Riflemen as they posed together in Charleston in 1865, shortly after the war was over. This copy of a tintype appeared in the *Charleston Daily Mail*, December 7, 1952. They are left to right, back row: Major Thomas Broun, Colonel Thomas Smith, Major Sam A. Miller, Colonel Tomas E. Fife (not listed on the Riflemen's 1861 roster), Captain Nicholas Fitzhugh; seated: Dr. Joseph F. Watkins, Lieutenant William Quarrier, Captain Richard Q. Laidley and Captain John Swann. *CHARLESTON DAILY MAIL*

Elm Grove, the Craik-Patton House

In 1828 James Craik, a young lawyer from Alexandria, Virginia, settled in Charleston to become the rector of St. John's Episcopal Church. He married Juliet Shrewsbury and in 1834 built the Greek Revival house known as Elm Grove. James Craik was the grandson of George Washington's personal physician and the son of Washington's secretary.

Thirty years later, Patton bought Elm Grove, which stood in the vicinity of the present Dunbar Street and the old Kanawha Valley Hospital. He lived there with his wife until he entered the Confederate Army in 1861. Their son, the father of World War II general George S. Patton, was born in Elm Grove. Mrs. Patton and the children left Charleston during the war to settle in Goochland County, Virginia, and Elm Grove was sold to Andrew B. Hogue. In 1907 the house was moved to 1316 Lee Street.

In 1971 the National Society of Colonial Dames of America in West Virginia moved the house to its present site at Daniel Boone Park and restored it to its former 1834 appearance.

The Craik-Patton house at its original location, where Dunbar Street intersects Virginia Street.
COURTESY PAUL VAUGHAN

(Below left) General Henry Alexander Wise, former governor of Virginia, and commander of Confederate forces in western Virginia at the start of the war. On June 26, 1861, Wise arrived in Charleston with 12 soldiers to recruit men into the Confederate Army. LC

(Below right) General Jacob D. Cox, a Canadian by birth and lawyer by profession, commanded the Ohio troops who were ordered into the Kanawha Valley in June 1861.
COURTESY MUDD LIBRARY, OBERLIN COLLEGE

In 1861 Charleston was the county seat and the center of trade and commerce for the Kanawha Valley. The James River and Kanawha Turnpike passed through the town, connecting the Ohio River with Lewisburg in Greenbrier County and the Shenandoah Valley of Virginia. This conduit to Ohio in the west and the Virginia valley to the east would dictate events in the Kanawha Valley throughout the war.

Approximately 1,500 people lived in Charleston in 1861, and the county population of 16,000 was mainly concentrated along the Kanawha River from Coalsmouth (St. Albans) to Malden and Cedar Grove. Salt was still the most important resource in the area and was sought after by both sides.

The riverfront housed most of Charleston's businesses along Cox's Lane (present day Capitol Street) that stretched back toward the hills. Several large buildings were in the "downtown" area: a branch of the Bank of Virginia at the corner of present-day Capitol Street and Kanawha Boulevard, the "Kanawha House" at the corner of Summers Street and Kanawha Boulevard, the old courthouse on its present site, and Mercer Academy near the corner of Hale and Quarrier Streets. Several churches, including the Asbury Chapel of the Methodist Church, the Presbyterian Church, and St. John's Episcopal Church were established in this area.

The Kanawha Valley was first occupied by a small Confederate army commanded by Brigadier-General Henry A. Wise, an ex-governor of Virginia. He led his troops over the mountains from Lewisburg, and marched into Charleston on June 26, 1861. His purposes were to recruit soldiers for his "Wise Legion," and, if possible, to expand the authority of the Confederate government to the Ohio River.

Wise's troops, which consisted primarily of the Richmond Light Infantry Blues and some cavalry units, set up their headquarters on the Littlepage farm at Kanawha Two-Mile. The local militia units were pressed into Confederate service, and they established their headquarters on the farm of William and Beverly D. Tompkins at Coalsmouth, slightly west of the mouth of Coal River near Tackett's Creek. Tompkins' spacious, antebellum mansion, known as Valcoulon, was used as the headquarters for Colonel George S. Patton and Christopher Q. Tompkins, commander of Virginia volunteers.

The federal authorities closely followed the occupation of the Kanawha Valley because they believed it was dangerous to the state of Ohio. The citizens in the northern part of western Virginia asked the commander of the Union troops in Ohio, General George B. McClellan, to occupy their area and drive out the southern troops concentrated there.

At the beginning of the war Colonel Christopher Q. Tompkins was a commander of Confederate forces in the Kanawha Valley. Before the war he was a retired army officer who had moved to the Gauley Bridge area, built a fine home and was active in the coal business.
COURTESY VIRGINIA STATE LIBRARY

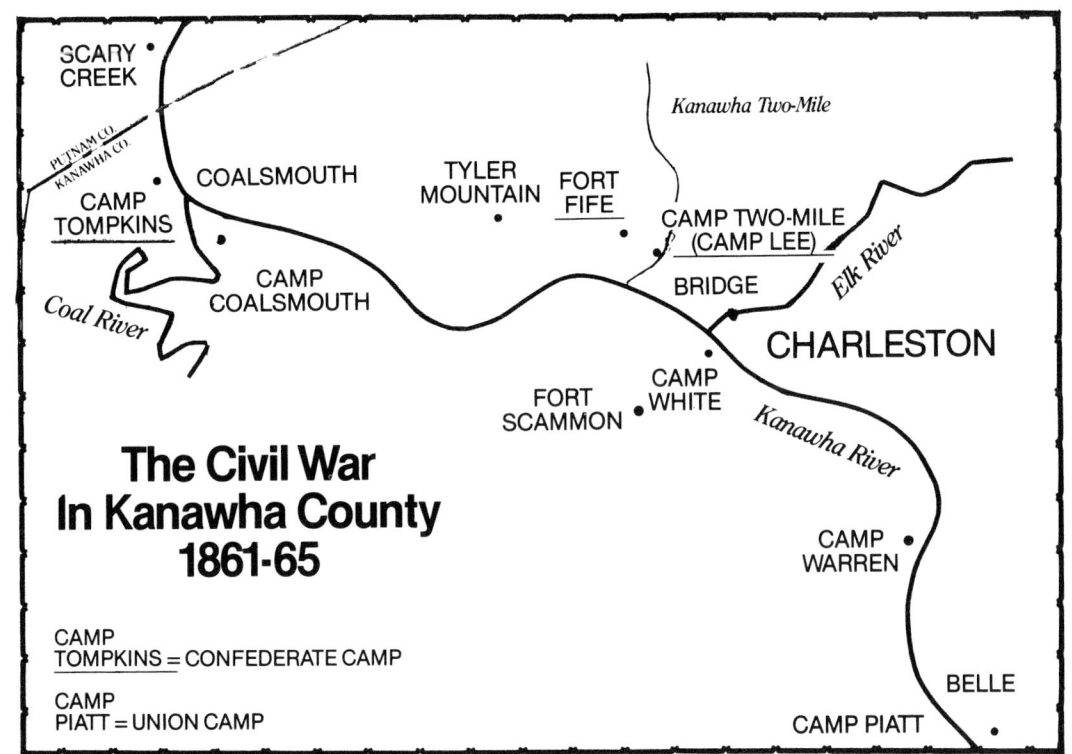

The Littlepage Stone Mansion was built in 1845 by Adam Littlepage. Today it is used as an office for the Charleston Housing Authority. COURTESY MRS. JOHN T. MORGAN

A post-war view of the apple orchard at Camp Two-Mile. The Confederates established the camp on the farm of Adam Brown Dickinson Littlepage, along Two-Mile Creek. The military camp extended from the Kanawha River to the junction of the Ripley-Ravenswood road and the Point Pleasant road (present West Washington Street). It is now the site of the Orchard Manor housing development. COURTESY MRS. JOHN T. MORGAN

In 1861 Mrs. Rebecca Littlepage, mistress of the Littlepage Mansion, denied entrance to the house by General Wise, who threatened to blow it up by cannon fire. COURTESY MRS. JOHN T. MORGAN

Pryce Lewis, glass in hand, toasts Colonel George S. Patton during their meeting at the Valcoulon Mansion, Camp Tompkins. Sam Bridgeman, Lewis' assistant and traveling companion, looks on from the left. FROM ALAN PINKERTON'S *SPY OF THE REBELLION*

Pryce Lewis, a Union spy employed by Alan Pinkerton, spent time in the Kanawha Valley prior to the Scary Creek battle obtaining information on Confederate troops and their fortification. He posed as an English tourist and was befriended by Colonel Patton and Colonel Tompkins, but was rebuffed by Wise when he tried to get a pass to travel to Richmond. Although he eventually made it back to Union lines in Ohio, he was too late to give any useful information to General Cox, who had already fought at Scary Creek.
COURTESY MARY LEWIS COLLEGE

Valcoulon, an antebellum mansion on the farm of William and Beverly Tompkins at Coalsmouth, was the headquarters for Colonel George S. Patton before the Battle of Scary Creek. It is on the site of the present day Valley Drive-In movie screen, just off Route 35 and 60 near St. Albans. COURTESY GARLAND ELLIS

A first sergeant in the 8th Virginia Cavalry sent to a Miss Sallie Young in Teays Valley, Putnam County, the following poem he had written about Wise's retreat.
ROY BIRD COOK COLLECTION, WVU

WISE'S RETREAT FROM HAWKS NEST

Should old c   uaintence be forgot
And never   ught to mind
To think old   e had run away
And left o   g behind

He stole awa   last old goose
He eat the _____ cow*
He did not sp_____ horse*
But left one

He used up all the oats and corn
He fed up all the hay
And when the eleventh came in sight
Old Wise he ran away

He ran so fast he could not stop
For valley and for hill
He had no time to call around
To pay his washing bill

And when old Gabriel blow his horn
And the devil claim his own
May he throw wide his arms
To welcome old Wise home

And when he takes old Wise below
With Jenkins and his host
May he, with fear and trembling
No longer swear and boast

When Floyd comes home to meet him
Which he is sure to do
May the devil and his angels
Put both the traitors through

But, good devil, be you careful
And give them all they need
Or, by the great old Moses
They'll get mad and secede

Watch Floyd in every movement
Be sure to guard him well
For if you don't be careful
He'll steal Wise out of h-ll.

*Illegible

In early July, a part of Cox's troops travelled by road into Putnam County, while the remainder came by steamboat up the Kanawha River and unloaded at Poca.

When the two armies were opposite each other, the inevitable battle took place at the mouth of Scary Creek, just over the county border in Putnam County. The first Kanawha County soldier killed in the battle, James Clark Welch, is now buried in Spring Hill Cemetery. Colonel George S. Patton, commander of the Confederate troops, was severely wounded but lived to fight for three more years.

The Confederates claimed that they won the battle, but their victory was short-lived. Union forces, under McClellan's command, threatened to move down toward Charleston after their victories at Philippi and Rich Mountain. Cox's troops, now reinforced, were still in the valley. Wise recognized that his troops in the Kanawha Valley could easily be caught in a pincher movement and decided to abandon the valley and pull back toward the east.

On the night of July 24, only a week after the "victory at Scary Creek," the Confederates pulled out of Charleston and headed east to Gauley Bridge. They partially damaged the Elk River bridge in Charleston, hoping to impede a Union advance, and burned the strategic covered bridge that crossed the Gauley River at Gauley Bridge. Their actions effectively stopped any Union advance beyond the Gauley.

Meanwhile, 700 Confederate troops boarded the steamboat *Julia Maffitt* and, as fast as possible, headed upriver to join Wise's retreat. Near Dunbar, Yankee troops on shore opened fire on the boat and forced it to the opposite shore. The pilot, Philip Doddridge, set the boat on fire and the troops were forced to set out on foot to the east.

On July 25, Cox moved his troops into Charleston without firing a shot, and quickly secured the area all the way to Gauley Bridge, where he set up a large supply base. The Federal headquarters were set up in the Lewis home at the corner of the present-day Capitol and Lee streets. Charleston's mayor, Jacob Goshorn, surrendered the city and then fled south until the end of the war.

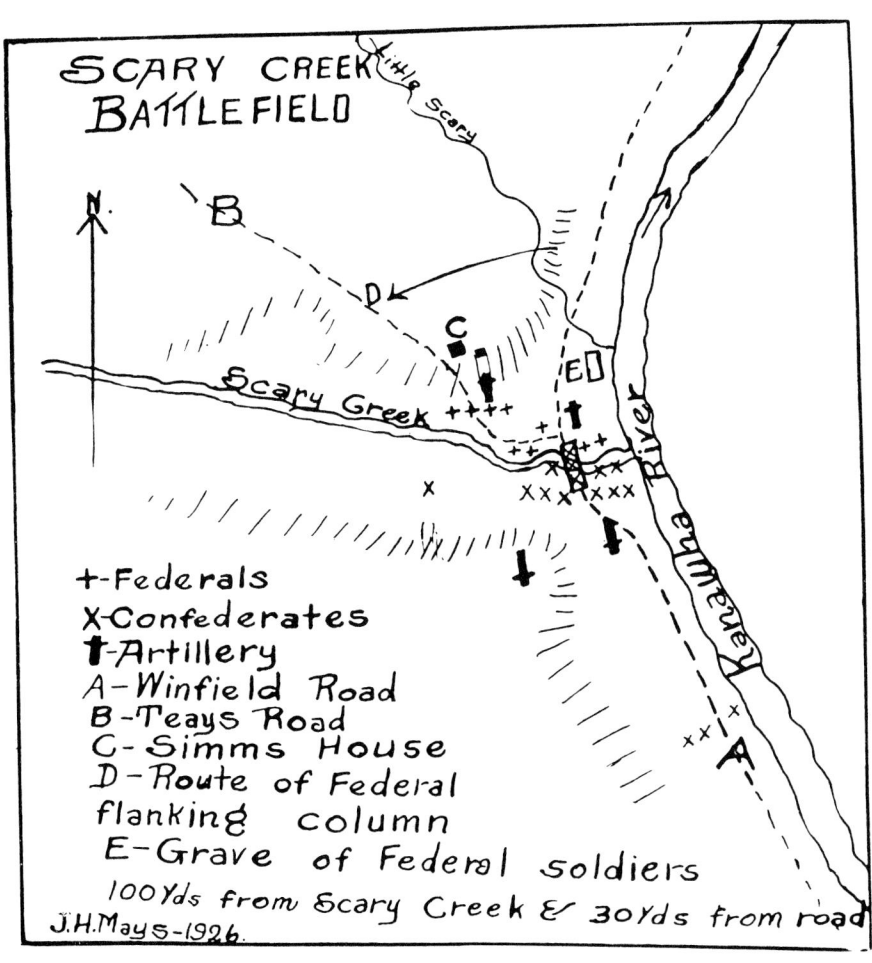

SCARY CREEK BATTLEFIELD MAP—As drawn by Confederate veteran James H. Mays in 1926.

Wise's troops used the Absalom Bowen Tavern (Six-Mile House) at Tyler Mountain as a source of drinking water in 1861. COURTESY BOWEN HEIRS

The Bowen Tavern today still looks like it did during the war, although its outer walls have been stuccoed. It is one of the few pre-Civil War homes in the Tyler Mountain area still standing.

COURTESY GARY BAYS

Morgan's plantation kitchen, which was used as a hospital after the Battle of Scary Creek. It was originally on John Morgan's farm in Putnam County but was moved in the 1960s to the St. Albans riverside park on Route 60.

The grave of James Clark Welch, one of four confederate soldiers killed at the Battle of Scary Creek. He is buried in the family plot at Spring Hill Cemetery in Charleston.
COURTESY GARY BAYS

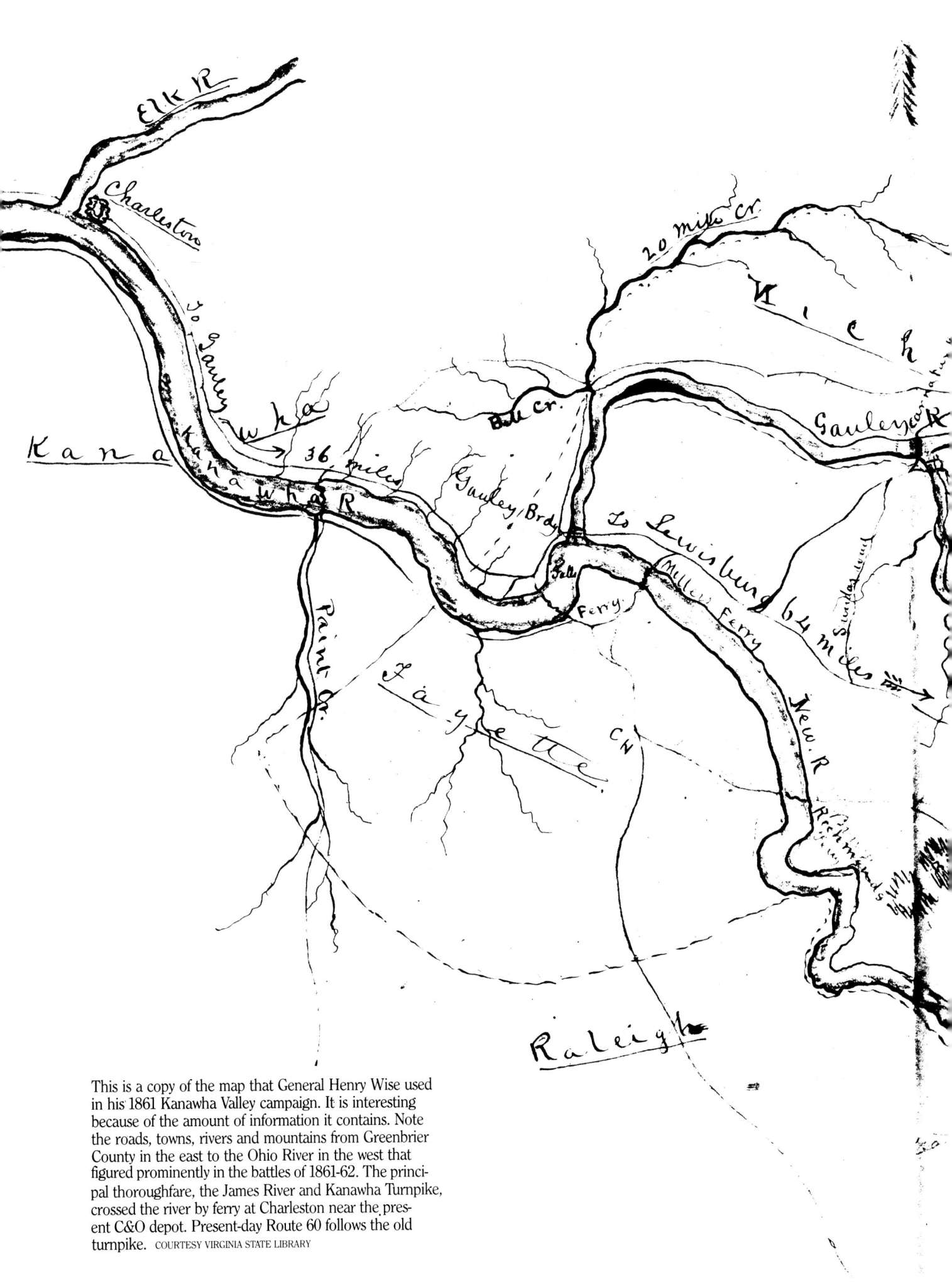

This is a copy of the map that General Henry Wise used in his 1861 Kanawha Valley campaign. It is interesting because of the amount of information it contains. Note the roads, towns, rivers and mountains from Greenbrier County in the east to the Ohio River in the west that figured prominently in the battles of 1861-62. The principal thoroughfare, the James River and Kanawha Turnpike, crossed the river by ferry at Charleston near the present C&O depot. Present-day Route 60 follows the old turnpike. COURTESY VIRGINIA STATE LIBRARY

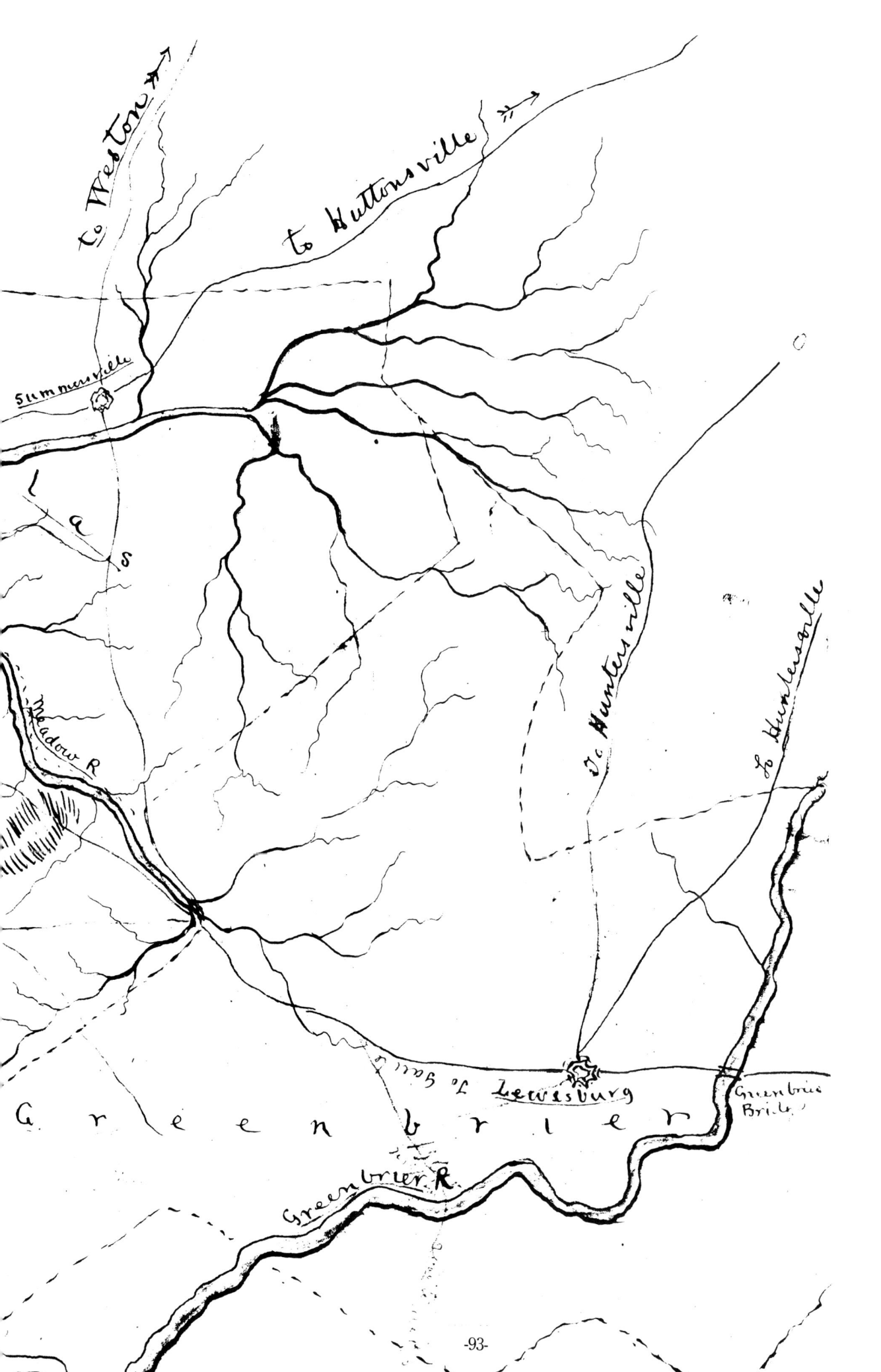

Steamboats were important during the war for transporting troops and supplies along the river from Ohio to the Kanawha Valley. BATTLES AND LEADERS OF THE CIVIL WAR.

On December 20, 1861, the first military execution in western Virginia—and one of the first of the war—took place on Charleston's West Side. Private Richard Gatewood of Company C, 1st Kentucky Infantry, was stationed at Gauley Bridge under General Jacob Cox's command, when he was court-martialed for desertion, threatening an officer and assaulting a fellow soldier. General Cox personally took charge of the execution in the interest of maintaining discipline among his troops.
AUTHOR'S COLLECTION

General George B. McClellan commanded the Union troops in western Virginia, including the Kanawha Valley, at the start of the war. AUTHOR'S COLLECTION

The Kanawha Valley was occupied by Union troops for over a year while great battles were raging to the east in Virginia. With Union troops in control of the most strategic portions of western Virginia, the citizens voted on October 24, 1861, to formally create a new state that was composed of the western Virginia counties. "Kanawha" was the proposed name for the new state.

The county overwhelmingly approved the creation of the new state; only one vote was cast against it. Because most of the men with southern sympathies had left, Union troops occupied the area, and women could not vote, it is quite understandable that the vote was 1,039 to one for statehood.

During the first Constitutional Convention at Wheeling in November 1861, Kanawha County lost out on naming the state after itself and West Virginia was officially adopted as the name of the proposed state. The new state entered the Union on June 20, 1863.

After approximately one year and two months of Union occupation and relative peace in the county, the war came back into the lives of the citizens for a brief time. General Joseph A.J. Lightburn from Lewis County was in command, although some of his troops had been transferred to Virginia. General Robert E. Lee directed General W.W. Loring, the Confederate commander who was stationed at Pearisburg, Virginia, to invade the Kanawha Valley, capture it, and use it as a base to recover Trans-Allegheny Virginia. Because the South was short of salt, the salt supply at Kanawha Salines was a deciding factor in this operation.

September 1, 1862, Loring marched with 4,000 troops to Fayetteville. The September 11 battle there resulted in an unexpected Union rout. Lightburn ordered a general retreat and called in his outposts at Ansted and Summersville, thus opening up the entire Kanawha Valley. He retreated down the Cotton Hill road near Gauley Bridge to Marmet, while the main body of his troops retreated down the Kanawha Turnpike in a wagon train 13 miles long. His army finally rejoined at Charleston to defend the city.

Early the morning of September 13, the first units of Loring's army arrived in Charleston in the vicinity of the University of Charleston. After an all-day battle, Lightburn retreated toward the Ohio River, cutting the cables on the bridge over the Elk River at Charleston. Loring did not pursue him.

(Left) General Joseph A.J. Lightburn, a native of Lewis County, was Union commander in the Kanawha Valley until Confederate troops forced his retreat in September 1862.
AUTHOR'S COLLECTION

(Right) General W.W. Loring was the last Confederate commander to invade and occupy the Kanawha Valley. His stay didn't last long.
AUTHOR'S COLLECTION

Newspapers of the Civil War era. The *Kanawha Valley Star* was founded at Buffalo, Putnam County, in 1855 as the *Star of the Kanawha Valley*. It moved its office to Charleston in 1857 and expounded the Democratic, pro-Southern cause. The publisher was John Rundle, who, as a member of the Kanawha Riflemen, joined the Confederate army in 1861. Union troops confiscated his press when they occupied Charleston in July 1861. Only two copies are known of *The Guerilla*, which was published in Charleston during the Confederacy's short occupation of the Kanawha Valley in September 1862. The *Charleston Daily Bulletin* was published in 1864 by E. T. and S. Spencer Moore and contained much war news and advertisements. The Moore Brothers were also job printers and dealers in newspapers, including *West Virginia Journal*, periodicals and stationery supplies. All newspapers are on file at the West Virginia State Archives.

THE GUERILLA.

DEVOTED TO SOUTHERN RIGHTS AND INSTITUTIONS. — No. 2

CHARLESTON, VA., SEPTEMBER 29, 1862.

...E GUERILLA,
...UBLISHED EVERY AFTERNOON
...the Associate Printers.
...—TEN CENTS per copy, or FIFTY CENTS
...k.

For the Guerilla:

...NES ON THE MARCH.

...soldier lay on the frozen ground,
...ith only a blanket tightened around
His weary and wasted frame;
...own at his feet the fitful light
...f fading coals, in the freezing night,
...ell as a mockery on the sight,
A heatless, purple flame.

All day long with his heavy load,
Weary and sore, in the mountain road,
And over the desolate plain;
All day long through the crusted mud,
Over the snow, and through the flood,
Marking his way with a track of blood,
He followed the winding train.

Nothing to eat at the bivouac,
But a frozen crust in his haversack,
The half of a comrade's store—
A crust that [illegible]
Some pampered spaniel might have passed,
Knowing that morsel to be the last
That lay at his master's door.

No other sound on his slumber fell,
Than the lonesome tread of the sentinel,
That equal, measured pace,
And the wind that came from the cracking pines
And the dying oak, and the swinging vine,
In many a weary, weary line,
To the soldier's hollow face.

But the soldier slept, and dreams were bright
As the rosy glow of his bridal night,
With the angel on his breast;
For he passed away from the wintry gloom,
To the pleasant light of a cheerful room,
Where a cat sat purring upon the loom,
And his weary heart was blest.

His children came—two blue-eyed girls,
With laughing lips, and sunny curls,
And cheeks of ruddy glow—
And the mother pale, but lovely now,
As when upon her virgin brow,
He proudly sealed his early vow,
In the summer, long ago.

But the *reveille* wild, in the morning gray,
Startled the beautiful vision away,
Like a frightened bird of the night;
...it seemed to the soldier's misty brain
...that sounded again,
... uneasy pain,

LATEST NORTHERN NEWS.

We clip the following accounts of the fight at Fayette C. H., on the 10th instant, and the exodus of the enemy from the Kanawha Valley, from the Cincin... *Commercial* of the 19th:

THE LATE BATTLE AT FAYETTE C. H.

From all I can learn, the only regiments engaged in the battle of the 10th inst. were the 34th and 37th Ohio. The Thirty-fourth was raised by Col. Don Piatt, and will be best known as the Piatt Zouaves. It is now commanded by Col. Toland, an officer who abundantly proved his military skill and capacity in the late engagement. The Zouaves fought desperately, and displayed an amount of courage and determination worthy of veterans. They met the rebels outside the fortifications of Fayette, while less brave men would have remained inside, and their long list of killed and wounded tell how manfully they battled for the cause of liberty. The force contending against them numbered not less that 7,000, at least half of which attacked them especially, while the others attempted the capture of the earthworks. The conduct of the 37th is spoken of in terms of highest praise. They [illegible] the enemy [illegible] drawing them into cross-fires and [illegible] tifications, drawing them into cross-fires and ambuscades, and reducing their ranks terribly each time.

The loss of the 37th was small, and I have as yet been unable to obtain a list of those of its members who were injured. I sent by telegraph to-day the names of all the wounded of the 34th. The list of killed has not yet been made out; it will number about fifteen perhaps more. Of the wounded very few are considered dangerous. A majority of the wounds are in the lower limbs. All the necessary amputations have already been made, and were noted in my dispatch yesterday. Capt. Hatfield, of company A, it is feared will not recover. He was shot through the hip, receiving a wound very much similar to that received by Gen. Nelson, at Richmond, Ky. The surgeon said to-day that the Captain's case was more hopeful than at first; that he had not lost any thing in three days, and might possibly live. His wife and several friends are here to nurse and care for him. He is highly esteemed as an officer by superiors and inferiors.

Col. Toland escaped uninjured. He was at the head of his regiment during the battle, and had two horses shot under him.

The wounded Zouaves are well cared for. They are all in the general hospital, about a mile from the city—a building put up expressly for the purpose for which it is used, and admirably adapted to it. I have never seen a cleaner hospital or one where the ... of the sick are better attended to.

EXODUS FROM THE KANAWHA.

During the past few days the Kanawha and Ohio rivers, between this point and Gauley, have been full of flatboats, batteaux, skiffs, rafts, and all manner of buoyant conveyance, laden with the families of Unionists, who find themselves compelled to flee on the approach of the Confederate army, fearing the rebel General will carry into execution his recently made threat to hang every citizen "Yankee" he found in the Kanawha Valley. Hundreds of people who two years ago, were the quiet possessors of large farms, are now driven away from home in a condition bordering on destitution. Unable to remove their farm stock, they are obliged to leave behind them what they depended on for subsistence during the coming winter. Arriving at Gallipolis, or elsewhere, most of them have to seek a charitable home among strangers—a few only, comparatively, have relatives or friends to live with. It is a pitiable sight to see families sent adrift, with their little lots of household furniture, to find a home, they know not where—and all because their father or husband would not renounce his allegiance to the Government of his fathers. The rebels in Western Virginia have declared themselves unsatisfied with anything less than armed resistance to the Federal [illegible] the part of citizens whom they meet in their raids. It will not do to say you have not taken sides either way, or that your sympathies only are with one side or the other. They demand active participation in their cause, and "confiscation," robbery and outrage are the punishments for Federalism. The whites are not the only emigrants from the Kanawha Valley. The negroes have absconded in hundreds, and few less than a thousand have left their disloyal masters to inquire as to their whereabouts and wonder at the answer. The darkies have constructed the most ingenious kind of sailing craft, and in the efforts to elude the rebel advent, which they have learned to dread greatly, have entrusted themselves to the most fragile of home-made vessels. I heard an escaped contraband say, today, that he came down the Kanawha fifty miles on a log, but that he would rather drown than remain with his master, who is in Loring's army and is expected home in a few days.

The rebels, the darkies say, have threatened death to the negroes of the Kanawha Valley, whom they accuse of having kept the Federal forces posted as to Confederate movements coming within their knowledge. The acts and orders of some of our Generals ought certainly to acquit the colored race of the charge of acting as spies for us. There is certainly a conflict of opinion on the subject between the Napoleons of the two sides. General Halleck holds that negroes give information to the rebels, and issues his ... that they be excluded from th...

THE GUERILLA.

Monday Evening, - - - - - - Sep. 29

☞ Owing to the non-arrival of the mail, up to the hour of going to press, we are without the latest Eastern news.

LINCOLN'S DESPERATION, &c.

LINCOLN seems to be getting to the last stages of infamy and despair. Baffled and defeated at every point, he is now writhing under the punishment he promised us. In the last Cincinnati papers is published his fiat, giving notice that he will, on the first of January, 1863, cause to be emancipated all slaves, or persons of African descent, who shall then be in the employ of any person residing in any State still in rebellion against the United States; and that all officers of the army and navy are commanded ... show proper respect to the negroes, as freemen, and that they are to assist them in their endeavors to throw off the shackles ... slavery.

To try still more to quench his hellish ...rst, he intends violating openly his faith, ...sending the prisoners we recently paroled ... Harper's Ferry to Minnesota, to fight the ...ians, who are giving him much trouble ...e, and thereby relieving the troops there, ...hat they can be brought to Washington. ...ere are the 600 and 300,000 that would ...p out the last vestige of rebellion in ...y days? This looks as if they were ... wanting. Poor Abe, like a drowning ... has for the last month been grasping ...ery little straw, but all has been of no ... and he is now in the last struggles of ... with not the least hope to cheer him ... last moments.

... North seems fully aware of the great ...ey have sustained in having to give ... Kanawha, and are free to acknow... ...he great importance of its acquisition ... cause. They are bitter against their ...ment for having withdrawn the ... and acknowledge that we have de... in a week what it took millions of ... and an army of fifteen or twenty ...d men fifteen months to accomplish. ...em to have no hopes of attempting ... it this season, at least, as they are ...eed of every available man in Ken... ...d Maryland; but let them come ... in what force they please, we have ...ut that they would be made to re... full style, the Lightburn double-...

...ave boys have much to congratu... ...selves upon in the good service ... rendered our cause.

...ERE will be a meeting of the salt ...re to-day, and it is to be hoped ...x some established and reasonable ...is much-needed article.

☞ THE STREETS of Charleston are again becoming gay. A great many merchants have re-opened their stores to the public.—Others, however, still keep themselves and their goods shut up in the dark, because they have some scruples about taking Confederate money, &c. We hope they will soon come to their senses, and show that they appreciate their deliverance from the Northern vandals, by immediately opening their stores and offering their goods at the same rate they sold to the Yankees. And it is well here to add, that it is a great wrong and outrage, and speaks poorly for any one to take advantage of his fellow-being in adversity.

☞ PIERPOINT, becoming frightened at the recent audacity of the rebels in polluting his soil, taking his salt works, &c., recently made a visit to Cincinnati in his "Scotch cap," for the purpose of getting aid to punish the audacious and impertinent rebels.—He was met with the happy intelligence, that every available man was needed for the same purpose in Maryland and Kentucky; but as soon as that was finished, he should have immediate assistance to accomplish his purpose. With this happy consolation, he has returned home, no doubt feeling much easier in mind and body.

☞ THE ENEMY, about six or seven hundred strong, came up day before yesterday, to Gen. Jenkins' position, with the evident intention of attacking him, but one shot from our cannon was sufficient to cause the same old "scare" to come upon them, and they immediately skedaddled, and have not been heard from since.

TRIBUTE OF RESPECT.

HEAD'QRS OTEY BATTERY,
Camp near CHARLESTON, Kanawha Co.,
September 23, 1862.

WHEREAS, in the all-wise providence of God, our comrades, Sergeant SPEAR NICHOLAS, CURTIS CHAMBERLAINE, GEO. M. LEFTWICH and HENRY SMITH, have been taken by the hand of death from the ranks of our company, and the scenes in which we loved to mingle with them—

Resolved, That while we bow submissively to the Divine will, in removing from our midst these, our brethren in arms, yet we cannot but mourn the loss of those who were kind in all their relations with us, faithful in the discharge of all their duties, and willing to do and suffer in behalf of their country.

Resolved, That we, as a company and as individuals, do sincerely sympathize with the parents and friends of the deceased, and most cheerfully record our testimony that they fell on the field of battle (Fayette C. H., September 10, 1862,) whilst nobly contending for the rights and liberties of their country.

Resolved, That the foregoing be published in the Richmond *Dispatch* and *Whig*, and copies be sent the families of the deceased.

By order of the Company.

WM. A. HART,
R. G. HARPER,
T. M. NIVEN,
J. R. PERDUE,
A. A. FARLEY. } *Committee.*

Sept 29--1t

BY TELEGRAPH.

From the Cincinnati Commercial. Sept. 25.

Gen. Buel's Arrival in Louisville.

LOUISVILLE, Sept. 24, near midnight.—Gen. Buell has just arrived.

Gen. Nelson has just issued an order permitting, to-morrow, a general resumption of business, the issuing of passes to loyal citizens, and the discharge of all enrolled citizens from duty.

The enemy seems to be concentrating at Bloomfield. About 12,000 of them were seen this morning beyond Salt river, on the Bardstown road.

FROM WASHINGTON.

WASHINGTON, Sept. 24.—Intelligence from McClellan is meagre in quantity, and uninteresting. No active movements have occurred within the last day or two, his operations being chiefly confined to reorganizing the army, and other preparations necessary to finishing the rebel rule in Virginia.

Gen. Thomas Morris has been appointed a Brigadier General, and it is reported that he has been assigned to the command of Western Virginia.

THE LONDON TIMES ON THE AMERICAN WAR.

The following is a copy of the leading editorial of the London *Times*, July 22, 1862. In the events that have since transpired, the *Times* will find additional force to its remarks:

Nothing is so melancholy as forced merriment, and sorrow never wrings the heart more bitterly than when affliction or anxiety is compelled to assume the appearance of rejoicing. There is a play of the old dramatist, John Ford, called the *Broken Heart*, in which the heroine is compelled to go through a solemn dance, although in the course of it she is told that her father is dead, that her dearest friend has committed suicide, and that her lover is murdered. She goes through the dance, and drops down dead at the close. Something similar to this must have been the mental torture endured by a large portion of the American public during the festivals and rejoicings which commemorate the 4th of July, the never-sufficiently-to-be-praised and never-sufficiently-to-be-violated Declaration of Independence. How flat, stale and unprofitable must have sounded the conventional eloquence and worn-out enthusiasm which celebrated war and quarrels, the remembrance of which out to sleep in the graves of those who made them! How jarring the music, how pale the fire works, how wearisome the processions to mothers and sisters, to wives and daughters, tormented with the well-grounded apprehension that in the bloody swamps of Virginia were lying those most dear to them on earth—happy, indeed, if dead, but only too probably lingering out the last remnants of existence under the chilling dews of night, consumed by thirst and fever, in all the agonies that wait on the wounded, abandoned by a retreating, and trampled on and disregarded by a pursuing army! Was there no one to ask whether the cause in which all this blood was shed be indeed the cause of independence; whether the North can really identify the grounds of the present quarrel with tha...

CHARLESTON Daily Bulletin.

Vol. I. No. 11. } Charleston, W. Va., June 13, 1864. { 7 o'clock, Evening.

MOORE & BROTHER, Publishers.
OFFICE, "BANK OF THE WEST" BUILDING.

Terms (in advance).

For Single copy,	5 cents.
For One Week, delivered by carrier,	25 "
For One Month, " "	$1 00

RATES OF ADVERTISING.

One Square (10 lines), or less, one insertion,	50 cents.
" " " one week,	$1 00
" " " one month,	3 00
Two Squares, one month,	5 00

Monday, June 11, 1864.

Thurman's Guerrillas.—Their Captain Captured.

The train, consisting of half a dozen old and empty wagons, sent out with 35 men of the O. N. G. as a guard, for the purpose of gathering up the broken-down wagons on the road between Gauley and Meadow Bluff, met with misfortune on Friday morning near Sewall Mountain.

The wagon-master, Dan. Lee, of the 12th Ohio, hearing of the presence of Thurman's guerrillas when at the foot of Sewall, proposed to leave the train with a guard, and with the rest of the force go up to the top and see if any were to be found. Some eight of them, having horses, were in the advance,—the infantry following as fast as they could, when, arriving on top of Big Sewall, they saw two mounted rebels and charged upon them. But these were a bait, and four of our boys, including the wagon-master, soon found themselves surrounded by Thurman's entire company, who, upon their refusing ... fired upon ...

The guerrillas followed as far as where the train had been left, but being disappointed in finding any plunder there, they burned the wagons and returned.

Two of the members of the 23d O. V. I., belonging to the train, having secreted themselves until the following day, were fortunate enough, having merely side-arms, to capture Capt. Bill Thurman, the notorious leader of this gang. He is now here under guard.

☞ Late intelligence from General CROOK is to the effect that he is operating disastrously to the rebels. How and where, it is not deemed proper to publish at present.

BY TELEGRAPH.

THIS MORNING'S DISPATCHES.

Grant changing his Base.
Official Advices from Sherman.
FURTHER FROM BUTLER.
Gen. Smith driving Marmaduke.
A Battle near Cynthiana, Ky.

CINCINNATI, June 13.

News from Grant's army indicates that the base of supplies is being transferred from White House, and by this time probably the Headquarters are on James river.

This means an attack on Richmond from the south-west. The position, if ... will enable Grant to cut ... compel Lee to ...

3

DAILY BULLETIN.

BY TELEGRAPH.

Fort Darling Captured!

The Enemy Repulsed by McPherson, leaving 2500 on the field!

Morgan Repulsed at Frankfort!

BURBRIDGE ROUTS MORGAN AT CYNTHIANA!

From General Butler.

NEW YORK, June 13, 1864.

The Herald's correspondent sends the following:

WHITE HOUSE, June 11.—News from the front this morning is most cheering. Two officers who have just arrived here, bring the joyful news of the capture of Fort Darling.

An order conveying this intelligence was read to the army last evening, and the cheers of our soldiers could be heard miles around.

From General Sherman.

NEW YORK, June 13, 1864.

The attack on McPherson proved very disastrous to the enemy. The rebels came on in two divisions, with great resolution, but were met with a very destructive fire of artillery and musketry. The fight continued for nearly an hour, when the enemy retreated, leaving the field covered with their dead and wounded, numbering nearly 2500.

After five days' fighting, principally on his own hook, McPherson has closed upon our right wing, enabling us to make important movements.

Latest from Morgan.

LOUISVILLE, KY., June 12.

Dr. Whaler, U. S. Mail agent, who has been at Frankfort during the seige, left there at 4:30 this morning, and reports that fighting commenced at 6 o'clock Friday evening, lasting till dark, and continued at intervals during the night; the enemy approaching from Georgetown, in two forces, aggregating 1200. Seven hundred entered Old Frankfort, and five hundred entered New Frankfort. They had no artillery.

A small 4-pounder had been placed below the fort to protect our rifle-pits, which was captured by the rebels, but was subsequently retaken.

On Saturday firing continued from 7 o'clock in the morning to 3 o'clock in the afternoon, with short intervals. The rebels made two ... the day for the surrender of the fort; the rebels abandoned the attack at 4 o'clock on Saturday afternoon.

By 7 o'clock in the evening they were moving eastward. Our loss was 6 wounded, one of whom seriously. The rebel loss is unknown.

The fort was garrisoned by 150 Federals, only 12 of whom were soldiers.

No injury was done to Frankfort, except burning the barracks and a bridge 3 miles northward.

Capt. Dickson, of Gen. Burbridge's staff, telegraphs to Gen. Ewing at Lexington at 9:35 P. M., that Burbridge completely routed Morgan's command at Cynthiana this afternoon.

Advertisements.

GATES & WHITTEKER,
PHOTOGRAPHERS,
Having recently purchased HOVER & BOWYER'S Gallery,
Front Street, opposite the Post-office,
Up Stairs. CHARLESTON, W. VA.,
Will continue to take PHOTOGRAPHS, AMBROTYPES, or any other class of pictures, in superior style.

INMAN HOUSE,
Corner Front St. and the Ferry,
Charleston, W. Va.
R. W. INMAN, Proprietor,
WOULD remind the public that he is ever ready and happy to administer to the comfort and stomachs of all who may favor him with their patronage. He has fitted up his old stand again, corner of Front St. and the Ferry, where he will welcome all his old friends and customers.

BANK OF THE WEST,
Opposite the Steamboat Landing,
Charleston, West Va.,
BUYS and sells Exchange, Discounts Paper, Receives Money on Deposit, Checks on New York, Cincinnati, &c., buys and sells Uncurrent Money, Gives the Highest Price for Certified Accounts, &c., &c.
W. J. RAND, *President.*
JNO. CLAYPOOL, *Cashier.*

MOORE & BRO.,
Printers,
AND DEALERS IN
Daily Papers, Periodicals, &c.
Job Printing
OF EVERY DESCRIPTION
DONE WITH NEATNESS & DISPATCH.
Blanks, Cards, Bill Heads, Tickets, Circulars, Envelopes, Posters, &c., &c.,
In Every Style, at Low Prices.
Office in the "Bank of the West" Building.
We keep a supply of fine Letter and Commercial Note Paper, Envelopes, Cards, &c., constantly on hand. ... at 75 cts. a hundred.

Thomas E. Jeffries, who as a boy witnessed the battle from Cox's Hill (near Spring Hill Cemetery above Piedmont Road), gave a vivid account to a Charleston newspaper in 1926. He wrote that the night before the battle, "came a night when a steady stream of wagons passed down Kanawha Street and crossed Elk River." He saw a stream of people going toward the hill (Cox's Hill) and added that residents "had been warned that the town was to be set on fire and shelled by retreating feds."

From his hill vantage point, he described the battle. "The Kanawha Hotel, Bank of Virginia, Brooks store, Methodist Church, large ware room on the corner of Capitol and Virginia and the Mercer Academy were all on fire. With no wind, the black smoke settling made it look like the greater part of the town was afire.

"The Federal Army had passed down, but we could still see them both in the field and on Kanawha Street, all headed for the old suspension bridge at Lovell Street. Behind the main body, could be seen stragglers, at times 10 or 12, then smaller groups until, finally, one straggled along by himself.

"The first of the Confederates we saw was a small cannon pulled by a large mule. They called it a jackass battery...

"While we were watching the little gun, a squad of Confederate skirmishers suddenly appeared, coming up the hill. I had on a blue flannel suit and blue cap, and Hawkins (his friend) had on a blue coat and cap.

"When we saw them, we jumped up and they, thinking we were Federal soldiers, fired at us. Fortunately, the bullets cut the leaves over our heads.

"I lost all interest in things down in the bottom and started up the hill on high, and never stopped until I got into a crowd of women behind the hill."

After the battle, Jeffries described the scene. "I saw several dead Confederates lying on the grass next door to us. One body was covered up, and they said his head was shot off.

"Several federals were killed in a field near what would be the eastern corner of Brooks and Washington streets. One man was killed near the corner of Lee and Broad streets."

Six weeks later the Confederates were in turn driven out of the valley, never to return. For the remainder of the war, Kanawha County was in the hands of Union troops while the Civil War raged to the east and west of western Virginia. Area residents were to see several retreating Federal raiding parties passing through the Kanawha Valley, but there was never any real threat of the Confederates returning.

The suspension bridge across Elk River was dropped into the river by retreating Federal troops during the Battle of Charleston on September 13, 1862. Called the Lovell Street Bridge—the first one to span the river—it was rebuilt after the war. It collapsed in 1904, killing several people. The site is now occupied by the Washington Street Bridge. The mountain in the background is obviously a figment of the artist's imagination.

AUTHOR'S COLLECTION

GENERAL ORDER.

**HEAD QUARTERS,
DEPARTMENT OF WESTERN VIRGINIA,
Charleston, Va., Sept. 24, 1862.**

General Order, No.

The money issued by the Confederate Government is secure, and is receivable in payment of public dues, and convertible into 8 per cent. bonds. Citizens owe it to the country to receive it in trade; and it will therefore be regarded as good in payment for supplies purchased for the army.

Persons engaged in trade are invited to resume their business and open their stores.

By order of **MAJ. GEN. LORING.**

One of General Loring's orders during his brief occupation of Charleston in September 1862. SWV

TO THE LOYAL CITIZENS OF THE KANAWHA VALLEY.

The 8th REGT. VA. VOL. INFANTRY has returned to the Kanawha Valley. This regiment served as the advance guard of Fremont's army in the Valley of Virginia, and was several times complimented by Gen. Fremont in General Orders, for its gallantry in action and behavior on marches. Afterwards it became a part of Sigel's corps, and after performing an honored part in the bloody campaigns of the Rappahannock, and participating in the Bull Run fight, it hastened back to Western Virginia, eager to assist in driving the rebel hordes from their homes and yours.

Having been in service nearly eighteen months, its ranks are much thinned. Half its term of service has expired, and you are now appealed to, to come forward and volunteer to fill up the ranks for the rest of the term.

All who wish to enter the service of their country, with veteran troops, and under officers of experience and tried courage, have now a glorious opportunity. You will receive the same pay, bounty, clothing, &c., as in any other regiment. Come on, then, loyal men of Virginia! Range yourselves side by side with your friends and brothers, and drive the ruthless Rebels from your soil!

COALSMOUTH, Dec. 7, 1862.

A poster issued at Coalsmouth (St. Albans) in December 1862 recruiting new members for the 8th Regiment of Virginia Volunteer Infantry (Union). WVU

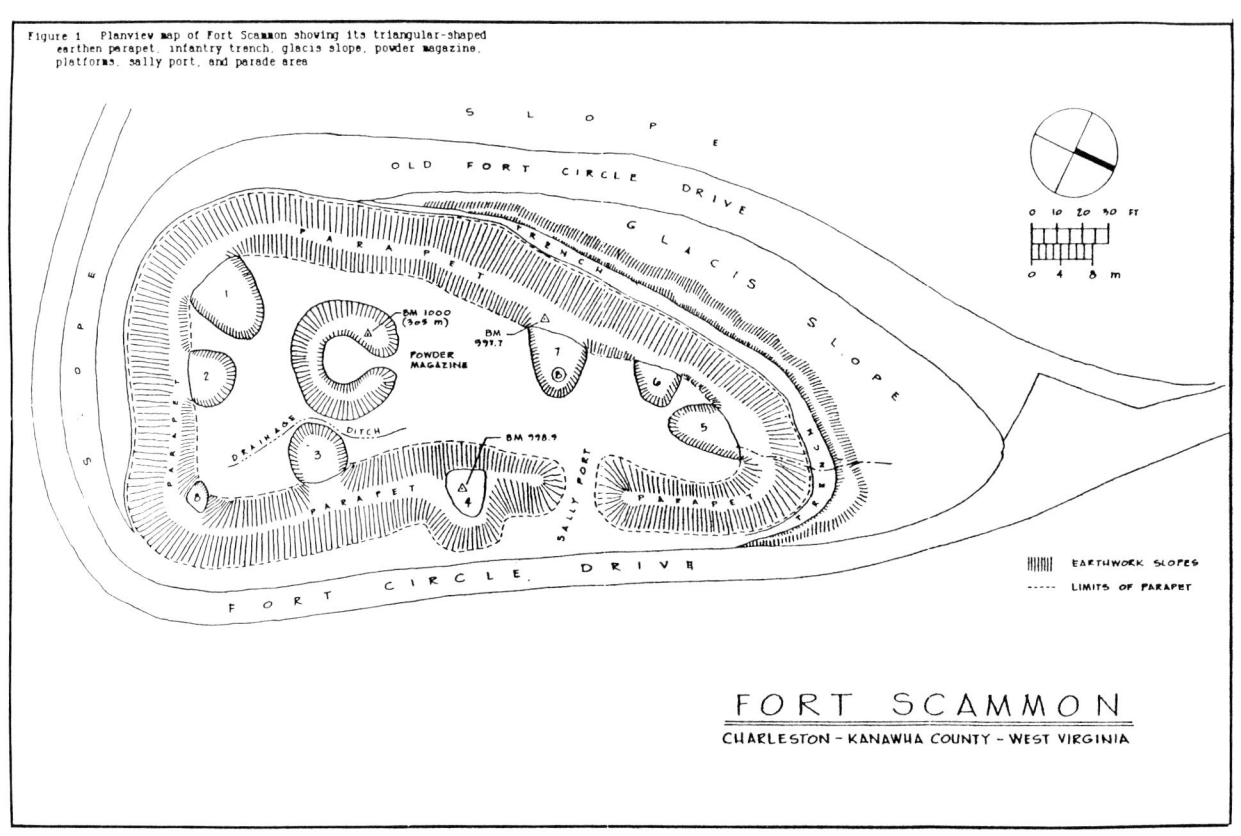

Figure 1 Planview map of Fort Scammon showing its triangular-shaped earthen parapet, infantry trench, glacis slope, powder magazine, platforms, sally port, and parade area
SLOPE
OLD FORT CIRCLE DRIVE
GLACIS SLOPE
PARAPET
TRENCH
POWDER MAGAZINE
DRAINAGE DITCH
SALLY PORT
FORT CIRCLE DRIVE
EARTHWORK SLOPES
LIMITS OF PARAPET
FORT SCAMMON
CHARLESTON - KANAWHA COUNTY - WEST VIRGINIA

COURTESY PAUL MARSHALL & ASSOCIATES

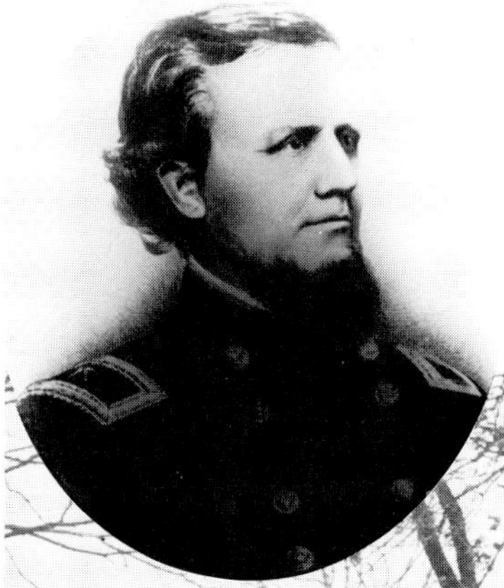

Colonel Eliakim P. Scammon. He was captured in 1864 by Confederates at Red House in Putnam County. USAMHI

Fort Scammon atop Fort Hill on Charleston's southside. It was named for Colonel Eliakim P. Scammon, commander of the 23rd Ohio Regiment, stationed at Charleston in 1863-64. The troops were actually quartered at Ferry Branch at the base of Fort Hill (now the site of gasoline storage tanks), and they probably built the fort out of boredom. By 1863 the threat of the war had passed by the Kanawha Valley. Restoration work and an archaeological investigation have been performed on the site in recent years.

DEAD END

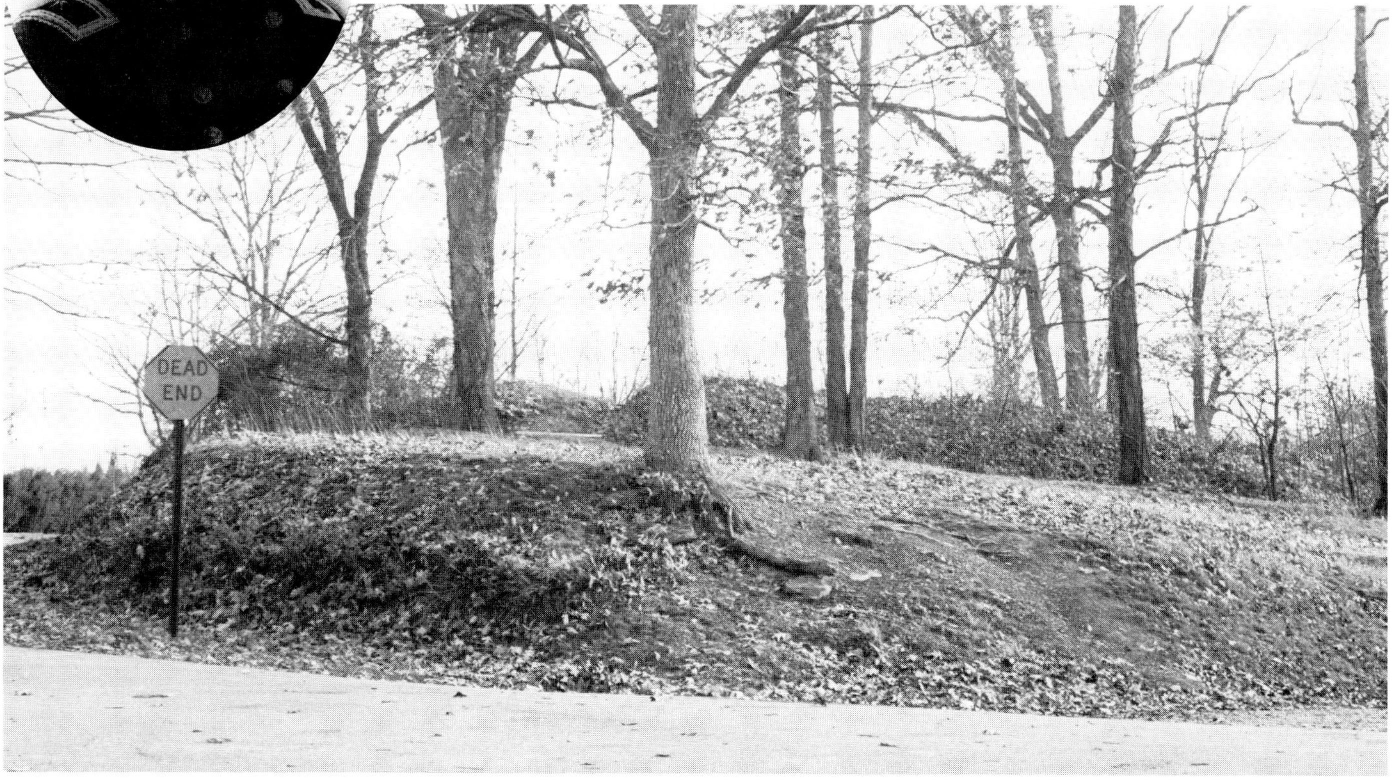

Photos and drawings from the Civil War era in Charleston are rare. This rather idyllic scene was painted in 1863 by Margaretta Doddridge, from a vantage point near what is now Morris Street. It shows a Union Army camp (Camp White) on the south side of the Kanawha River, around the Ferry Branch outlet just upriver from the present C & O railroad station.
AUTHOR'S COLLECTION

The 23rd Ohio Volunteer Infantry band in Charleston in 1863. It is one of the few photos taken during the war in Charleston known to exist. The building in back of the band is the Bank of Virginia, at the corner of present Virginia and Summers streets. It was burned during Lightburn's retreat in 1862. RBHL

1863.

THE DRAFT!
List of Those Drafted in 1st Sub-District, Kanawha Co.

Stephen Rigg, C. Jarrett, Joseph Stephenson, Isaac G. Wills, Wm. L. Keeney, John P. Whitlock, Joel Smith, A. P. Fry, A. E. Summers, Wm. H. Hamilton, George Pfeifer, John W. Dawson, Wm. L. Young, Henderson Hostick, Wm. C. Acord, Davis James, Nathan Hoctor, Arthur Allen, Patrick Scarrin, M. Woody, James P. Wills, H. C. Glover, Edward Smith, E. P. Young, Wm. Hudnal, Lewis Burns, Edward Morning, J. M. Derrick, J. B. Clendenin, G. W. Tate, Franklin Gaston, Wm. H. Neckers, Fielding Bonham, Wm. Robine, Elias Kend... , John D. V..., Samuel H. Taylor, T. J. Garder,

George Stocton, Wm. H. Osborn, Benj. L. Boggess, John Hodges, P. Morgan, Beverly Lewis (col.), R. J. Morris, Theodore Robinson, Wm. Baker, A. H. Morris, Edmund Newhouse, John Dillon, Michael Armentrout, Robert Calell, Wm. Barker, Cooper's Creek. James Cliff, Wm. Martin, C. C. Coon, Wm. Fox, Charles Spencer, James Barton, Washington Brawly, James H. Kenison, G. W. Groves, James E. Kendall, James B. Smith, Charles Cozens, (col.) Nathan Hannah, Enoch Coburn, Michael Ford, T. H. Noyes, B. A. Melton, Lewis R. Kirk, Spencer Proctor, Wm. J. Bryant, Wm. Lanham, Abner Nickols, Wm. K. Givens, Wm. Brown,

James M. Britt, Cornelius Bow, Wm. Dawson, Delacy Casdorph, Patrick Gaughan, John Ward, (col.) Frank Shrewsbury, Wm. H. Tully, (colored) James M. Witherow, ... More, Berry Proctor, John F. Hubbard, James L. Guthrey, Wm. Cavender, John Lockhart, John Stinson (col.), Wm. G. Burgess, Henry Crowder, H. W. Coster, Jef Milam, Morrison Bailey, John D. Martin, I. C. Vandine, L. H. Hamilton, Patrick Flaherty, James Curry, Lafayette Wells, (col.) Joseph Layton, George Williams, Wm. J. Parish, James Payne, Marshall Payall, Wm. G. Brown, James Crowder, Franklin Hamilton, Lewis Woods, George L. Mitchel, Wm. Lynch, Elias Kendall, Samuel H. Baily, Collin Griffith, Willie Kline, Wm. James, James McMahan, Jacob Plumly, John Shaffer, Mobery Smith, Austin Burgess, John Tully, J. W. Oaks, Thomas McCloud, O. A. Thayer, Michael Waylen, James Lanham, Lewis Allen, (col.) Benonic Surratt, G. W. Sandford, Wm. Ransom, Benj. F. Ballard, Wm. L. Hicks, John Buckell, Charles M. Honaker, Hamilton S. Adkins, Marion Britt, Patrick Dorsey, Nathaniel King, A. J. Boggess, B. K. Shepherd, Reuben Proctor, A. B. Clark, Shadrick Hudnal, M. W. Young, James Wilson, G. B. Givens, Franklin Fisher, Volentine Wehrle, Washington Lurboy, Sylvester Hammock, Thomas C. Smails, Columbus Franklin, Cyrus Corey, Lewis Sims, Newton Smith.

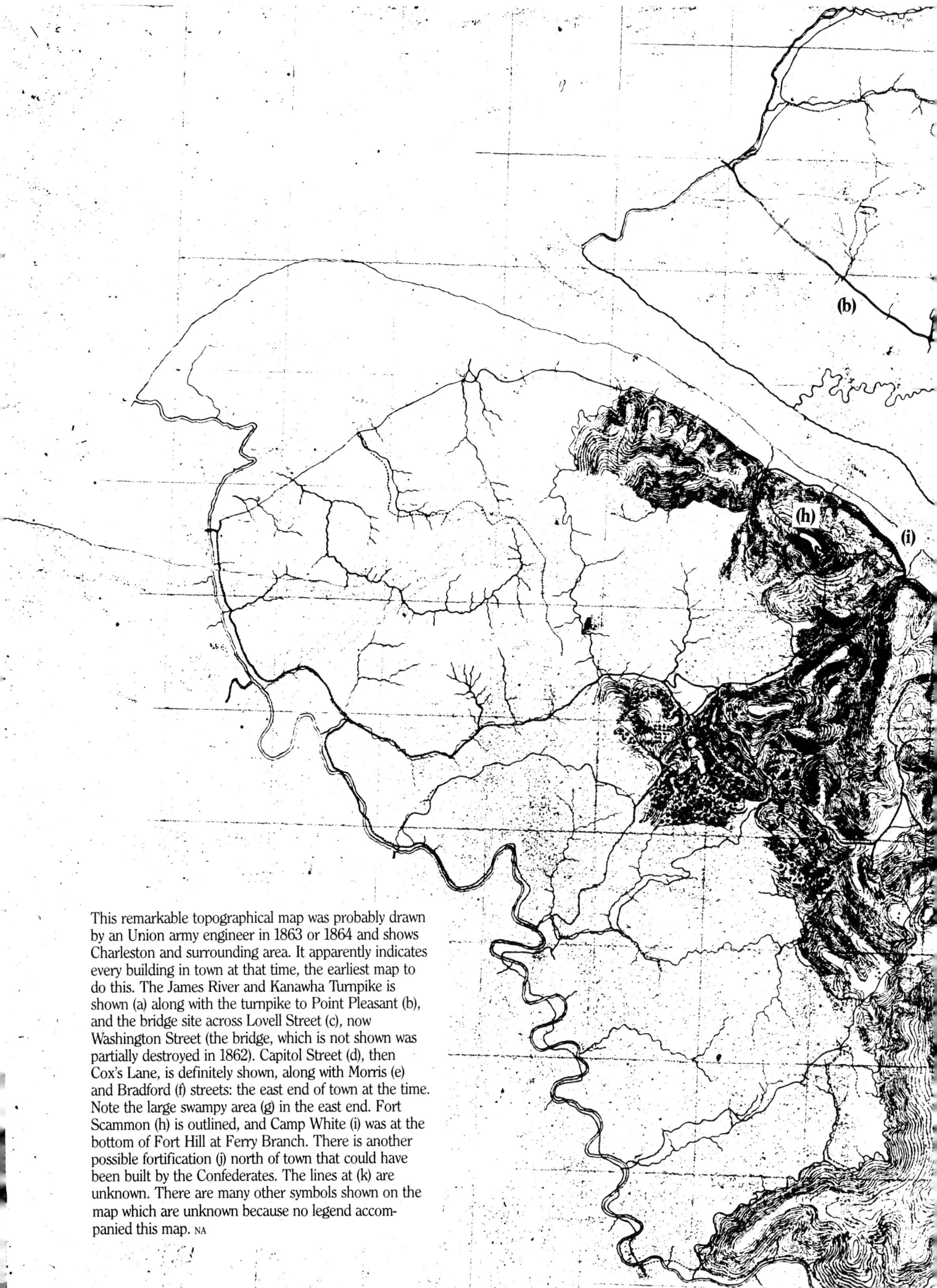

This remarkable topographical map was probably drawn by an Union army engineer in 1863 or 1864 and shows Charleston and surrounding area. It apparently indicates every building in town at that time, the earliest map to do this. The James River and Kanawha Turnpike is shown (a) along with the turnpike to Point Pleasant (b), and the bridge site across Lovell Street (c), now Washington Street (the bridge, which is not shown was partially destroyed in 1862). Capitol Street (d), then Cox's Lane, is definitely shown, along with Morris (e) and Bradford (f) streets: the east end of town at the time. Note the large swampy area (g) in the east end. Fort Scammon (h) is outlined, and Camp White (i) was at the bottom of Fort Hill at Ferry Branch. There is another possible fortification (j) north of town that could have been built by the Confederates. The lines at (k) are unknown. There are many other symbols shown on the map which are unknown because no legend accompanied this map. NA

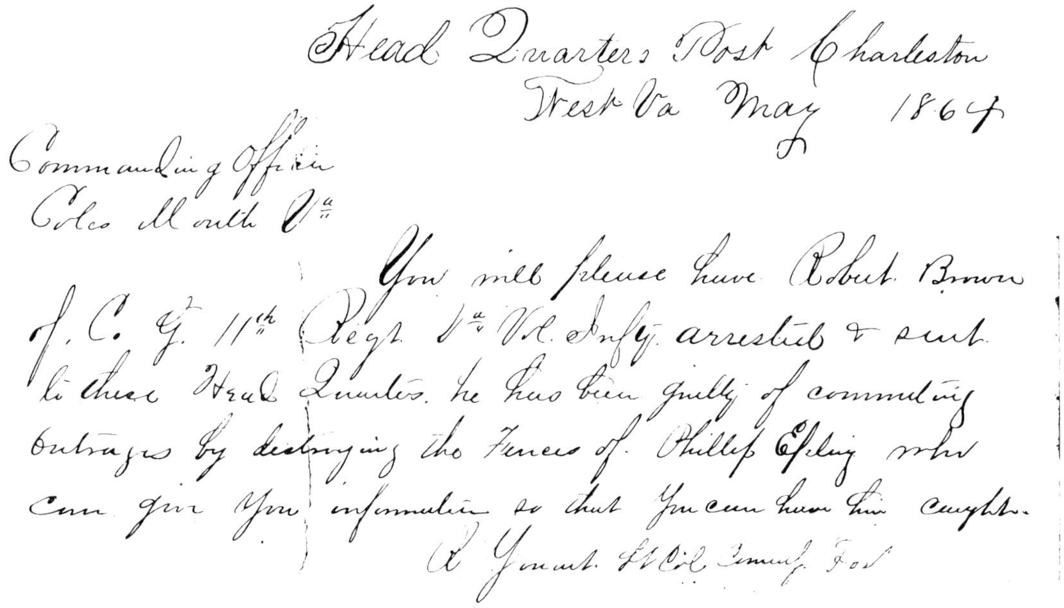

Head Quarters Post Charleston
West Va May 1864

Commanding Officer
Coles Mouth Va

You will please have Robert Brown of C. G. 11th Regt Va Vol. Infy. arrested & sent to these Head Quarters. he has been guilty of committing outrages by destroying the Fences of Phillip Epling who can give you information so that you can have him caught.

R Yount Lt Col Commg Post

You will please have Robert Brown of C. G. 11th Regiment. Va. Vol. Infantry. arrested & sent to these Head Quarters. He has been guilty of committing outrages by destroying the fences of Phillip Epling who can give you information so that you can have him caught.

R. Yount, Lt. Col. Commg. Post

AUTHOR'S COLLECTION

Two envelopes from the Civil War era. The bottom one was sent to Mr. E. A. Brown of Company C, 26th Regiment O.V.I. in Charleston, Western Virginia. The opposite was postmarked from Kanawha Court House, the name used by the post office in Charleston until 1879. AUTHOR'S COLLECTION

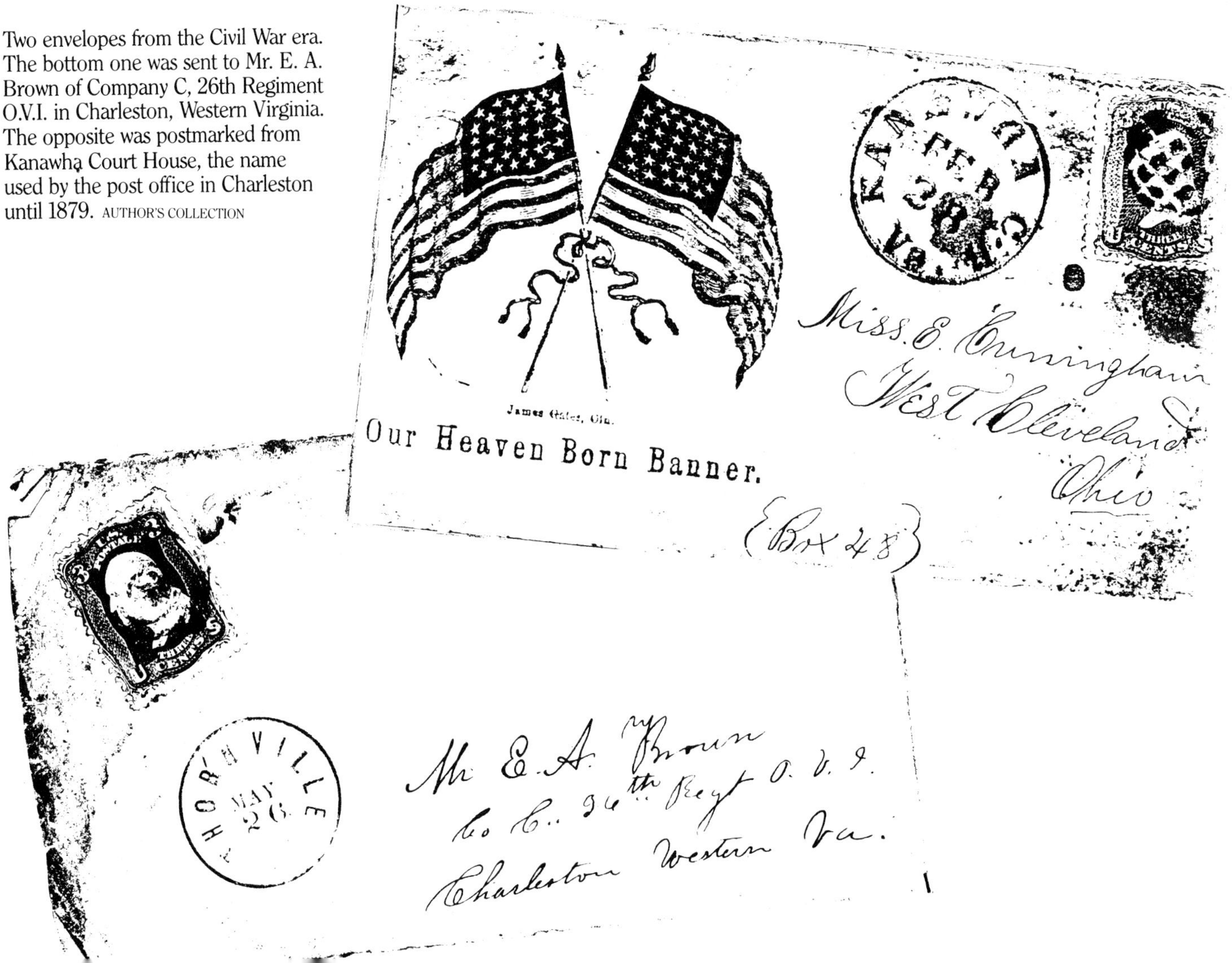

Two future presidents of the United States were stationed for a time in Charleston while serving with the 23rd Ohio Volunteer Infrantry. Rutherford B. Hayes, President from 1877 to 1881, was a colonel, and William McKinley, President from 1897 to 1901, was a lieutenant. They were stationed briefly at Camp White at the mouth of Ferry Branch, and at Fort Scammon atop Fort Hill in 1863. COURTESY RBHL AND CARINFEX FERRY STATE PARK

Reunion of the 23rd Regimental Band of the Ohio Volunteer Infantry Regiment at Lakeside, Ohio, in August 1885. The regiment was commanded by Col. Eliakim P. Scammon in 1861. It spent considerable time in the Kanawha Valley in 1863 and 1864. These members are probably the same ones in the band photo on page 101. RBHL

C&O engine terminal at Handley with road engines and switchers present, July 1955. The locomotive in the center is #1648 of the famous H-8 class, which is widely regarded as the finest steam engine ever built. These giants with their twelve driving wheels ran the steep grades from Handley to Clifton Forge, Virginia. One of these same engines is on display at the Henry Ford Museum in Dearborn, Michigan. At the time this photo was taken, in 1955, diesels had generally deposed steam as king of the rails! The locomotive on left is a switch engine. The structure with the peaked roof is a coaling tower. The locomotive tender was pulled under this tower and coal for the engine was dumped into the tender. The locomotive on right is a 2700 Kanawha class, an excellent high speed freight engine.

COHS. PHOTO BY GENE HUDDLESTON

Chapter Seven
The Railroads

It is hard to believe that mainline railroads did not cross Kanawha County until four years after the golden spike was driven at Promontory Point, Utah in 1869, linking the east and west coasts. For many years, a railroad that crossed the rugged Allegheny Mountains to the Kanawha Valley had been envisioned, and until the Civil War halted rail development, the rails had actually reached Covington, Virginia. Although two railroads of sorts had been built up Field's Creek and Paint Creek in the 1850s, they were crude operations that used animals to pull cars along wooden rails capped with iron.

Once the Chesapeake & Ohio (C&O) reached the county, however, the coal operators could get their product to market. Short line railroads soon started edging their way up the many tributaries of the Kanawha River, so companies could tap the rich deposits of coal. The Kanawha and Michigan (K&M) Railroad reached Charleston in 1884, and by acquiring the Charleston and Gauley Railway, extended to Gauley Bridge in 1893. The New York Central, which became Penn Central and later Conrail, eventually absorbed the K&M.

Although several railroad schemes were proposed for the Coal River drainage, it took several failures and many different owners before rails reached from St. Albans to Boone County to tap the huge coal deposits. The Black Jack Line, which became the Charleston, Clendenin & Sutton (CC&S) Railroad in 1890, laid track on Elk River. Henry Gassaway Davis, a powerful timber and railroad baron, took over the CC&S in 1904 and incorporated it in his Coal and Coke Railroad. This provided a rail link from Charleston to Elkins, and connections with the Western Maryland and Baltimore & Ohio lines to the north. The Baltimore & Ohio Railroad later took over this line.

The Virginian Railroad was built in the early 1900s to tap the rich coal fields of southern West Virginia. The railroad reached Deepwater on the Kanawha and then leased the C&O rails into Charleston.

Chesapeake & Ohio Railway

The C&O constructed their railroad through Charleston on the south side of the river. The last spike was driven about one mile east of the Hawks Nest Station in Fayette County on January 29, 1873, and that evening the sound of a train whistle pierced the air east of Charleston as the C&O train made her first run from Richmond to Huntington. This prompted a great celebration in Charleston. Boxes, barrels, and wood were burned in a huge bonfire on the river bank in front of Hale House and roman candles, skyrockets, and other fireworks were touched off to make this a loud and brilliant affair.

With its steam engine huffing and puffing, the train moved down the valley at about 20 miles an hour. It rumbled to a halt at the site of the present C&O station about 9:10 p.m., and the whistle blew again and again as cheers rose from both sides of the Kanawha in a celebration that lasted about a half hour. Finally the train, under clouds of smoke, moved slowly forward to resume its grand journey toward Huntington.

For years, passengers were ferried across the Kanawha River to the downtown area at the foot of Capitol Street. Forty-six years later, railway passengers crossed over the Kanawha to the business district on the newly constructed South Side Bridge.

When the C&O lines shipped freight into Charleston, it was ferried across the Kanawha to the Kanawha & Michigan Railroad, then transported to the C&O freight depot on the north side of the city. This connection was eliminated in 1907 when the C&O opened a modern railway bridge across the river that connected its Elk yard at South Charleston with the wholesale district in Charleston.

Coal is still a major commodity for the C&O but most of the short lines into the coal fields have been abandoned. Although passenger service is no longer a major part of the railroad business, Amtrak continues to travel through the county on its Washington-Cincinnati run.

PROGRAMME
OF
Ceremonies attending the Breaking of Ground for the Chesapeake & Ohio Railroad, in West Virginia, on Thursday, April 7th, 1870,
OPPOSITE CHARLESTON.

The United States Artillery, now at Charleston on special duty, under command of Col. Miller, will form at 2 o'clock P. M., on the wide pavement next above the public landing, headed by the Charleston Brass Band. It will then escort the Governor of the State, with other Executive officers, the Committee of Arrangements, the Chaplain and Orators of the Day, the Mayor and Council of Charleston,—all under Col. A. B. Jones, Marshal of the Day,—to the point on the opposite side of the river designated for the following ceremonies:

1st. Music by the Charleston Brass Band.
2d. The meeting will be called to order by one of the Committee of Arrangements.
3d. Prayer by the Rev. J. C. Barr.
4th. Anthem.
5th. Speeches by S. A. Miller, James H. Nash and T. B. Swann.
6th. Music by the Band.
7th. The shovel prepared by the Committee of Arrangements will be given by the Contractor to Col. Kuper, Engineer in charge, who will hand the same to Capt. Parsons, representative of the Chesapeake and Ohio Railroad, who, accompanying the same with a brief address, will deliver it to the Governor of West Virginia.
8th. Address by the Governor, followed by the breaking of ground by him.
9th. A national salute by Col. Miller's Artillery, and the Star Spangled Banner by the Charleston Brass Band.

Fireworks at 8 P. M.

COMMITTEE OF ARRANGEMENTS.
GEORGE JEFFRIES,
JOHN S. CUNNINGHAM,
J. W. CRACRAFT,
V. A. GATES,
A. B. JONES,
JOB E. THAYER,
JOHN SLACK, SR.,
CHARLES HEDRICK,
C. W. SMITH,
WM. H. HOGEMAN,
CHARLES FERRILL,
J. M. LAIDLEY.

Stoves, Tin-ware, Lamps, Cutlery, &c., at D. Goshorn's, at city prices.

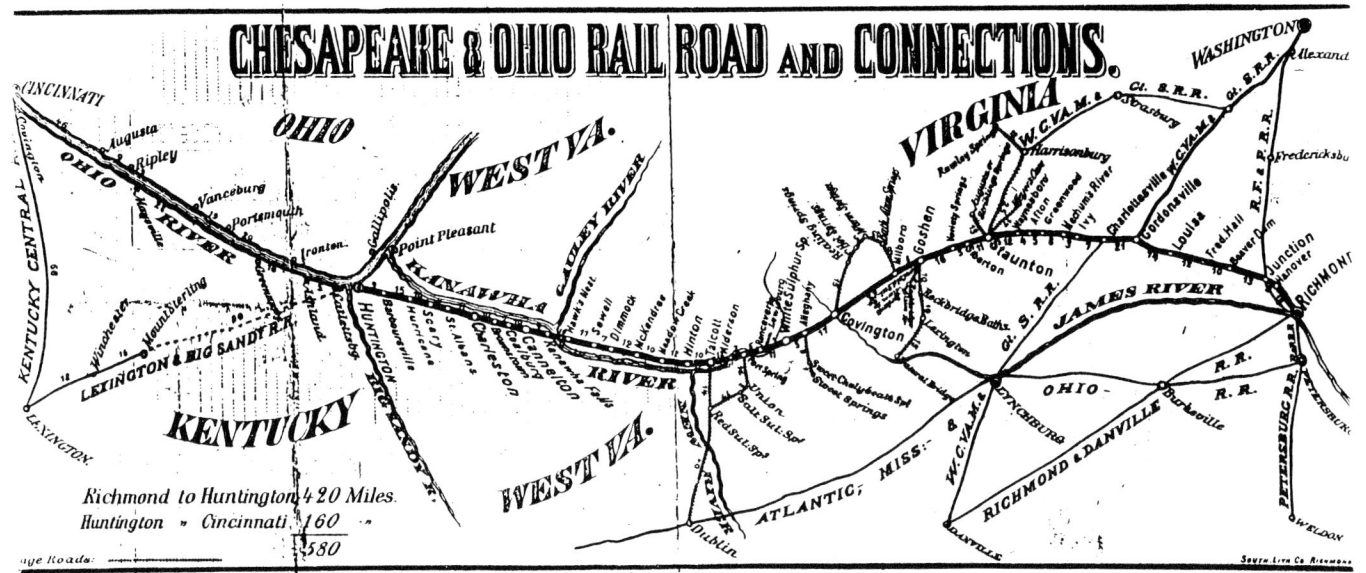

1873

The C&O's first depot on the south side was a frame building as shown at the south end (right) of the South Side Bridge. This was replaced in 1905 by the present depot. This scene was taken around 1892-95 as Sacred Heart Catholic Church's tall steeple has not yet been built (1896) and the bridge was completed in 1891. Notice the toll booth on the north (left) end of the bridge. COURTESY DAVE MOORE

C&O Station at Charleston in 1910. This station was opened in 1905 to take the place of the original frame building. Amtrak still uses the building, but it is now privately owned. At the east end of the structure was an elevator that ferried freight and baggage to the level of the southside bridge. The concrete ramp leading from the bridge and standing next to the station was built about 1930. Until that time access to MacCorkle Avenue from the bridge required a descent down the hillside on what was later called Justice Row. The road crossed the C&O mainline—a dangerous situation—so the ramp was built in the interest of safety as well as convenience. COHS

A Chesapeake & Ohio Railroad Album

MacCorkle Avenue looking west at the C&O station, early 1930s. This is probably an excursion trip judging from the large crowd and the small switch engine, which is about to couple on to the rear of the coach. KCL

C&O, K-1, #1120 with westbound freight at Marmet, 1946. The rather strange looking appliances on the boiler front were air compressors which provided air for the brakes. C&O preferred to mount them on the front.
COHS. PHOTO BY T.L. WISE

C&O, K-3A, #2320 at the St. Albans yards, 1949. Notice the Dailey Bros. Circus train in the background.
COHS. PHOTO BY T.L. WISE

The 2700 Kanawha-type, 2-8-4 steam locomotive of the C&O, heading east from the foot of the Patrick Street Bridge, circa 1940s. These engines were noted for their speed and reliability in handling fast freights. This is probably the fast freight known as #92, the "Kanawha Dispatch." Note the low mounted headlight which was a C&O trademark. CN

A huge Mallet-type, C&O locomotive that was wrecked on Coal River in 1955. This engine was especially suited for the sharp curves of the branch line coal-hauling runs. A total of 12 driving wheels provided great motive power. CN

The ill-fated C&O steam turbine locomotive at Charleston in 1949. This locomotive used a conventional boiler to make steam, which was then utilized by a turbine. The turbine drove generators which created electricity, so in fact this was a coal burning turbine electric locomotive. Developmental problems and the arrival of the diesel doomed this attempt to couple technology to a coal burning steam system. It is entirely possible that this locomotive could be a success today given the high cost of diesel fuel. In this photo members of the public are being allowed to tour the locomotive cab.
COHS. PHOTO BY T.L. WISE

The Friendship Train with food for foreign countries rolls through Charleston in 1949. This was an effort to feed starving millions in war-torn Europe. COHS.

A Sperry Rail Service Detector Car #123 at the Charleston depot, 1949. This car was used for many years on the C&O line. Its purpose was to discover fractures or breaks in the rails, thereby averting possible accidents. COHS

C&O, H-8, #1648 on the turntable at Handley, July 1955. The turntable was a necessity for steam engines, and it was one of their weaknesses since diesels could run either direction with no problem. The great H-8 was one of the largest and most powerful railroad locomotives ever built. COHS. PHOTO BY GENE HUDDLESTON

C&O, A-16S, #293 with Brill Gas Electric at St. Albans station, 1949. This little engine, which was quite old in 1949, served the Coal River branch. Although she had only four drivers, their great diameter made her capable of considerable speed. COHS. PHOTO BY T.L. WISE

C&O, RSD-S, #5591 on Cabin Creek line at Leewood, 1954. These diesels, although lacking any personality, banished the legendary steam locomotives and did considerable damage to West Virginia's coal market.
COHS. PHOTO BY GENE HUDDLESTON

Coal hauling has been the mainstay of West Virginia and Kanawha County railroads for over 100 years. This long train pulled by a H-6 mallet #1492 brings a coal train to Handley from Cabin Creek in 1956. This was the twilight of steam as diesels had largely taken over the C&O by then. Due to an economic upturn in 1956, many steamers were brought out of storage, but their days were numbered. COHS

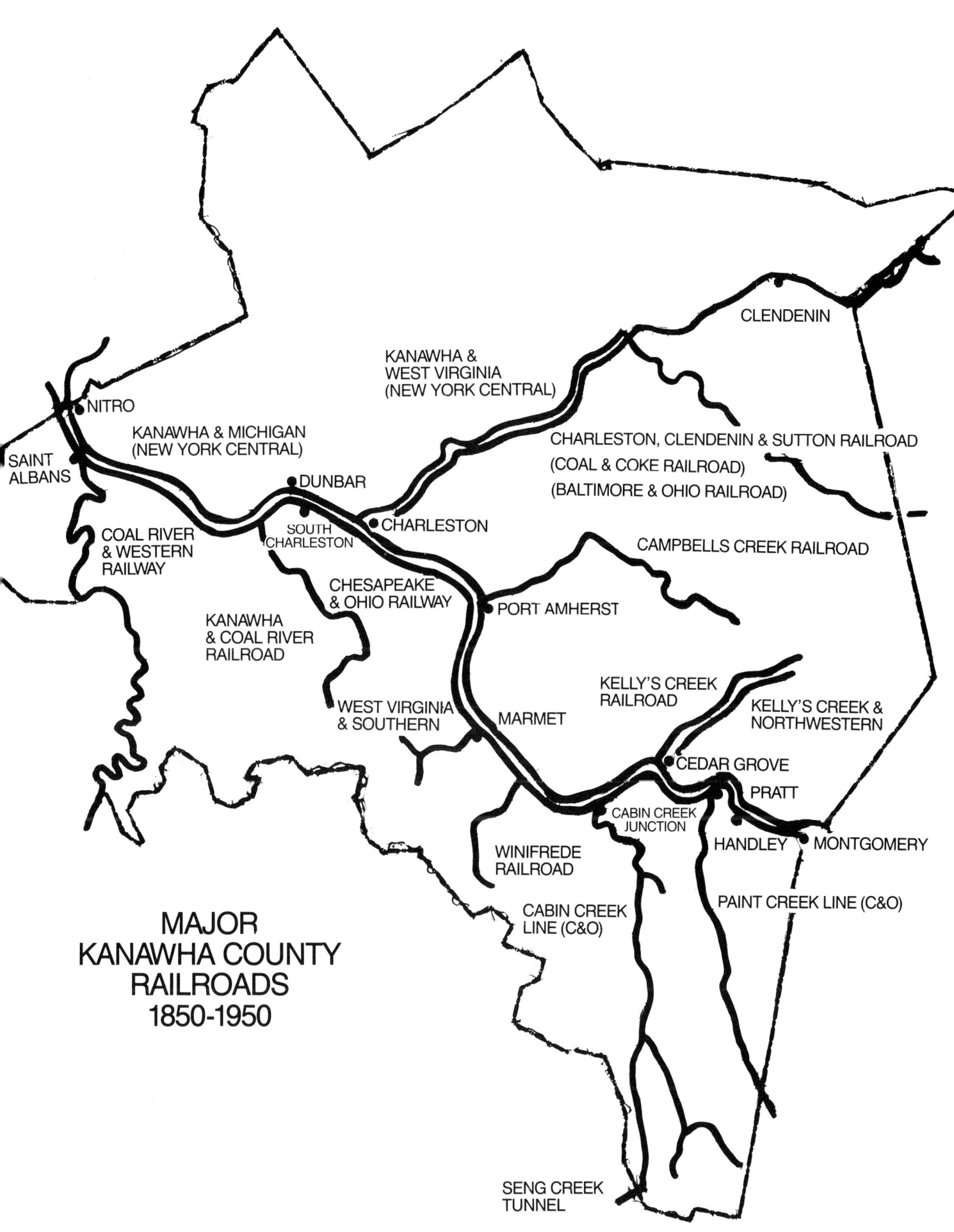

CHESAPEAKE & OHIO RAILROAD TIME-TABLE No. 31.

(SUNDAYS EXCEPTED, UNLESS OTHERWISE STATED.)

MAY 5th, 1873.

GOING WEST.

MILES	STATIONS	No. 1. Mail	No. 3. Cincinnati Express	No. 5. Accom.	No. 7.
		A.M.	P.M.	P.M.	
	Richmond	8.30	10.00	5.10	
9	Atlee's	8.55		5.40	
12	Ashcake	9.05*		5.50*	
15	Peake's	9.10		5.56*	
18	Hanover	9.20		6.05	
21	Wickham's	9.28		6.13*	
23	South Anna	9.34*		6.20*	
	Garnett's				
27	Junction	9.46	10.50	6.30*	
30	Anderson's	9.55*		6.40*	
33	Noel's	10.10		6.50	
35	Hewlett's	10.15*		6.55*	
40	Beaver Dam	10.27		7.10	
43	Green Bay	10.34		7.15*	
45	Bumpass'	10.39*		7.20*	
47	Buckner's	10.44*		7.25*	
50	Frederick's Hall	10.52		7.35	
56	Tolersville	11.07		7.50	
61	Louisa	11.22		8.05	
67	Trevilian's	11.33		8.15	
73	Melton's	11.50		8.35	
78	Gordonsville	12.17d	12.40	8.45	
81	Lindsay's	12.30			
83	Cobham	12 48			
90	Keswick	1.06	1.14		
93	Shadwell	1.15			
97	Charlottesville	1.29	1.33		
104	Ivy	1.50			
107	Mechum's River	1.58			
115	Greenwood	2.20			
120	Afton	2.38			
124	Waynesboro'	2.50			
129	Fishersville	3.07			
136	Staunton	3.35	3.45		
144	Swoope's	3.55			
147	Siberton	4.03*			
152	No Mountain	4.15			
	Variety	....			
153	Elizabeth	4.25			
155	Pond Gap	4.30*			
159	Craigsville	4 40*			
164	Bell's Valley	4.52			
168	Goshen	5.02	5.08		
176	Millboro'	5.20			
188	Longdale	5.50*			
192	Clifton Forge	6 00*			
195	Jackson's River	6.10*			
205	Covington	7.00s	7.00b		
211	Callaghan's	7.12*			
222	Allegheny	7.55			
227	White Sulphur	8.05	8.03		
238	Ronceverte		8.30		
244	Fort Spring	P. M.	8.46		
251	Alderson		9.05		
262	Talcott		9.35		
273	Hinton		10.05		
285	Meadow Creek		10.41		
295	McKendree		11.11		
307	Dimmock		11.47		
313	Sewell		12.05		
324	Hawk's Nest		12 40		
326	Laurel	A. M.			
333	Kanawha Falls	6.30	1 40d		
337	Loup Creek	6.10*	1.50*		
343	Cannelton	7.00	2.03		
348	Paint Creek	7.15*	2.16*		
353	Coalburg	7.30	2.28		
360	Brownstown	7.50	2.46*		
364	Alden	8.02	2.55*		
369	Charleston	8.20	3.10		
375	Spring Hill	8.38*	3.23*		
382	St. Albans'	8.55	3.40		
385	Scary	9.07*	3.48*		
389	Scott	9.20*	3.57*		
395	Hurricane	9.40	4.12		
403	Milton	10.00	4.30		
410	Barboursville	10.30	4.52		
417	Guyandotte	10.49	5.10		
			P. M		
421	Huntington	11.00			
	(Steamer)	A. M.			
571	Cincinnati		6.00		
			A. M.		

GOING EAST.

STATIONS	No. 2. Mail	No. 4. Cincinnati Express	No. 6. Accom.	No. 8.
		P.M.	P.M.	
Cincinnati		4.00		
(Steamer)		A. M.		
Huntington	3.20	10.00		
Guyandotte	3.30	10.13		
Barboursville	3.55	10.30		
Milton	4.30	10.50		
Hurricane	4.52	11.06		
Scott	5.10	11.20		
Scary	5.22*	11.30*		
St. Albans'	5.35	11.40		
Spring Hill	5.52*	11.55*		
Charleston	6.10	12.10		
Alden	6.30	12.23*		
Brownstown	6.40	12.34*		
Coalburg	7.03	12.50		
Paint Creek	7.15*	1.03*		
Cannelton	7.32	1.17		
Loup Creek	7.50*	1.30*		
Kanawha Falls	8.00	2.00d		
Laurel	P. M.	2.21		
Hawk's Nest		2.30		
Sewell		3.02		
Dimmock		3.10		
McKendree		3.55		
Meadow Creek		4.25		
Hinton		5.05		
Talcott		5.30		
Alderson		6.00		
Fort Spring		6.18		
Ronceverte	A. M.	6.35		
White Su'phur	5.55	7.00		
Alleghany	6.10	7.15		
Callaghan's	6.48			
Covington	7.20	8.38s		
Jackson's River	7.44*			
Clifton Forge	7.53*			
Longdale	8 00*			
Millboro'	8.35			
Goshen	8.50	10.08		
Bell's Valley	9.00			
Craigsville	9.15			
Pond Gap	9.25			
Elizabeth	9.30			
Variety	....			
No Mountain	9.45			
Siberton	9.53			
Swoope's	10.00			
Staunton	10.25	11.30		
Fishersville	10 43			
Waynesboro'	10.55			
Afton	11.05			
Greenwood	11.25	12.15		
Mechum's River	11.41			
Ivy	11.50			
Charlottesville	12.15	12.55		
Shadwell	12.22	1.02		
Keswick	12 30	1.10		
Cobham	12.50			
Lindsay's	12.58			
			A. M.	
Gordonsville	1.30d	1.42	6.50	
Melton's	1.42		6.58*	
Trevilian's	1.55		7.14	
Louisa	2.08		7.25	
Tolersville	2.22		7.39	
Frederick's Hall	2.38		7.55	
Buckner's	2 45*		8.02*	
Bumpass'	2.51*		8.08*	
Green Bay	2.58*		8.13*	
Beaver Dam	3.04		8.20	
Hewlett's	3.15*		8.30*	
Noel's	3.25		8.40	
Anderson's	3 33*		8.50	
Junction	3.40		8.56	
Garnett's				
South Anna	3 55*		9.09*	
Wickham's	4.00		9.13	
Hanover	4.08		9.20	
Peake's	4.15*		9.30*	
Ashcake	4 21*		9.35*	
Atlee's	4.30		9.45	
Richmond	4.45	4.30	10.15	
	P. M.	A. M.	A. M.	

*Stops only on signal. †Leaves Richmond daily except Saturday. Trains do not stop where time is not given.
b—Breakfast. d—Dinner. s—Supper. ††Leaves Huntington daily except Sunday.

STAGES CONNECT

At STAUNTON for Augusta or Stribling's Springs, Rawley Springs, Weyer's Cave and Harrisonburg.
At GOSHEN for Rockbridge Alum, Jordan's Alum, and Cold Sulphur Springs, Rockbridge Baths, LEXINGTON and Natural Bridge.
At MILLBORO for Bath Alum, Hot, Healing, and Warm Springs.
At COVINGTON for Healing and Hot Springs.
At ALLEGHANY for Sweet Chalybeate and Sweet Springs.
At TALCOTT for Red Sulphur Springs.
At KANAWHA FALLS for Raleigh C. H.

☞ W. C. V. M. & G. S. R. R. Trains connect at Gordonsville for WASHINGTON and NORTH, and at Charlottesville for LYNCHBURG and SOUTH.

☞ Connect at HUNTINGTON with steamers FLEETWOOD and BOSTONA DAILY, (except Sunday) for CINCINNATI.

Note that in 1873 the traveller got off the train in Huntington and boarded a steamboat to go on to Cincinnati as the railroad did not then go on to Ohio.

THE VIRGINIAN RAILWAY

CORRECTED TO MAY 28, 1929

Condensed Through Schedule Between Norfolk, Roanoke, Va., Princeton, Charleston, W. Va., Huntington, W. Va., and Ashland, Ky., in connection with Chesapeake & Ohio Railway.

[Virginian Railway condensed through schedule table]

WESTERN UNION TELEGRAPH COMPANY TELEGRAMS for transmission over the wires of the WESTERN UNION TELEGRAPH COMPANY accepted at public telegraph stations of the Virginian Railway. NIGHT LETTERS of fifty words or less handled at the regular rate for a ten-word day message. DAY LETTERS, fifty words, at rate of one and a half tolls for ten-word day message.

RAILWAY EXPRESS AGENCY
Operated On The Virginian Railway.
GIVE THEM YOUR EXPRESS SHIPMENTS.

Table 79—CHARLESTON AND SWISS.

[New York Central System table, July 7, 1929, Charleston to Swiss schedule]

+ Coupon stations; § Telegraph stations.
Trains marked * run daily.
† Daily, except Sunday.
§ Sunday only.

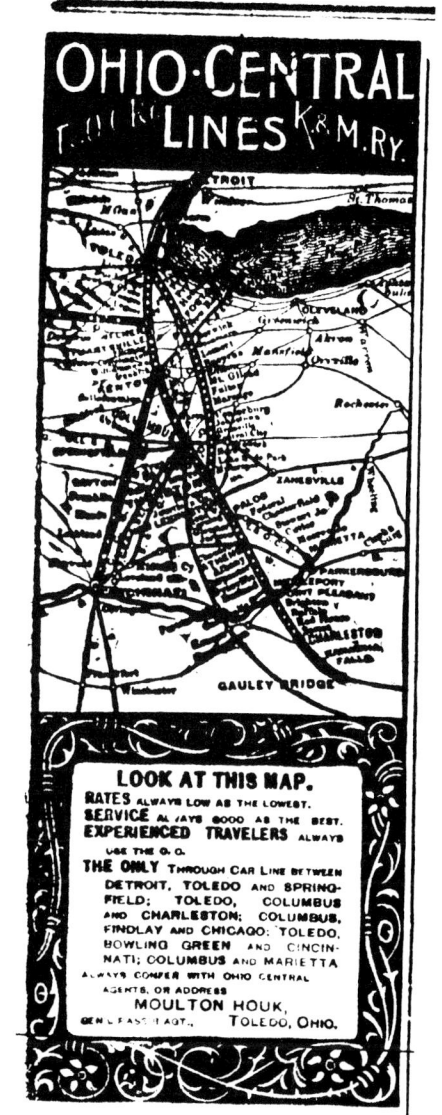

Charleston, Clendennin & Sutton Railroad Company.

PASSENGER TIME TABLE.

In Effect February 18, 1897.

Trains Run on Eastern Standard Time. (Charleston Time.)

NORTH BOUND.			SOUTH BOUND.	
No. 5 Passenger. Sundays Only.	No. 1 Passenger. Daily Except Sunday.	STATIONS.	No. 4 Passenger. Daily Except Sunday.	No. 6 Passenger. Sundays Only
LEAVE A. M.	LEAVE A. M.		ARRIVE P. M.	ARRIVE P. M.
9 30	7 30	CHARLESTON	4 50	4 55
9 48	7 48	Mill Creek	4 38	4 36
9 52	7 52	Masons	4 35	4 32
9 56	7 56	Indian Creek	4 28	4 28
10 04	8 04	Jarrett's Ford	4 17	4 20
10 10	8 10	Blue Creek	4 11	4 14
10 19	8 19	Rich Creek	4 02	4 05
10 23	8 23	Falling Rock	3 58	4 01
10 28	8 28	Leatherwood	3 54	3 56
10 33	8 33	Clendennin	3 48	3 51
10 39	8 39	Morris Creek	3 42	3 45
10 41	8 41	Blyth	3 40	3 45
10 44	8 44	Queen Shoals	3 33	3 40
10 53	8 53	Porters	3 24	3 31
11 01	9 01	King	3 16	3 23
11 09	9 09	Dulls	3 08	3 15
11 19	9 19	Laurel	2 59	3 05
11 35	9 35	Big Sycamore	2 44	2 49
11 45	9 45	Yankee Dam	2 33	2 35
11 53	9 53	Middle Creek	2 26	2 31
12 01	10 04	CLAY COURT HOUSE	2 15	2 20
		MOUNT PISGAH		
P. M. ARRIVE	A. M. ARRIVE		P.M. LEAVE	P.M. LEAVE

J. Wainwright, General Manager.

Chas. K. McDermott, Superintendent.

Chesapeake & Ohio Railway

Schedule in Effect October 11, 18--
CENTRAL STANDARD TIME
EAST BOUND TRAINS
9:26 a. m.—No. 14, daily, for Clifton Forge and local stations.
3:27 p. m.—No 16, daily except Sunday, for Hinton and local stations.
5:29 p. m.—No. 2, F. F. V. Limited, arrives Washington 6:47 a. m., New York 19:43
1:45 a. m.—No. 4, daily, arrives Washington 3:48 p. m., New York 9:08 p. m.
WEST BOUND
1:55 a. m.—No. 1, Cincinnati Fast Line, daily, arrive Cincinnati 8.00 a. m., Louisville 11:00 a. m.
6:55 a. m.—No. 15, daily except Sunday, for Huntington.
12:13 p. m.—No. 3, F. F. V. Limited, daily arrives Cincinnati 6:00 p. m., ----- Ky., 6:15 p. m., Louisville Lexington
4:10 p. m.—No. 13, daily for Huntington and -----

COAL RIVER & WESTERN RY. CO.

In Effect Saturday, December 19th
1903 — 7 a.m.
Trains Run on Central Standard Time.

Southbound No. 1 Passenger Daily Ex. Sunday Leave A.M.	STATIONS	Northbound No. 2 Passenger Daily Ex. Sunday Arrive P.M.
11:55	St. Albans	2:28
12:02	Indian Creek	2:21
12:05	Calvert	2:18
12:14	Ferrell	2:09
12:19	Upper Falls	2:04
12:25	Island Ck.	1:58
12:36	Fuqua	1:48
12:40	Crooked Ck.	1:44
12:43	Alum Ck.	1:41
12:47	Fks. of Coal	1:36
P.M. Arrive		P.M. Leave

(Their first train schedule from the Charleston Daily Mail, December 18, 1903).

CORRECT TIME CARDS 1895

Arriving and leaving time of all Passenger Trains on all Railroads at Charleston:

C & O. RAILWAY.

Central Time.

EAST		WEST	
No. 14, Leaves	8:28 A. M.	No. 1, Leaves	2:06 A. M.
" 16, "	3:42 P. M.	" 15, "	8:00 A. M.
" 2, "	5:29 P. M.	" 3, "	11:36 A. M.
" 4, "	1:15 A. M.	" 13, "	4:57 P. M.

K. & M. RAILROAD.

Central Time.

NORTH.		SOUTH.	
No. 1, Leaves	6:20 A. M.	No. 16, Leaves	9:30 A. M.
" 11, "	12:10 P. M.	" 10, "	4:05 P. M.
" 15, "	3:55 P. M.	" 2, Arrives	11:20 P. M.

C. C. & S. RAILROAD.

Standard Time.

NORTH.		SOUTH.	
		No. 2, Arrives	9:20 A. M
		" 4,	6:00 P. M

KELLEY'S CREEK & NORTHWESTERN RAILROAD CO.

J. A. PAISLEY, President.
G. W. WILCOX, Asst. to President and Asst. Secretary, 800 Western Reserve Building, Cleveland.
E. G. MATHIOTT, Vice-President, 800 Western Reserve Building, Cleveland.
C. S. PAISLEY, Treasurer.
A. D. MURRAY, Secretary. Charleston, W. V.
J. H. MOYLE, Traffic Manager, 800 Western Reserve Building, Cleveland, O
LESTER RIDENOUR, Auditor, Charleston, W. Va

Pas'nger	Mls	March, 1929.	Pas'nger	
		LEAVE	ARRIVE	
†6 30 A M	0	Cedar Grove	5 00 P M	
6 40	2.1	Buff Lick		
6 45	3.4	Ward	4 55	
7 00 A M	6.7	Lewis	4 25	
		ARRIVE	†4 15 P M	
			LEAVE	

† Daily except Sunday.

STANDARD—Eastern time.
Connection.—At Cedar Grove, W.Va.—With New York Central R. R. (Ohio Central Lines).

-115-

Crew at the Handley shop in the 1920s. SWV

Kanawha and Michigan engine of train #34, which was wrecked near Hugheston, November 5, 1910.

COURTESY KANAWHA COIN SHOP

The last B&O steam train in Charleston, probably in the mid 1950s. The location is near the north end of Capitol Street in the old yards. The engine is a 2-8-2 type and ran up Elk River. CN

Montgomery Station on the C&O mainline, 1909. This station was typical of all the stations on the mainline. KCL

The new C&O depot on Fourth Street in St. Albans was built in 1906, replacing the 1871 depot, which was converted into a freight depot. PM

Abandoned railroad tunnel in the Blue Creek area. TH

The Kanawha and Michigan Railway

The Kanawha and Michigan (K&M) Railway Company was chartered on April 23, 1890, as a successor to the Kanawha Ohio Railway Company. By 1888, two years before the takeover, the Kanawha and Ohio had laid a 58-mile main line from Charleston to Point Pleasant. The tracks were laid in 1884 just below Capitol Hill, approximately parallel to Piedmont Road. At that time, rolling stock consisted of 14 locomotives, 11 passenger and baggage cars, 513 freight cars and 17 other cars.

The same year it acquired the Kanawha and Ohio Railway, K&M bought the Charleston and Gauley Railway. By 1898 the K&M reported a 30-mile extension from Dickinson's to the C&O at Gauley Bridge that didn't include the properties it acquired from the Kanawha and Ohio. Although the K&M was still independently operated at this point, its stock was controlled by the Toledo and Ohio Central Railroad.

By 1898 the K&M equipment fleet was not much larger than the 1888 K&O fleet. Business must have increased substantially, however, because in 1903, the K&M reported 43 locomotives, 16 passenger equipment cars, 4,079 freight cars (about three-quarters of which were open-top) and 55 other cars. The only new trackage reported was the 5-mile Smithers Creek Branch in West Virginia.

Between 1903 and 1910, the K&M was controlled first by the Hocking Valley, and later by the Lake Shore and Michigan Southern Railway and the Chesapeake and Ohio, although the railway was independently operated during this period. By 1910 the locomotive fleet had increased to 52 and the number of freight cars now stood at 4,951. Business continued to increase, and by 1914 the railroad had 71 locomotives, 30 passenger equipment cars, and 5,789 freight cars, over 5,000 of which were open-top design, an indication of the heavy coal traffic on the K&M.

The Seng Creek Tunnel, which connected the Paint Creek line at the southern tip of the county with the Coal River area in Boone County, is about a mile long. For years coal trains rumbled through its portals. TH

When the Chesapeake and Ohio and the Lake Shore and Michigan Southern transferred their holdings in 1914, stock control of the K&M once again passed to the Toledo and Ohio Central (T & O.C.) Railway. Independent operation of the railroad came to an end on January 1, 1922, when the K&M leased its properties to the T & O.C., which in turn transferred the leaseholds to the New York Central. The K&M existed as a non-operating company until June 1938, when it merged with the Toledo and Ohio Central. The T & O.C. merged later with the New York Central on June 30, 1952.

There are very few extant photos of the Kanawha and Michigan Railroad that served the county for many years, until being absorbed into the New York Central System and later Conrail. This rather poor-quality photo was taken at the K&M depot at the north end of Broad Street and shows men boarding an excursion train. Notice the man in the center carrying a trombone. RA

The Kanawha and Michigan depot at the north end of Broad Street was built in 1897 and demolished in 1975 to make way for the interstate ramp. AUTHOR'S COLLECTION

Short-line Railroads

Winifrede Railroad

It was many years before the major railroads crossed over the mountains to establish dependable rail transportation in Kanawha County, but eleven years before the Civil War, a railroad of sorts was operating in the county. An Englishman, Ralph Swinburn, was instrumental in building a railroad up Field's Creek in 1850. A former assistant to Robert Stephenson, who was the father of steam locomotives, Swinburn was employed in 1850 by the Field's Creek Coal Company to construct a railroad capable of hauling coal to the Kanawha River. Swinburn developed a gravity-type of rail system that used timber rails topped with metal strapping as a running surface. After a run, oxen towed the makeshift cars back to the mine. In 1854 the company imported a 15-ton steam locomotive from England, and shipped it to the Kanawha Valley.

The railroad operated until just before the Civil War, the company changing its name to Winefrede Mining and Manufacturing Company. After the rails and roadbed underwent massive reconstruction in the 1870s, the Winifrede Railroad operated at a profit until the 1920s, when the declining coal market forced the railroad and coal company to close. In 1930, however, the company resumed operations under the name Winifrede Colleries.

For many years, the railroad operated a "school train" in addition to its regular passenger and freight business. Roads in the rural areas were poor and the railroad offered the only easy means of transportation. Once again, however, declining coal revenues forced the railroad to close in the 1980s. The Winefrede area can be proud of its 130-year history of railroads.

Charleston, Clendenin and Sutton Railroad, up Elk in 1897. KCL

The Winifrede Railroad purchased this Baldwin engine #4 in the 1920s from the defunct West Virginia and Southern at Marmet to pull its passenger and school trains. COURTESY JOHN INGRAHM

Engine #4 on the West Virginia and Southern Railroad.
COURTESY JOHN INGRAHM

West Virginia & Southern Railroad

An early charter was granted to the West Virginia & Southern Railroad to build 125 miles of track across southern West Virginia, although only four miles were actually constructed from Hernshaw to haul coal to the C&O mainline at Marmet. Construction began in 1884, but the first coal was not transferred until 1896. A standard-gauge shortline built with 60-pound rail, the railroad operated two steam locomotives, a passenger car and an assortment of seven-ton wooden hopper cars. A marginal operation from the beginning, the operation closed in the mid-1920s because of the diminishing quality of coal and sagging market conditions.

Kanawha and Coal River Railroad

In 1892, the Kanawha and Coal River Railroad was built from the C&O mainline at the mouth of Davis Creek to the Davis Creek headwaters in the present Kanawha State Forest. The only access to this remote area of the county, the railroad hauled out coal and timber for the Black Band Mining and Manufacturing Company that was owned by the Anheuser Busch Brewing Company. In the summer of 1894, the railroad was extended about one mile up Dunlap Hollow to haul out the large white and chestnut oak logs. Several schools, churches, stores, and a post office were built in the town of Clifton that was founded in the upper end of Davis Creek.

In 1907, when the Black Band Mining and Manufacturing Company closed, the railroad was abandoned, and most of the people moved away from the area. The railroad, however, was rebuilt after World War I, and it operated for about a year, removing all the mining machinery and other scrap iron. Afterward, the rails were removed, and the railroad grade was turned over to the County for a road.

D.G. Courtney's Frogs Creek Logging Railroad and the barrel stave mill located at the northwestern tip of Kanawha County. Engine No. 1 ran to Raymond City in Putnam County, circa 1892. COURTESY ANDREW TRUSLOW

The Campbells Creek Railroad

The Campbells Creek Railroad extended from Dana on the Kanawha and Michigan Railroad to Putney up Campbells Creek, a distance of 12 miles. In 1902, the railroad was extended to Putney where it transported coal, timber and passengers to the Kanawha River.

The railroad scheduled two passenger trips daily, which stopped at Spring Fork, Coal Fork, Midway, Rensford, Tad, Rattlesnake, Cinco, Eightmile, Annfred and Putney. Because the line stopped at Putney, the trainmen had to back out of Point Lick after the Rensford stop, then the engine changed a mile below Putney at Mill Hollow, and the cars were pushed up to the Putney Station.

On Friday, December 29, 1950, when engineer George "Skinner" Morton brought the engine and a single passenger car into the Reed yards at 5:20 p.m., over 40 years of passenger service and mail delivery to eleven mining communities on Campbells Creek ended. The railroad, however, transported coal until 1961.

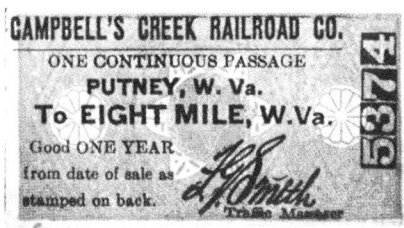

Campbells Creek Railroad

Wreck at mouth of Campbells Creek, early 1920s.
COURTESY DALE KELLY

Passenger train at Tad on the Campbells Creek Railroad.
COURTESY MAYWOOD HACKNEY

Engine #5 of the Campbells Creek Railroad.
COURTESY AMHERST INDUSTRIES

Passenger train at Annfred on Campbells Creek Railroad, 1948. COURTESY TOM STAMPER

A railroad barn from the 1880s at the mouth of Campbells Creek. The barn was used by the Campbells Creek Railroad. TH

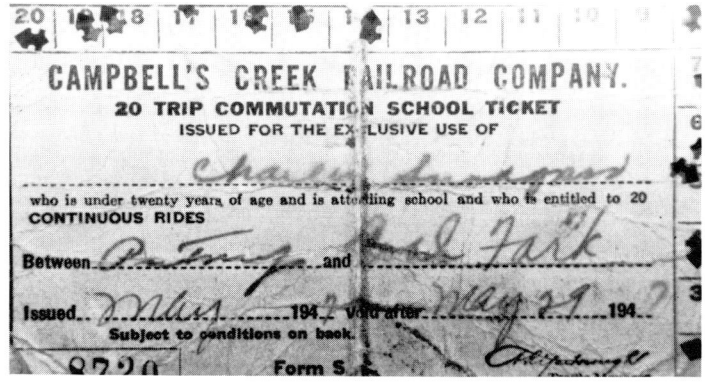

COURTESY CHARLES SNODGRASS

Kelly's Creek Railroad

The Kelly's Creek Railroad had a long tenure beginning in 1895, when it travelled between Cedar Grove and Big Mountain. The new railroad was financed by Charles Cameron Lewis, the primary investor, and financial backing was also provided by Collis P. Huntington, the famed railroad builder. Later, the railroad extended the tracks seven miles to haul coal from Mammoth to the Kanawha and Michigan tracks at Cedar Grove. After the railroad went through several owners, labor strife in the 1930s, and World War II, W.H. Warner Company was the final operator until the railroad closed down in 1964 because the mineable coal in the area was exhausted and the nations' railroads were converted to diesel.

Kelly's Creek & Northwestern Railway

The Kelly's Creek & Northwestern Railway (KC&NW), owned by the Valley Camp Coal Company, was constructed in 1902. Extending northward up Kelly's Creek from Cedar Grove to Ward, the railroad line served the mines of the parent company exclusively. Originally the track extended about seven miles, but when the neighboring Kelly's Creek Railroad was abandoned in 1964, the KC&NW picked up three additional miles of track and another mine. The only commodity this railroad carried was coal, and plenty of it. On a daily basis, about 150 cars interchanged with the New York Central at Cedar Grove and the coal was then transferred to barges headed for power plants in the Kanawha River and Ohio River basins.

With good supervision and management practices, the KC&NW operation was profitable for its owners. There were two crews a day on the railroad for many years, one by day and the other by night.

The KC&NW relied on a fleet of 40-ton outside-braced hoppers that they obtained from the C&O Railway to transport coal to the tipple at Cedar Grove. The railroad also provided transportation for the Valley Camp miners in three unique arch-roofed cars, similar to those used during the Civil War.

Currently, the KC&NW is one of the few remaining short line railroads in West Virginia. The area that it serves has changed drastically. Gone are the many mines on Kelly's Creek, the monstrous crane at Cedar Grove that stockpiled coal, the wooden barges that transported coal to markets, and the interchange with the New York Central. The Kelly's Creek & Northwestern, however, is alive and prospering by delivering the black diamonds to market.

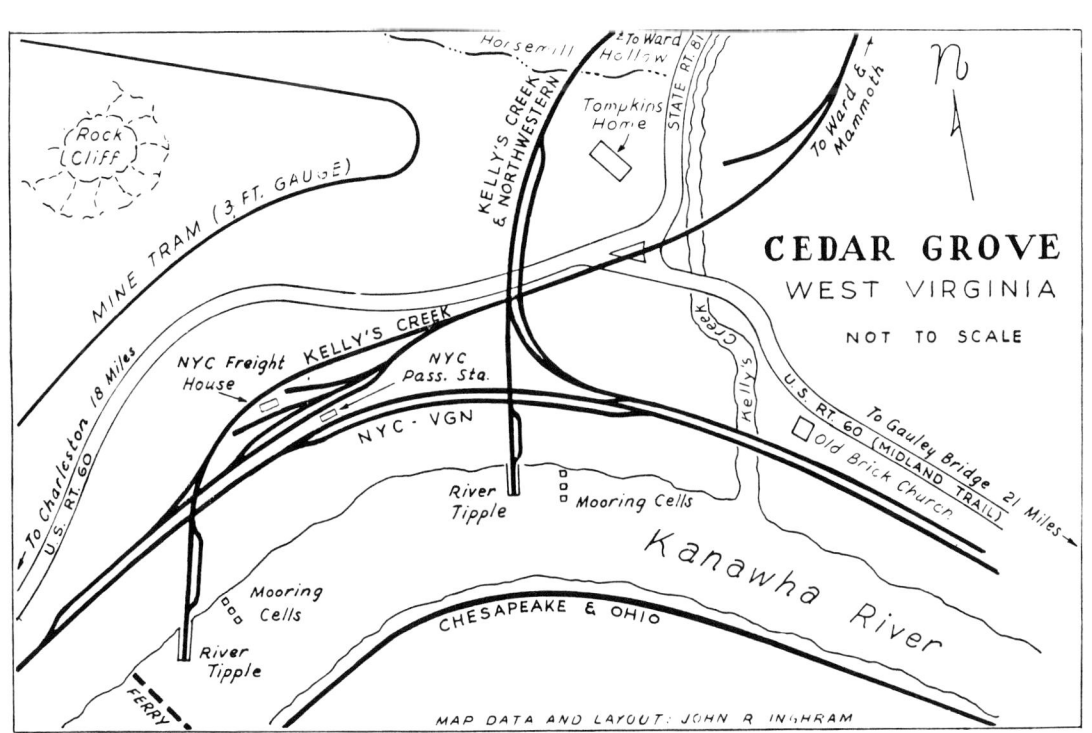

Engine #1 on the Kelly's Creek & Northwestern Railroad.
EG

Coal cars of the Kelly's Creek & Northwestern Railroad.
EG

Charleston, Clendenin & Sutton Railroad

In 1890 a group of local businessmen chartered a railroad that ran up the Elk River from Charleston to Clendenin and to Sutton in Braxton County. First called the Black Jack line, the line became known as the Charleston, Clendenin & Sutton Railroad, and by 1904 the tracks reached the county seat of Clay County. Two years later, Senator Henry Gassaway Davis purchased the railroad, which he reorganized under the name Coal and Coke Railroad. Davis rebuilt the railroad and extended the tracks to Elkins in Randolph County, where it connected with the Western Maryland and Baltimore & Ohio railroads. The Baltimore & Ohio acquired the railroad in 1917, which extended the B&O line into Charleston.

RIGHT: A July 4, 1917, excursion train on the Kelly's Creek & Northwestern Railroad. The engine is complete with bunting and a kerosene head lamp, and merrymakers peer from the coach windows. The ribbed front bumper was known as the cow-catcher as it was intended to scoop up and throw aside any animal unwise enough to stand on the tracks. COURTESY JOHN INGRAHM

Cabin Creek Line

Built in 1890, the Kanawha Railway Company's line from the C&O at Cabin Creek Junction to Cane Fork and Acme was the first rail line constructed along Cabin Creek. The C&O was interested in purchasing this coal line, and on January 31, 1902, the Kanawha Railway Company was sold to the C&O.

Immediately after the sale, the C&O expanded the line to reach the vast coal reserves in Cabin Creek. Lines from Cabin Creek toward Kayford and Decota were completed in 1903, and additional branch lines were built to the many coal mines that opened in the area. In the same year, work began on the extension to the Big Coal River line, which was completed in 1905. The line extended from Leewood to Lawson, above Whitesville, via the Seng Creek Tunnel. During the next decade, additional extensions were built in the Big Coal River area, most notably the Big and Little Marsh Fork branches. In 1910 the C&O bought a plot of land near Eskdale where they built the Cane Fork yard and engine facility, which included a yard office, watering facilities, a 50-ton cylindrical coal dock, and a large two-track engine house. In later years, a railroad YMCA and a miniature golf course were built near the yard for the crews who brought the trainloads of empty coal cars that were sent to the mines.

As the coal industry grew, the population of the area increased, and coal towns, such as Miami, Ohley, Eskdale, Ronda, Sharon, Dawes, Leewood, Kayford, Decota, Carbon, Giles, and Red Warrior sprang up.

The coal business was booming and so was coal transportation on the railroad.

As the coal industry boomed, the railroad expanded to meet the growing transportation need. The typical passenger train consisted of two passenger cars, an express car and a mail baggage car, and some days there were so many passengers that people had to stand in the aisles. On many occasions, the conductor had to ask the engineer to go slow so he had enough time to collect his passenger fares. Passenger service was offered from Boone County, down to the main line at Cabin Creek Junction, via the Seng Creek Tunnel. This service was cut back in 1919, however, when the Big Coal River Line was completed.

When the Coal River Line was finished in 1919, the railroad discontinued using the Seng Creek Tunnel for regular freight operations, except to ferry engines from Elk Run Junction to the Cane Fork engine house for monthly inspections. These regular runs were made until the late 1950s, when the C&O closed its steam operations. The tracks in the tunnel were removed and a road was built on the abandoned right-of-way.

Diesel engines first came to Cabin Creek in the early 1950s, when they were placed on the inbound trains from Russell, Kentucky. During this time, both steam and diesel engines came into Cane Fork on these runs.

The decline of the coal business in the 1970s spelled doom for the railroad, and as market conditions worsened, many coal companies closed down and moved elsewhere. Although yard clerks and crews were still stationed at Cane Fork during these slack periods, by 1980 the Chessie System had decided to close the Cane Fork yard.

The Kanawha & West Virginia Railroad

The Kanawha & West Virginia Railroad connected with the Kanawha & Michigan Railroad at Charleston, and extended up the north bank of the Elk River, 13½ miles to the mouth of Blue Creek, and then crossed Elk River at Blue Creek and extended to Blakely in Clay County, a distance of 33½ miles. It was an important coal and timber road, and was projected to Curtin on the Richwood Branch of the B&O Railroad. It was completed to Blakeley in 1907.

Facing west, the C&O station at Cabin Creek Junction, 1935. EG

Steam engine #279 along the Cabin Creek Line, 1912. EG

Building railroad grade on Cabin Creek, around the turn of the century. EG

Scene of runaway, and fatal accident of engine #270, September 23, 1905, at Cherokee on Cabin Creek (now Leewood). Engineer J.W. Parnell and Fireman R.G. Saunders were thrown 70 feet and killed instantly. Total damage was $8,500. EG

Paint Creek Line

Although the C&O railroad came through Paint Creek in 1872, when the tracks from Huntington to Richmond were built, it wasn't the first railroad in the area.

The first railroad in Paint Creek was built by the Paint Creek Coal and Iron-Mining Manufacturing Company. It was a 5-foot broad gauge track that was built along the creek in 1853-1854. Ralph Swinburn, who previously built the Winifrede Railroad, located and constructed the line, which was laid with wooden rails that were spiked on top with handmade scrap iron spikes. Wooden trestles and bridges were built to cross Paint Creek, and the line ended at the river in the east end of Dego (Pratt), where the coal was then transferred to barges.

The railroad's locomotive was built in Richmond by Tredegar Iron Works. To transport the engine to Paint Creek, the engine was shipped on a barge from Richmond to New Orleans, then up the Mississippi, Ohio, and Kanawha rivers to the mouth of Paint Creek. The trip, however, was in vain. The engine was too wide for the newly built trestle, and if the trestle was widened, it would have weakened the structure and made it unsafe for heavy loads. The engine was returned to Richmond, and mule teams were used for any hauling on the railroad. This lasted for six or seven years, until the operation was abandoned.

On April 28, 1884, the Kanawha and Paint Creek Railroad was formed to build a railroad along the eastern bank of Paint Creek. Reorganized in 1885 as the Kanawha and Paint Creek Railway Company, the company constructed a small portion of the roadbed, but never laid tracks. The Kanawha and Pocahontas Railroad, which had incorporated in 1898, bought the Kanawha and Paint Creek Railway Company in 1902. They constructed a line on the eastern bank of Paint Creek, which was completed in 1905, and later extended from Paint Creek Junction to Keeferton. The C&O leased and then purchased the line in late 1905, and in 1917 the line was extended from Keeferton to Kingston.

As the railroad advanced up Paint Creek, the development of the coal industry took a big step forward. When Charles Pratt of New York came to the area, he built a large tipple, a machine shop and an office building in the east end of the town that has been named after him. To transport coal to the tipple, railroad tracks were built from Paint Creek and the C&O, part of which were on an elevated trestle.

As the railroad was extended south, more and more mines located near the line. A five-track yard was built two miles from the main line to weigh all coal cars that came out of the Paint Creek Branch. The westbound coal was then taken to a siding at Hansford, where it was picked up by a westbound train from Handley.

Coal mining was the main business on Paint Creek, and where there was a mine, there was a town nearby. Towns along the railroad such as Gallagher, Standard, Whitaker, Greencastle, Burnwell, Collinsdale, Mahan, Coalfield, Milburn, Westerly, Glen Huddy, and Kingston were founded by coal operators to house the miners and their families. The people of Paint Creek relied on the railroad to bring in the supplies they needed, for without roads, the railroad was their only means of transportation. The Paint Creek passenger train brought in the mail, and it took students to high school until 1949 when this service was discontinued.

Although the C&O mainline still depends on the coal business, many of the mines in the area have closed. Some of the many towns that were built along Paint Creek have almost vanished without a trace, and now that a road has been built, the towns that remain do not depend on the railroad as the primary means of transportation.

Handley

In 1875 Frank Love, John Smith, and J.B. Lewis came east of Pratt to Handley to begin a coal and gas business, the Wyoming Manufacturing Company. Seeing the need to develop a town, the company laid out the surrounding land and called the new town Handley after a company official. The company mined coal in the east and west ends of town, which was hauled from the mines to the river by a wooden rail car, called a buckjimmy, that held up to 15 tons of coal.

In early 1891 the C&O decided to expand its Montgomery facilities, and after searching for a new site, moved its operation from Montgomery to Handley on June 23, 1891. A roundhouse, bunkhouse, and engine facilities were built soon after the move, and in 1896 a large YMCA was constructed for railroad personnel. As the railroad expanded, a large yard was constructed to hold all the incoming coal cars, and soon the Wyoming Company used the railroad as its primary means of transporting its coal to market.

The developing railroad in Handley became an important part of the C&O operation. Trains stopped in Handley for new engines, more coal or water, and engines and freight cars were repaired in the roundhouse. The shop forces handled almost any job except for the major engine inspections, which were done in Huntington.

The population of Handley grew as more and more jobs became available on the railroad. Handley residents either worked in the coal mines or on the railroad, and as the size of the locomotives located at Handley increased, additional people were hired to enlarge the facilities. Every type of engine that the C&O owned came into Handley. Switching crews worked both the east and west ends of the yard to keep the coal moving, and crews stationed in Handley made runs to Paint Creek, Cabin Creek, and Winfrede Junction to bring the coal to Handley for classification into larger trains.

As the railroad operations changed, however, many of these functions were discontinued or moved from Handley, and the town no longer is a major railroad junction.

An early steam engine at Indian Creek just north of St. Albans on Coal River. COURTESY PM VIA MILDRED TROWBRIDGE

Coal River Railroads

Four attempts were made to construct a railroad along the Coal River before it became a reality, and each attempt was financially unsuccessful because the C&O Railroad quietly opposed the plans.

Col. Michael P. O'Hern first attempted to build the railroad in 1890. Although he had previously lost the bulk of his fortune in a transcontinental railroad venture, O'Hern began constructing the St. Albans & Coal River Railroad with his remaining capital. When O'Hern died in 1897, he was so deeply in debt that his daughter asked Judge J.B.C. Drew, the legal counsel, to sell all the estate's assets to pay off her father's debts.

Drew reorganized and renamed the corporation as the Coal River & St. Albans Railroad, and he raised $216,000 to purchase the bankrupt firm. Drew later raised some additional capital and changed the name of the corporation to the St. Albans & Boone Railroad Company. This company was also unsuccessful in getting beyond a grading right-of-way, so Judge Drew stepped in to form yet another corporation. The Pocahontas, Coal River & Kanawha Railroad Company, as it was named, had a unique approach to the terminal in St. Albans. It proposed to build a station at the mouth of Coal River to connect with the boat traffic on the Kanawha, and to run the railroad up "A" Street alongside the river. When they applied to St. Albans for a franchise, the mayor, U.S. Jarrett, realized the plan was impractical, so he had the council give the company a year to build the road from the mouth of Coal River across Main Street. It agreed that once this section was completed, a proper franchise would be granted. The company, however, was unable to work out any plan to cross the C&O Railroad and Ram's Horn Creek, and this requirement was never met.

In 1901 J.V.R. Skinner from Ohio and Senator Sproul of Pennsylvania formed the Coal River & Western Railroad Company because they wanted to develop their large holdings on the Coal River. They took over the defunct corporations' rights-of-way, and under Skinner's able leadership, freight and passenger service was soon extended up Coal River for about 20 miles.

In 1906 the C&O floated a $3 million bond issue, which it used to purchase the company and to extend their railroad line along both forks of Coal River. The first tracks that were laid along Coal River traversed the hilly part of what is now downtown St. Albans. The train crews encountered stiff grades of one percent inbound and two percent outbound, which caused a number of problems when coal was transported out of the Coal River Basin. Because of the alignment problems, the railroad had to use smaller engines that could only pull a limited number of loads.

As the number of coal trains coming out of the Coal River Subdivision increased, St. Albans soon became a railroad town. To meet the demand for services, a shop was built, water plugs were installed, and a 500-ton coal dock that spanned the two main tracks through St. Albans was constructed. The headquarters of the Coal River Subdivision was located next to the passenger station.

The present-day businesses in St. Albans still rely on coal. In the late 1960s, the Appalachian Power Company built the John Amos Power Plant that used coal to generate power. The C&O built a branch that ran along Bill's Creek from the main line at Scary Creek to bring in coal supplies. Known as the Bill's Creek Local, the railroad now makes at least two runs daily because the company uses the facilities at the power plant to transfer the coal from railcars to barges.

Campbells Creek Coal Company at the mouth of Campbells Creek (Dana) in the 1930s. The present Port Amherst facilities are along the river. swv

Chapter Eight

King Coal

Coal company script.

King Coal

Although coal was first noted in North America by Father Louis Hennepin on a journey down the Illinois River in 1679, John Peter Salley of Augusta County, Virginia, is credited with the first discovery of coal in what is now West Virginia. Salley was on an exploratory trip across the Allegheny Mountains in 1742 when he came to a small stream in the Kanawha area. There the exploring party found "a large plenty of coals, for which we named it Coal River." (The site is now located at Peytona in Boone County.)

Nothing was done with this discovery, however, until the early 1800s, when the manufacture of salt became a big business in the Kanawha Valley. For years wood was used in the process of drying out the salt brine which was pumped from wells, but with increased production the wood supply was soon exhausted. Coal, which was plentiful in the surrounding hills, was used as a substitute as early as 1817.

During the years preceding the Civil War, coal became more of an economic factor in the valley, and the first commercial coal company was incorporated on March 10, 1834. Slaves were even brought to some areas to mine the resource. Coal was shipped down the Kanawha River during periods of high water to Cincinnati and occasionally to markets as far south as New Orleans.

An 1836 state geological report by Professor William B. Rogers of the University of Virginia painted a glowing picture of the potential for coal development in the Kanawha Valley. But it was not until after the Civil War that out-of-state and foreign investors came into the valley, and bought stock in the various locally owned coal companies or founded their own.

Coal production in the valley was somewhat expanded when it was discovered that kerosene could be extracted from cannel coal, a variety of coal that existed in large deposits in the region. Until the discovery of underground oil reserves in Pennsylvania in 1859, cannel-coal oil was a substantial growth industry.

Transportation was a serious problem for the coal industry until the 1870s, when the Chesapeake and Ohio Railway finally laid its rails across the Alleghenies and down the Kanawha Valley to the Ohio River at Huntington. This opened up markets both east and west, and dozens of coal companies were subsequently formed. Branch lines snaked out into the previously isolated sections of the county and opened up vast, previously untapped coal fields.

Kanawha County's coal production first passed the million ton mark in 1889. By 1904 the production figure had reached 3.5 million tons. In 1915 it was more than 5.7 million tons, and by 1947 it had reached ten million tons.

Labor troubles have plagued the coal fields as long as they have been in existence. Dispute turned to violence in 1912 and 1921, with far-reaching effects on Kanawha County. The United Mine Workers was finally successful in unionizing county miners in the 1930s.

Kanawha County has been relatively free of the mine disasters common to the industry. On April 20, 1905, an explosion at the Kayford mine killed six miners. A mine fire at Villa near Charleston on May 20, 1918, caused the death of 13 miners.

The coal industry has always been an up-and-down kind of business. It was booming during the world war years, and has been depressed during times of economic slowdown. Today, while there is still substantial production in the county, it is with a very small work force and highly mechanized mining equipment. It is hard to say that coal is really "King" anymore.

> **Kanawha County had an estimated mineable reserve of coal of approximately six billion short tons as estimated by the West Virginia Geological Survey, sixth largest county reserves in the state. Only 635 million short tons have been mined in the first 100 years of record keeping (1883-1983).**
>
> —Department of Mines

Mine checks.

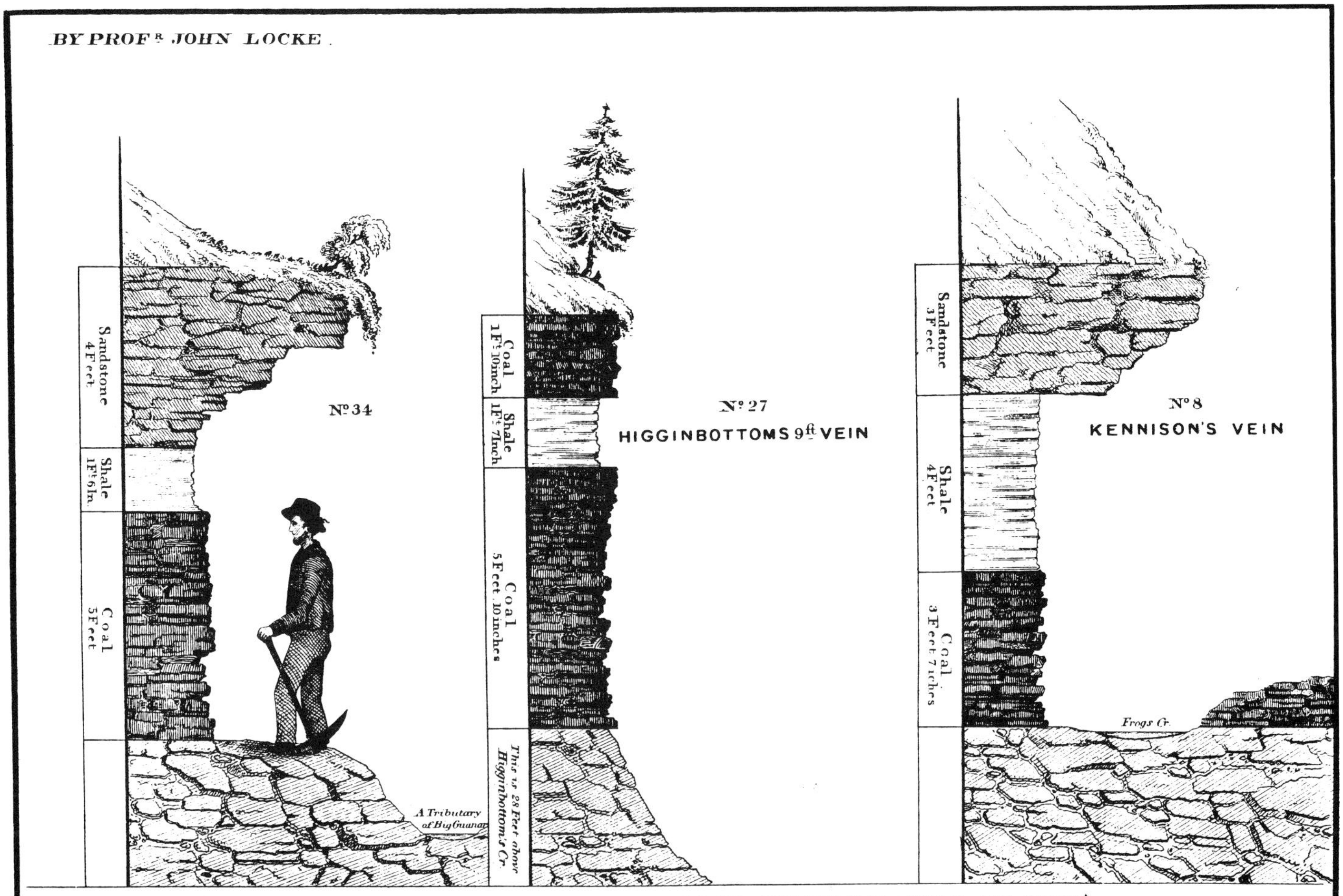

BY PROF. JOHN LOCKE.

Sandstone 4 Feet		
Shale 1Ft 6 In	Coal 1Ft 10 Inch	Sandstone 3 Feet
Coal 5 Feet	Shale 1Ft 7 Inch	Shale 4 Feet
	Coal 5 Feet 10 Inches	Coal 3 Feet 7 Inches

Nº 34

Nº 27
HIGGINBOTTOMS 9 ft VEIN

This is 28 Feet above Higginbottoms Cr.

A Tributary of Big Guanag.

Nº 8
KENNISON'S VEIN

Frogs Cr.

CROPPINGS OUT OF SOME OF THE COAL ON THE LANDS OF THE GREAT KANAWHA Cº

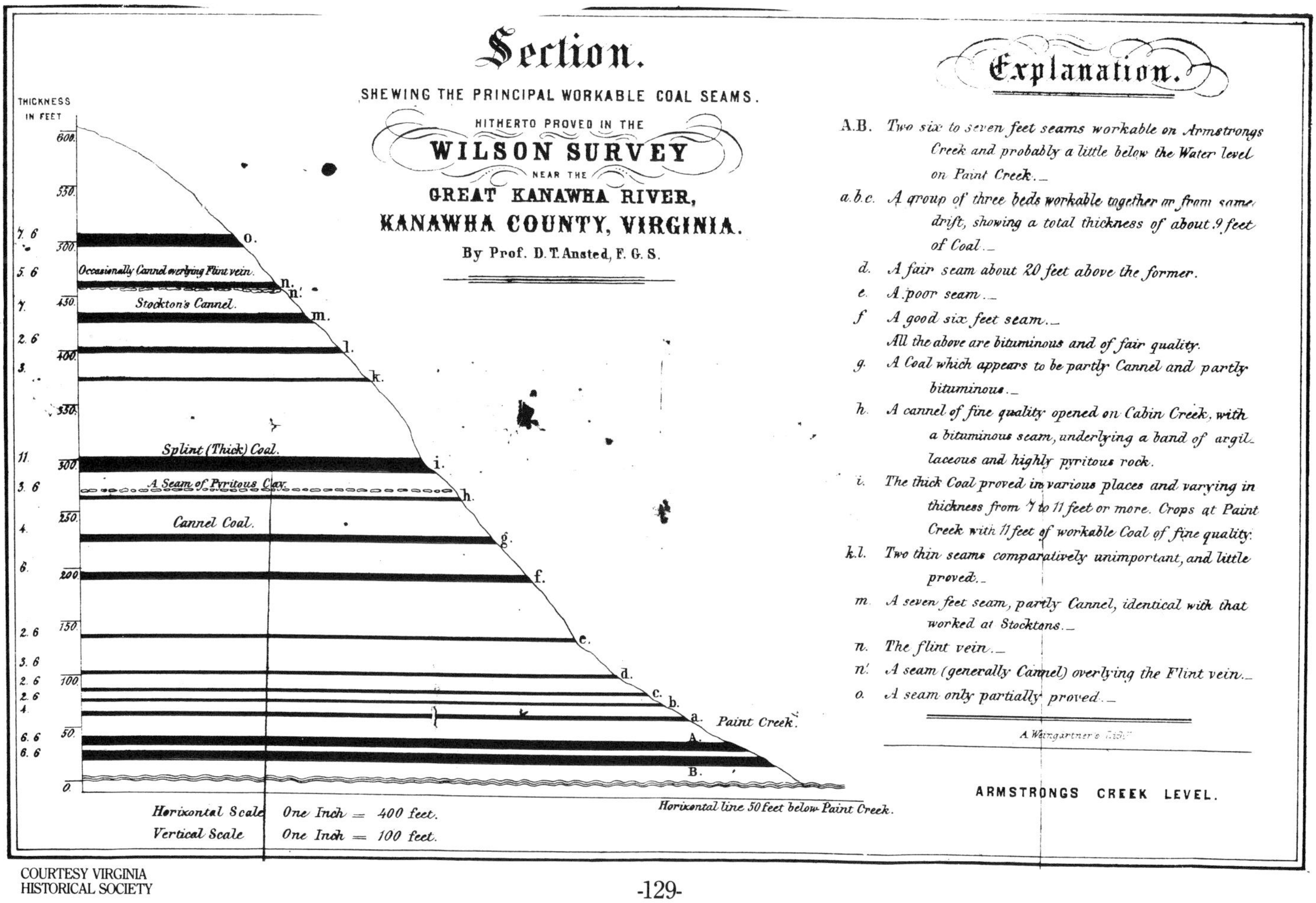

Section.
SHEWING THE PRINCIPAL WORKABLE COAL SEAMS.
HITHERTO PROVED IN THE
WILSON SURVEY
NEAR THE
GREAT KANAWHA RIVER,
KANAWHA COUNTY, VIRGINIA.
By Prof. D. T. Ansted, F. G. S.

Explanation.

A.B. Two six to seven feet seams workable on Armstrongs Creek and probably a little below the Water level on Paint Creek.

a.b.c. A group of three beds workable together or from same drift, showing a total thickness of about 9 feet of Coal.

d. A fair seam about 20 feet above the former.

e. A poor seam.

f. A good six feet seam.
All the above are bituminous and of fair quality.

g. A Coal which appears to be partly Cannel and partly bituminous.

h. A cannel of fine quality opened on Cabin Creek, with a bituminous seam, underlying a band of argillaceous and highly pyritous rock.

i. The thick Coal proved in various places and varying in thickness from 7 to 11 feet or more. Crops at Paint Creek with 11 feet of workable Coal of fine quality.

k.l. Two thin seams comparatively unimportant, and little proved.

m. A seven feet seam, partly Cannel, identical with that worked at Stocktons.

n. The flint vein.

n'. A seam (generally Cannel) overlying the Flint vein.

o. A seam only partially proved.

A. Weingartner's Lith.

THICKNESS IN FEET

600.
550.
7. 6   500.   o. — Occasionally Cannel overlying Flint vein.   n'. n.
5. 6   450.   Stockton's Cannel.   m.
7.   400.   l.
2. 6   k.
3.   350.
       300.   Splint (Thick) Coal.   i.
11.   250.   A Seam of Pyritous Clay.   h.
3. 6   Cannel Coal.   g.
4.   200.   f.
6.   150.   e.
2. 6   100.   d.
3. 6   c. b. a. Paint Creek.
2. 6   50.   A.
4.   B.
6. 6
6. 6   0.

Paint Creek.
ARMSTRONGS CREEK LEVEL.

Horizontal Scale   One Inch = 400 feet.
Vertical Scale   One Inch = 100 feet.

Horizontal line 50 feet below Paint Creek.

Cannel Coal

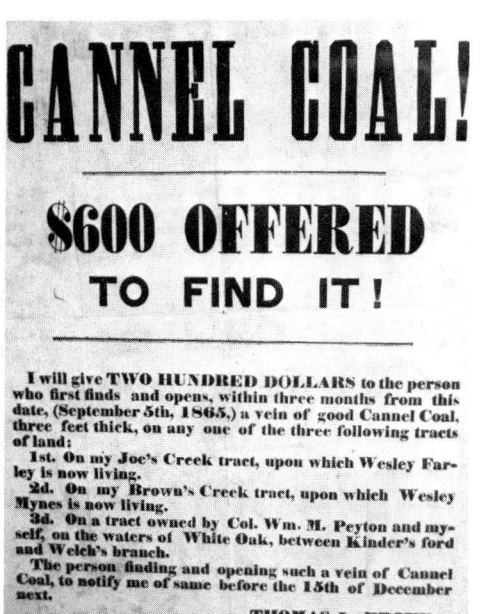

Cannel coal is formed from fossilized seeds and spores of plants, in contrast to the fossilized wood, bark, and leaves that form the more common bituminous coal. Cannel, in Scotland, means candle, and the coal was given this name because it could be lit with a match, and it burned with a long, bright flame. It is a hard, bituminous coal, and highly volatile.

Cannel coal was first discovered in 1848 in the Cannelton area along the Kanawha-Fayette county line by Colonel Aaron Stockton. Stockton was a tavern owner, coal operator, and salt producer, who pioneered the manufacture of oil from cannel coal. Other deposits were later discovered along Falling Rock Creek near Clendenin, Paint Creek, and Coal River in Boone County. Cannelton coal oil was shipped down the Kanawha River to a refinery at Maysville, Kentucky. Coal River cannel coal was shipped before any oil extraction. A refinery was later built at the Falling Rock Creek site about 1852.

Then, in 1859 underground oil was discovered in Pennsylvania. As oil fields developed there and in northern West Virginia, the demand for cannel oil dropped off, and soon thereafter the Civil War closed down all the mining activity in the county. Some cannel coal was mined after the war because its high and steady flame was preferred by city dwellers in the east at the turn of the century. The Falling Rock Creek refinery reopened in 1893, and stayed in operation until 1912.

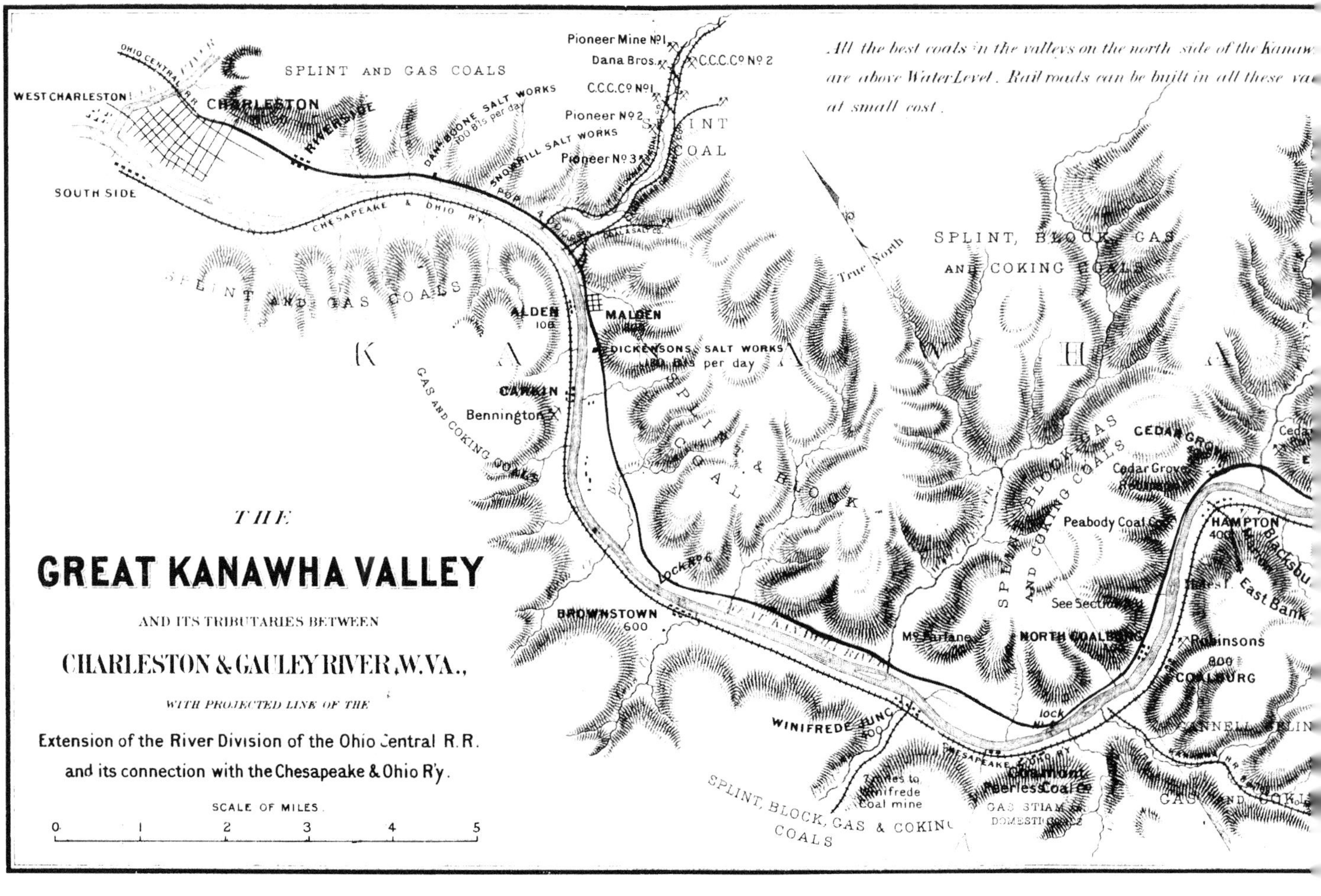

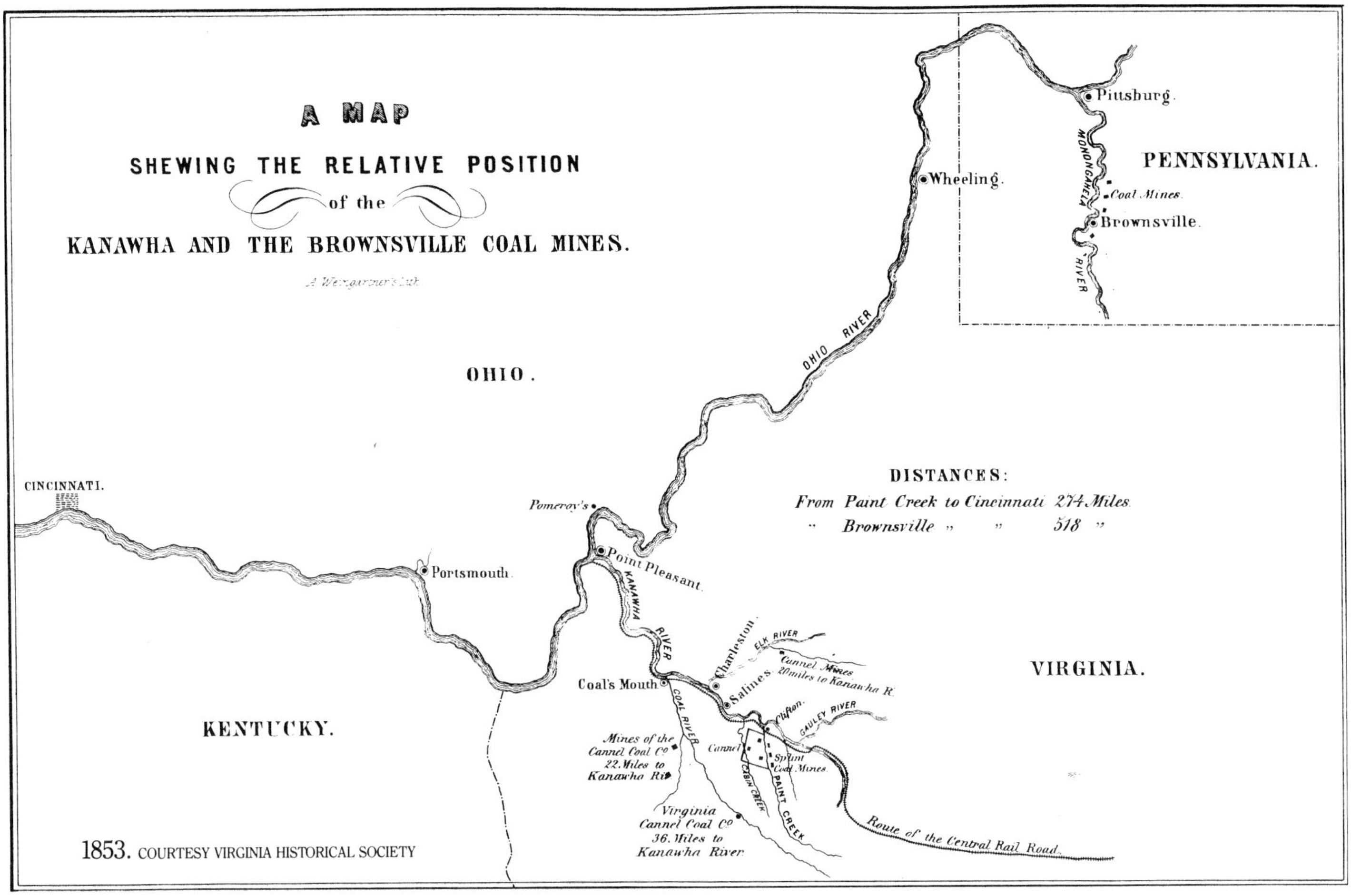

A MAP
SHEWING THE RELATIVE POSITION
of the
KANAWHA AND THE BROWNSVILLE COAL MINES.

OHIO.

CINCINNATI.

Pomeroy's
Point Pleasant
Portsmouth
Coal's Mouth
Charleston
Salines
Clifton

KENTUCKY.

Mines of the Cannel Coal Co. 22 Miles to Kanawha R.

Virginia Cannel Coal Co. 36 Miles to Kanawha River.

Pittsburg
Wheeling
Coal Mines
Brownsville

PENNSYLVANIA.

DISTANCES:
From Paint Creek to Cincinnati 274 Miles.
" Brownsville " 518 "

VIRGINIA.

Cannel Mines 10 miles to Kanawha R.

Route of the Central Rail Road.

1853. COURTESY VIRGINIA HISTORICAL SOCIETY

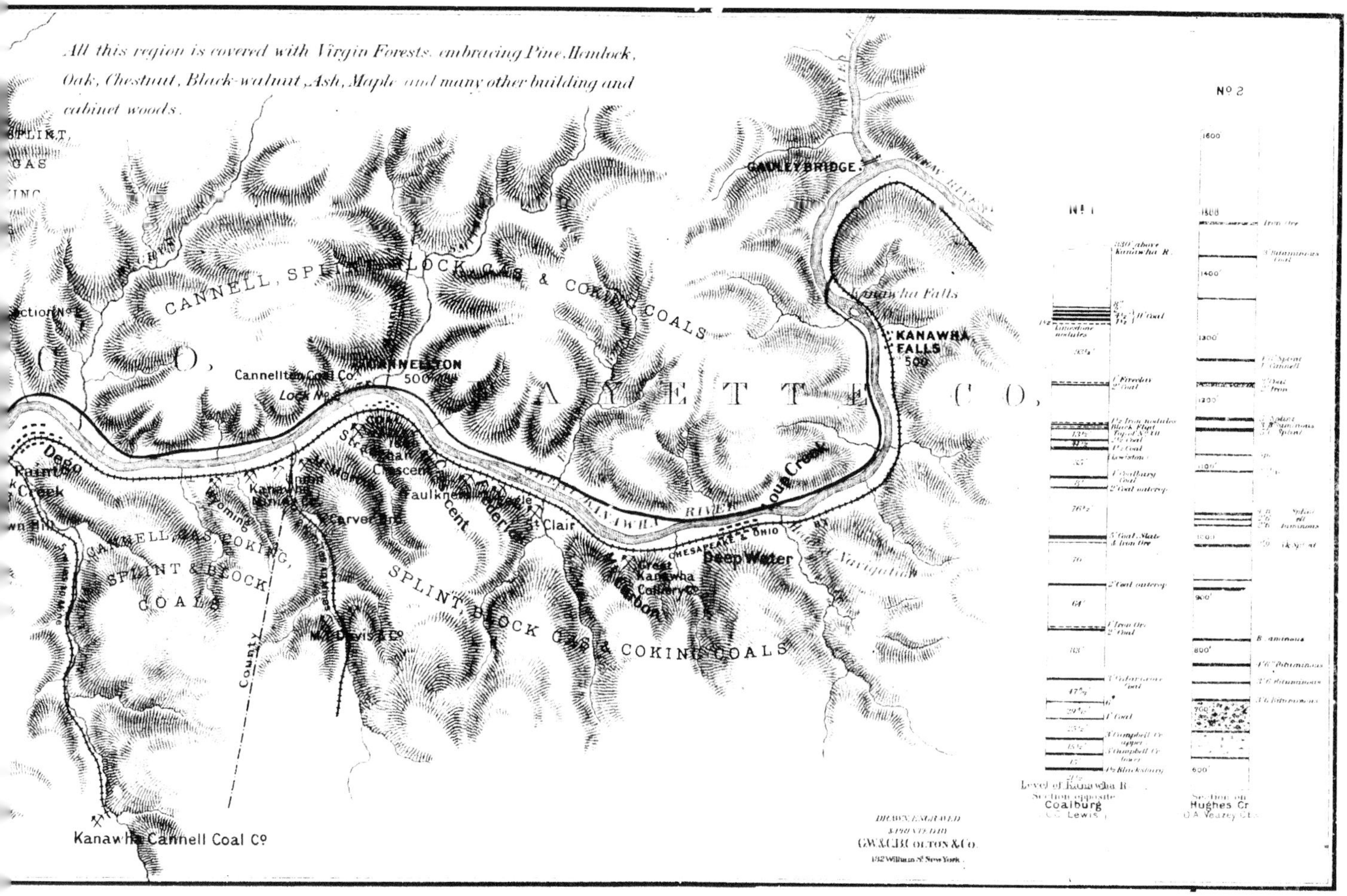

All this region is covered with Virgin Forests, embracing Pine, Hemlock, Oak, Chestnut, Black-walnut, Ash, Maple and many other building and cabinet woods.

GAULEY BRIDGE

CANNELL, SPLINT, BLOCK, GAS & COKING COALS

Cannelton Coal Co. CANNELTON

FAYETTE CO.

Kanawha Falls
KANAWHA FALLS

Deep Water

SPLINT, BLOCK, GAS & COKING COALS

Kanawha Cannell Coal Co.

Coalburg   Hughes Cr.

-131-

LEFT: The cannel coal refinery on Falling Rock Creek near Clendenin is perhaps the oldest refinery that remains in America. It was built in the 1850s to distill kerosene from cannel coal and slaves were used to mine the coal. The refinery produced kerosene until 1863. Although this 1950s photo shows the refinery buildings still standing, all that remains now is the large chimney. CN

RIGHT: The historic Falling Rock Creek refinery chimney now sits abandoned in the middle of the Falling Rock Creek road, a reminder of the once-great cannel coal industry.

Wooden coal barges at Charleston, 1890. WVU

Mine motor locomotive on a mountain near Cannelton in 1898. EG

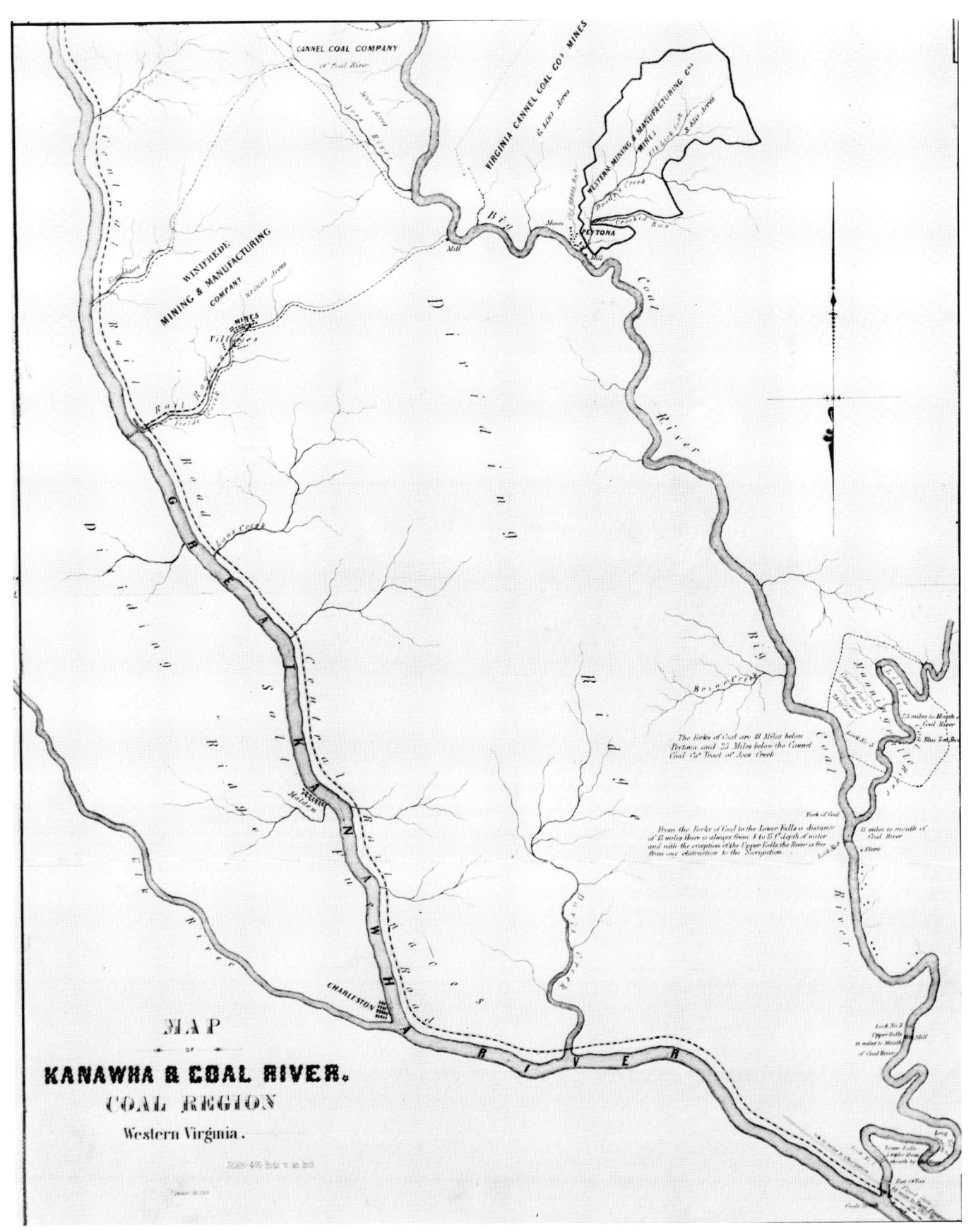

Map of the coal region around the Kanawha and Coal rivers in the 1850s. Note that a railroad is included along the Kanawha River. It was proposed before the Civil War but did not open until 1873. GS (LIBRARY OF CONGRESS, GEOGRAPHY & MAP DIVISION)

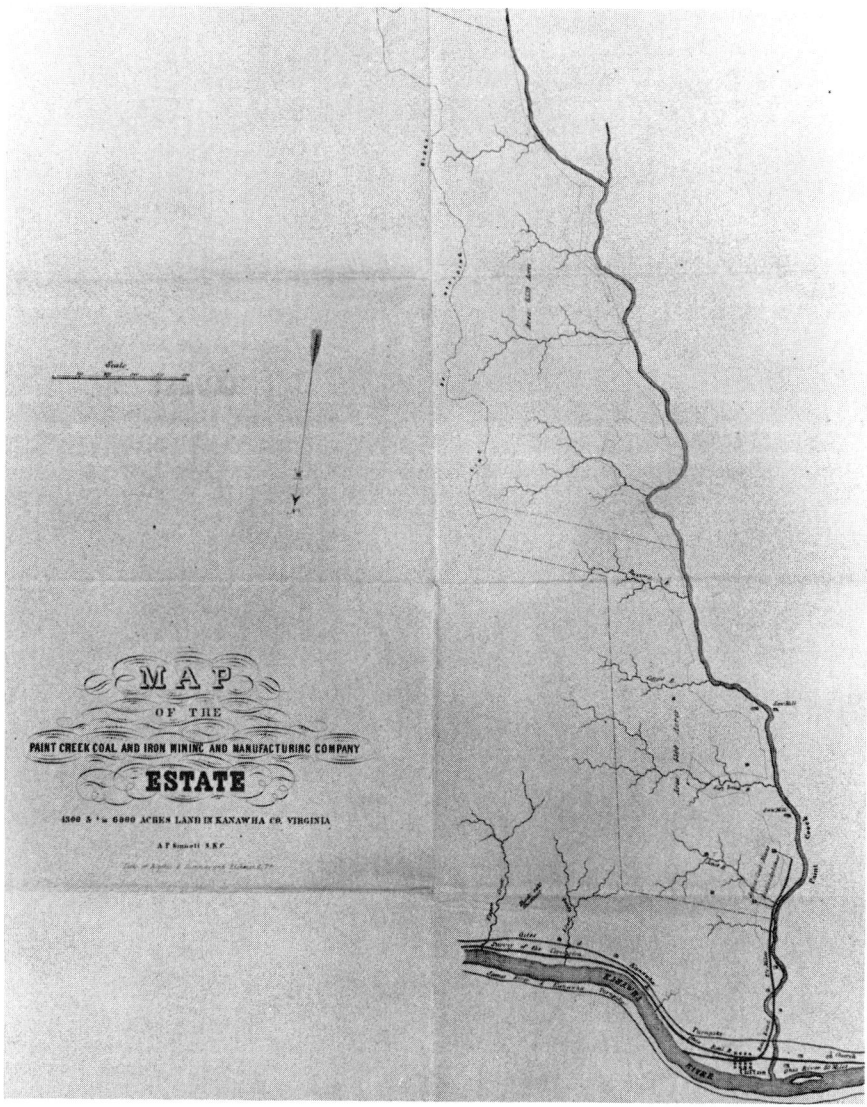

COURTESY VIRGINIA STATE LIBRARY

Campbells Creek Coal Companies

The Campbells Creek area was one of the earliest regions of the county to start coal mining because of its close proximity to the salt works. The Pioneer Coal Company was incorporated in 1855 and operated mines on Campbells Creek from 1871 to 1892. It was the first coal company in the valley to issue scrip.

Near the end of the Civil War, three brothers, George, J. Eugene and Stephen Dana, came to the Kanawha Valley and began operating coal mines on Campbells Creek. The Dana Brothers had soon built up a large business, which was known as the Campbells Creek Coal Company. The Campbells Creek Coal Company became an Ohio corporation on December 29, 1903, and it lasted for 49 years until it was dissolved on July 31, 1952.

In the meantime the Hatfield/Campbells Creek Coal Company was formed from the merger of the old Campbells Creek Coal Company and the Hatfield River interest in 1924. The Hatfield family had been pioneers in the coal on the river business, building the Hatfield Yard in Cincinnati the largest independent coal terminal on the Ohio River.

The Amherst Fuel Company, one of the earliest operators in the Logan County District, acquired the Hatfield/Campbells Creek Coal Company in 1950 extending its operations to the Kanawha District. The Hatfield purchase included, in addition to coal land, a fleet of towboats and barges, a short line railway, and an extensive retail coal-distribution establishment in Cincinnati.

Today, Amherst Industries continues as a fourth-generation family-owned and managed company, operating with its three subsidiary companies, Amherst Industries, Inc., Madison Coal and Supply Company, and the Landisville Railroad, Inc.

In the early 1900s, coal was hauled out of the mines by animals. This mine is at Putney. TH

Cleaning tracks at Putney at the head of Campbells Creek, 1940s.
COURTESY ETHEL HANSON

Motor Barn at Putney, 1915. TH

Workers of the Pinnacle Coal Company at Spring Fork on Campbells Creek in 1924. TH

Dixpont Coal Company store at Cinco. The store, which operated from 1935 to 1958, also served as a train station and post office.
COURTESY BOB PERDUE

Coal company shops of either Campbells Creek Coal Company or Hatfield Campbells Creek Coal Company. Behind the paddle wheel was the shop where lumber was planed for wooden barges. The middle building was the machine shop, and at the right was a supply house. COURTESY AMHERST INDUSTRIES

Main entry of the Campbells Creek Coal Company, July 12, 1901, at Putney. COURTESY BOB PERDUE

The old coal company store at Cinco on Campbells Creek. TH

Tipple remains at Putney are about all that is left of this once-thriving coal mining town. TH

The No. 4 mine of the Hatfield Campbells Creek Coal Company at Point Lick was a deep mine (No. 2 gas seam) that opened in 1924. Over 40 men were killed in this mine during the life of its operation. COURTESY AMHERST INDUSTRIES

Carbon Fuel Company's clubhouse at Decota. This large building burned down in about 1976. EG

The Eskdale store of the Wyatt Coal Company on Cabin Creek.
COURTESY JACQUELINE CASTO DAVIS

Typical Coal Towns

Some typical coal mining towns in the county were located ten miles up Cabin Creek. Eskdale, Leewood and Cane Fork thrived during the coal mining boom, from the 1870s when the C&O Railway punched through the mountains until the late 1950s when machines began replacing the thousands of men who were employed in the mines. By this time, the railroads converted to diesel fuel, which reduced the demand for coal. In addition, the labor struggles in the coal fields had forced many coal consumers to turn to oil for fuel.

In the 1880s the construction of the Cabin Creek Branch Railway opened the drainage up for development, and around 1902 the Leewood Colliery opened up a large mine that employed many workers. Soon afterward, coal company towns were established up and down the hollow, and stores, churches, schools, workers homes, and even YMCAs dotted the creek bottom and hillsides. In 1905 the railroad built a large railyard at the lower end of Eskdale called Cane Fork.

Because the coal miner has largely been replaced by the machines that can produce much more coal per man-hour, the hills of the Cabin Creek drainage, like Paint Creek and other coal mining areas, are much quieter today than in the old days.

Other towns in the Cabin Creek drainage—Dry Branch, Sharon, Miami, Dawes, Giles, Ohley, Decota, Kayford, Wevaco, Carbon, and Republic—are only a shadow of their former size.

Coal tipple at Decota along Cabin Creek.
COURTESY HOY O. YOUNG, JR.

Company store of the Cannelton Coal and Coke Co.
COURTESY KELLY BRATTON

The No. 2 tipple at the United Splint Mine.
COURTESY HOY O. YOUNG, JR.

Miners' houses at United, located on Cabin Creek above Decota.
COURTESY HOY O. YOUNG, JR.

A Ward Community Scrapbook

Scenes from the coal mining community of Ward, three miles up Kelly's Creek from Cedar Grove. EG

The community church was dedicated on May 15, 1919. It closed in 1970 and was dismantled.

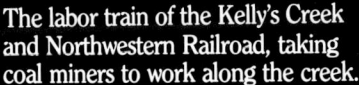

The park and clubhouse.

The community hall, built in 1922 at a cost of $70,000. It burned down in 1947.

The labor train of the Kelly's Creek and Northwestern Railroad, taking coal miners to work along the creek.

Burnwell during the heyday of coal mining in the 1920s. The company store, which still stands, is on the right. The YMCA, on the left, and the rows of houses are all gone.

COURTESY IMPERIAL COLLIERY COMPANY

The Imperial Colliery Company store in the old coal mining town of Burnwell on Paint Creek. The main mine closed in the late 1940s, and this area is largely deserted today. However the store, which was built in 1903, still serves the few remaining residents and visitors in the area.

MIDDLE: COURTESY DAVID BOULDIN, ST. ALBANS
BOTTOM: CN

The typical living conditions of coal miners, not only in Kanawha County but throughout the state and in Appalachia. These scenes were taken in 1946 at the Wyatt Coal Company's operation at Sharon, Kanawha County. These houses were of the "Jenny Lind" type, consisting of board and batten construction. The walls consisted of wooden planks with narrow strips covering the joints. This was the basic type of construction in many coal camps because it was inexpensive. NA

William Henry Edwards, born in 1822 in New York, became interested in surveying coal in the Kanawha Valley. He acquired thousands of acres of coal lands along Paint Creek in the late 1840s and settled in Coalburg where he opened his first mine in 1853. Edwards later became president of the Ohio and Kanawha Coal Company. He was also interested in scientific and literary pursuits.
SWV

The proclamation of martial law in Kanawha, Boone, Raleigh and Fayette counties issued by Governor W.E. Glasscock on February 10, 1913.
PM

Our Coal Business.
OVER 42 MILLION BUSHELS SHIPPED FROM THE GREAT KANAWHA MINES BELOW KANAWHA FALLS DURING THE LAST YEAR, BIG INCREASE OVER FORMER YEARS.
[From the Kanawha Gazette.]

A statistical report recently made at the U. S Engineer office in this city, of the amount of Coal shipped from mines on the Great Kanawha during the past year is a very gratifying one, showing a decided increase in the business both by river and by railroad. The statement was compiled to accompany the annual report of Mr. A. M. Scott, Resident Engineer of the Great Kanawha Improvement, to Col. Wm. P. Craighill, the officer in charge. It was derived (like the Great Kanawha coal statements for several years past, published in the annual reports of the Chief of Engineers), from statistics furnished to the U. S. Engineer office from every coal mine in the Valley and is regarded as accurate. It shows the total amount shipped from the Valley, below the Falls, during the year ending June, 1887, was 42,394,270 bushels. Of this 23,233,347 bushels went out by river and 19,160,896 by rail.

The report for the year before, being to June, 1886, was the largest up to that time, showed the total shipment for that year to be 31,815,358 bushels; of which 17,861,613 was by river and 13,953,745 by rail.

It appears that during the past year the output of coal on the Great Kanawha has increased fully 33 per cent. over any previous year. Over 10½ millions bushels more coal was shipped than in any year before.

It will be noticed, too, that this increase is about equally divided between the shipments by river and by railroad.

Strife in the Coal Fields

The history of the mine wars and union strife in West Virginia is reminiscent of the warfare in Europe prior to and during World War I. For years the insurrection and rebellion in the coal fields turned the state into an armed camp. The struggle of miner against coal operator could be called West Virginia's second Civil War. It eventually involved county and state politicians, the U.S. Army, and even the President of the United States.

During the main period of conflict, from 1912 until 1921, labor violence erupted throughout the state. Political influence was rampant, from the local level all the way to the state legislature. At one point there was even a threat to take over the capitol in Charleston. The justice system in the state was stretched beyond its capacity to serve its citizens.

The expansion of the railroads in the late 1800s opened up the vast coal fields of the state to major exploitation. The entrepreneurs who took advantage of this new accessibility were for the most part a hardy breed and fiercely independent. Many became large operators, "coal barons," and their power and influence was widespread.

The miners, however, did not share in the operators' new found wealth. Thousands of workers and their families had poured into the state, mainly from Europe and the South, with the opening of the coal fields. They often were forced to live in company towns, usually in substandard housing, and at times to buy only from the company stores. There were great inequities in the way the miners were treated and paid. It was only natural that conflict would arise between the miners and the mine operators under these conditions.

To protect their holdings, the operators hired mine guards, frequently from the Baldwin-Felts Detective Agency in Bluefield. Supposedly these guards were employed to maintain law and order in the camps; the law of the camps, however, was at times in direct conflict with the established law enforcement in the counties, who were usually allied with the operators. In reality, the guards were there to keep the miners from joining the union or causing trouble in the camps.

If a miner showed an interest in the union, he was considered an agitator and usually fired and blacklisted in all the other mining camps in the area. One method of keeping the union out of the coal fields was to compel miners to sign a document known as a yellow-dog contract before going to work. This simply stated that the prospective worker was not a member of nor would become a member of the United Mine Workers of America (UMWA). (Unions were also recognized in many contracts, but for a limited time period.)

The struggle to unionize all the mines in West Virginia continued until 1933, when Roosevelt's New Deal legislation forced the coal operators to allow the union into the mines. For over three decades, the battle between labor and management was waged in the state, with hundreds of men killed, thousands evicted from their homes, and coal production halted for months as a result.

It is a sad chapter in the state's history, and in the history of Kanawha County.

Paint Creek and Cabin Creek

A major event in the 38-year fight to unionize all of Kanawha's coal mines occurred along Paint and Cabin creeks, just south of Charleston. In April 1912, 7,500 miners at approximately 100 different mines went on strike. Most of the Kanawha River coal fields were already unionized; but for years, the operators along the two creeks had resisted the union.

The miners made several demands to the operators: (1) blacklisting was to be halted; (2) the miners were to be allowed to unionize; (3) cribbing was to be stopped; (4) scales were to be installed at each mine to give the miners an accurate tonnage weight; (5) compulsory trading at company stores was no longer to be allowed, and (6) docking penalties were to be determined by two check-weighmen, one of whom was to be employed by the miners.

All of the demands were refused, and a bitter strike ensued. Baldwin-Felts detectives were hired by the operators to break the strike. Striking miners and their families were evicted from their company-owned homes, and scab (nonunion) labor, including immigrants, were brought in to reopen the mines.

The West Virginia Legislature conducted an inquiry, however no action was taken and the coal operators set up pillboxes and fortifications in the fields in anticipation of armed conflict. A U.S. Senate committee investigated the strike, and found much evidence of abuse against the miners.

At the height of the confrontation, eighty-two-year-old Mary Harris "Mother" Jones, a fiery union organizer, appeared on the scene. She gave a speech on the state capitol grounds, in which she advocated armed aggression by the miners to rid the creeks of the hated mine guards. Governor William Glasscock, whom Mother Jones violently denounced, tried to arbitrate a settlement, but both sides rejected his proposals.

Both the miners and the mine operators armed themselves for the inevitable confrontation. Several guards were killed, and small skirmishes occurred up and down the creeks. A larger battle took place at Mucklow, on Paint Creek, in which at least sixteen guards and miners were killed.

On September 1, 1912, union miners from the area joined the strikers; over 6,000 armed men converged on Cabin Creek for a showdown. The days of 1861-65 appeared to be recurring the next day when Governor Glasscock put the strike area under martial law and sent in 1,200 militia. Both the guards and strikers were ordered to disarm, and military courts were established. The miners were prohibited from assembling in large numbers. Mother Jones reappeared, attempting to read the Declaration of Independence to a group of strikers. The old woman was arrested but soon released.

On October 15 martial law was lifted. Soon afterward, some of the soldiers joined forces with the mine guards, and early in November things heated up once more. Scab workers were fired upon, as were the trains transporting coal from the area, and the strikers soon had the upper hand. The governor reissued the martial law order on November 15. Military councils were reestablished and many strikers jailed. The second order came to an end on January 10, 1913, but nothing had been settled.

Searching passengers on Train #13 at Pratt, 1912. PM

The state militia at Pratt in 1912. PM

A sick soldier en route to a Red Cross tent at Pratt. PM

Soldiers with rifles and machine guns on the firing line at Paint Creek. SWV

Baldwin-Felts guards on Paint Creek, along with a pet bear. SWV

Encampment of the state militia, which was called into Paint Creek in 1912 to enforce martial law. WWU

Strife on Cabin Creek & Paint Creek

ALL PHOTOS FROM THE
B.E. ANDRE COLLECTION

Mine guards at Cabin Creek Junction the day before martial law was declared, September 1, 1912.

Troops detraining at Mucklow on Paint Creek.

Troops detraining at Cabin Creek with a patrolling mine guard in the foreground.

The troops' camp life was under wartime conditions during the 1912-13 mine wars.

Gov. Henry D. Hatfield settled the Paint Creek strike in 1912. SWV

In February 1913 an armored train equipped by the coal operators with machine guns sped by the strikers' tent city and fired upon the inhabitants. One miner was killed, several wounded. Three days later the third martial law order was issued and military courts once again instituted. Mother Jones was again arrested and this time sentenced to twenty years in prison.

Rumors about the situation abounded, including one that the miners would march on Charleston to demand action by the legislature. The residents of Charleston were thrown into a panic, and the area around the capitol was fortified against such a possibility. The march never materialized; the reaction to it, however, was a good example of the state-of-siege mentality under which the citizens in this part of the state were living at the time.

The tension continued until March 4, 1913, when Dr. Henry D. Hatfield was inaugurated as governor. Hatfield immediately traveled to the strike area. He ordered civil rights restored to the miners, abolished the hated military courts, freed Mother Jones, and imposed peace on both sides of the conflict. The struggle along the creeks had finally come to an end.

This remarkable collection of guns and ammunition on the capitol lawn was gathered by state police in the Paint Creek area, after the first declaration of martial law on September 2, 1912. Note Hale's Quarrier St. Hack Station in the background. WVU

The old capitol grounds looked like an armed camp during the 1912 miners' strike. The boxes contained thousands of rounds of ammunition. This photo is at the location of Stone and Thomas. A careful examination of these photos will reveal heavy colt machine guns, which were owned by mine owners. RA

Tents, on Cabin Creek, of striking miners who were forced from their company homes in 1912. Some of the miners and their families lived in these tents for over a year.
COURTESY JACQUELINE CASTO DAVIS

Camp of troops at the mouth of Paint Creek, near Pratt, 1912. swv

Mary Harris "Mother" Jones, the firebrand of the coal fields in the early 1900s, was born in 1837 in Cork, Ireland. As a young woman she taught school in Memphis, Tennessee, and worked as a dressmaker in Chicago. Her husband and children died in the Memphis yellow fever epidemic of the 1870s; it was then she became active in the labor movement, dedicating her life to improving conditions for American workers. She traveled all over the United States as a labor organizer.

Mother Jones participated in strikes in Colorado and West Virginia mines, for which she was arrested and jailed many times. In 1919, when she was almost ninety years old, she delivered a violent speech from the state capitol steps in Charleston, calling Governor Cornwell several unprintable names. The *Charleston Daily Mail* referred to her as "that disreputable old woman."

A highly controversial figure, Mother Jones was even accused of working for the coal companies at the same time that she was calling upon the miners to strike. There is no doubt, however, that she has earned a place in the history of labor reform in the United States. She died in 1931. swv

Mrs. Carney's boardinghouse, which still stands in Pratt, was used to house Mother Jones during the miners' strike in 1913.

The 1921 Armed March

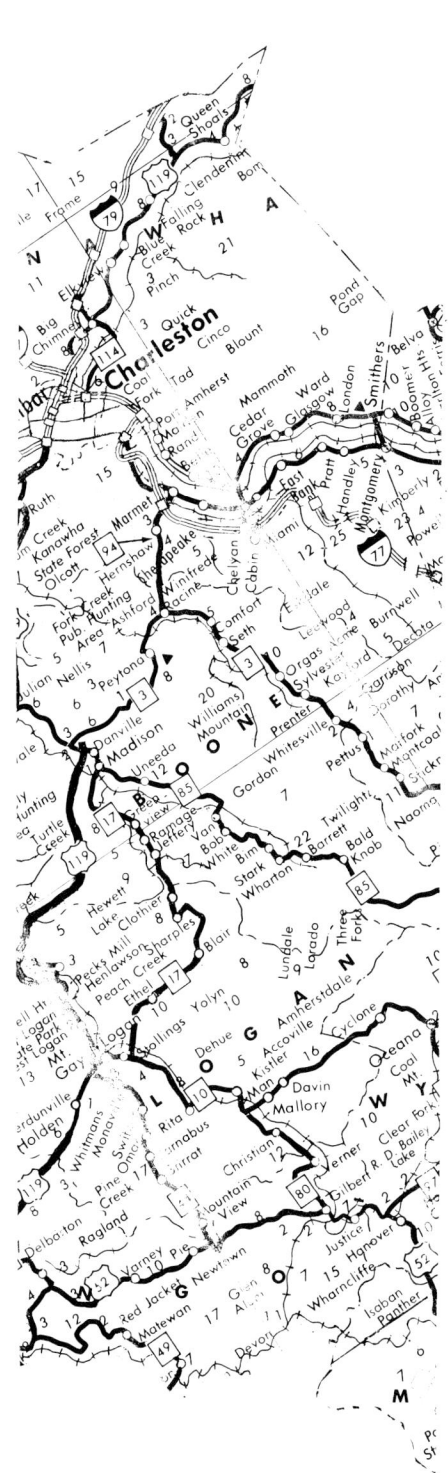

Of all the coal counties in West Virginia, none was more corrupt than Logan County. From 1913 until 1934, Don Chafin, who served first as county assessor and later as sheriff, ruled the county along with hundreds of his "special appointed" deputy sheriffs, who acted as his personal mine guards. Chafin successfully kept the UMWA out for many years, virtually controlling the lives of everyone in the county. He essentially had his own "feudal kingdom" in the heart of the coal fields.

The United Mine Workers of America had organized the mines in the Kanawha and New River fields and was determined to do the same in Logan County. In August 1919, union miners armed themselves, and over 5,000 men began a march to Logan County to wrest control of the mines from Chafin and his guards. Upon the threat of federal troops made by Governor Cornwell, however, the miners disbanded. The legislature was called upon to investigate Logan County corruption, but no action was taken. The legislature was controlled at that time by the coal companies; so this came as no surprise.

By 1921 conditions had worsened in the county. The union, under the leadership of Frank Keeney, urged the miners from the 1919 march to rally at the capitol in Charleston. Mother Jones was there again, giving an inflammatory speech denouncing the governor and the coal operators. A few days later Keeney asked the miners to gather their arms and meet at Lens Creek near Marmet to begin a second march to Logan County. Their objectives: to hang Chafin, organize the mines, and liberate adjacent Mingo County from the martial law that had been imposed upon it in the wake of the violence there.

This was insurrection. Governor Morgan requested federal troops from President Warren G. Harding. General H.H. Bandholtz and his troops were sent to the scene from Washington to urge the miners to abandon their march. After he was able to enlist the help of Keeney, Bandholtz succeeded in defusing the situation.

A short while later, there was an alleged attack upon a group of miners by Chafin's deputies and the state police. William Blizzard, the president of UMWA Subdistrict No. 2, organized his men and once again they headed toward Logan County. Chafin assembled his "army" to meet the miners. All the necessary ingredients were present for a genuine civil war.

The scene of battle would be Blair Mountain in Logan County, a natural barrier to access to Logan County. Chafin set up breastworks on its summit to protect his army of three thousand men. An attacking force of over 3,000 miners met Chafin's army of men, and for several days a heated battle was waged, and machine guns were used by both sides. Many of the participants were veterans of World War I, and this was as real a battle as any they had fought.

The governor again requested federal assistance. General Bandholtz brought 2,000 troops and by September 3 he had the situation under control. The miners were disarmed and dispersed, and Chafin's men ordered back to Logan County. There were numerous casualties on both sides, but no accurate count was ever taken. In Charleston, army bombers that were flown in from Washington, D.C., under the command of Brigadier General Billy Mitchell were put on alert to assist the troops if called upon. In Mitchell's words, he "would use gas if necessary." Luckily this was not to be the case.

Hundreds of miners and union officials were indicted and jailed. Four officials, Frank Keeney, Fred Mooney, Bill Petry, and William Blizzard, were eventually taken to Logan County and jailed to await trial. Because of local sentiment, the trials of hundreds of prisoners were moved to Jefferson County in the state's Eastern Panhandle. It was ironic that the Jefferson County Courthouse, the scene of John Brown's treason trial in 1859, would be the site for these trials.

As with other trials in the state, justice was "bent" by both sides. The county was crowded with people trying to influence prospective jurors. Blizzard was acquitted on the basis of testimony from many of his codefendants, but one man was convicted of treason. In later years, Blizzard became president of District 17 of the United Mine Workers of America in Charleston and a powerful union leader in the state.

By this time the county was so divided in its opinions concerning the union that a fair trial was not possible for anyone. Justice was attempted by sending the defendants first to Greenbrier County and later to Fayette County, but it appeared to be impossible to obtain a fair hearing anywhere in the state. Over two years and thousands of dollars were spent without resulting in the conviction of any of the union members.

Brigadier General Mitchell's planes at the Kanawha City airfield during the 1921 miners' strike. They are lined up along what would became Mac-Corkle Avenue. The tents were probably set up for the aircrews. LC

Brig. Gen. Billy Mitchell.
COURTESY U.S. AIR FORCE

Mitchell's Martin MB-2 bombers and tent camp at the Kanawha City site, 1921. One of the bombers crashed in Nicholas County while returning to Langley, Virginia, killing all but one of the crew. LC

Closeup of the Martin MB-2 twin-engine bombers. RA

Leaders of the march to Logan and Mingo counties in 1921. From left: William Blizzard (SP), president of UMWA Sub-district 2; Fred Mooney, secretary-treasurer of District 17; William Petry, vice-president of District 17; and C. Frank Keeney, president of District 17. These men were later tried for treason for their part in the so-called miners' insurrection. WVU

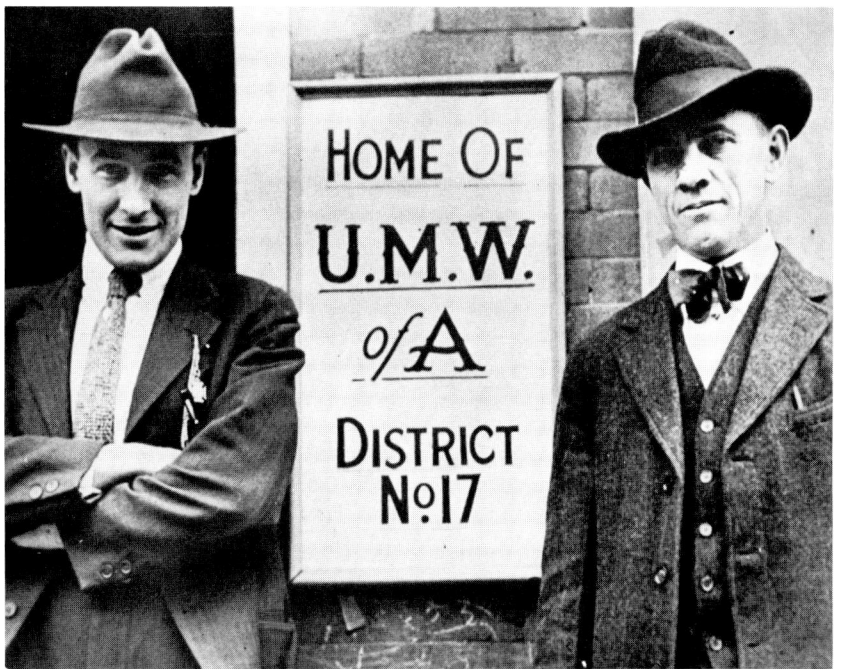

District 17 of the United Mine Workers of America was, and still is, headquartered in Charleston. During the labor unrest in 1921 Fred Mooney, left, the secretary-treasurer, and Frank Keeney, right, president of the district, were leaders of the union. SWV

The tents of striking miners in the Paint Creek area. BETTMAN ARCHIVE

Striking miners and their families march at Ward in August 1931. Six hundred miners and their families faced eviction from their company-owned homes. Sixty families were actually evicted and their belongings put in a field, until a wealthy society woman, Mrs. Ethel Clyde from New York, posted a bond to guarantee payment of rent. Strike breakers were imported by mine owners, who were protected by armed guards and state police—a throwback to the 1912 and 1921 strife.
UPI/BETTMANN NEWSPHOTOS

John L. Lewis, the head of the United Mine Workers of America, had a profound effect on coal mining in Kanawha County as well as the entire region. During his long tenure as president he fought relentlessly for the welfare of miners, which created a great deal of strife in the coal fields. SWV

United Mine Workers of America

The United Mine Workers of America (UMWA) was formed on January 25, 1890, by the merger of two rival coal miners' unions that had been competing for ascendancy for 50 years. The need for one strong union to represent the miners in the coal fields was tremendous. Miners worked long hours in hazardous, back-breaking conditions, often beginning as young children. John Mitchell, the first UMWA president, worked to abolish child labor and establish the eight-hour workday.

John L. Lewis, the union's legendary leader, became its president in 1920 and ruled with an iron hand for the next 40 years. During this time, the union achieved a guaranteed eight-hour day, national wage agreements, and much-needed safety legislation.

The fight to organize the southern coal fields in West Virginia was a Herculean task. Violence against union supporters was common, with eviction of the miners from company-owned houses the order of the day for strikers and sympathizers.

The violence ended with the passage in 1933 of the National Industrial Recovery Act, legislation that gave workers the right to join the labor organization of their choice. Miners joined the UMWA in record numbers; in only one year the membership increased by 300,000.

Arnold Miller, a native of Kanawha County, was elected the UMWA's president in 1970. During his administration, which coincided with the coal boom of the seventies, the union won cost-of-living increases, more benefits, and the return of the coverage that had been cut from the Welfare and Retirement Fund. An increased emphasis on democratic reforms resulted in the establishment of the right of the rank and file to vote on their contracts. Safety measures were also toughened. Nineteen sixty-nine saw the passage of the Federal Coal Mine Health and Safety Act, and in 1974 the miners won the right to refuse unsafe work.

Miller was forced to retire due to ailing health in 1979, two years before his term was to expire.

Arnold Miller (1923-1985) was born in Leewood and went to work in the mines when he was 16. Miller became president of the United Mine Workers of America in 1970, the only person from West Virginia to hold this high office. CN

Chapter Nine
Industry

Carbide's original plant was located along the Elk River in Clendenin. A small gasoline plant on the site owned by Jackson and Koontz was purchased and a division of the Linde Air Products Co. was established under the name Carbide and Carbon Chemical Corp. Several chemical products were made from the natural gas that passed through the plant. SWV

The Magic Valley

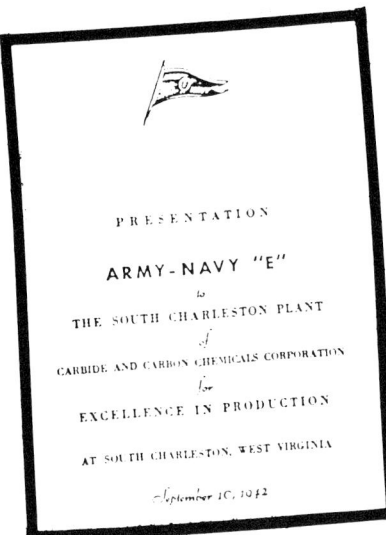

Panorama of Carbide's first plant in 1923. The plant is to the left, the town of Clendenin to the right. Oil pumping rigs can be seen at several locations. One of the plant's original buildings is still standing.

COURTESY MRS. LOWELL WARNER

Over the years, the underground deposits of salt brine attracted the coal, oil, natural gas, and chemical industries to the area which made Kanawha County a leader during the industrial age. Salt was a major industry until 1861, and a decade later the great coal mining era began when the railroads forged their way west in the 1870s. The vast chemical industry, the dominant economic force in the county today, moved into the Kanawha Valley after 1900 to tap the rich salt, gas, and coal resources. Although some chemical products were produced in the area before the turn of the century, they were simple compounds from local cottage industries. As products became more complex, however, large plants that used a variety of resources moved into the valley. As these plants used more and more advanced technology to produce sophisticated new products, the Kanawha Valley became internationally known as "The Magic Valley" and "The Chemical Center of the World."

The chemical industry had its beginning when a carbon black industry developed in 1915, because of the vast deposits of natural gas in the area. Carbon black, which is produced from natural gas, was used to manufacture rubber tires. Oscar Nelson, a native of Sweden, helped form the United Carbon Company, which became the largest carbon producer in the world. In 1916 a plant was established near the rapidly expanding oil and gas fields in Clendenin. Years later the company moved out of West Virginia.

The chemical industry got its real boost at the beginning of World War I, when shipments of chlorine and certain alkaloid products from Germany were cut off. In 1914 and 1915, the Rollins Chemical Company and the Warner-Klipstein Company set up small plants in the South Charleston area to produce these two important chemicals. The companies reorganized after the war: in 1923 Rollins became the Barium Reduction Corporation; in 1925 Warner-Klipstein became The Westvaco Chlorine Products Corporation, which merged with Food Machinery Corporation in 1948 to form FMC Corporation.

At the time South Charleston was becoming a major force in the nation's chemical industry, a small company named The Carbide and Carbon Chemical Company that moved to Clendenin from Buffalo, New York, in 1920, moved next door to the old Rollins plant to be close to a source of chlorine. Chlorine was needed to manufacture antifreeze, which is still produced at the plant. The company purchased Blaine Island, a large flat island in the Kanawha River, where it built a large plant in 1928. Now named Union Carbide, the company produces a variety of products at plants in South Charleston and Institute, and has developed into one of the largest chemical complexes in the world. Over the years, the small town of Belle has also become a major chemical center. The Belle Alkali Company began producing chlorine and caustic soda in 1921, and pioneered the manufacture of synthetic ammonia and chloroform. The company later became the Diamond Alkali Company and is now a subsidiary of the Diamond Shamrock Company.

In 1926 the giant E.I. Dupont de Nemours Company met the need for a dependable source of nitrates, when it began manufacturing ammonia. Using a French process called "The Claude Process," the company produced synthetic ammonia in the plant they established in Belle, where coal, river transportation, and workers were available. In 1932, the E.I. Dupont de Nemours Company opened the first commercial urea plant in the country at Belle, and from 1939 to 1947 all the nylon produced in the Western Hemisphere came from Belle. A number of other products have been produced at Dupont's large Belle plant.

The undeveloped Blaine Island and the Carbide and Carbon Chemical Company's main plant at South Charleston. Carbide (later the Union Carbide Corporation) moved its plant from Clendenin to this site in 1925, to be close to a source of chlorine for its manufacture of antifreeze. Three years later, Blaine Island was developed. swv

Union Carbide's plant in South Charleston, which stretches for several miles along Route 60 and covers Blaine Island, is the largest industrial complex in Kanawha County. It produces many raw and finished chemical products which are shipped throughout the world. The company established a large technical center in South Charleston some years ago for the development of new procedures and products, circa mid-1930s.
COURTESY COLUMBIA GAS TRANSMISSION CORP. AND WVU

An early view of the industrial area at Belle before the Dupont plant was built. The facilities shown are the Sharples Solvents Corporation, Belle Alkali Company and Layote Inc., 1920s. KCL

A late 1920s panorama of the Dupont Ammonia plant. COURTESY DALE KELLY

Two views of the Belle Alkali and Sharples Solvents plants in the late 1920s and 1931. Sharples closed in 1932. COURTESY COLUMBIA GAS TRANSMISSION CORP. & GS

The Dupont Ammonia plant in the late 1920s and 1931.
COURTESY COLUMBIA GAS TRANSMISSION CORP. & GS

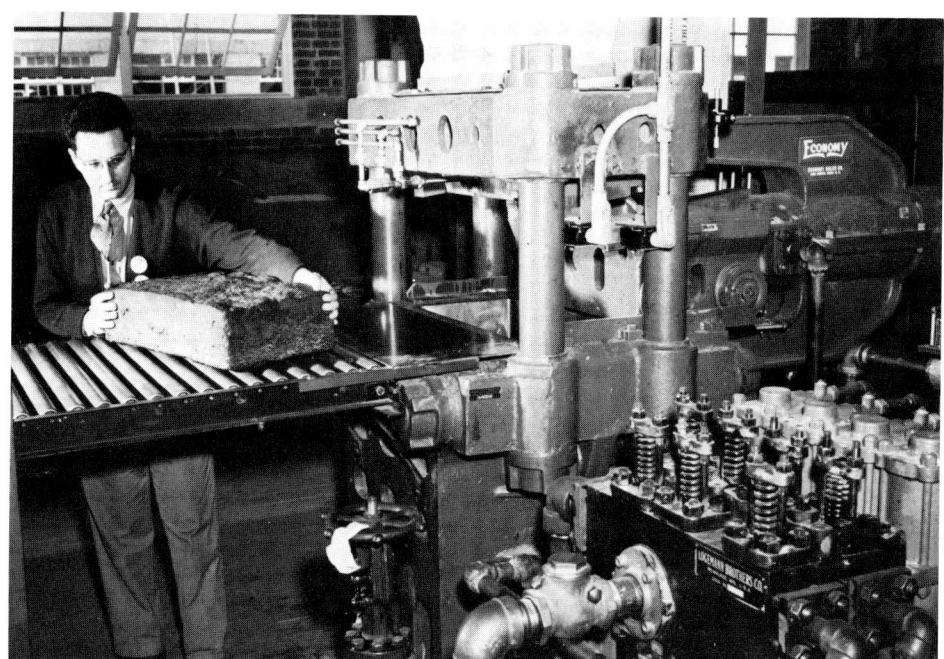

These three views show the important rubber manufacturing facility built in the Institute area in 1941. Natural rubber imports had been sharply curtailed at the beginning of World War II. Because of Japanese conquests in the Pacific by 1943, when these photos were taken, the plant produced over 75 percent of the major ingredients of the manufacture of synthetic rubber. These large 30,000-gallon tanks held styrene, the main ingredient in the rubber process. A bail of synthetic rubber weighed 75 pounds when it came from the dryer at the adjacent United States Rubber Company plant. This complex, like others in the Kanawha Valley, was absolutely vital to the U.S. war effort. Close attention was paid to security because of the danger of sabotage. The plant closed in September 1953. LC

Views of the Kanawha River Salt and Chemical Company's plant at Belle about 1919. This plant was a subsidiary of the Pure Oil Company which had a refinery at Cabin Creek. This plant utilized the natural gas deposits of the area in the production of salt, bromine compounds and calcium chloride. At the end of World War I the plant closed because of the great demand for natural gas as a consumer fuel. Besides the plant, 22 workers houses, a clubhouse and company owned grocery store made up the plant community. This area is completely built up now with residences and commercial concerns.

COURTESY MR. AND MRS. ADRIAN EDWARDS

Nitro also had its share of chemical plants. In 1921 four employees of the Goodyear Tire and Rubber Company formed the Rubber Service Laboratories, which supplied chemicals to the rubber industry. Monsanto Chemical Company of St. Louis purchased the plant in 1929, and over the next few decades, the plant was greatly expanded, using many raw materials from West Virginia. The Ohio-Apex Company, which was founded in 1934 and taken over in 1950 by the FMC Corporation, was a large producer of chemical plasticizers. American Viscose Corporation took over the Nitro Pulp Mills in 1921 and became the largest producer of viscose rayon staple fiber in the country.

Throughout the years, some of the other chemical plants in the area have been the Vanadium Corporation of America, Cardox Corporation, J.Q. Dickinson and Company, Linde Air Products Company, and National Lead Company.

The production of glass was another major industry in the Kanawha Valley. In the early 1900s the glass companies were the Banner Window Glass Company and the Dunkirk Glass Company in South Charleston, the Dunbar Flint Glass Company, and the Whittemore Glass Company in Dunbar. Because of the unlimited supply of cheap gas, the Libby Owens Company and the Owens Bottle Company opened their plants in Kanawha City in 1917. Eventually, the Libby Owens and Owens Bottle companies purchased all of the other plants in the area, and by 1929 Kanawha City was one of the largest glass producing areas in the world.

The oil and gas industries played a predominant role in the industrial history of the county. Long before anyone knew anything about the phenomenon, natural gas seeps were common along the Kanawha River. In 1815 James Wilson inadvertantly drilled the first gas well at "burning springs" when he was looking for a salt brine deposit. His crew hit a gas pocket, which caught fire and flames shot into the air. In 1841 salt producer William Tompkins of Malden struck gas in one of his salt wells and piped it to his salt furnaces, the first person in the country to use the gas for manufacturing purposes. Before the Civil War, gas was found as a result of drilling for salt brine; it was several decades before gas was recognized as a reliable source of fuel and light.

Michael Owens, a native West Virginian, invented several machines for glass-making that revolutionized the industry. By 1929 the Owen-Illinois Company had built the world's largest glass bottle plant in Kanawha City, across from the Libby-Owens-Ford plate glass plant. The huge Owens Automatic Bottle Machines had as many as 15 arms. Each arm held a blank mold that shaped a slug of molten glass when it was dipped into the furnace. This machine turned out thousands of bottles in a 24-hour period. The plant closed in 1980. KCL

Scenes at the Banner Glass Plant in South Charleston, 1920. The plant was opened in the small town of South Charleston in 1906 and produced sheet glass made by hand. Before it closed in 1920, the glass was hand blown, but when machinery was invented to do this the plant sold its property to a local chemical company. The FMC plant was located at the old glass plant property for many years. Most of the Banner employees were brought over from Belgium and many of their descendants still live in the valley. ww

The Libby-Owens-Ford sheet glass plant and the Owens-Illinois Bottle Plant at the upper end of Kanawha City. The Libby-Owens Company built the first six units of the plant in 1916 and 1917. It added six more units in 1918 and 1923, making this the largest sheet glass plant in the world. Ford Motors purchased an interest in the company in 1929 and it was thereafter called Libby-Owens-Ford. The plant made plate, window, windshield and non-shatterable glass. Most of its raw materials, white silica, sand, salt and natural gas, were obtained within seventy-five miles of Charleston. The Owens Bottle Company located its factory at the same site in 1917. It merged with the Owens-Illinois Company in 1929 and became the largest bottle making plant in the world, manufacturing bottles, fruit jars, and after 1933, beer bottles. The bottle plant closed in 1964, the glass plant in 1980. The bottle plant is still in use as an industrial park, the sheet glass plant was torn down and is now occupied by the Kanawha Mall. COURTESY OF COLUMBIA GAS TRANSMISSION CORP.

An Owens Automatic Bottle Machine in operation. These huge machines, massive in construction and yet amazingly intricate in detail, were capable of turning out thousands of bottles in a day. A machine might have as many as 15 arms, each holding a "blank" mold with which to dip into the furnace and gather a "slug" of molten glass, in somewhat the same manner as the hand craftsman gathers glass by hand on the end of his blowpipe.
KCL

Inspecting beer bottles as they came off the line at the Owens Bottle plant.
KCL

Libby-Owens-Ford plant facing MacCorkle Avenue in 1950. CN

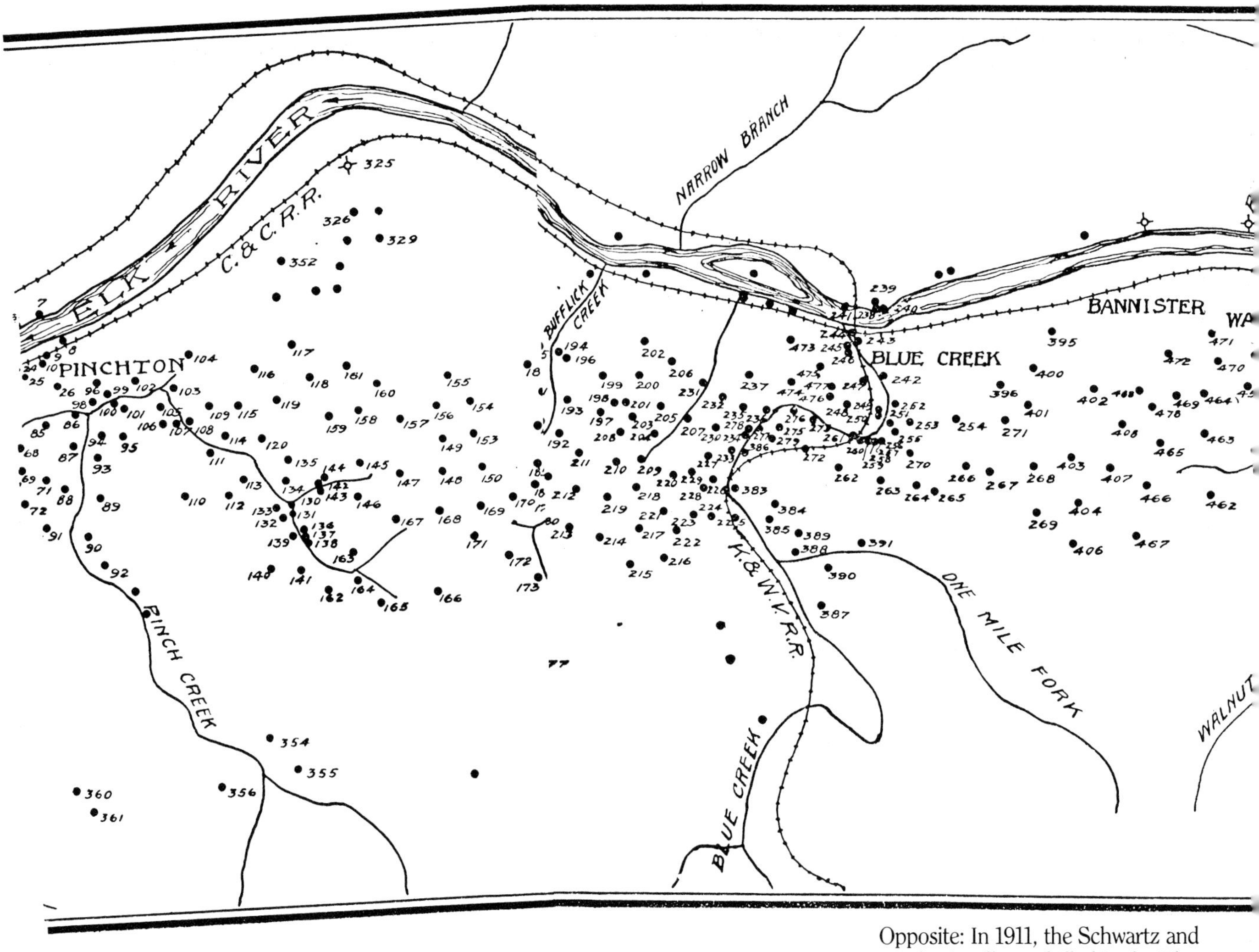

An abandoned oil well derrick in 1938, probably in the Blue Creek area. The early wells were all drilled by the cable-tool method, with wooden derricks. LC

Opposite: In 1911, the Schwartz and Barth #1 well was drilled in the Blue Creek area near Elk River. This was the largest oil pool in the county and by 1936 800 wells were producing. The field at Pinch boomed in 1917 and 1918. These photos show the area around Blue Creek about 1914 at the height of the oil boom. The large island just downstream from the railroad bridge across the Elk River into Blue Creek is now used by a church group as a recreational site.
COURTESY DR. A.C. DIXON

Where there is natural gas there is usually oil, and oil too, was discovered in 1807 as a result of drilling for salt brine. The early salt makers considered oil a nuisance and they let it flow into the Kanawha River, which the boatmen nicknamed "Old Greasy." Eventually, the improvement of salt well drilling techniques along the Kanawha provided the know-how for the oil drilling industry.

The search for oil deposits began in earnest around the turn of the century, and the Porters Creek pool on the south side of Elk River, 35 miles northeast of Charleston, was one of the earliest discoveries. In 1909 the Elk River Oil and Gas Company discovered the Hackberry field while drilling for gas in the Falling Branch Creek area along Elk River, the first oil of commercial value in the county. More than a dozen oil fields were discovered in the next few years: the Walton field that was 25 miles northeast of Charleston, the Kelly's Creek field, the Cabin Creek field, and fields in the Elk District. In 1911 the Schwartz and Barth #1 well was drilled in the Blue Creek area. Eventually, over 1,000 wells were drilled in the area, in an oil industry boom that lasted for several years. Wells were drilled all over the Blue Creek drainage and downriver in the Pinch area. Refineries were built at Cabin Creek and near Clendenin, which became an oil boom town. For a time, Kanawha County was one of the largest oil and gas production centers in the world.

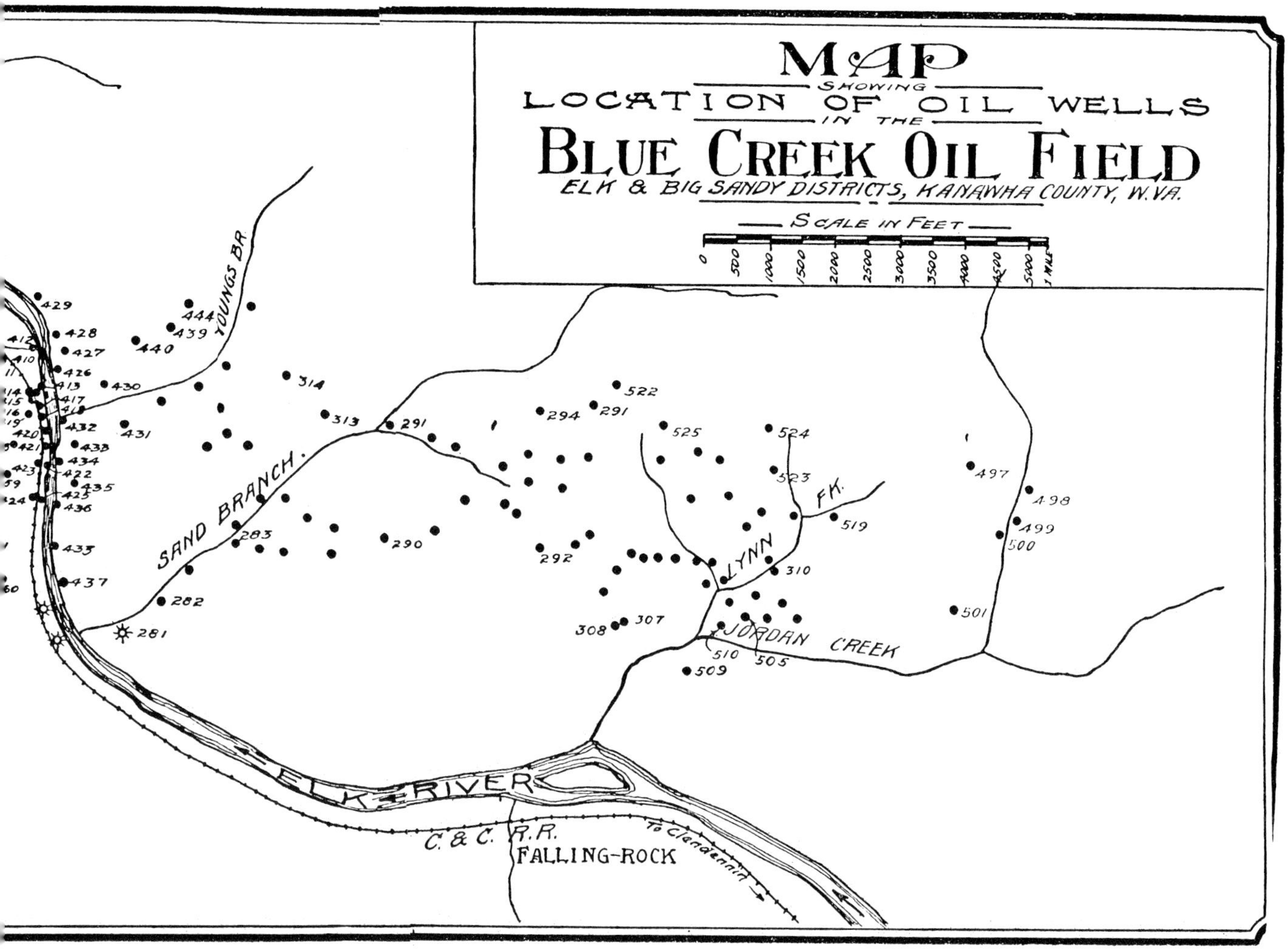
MAP
SHOWING
LOCATION OF OIL WELLS
IN THE
BLUE CREEK OIL FIELD
ELK & BIG SANDY DISTRICTS, KANAWHA COUNTY, W. VA.
SCALE IN FEET
0 500 1000 1500 2000 2500 3000 3500 4000 4500 5000 1 MILE
YOUNGS BR.
SAND BRANCH
LYNN FK.
JORDAN CREEK
ELK RIVER
C. & C. R.R.
To Clendennin
FALLING-ROCK

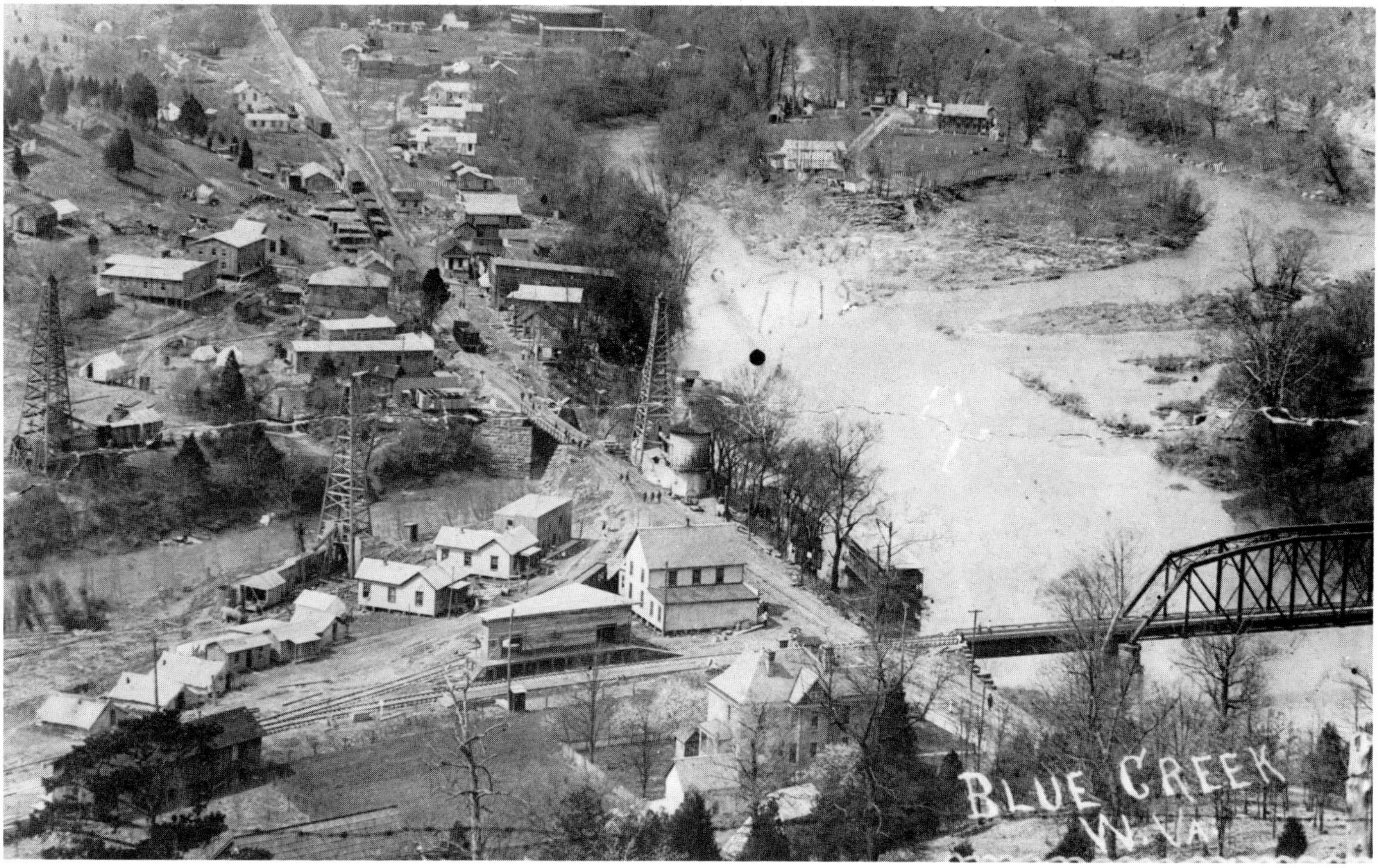
BLUE CREEK
W. VA.

The Dawes field on Cabin Creek was one of the best producing pools of oil in southern West Virginia. SWV

A blowout of an oil well in the Pinch area, 1947.
COURTESY COLUMBIA GAS TRANSMISSION CORP.

An early drilling crew in the county oil and gas fields. KCL

Blue Creek Oil Field Scenes

Drillers.

Engine of the Coal and Coke Railroad.

Oil storage tanks.

Derrick crew.

Casing crew.

Casing crew.

ALL PHOTOS COURTESY DR. A.C. DIXON

The county's largest refinery was located along Elk River just south of Clendenin. The Elk Refinery Company produced several grades of gasoline which included rubber solvent gasoline, aviation fuel, automotive gasoline, varnish maker's and painters' naphtha, dry cleaners' fluid and turpentine. It also produced fuel oil, motor oil, lubricating oil, fine wax, petroleum jelly and vaseline. Its largest product was "Crystal White" gasoline which was sold at retail outlets for many years. The plant has been closed for many years and lies in ruins. COURTESY COLUMBIA GAS TRANSMISSION CORP.

Pure Oil Company's Cabin Creek refinery in 1931. It refined exclusively high amber oils. Its best known product was tiolene oil, and it also refined aviation and automotive gasoline, kerosene, lubricating oils and paraffin wax. It too is closed and lies in ruins. A sawmill operates on its property now. GS

Hope Natural Gas Company's gas compressor station below the Cabin Creek Junction in 1931. GS

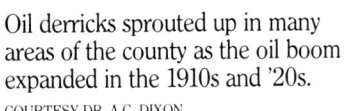

Oil derricks sprouted up in many areas of the county as the oil boom expanded in the 1910s and '20s.
COURTESY DR. A.C. DIXON

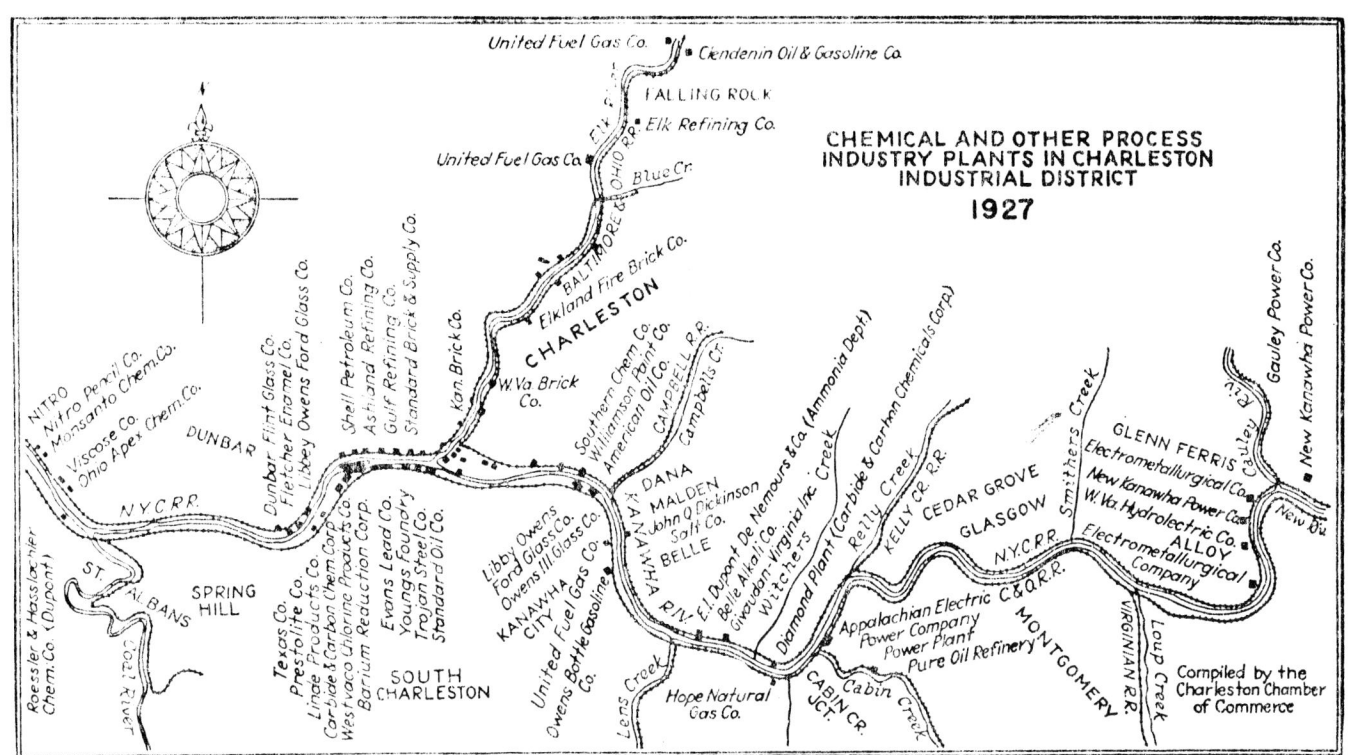

Jack Liming of Clendenin reconstructed this cable tool drilling rig on his farm. It is probably the only operating rig of its type left in the state. Until the rotary drilling rigs took over, cable tool rigs developed all of West Virginia's early oil and gas fields. This drilling process was an outgrowth of the early salt brine drilling in the Kanawha Valley.

An old oil well pumping rig near Clendenin.

Remains of the old oil drilling equipment are in evidence in many of the oil fields of the county. These photos were taken in the Blue Creek and Mill Creek oil fields.

COURTESY CLAYTON SPANGER & TODD HANSON

In 1917 the U.S. Government decided to build a massive factory on a site in South Charleston, to produce armor plate for U.S. Navy ships. This picture, taken on August 25, 1919, shows the nearly-completed machine shop in the far background, construction of the open-hearth building, and the foundations for the forge and furnace building in the foreground. KCL

At the beginning of World War I, the federal government searched the country to find locations for huge war-related industrial plants. In 1917 South Charleston was picked as the site for a large ordnance plant, which made armor plate, gun forgings and projectiles for U.S. Navy ships. Although almost 200 million dollars was spent to build a plant on a 210-acre site, the plant was not completed until after the end of the war and it closed in 1922. It was reactivated, however, in 1939 and the plant made important contributions to the World War II effort. The buildings are now leased to numerous industrial concerns.

Around the same time South Charleston was chosen as the site for the ordnance plant, the government selected a large flat site along the Kanawha River, where Nitro is presently located, to construct the largest explosives factory in the world. The name of Nitro, in fact, was derived from nitroglycerin, an ingredient in the explosives process. The government picked the valley location because of its security from coastal attacks, and the availability of rail and water transportation, and raw materials. Ground was broken in December 1917 and, remarkably, the plant was finished in eleven months. Over 100,000 people worked on the plant's construction; by the time Explosive Plant "C" was shut down at the end of World War I, the town housed over 23,000 people.

On November 3, 1919, the Charleston Industrial Corporation (C.I.C.) was formed to redevelop the enormous industrial complex—the beginning of today's industrial bases in the Nitro area. Although nothing remains of the original plant, hundreds of the workers houses in Nitro are still in use.

Panorama view of the armor plant and South Charleston, April 2, 1922.
COURTESY MRS. LOWELL WARNER

-168-

An aerial view of the South Charleston Ordnance Plant on September 22, 1941. The plant played an important role in the defense build-up before and during World War II. It produced gun-barrels for the U.S. Navy, from 20mm to 6-inch cannon as well as torpedo parts. By 1955 the plant was no longer needed, and it was subdivided and leased out to many different industries. NA

Interior view of the massive forge and furnace building in December 1920. KCL

The Naval Ordnance Plant in 1931. GS

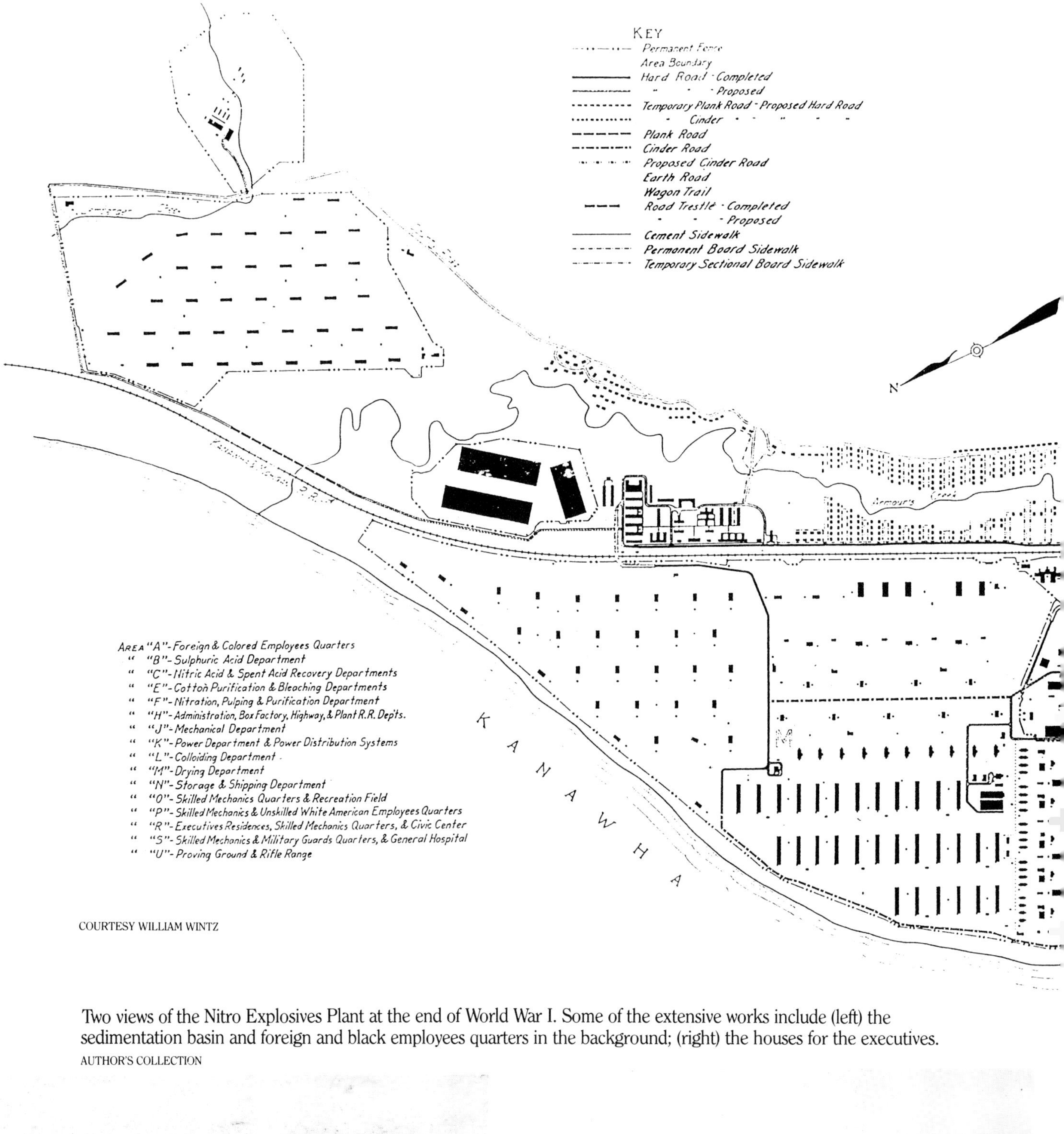
KEY
Permanent Fence
Area Boundary
Hard Road - Completed
" " - Proposed
Temporary Plank Road - Proposed Hard Road
" Cinder " " " " "
Plank Road
Cinder Road
Proposed Cinder Road
Earth Road
Wagon Trail
Road Trestle - Completed
" " - Proposed
Cement Sidewalk
Permanent Board Sidewalk
Temporary Sectional Board Sidewalk
N
Armour's Creek
K A N A W H A
M
AREA "A"- Foreign & Colored Employees Quarters
" "B"- Sulphuric Acid Department
" "C"- Nitric Acid & Spent Acid Recovery Departments
" "E"- Cotton Purification & Bleaching Departments
" "F"- Nitration, Pulping & Purification Department
" "H"- Administration, Box Factory, Highway, & Plant R.R. Dep'ts.
" "J"- Mechanical Department
" "K"- Power Department & Power Distribution Systems
" "L"- Colloiding Department
" "M"- Drying Department
" "N"- Storage & Shipping Department
" "O"- Skilled Mechanics Quarters & Recreation Field
" "P"- Skilled Mechanics & Unskilled White American Employees Quarters
" "R"- Executives Residences, Skilled Mechanics Quarters, & Civic Center
" "S"- Skilled Mechanics & Military Guards Quarters, & General Hospital
" "U"- Proving Ground & Rifle Range

COURTESY WILLIAM WINTZ

Two views of the Nitro Explosives Plant at the end of World War I. Some of the extensive works include (left) the sedimentation basin and foreign and black employees quarters in the background; (right) the houses for the executives.
AUTHOR'S COLLECTION

Explosives Plant "C."
GENERAL VIEW. SEDIMENTATION BASIN & AREA "A" IN FOREGROUND

Explosives Plant "C."

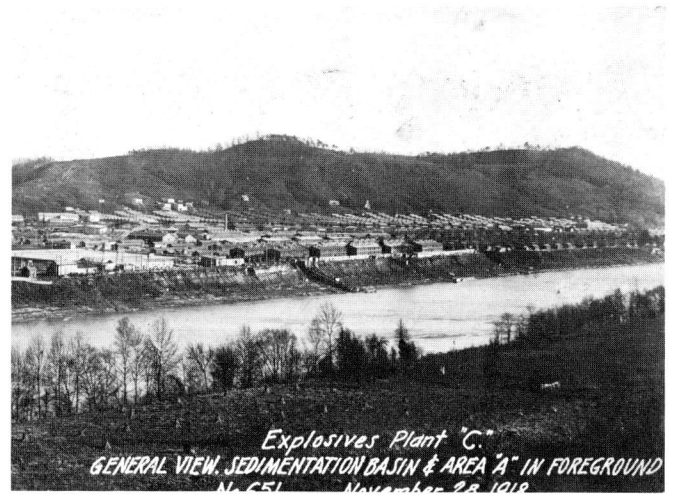

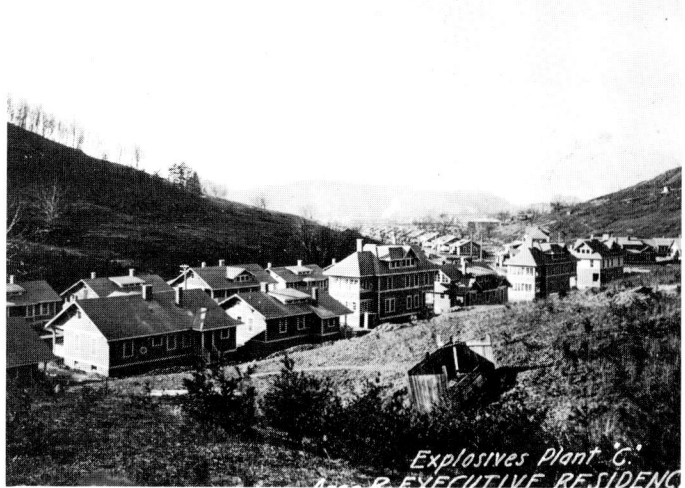

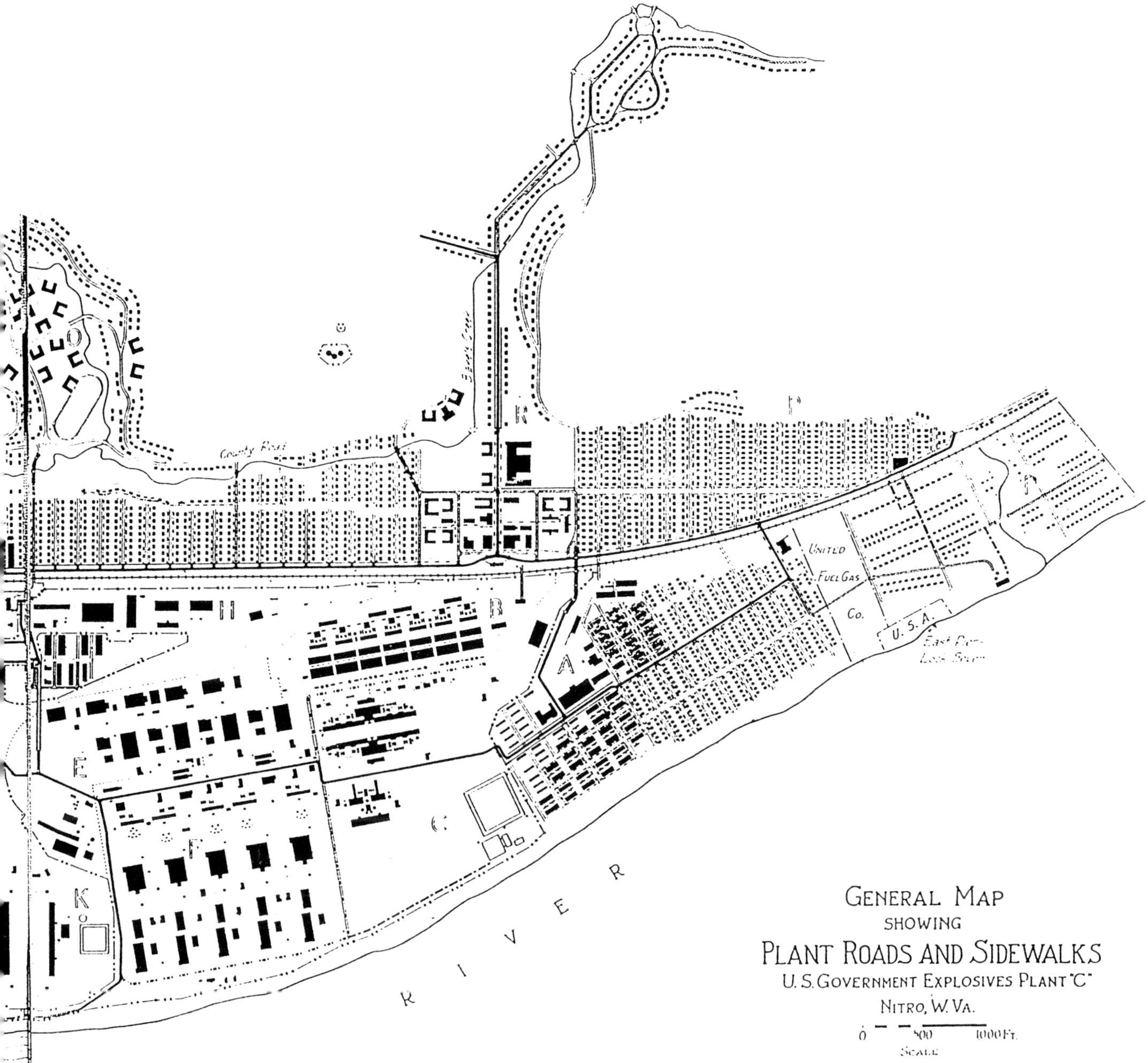
General Map
showing
Plant Roads and Sidewalks
U. S. Government Explosives Plant "C"
Nitro, W. Va.
Scale
United
Fuel Gas
Co.
U. S. A.
River

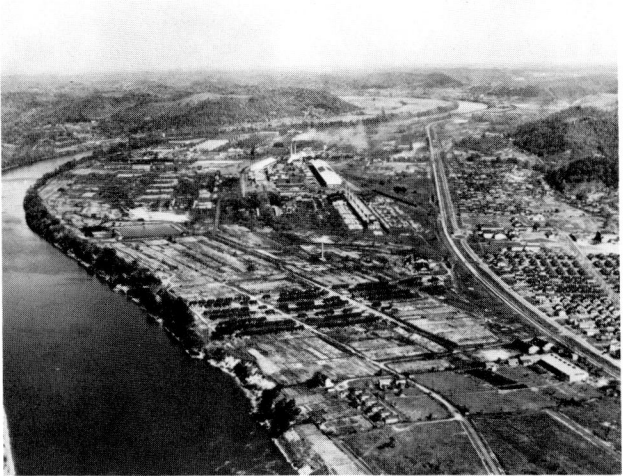

Much of the Nitro Explosives Plant had been demolished by the time this photo was taken in 1931, but the workers houses are still standing and are still in use today. GS

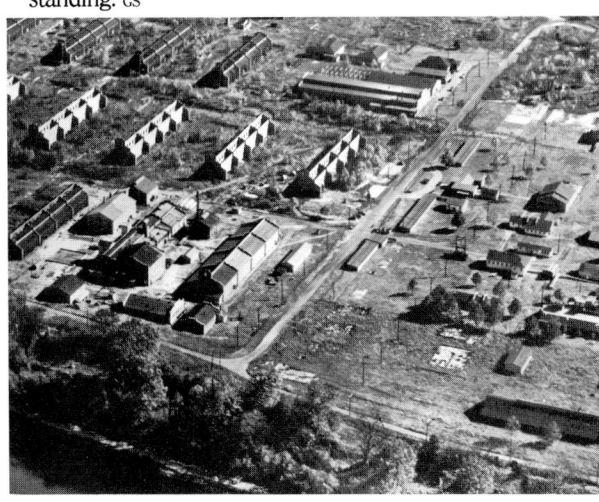

The Nitro Pencil Company in the lower left occupied part of old buildings left over from the explosives plant. This is a 1931 view showing many of the old buildings still standing. GS

Panoramic views of Explosives Plant "C" at Nitro, November 1918. The top photo shows the southern portion of the plant and hundreds of workers houses. These houses were some of the first premanufactured homes in the country. Made by Minter Homes in Huntington, they were shipped flat to Nitro and rebuilt. Many are still in use. The bottom photo shows Area "M." The long chutes extending from the tall silos in the middle were built for rapid emergency exits by workers. The manufacturing process for the explosives was extremely dangerous and all the structures were widely separated so that if one exploded there would not be a chain reaction. ww

Some of the earliest manufacturing concerns in the county were mainly engaged in some aspect of the lumber business. The salt industry stimulated the manufacture of flatboats, and barrels, which were used to ship salt to western markets. At one time, the county was the barrel-producing capitol of the world. In 1832 David Ruffner erected the first steam sawmill in the valley. Several years later, sawmills and furniture factories operated from St. Albans to Marmet, and these thriving businesses up and down the valley were fast denuding the hills of their virgin forests.

Many other industrial concerns started or moved to the Kanawha Valley because of the availability of transportation and raw materials. The Kelly Axe and Tool Company, adjacent to the Patrick Street Bridge, became the largest factory of its kind in the world. The Kanawha Manufacturing Company, which was incorporated in 1902, became one of the largest producers of coal mining cars in the world. The Ward Engineering Works on Charleston's south side was world-renowned for its marine boilers and towboats.

The Kanawha Woolen Mills, founded in 1874, produced yarns, flannels, jeans, and blankets. In 1902 the Charleston Manufacturing Company began making work clothes. A year later, the Kanawha Brewing Company opened. The South Side Foundry was founded at Malden in 1867, and it moved to a site near the C&O station in the 1870s. The Foundry produced equipment for the coal mines, coke ovens and other industries in the area.

By 1931, when this photo was taken, the Dickinson property above Malden was the last available large industrial site. The area is still largely farmland. GS

Monument erected by the West Virginia Oil and Natural Gas Industry on the grounds of Dupont High School to commemorate the discovery and use of natural gas in the area.

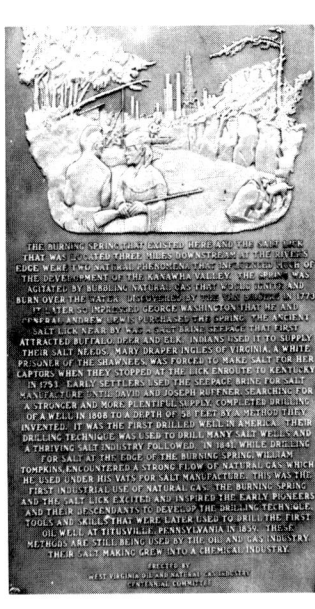

Grist mills have also been important to the business life of the county. The first of these was probably built at Upper Falls on Coal River in 1802. In 1817 Edmund Price built a mill on Elk Two-Mile. A mill at Mill Creek Falls near Meadowbrook Hills was reportedly in use by 1820. At Lower Falls of Coal River, a water-powered carding mill was in operation by the early 1800s. In 1860 this facility was converted to a grist mill by John Karl Sattes. The foundation stones of this old mill can still be seen at Lower Falls.

Today the county is still in the forefront of the nation's industrial progress. There have been many changes throughout the years, but the basic necessities for production are still available here: good rail and river transportation, raw materials, and a stable work force.

The Old Sattes Mill

A grist mill was built as early as 1802 at Upper Falls on Coal River by Joseph Thompson. John Karl Sattes, a German immigrant, bought property along Lower Falls in 1855 and replaced the small mill at the falls with a large three-story one in 1860. The Sattes mill survived the great 1861 flood and Civil War actions and served the needs of people from as far away as Montgomery and Huntington for 56 years. A flash flood in 1916 closed the mill and it was dismantled in 1922. Foundation stones can still be seen at Lower Falls.

COURTESY MRS. MARGARET STRYKER

An old sawmill in the Clendenin area. Note the oxen used to pull the logs to the mill. KCL

The branch line railroads that branched out to many of the hollows not only hauled out coal but in the early 1900s much timber was also transported. This is H.C. Dickinson's lumber train in 1901, probably in the Campbells Creek area. COURTESY EVA HENDERSON

A timber crew and their peaveys used to turn the logs. TH

Band sawmill at Burnwell about 1905. Note the Climax type locomotive, "The D.G. Courtney No. 2."
COURTESY ANDREW TRUSLOW

Band sawmill at Spring Hill, 1911. It was located about where the Interstate bridge crosses the Kanawha River.
COURTESY ANDREW TRUSLOW

Charleston had the distinction for many years of having the largest plant in the world for the manufacture of axes and hatchets. In 1904 W.C. Kelly moved his axe factory to a site on Patrick Street from Alexander, Indiana. The abundance of natural gas, other raw materials and transportation facilities brought him here. The Kelly Axe and Tool Company was the largest metal working plant in the area, and by 1912 it had absorbed all 17 plants of The American Axe and Tool Company and consolidated all manufacturing at the Charleston plant. It was located on 41 acres and ran 24 hours a day, employing over 700 and producing 40,000 finished tools per day. The True Temper Corp. took over the company many years later and continued manufacturing until 1980 when it closed down. The site is now occupied by the Patrick Street Plaza. CN

Three of Dunbar's industries in 1931. Fletcher Enamel Co., Dunbar Glass Co. and Libby-Owens Sheet Glass Co. GS

A large brick manufacturing plant was in operation on the banks of the Elk River in 1931. It was called Standard Brick and Supply Co. GS

Ward Engineering Works

The Charles Ward Engineering Works, one of the most important manufacturers in the Kanawha Valley, was established by Charles Ward, a young English engineer who emigrated to Charleston in 1871. Ward originally helped establish the first city gas works, and later he started producing a new boiler for river steamboats. By the 1880s the Charles Ward Engineering Works, located on the Kanawha River just west of the C & O depot, became one of the largest national manufacturers of the new water-tube boiler. Charles and his son, Ed, who joined the business in the 1890s, sold boilers for both river and ocean steamers and many of Ward's boilers were used in United States Navy ships.

In 1893 the Ward Engineering Works built their first boat, the *Mascot*, which was an inspection boat for the U.S. Engineering Corps. One of the first boats that used a propeller drive rather than a paddle system, the *Mascot* was the first of many boats built by the Ward Engineering Works. Over the next three decades, the firm launched towboats, tugs, and even ocean-going vessels into the Kanawha River.

When Charles Ward died in 1915, his son, Ed, took over the business. Business, however, waned during the Great Depression and because he had no male heirs to take over the reins, Ed closed the company in 1931. Only the boats remained, for many years, as a testament to the proud tradition of the Charles Ward Engineering Works.

At the height of business, the Charles Ward Engineering Works employed over 100 skilled craftsmen. WVU

The *Wild Goose*, one of many towboats built by Ward, on its trial run, September 25, 1926. WVU

Charles Ward, founder of the Charles Ward Engineering Works. WVU

Ward Engineering had a large plant on the southside that was greatly expanded after 1900. WVU

The Ward's largest boiler, the Royal Arch model boiler, could power a large battleship. WVU

A christening party to celebrate the launch of the *Indiana*, a 200-foot towboat. Governer William A. MacCorkle is second from left. WVU

Gravely Motor Plow and Cultivator Company's plant in Dunbar. In 1920 a local man, B.F. Gravely of Gravely & Moore Photographers, invented a low-cost, light, one-wheel plow that revolutionized the home garden industry. His plant was established in Dunbar and plows were shipped worldwide. The company is still in business but moved out of the state in the 1960s. COURTESY OVA TOLLEY

Interior view of the Gravely factory showing one-man garden plows, ready for shipment. SWV

-177-

Kanawha Valley Traction Company employees at the Virginia Street car barn, 1906. KRTA

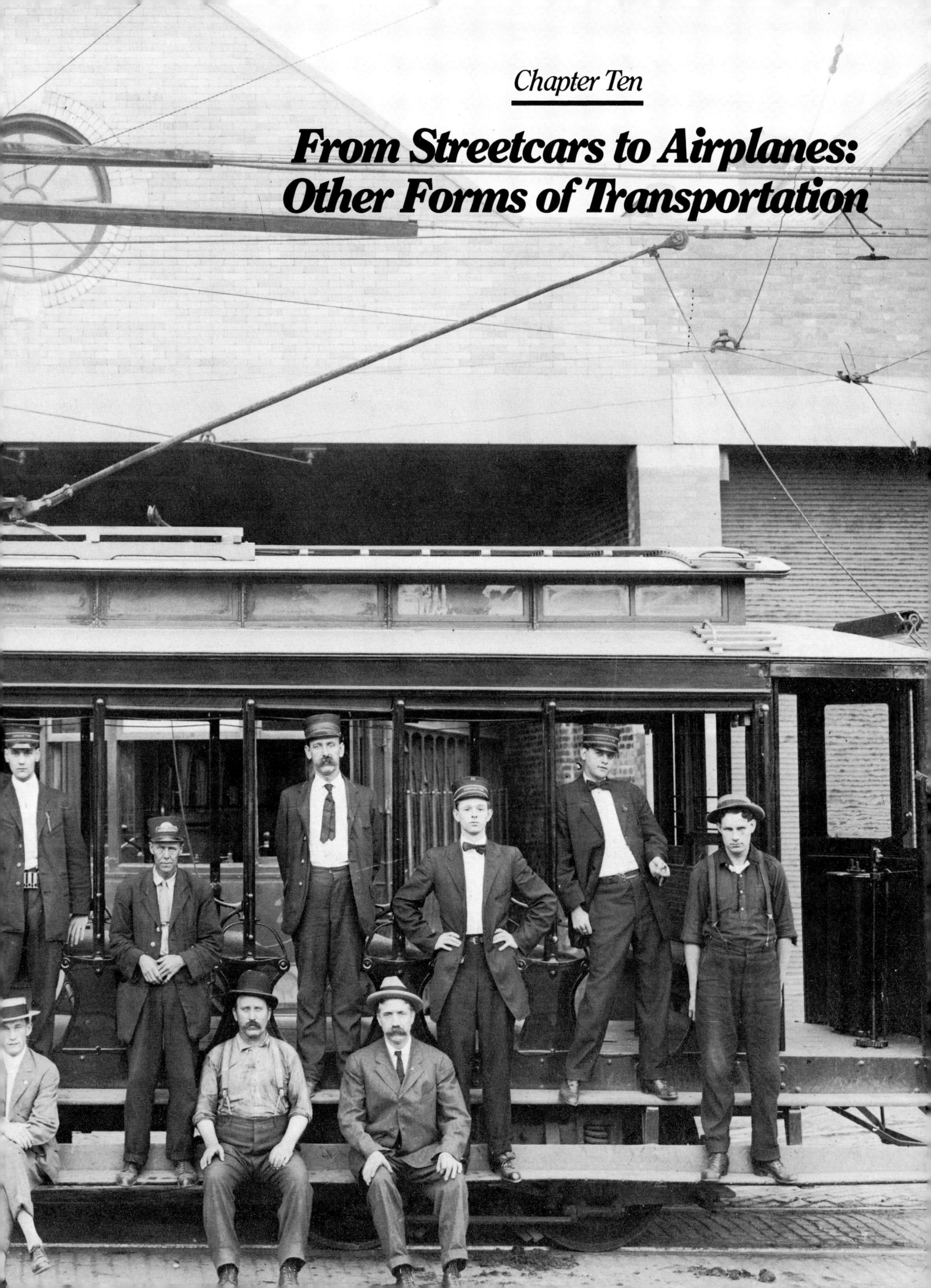

Chapter Ten
From Streetcars to Airplanes: Other Forms of Transportation

Other Forms of Transportation

From Streetcars To Buses

Like river transportation and the railroads, the intercity transportation that developed in the late nineteenth century dramatically altered the business and social life of Kanawha County. Horse-drawn streetcars were established in 1888 that travelled in a loop through the downtown area of Charleston. A second line was soon developed that travelled into West Charleston, crossed the Virginia Street bridge and continued to Patrick Street. Another extension was established along Washington Street to the city limits at Bradford Street.

W.W. Hazard acquired the horse-drawn line in 1898. Under his newly formed Charleston Traction Company, Hazard electrified the entire system. By 1903 the new company moved the tracks from Kanawha Street one block over to Virginia Street, then extended the streetcar line further east over a new landfill area. An old mule car route that crossed Elk River at Dryden Street to the west side was electrified and the company built a car barn and power plant in the 100 block of Virginia Street West.

The street railway system changed ownership several times in the early 1900s, including the purchase by former U.S. Senator William E. Chilton. The Edgewood line, which ran along Tennessee Avenue and West Virginia Street and north on Edgewood, was established in 1907, and the South Charleston line ran from Central Avenue and crossed the Kanawha River on the C&O railroad bridge in 1908.

In 1910 Chilton, F.M. Staunton, former governor W.A. MacCorkle and others formed the Charleston Interurban Railroad Company. With the infusion of capital, the new company greatly expanded the streetcar line over the next few years. In 1912 the South Charleston line was extended to St. Albans, and a line was started from Charleston to connect the new town of Dunbar; the Kanawha City bridge was built in 1915; in several stages, the line was extended to Cabin Creek in 1916.

Three streetcar loops were established within the limits of Charleston. The inner loop ran up Quarrier Steet to Brooks, out Brooks to Smith, down Smith to Capitol Street. The middle loop ran up Virginia Steet to Ruffner Avenue, out Ruffner to Washington, down Washington to Capitol Street. The outer loop ran up Washington and Virginia streets from Capitol to Duffy Street. The car going up Virginia would return down Washington and the Washington car would return to Capitol down Virginia Street.

In the 1920s, jitney buses, some of which were actually touring cars, also provided service to the intercity and to some outlying areas.

When buses came into prominence, the days of streetcars were numbered. In 1924 the Midland Trail Transit Company was formed to provide bus service because of the rapid development of paved roads. Owned by Arthur M. Hill and the Charleston Interurban Railroad Company, the company first started bus service on Crescent Road in 1925, followed by routes to Piedmont Road and South Hills. When the Capitol moved to its present location in 1932, a new center of employment was established that was separate from the downtown. Bus routes soon connected both areas together.

The Interurban Railroad went into receivership in 1933, and it was replaced by the Charleston Transit Company, controlled by Hill, in 1935. When streetcars were discontinued in mid-1939, bus service expanded tremendously. Routes were established all the way to Montgomery, St. Albans and Nitro, and several other bus lines were purchased. By the start of World War II, there were bus routes to all of Kanawha Valley inside the county lines. In 1971 the entire bus line was absorbed into the new Kanawha Valley Regional Transportation Authority, which is owned by the county.

KRTA

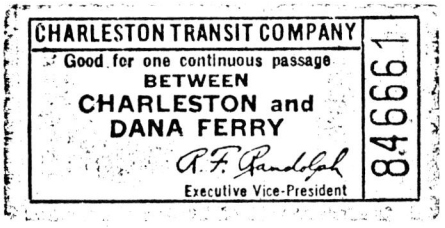

The Charleston Traction Company was organized in 1898 to acquire and electrify the horse railway. The company was bought by J.C. Sproul about 1902, so this photo must have been taken right after the turn of the century. RA

Street car operators of the CIRR inside the Virginia Street car barn, 1920s. KRTA

A 1906 view of streetcar employees in front of the Virginia Street car barn. At this time, the Kanawha Valley Traction Company was probably owned by J.C. Sproul of Pennsylvania, whose local associates included former U.S. Senator William E. Chilton. KRTA

One of Charleston's streetcars, about World War I. RA

An inner-loop street car on Virginia Street, late 1920s. KCL

The car barn on Virginia Street West, owned by the Charleston Interurban Railroad Company. Built in 1903, this building is now occupied by the Goodwill Industries. KCL

The St. Albans station of the Charleston Interurban Railroad Company, 1920. KCL

The old bus station was downtown at the corner of Virginia and Alderson streets, across from Woodrums Furniture Store. This building was the station for the Charleston Interurban Railroad Company, later the Charleston Transit Company, the Blue and Gray Bus Line, and finally the Atlantic Greyhound Lines. Charleston Transit moved to their new office on the west side in 1950. COURTESY KELLY BRATTON AND KCL

Line crews were constantly called to service the electrical lines for the Interurban Railroad Company. KRTA

A line truck of the Charleston Interurban Railroad (CIRR) Company, 1930. KRTA

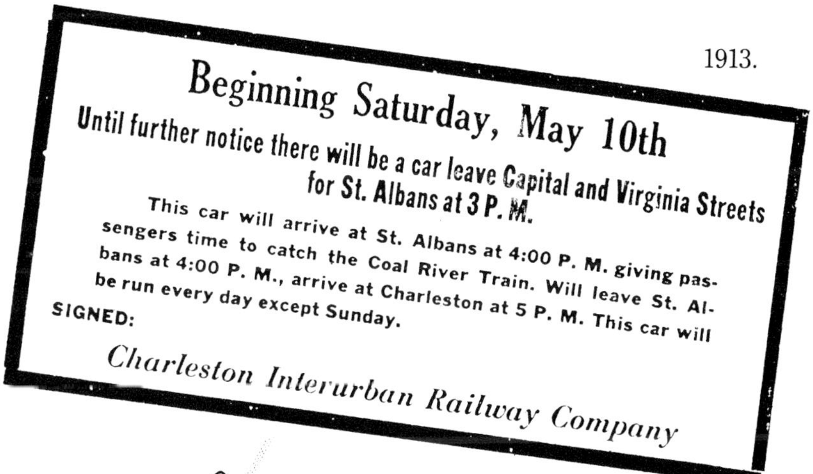

1913.

Beginning Saturday, May 10th

Until further notice there will be a car leave Capital and Virginia Streets for St. Albans at 3 P. M.

This car will arrive at St. Albans at 4:00 P. M. giving passengers time to catch the Coal River Train. Will leave St. Albans at 4:00 P. M., arrive at Charleston at 5 P. M. This car will be run every day except Sunday.

SIGNED:

Charleston Interurban Railway Company

CHARLESTON 1934

- ——— C.I.RR. STREETCAR ROUTES
- xxxxx FORMER ROUTE OF DUNBAR LINE
- ——— C.I.RR. BUS ROUTES
- .... INDEPENDENT BUS ROUTES

ONE MILE

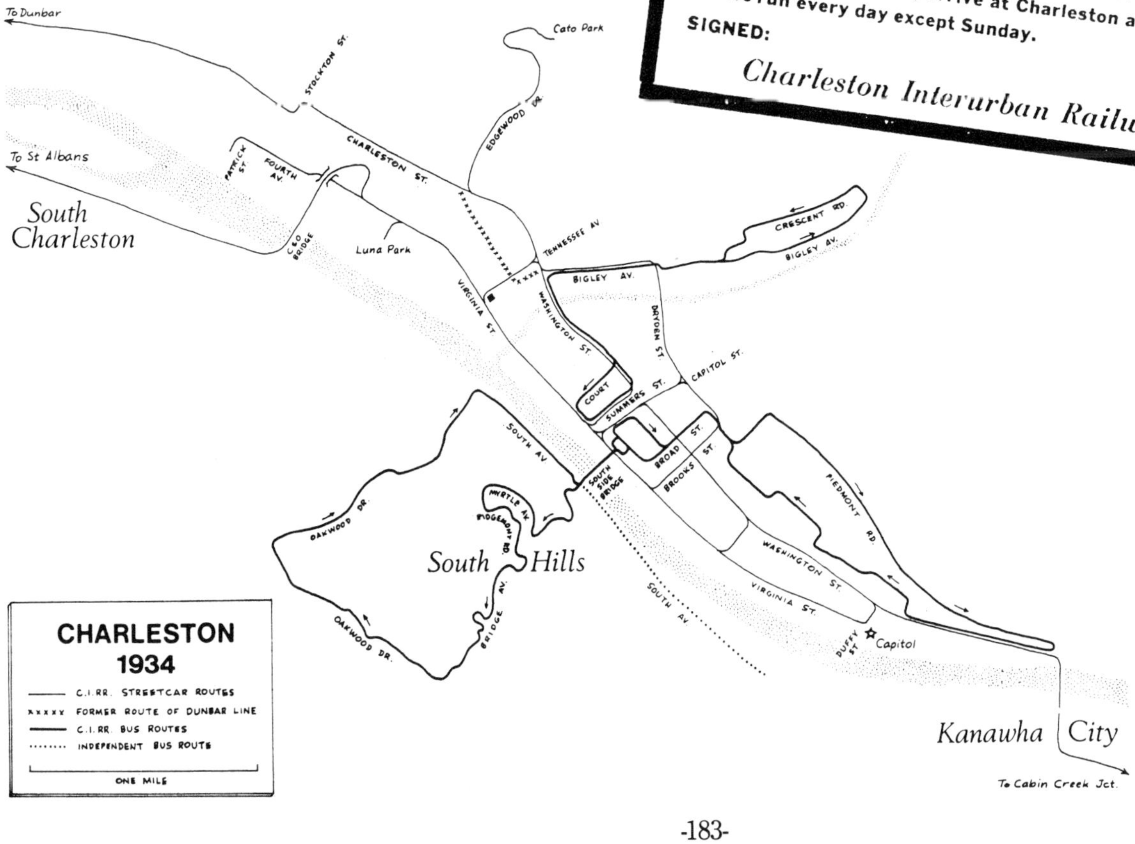

A Charleston Transit streetcar, the "Kanawha," on July 1, 1939. This may have been the valley's last streetcar, as streetcar service was discontinued in 1939. KRTA

The trailer bus in this photo was used after streetcars were taken out of service in the late 1930s. They were aptly named "cattle cars." KRTA

Yellow Coach buses, model 740, parked in the car barn in 1940. Powered by new diesel engines, these buses had a red body, grey roof and a white belt. KRTA

Charleston Transit Company's first scheduled bus service to St. Albans began on June 20, 1939. KRTA

Charleston Transit buses at the old Virginia Street car barn in the late 1940s. In May 1950 the company moved to a new square-block building on Fourth Avenue and Stockton Street. The Kanawha Valley Regional Transportation Authority still uses the facility. KRTA

A 1930 Blue and Gray Lines bus, the forerunner of Atlantic Greyhound Lines, beside the governor's mansion on Duffy Street.
SWV BOLLINGER COLLECTION

...the same vintage bus, only taken in 1935, on the Campbells Creek Road underpass at high water. By this time, Blue and Gray Lines had been absorbed by the Atlantic Greyhound system.
SWV BOLLINGER COLLECTION

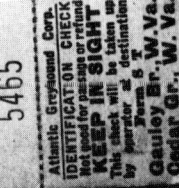

An Atlantic Greyhound Lines bus on Duffy Street, 1935. The cities served by the bus line, as stated on the side of the bus, include: Miami, Jacksonville, Pittsburgh, Cincinnati, Detroit, Chicago, Atlanta, Washington and Richmond.
SWV BOLLINGER COLLECTION

Atlantic Greyhound Lines

Arthur M. Hill formed the Midland Trail Transit Company in 1924 by merging the White Transportation Company and the Huntington-Charleston Motor Bus Company. Hill was involved with the Charleston Interurban Railroad Company, and in the 1930s he was president of the Charleston Transit Company. In 1926 Hill combined his Midland Trail, Blue and Gray and Old Dominion lines to form the Atlantic Greyhound Lines that became one of the largest bus companies in the South and the largest subsidiary of the Greyhound Corporation.

Greyhound buses with a state police escort, on Kanawha Street in front of the State Capitol, 1937. These police cars were Ford V-8 roadsters used because of their great speed and visibility.
SWV BOLLINGER COLLECTION

The Greyhound bus terminal on Summers Street opened January 30, 1937. The terminal served thousands of customers for more than 40 years before it was demolished in 1980. SWV BOLLINGER COLLECTION

A fleet of taxis on Kanawha Boulevard opposite the Virginia Street bridge, about 1940. SWV BOLLINGER COLLECTION

Trails and Roads

The earliest travel routes were blazed by herds of deer, elk, buffalo and other fur-bearing animals who wore trails to the springs and salt licks in the area. The Indians also used these trails when they hunted game to provide food and clothing. Best suited for travel on foot or horseback, these trails were later widened by the settlers who removed logs and other obstructions as they crossed the trails into the area.

After the Revolutionary War the government of Virginia considered a proposal for improving the travel facilities and the commerce between eastern and western Virginia that later became the James River and Kanawha Turnpike. George Washington, who was principally interested in building a canal, was the leading exponent of the route. He influenced the legislature to pass an act that incorporated the James River Company, and in 1785 the legislature authorized the company to construct a "state road" for wagons.

The road was built to the navigable waters of the Kanawha in 1790, and to the Ohio River in 1800. In October 1785 the legislature authorized the construction of a wagon road at least 30 feet wide from Lewisburg to the lower falls of the Kanawha. Although the road that was built in 1786 was probably narrower than specified, it was the first wagon road from the east to the navigable waters of the Kanawha. By 1791 the Morris Settlement that was 20 miles above the mouth of the Elk at Kelly's Creek became the terminal point for overland traffic headed west to Kentucky and the Ohio River. So many flatboats were built and launched from this point on the Kanawha that is now Cedar Grove, the area became known as the "bote yards."

The legislature authorized the extension of the wagon road to the Ohio in 1787. Using surveys provided by the Kanawha County Court in 1802, a road was constructed by 1804. That year mail was carried from Lewisburg to the Scioto salt works in Ohio, and by 1807 mail was delivered from Lewisburg to Chillicothe, Ohio. By 1808 many Ohio and Kentucky drovers travelled the Kanawha route to find a market for hogs and other livestock, and in February 1, 1809, tolls were authorized for the road.

Kanawha Republican

CHARLESTON, KANAWHA COUNTY, VIRGINIA,

SEPTEMBER 8, 1847.

☞ 1847! ☜

REESIDE'S
U. S. MAIL LINES
ARE NOW RUNNING
Between Charleston and Guyandotte, Va.
AND
Between Charleston and Point Pleasant, Va.
OFFICE, Kanawha House, Charleston,

Leaves Kanawha House, Charleston, every Sunday, Wednesday and Friday mornings.
Returning, leaves Hale's Hotel, Point Pleasant, every Tuesday, Thursday and Saturday mornings.
There is a line running from Charleston to the Salines every evening, leaving after the arrival of the stages from the West, and leaving the Salines every morning in time to connect with the stages for the West.
June 30, 1847.

The James River and Kanawha Turnpike was the major thoroughfare that connected the Ohio River with tidewater Virginia. The wagon road started at the end of the canal at Buchanan, Virginia, crossed the Allegheny Mountains, and followed the Kanawha River to Charleston. The road crossed the Kanawha River at Charleston, and headed west through Teays Valley to Guyndotte on the Ohio River. U.S. Route 60 generally follows this old route.

The Virginia General Assembly chartered the Kanawha Turnpike in 1819 as an extension of the James River and Kanawha Canal that was owned by the James River and Kanawha Company. The company extended the turnpike little by little, intending to end the turnpike at the head of navigation on the Kanawha River. But by 1825 the road was finished to Gauley Bridge. Two years later, the road reached Charleston, and by 1829 it was extended to the Ohio River.

In 1835 the stockholders of the turnpike consolidated the eastern and western sections into one company, and Ezra Walker, the toll keeper in the Charleston area, collected tolls from the road for many years. In May 1837, a flood severely damaged the road and washed out 11 of 40 bridges. Bridges were reconstructed over many of the major streams along the route including the Coal River bridge at Coalsmouth in 1849 and the Gauley River bridge in 1850. Both of these large covered bridges were later burned by Confederate troops in 1861.

In the 1850s the increased river traffic and the completion of the Virginia Central Railroad as far west as Covington, Virginia, diminished traffic on the wagon road. The road rapidly deteriorated, and during the Civil War it was not maintained at all.

The new state of West Virginia inherited this thoroughfare, which continued to be the major east-west route through the southern part of the state, until the interstates were completed in the late 1970s and early 1980s. Designated now as Route 60, the road was first paved between Huntington and Charleston in 1923.

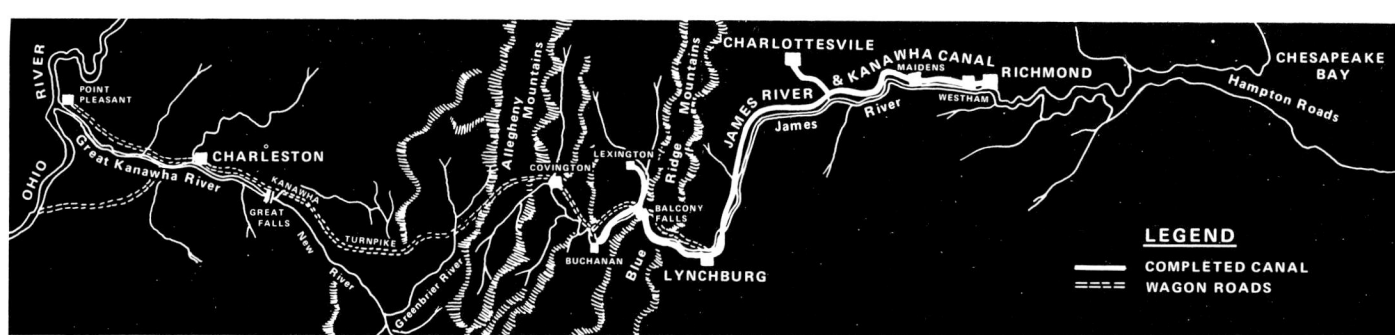

The James River and Kanawha Turnpike was a toll road until 1875. Some tolls in effect in 1809 were:

Wagon, team and driver, 25 cents

Four-wheeled riding carriage, 20 cents

Cart or two-wheeled, 12½ cents

Man and horse, 6¼ cents

Cattle per head, ¼ cent

Sheep or hogs, per score, 3 cents

The Giles-Fayette-Kanawha Turnpike was chartered in 1837 and completed in 1848. Passing through what are now the towns of Beckley, Mount Hope, Oak Hill and Fayetteville, the road joined the James River and Kanawha Turnpike at Kanawha Falls. From there it followed the south bank of the Kanawha River, crossed Fayette County to Montgomery at the Kanawha County line. The Charleston-Ripley-Ravenswood Turnpike opened in 1848, which was extended to Parkersburg in 1861. More roads were built that generally followed water courses, although roads did not reach some of the more isolated areas until the mid-twentieth century. A paved road to Logan was not opened until 1927, and the capital was finally connected to Winfield in 1930 and to Hamlin in Lincoln County in 1933. In the late 1920s and 30s, more and more of the important traffic arteries were paved, and today the interstate highways that bisect the county provide easy access to all areas of the country.

Caldwell and Surbaugh established the first stage line between Charleston and Lewisburg, which made a trip a week by January 1827. The fare was $7.00 and seats were on a first-come, first-served basis. The weekly run was extended to Catlettsburg, Kentucky, when the road was built to the Big Sandy River, and branch lines were added as the roads were improved. In the early 1830s stage connections went to Sutton by way of Lewisburg, and to the steamboat landings at Guyandotte on the Ohio River, via Barboursville. Established mail routes soon enabled the stage company to run daily, and as improvements were made it permitted stages to cover 75 to 80 miles in a day. By 1832 passengers could travel to Lexington, Kentucky, or transfer to Caldwell's line at Lewisburg, which extended east through White Sulphur, Salt Sulphur, Sweet Springs, and Fincastle in eastern Virginia.

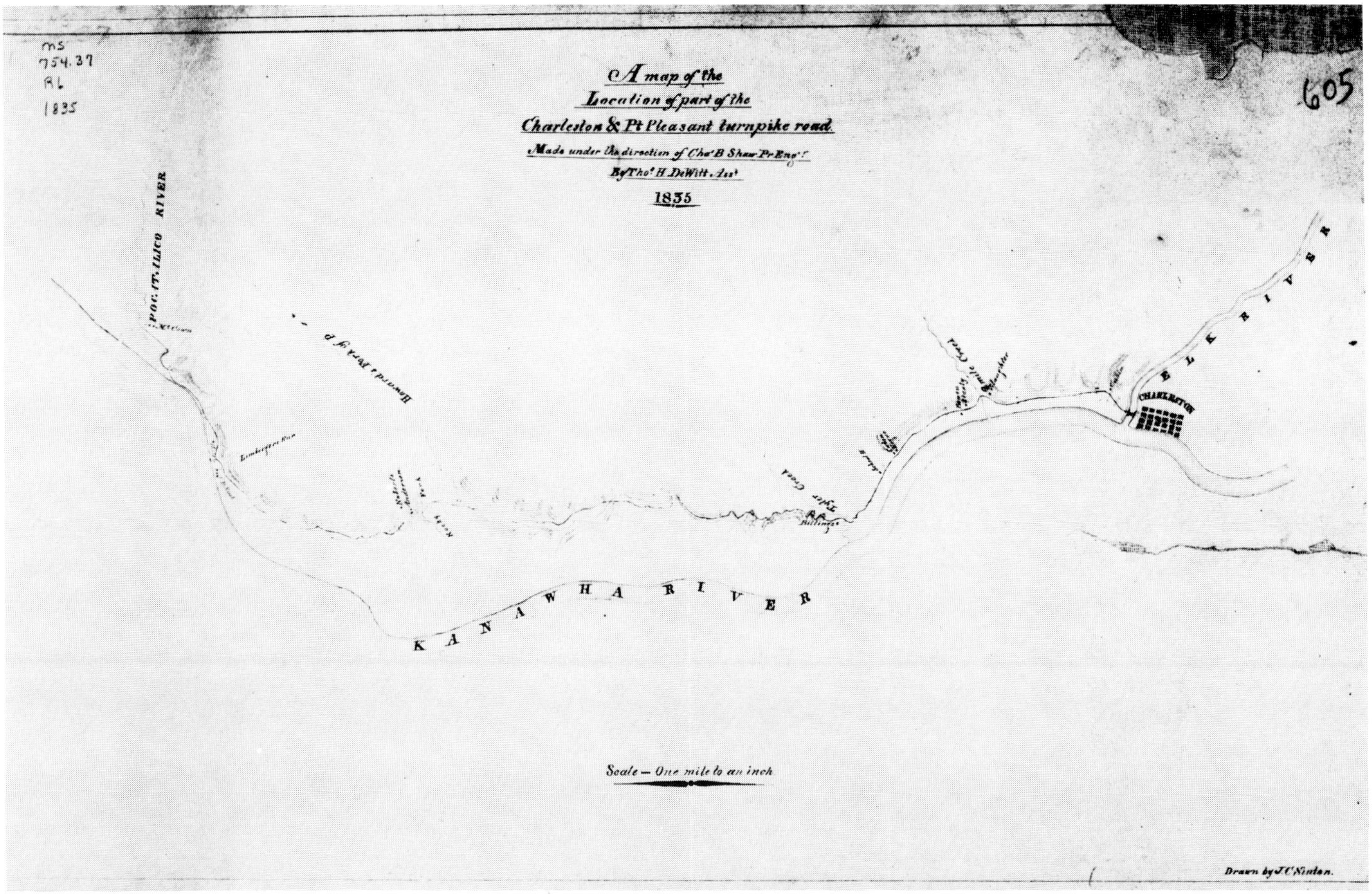

COURTESY VIRGINIA STATE LIBRARY

The County's First Automobiles*

*From a 1961 newspaper story by B.E. Andre.

The first car in Kanawha County was a Foster Steam Buggy that was manufactured in Massachusetts and sold in 1901 by John Wanamaker's store in Philadelphia to Dr. Fleetwood Butts, an adventurous young dentist in Charleston. Butts learned about the buggy from a friend who had seen the car in Wanamaker's window in Philadelphia. Butts immediately took a train to Philadelphia and bought the car, which he shipped to Charleston by train.

When the Foster arrived in Charleston, Dr. Butts and a crowd of friends went to the C&O depot to unload it. Called a "steam buggy," the car was powered by steam from a small boiler that was heated with a kerosene-fed flame. Once one got up a head of steam, he was on his way at a speed up to fifteen miles an hour. One can only imagine how excited the people were about the strange new contraption that roared around the few paved streets.

A man surnamed Neore, who lived in the Ruffner Hotel, owned the second car in the county. The car was a small French model called the deDion Bouton that was powered by a gasoline engine. The third car in the county was an unusual, three-wheeled car named the Knox that was steered with a tiller. David Collins, a timber operator on Elk River, brought the car to Charleston but he soon tired of it.

The Foster Steam Buggy owned by Dr. Fleetwood Butts. RA

In the next few years, Oldsmobiles, Maxwells, Stanley Steamers, White Steamers, Franklins, Reos, Stutz Bearcats, and the ever-popular Model T Fords, and later Model A Fords travelled the streets and roads of the county so frequently that they were no longer a novelty item.

Andre Buys Truck In Chicago; Drives Here

Hauls Seven Motorcycles From Milwaukee to Charleston in Truck Bought For Purpose.

When B. E. Andre, local motorcycle distributor on Hale street, was unable to secure deliveries of motorcycles, he immediately repaired to Chicago where he bought a two-ton all-American truck, and ran it over to Milwaukee. There he loaded it with seven Harley-Davidson motorcycles, some of which will be used by state police, and three side cars.

Andre then turned his new truck toward home, making the trip in less than four days and a half, the last day of which was spent on the roads between Charleston and Huntington.

He left Milwaukee at 3:10 Thursday afternoon and arrived in Charleston Monday evening at 8. He said he encountered nothing but good roads from Milwaukee to Chillicothe, but that difficulties began Monday morning when he pulled out of Huntington.

His route was: Milwaukee to Chicago to Valprasio to Bass Lake to Richmond, all in Indiana, to Dayton, O., to Chillicothe, to Portsmouth to Huntington to Charleston.

Charleston Gazette, May 27, 1920.

This may very well have been one of the first attempts at interstate trucking. In 1920 the railroads carried most of the freight and the rural roads were often mud quagmires. Photo on Virginia Street near Court.

Motorcycles on Virginia Street directly across from the courthouse, circa 1920. RA

A Sunday outing of motorcyclists posing on the old Elkview bridge that crossed Elk River, circa 1920. The building in the background is the Elkview store, which burned in 1962. This bridge is still standing but traffic has been rerouted to the new bridge adjacent to it. RA

The Bender Bridge crosses Fourmile Fork from the south entrance of the 2,265' Memorial Tunnel on the West Virginia Turnpike. Completed in 1954, the turnpike traversed approximately 40 miles through the southeast corner of the county, and provided easier access from Charleston to Beckley, Princeton and Bluefield. The tunnel and bridge have been bypassed by a tremendous cut and fill project, and the turnpike upgraded to a four-lane interstate, (I-77). COURTESY BETTMANN ARCHIVE/NEW YORK

In the early days of automobile travel, one had to have some detailed directions to travel on the few maintained roads of the state. There were few road signs and in many places, what road there was, usually followed the natural contour of the ground. This 1915 guide gives a good indication of the directions one would need to go from Charleston to Parkersburg, an all-day trip if not more. RA

Construction of the West Virginia Turnpike in the Kanawha Valley, early 1950s. KCL

The solid black lines on this 1923 road map show all the paved roads in the county.

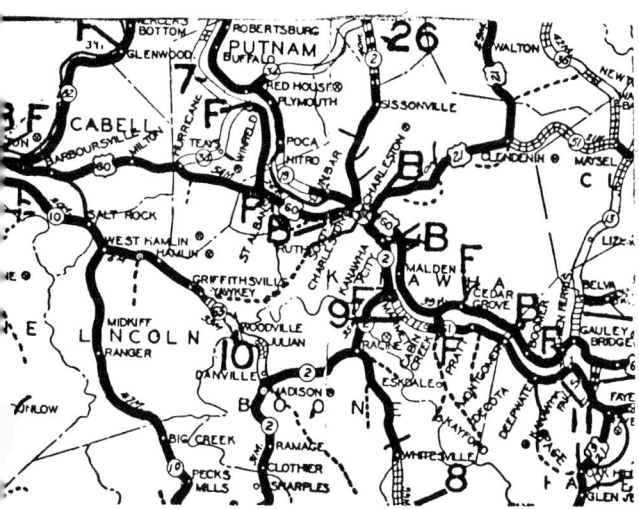

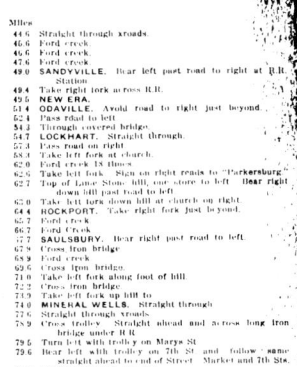

Aviation History

Paul Peck is shown at the controls of his biplane on June 26, 1912, at Charleston. Peck, from Ansted, was the first pilot to fly an airplane from a landing field in the state. Using the old South Charleston ballpark in 1912, he took off, cleared a fence and cornfield and landed minutes later in a terrific rain storm. He is also credited with flying the first airmail flight in the United States and was the first to fly over the U.S. Capitol building. He died in an air crash in 1912. COURTESY EAGLE AVIATION

An early biplane at the Kanawha City landing field in 1927. This field, near the present 35th Street bridge, was in use until Wertz Field in Institute went into operation in 1930.
COURTESY EAGLE AVIATION

Close-up view of *Waco* and *Aeronica* seaplanes at Glen Clark's base on the Kanawha River at the city levee in the 1930s. Clark operated this base for many years and many of today's local pilots learned to fly here. COURTESY EAGLE AVIATION

A very early biplane on a ballfield in the east end of South Charleston. Note the chain drive on the twin pusher propellers. COURTESY MRS. FOREST BARKER

The county's first airport was established on a level area at Institute in 1930. It was named Wertz Field for the then mayor of Charleston, W.W. Wertz. The city lacked the funds to develop and operate the field so it was leased to West Virginia Airways, Inc., a group of local businessmen. It was operated this way until 1942, when the government took over the field for a synthetic rubber plant. In October 1933, American Airlines opened passenger service between Washington and Chicago via Charleston. Pennsylvania Central Airlines (later Capital Airlines) opened service in 1935. By the late 1930s the field was inadequate for the larger passenger planes coming into use. TOP: Apparently some sort of aviation meet at Wertz Field about 1936. BOTTOM: Wertz Field with the buildings of West Virginia State College to the right, 1939. COURTESY EAGLE AVIATION

A modern administration building was constructed in the early 1930s to service the scheduled airlines. swv

Famous aviators Wiley Post and Harold Gatty toured America following their record-breaking 1931 around-the-world flight. Here the famous Lockheed model 5B Vega, named *Winnie Mae,* is parked at Wertz Field. swv

Inauguration of Air Express service from Wertz Field in 1935. Governor Guy Kump is second from right.
COURTESY EAGLE AVIATION

COURTESY DR. CHARLES C. QUARLES

A heck of a way to land an airplane. Sometime in the 1940s one of the seaplanes based on the Kanawha River got caught in electrical wires. This site is at the corner of Kanawha Boulevard and Delaware Avenue. In 1987 the tree is still there! KCL

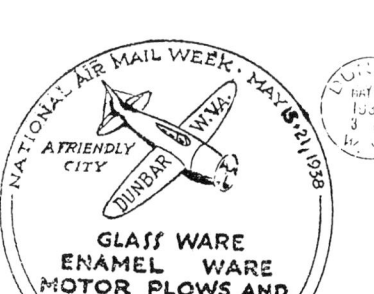

COVERS COURTESY RICK HAMILTON

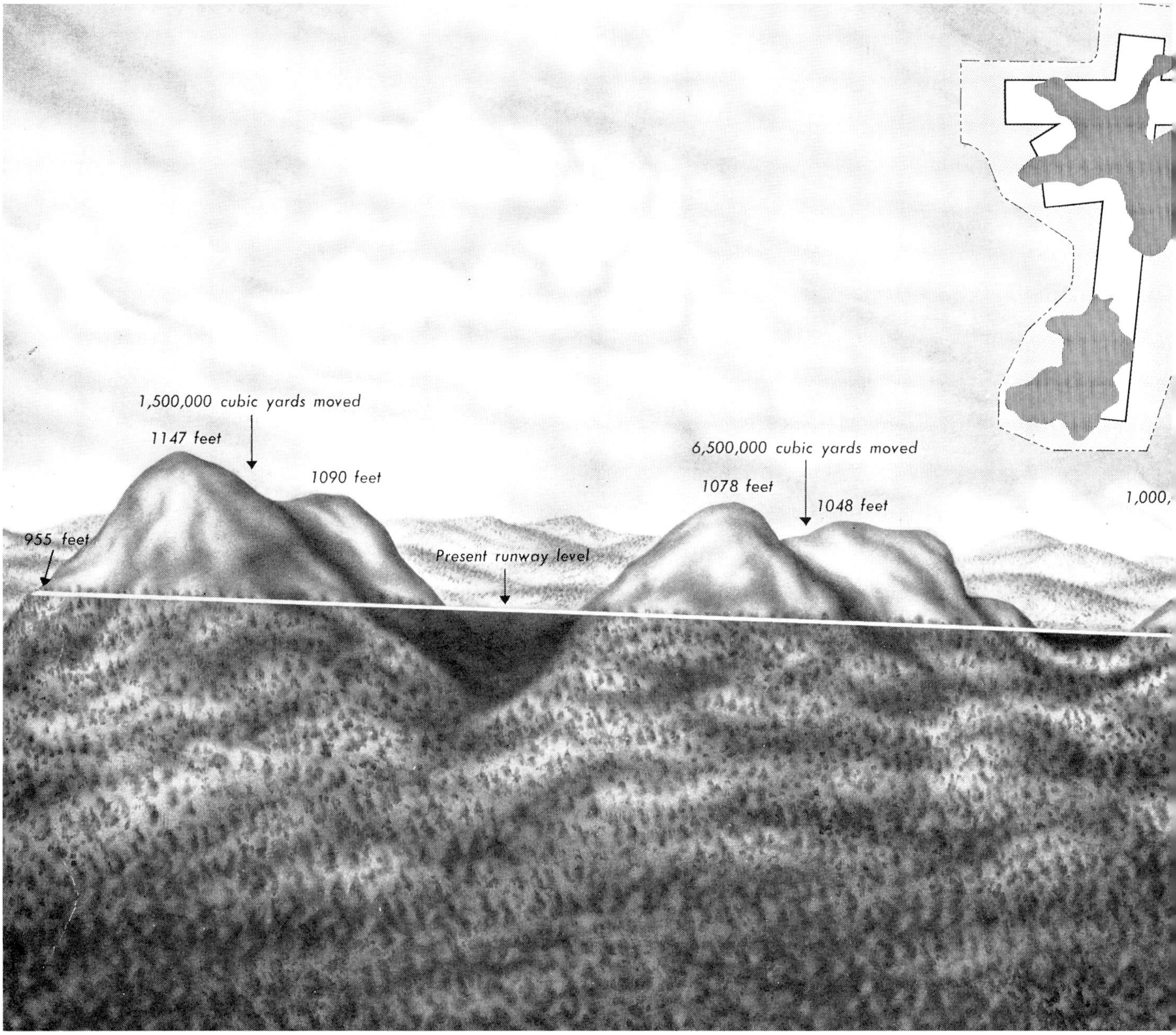

955 feet • 1,500,000 cubic yards moved • 1147 feet • 1090 feet • Present runway level • 6,500,000 cubic yards moved • 1078 feet • 1048 feet • 1,000,

Ground-breaking for the new Kanawha Airport on October 18, 1944, on Coonskin Ridge. This was the beginning of the present Yeager Airport. COURTESY EAGLE AVIATION

Looking northwest in September 1945, shows extensive area over which grading and filling was spread out. The Meadowbrook Road is at right. COURTESY EAGLE AVIATION

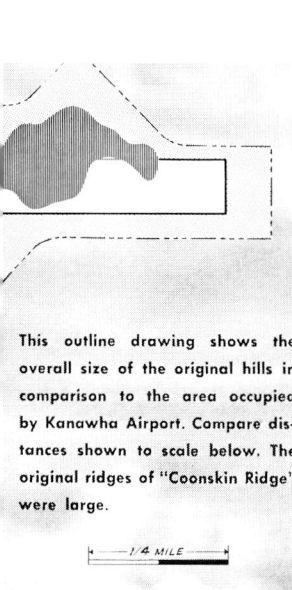

This outline drawing shows the overall size of the original hills in comparison to the area occupied by Kanawha Airport. Compare distances shown to scale below. The original ridges of "Coonskin Ridge" were large.

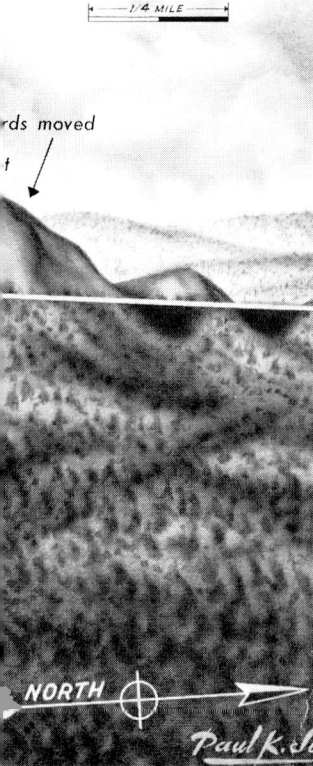

Accurately drawn from original maps by Louis Hark, airport engineer, this drawing by Paul K. Jordan portrays the original profile of Coonskin ridge as it appeared from the eastern approach. All heights indicated are "above sea level." Note the gradual slope of the runway which extends over a mile in length. The inset drawing shows the great extent of the projecting hills and the area they occupied over and above the present runway level. COURTESY YEAGER AIRPORT

One year later, paving began at the intersection of runways one and two. COURTESY EAGLE AVIATION

This scene from late 1947 or early 1948 shows the completed hangar and other base facilities. The main terminal construction had not yet begun. P-51s of the newly formed West Virginia Air National Guard unit are lined up on the parking ramp.

This view from the early 1950s shows the completed airport and terminal facilities. COURTESY EAGLE AVIATION

COURTESY RICK HAMILTON

An aerial view of Kanawha Airport, showing the new terminal that opened in 1950. COURTESY EAGLE AVIATION

Famous aviator Chuck Yeager and his father at Kanawha Airport, October 11, 1948, in front of his F-80 jet. Yeager, originally from neighboring Lincoln County, was a fighter pilot in World War II, the first man to fly faster than sound and America's most famous test pilot for many years. General Yeager, who now lives in California, attended the ceremonies at Kanawha Airport in 1984 when the airport was renamed Yeager Airport, the first airport to be named for a living American aviator. On this 1948 visit to Charleston, Yeager stunned the spectators at the Kanawha River boat races by unexpectedly flying his F-80 beneath the South Side Bridge. CN

Capital Airlines (formerly Pennsylvania Central Airlines) first provided passenger service to Wertz Field in 1935. The airline provided service to Kanawha Airport for many years. This DC-6 is parked in front of the terminal in the mid-1950s. CN

-198-

LEFT: P-51s at Kanawha Airport in 1950. An Eastern Airlines DC-3 can be seen in front of the original terminal. COURTESY J. KEMP McLAUGHLIN

RIGHT: World War II vintage P-51 fighters of the 167th Air National Guard Unit stationed at Kanawha Airport fly over Charleston in 1948. COURTESY J. KEMP McLAUGHLIN

Brigadier General James Kemp McLaughlin. COURTESY JAMES K. McLAUGHLIN

West Virginia Air National Guard

After World War II, Air National Guard units were formed throughout the United States to provide a backup pool for the regular Air Force. West Virginia's unit was formed in 1947 at the new Kanawha Airport under command of Colonel J. Kemp McLaughlin. Their first planes were World War II vintage P-47 fighters. The next year, 38 P-51D fighters were acquired. A few months after the beginning of the Korean War in 1950, the unit was called to active duty and joined the 123rd Fighter/Bomber Wing. It furnished airplanes and pilots to Korea but most of the group was sent to an air base in England. It was activated for 21 months. In 1952 the group was reformed again as a guard unit at Charleston with P-51s and known as the 167th Fighter/Bomber Squadron. In 1955 the 167th was transferred to Martinsburg and the 130th Air Re-Supply Group was activated at Charleston with C-46s and SA-16 flying boats. In 1975 the unit received their first C-130 Hercules, the predominant cargo airplane in the Air Force Inventory. The 130th Air Re-Supply Group has flown around the world since 1975 providing valuable service for the regular Air Force. McLaughlin, who received his baptism in combat flying B-17s over wartime Germany, retired in 1977. He also served six years as a Kanawha County Commissioner.

A tragic airplane accident occurred near the Kanawha Airport on April 9, 1951, when a West Virginia Air National Guard C-47 attempting to make a landing at the airport crashed into a nearby mountain, killing 19 airmen on board. Two airmen died later. CN

Although views of Charleston's waterfront are common, this 1894 photo from a glass negative is exceptionally fine. It shows the original center section of the courthouse (A), the old city hall (B), the landmark St. Albert Hotel (C), the Union School (D), the post office (E), the state capitol (F) and the premier hotel of the time, the Ruffner (G). The river on this day is glassy calm. From the looks of the trees it must be winter or spring. A magnifying glass will reveal a man applying roofing tar to a building on the waterfront just east of the St. Albert Hotel. COURTESY DAVE MOORE

E F G

Chapter Eleven
Life in the County: 1865-1918

This unusual view of downtown Charleston, circa 1920, looks west. Quarrier Street is in the middle of the photo, dead-ending at the Charleston National Bank building. The back of the capitol annex is to the extreme right; the heating plant for the capitol building is next to it. The Masonic Temple can be seen just to the left of Quarrier Street. The top of the Union Building can be seen just left of the Masonic Temple. The corner of Virginia and McFarland streets is to the extreme left. COURTESY MRS. LOWELL WARNER

Life in the County: 1865-1918

When the Civil War finally ended, in April 1865, Charleston residents celebrated by holding a parade down Cox's Lane (now Capitol Street). The April 12, 1865, issue of the *West Virginia Journal* reported that Colonel J.H. Ohley led the parade, followed by the first New York Veteran's Cavalry Band, soldiers and citizens of the Kanawha Council, an old hearse with "secession" painted on both sides, and a wagon with an effigy of Jefferson Davis hanging from a "sour apple tree."

Unlike the rest of the vanquished South, the end of the war did not bring about the harsh realities of reconstruction life in Kanawha County, but nevertheless the terrible conflict profoundly changed the area. The new state of West Virginia was born out of the strife, and West Virginians were no longer tied to their eastern neighbors. The citizens of the western part of Virginia had always felt separate from the eastern Virginians and now they were on their own.

Additional changes were on the horizon. There were no longer slaves to work in the salt industry that was devastated by the war and the discoveries of salt deposits farther to the west. The wealth of the county's old families and new entrepreneurs that once depended on salt was replaced by the emerging timber and coal industries.

In the 1870s, the financial fabric of the county was also changed by the extension of the C&O Railway through the Kanawha Valley, and the construction of branch lines into the drainages. As the railroads provided easy transportation to both eastern and western markets, coal became king.

Kanawha Salines became just another small village in the valley, as Charleston increased in size and stature to become the dominant town in the county, and eventually the state. Charleston's predominance was augmented when the state capitol was moved from Wheeling to Charleston in 1870. Dr. John P. Hale and others put up the money to build the first capitol building at a site on Cox's Lane far in from the main part of town which was along the Kanawha River. Hale would also build his Hale House in 1872, second only to the capitol building in size, and one of the finest hotels in the new state.

Several large churches were constructed in the 1870s; the Cotton Opera House and the Union School were opened in 1870. John Brisben Walker, a young industrious businessman, bought a large tract of land on Charleston's West Side in 1870. Walker laid out streets and lots, and then heavily promoted his development, Elk City. In 1873 he built the Keystone Bridge over Elk River to tie Elk City to Charleston.

A constitutional convention, the second in the new state's history, was held in Charleston from January 16 to April 9, 1872, and John A. Warth and Edward B. Knight represented Kanawha County. The convention was first held in the capitol, and was then moved to the Asbury Chapel.

Five years after Charleston was chosen as the state capitol, the state legislature again decided to move the capitol to Wheeling. This vacillation between sites finally ended in 1877, when a statewide election was held to select a permanent capitol site. Charleston won the election (Wheeling wasn't even on the ballot), and eight years later, the state capitol was moved to its permanent home in the Kanawha Valley.

American life radically changed in the decades between the end of the Civil War and the beginning of the 1900s. Inventions and civic improvements were rapidly improving the standard of life in the country. In Kanawha County, citizens benefited from innovations such as Hale and Levi's first brick pavement on Summers Street, horse-drawn and later electric street cars, natural gas-lit street lamps, improved water, gas and electric service, the telephone, improved medical facilities, railroads, the first bridge across the Kanawha in 1891, and finally the automobile and the airplane.

The industrial growth in the county was rapid from the end of the nineteenth century through World War I. In 1883 Will, Fred and Arch Staunton established one of the first ice manufacturing plants in the country. Known as the Diamond Ice Factory, it was built in Charleston. Glass manufacturing came first to South Charleston and then to Kanawha City. Ward Engineering Works opened a boat yard on Charleston's south side, Kelly Axe moved in on the west side, and other plants that manufactured wood products, woolens, and other items were established up and down the Kanawha Valley. Before World War I, the fledgling chemical industry was expanded when large, war-time industrial complexes were built in South Charleston, and in the new town of Nitro at the county's western border.

John E. Kenna was one of the most prominent citizens of the county in the late 1800s. He was born in 1848, served in the Confederate Army and admitted to the bar in 1868. He was elected county prosecuting attorney in 1872, a judge in 1875, a U.S. Congressman in 1876, 1878, 1880 and 1882 and a U.S. Senator in 1883 and 1889. He led the fight to make Charleston the state capitol. He died in Washington D.C. at the age of 45. swv

Henry Gassaway Davis left his mark on Charleston in a number of ways. He was a very successful coal, timber and railroad baron who donated property and money for the Davis Child Shelter and the YMCA. He was a candidate for vice-president of the U.S. in 1904 as the running mate of the unsuccessful Democrat, Alton B. Parker. swv

Oil and gas deposits were discovered in Blue Creek, Paint Creek and Cabin Creek, and their rapid development created a boom in these areas, and over the next few years spawned other related industries. By the start of World War I, Kanawha County lead the nation in coal, oil and gas production, and it was beginning to be known as a center for industrial production.

In 1884 Charleston built the first city hall at its present location, and in 1892 the county opened its magnificent new stone courthouse. The federal government built a new post office in 1884, and again in 1911 on the same site. The Hale House burned down in 1885 and the new Ruffner Hotel was built in its place. Other hotels were built in Charleston, which was rapidly becoming the retail and wholesale center for southern West Virginia. On its centennial in 1894, Charleston had a population of 8,000, the third largest city in West Virginia, behind Huntington and Wheeling. Several years later, the city's boundaries were extended to include the Upper Ruffner area to Michigan Avenue to the east, and Walker's Elk City development to the west.

On July 4, 1891, a tragic accident occurred when a Kanawha and Michigan train with two loaded passenger cars left the Charleston station for a picnic in Putnam County. At a trestle crossing near Dunbar, the engineer noticed that the trestle was on fire, and he sped up the train to cross it. The engine and mail car made it across, but the two passenger cars toppled over the side of the weakened trestle and plunged into a ravine 20 feet below. Sixteen passengers were killed and about 50 were injured in the worst train wreck in the county's history.

Democratic and Conservative Platform.

Resolutions adopted by the Democratic and Conservative Senatorial Convention for the Seventh Senatorial District, held at Charleston, on Wednesday, September 27th, 1871.

The Democratic and Conservative party of the Seventh Senatorial District, in Convention assembled, desirous of redeeming the pledges of reform which they have given, and believing that no measures of reform will be permanent and effective that do not go the root of the evil under which we have suffered—a bad constitution—present the following platform of principles for the honest consideration of the voters of the Seventh Senatorial District:

1. We are in favor of such a change in the County and Township organization of the State as will secure simplicity, economy and honesty in county administration. We believe that a reduction of the number of useless office-holders and a more rigid accountability of those who have the levying, collection and disbursement of the public taxes, will accomplish this.

2. We are in favor of making the Judiciary a free and independent department of the government; and placing it beyond the influence and control of the Legislature.

3. We are in favor of constitutional guarantees to a liberal and effective free school system; providing at the same time for its honest and economical administration.

4. We are in favor of a constitutional prohibition against the use of the credit of the State in the construction of works of internal improvement.

5. We are in favor of a prohibition in the constitution against the enactment of test oaths and proscriptive legislation.

6. We are in favor of equal and fair representation in the government, based upon population.

7. We are in favor of taxation based upon property, and believe that no capitation tax should be imposed, which will bear oppressively upon the people.

8. We believe that the Legislature should meet only once in two years, and that the time thereof should be occupied in the enactment of wholesome laws for the general good, and not in private and class legislation. Relief should be given in individual cases, by the courts, under the provisions of general laws.

We believe that a wise reform of the constitution upon these principles will greatly conduce to the welfare and honor of the State.

Democratic and Conservative Ticket.

For Senator from 7th Senatorial District,
Dr. M. R. HEREFORD, of Nicholas.

For Delegates to Constitutional Convention from 7th Senatorial District,
NICHOLAS FITZHUGH, of Kanawha,
ALONZO M. CUSHING, of Mason.

Kanawha County Ticket.

For Delegates to Constitutional Convention,
JOHN A. WARTH,
EDWARD B. KNIGHT.

For House of Delegates,
Dr. A. E. SUMMERS, and
JOHN D. LEWIS,

For Superintendent of Free Schools,
WILLIAM L. HINDMAN.

Democratic State Ticket.
Election October 14, 1884.

For Governor,
E. WILLIS WILSON,
Of Kanawha County.

For Auditor,
PATRICK F. DUFFEY,
Of Webster County.

For Treasurer,
WM. T. THOMPSON,
Of Cabell County.

For Attorney General,
ALFRED CALDWELL.
Of Ohio County.

For Superintendent of Free Schools,
B. S. MORGAN,
Of Monongalia County.

For Judge of Supreme Court of Appeals,
A. C. SNYDER,
Of Greenbrier County.

For Judge of Supreme Court of Appeals for unexpired term of A.F. Haymond,
SAMUEL WOODS,
Of Barbour County.

For Senator—9th Senatorial District.
WM. H. HOOVER,
Of Webster County.

Democratic County Ticket.

For House of Delegates,
J. H. FERGUSON,
A. H. WILSON,
PHILIP GOLDEN.

For Clerk of Circuit Court,
SAM'L D. LITTLEPAGE.

For Clerk of the County Court,
W. B. DONNALLY.

For Sheriff,
R. R. DELANEY.

For Prosecuting Attorney,
W. E. CHILTON.

For Assessor—Lower District,
I. C. VANDINE.

For Assessor—Upper District,
A. T. CABELL.

For Surveyor,
A. P. SINNETT.

For Commissioner of County Court,
JOHN LEONARD.

Malden District Ticket.

For Justices,
J. S. RUFFNER,
JAMES R. ROBERTS.

For Constables,
CHAS. F. SPRIGGLE,
JAMES D. GARDNER.

Constitutional Amendment, Section Seven, Article Four,
For Ratification.

City of Charleston.
Democratic Municipal Ticket.
Election, March 14, 1881.

FOR MAYOR,
R. R. DELANEY

FOR RECORDER,
DAVIS H. ESTILL.

FOR SERGEANT,
E. M. STONE.

FOR TREASURER,
C. C. LEWIS.

FOR COUNCILMAN,
First Ward..............
Second Ward..............
Third Ward..............

People's State Ticket.
Election, October 14th, 1884.

FOR GOVERNOR,
EDWIN MAXWELL.
Of Harrison County.

FOR AUDITOR,
J. H. BURTT,
Of Ohio County.

FOR TREASURER,
S. W. STURM,
Of Marion County.

FOR ATTORNEY-GENERAL,
JOHN A. HUTCHINSON,
Of Wood County.

FOR SUPERINTENDENT OF FREE SCHOOLS,
J. N. KENDALL,
Of Ritchie County.

FOR JUDGE SUPREME COURT OF APPEALS
W. H. H. FLICK,
Of Berkeley County.

FOR JUDGE SUPREME COURT OF APPEALS
For Unexpired Term of A.F. Haymond
J. H. BROWN,
Of Kanawha County.

FOR SENATOR—9TH SENATORIAL DISTRICT
J. W. MORRISON, JR.,
Of Braxton County.

People's County Ticket.

FOR HOUSE OF DELEGATES,
H. C. McWHORTER.
JAMES B. FLEMING.
A. A. ROCK.

FOR CLERK OF THE CIRCUIT COURT,
SAM'L. D. LITTLEPAGE.

FOR CLERK OF THE COUNTY COURT,
CHAS. B. SMITH.

FOR SHERIFF,
L. H. EWART.

FOR PROSECUTING ATTORNEY,
W. E. CHILTON.

FOR ASSESSOR—LOWER DISTRICT,
J. B. MAIRS.

FOR ASSESSOR—UPPER DISTRCT,
A. T. CABELL.

FOR SURVEYOR,
SYLVESTER CHAPMAN.

FOR COUNTY COMMISSIONER,
W. B. CALDERWOOD.

Malden District.

FOR JUSTICES,
R. E. PUTNEY,
JOHN BRACKER.

FOR CONSTABLES,
WM. ABBOTT,
WM. H. YOUNG.

Constitutional Amendment, Section Seven, Article Four.

FOR RATIFICATION.

"At present, streets have been extended in all directions...as fast as they opened they have been built up with neat, elegant and in many cases expensive residences. During the past two years alone, the number of new houses most probably would be between 300 or 400."

—David Hunter Strother, The Capitol of West Virginia and the Great Kanawha Valley; Advantages, Resources and Prospects, 1872

The worst flood since 1861 hit Charleston and surrounding towns on February 23, 1897. The Cabin Creek area experienced another disastrous flood in 1916 that wiped out many homes and businesses. The Elk River suspension bridge, built in 1852, fell into the river on an icy December morning in 1904, killing two schoolchildren and a number of horses.

In the years before World War I, the population of the county and the city almost doubled in size from 1900. By 1910 Charleston had miles of paved streets, electric street cars, 13 schools, 38 churches and four first-class hotels. The city's first skyscraper, the Alderson-Stephenson Building (Union Building), was built in 1911. Luna Park opened in 1912, and the Kanawha City Bridge built in 1915 opened up this vast flat area for development. Other parts of the county, including St. Albans, South Charleston, Handley, and Clendenin were also rapidly increasing in size.

This building was located on the south side of Kanawha Street, four lots east of Capitol Street. Upstairs was the Jeffrey Manufacturing Co., which served the coal industry. D.W. Patterson's window carries an advertisement for transatlantic ship passage via the Anchor Line from New York to Glasgow. The car is a 1904 Model Oldsmobile with a steering tiller instead of a wheel. The Daily Mail moved its office sometime after 1904, when this picture was taken. All the buildings on the south side of Kanawha Street were demolished in the late 1930s for construction of the boulevard.
COURTESY CHUCK GARDNER

Corner of Virginia and Summers streets, 1907. Building in the background is the Kanawha Hotel. RA

Hale House was Charleston's and the state's finest hotel when it was built in 1872 by John P. Hale. It was second in size only to the state capitol building. It had 100 bedrooms, but only one bathroom. Built at a cost of $150,000 on the corner of Kanawha and Hale streets, it would host people from all over the world until burning down in 1885. The elegant Ruffner Hotel was built in its place.

COURTESY OTIS K. RICE

Hale House Dance.

You are Respectfully Invited to attend a Dance to be given at the

Hale House, Friday, Aug. 19, 1881.

JARRETT & ESTILL'S CITY DIRECTORY.

HALE HOUSE,
Charleston, W. Va.

The Leading Hotel of the City

Complete in all its Appointments

FOR THE

COMFORT AND PLEASURE OF ITS GUESTS.

Telegraph & Express Offices in Hotel.

LARGE AND WELL ARRANGED

SAMPLE ROOMS
FOR
Commercial Travelers.

BILLIARD ROOM WITH NEW AND ELEGANT TABLES.

Board $2.00 Per Day.

E. O. PEYTON, *Superintendent.*   J. M. FITZ, *Proprietor.*

Merry Christmas!   Merry Christmas!

HALE HOUSE,

FITZ & WOODWARD, Prop'rs,

CHRISTMAS DAY.

SOUP.
CREME OF CHICKEN.

BOILED.
SUGAR CURED HAM, WINE SAUCE.   LEG OF MUTTON, CAPER SAUCE.
TURKEY, OYSTER SAUCE.

ROAST.
RIBS OF BEEF.   TURKEY DRESSED WITH OYSTERS,
LOIN OF MUTTON,   SHOAT.

ENTREES.
BEEF TONGUE, TOMATO SAUCE.   ESCOLLOPED OYSTERS.
MACARONI AU GRATIN,
BEEF A LA MODE,   CAICKEN SALADE.

COLD DISHES
BEEF,   SHOAT.
HAM,
MUTTON.
PRESSED CORNED BEEF.

VEGETABLES.
POTATO CROQUETTES,
STEWED TOMATOES.
BAKED SWEET POTATOES.
CORN,   LIMA BEANS,

RELISHES
WORCESTER SAUCE,   MIXED PICKLES.   CHOW CHOW.
FRENCH MUSTARD,
CELERY,   CRANBERRY SAUCE.

PASTRY AND DESSERT
PEACH ICE CREAM.   ENGLISH PLUM PUDDING, WINE SAUCE.
MINCE PIE,   APPLE PIE.   BLACKBERRY PIE.
FRUIT CAKE,   POUND CAKE.   LADY CAKE,   JELLY CAKE.
BANANAS,   PECANS
LAYER RAISINS,
FILBERTS,   CRACKERS.   CHEESE,   COFFEE.

Evening Call.

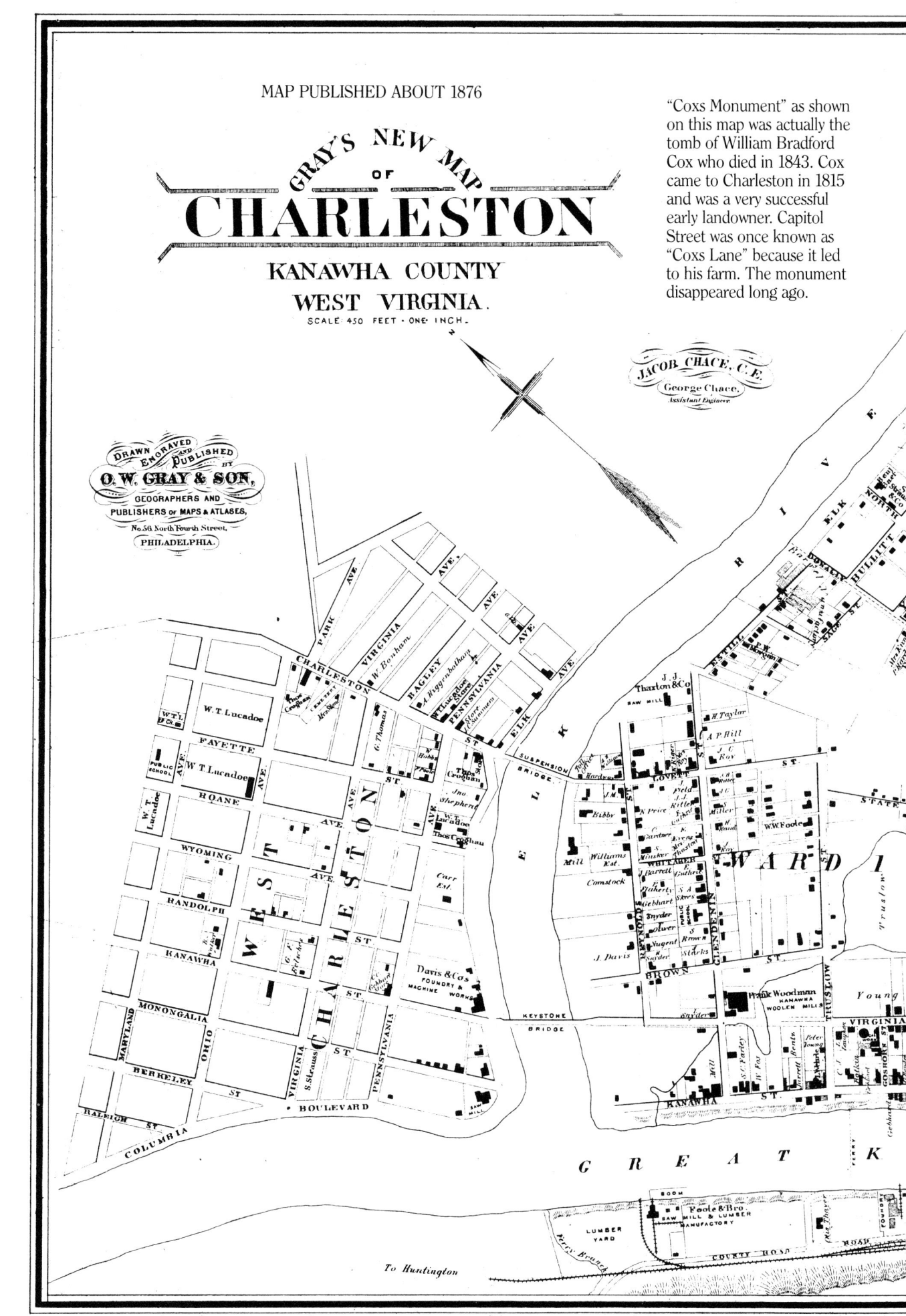

MAP PUBLISHED ABOUT 1876

GRAY'S NEW MAP OF CHARLESTON KANAWHA COUNTY WEST VIRGINIA.
SCALE: 450 FEET - ONE INCH.

"Coxs Monument" as shown on this map was actually the tomb of William Bradford Cox who died in 1843. Cox came to Charleston in 1815 and was a very successful early landowner. Capitol Street was once known as "Coxs Lane" because it led to his farm. The monument disappeared long ago.

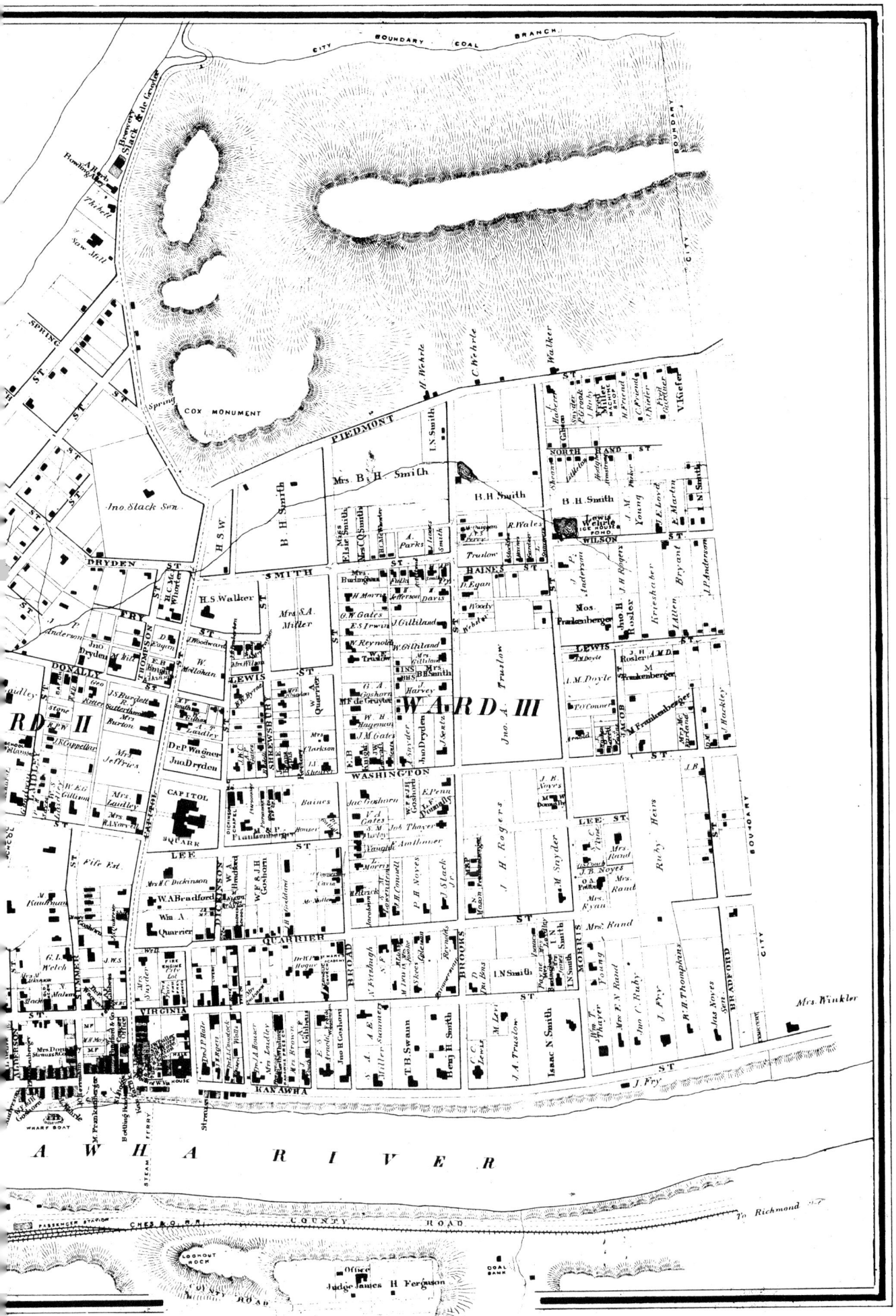

John Brisben Walker (1847-1931) purchased a large tract of land on Charleston's west side, laid out town lots and connected his new development to downtown Charleston via the Keystone Bridge across Elk River. Walker established the *Charleston Herald* in 1870. He left Charleston in 1873 and pursued careers as a newspaper editor, rancher, owner of *Cosmopolitan* magazine and manufacturer of steam automobiles.
COURTESY OTIS K. RICE

William MacCorkle (1857-1930) left his mark on Kanawha County in a number of ways. Born in Virginia and raised in Missouri, he moved to Charleston in 1879 to practice law. He was elected governor of the state in 1893 and U.S. Senator in 1910. He was involved in the early street car system, Kanawha City development, banking and other business enterprises. In 1905 he built Sunrise in South Hills. SWV

LOTS
IN THE
CITY OF CHARLESTON.
THE CAPITAL OF WEST VA.

5,000 INHABITANTS.

GROWING LIKE A WESTERN TOWN.

Cheap Lots for Laborers and Mechanics, within half a mile of Capitol building,
40x130 feet—Price $250.

Next grade of Lots within one-fourth mile of Capitol building,
50x105 feet—Price $400.

Choice Residence Lots on Virginia street, the grand street of the city,
Lots 193 feet deep—Price $20 per front foot.

Magnificent Lots with river frontage, clear outlook upon river and railroad, no structure to intervene rare and choice,
Lots 250 feet deep—Price $50 per front foot.
Alleys in rear of all Lots.

TERMS GUARANTEED TO SUIT.

Any one who will agree to build a house on any of the above lots to suit the surroundings, can purchase on *five annual payments with interest from date of purchase* and NO CASH.

Valuable coal property on south side of Kanawha river, within one mile of Charleston and one-fourth mile of C. & O. R. R., for sale at $20 per acre, on easy terms, or for lease on royalty.

Timber lands of choicest quality on Elk River, convenient of access.

Large interests in extra-valuable coal lands on Kanawha River in process of partition.

This is not an agency. Am selling my own property. No delay to consult other parties. Titles unquestioned. Can suit in property, terms and title if anybody in Kanawha can.

Isaac N. Smith,
Charleston, Kanawha Co., W. Va.

The only known interior views of The Arcade in downtown Charleston. It was built in 1895 by John T. Cotton and E.W. Wilson. Cotton had earlier built the Cotton Opera House and Wilson, his son-in-law, was elected Governor of West Virginia in 1884. The building was unique—it had a two-story atrium interior which allowed light in through panels of iron-framed glass supported by iron trusses. The building remains virtually unaltered. PM

The Evening Call.

VOL. 2.   CHARLESTON, W. VA., FRIDAY, FEBRUARY 23, 1883.   NO 219

THE EVENING CALL.
SWANN & WARREN.

LOCAL TIME TABLE.

The following local time table took effect on the Chesapeake & Ohio Railway Sunday December 24, 1882, at 10 A. M:
WESTWARD.—No. 3, arrives 7:22 A. M.
" No. 5, 2:50 P. M.
EASTWARD. No. 4, 7:22 A. M.
" No. 6, 12:45 P. M.

☞ All the trains run by Washington city time, which is 18 minutes faster than Charleston time.

ANNOUNCEMENTS.

☞ All Announcements for office must be paid for before insertion.

FOR MAYOR.

At the earnest solicitation of many friends I hereby announce myself as a candidate for the office of Mayor of the city of Charleston, subject to the action of the Republican Primary, to be held on February 24th next.
LOVELL C. GATES.

Please announce J. D. Baines as a candidate for the Mayoralty. We hardly think it necessary to assure the people of Charleston that Mr. Baines will fill the place faithfully and well. HIS FRIENDS.

I respectfully announce myself as a candidate for Mayor of the City of Charleston at the coming election, subject to the action of a Citizens' Mass Convention. I pledge myself to institute and practice a progressive reform policy if elected.
JOHN S. BURDETT.

FOR CITY SERGEANT.

I announce myself as a candidate for City Sergeant, subject to the decision of the voters of the city of Charleston.
ALEX SUMMERS.

By the request of many friends, I hereby announce myself as a candidate for the office of City Sergeant, subject to the decision of the citizens, If elected I will give good bonds and discharge my duties faithfully.
J. C. HERMANN.

I am a candidate for the nomination for City Sergeant in the Citizens' Convention. I am not the candidate of any party, clique or ring, but want the office, because I am prepared to attend to its duties. I would give strong security and do my whole duty to the people.
Very Respectfully,
ALE. W. BURNETT.

FOR CITY RECORDER.

At the solicitation of many friends, Wm. Fox, Jr., has consented to become a candidate for City Recorder, subject to the decision of the Republican primary election. This announcement is endorsed by both Republicans and Democrats. MANY FRIENDS.

We respectfully announce J. T. Brodt as a candidate for the office of City Recorder. Mr. Brodt has heretofore filled the office to the satisfaction of our citizens, and we feel confident that he will, if elected, faithfully perform the duties of the office.
MANY CITIZENS.

I hereby announce myself as a candidate for re-election for the office of City Recorder, at the ensuing municipal election.
D. H. ESTILL.

I hereby announce myself as a candidate for City Recorder to be voted for at the coming city election. If chosen for this office, I will transact all business faithfully and satisfactorily. JIM CARR.

CITY TREASURER.

C. C. Lewis is announced as a candidate for City Treasurer.
BY MANY FRIENDS.

W. W. TOMPKINS, M. D.
PHYSICIAN & SURGEON.
CHARLESTON, W. VA.

Office in Lawrence Block, Capitol St.

☞ Prompt attention given to calls day and night.

SCRAPS.

The postoffice at Liberty, Putnam county, has been abolished.

The candidates are treating, and the dead-beats are beating.

The damage on the O. C. Railroad is not as bad as thought to be.

Baylus Cabe, of Scott's Depot, has been granted a patent on a car coupling.

Fred Gardner informs us that he is not a candidate for Councilman from the Third Ward.

The Republican candidates will battle with the ballots to-morrow. The candidates are working hard to-day in order to see who will come out of the wreck whole.

The Western Union Telegraph line, between this city and Pt. Pleasant has been repaired. It was broken in several places and held under the water by drifts.

We understand John R. Couch, a farmer of Mason county and brother of our fellow-citizen Geo. S. Couch, met with heavy losses by the recent floods. He lost all of his last year's crop besides his barns.

The many friends of Mrs. Guthrie, who lived in North Charleston, will regret to learn of her death, which occurred this morning. Deceased was one of our older citizens and was highly respected by all who knew her.

The Point Pleasant Register says:
"The engineer corps of the Ohio River Railroad reached this place on yesterday morning. Their line runs along the Ohio river all the way from Parkersburg to this place, its terminus."

A new poet has come upon the horizon in the person of Bro. Lacy, of the Huntington News. He got off some villianously good hog poetry this week, and published it in his paper. We wish he would come up to our city and drive away our hogs with his poetry.— It is sure shot at long range.

We understand that a company is being organized in Wheeling to manufacture scales patented by Geo. W. Craig, formerly a resident of Mason county, but now a resident of this city. The scales are said to be superior to any now made. We hope that Mr. Craig has struck luck, as he deserves it.

Yesterday afternoon Drs. Barber and Comstock, of this city, amputated a leg of Brown Burford, son of Kemper Burford, who resides on Rocky Fork, of Poca. The leg was amputated about the middle of the thigh. Mr. Burford has been suffering with cancer for some time, which necessitated the surgical operation. The amputated limb was brought to the city by Dr. Barber.

New dress goods constantly arriving at 5c Store. The prices will be the lowest in this city, every time.

Venetian damask table linen at 5c. Store. Colors warranted.

Best value in linen towels in Charleston at 5c. Store.

FOUND—A valuable key, which the owner can have by calling at this office and paying charges.

For the nobbiest hat in the city go to Harmison's New Clothing House.

FOR SALE.—A fire-proof Diebold safe, nearly new, and in good condition. Apply at this office.

PERSONAL.

Joe Silverman, of Galipolis, everybody's friend, is at the Hale.

Mrs. Wm. Estell, who has been sick for several weeks, is convalescing.

A. Barlew has returned home from a trip to the Sunny South looking well.

Jas. S. Atkinson, deputy U. S. Marshal, has returned from Jackson county.

Chas. Wilcox, who has been engaged in business in Alabama for sometime past, has returned.

Mrs. Wm. Wright and Miss Ferguson, who are visiting relatives in New Orleans, will return home in a few days.

Nonpareil Henderson is going to Richmond next week. The lunch routes will suffer while our esteemed friend is in the ex-Capitol of the South.

Capt. J. M. Fitz, proprietor of the Hale House, and family are visiting friends in Staunton. Capt. Cartmell is the handsome manager during the boss' absence.

Best muslin for the money in this town at 5c. Store.

Standard Prints of best makes and styles at 5c. Store, at their well known low figures.

New fancy brocade ribbon at 5c. Store.

They always sell ribbons at 5c. Store way down in price.

A genuine bargain in bedspreads at 5c. Store.

LOST.
A part book sleeve button (the button.) Finder please return to Phil. Frankenberger.

If you want a nice collar, cuff, scarf or anything usually kept in a first-class clothing house go to Harmison's. wedpt

Go to Crigg's for Mason county mutton.

Good navy jeans pants, lined through and through, at $4 at Harmison's Clothing House.

Largest assortment of glassware in W. Va. can be found at 5c. Store.

New branded chamber sets at 5c. Store.

House keepers all go to the 5c. Store, as they keep everything and sell at reasonable figures.

CARD NOTICE.
I am not a candidate for Councilman from the Second Ward, as I do not wish it; thanking my friends. I respectfully decline in favor of James F. Brown, who has heretofore served the City so faithfully.
w20rw VAL KIEFER, Sr.

For the best of ginger ale call at Rummel's manufactory, wholesale or retail.

FOR SALE.—A portable steam saw mill, in first-class order and with all the attachments. Apply to
HENRY WHITTEKER.

If you want to save from $2 to $5 on a suit of clothing go to Harmison's Clothing House.

FOR SALE.—A residence with 12 rooms, on a lot 118 x 8 feet. Will be sold for half cash, balance in one and two years. Apply to Editor CALL.

Social Entertainment at State Street M. E. Church.

The ladies of Section A, return thanks to a generous public for their patronage at the social last evening. The musical and literary entertainment in connection therewith was a decided success. A few deserve special mention. Miss McChesney, the little daughter of the Front street merchant, recited on Indian legend, which showed her to be far advanced for one of her age, and the great applause which followed indicated the feelings of the audience. The Ewart Band discoursed some of their sweetest and best music, which made all hearts glad. The instrumental duet "Take Back the Heart" by Miss Margie and Master Charlie Ewart was exceptionally good and received hearty applause. Solo and chorus by Mr. Will Moore and others, same by Miss Blandon and others, solo by Miss Mema Gates, quartette by Mr. Spargo and others, instrumental duet by Misses Martin and Shideler, solo by Mr. Lewis, and two or three readings completed the programme. Oysters, ice-cream and cake were slaughtered badly. In short, success expresses the idea. Proceeds $35 53.

A magnificent suit of clothes for $5 00 at the Variety Store of R. W. Workman.

SHIRTS! SHIRTS!!
Percale shirts, with two collars, only 50c. Good white shirts, Sine flax refused Laundried, at 75c, by R. W. WORKMAN.

Cincinnati Enquirer : The trial of Craft and Neal is costing the State of Kentucky a trifle of $3,000 a day. Almost as bad as a flood.

Portsmouth Times : The trial of Craft and Neal still drags along. It looks as if Blackburn & Co. are determined to clear them if possible. It is remarked that some one has employed the Lexington lawyer, who has money, to defend them.

☞ For bargains in Boots and Shoes go to R. W. Workman's Variety Store, Botkin Building.

If you want a nice bedspread for $1, that sells everywhere for $1.25, call at R. W. Workman's.

SEED OATS! SEED OATS!!
We have just received a large supply of black and white seed oats, which can be had at our mill cheap.
MORGAN MILL CO

FOR SALE.
I have several thousand fire brick, for sale suitable for setting boilers, grates, &c. Inquire at the foundry on Elk, or store on Front street, opp. St. Albert.
GEO. DAVIS.

Old age is honorable, but when kicked out for being too old like Lewis Wehrle's Boom Bonded Bourbon Whiskey has been by Uncle Sam, it is too hard and you should sympathize with old age by giving Mr. Wehrle a call.

For Sale.
Three draft horses; two sets harness, and two wagons—all in good condition. Enquire of Snedor & Burdett for terms.

Fresh butter, 20c. at Shrewsbury & Shorrock.

BOOKS! BOOKS!! BOOKS!!!
A large variety of books for young and old just received at Mrs. Donnally's.

Fresh extra select oysters received daily at Schwartz's.

JARRETT & ESTILL'S CITY DIRECTORY.   23

THE NEW ERA.

TRUNKS & VALISES

TRADE WITH

B. GALLENBERG,

Best and Cheapest Place

FOR

EXCLUSIVE LINE OF

GENTS' FURNISHING GOODS!

LATEST STYLES

HATS, CAPS

UMBRELLAS, &C.

REMEMBER THE PLACE.

Opposite Public Landing,   Charleston, West Va

---

30   SHEPPARD'S CHARLESTON DIRECTORY.

JAMES H. ROGERS,

FIRST STREET,

Charleston, W. Va.

DEALER IN

DRUGS, MEDICINES, CHEMICALS, FINE TOILET SOAPS, FANCY HAIR AND TOOTH BRUSHES, PERFUMERY AND FANCY TOILET ARTICLES, TRUSSES AND SHOULDER BRACES, GARDEN SEEDS, PURE WINES AND LIQUORS FOR MEDICINAL PURPOSES, PAINTS OILS, VARNISHES & DYE STUFFS, LETTER PAPER PENS, INK, ENVELOPES, GLASS, PUTTY, OIL, LAMPS AND CHIMNEYS,

Physicians Prescriptions Accurately Compounded.

Assembly Rooms' RESTAURANT,

WILLIAM GRAMM, PRO'R.

Cor. Kanawha & Summers,

[UP STAIRS.]

SELECTED OYSTERS STEWED — GAME HOT COFFEE SARDINES — PIGS FEET

OYSTERS, FISH, GAME,

And all the Delicacies of the Season

CONSTANTLY ON HAND.

Office Saloon—In the Basement.

Choice Wines, Liquors, Cigars, &c.

E. J. HANEY, SUPERINTENDENT.

W. B. WATKINS & CO.

WHOLESALE AND RETAIL DEALERS IN

SUGAR MOLASSES, TEAS, COFFEE SPICES,

Cigars, Smoking and Chewing Tobacco, Nuts, Fish, SOAP, CANDLES, DYE-STUFFS, STARCH, SALARATUS, SODA, FRUITS RICE, CORDAGE, WRAPPING PAPER AND TWINE,

AND ALL KINDS OF GROCERIES.

HIGHEST CASH PRICE PAID FOR ALL COUNTRY PRODUCE.

Front Street,   CHARLESTON WEST VA

THE KANAWHA DAILY,

The Daily is furnished at the following rates:

One year, - - - - $6.00
Six months, - - - - 3 00
Three months - - - 1.50

The KANAWHA DAILY is published in the interests of the State, regardless of politics.

KANAWHA PUBLISHING CO.

Charleston, West Va.

BOGGS AND RANDOLPH.

WHOLESALE AND RETAIL DRUGGISTS.

DEALERS IN

DRUGS, MEDICINES, PAINTS, OILS VARNISHES, &C., &C.,

Particular attention given to orders from Physicians and Merchants in the country.

Kanawha Valley Bank Building.

Charleston West Va.

H. POINDEXTER.   A. A. PRESTON.

POINDEXTER AND PRESTON.

[Opposite First National Bank.]

WHOLESALE AND RETAIL DEALERS IN

GROCERIES AND TOBACCO.

AGENTS FOR

CHOICE BRANDS, VIRGINIA CHEWING AND SMOKING TOBACCO.

CHARLESTON, W. VA.

Produce sold on commission.

No Wharfage Charged on Goods Shipped by Us.

Charleston, W. Va. Dec 1893

M Kanawha Presby Church

Bought of **GEO. W. GATES,**

— DEALER IN —

Hardware, Glass, Sash, Blinds, Doors,

FLUE AND SEWER PIPE, FIRE BRICK AND FIRE CLAY, LIME, CEMENT AND PLASTER,

BUILDING MATERIALS.   FARM AND GARDEN SEEDS.

10 PER CENT INTEREST CHARGED ON BILLS PAST DUE.   No. 31 COR. SUMMERS AND VIRGINIA STREETS.

---

90   Woodrow & Barbour's City Directory.

PHIL. FRANKENBERGER,

The

ONE PRICE CLOTHIER,

Warrants Every Article as Represented

STRICTLY ONE PRICE TO ALL.

No deviation allowed. Best goods at lowest prices.

Don't fail to call if in need of anything in his line.

Sign "Big Hat."   CHARLESTON, W. VA.

E. A. ANDRE,

PRACTICAL and THEORETICAL MUSICIAN.

TEACHER OF

Harmony and Piano and all Instruments in the Orchestra and Band.

CHARLESTON, WEST VA.

---

18   SHEPPARD'S CHARLESTON DIRECTORY.

MAMMOTH CLOTHING EMPORIUM.

M. KAUFMANN,

WHOLESALE AND RETAIL DEALER IN

Clothing and Gents' Furnishing Goods,

TRUNKS, VALISES AND TRAVELING BAGS.

COR. KANAWHA & SUMMERS STREETS.

— ALSO —

Dealer in Clothing, Boots, Shoes, Trunks, and General Assortment of Goods in my Line, on Kanawha Street, third door above Court House.

M. KAUFMANN,

CHARLESTON, W. VA.

☞ Special inducements offered to Wholesale Dealers.

MAY, 1874!

GREAT SALE OF LOTS.

THE undersigned will sell Five Hundred Town Lots, at the City of Coalsmouth, Kanawha County, W. Virginia, on the premises.

TERMS:

One-eighth cash, residue, seven equal annual payments, bearing interest. Deed with general warranty, and lien retained till paid.

T. B. SWANN,

CHARLESTON, W. VA

-210-

All claims for damages must be made within Ten Days.   Legal Interest charged on all accounts past due.   No wharfage on goods shipped by us.

Charleston, W. Va. May 31 1893

M Kanawha Presby- Church

Bought of **N. S. BURLEW,**
WHOLESALE AND RETAIL DEALER IN
GENERAL HARDWARE, IRON AND NAILS
Steel Plows, Blacksmith and Harvest Tools, Sash, Doors, Blinds Etc.
OPP. PUBLIC LANDING.
Nails and Horse Shoes CASH.

GEORGE RITTER & CO.
MANUFACTURERS OF
TIN, COPPER & SHEET IRON WARE,
AND DEALERS IN
COOK STOVES, HOUSE FURNISHING GOODS,
AGENTS FOR
Celebrated Cook Stove "Arlington"
CHARLESTON,
Kanawha County, West Va.

WILLIAM PARSONS,   WATSON EASTWOOD
J. W. M. APPLETON.   S. MINKER.
PARSONS, APPLETON & CO.,
KANAWHA MILLS,
AND LAUNDRY.
MANUFACTURERS OF
Flour, Meal, Woolen Goods,
Dealers in Coal, and General Merchandise,
CHARLESTON W. VA.

Terms

T. O. Charleston, W. Va., May 1 1893

M Kanawha Presbyterian Church

To **Elk Foundry and Machine Co.** Dr.
—Proprietors of—
Foundry, Stove Works and Machine Shops,
(Formerly Davis' Foundry, near Mouth Elk River.)
MANUFACTURERS OF
CASTINGS OF ALL KINDS IN IRON AND BRASS.
—Works in Elk City.—

1840.   ESTABLISHED.   1840.
The Old Reliable Democratic Newspaper
THE KANAWHA REPUBLICAN
For 1872 contains fifteen columns reading matter, and is one of the most interesting journals in the State. Subscription price only $2.00 per annum. The Book and Job Printing Office of the Republican is one of the best in this section of the country. Work done as well as in any other office.
CENTERS & DENNIS,
Proprietors.

J. C. WOLF & SON.
MANUFACTURES OF
TIN AND SHEET IRON WARE,
AND DEALERS IN
STOVES, HOLLOW WARE,
JAPAN & BRASS WARE, &C.,
Front Street, below Steamboat Landing,
CHARLESTON, WEST VA.

All kinds of JOB WORK promptly attended to.
Special attention given to ROOFING.

M   Charleston, W. Va.,   18

BOUGHT OF **J. BIBBY & BRO.,**
WHOLESALE AND RETAIL DEALERS IN
FLOUR, CORN, CORN MEAL AND GRAIN.
CASH PAID FOR GRAIN.

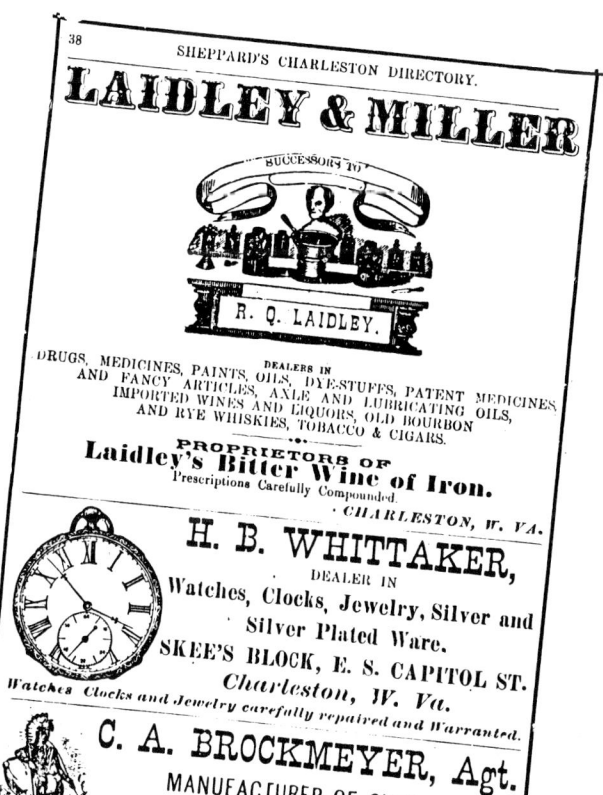

-211-

This imposing building housed the Kanawha Brewing Company. The business was established in 1903 on Bullitt Street. PM

For many years the K&M ticket office was next to the old Burlew Opera House building. KCL

Baird Hardware at 402 Charleston Street (now West Washington Street), early 1900s. COURTESY DANIEL DAVIDSON

The restored One Bridge Place adjacent to the South Side Bridge was built in 1897 by Lewis, Hubbard & Co. to replace their original building, destroyed by fire. It became the warehouse of Guthrie, Morris and Campbell & Co. in 1943. KCL

The Lowenstein Building at 223 Capitol Street was built in 1900 by S.M., Louis and Moses Lowenstein for their hardware business.

Some of Charleston's oldest buildings on Capitol Street. The buildings date from the 1890s. The building to the left housed Scott Brothers Drug Store at one time. The next building is the old Washburn Hotel, which also occupied a portion of the building to the left. The building to the right is the Mary Block, which housed S. Spencer Moore Co. KCL

The oldest business in Charleston under the same ownership, the S. Spencer Moore Co. was a fixture on Capitol Street for many years. Established in 1863 on Kanawha Street, it moved to the Cotton Opera Building on Capitol Street in 1872, to the Midelburg Building on Summers Street in 1884 and to its last location about 1890. The business closed in 1987.

At the turn of the 20th century the motorcycle competed with the automobile for the affection of the American motorist. Motorcycles were simple to maintain and could not be stopped by knee-deep mud. B.E. Andre is shown here in shirtsleeves in the doorway of his shop at 911 Quarrier in 1916. This site is now occupied by the city parking building. RA

One of Charleston's most well-known businesses was Joseph Popp, harness maker, at 613-15 Kanawha Street. The business started in 1885 and continued for over 70 years. KCL

The Idle Hour Billiard Parlor at 713 State Street.
COURTESY DOUG BUMGARTNER

Interior of a tea room that once did business in the Kay Jewelers building next to O.J. Morrison's on Capitol Street. PM

A very rare view of Charleston from Capitol Hill looking south. This exceptionally clear photo taken about 1905 shows the West Virginia capitol—the steepled building on the right—and its domed annex (later the library). Shrewsbury Street is visible at the left. It ran south to the old First Baptist Church, whose tower faces Washington Street. At the far left, the steeples of St. John's Episcopal Church and the Sacred Heart Catholic Church appear. The pillars of Governor MacCorkle's home "Sunrise," far away in the south hills, are on the right. The tops of freight cars on the K&M Railroad tracks next to Smith Street can be seen along the bottom of the photo. KCL

This 1905 photo, taken when old Charleston was in full bloom, depicts the fine homes of the residential district along the north end of Summers Street. Union School is visible in the center of the photo. Virtually everything in this picture has been replaced with new structures. KCL

A view to the west from Capitol Hill in 1905 showing the so-called "Triangle District," which was chiefly residential. Of particular interest is the roundhouse and locomotive servicing facilities of the CC&S Railroad. The circular device in the lower center is a railroad turntable which allowed the locomotives to be turned around and directed at whatever track was desired. Urban renewal and the interstate highway has transfigured most of the area. KCL

A 1905 view of Charleston along the Elk River. This photo is full of detail and gives a splendid look at a little photographed neighborhood. The large building near the center is the Kanawha Brewing Company on Bullitt Street whose product "wet the whistles" of thirsty customers for years. Just to its left are the twin bridges across Elk River. The nearest is the K&M Railroad bridge; the other is the interurban streetcar bridge. Just above them appears the smokestack of the interurban electric power house. In the lower part of the photo are the busy railroad tracks of the Charleston, Clendenin & Sutton Railroad, which later was taken over by the B&O. Note the small locomotive in the lower right corner going about its work with a trail of steam and smoke. KCL

Kanawha Street between Hale and Capitol about 1905, looking west. This interesting photo shows the pointed spire of the old Kanawha Valley Bank building (northwest corner of Kanawha and Capitol) being disassembled to prepare for new upper floors. The delightful circular street lights over the intersection can be clearly seen as well as the "Cotton Block" building which housed Beller's saloon. The Cotton Block was built in 1884 and still stands although the tempo of traffic on Kanawha Boulevard is considerably faster than it was in the horse-and-buggy days captured by this shot. KCL

When the Union Building was built by the Moore Construction Company in 1911, it was the largest commercial building in the city. Originally called the Alderson-Stephenson Building, the Union Trust Building, and finally the Union Building. It was the only building left on the south side of Kanawha Street, when the Boulevard was constructed in the late 1930s.
COURTESY MOORE CONSTRUCTION COMPANY

A most interesting river front view of Charleston's skyline in 1904. The large spired building on the right is the Ruffner Hotel. The spired building to the left is the Kanawha Bank. Both roof lines were altered in later years. The steamboat *Liberty* is docked at the city levee. KCL

Scott Brothers Drug Store

In the 1890s the Scott Brothers Drug Store was located at 124 Capitol Street. They built their permanent building on Capitol and Fife streets in 1892 but didn't move their business to it until 1914. The business lasted into the 1950s. After that the downstairs was occupied by a bakery. The building is now owned by the First Empire Federal Savings and Loan Association. SWV

Mr. Ray, manager of the drugstore, with photos of the Scott brothers, Winfield D. and George W. KCL

ICE CREAM 15 CENTS
Vanilla   Chocolate

ICE CREAM SODA 15 CENTS

FLAVORS

Chocolate Coffee Orange Strawberry Raspberry
Pineapple Vanilla Lemon Ginger
Red Cherry Sarsaparilla

PHOSPHATES ALL FLAVORS 5 CENTS

CRUSHED FRUITS

Pineapple 15c   Cherry 15c   Peach 20c

FANCY SUNDAES

North Pole - - - 20c   Marsh Mallow - - - 15c
Lover's Delight - - 20c   Maple Nut - - - 15c
Banana Special - - 25c   Malted Milk - - - 15c
Nut Chocolate - - 20c   Chocolate - - - 15c
Merry Widow - - 15c   With Whipped Cream - 20c
Double Sundae - - 20c   Peach Melba - - - 25c
Pineapple Special - 25c   Buffalo - - - 20c
Bitter Sweet - - 20c   Butter-scotch - - - 20c

EGG DRINKS

Egg Chocolate 20c   Egg Coffee 15c
Egg Malted Milk 20c   Egg Phosphate 15c
Egg Lemonade 20c   Egg and Milk 15c

PARFAIT

Cafe 20c   Chocolate 20c   Pineapple 20c   Nut 20c
Maple Nut 20c

FANCY MIXED DRINKS

Chocolate Frappe 20c   Malted Milk 15c
Chocolate Milk 10c   Grape Juice High Ball 15c
Frosted Chocolate 20c
Whipped Chocolate Milk 10c

MILK SHAKES ALL FLAVORS 15 CENTS

LEMONADES

Plain 10c   White Rock 20c
Egg 20c   Fruit 20c
Grape 15c   Mint 15c

LIMEADES

Plain 10c   Grape 20c

MISCELLANEOUS DRINKS

Root Beer 5c   Coca Cola 5c   Cream de Menthe 5c
Ginger Ale, C. & C., per Bottle - - 25c
Ginger Ale, Sheboygan, per Bottle - 15c
Grape Juice, per Bottle - - - 10c
Orange Juice - - - 10c

MINERAL WATERS

White Rock 15c   Red Raven 15c
French Vichy, per Bottle 20c

FOR HEADACHE 5 CENTS

Bromo Seltzer   Hicks' Capudine

Banks

The origin of this banknote is a mystery, as there is no indication of a Bank of Charleston prior to the Civil War.

1920s interior of the Kanawha National Bank at the northeast corner of Capitol and Virginia streets. This bank merged with another during the 1930s and the building was renamed the Security Building. This view shows the area that in later years was Frankenbergers' sales floor. It is now occupied by the Charleston Chamber of Commerce. KCL

The Kanawha National Bank Building stood at the northeast corner of Capitol and Virginia streets until it was torn down about 1914 to make way for the present Security Building. KCL

The Citizens National Bank Building on the southeast corner of Capitol and Quarrier streets. It still stands today, although much of the fine architectural trim has been removed over the years. SWV

Kanawha Valley Bank

Kanawha County's oldest existing bank was organized on April 8, 1867, by the Dickinsons and others. The three buildings shown here were all at the corner of Kanawha and Capitol streets. The first building (upper left) was the rebuilt Bank of Virginia. The second building (upper right) was built in 1870 and the third building (opposite) in 1894. This building was extensively remodelled in 1911 and was torn down in 1963. The bank moved to its second location in 1930 and its present location in the 1970s.
COURTESY KANAWHA VALLEY BANK & PM

The staff of the Kanawha Valley Bank in 1922. John L. Dickinson, president, is the white-haired man in the front row. COURTESY MRS. SARAH BING

The Kanawha Valley Bank Building shortly after completion in 1930. For many years this building was the tallest in the state and the pride of the city. LC

Early construction of the Kanawha Valley Bank showing the circular walks of the previous capitol building, which burned down. KCL

Foundation excavation for the Kanawha Valley Bank, looking west. KCL

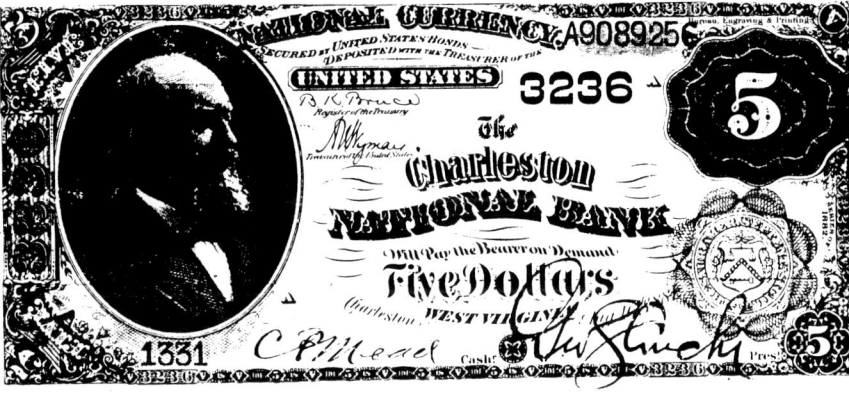

First five-dollar bill issued by the Charleston National Bank on August 16, 1884. It was signed by George Stribling Couch, Sr.

Upper left: The Charleston National Bank was organized in 1884. The bank's first location was on Kanawha Street. Its second location was on Virginia Street, currently the location of Arthur Treachers. The third location was on Capitol Street at KB&T's previous location, and the fourth location from 1906 to 1969, opposite the present public library. McDonalds now occupies this site. SWV

Upper right: The Kanawha Banking & Trust Company (now the United Bank) was organized in 1901. Its first location was 13 Capitol Street. C.C. Lewis, Sr. was the bank's first president. The bank moved to the corner of Capitol and Quarrier streets in 1903 and in 1918 to its large quarters opposite the present public library. The present bank building was built in the 1980s. AUTHOR'S COLLECTION

Coyle & Richardson Department Store at the corner of Lee and Capitol streets, 1915. In later years this building was occupied by the National Bank of Commerce. KCL

Victory Bond parade in 1918. Looking west on Virginia street from Capitol Street. Note the Arcade Building in the upper center. All the buildings on the right are still standing; those on the left were razed in 1962 for construction of the Charleston National Bank.
COURTESY MRS. KATHERINE KELLER

World War I was a time of great patriotic fervor in Kanawha County, and the many war-related industries in the valley brought the war close to home for the citizens. Hundreds of men enlisted soon after the United States entered the war on April 6, 1917, and Victory Loan parades and rallies raised thousands of dollars for the war effort in 1917 and 1918. The top left photo shows a bond parade on Virginia Street with the old Woodrum Furniture store in the background, the top right photo shows a parade down Kanawha Street, and the opposite photo was taken of a parade down Virginia Street. At the end of the parades, a rally was usually held extolling people to purchase bonds for the war effort. Famous entertainers and war heroes travelled throughout the country to appear at these rallies. Kanawha County provided 4,371 men to the armed forces. Of these, 120 were killed or died of diseases contracted during the war. WW & RA

Captain Timothy L. Barber, a native of Charleston, graduated from the Medical College of Virginia. He was the son of Dr. T.L. Barber, who established Kanawha Valley Hospital. The younger Dr. Barber set up his practice in Charleston. When America entered World War I, Dr. Barber established an Ambulance Unit composed mostly of Charleston natives. He later transferred to the 313th Infantry and was sent to France. In October 1918 Dr. Barber was severely burned by an explosion in a bomb crater that had been mined by the Germans. He died on October 10. His loss was deeply felt by the citizens of Charleston.

This remarkable photo taken in 1908 at the corner of Capitol and Quarrier streets shows a crowd waiting for a circus parade in the distance. A steam calliope can be seen down Capitol Street. Notice that Scott Brothers Drug Store was located south of Quarrier Street at this time. The lawn of the old post office is on the left. swv

This very rare photo shows George Beller's first saloon and billiard parlor in 1889 at its location in the St. Albert Hotel on Kanawha Street. COURTESY CLAUD KELLER

George Beller's Saloon occupied 812 Kanawha Street from 1890 to 1914. It was unquestionably Charleston's foremost tavern and a first-class establishment in every respect. "Uncle" George, as he was known, insisted on strict propriety and many of the city's best people were often seen here. The white towels hanging from the bar were for customer use in the event a glass of beer overflowed. The bar and all of Beller's fittings were the finest in the area. COURTESY CLAUD KELLER

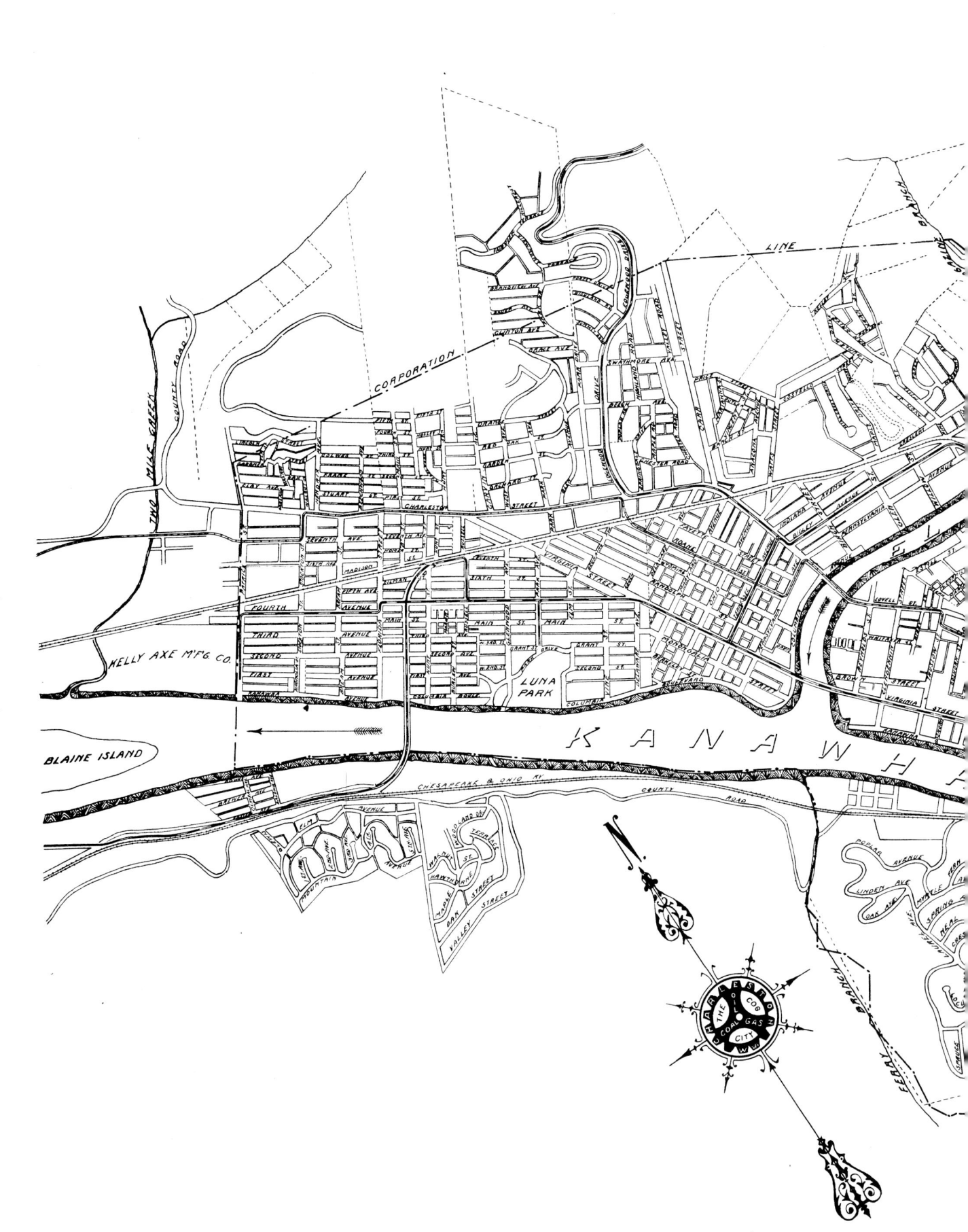

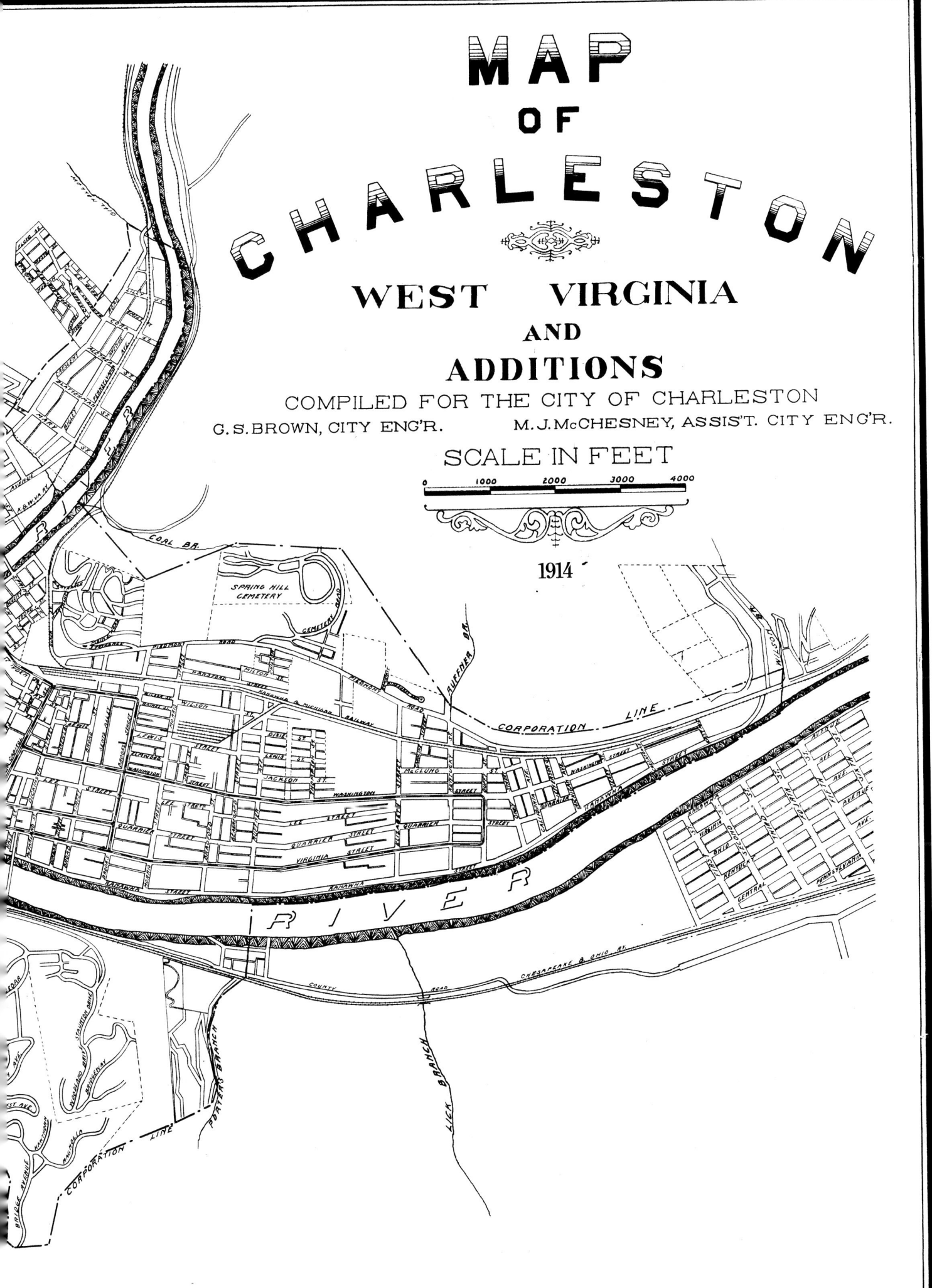

The work on the exterior was almost finished by March 31, 1931. The one-story connections between the wing and the center portion were done and the dome is taking shape. The Governor's Mansion on Duffy Street is on the right. The main part of the capitol building was 558 feet long; the House and Senate chambers on each end would stretch 495 feet from the main unit. The driving lanes built between the wings have been replaced with a circle and fountain. swv

Chapter Twelve
The Moving Capitol

No. 64 Taken 3-2-31
West Virginia State Capitol
Main Building
Cass Gilbert, Architect

The Moving Capitol

The site of West Virginia's capital has had a very interesting history, in which Charleston has figured very prominently.

When the state was formed on June 20, 1863, Wheeling was chosen as the capital city because it had hosted two constitutional conventions and was most influential in the formation of the new state. In addition, it was fairly secure from the ravages of civil war that threatened other parts of the state. Finally, Wheeling was a transportation hub on the mainline of the Baltimore and Ohio Railroad and one of the major stops on the National Road.

However, with the end of the Civil War in 1865 and a return to normalcy, citizens of West Virginia started to question Wheeling as a permanent capital site.

The First Move

Four years after the end of the war, Charleston citizens met to promote the moving of the capital to their city. Their actions prompted the West Virginia Legislature, meeting in Wheeling, to approve the move to Charleston effective April 1, 1870. Charleston citizens pledged $50,000 toward the cost of building a permanent capitol building. At a formal meeting in May 1869, the Charleston citizens chartered the Statehouse Company and issued stock for $100,000. Alex T. Laidley and J.A. Lewis sold the company a tract of land on Capitol Street (just north of the Lee Street Triangle) for $5,000, and on November 3, 1869, the cornerstone was laid. The final cost of building the capitol amounted to $80,000.

When the steamboat *Mountain Boy* docked at Charleston four months later carrying Governor William Stevenson and the state papers, the capitol building was not ready. Instead, the governor and his staff had to conduct state business from several buildings and churches until December 20, 1870, when the capitol was completed.

Bottom: The first state capitol building in Charleston was completed on December 20, 1870. It was 138 feet long, 56 feet deep and 140 feet high from the base to the tip of the steeple. The first story housed offices and committee rooms; the second, the Hall of the Senate and House of Delegates, committee rooms and clerks' offices; the third, the Supreme Court, the Federal Court, clerks' offices, jury rooms and a library. The building stood north of the Lee Street Triangle site and was demolished in 1880 for construction of the second capitol building. WVU

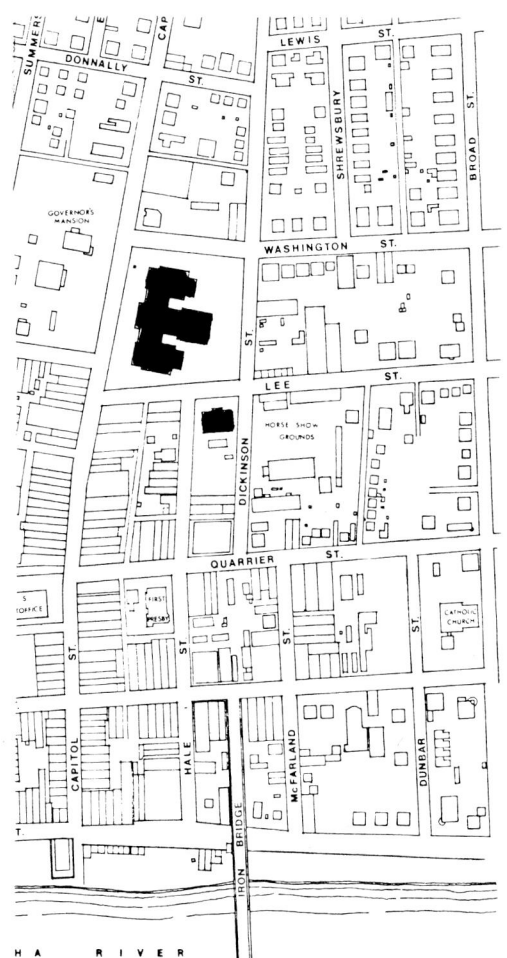

The Second Move

Five years later, the state legislature did a turnaround and voted to return the capital to Wheeling. The act passed on February 20, 1875, but a month later several prominent Charleston businessmen succeeded in getting a court injunction against the move. The case went to the State Supreme Court but Charleston lost. Even the governor was against the move.

Once again the governor and state papers were put aboard a steamboat and they traveled up to Wheeling, where a new capitol building had been constructed at the cost of $100,000.

The second move, however, was not the end of the story. In 1877 a state-wide election was held to vote for a permanent capital site. Ironically, Wheeling was not even on the ballot. Charleston won out over Clarksburg and Martinsburg and the capital was permanently moved to Charleston in 1885.

"The members of the Legislature are not so...fastidious that they cannot be well accommodated here. We have no doubt that even the members from Ohio County will find as good beef, whiskey, and wine, with as much genuine hospitality and refinement in Charleston, as they have been accustomed to in Wheeling."

George W. Atkinson, Editor
West Virginia Journal
1871

The *Mountain Boy* carried the governor and state papers from Wheeling to Charleston for the government transfer in 1870. WVU

The *Chesapeake* was used to transport Governor Emanual Willis Wilson and state officials from Wheeling to Charleston in 1885. WVU

West Virginia's second capitol building in Charleston was completed in 1885 for a cost exceeding $350,000. Eventually, a cannon and several statues were placed on the grounds. This building stood 36 years until it was destroyed by fire on January 3, 1921. KCL

The Third Move

Once again the governor and the state papers were sent down the Ohio River and up the Kanawha to Charleston. This time the *Belle Prince* docked at Charleston on May 3, 1885, with a barge in tow containing state property. The *Chesapeake* also docked with state officials, including Governor Emanuel Willis Wilson, aboard.

The old capitol building was demolished and a new building, costing in excess of $350,000, was erected on the same site. The new capitol stood an impressive three stories high, 230 feet long, with a clock tower that rose 194 feet high. The building contained 85 rooms. In 1903 an annex was built across the street that later housed Morris Harvey College and the Kanawha County Public Library until it was demolished in 1966 to make way for Commerce Square.

The new capitol building was the seat of government for 36 years until it was destroyed by fire on January 3, 1921. Law librarian James Arthur Jackson, working in the capitol annex, first saw the flames. In a short time, the building was completely gutted and a falling chimney killed fireman Captain Oscar Thaxton. Many people assumed that the fire started in a cache of guns and ammunition that had been seized from striking coal miners in 1919 and was stored in the top floor of the building.

After the fire, many buildings in town were used to conduct state business, including the YMCA and several churches. However, workers quickly cleared the rubble away and constructed a large 166-room structure, nicknamed the "pasteboard capitol," at the site of the Daniel Boone Hotel (now the 405 Capitol Building).

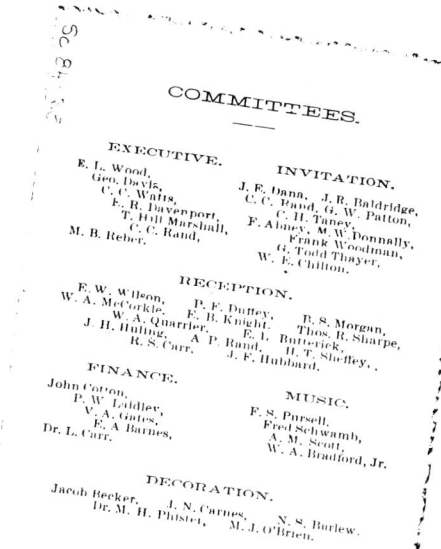

Invitation to the opening of the new capitol building on January 5, 1887. SWV

An 1897 scene on the capitol lawn facing Capitol Street.
COURTESY MRS. ROBERT W. LAWSON, JR.

The Historical Room in the old capitol building housed much of the state's historical artifacts. The State Bureau of Archives and History was established in 1905 with Virgil A. Lewis as the first state historian. WVU

West Virginia governors had to provide their own housing until 1893, when the Legislature honored Aretas B. Fleming's request for $22,000 to purchase an official residence. His successor, William A. MacCorkle, bought a frame dwelling on Capitol Street across from the state capitol. Eight governors lived here before the present mansion was completed in 1925. The AT&T building is now at this site. WVU

When the annex was completed the state museum was moved to its third floor. This fateful move was most fortunate since the capitol fire of 1921 would have destroyed the entire collection. swv

The Capitol Annex, which was completed in 1903, is shown completely covered with ivy in 1925. It housed the offices of the auditor and treasurer, the Supreme Court of Appeals, the State Law Library, the adjutant general and the Department of Archives and History. However, the state offices vacated the building when the new capitol was completed. The building then housed Morris Harvey College on the upper floors from 1935 to 1947 and the Kanawha County Public Library from 1928 to 1964. The old Capitol Annex was demolished in 1966 when Commerce Square was constructed. swv

Top: A dramatic view of the fire. SWV

Fire January 3, 1921

Top Center: The steeples on the capitol were gutted by the fire. The statue of the Union Soldier, in front of the building, now stands on the east end of the present capitol. WVU

Opposite: On January 3, 1921, a large crowd gathered to watch West Virginia's capitol burn. The building on the right, the old National Bank of Commerce, is still standing. The capitol annex can be seen at the rear of the building.
WVU, R.B. COOK COLLECTION

Cooling down the rear of the building. RA

Like a scene from a Wagnerian Opera, the fires glow through the gathering darkness. In a short time the citizens of the city had lost their most majestic building. RA

Not much remained of the capitol's contents the day after the fire. KCL

Ammunition stored in the capitol attic discharged in the holocaust, which sent spectators scattering. Witnesses recalled how the old familiar tower clock continued to chime up to the moment the structure collapsed.

Interior of the burned out capitol building. RA

Officials examine a safe holding documents from the pasteboard capitol fire on March 2, 1927. Contents of the various safes salvaged were charred but not destroyed. KCL

Two views of the temporary capitol erected soon after the January 3rd fire on the site of the Daniel Boone Hotel (now 405 Capitol Building). It was nicknamed the "Pasteboard Capitol" because of the wooden materials used in its construction. It cost $225,000 to erect this building, and it too was completely destroyed by fire on March 2, 1927.

COURTESY TERRY LOWRY & KCL

Fire
March 2, 1927

Remains of the "pasteboard capitol." The building in the background is the original Diamond Department Store, which was later added to and is still standing. KCL

Firefighters spray the smoldering ruins of the destroyed building. KCL

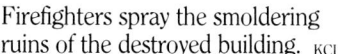

The Fourth Move

"Behold in this Capitol a monument to West Virginians of yesterday, today and tomorrow," Governor William G. Conley said at the June 20, 1932, dedication of the new $10 million capitol building. For after several moves between cities and three different structures in Charleston, the state finally had a permanent site for the seat of government.

The state purchased a tract of land along Kanawha River in the east end of Charleston and started construction in early 1924 on a four-story capitol. This building was designated as the west wing of the capitol, and was completed in March 1925.

Cass Gilbert, a noted architect who had designed many prominent buildings in New York City, was hired to design West Virginia's new capitol. In July 1926 the construction of what is now the east wing of the capitol commenced and, a year and a half later the government offices moved in. In the meantime, the old pasteboard capitol building had burned down, and it was fortunate that both wings were complete.

It took a special levy enacted by the legislature in March 1929 to authorize construction of the main capital structure. Amidst a great deal of criticism, the George A. Fuller Company began work on March 6, 1930. The entire country was in the throes of the Great Depression and many people felt that the building would cost too much. The construction, however, was already under way and it was decided to go ahead and finish it. Controversy arose again when the public learned that the architect's plans called for a dome covered with gold leaf instead of the more commonly used stone. Gilbert insisted that gilding the dome would cost less in the long run and finally his idea prevailed.

The massive gold dome we see today is 292 feet in height, slightly taller than the nation's capital but slightly smaller in diameter. Inside hangs a 4,000-pound chandelier of beveled crystal that was made in Czechoslovakia.

The present capitol complex is one of the most impressive structures in the United States. Since 1932, five additional buildings have been built around the capitol building and a circular driveway and fountain were constructed between the two wings of the capitol building itself.

Eight governors had lived in the original governor's mansion, an old frame dwelling on Capitol Street across from the downtown capitol building. After the 1921 capitol fire, the legislature passed a sales tax for construction of a new, permanent capitol building and appropriated $100,000 for a new governor's mansion. A tract of land that faced Kanawha Street was purchased adjacent to the site of the new capitol. Charleston architect Walter F. Martens designed the new governor's mansion at a final cost, including furnishings, of $200,000. The building was completed in 1925, during the term of Governor Ephraim Morgan.

The thirty-room mansion provides living quarters for the official family and is often the place where official state social gatherings are held. In 1965 the mansion was renovated and in 1977 it was redecorated by Governor and Mrs. John D. Rockefeller IV as a personal gift to the state.

Total cost for the State Capitol Building, completed in February 1932 was $9,491,180.03.

Twelve houses were moved across the Kanawha River on barges in 1923 to make way for the new capitol building. They were moved to the riverbank, transferred to built-up barges rented from coal companies and towed across to sites on 20th Street in South Ruffner. Each house cost about $3,500 to move. SWV

Houses, lined up like toy soldiers, are being skidded toward the river and eventual relocation. SWV

The Capitol Building Commission in January 1932. The architect for the capitol, Cass Gilbert, stands fourth from the right in the front row. Governor William G. Conley, under whose administration the capitol complex was completed, is to his left. Senate President, M.Z. White, stands at far left, House Speaker William J. Cummins, with watchchain, is fifth from left. SWV

An early photograph of excavation for the west wing of the capitol taken on January 15, 1924. Notice that some house foundations are still evident. SWV

When this photo was taken in April 1924, structural steel for the west wing was being erected. Large cranes were moved onto the site by a rail siding off California Avenue. SWV

An immense steam pile driver at work on the east wing of the capitol, August 27, 1926. The west wing can be seen in the background.
SWV

The cornerstone for the east wing was laid by Governor William A. MacCorkle (light coat and goatee) on November 30, 1926. The west wing had been completed and occupied more than a year before. Construction on the main part of the capitol would not be started for almost another four years.
SWV

The east and west wings were completed in 1925 and 1927 respectively. This view is looking toward Washington Street (to the right).
SWV

Construction of the main part of the present capitol building was started on March 6, 1930, by the George A. Fuller Company, builders of the west wing. The Fuller Company built a temporary rail line to bring in tons of gravel, cement, steel, limestone and marble needed for construction. The east wing is just visible on the left. SWV

Construction advances. (Top) November 15, 1930. (Bottom) January 2, 1931. SWV

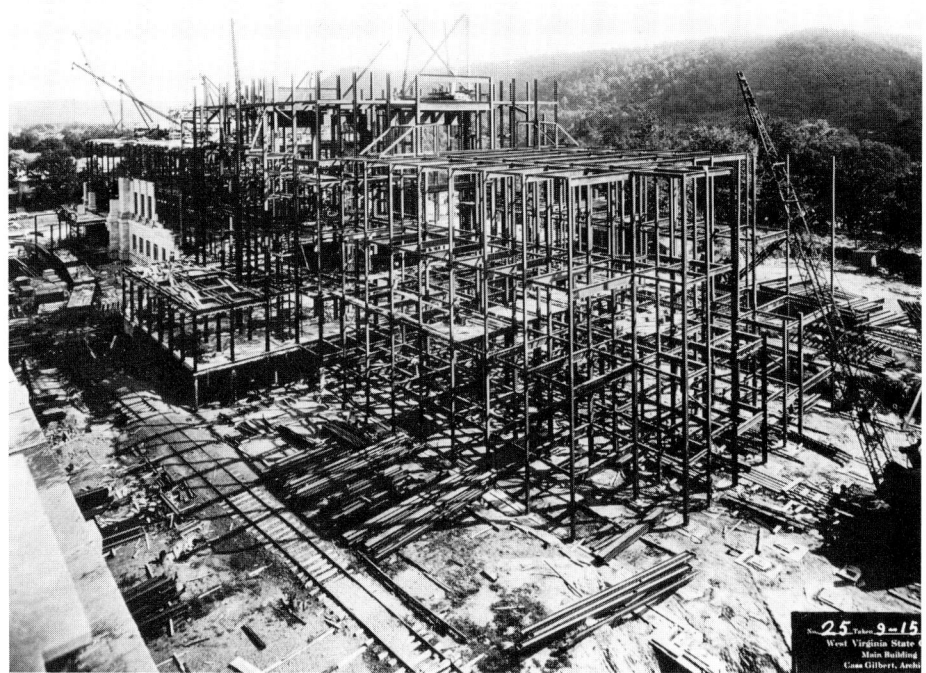

The enormous steel shell of the central portion was almost complete by September, six months after groundbreaking. The outside facade is just starting to take shape. The dome structure has not yet been formed. This view is looking to the south. SWV

Interior construction of the House chambers in April 1924. Many ornate marble carvings made by skilled stone masons appear throughout the building. SWV

Interior of the dome, April 1931. It stands 292 feet above ground level, which is slightly taller than the U.S. Capitol. SWV

Bottom right: A beveled crystal chandelier hangs on a 54-foot gold chain from the dome's ceiling, which is 185 feet high from the ground floor. Once every five years the chandelier is lowered for cleaning and replacement of crystals, a job that takes two days. SWV

Interior of the capitol looking down from the dome upon completion in 1932. SWV

By September 1932, it was business as usual in the completed capitol building. At the insistence of architect Cass Gilbert, the dome was gilded for the sum of $23,700. SWV

The completed three-unit capitol complex on February 7, 1932. Some houses, since removed from the grounds, can still be seen to the side and front of the building. The landscaping would come later. Kanawha City, largely undeveloped at this time, spreads out in the distance. swv

Many programs and ceremonies were held on the steps of the newly completed capitol steps in the 1930s. The top photo shows a parade heading down Quarrier Street and turning on Duffy Street toward Washington Street. SWV, BOLLINGER COLLECTION

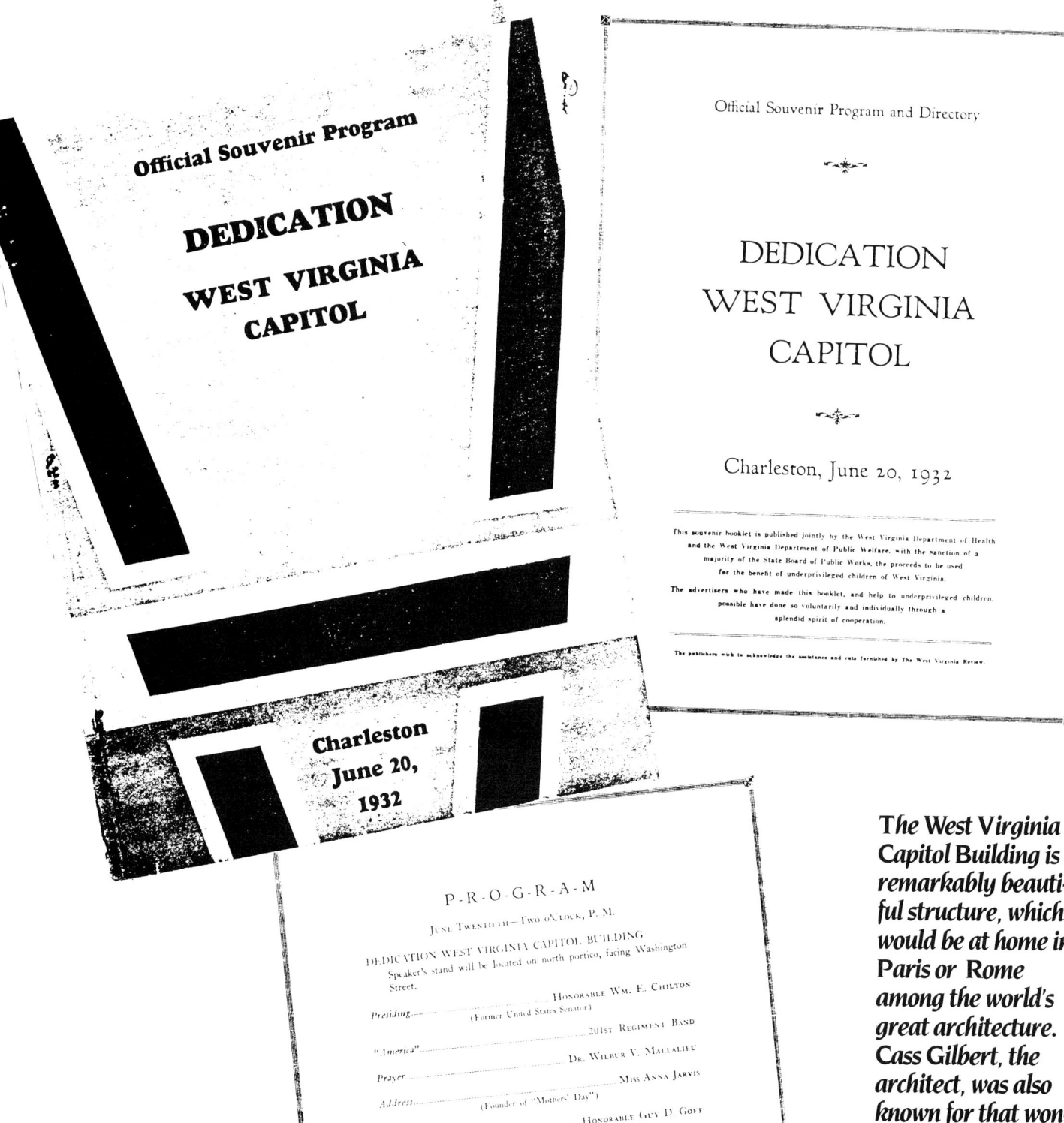

The West Virginia Capitol Building is a remarkably beautiful structure, which would be at home in Paris or Rome among the world's great architecture. Cass Gilbert, the architect, was also known for that wonderful early New York skyscraper, the Woolworth Building.

Cost of New Capitol

The net cost to the taxpayers in property taxes for the completed capitol was $6,412,373.60.

The following is a condensed statement of all receipts and disbursements incident to its construction:

Expenditures

Purchase of new site	$ 2,211,825.43
(Including expense of grading and sundry expenses in preparing for construction)	
Office Building, Unit No. 1	216,967.66
(Total cost of construction)	
Office Building, Unit No. 2	254,525.94
(Total cost of construction)	
Capitol Building, Main Unit, and interest	6,807,861.00
(Total cost of construction)	
Total cost of new capitol	$ 9,491,180.03

Receipts from Sale of Old Capitol Site, Insurance, etc.

Received from sale of old site, etc.	$ 1,551,000.00
Received from sale of old annex	501,256.59
Received from sale of site of old temporary capitol and mansion	352,223.84
Insurance on old buildings and contents	533,455.23
Received from sale of houses on new site	104,586.52
Interest received on deferred payments	36,284.25
	$ 3,078,806.43
Total cost of new capitol	$ 9,491,180.03
Less total salvage from old capitol	3,078,806.43
Net cost to taxpayers	$ 6,412,373.60

The amount authorized by the Legislature to be expended in erecting the Main Capitol Unit was $5,000,000.00. The amount actually expended was $4,627,278.00, or $372,722.00 less than the amount authorized.

Thirteen

A rendering of the new Executive Mansion designed by Walter F. Martens—Architects of Charleston.

If one were to imagine having just arrived in Charleston on a steamboat from Cincinnati or Pittsburgh, this 1900 scene looking north on Capitol Street from Kanawha Street would have been your first view of the downtown area. The intersection of Capitol and Virginia streets can be seen near the center of the photo. Virtually every building in this scene has passed on into the realm of memory—those on the left taken by 1962 Urban Renewal and on the right by the Terminal Building and other later construction. Little did these two gentlemen realize that their walk down Capitol Street would be seen nearly 100 years later by the thousands of readers of this book! KCL

Chapter Thirteen

Streetscapes

Capitol Street Scenes

Looking north from the present Kanawha County Public Library at the corner of Capitol and Quarrier streets, circa 1906. AUTHOR'S COLLECTION

Looking north from the corner of Capitol and Kanawha streets featuring the old Kanawha Valley Bank Building, circa 1900. KCL

South Capitol Street from the front of the present Kanawha County Public Library around the turn of the century. The S. Spencer Moore Co. is on the left. KCL

The view north from a window of the newly built Union Building on Capitol Street, circa 1912. The state capitol building can be seen in the distance. KCL

The pavement of Capitol Street has rung with the cadence of marching soldiers, the rumble of streetcars, the rude rattle and roar of the first automobile, the stamping of circus elephants, the tragic wail of fire engines, and even the lapping of water as early floods submerged the area. Millions have passed by, the great and the near-great, but mostly just ordinary, hard-working people going about the business of life.

Capitol Street's name was chosen because it bordered the front of the capitol building of West Virginia. Long, long ago it was known as Cox's Lane and Cross Street.

An early 1900s view of Capitol Street looking south. The building on the extreme right is Lowenstein and Sons Hardware. Most of these buildings are still standing. KCL

Note the interesting hoop-like street lights in this photo taken about 1907 at the intersection of Capitol and Virginia streets. The lights are composed of dozens of small bulbs that were fixed to these hoops at each intersection. The building on the corner is now the site of Security and Chamber of Commerce Building. KCL

Taken around 1906 at the corner of Capitol and Virginia streets with the Kanawha National Bank in the background, this photo shows one of Charleston's "finest" wearing a "bobby" style helmet. RA

This building on the corner of Quarrier and Capitol streets in the 1900s was the first home of the Kanawha Banking and Trust Company. The building next to it burned down in the 1980s. KCL

For more than 100 years, Charleston's commercial hub has been Capitol Street, and these seven short blocks represent the stage along which the colorful century-long drama of local history has paraded.

The S.S. Kresge store was located in the Lowenstein Building at the corner of Capitol and Fife streets, now Brawley Walkway, in 1939. PM

The first block of Capitol Street about 1930. The left side of the block is now occupied by the Charleston National Bank Building. PM

The third block of Capitol Street in 1939, featuring the old Charleston National Bank building and the Woolworth's store that burned down in 1949. PM

Taken shortly after its completion in 1894, the "Savage" house has been a familiar sight to Charlestonians for nearly a century. Located on the brow of Capitol Hill at the north end of Capitol Street, its silhouette stands out in sharp relief against the sky (see page 279). It is presently being restored by its owner, Mr. Jim Neff. KCL

Capitol Street was once the hub of activity in Charleston, and shoulder-to-shoulder crowds were common, especially during the Christmas season. The top photo was taken about 1940, the middle, ten years later. KCL

Capitol Street looking south, 1946. KCL

Nighttime parade down Capitol Street, late 1940s. KCL

Capitol Street, late 1930s. KCL

Capitol Street was still a place to shop when this 1960s photo was taken. KCL

TOP LEFT: Paving near the front of the present Kanawha County Public Library, in the early 1900s. The gabled building in the distance currently houses the Rite Aid store. KCL

TOP RIGHT: Paving Capitol Street in the first block off Kanawha Street. PM

BOTTOM: Workmen laying brick paving in a bed of sand over wood planking on Quarrier Street from the Capitol Street intersection. PM

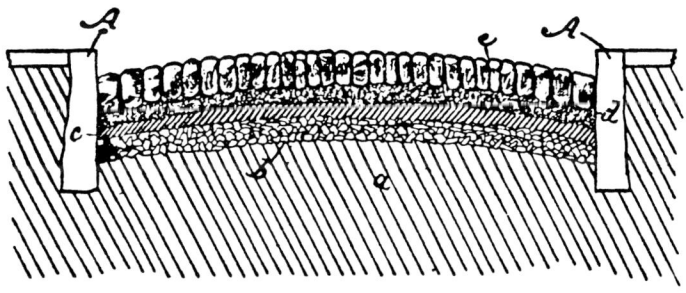

About 1870, a small section of brick pavement, approximately 30 feet square, was laid over a mud hole in front of V.A. Gates' store on Summers Street, as a private experiment. Documented as the first brick pavement in the United States, this new method of street improvement was invented by Mordecai Levi with financial backing from Dr. John P. Hale. The method was explained to the West Virginia Road School at Morgantown in 1917:

> The street was graded to about nine inches below the finished grade and the subgrade well-rolled with a large stone roller about like those used for lawn rollers 25 years ago only larger. Then upon the subgrade was placed about three inches of sand and the sand was shaped to form the finished crown of the street by means of a template very similar to those used at the present time in the construction of concrete streets. Upon this a layer of one inch oak boards, which had first been dipped in hot tar; these boards were placed lengthwise of the street and after being laid were rolled to a solid bearing. On top of these boards was spread another layer of sand about one and one-half inches thick, which was rolled with a light roller and then shaped to the form of the crown with the template. The bricks were then laid on this layer of sand, and after being thoroughly rolled were covered with a thin layer of sand, part of which was swept into the joints, and the remainder allowed to wear off."

The first brick pavement in the United States was laid on Summers Street about 1870 as an experiment. The entire block between Kanawha and Virginia streets was paved by the city in 1873. This is a cross-section of the pavement which was invented by Mordecai Levi, who was backed financially by Dr. John P. Hale.

-257-

Kanawha Street Scenes

Looking west from the corner of Kanawha and Summers streets in 1917. KCL

Looking west down Kanawha, from the intersection of Kanawha and Summers streets. Frankenberger's original store is the closest building. Note the multiple phone wire that was used in the 1890s.
COURTESY MRS. ROBERT W. LAWSON

A view of Kanawha Street from a window in the Union Building. The buildings on the riverbank were removed during the construction of the boulevard in the late 1930s. KCL

The corner of Capitol and Kanawha streets, just after the turn of the century. Note the 1904 curved-dash Oldsmobile just left of the boy with the paper. In just a few short years, these "new-fangled" machines would be common on the streets of Charleston. AUTHOR'S COLLECTION

Kanawha Street between Summers and Capitol streets, 1920s. All the buildings on the left side of the street were removed by Urban Renewal and replaced by the Charleston National Bank. The building across from the Kanawha Valley Bank is now called the Terminal Building. KCL

The corner of Brooks and Kanawha streets, facing east, circa 1910. KCL

BOTTOM RIGHT: Looking west on Kanawha Street near the intersection with Laidley Street in 1917. The tall building on the right is the ornate St. Albert Hotel. KCL

OPPOSITE TOP: The newly completed Kanawha Boulevard in 1940. Partially funded by the WPA, the project cost $3.5 million, and it completely transformed the appearance of downtown Charleston. The west section, which ran from Court Street to Delaware Avenue, including the Elk River bridge, was completed in 1938, and the extensions to Patrick Street and the Kanawha City bridge were finished two years later. Note the statue of justice on the courthouse. NA

Lee Street in the 700 block was formerly called State Street because it ended at the statehouse lawn on Capitol Street. Taken during Warren Harding's presidential campaign in 1920, this photo shows in the distance the capitol building that burned down in January 1921. The Virginian Theater was next to the Virginian Hotel. Most of the other buildings pictured are still in existence. SWV

OPPOSITE LEFT: The construction of Kanawha Boulevard near Elk River in 1938. KCL

OPPOSITE RIGHT: Kanawha Street, looking west, near Morris Street, circa 1900. KCL

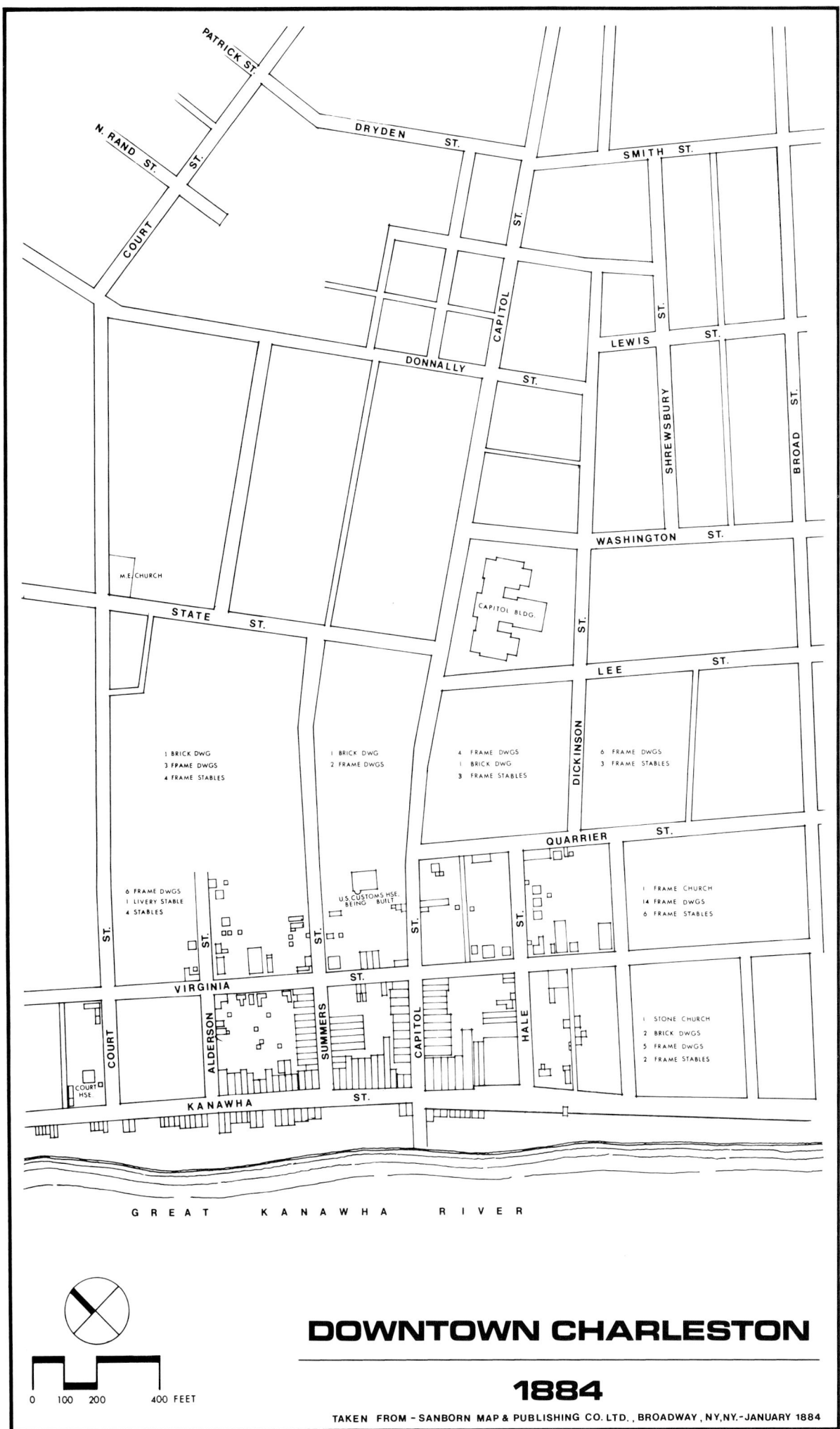

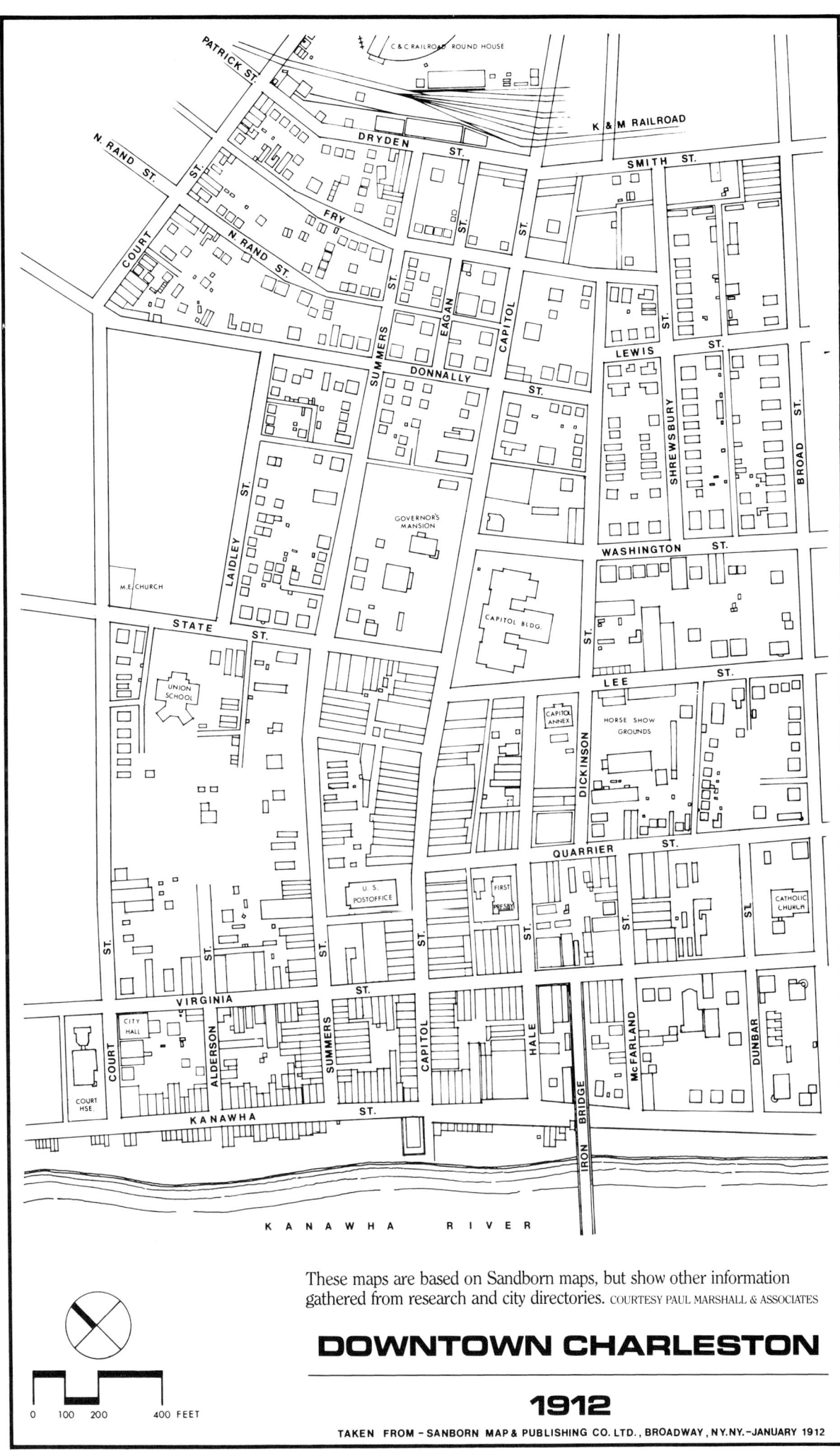

DOWNTOWN CHARLESTON

1912

TAKEN FROM - SANBORN MAP & PUBLISHING CO. LTD., BROADWAY, N.Y. NY.- JANUARY 1912

These maps are based on Sanborn maps, but show other information gathered from research and city directories. COURTESY PAUL MARSHALL & ASSOCIATES

The walkway next to the Federal Building that connected Capitol and Summers streets. In 1958 an extension of Quarrier Street was built through here. CN

TOP: Looking east on Quarrier Street near Capitol, about 1940. The Rialto Theater (now the Morrison Building) opened in 1917. By this time the streetcar tracks had been taken up and the street paved over. KCL

ABOVE: Facing west on Quarrier Street at Dunbar Street about 1940.
COURTESY COLUMBIA GAS TRANSMISSION CORPORATION

Many of Charleston's streets were joined out of two or more streets. Modern-day Lee Street, for instance, was once called State Street from Truslow to Capitol where it ended at the statehouse grounds. After the capitol burned in 1921, city fathers joined State Street to Lee Street, right through the old capitol yard. This explains the triangle at Lee and Capitol; the triangle is actually the southwest corner of the old statehouse lawn.

Virginia Street at Capitol, looking west, in 1939. SWV

The view east from the corner of Washington Street West and Tennessee Avenue, 1940. The building on the right was formerly a bank.
COURTESY STATE DEPARTMENT OF HIGHWAYS

Taken from the new post office, this photograph of the corner of Washington and Dickinson streets in 1940, shows St. Marks United Methodist Church, the Firestone store and the K of P Hall. TH

An early 1940s photograph of Charleston Street, now West Washington Street, near Stockton Street. RA

This view is Patrick Street in the late 1930s. Until the 1960s, this area was Charleston's principal farmers' market outlet. RA

Charleston Street (now West Washington Street) near Tennessee Avenue in the early 1900s. RA

West Washington Street looking west, 1915.
COURTESY C & P TELEPHONE MUSEUM

The road from Charleston to Montgomery went through Marmet in 1915. This is now Route 61.
COURTESY C & P TELEPHONE MUSEUM

The Lee Street Triangle, which was actually the southwest corner of the old capitol lawn in 1949.
COURTESY COLUMBIA GAS TRANSMISSION CORPORATION

Bridge Road leading to South Hills, 1897.
COURTESY MRS. ROBERT W. LAWSON, JR.

The eleven-hundred block of Virginia Street looking west, 1897. The Virginia Street Temple's two cupolas are visible on the left. COURTESY MRS. ROBERT W. LAWSON, JR.

When this sign was posted in the early 1900s, automobiles were still a novelty in Charleston. SWV

Looking north from the corner of Greenbrier and Washington streets, 1925.
COURTESY WEST VIRGINIA WATER COMPANY

Washington Street West at Woodward Drive (U.S. 35), 1948. COURTESY STATE DEPARTMENT OF HIGHWAYS

MacCorkle Avenue at 41st Street in Kanawha City, July 1948. COURTESY STATE DEPARTMENT OF HIGHWAYS

Summers Street looking northeast from Post Office Square, 1930s. PM

Summers Street on a rainy night in 1954, looking south. The Kearse Theater on the right opened in 1922. CN

Post Office

TOP: This 1890 view shows the capitol building built in 1885, the U.S. Post Office and several churches. The old 1817 courthouse is just out of view on the left. Because the South Side Bridge was not constructed until 1891, a ferry service still provided service across the river. The city levee and some old barges can be seen on the river. Most of the large buildings in the downtown area have not yet been built.

ALL PANORAMA PHOTOS COURTESY GEORGE HUBBS

Ruffner Hotel | Capitol Building | Dr. John P. Hale Home

BOTTOM: By 1920 the Charleston skyline had changed considerably. The South Side Bridge was completed in 1891, and the capitol annex completed in 1903, although the capitol building would be destroyed in 1921. The Ruffner Hotel changed its facade and many of the large downtown buildings, most of which still stand, were completed. The old Red Cross building is next to the 1911 Union Building, and the city levee was completely rebuilt. Many new buildings were built along Kanawha Street, and the numerous houseboats indicate that there was still a good deal of activity on the river.

TOP: Thirty years later Charleston's skyline had changed considerably because of the completion of the Kanawha Boulevard in 1940. The new South Side Bridge was constructed in 1937.

BOTTOM: This contemporary view of Charleston's skyline is presented here as a comparison to the previous views. High-rise buildings and Interstate highway construction have changed the look of Charleston again. Fifty years from now, it will be interesting to see what further changes have been made.

Looking west down State Street during the 1897 flood.
CN

Chapter Fourteen

Flood and Fire

Flood and Fire

The waters now rose about these high banks and flooded the town itself, being four or five feet deep in the first story of dwelling houses built in what was considered a neighborhood safe from floods.

There was enormous waste and loss, but we managed to keep our men in rations, and were better off than the Confederates.

—General Jacob Cox, Commander of Union forces in the Kanawha Valley commenting on the September 1861 flood.

Because of the rugged, mountainous terrain and the lack of flood control systems in the numerous hollows throughout Kanawha County, disastrous flash floods have occurred through the years. The Kanawha River flooded fairly frequently before locks and dams were built on the river and its tributaries in the late 1890s.

The highest recorded flood on the Kanawha River occurred in September 1861 when the water crested at 46 feet. Water covered most of the small town of Charleston and caused considerable damage to the salt works in the Malden area and to the navigational aids that were installed in the Coal River just before the Civil War.

Another disastrous flood occurred in February 1897, when water crested at 42 feet, the second highest water level recorded. Water inundated most of the downtown area and covered the state capitol grounds from Dickinson Street almost to Quarrier Street and up Virginia Street almost to Summers Street. Because of a slight depression in the back end of town, the Kanawha and Michigan Railroad yards were entirely under water.

The 1897 flood brought on a great deal of suffering that was accentuated by the cold weather and poor distribution of food. Men in boats did a thriving business; one man hauled the legislators from the capitol through the flooded streets to their hotels.

In 1899 the Kanawha River crested at 41.3 feet and in 1900 waters reached 39 feet. When the Kanawha Boulevard was completed in 1940, and flood control dams were built on the Bluestone, Elk and Gauley rivers, the threat of widespread flooding greatly diminished.

Many flash floods have devastated the heavily populated hollows in the county, especially in the coal fields. In addition, highways, railroads, and industrial concerns have been built near the narrow waterways, which make flash flooding more probable and more destructive during heavy rainfall.

One such flood on August 9, 1916, in the Cabin Creek drainage area, destroyed many miles of railroad track, rolling stock, houses and buildings. The photos in this chapter attest to the flood's ferocity. Paint Creek experienced a terrible flood on July 10, 1932, when water crushed homes, bridges and coal facilities, killing 21 people.

In the Kanawha Valley on July 19, 1961, a flash flood wreaked havoc, killing 21 people and causing property damage in the millions of dollars. Charleston's west side and areas east of town were especially hard hit.

Most of the communities in Kanawha County have experienced devastating fires in the past 200 years. Charleston's worst early fire took place on January 19, 1874, when the business block bounded by Kanawha, Summers, Virginia and Capitol streets was destroyed. The total damage estimate was $85,000.

The two state capitols burned, one in 1921 and the other in 1927. The biggest fire in Charleston since the 1921 capitol fire was on January 27, 1946, when a city block on Virginia Street were consumed by flames. Four people were injured and ten office and warehouse buildings worth more than one million dollars were destroyed. The fire apparently started in The Rose City Press building on the corner of Virginia and Hale streets.

The greatest loss of human life was on March 4, 1949, when seven firemen died in the ruins of the Woolworth's fire near the corner of Capitol and Quarrier streets.

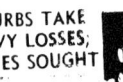

Ruffner Brothers Fire, November 9, 1907

Cleaning up the debris after the November 1907 fire.
COURTESY MOORE CONSTRUCTION COMPANY

On November 9, 1907, a fire broke out in the Ruffner Brothers Wholesale Grocery on Kanawha Street, adjacent to the Ruffner Hotel. A fireman and a clerk were killed. The business loss was over $35,000. TOP LEFT: The rear of the building on Virginia Street. BOTTOM LEFT: Kanawha Street and the Ruffner Hotel. BOTTOM RIGHT: Looking east on Kanawha Street, with the pumper at the Hale Street corner. People can just barely be seen on the South Side Bridge ramp, on extreme right. RA

Fire at the church on the corner of Dickinson and Washington streets, in the 1930s. This building was later used as the Kanawha Players workshop and is now the site of the main post office. KCL

The most destructive fire in Charleston's history occurred in January 1946 when several large buildings adjacent to the South Side Bridge on Virginia Street burned. Fortunately, no one was killed. The Ruffner Hotel barely escaped destruction, and windblown ashes were carried as far as Kanawha City. The near-zero temperature actually froze the water in the hoses and icicles formed on firemen's helmets. The Empire Federal Savings and Loan's drive-in facility is now at this location. CN

The old capitol annex—later the Kanawha County Public Library—caught fire on December 27, 1966, during its demolition to make way for Commerce Square. CN

At the corner of Capitol and Quarrier streets a crowd stands awe-struck as fire destroys Woolworth's store. The fire engine is a Seagrave Pumper. CN

The Woolworth's fire on Capitol Street. An American La France Aerial Tiller ladder truck is being rolled into position. This vehicle had a steering wheel in the rear that made it easier to negotiate narrow city streets. CN

Charleston's most tragic fire took place on March 4, 1949, when the Woolworth's building on Capitol Street caught fire. Seven firemen perished when the wooden floor collapsed into the basement. The seven firemen who gave their lives were: J.P. Little, George Coates, Freddie Summers, Frank Miller, Dick McCormick, Frank Sharp, and E.C. Pauley. Thirteen firemen were injured and damage was over $1 million. The Kresge building next door had severe water damage. CN

The Great 1897 Flood

During the 1897 flood, the river rose to 42 feet. This level was four feet lower than the record 46 feet of the 1861 flood, the highest in the history of the Kanawha River. Water backed up in the low areas of the Kanawha and Michigan yard, and covered the downtown area around the capitol building.

Looking east from capitol at the flooded railroad yards.
SWV

Looking at the Kanawha and Michigan Railroad yards from the Capitol Hill area. The state capitol is in the background. This is not the Kanawha River, but a low area next to the mountain that flooded periodically. Interstate 64 now covers the site. SWV

Looking west on State (later Lee) Street near Laidley Street. The Union School dome can be seen at left.
COURTESY TERRY LOWRY

Looking south down a flooded Broad Street. Sacred Heart Church can be seen in the distance.
COURTESY CARNETTA BRITTON

A flood scene near the north end of Broad Street. The prominent house on the hilltop is the Savage Home, which still stands but is partially hidden by trees. The Interstate now covers most of this flooded area.
COURTESY CARNETTA BRITTON

The flooded Kanawha and Michigan Railroad yards, now Conrail.
COURTESY CARNETTA BRITTON

The corner of Capitol and State (Lee) streets with the capitol building in the background. The children are obviously enjoying this act of Mother Nature. CN

The corner of Capitol and Fife streets with the capitol building in the background. CN

Corner of Capitol and Virginia streets, 1897. The building in the distance now houses The Cheers restaurant. KCL

Flood waters covered much of the industrial concerns close to the Kanawha River. WW

The Cabin Creek Flood

The greatest disaster in the Cabin Creek area was the flood of August 9, 1916, which came on so quickly and with such fury that several lives and a great deal of property were lost. Caused by a cloud-burst on the watershed between the headwaters of Coal River, Cabin Creek and Paint Creek, the flood inundated each of these valleys, but Cabin Creek was the most severely affected.

Early in the morning of August 9, the water reached Cane Fork, Eskdale and other valley communities, and it kept rising until noon, when the valley was flooded from hill to hill. The flood took people by surprise, and, panic-stricken, they grabbed what belongings they could and rushed for the hills. Many of them returned that evening after the flood had subsided, to find their homes had washed away.

The flood destroyed the railroad in many places, like the yard at Eskdale, where box-cars were piled up like so many store boxes. This further aggravated the suffering caused by the flood because food could not be shipped into the Cabin Creek area.

Cabin Creek Flood, August 9, 1916

PHOTOS COURTESY LANGDON MORRIS

The Kanawha River flood at Winifrede, May 22, 1901.
GS via JESSE P. HUGHES

1932 flood on the Elk River that covered much of Clendenin.
COURTESY HENRY YOUNG, CLENDENIN

A disastrous flash flood hit Paint Creek on July 10, 1932. More than 100 homes were partially or totally destroyed and 22 people were killed. A number of people died of disease after the flood waters receded. COURTESY DENNIS DIETZ

The Kanawha River flood at the mouth of Cabin Creek on August 15, 1940. EG

The great flash flood of July 19, 1961, in the Charleston area caused 21 deaths and widespread destruction in the county. CN

Downtown Charleston in the late 1930s. This view was taken before boulevard construction started. Many buildings are still recognizable today. LC

Chapter Fifteen

Life Between the Wars: 1919-1941

Life Between the Wars: 1919-1941

Like the post-Civil War era, the end of World War I had an enormous effect on the citizens of Kanawha County. The carefree life of the 1920s, with prohibition and speakeasys, affected the county much the same as the rest of the country. Business was good in the Kanawha Valley, and industries were rapidly expanding, especially the chemical industry. The war-related industries in South Charleston and Nitro were no longer needed, and the Nitro plant shut down right after the armistice, before any gunpowder was actually shipped. The Naval Ordnance plant in South Charleston closed down a few years later because international treaties limited the size of signatory navies.

Coal mining increased, although the terrible strikes and subsequent mine wars of 1912 and 1921 affected the production and employee relations for many years. It was not until 1933 that new government regulations allowed all the mines to unionize.

After the 1921 and the 1927 capitol fires, plans were made to build a magnificent new capitol at the very east end of Charleston. In 1920 Charleston's population had grown to over 39,000, and the county's had increased to 90,000. A new city hall was constructed in 1922, and many of the existing large banks and office buildings were built in the two decades between the wars.

The Depression of the 1930s hit all segments of life. Coal mining and manufacturing were down, and many people were out of work. Charleston, however, was not as severely affected as other parts of the country because of the diverse nature of its industries and its role as a hub for wholesale and retail commerce in the southern part of West Virginia. The Civilian Conservation Corps (CCC) set up camps near Hernshaw in the Kanawha State Forest area, and at Decota on Cabin Creek.

Many of the developments that citizens now take for granted were constructed during this trying time, such as the new South Side Bridge in 1937, and the Kanawha Boulevard in 1939-40. The Littlepage Terrace and Washington Manor housing developments, and other city and county government facilities were also constructed during the depression.

As defense spending rapidly increased in the late 1930s, the economy began to recover from the Depression. The county's industrial production increased, and production intensified at the South Charleston Ordnance Plant because of the world tensions which prompted the Federal Government to increase defense spending. President Franklin D. Roosevelt visited the ordnance plant on September 3, 1940.

Charleston's population climbed to 67,000 in 1940, while the county's total was 100,000. International tensions increased in 1940-41, which culminated with the December 7, 1941, attack on Pearl Harbor, and men from Kanawha County went to war with soldiers from the rest of the nation.

Many people in Charleston will remember Earl "Lightning" Harvey, who was a fixture on the city streets for many years selling local newspapers. He was featured in Ripley's *Believe It Or Not* on February 17, 1936. RA

Lions Club members rallying for a vote for bonds in 1922, near the old Capitol annex on Lee Street. The photo caption does not indicate what the bonds were for. Note the large building to the left, which was Billy Sunday's tabernacle and now is the site of the old Coyle and Richardson Building. KCL

The downtown skyline in 1897 (top) and 1906 (bottom). Note the differences by 1906. The riverbank has filled up, the Capitol Annex dome is visible, the Charleston National Bank building is complete and several new buildings have been built between the Ruffner Hotel and the bridge. The hotel's roof line has been altered and it appears that construction of the elevator is taking place. Note the toll booth at the north end of the bridge. The 1906 photo appears to have been taken during a period of high water as the waterfront buildings are partially submerged.
COURTESY MRS. ROBERT W. LAWSON, JR.

A good aerial view in the late 1920s. The new state capitol building in the background shows its two wings complete. CN

AUTHORS COLLECTION

KCL

COURTESY DOUG BUMGARTNER

The Ruffner Hotel at the corner of Kanawha and Hale streets were built in 1885 on the site of Hale House, which had burned down the same year. The building was a landmark in Charleston until 1970 when it was torn down. Sometime after 1900 the roof line was altered considerably and an elevator put in. Several times, in 1907 and 1946, the building was threatened by neighboring fires but it remained untouched. Later views are from the mid to late 1930s. KCL

Charleston's premier hotel in later years, the Daniel Boone, was built in 1929 by a group of city citizens. Over the years it housed many notable visitors to the city and many political confabs and decisions were made in its rooms. The 10-story building, now known as 405 Capitol Building, has been renovated into a unique office complex with an interior glass enclosed atrium and a 30-foot indoor waterfall.
COURTESY COLUMBIA GAS TRANSMISSION CORPORATION

Interior view of the massive kitchen of the Daniel Boone Hotel in 1950.
COURTESY COLUMBIA GAS TRANSMISSION CORPORATION

The Kanawha Hotel, now headquarters of the Charleston Job Corps Center, at the corner of Summers and Virginia streets about 1905. Its upper floors and roof were rebuilt after a fire. John F. Kennedy held his West Virginia primary victory celebration here in 1960. AUTHOR'S COLLECTION

A West Side gas station on Virginia Street. The Interstate now covers this area. KCL

Kanawha Street looking west showing the courthouse and Kanawha Furniture Company, circa 1920s. KCL

West Side Confectionery, 1920.
COURTESY WILLIAM GOEBEL VIA WVU

Interior of Alford's Store at Poca, 1925.
COURTESY WILLIAM GOEBEL VIA WVU

The P.E. Holz meat market was located at 713 Virginia Street. SWV

Palmer's Shoe Store, now located on Capitol Street, began operations in 1892 as Palmer & Thomas on Kanawha Street. In 1900 it moved to a site on Capitol Street a few doors from its present location. For years the store was called Palmer's Walk Over for the type of shoes it sold. COURTESY BILL PALMER

Demolishing the Burlew Opera House about 1920 to make way for O.J. Morrison's Department Store building. Part of the old building's walls were incorporated into the new building Scott Brothers Drug Store is to the left. swv

The Scott Brothers Drug Store, the Kay Jewelry Company and O.J. Morrison Department Store in the 1920s. The Scott building was built by the Scott Brothers in 1892 but not occupied by the drugstore and soda fountain until 1914. The pressed brick building is designed in high Victorian Queen Anne-Renaissance style with a unique corner turret. It has been renovated and is now occupied by Empire Federal Savings and Loan. The Kay Jewelry building has also been renovated. O.J. Morrison bought the old Burlew Opera site, tore it down and built this building in 1920. When he built his five-story store at the Burlew site, it was hailed as the most modern store building in the state. At one time, he had 15 stores around the state but the last one closed its doors in 1986. swv

Early tire shop and gas station in Charleston, 1930s. SWV

Dickinson (Quincy Store) in 1935. It was a gas station, IGA store and post office. TH

The *Charleston Daily Mail* and *Charleston Gazette* building on Virginia Street before additions were built. The *Daily Mail* was located across the street before the new building was built. The early delivery truck is at this location. The *Gazette* was founded in 1888 as a Democratic paper; the *Daily Mail* in 1893 as a Republican paper. The county's first newspaper, the *Kenhawa Spectator*, appeared in 1820. Although dozens of papers made their appearance through the years, most lasted only a short time. KCL

View looking south on Summers Street just beyond Brawley Walkway (Fife Street), circa 1940s. CN

View looking south on Summer Street just above the Capitol Theater. This is now the southwest corner of Summers and Quarrier streets, although Quarrier did not run west beyond Capitol Street in the 1940s. "Jacks Place" will be remembered by auto enthusiasts for its wide range of auto accessories. This building is now occupied by the Union Mission. CN

Quarrier Street just west of McFarland Street about 1938. Reeves was a prominent early supermarket renowned for its quality foods. The site is now a parking garage. CN

The Sterrett Building on Capitol Street was built in the early 1890s for Sterrett Brothers Dry Goods store. For years it housed the J.C. Penney Company until it moved farther down Capitol Street. SWV

Kroger's warehouse on West Washington Street, early 1930s. KCL

This well-known landmark stood at the west end of the Kanawha City Bridge for many years. The Gold Dome Drive-Inn was memorable for its dome that was circled by a number of little pigs which appeared to be running. At night the dome was lit up by neon. Piedmont Road is in the background, Washington Street in the foreground. SWV

The Eagle Sandwich Shop at the corner of Washington and Morris streets about 1937. Mr. George Jacobs, next to the cash register, was the owner. This photo was taken on introduction of the first canned beer. Since the business was just down the street from Charleston High School, the students were put on notice as to what they could and couldn't do. SWV

Situated on a hilltop above Charleston for better reception (circa early 1920s), this may be the city's first radio receiver. B.E. Andre, an early radio pioneer in the area, has his hand to his head. The first commercial radio station in the county, WOBU, was established about 1930. The antenna was at Davis Creek and studios in the Fleetwood Hotel on Capitol Street. The call letters were changed to the present WCHS in about 1940. WGKV was the second station on the air. RA

Valley Bell Dairy Company's predecessor was the Lewis Brothers Dairy at the corner of Court and Ross streets. The company moved to its present location on Roane Street in 1918. SWV

During the war the Valley Bell Company took some of their old milk wagons, fitted them with rubber tires and horse power and delivered milk. This saved wear and tear on their trucks and reduced gasoline consumption. SWV

The other large dairy company in the valley was Blossom Dairy. The business was founded in 1937 by Sam Sloman and closed in the 1960s. SWV

Boy Scouts handed out the 1918 C&P telephone directory from the company's Hale Street office. They also apparently gave out leaflets promoting "Liberty Loan" war bond sales. KCL

For many years the C.A. Potterfield Drug Company occupied the southeast corner location at Virginia and Capitol streets. SWV

Much activity was centered around "The Block." The Elks Club was located here, and was host many times to the Elk Conventions. This late 1930s photo is one such occasion. The Garnet High School Band is forming in the background by the school for a parade. JR

The Ferguson Hotel building in the 1930s. It was constructed in 1922 with 70 rooms, a theater, cafe, assembly hall, billiard parlor, and barber shop. It was located on Washington Street between Broad and Shrewsbury streets and was torn down in 1966. Part of the Holiday Inn occupies the space today. JR

Ferguson's Special Football Day Menu

Lincoln vs. W. V. C. I.
November 5, 1926
Charleston

FOOTBALL DOLLAR DINNER
Fried Chicken with Cream Gravy
Candied Sweet Potatoes
Green Peas in Cream
Stewed Tomatoes
Mexican Salad with Green Peppers
Fresh Apple Cobbler or Ice Cream
Coffee Tea Milk

FERGUSON 75 CENT DINNER
Roast Beef, Roast Pork or Salmon Croquettes
Mashed Potatoes
Stewed Tomatoes
Cold Slaw
Rice Pudding or Ice Cream
Coffee Tea Milk

SOFT DRINKS
Wiedeman
Budweiser _____ 10
Nu Grape _____ 20
Orange _____ 5
Coca Cola _____ 5

ALA CARTE
Fried Half Chicken
Best T Bone Steak _____ 75
Roast Beef _____ 75
Roast Pork _____ 40
Salmon Croquettes _____ 40
Pork Chops (2) _____ 35
Veal Chops (2) _____ 50
Cold Ham with Potato Salad _____ 50
Fish _____ 40
Oyster Stew, Half _____ 30
Oyster Fry, Half _____ 40

SANDWICHES
Combination 25 Chicken, cold 35
Cold Ham 10 Hot Ham 15
Fish, large 25 Club, large 65
Roast Beef or Pork _____ 20
Egg _____ 10 Cheese _____ 10

SALADS
Salmon _____ 30
Chicken _____ 65
Shrimp _____ 50
Combination _____ 35
Potato _____ 25

DESERTS
Pie 10, Cake 10, IceCream 10

Anderson H. Brown, crusader for business opportunities and civil rights for blacks in Kanawha County and the owner of the main building at Washington and Shrewsbury streets, the cornerstone of "The Block." JR

A 1953 portrait of the late G.E. "Cap" Ferguson, owner of the Ferguson Enterprises. JR

Mr. C.H. James, Sr., founder of C.H. James and Son Wholesale Fruits and Produce Company in 1916. Mr. James, with his three brothers, had entered the world of business as foot peddlers in 1883. JR

In the early teens, C.H. James made deliveries with mule drawn wagons, and operated out of a Summers Street storefront. JR

C.H. James and his son, E.L. James, Sr., stand in front of their new building at Virginia Street and Park Avenue in 1916. JR

In this 1933 photo, Mr. R.C. Barnes stands in front of his second Q-Ball Inn, located on Washington Street East between Jacob and Bradford streets. His first business in the 1920s was located on Summers Street, between Kanawha and Virginia streets. The little boy is Charles Cunningham. JR

During his campaign against Franklin Delano Roosevelt, President Herbert Hoover spoke for a few minutes to 20,000 people at Laidley Field on October 22, 1932. He was welcomed with a 21-gun salute. SWV AND KELLY BRATTON

West Virginia's candidate for president, John W. Davis of Clarksburg, stopped at Charleston's C&O depot on September 25, 1924, on his campaign against Calvin Coolidge. SWV

A good 1931 aerial view of the river, South Side Bridge, C&O station and Ward Engineering Works. GS

Elk River area in 1931, showing the Washington Street Bridge. Morgan Lumber & Manufacturing Company and the West Virginia Sand and Gravel Company (both on the west bank). Note the sunken barge at the bottom. GS

Elk River area in 1931 showing the Virginia Street Bridge. GS

Kanawha Boulevard followed the same path as the old James River and Kanawha Turnpike. This famous road saw many famous people of history pass along its course—Henry Clay, Andrew Jackson, Rutherford B. Hayes, and William McKinley. When the five miles of the boulevard were constructed in 1939-40, it was considered one of the greatest waterfront projects in the world. Engineers have compared the volume of earth and stone moved as equal to the building of the great pyramid of Cheops in Egypt —over 938,000 cubic yards! Much of the fill was dredged from the river itself and most of the stone for stabilization was quarried on the Elk River. Nearly 26,000 cubic yards of concrete was used. The total cost of this magnificent riverfront thoroughfare was $3,500,000.

At the start of construction of Kanawha Boulevard in 1937, the home of Mrs. Curtis Dawley at 1301 Kanawha Street was moved onto coal barges and towed across the Kanawha River to its new site at 4906 Kanawha Avenue in Kanawha City.

The old city levee before and during construction of the Kanawha Boulevard. All the buildings on the river side of Kanawha Street were removed except the Union Building at the end of Capitol Street. AUTHOR'S COLLECTION

The unmistakable profile of President Franklin D. Roosevelt as he inspected the naval armor plant at South Charleston on September 3, 1940. Riding in the car with him are Senator Matthew M. Neely to his right and Governor Homer A. Holt to his left. The plant was built during Roosevelt's tenure as assistant secretary of the Navy in 1917. After the inspection, the President's party crossed the Patrick Street Bridge, rode up the new Kanawha Boulevard to the South Side Bridge to the C&O Station where he boarded his train for the return trip to Washington. Roosevelt had visited Charleston twenty years before when running for vice-president. He rode the train to the K&M depot on Broad Street and spent some time campaigning in the city. On his 1940 visit the President was accompanied by his wife, Eleanor, who visited the state capitol, spoke briefly from the steps of that building and had lunch with Mr. and Mrs. Arthur Koontz at their South Hills home. This beautiful Cadillac was one of FDR's special vehicles. It was carried on the train for his use at each stop. Note the license tag, U.S.S.S.—United States Secret Service. COURTESY AP/WORLD WIDE PHOTOS

D. Boone Dawson served as mayor of Charleston from 1935 to 1947, through the Depression and World War II. He had a profound impact on developments in Charleston.
COURTESY CITY OF CHARLESTON

Camp P-39 of the Civilian Conservation Corps at Decota on Cabin Creek, 1935. This was a private CCC camp established on coal company land in 1933 to employ area coal miners who were out of work. Enrollees came from Ohio, others parts of West Virginia, and the immediate area. Their work involved forest fire fighting, fire hazard reduction and state nursery production. The camp closed in 1939 or 1940 and a few houses are now located on the site just below the Decota School.

COURTESY CHARLES SMOOT, DRY BRANCH

The majestic Union School that was built in 1870 on State (Lee) Street, was the first school building erected in the county. The building also housed the county's first high school in 1876. The building was eventually torn down and the Fruth School built in its place in 1932.
COURTESY MRS. ROBERT W. LAWSON, JR.

Chapter Sixteen

Teaching the Mind

Education in the County

Primary schools in Kanawha County can be traced back at least to 1798, when a school is known to have been in existence at present Cedar Grove. The first primary schools were supported by private subscription in Kanawha, as in other Virginia counties, and were available only to children whose parents paid the required tuition. After 1810 the Literary Fund of Virginia paid tuition for children whose parents were too poor to send them to school. In 1829 the Virginia legislature passed a law allowing counties to establish free public schools, but Kanawha was not one of the counties to take advantage of it.

About 1820 Ezra Walker opened the first school in the Malden district in a building erected by Lewis Ruffner. Although records have not been found to indicate exact dates, schools were also established early on in the districts of Elk, Poca and Big Sandy. Mrs. Stephen Teays established the first St. Albans school in 1820 in a large, log church on the west side of Coal River. By 1826 there were 16 schools for indigent children in the county, although the number varied greatly until 1847.

In 1847 the Virginia legislature enabled the counties to vote for public schools and to levy taxes to pay for them, but several salt makers in Kanawha County refused to pay a school tax, which limited school funds and student participation. In 1863, however, the new West Virginia constitution mandated the creation of a public school system in the state. Under the state township plan, Charleston residents established a Board of Education, which divided the town into two districts that were separated by Truslow's Branch. The Upper District established a school in the Asbury Chapel in 1864, and other districts in the county established schools in whatever buildings they could find, sometimes private homes.

Although education was not a high priority, in 1870 the Charleston citizens were finally persuaded to build their first school at a cost of $9,000. Situated on State Street, the Union School was in use when the first high school in the county was established there in 1876.

The Charleston school system was rapidly expanded under the leadership of George S. Laidley, who was Charleston's superintendent of schools from 1878 to 1922, except for the years between 1881 and 1883. Laidley had previously been the principal of the first high school at Union School in 1876.

The 1933 county unit plan, under which all school systems in the state now operate, greatly increased the progress of education in the county. The county's Board of Education survived the financial crisis of the Great Depression, wartime restrictions, and more recently, the school textbook controversy that made national headlines in 1974.

Black children were educated separately from white children. By 1865 the Tinkerville School was opened in Malden, which was attended by Booker T. Washington. Garnet School was erected in 1889, and other black grade, junior high and high schools were soon established until a Supreme Court ruling ended school segregation in 1954.

In 1867 the Sisters of Saint Joseph started a parochial school in Charleston, which was open until 1895. The Franciscan Sisters reopened the school in 1903 as the Sacred Heart School. Charleston Catholic High School opened in 1923, and currently several other Catholic schools exist in the county.

George S. Laidley (1855-1938) was the superintendent of city schools for 42 years, and was the most influential person in the early development of the city school system. After receiving a degree from West Virginia University, Laidley was principal of the county's first high school that was established at Union School in 1876. He was also instrumental in the formation of the present Kanawha County Public Library. Laidley Field is named in his honor.

COURTESY OTIS K. RICE

Grade 3A at the Union School in 1909.
COURTESY RICK HAMILTON

Private schools, funded by subscription, have been established in the county for years. Prior to the Civil War, Henry Ruffner opened the Mount Ovis Academy for young men in the hills above Malden. Mrs. Eckstein opened a school for young girls in 1823, and several churches had schools in the early nineteenth century. In 1880 Major Thomas F. Snyder founded the Kanawha Military Institute on State Street as a high school that prepared young men for the Virginia Military Institute, the University of Virginia, and other institutions of higher learning. Students learned basic soldiering skills, in addition to the normal high school courses. The school, however, was not open for many years. Private schools that provide specialized instruction or adhere to certain religious ideals still exist in Kanawha County.

COURSE OF INSTRUCTION

AND

RULES AND REGULATIONS

FOR THE

UNION SCHOOL

OF THE

CITY OF CHARLESTON,

WEST VIRGINIA.

Approved Nov. 2, 1878.

SCHOOL COMMITTEE:

JOHN W SENTZ, D MAYER, W I OAKES

CHARLESTON, W. VA.:
JOURNAL JOB PRINTING OFFICE, OPERA BUILDING.

1878.

8 RULES AND REGULATIONS

RULES AND REGULATIONS.

GENERAL POWERS AND DUTIES OF THE SUPERINTENDENT.

1. He shall have the *general supervision*, classification, and management of the Schools, and of the School property.

2. He shall visit and examine each and all of the Schools personally, as often as practicable, and give attention to their organization; and shall aid and direct Teachers in the proper classification of their pupils, and may *promote* or place in a lower grade upon examination. And he shall direct the Teachers to make such changes as shall seem best calculated to give greater efficiency to the Schools.

3. He shall kindly and plainly point out to the Teachers any faults or defects in modes of instruction or management which he may consider calculated to interfere with the prosperity of the school.

4. He shall hold Teachers' Meetings weekly, or as often as he may deem necessary; and he shall keep the School Committee informed of the condition of the several schools, and any changes required in the same; and whenever he doubts the qualifications, efficiency, or fitness of a Teacher, he shall report the same to the School Committee.

5. He shall prepare the Monthly Pay-Roll of Teachers, and shall monthly make to the School Committee a general report of the School. He may hear recitations, and conduct any examinations he may deem proper; and when not occupied by his other duties, he shall assist in teaching the High School.

FOR THE UNION SCHOOL. 9

DUTIES OF TEACHERS.

1. They shall preserve neatness and order in the school-rooms, and give vigilant attention to the ventilation and temperature of the same, causing the rooms to be frequently opened and aired. They shall always ventilate, except in *Summer, by lowering the upper sash* of the window; and on no account to suffer the children to sit in draughts of cold air: and, as a general rule, to cause all the windows to be opened for the free admission of air at recess, except in extreme cold weather.

2. It shall be the duty of the Teacher, at the close of each school day, to notify the parent or guardian of every pupil, without exception, who was absent or tardy. The first and second notices may be sent by a pupil, but the third shall be carried by the Teacher in person, or sent through the mail.

3. It shall be the duty of any Teacher who may intend to resign, to give two weeks' notice before such resignation shall be accepted, unless specially relieved by the School Committee. And any Teacher may be discharged at any time for improper conduct, incompetency to teach or to govern his School, unfaithfulness in the performance of his duties, disregard for the rules of the Schools or the requirements of the Superintendent, or the want of success, which is necessary to the progress of the School.

4. Teachers shall at all times exercise a firm and judicious discipline, and punish as sparingly as may be consistent to secure obedience. The following modes of punishment are regarded as unobjectionable: Reproof, properly and kindly administered, in private or before the School, according to the nature of the offence; deprivation of privileges, as recesses, &c.; restraint, and when other means have failed, corporal punishment: and when the *rule* is used, it must be a *flexible wooden rule* not less than one and one-half inches wide, nor more than one-eighth of an inch in thickness, and not to be used upon the hands or about the head. Punishments are to be inflicted in the room by the pupil's Teacher, except in *special* cases, in which the Superintendent is to be the judge. For violent and determined insubordination, Teachers may report a pupil to the Superintendent

10 RULES AND REGULATIONS

5. Teachers having charge of Schools, must be present at their respective rooms at least fifteen minutes before school commences in the morning, and fifteen minutes in the afternoon. The hour for commencing school, in the morning, shall be fifteen minutes before nine o'clock, and fifteen minutes before two in the afternoon.

6. They shall attend regularly and promptly all Teachers' Meetings.

7. Each Teacher shall make out a schedule of his recitations at the beginning of the year, and shall furnish a copy thereof to the Superintendent, who shall likewise be notified of any changes in the same.

PUPILS.

1. The Public Schools of the city being established for the general benefit of the community, all pupils shall be admitted on equal terms, impartially instructed in the branches taught, enjoy equally all privileges of the schools, saving, however, the separate organization of the colored school, and be promoted from grade to grade upon the basis of *merit* and *proficiency* only.

2. No pupil shall be received or continued in the Public Schools, known to be affected with scarlet fever, small-pox, [redacted], whooping cough, measles, itch, spotted fever, [redacted], contagious inflammation of the eyes or scald head, or any other contagious disease, nor coming from a family where any of the above contagious or infectious diseases prevail.

3. Pupils must walk quietly through the halls and up and down stairs, and not remain in the hall or stairway at any time when their school-rooms are open.

4. Pupils must not throw stones or other dangerous missiles of any kind upon the school-grounds. They must not collect upon the school-ground more than one-half hour before the time for opening schools, nor must they remain after the sessions have closed.

5. No pupil, nor any one in daily connection with the school, will

FOR THE UNION SCHOOL 11

be permitted to use tobacco or any substitute for the same in the school-room or on the school premises.

6. Pupils guilty of defacing or injuring school property, shall be required to pay for all damages, the amount of which shall be estimated by the Superintendent.

7. No pupil shall be allowed to depart before the appointed hour of leaving school, except in case of sickness or at the request of parents or guardian, or for some pressing emergency, of which the teacher shall judge. Pupils whose recitations are imperfect, will be required to recite at such times as will be most convenient to the teacher, and may be retained fifteen minutes after the close of the forenoon session, and sixty at the close of the afternoon.

8. The pupil in the three primary grades who shall be absent ten half days in one month without valid excuse, and any pupil above the three primary grades who shall be absent eight half days in the same length of time, without good excuse, shall be suspended from school; such suspension to remain in force until satisfactory assurance is given that attendance will be punctual in the future. The Superintendent may reinstate a pupil once, but in case of a second forfeiture, he or she can be admitted only by special order of the School Committee. Three tardinesses shall be regarded as one absence, in applying this rule.

9. Upon the return of a pupil after any absence or tardiness, he or she shall bring an excuse in writing from his or her parent or guardian, stating "*that such absence or tardiness was necessary and with his consent.*" Such absence or tardiness shall thereupon be excused.

See above rules for punishment: "When a rule is used it must be a flexible wooden rule no less than 1½ inches wide nor more than 1/8 inch in thickness and not to be used on the hands or about the head!"

St, Albaas Graded School,

Report to parents of standing as to Scholorship, Industry, and General Deportment of Pupils in the Advanced Department for the 1st half of the Session of 1884 and 1885. 100 perfect.

THE NAME OF Marquess Lyle

GRADE FROM 0 TO 100.

1. Algebra........ 75
2. Arithmetic........ 85
3. Composition........ 95
4. Deportment........ 90
5. Geography........
6 Grammar........

U. S. History........ 85
Map Drawing........ 95
Industry........ 90
Orthography........ 80
Penmanship........ 99
Punctuality........ 99

Regularity of Attendance.

Respectfully,
H. W. HOVEY, A. M., PRINCIPAL.

JARRETT & ESTILL'S CITY DIRECTORY. 7

KANAWHA MILITARY INSTITUTE.

MAJOR THOS. F. SNYDER,
Professor Mathematics and Tactics, and Commandant of Cadets.

MAJ. W. P. EWING, M. D.,
Professor of Chemistry and Physiology and Surgeon.

CAPT. DAVID T. DUNCAN,
Professor Ancient and Modern Languages.

CAPT. W. F. SNYDER,
Assistant Instructor in Tactics.

Thorough Instruction in *Mathematics*, Ancient and Modern Languages, *Natural Science*, History, Literature, Tactics, and the preparatory *English* studies.

Especial inducements offered to young gentlemen preparing for our higher Colleges or Universities.

FIRST TERM COMMENCES ON THE
FIRST WEDNESDAY IN SEPTEMBER,
THE SECOND TERM BEGINS ON THE
THIRD WEDNESDAY IN JANUARY.

For further information, Address,
THOS. F. SNYDER,
Charleston, West Va.

1884

JARRETT & ESTILL'S CITY DIRECTORY. 103

Kanawha Military Institute.

Professors:
Thos. F. Snyder,   W. P. Ewing, M. D.,
David T. Duncan,   W. F. Snyder.

Roll of Cadets:

1. Snyder W. F. Captain.
2. Campbell C. M. 1st. Lieutenant and Adjutant.
3. Brabbin R. 2nd. Lieutenant.
4. Patrick G. S. 1st. Sergeant.
5. Ruffner A. 2nd. "
6. Putney J. 3rd. "
7. McChesney R. 4th. "
8. DuBois C. G. 1st. Corporal.
9. Smith H. B. 2nd. "
10. Hubbard J. 3rd. "
11. Loyd E. 4th. "

PRIVATES.

12. Alexander A. B.
13. Ashby W. L.
14. Barr W. B.
15. Bodkin Herman.
16. Brooks H.
17. Broun E. F.
18. Broun H. L.
19. Caruthers Ben. A.
20. Clarkson H. B.
21. Dickinson Wm.
22. Dryden Chas.
23. Farrar R. G.
24. Fife W. E.
25. Fisher F.
26. Flagg F. L.
27. Fry Henry
28. Goshorn Albert
29. Hoge Geo. W.
30. Hogue Wm. A.
31. Kaufmann L. E.
32. Kyle Geo.
33. Knight E. W.
34. Knight H. W.
35. Laidley Percy
36. Lewis C. C.
37. Lewis J. D.
38. Lovell Wm.
39. Loyd F. H.
40. McChesney H.
41. Morris Chas.
42. Norman C. W.
43. Peyton Jno. A.
44. Quarrier A. W.
45. Quarrier J. S.
46. Quarrier R. G.
47. Ruffner D. L.
48. Summers Geo. W.
49. Tompkins Prince
50. Thayer G. T.
51. Thayer W. T.
52. Thayer J. R.
53. Thayer J. J.
54. Ward C. E.
55. Winkler John
56. Whitehurst G. A.
57. Wyant E. J.

The Hillcrest Open Air School that was associated with the Hillcrest Sanatorium on Hillcrest Drive, overlooks downtown Charleston in the 1920s. COURTESY BOARD OF EDUCATION

The May Queen and her court at the Leewood School in 1944.
COURTESY MR. & MRS. F.L. CRAWFORD

The grade school at Ordnance Park, South Charleston, during a demonstration of good dental hygiene. COURTESY MRS. R.B. FRINCKE, TORANDO

Malden High School was housed in this building from 1922 to 1939, when the high school was consolidated with the new Dupont High School. The building was torn down in 1961. TH

Leewood Grade School on Cabin Creek.
COURTESY MRS. JACQUELINE CASTO DAVIS

The first Catholic grade school was on the old Dunbar property at Broad and Quarrier streets. This building was built in 1872 and closed in 1920. The Sacred Heart Grade School is now on this site. COURTESY SACRED HEART CHURCH

Kanawha School was built in 1907, and its 1915 annex now houses the Kanawha County Board of Education on Elizabeth Street. COURTESY BOARD OF EDUCATION

Kanawha County Secondary Schools

In 1876 the first county high school was established at Union School with George S. Laidley as principal. Although there were only two teachers, about 25 students were taught algebra, history, Latin, German, English, philosophy and geometry. The first graduating class was made up of Mary E. Jones and Mattie V. Brown.

The high school was moved in 1890 to the Mercer School, presently the site of Charleston High School. Several years later, the school moved back to Union School until 1904, when it occupied a new building on Quarrier Street that was built for the newly named Charleston High School. Charleston High School was moved in 1918 to a new building on the corner of Quarrier and Morris streets and in 1926 to its present building on Washington and Brooks streets.

Garnet High School for black students opened in 1908, and by the early 1920s Elkview, Clendenin, Dunbar, St. Albans, Malden, and East Bank had their own high schools. At the end of 1922, Kanawha County had seven high schools with an enrollment of 1,628 pupils. The Charleston Catholic High School, which had been in existence since 1923, was built in 1940 when the Catholic community raised money for the building. The number of students from the west side increased at Charleston High School, and finally in 1940, Stonewall Jackson High School was built on West Washington Street. Over the next few decades, high school enrollment increased when several new and consolidated schools opened in the county. The controversy about consolidating the Charleston high schools was finally settled in 1987, when ground was broken for the new Capitol High School at the old Meadowbrook Country Club site.

Commencement Exercises

Clendenin High School

on Friday evening

May the Thirtieth

Nineteen hundred nineteen

High School Auditorium

Junior high schools were first started in the county in 1915 with the establishment of Central Junior High School. Situated in the old Charleston High School on Quarrier Street in 1915, it was the first junior high established in West Virginia. Mabel Frances Gibbons, who was the principal from 1915 to 1938, was the first female junior high principal in the state. In 1918 the second junior high, Lincoln Junior High, was established in the old Lincoln Grade School on the West Side. Thomas Jefferson Junior High School moved in 1926 to the former Charleston High School building at Quarrier and Morris streets.

Four more city junior highs, Roosevelt, Woodrow Wilson, Chamberlain, and Boyd for black students, were built in the 1920s in addition to schools in Chelyan, Gallagher, Leewood, Pratt, Ward, Cedar Grove and other areas of the county.

Mercer School was built in 1888 on the site of the present Charleston High School. Although there is no record of when this building was torn down, the first Charleston High School was opened on Quarrier Street in 1904 and the present building was finished in 1926.
COURTESY MRS. ROBERT W. LAWSON, JR.

Mercer Grade School opened next to the YWCA on Quarrier in 1904. It was the first building erected for a high school in the county. Over the next six decades the building housed the Charleston High School, Central Junior High School, Mercer Grade School, and the Board of Education. In 1970 it was demolished to make way for a parking lot.
COURTESY BOARD OF EDUCATION

The 1904 sophomore class on the steps of the nearly completed Charleston High School on Quarrier Street. Nine boys and nine girls from this class graduated in 1906 RA

The Charleston High School band in 1921 posing in front of the school which later became Thomas Jefferson Junior High School. SWV

Construction of Charleston Catholic High School in 1940. The first Catholic high school in the county was opened in 1923 at the corner of Broad and Quarrier streets.
COURTESY SACRED HEART CHURCH

Kanawha County's second high school was Big Sandy District High School at Clendenin in 1911. The building is now used as a grade school. CPL

The original Garnet School, on the left, was erected in 1889 to educate black children. The building on the right was erected in 1908 as Garnet High School. Both schools were located on Jacob Street. The old grade school was replaced by the new Boyd Grade School, left in right photo, and the high school became Boyd Junior High in 1921. The new Garnet High School for black students was opened in 1928 on Dickinson Street. Because of the desegregation rule in 1954, Garnet was closed in 1956 and it now serves as a community education center for the Kanawha County School System.

SWV & KANAWHA COUNTY BOARD OF EDUCATION

Garnet High School on Dickinson Street.
COURTESY KANAWHA COUNTY BOARD OF EDUCATION

Garnet High "Girls," early 1900s. SWV

Garnet High School teachers about 1915. SWV

One of the county's oldest school buildings still in use, the Lincoln Junior High School at Lee and Delaware streets was built in 1890 as a grade school. CN

The first class of the Elkview High School in the C.I. Dodd Building, 1922. COURTESY DR. A.C. DIXON

Higher Education in Kanawha County

Higher education was first established in the county when the Mercer Academy opened in 1818 at the corner of Quarrier and Hale streets. Presently the location of the Morrison Building, the lot was donated by David Ruffner to the Presbyterian Church, which was built next to the Mercer Academy. Henry Ruffner was the first teacher at the school, which eventually offered post secondary courses in science, languages, mathematics, philosophy, and law. Union troops took over the Mercer Academy during the Civil War, and they burned the school during the Battle of Charleston in 1862. After the war, the building was repaired and used as a black church until it was reopened as a school a few years later. David Ruffner's heirs later repossessed the property, until the Charleston Board of Education took it over and removed the building in 1876.

The second Mercer School, which was no longer called an academy was built in 1888 on the present site of Charleston High School. The school was a high school for two years, and a grade school until 1903, when the third Mercer School was built on Quarrier Street. Although there is no record of the date the second Mercer School was torn down, it was gone when the new high school was built in its place in 1925.

In the 1870s the state legislature established six normal schools in the state but none were located in Kanawha County. Instead, high school graduates attended a variety of private schools that sprang up in the county in the late 1800s. The Charleston Female College was founded in 1874, but without the expected support from the Methodist Church of West Virginia, it was not open for long. Ten years later, Carbondale College opened at Big Chimney in 1884. Named for the carbon in the surrounding coal mines and supported by subscription, the school was founded by Timothy Nash in an old schoolhouse near the abandoned salt works in Big Chimney. Although the school was attended by students from the surrounding counties, it closed in 1887 because of insufficient funding.

Later known as Shelton College, the Coalsmouth High School was originated in 1872 by the Teays Valley Baptist Association. Originally located in the Town Hall School building in St. Albans, the school moved two years later to a new brick building on College Hill. In 1877 the school was renamed Shelton College in honor of T.M. Shelton, who donated a substantial amount of money to keep the college open.

Although the school finally closed in 1887 because of inadequate funding, its graduates included Senator William E. Chilton and Congressman Joseph H. Gainer. Several prep schools—St. Albans Latin School in 1906, and a boarding school for young ladies in 1915—subsequently used the facilities. By the 1940s the building was in great disrepair, and

Shelton College, formally called Coalsmouth High School, opened in 1874 at St. Albans, and provided a college education for the Kanawha Valley students until it closed in 1887 because of the lack of money and students. The former college is now a two-story residence on College Hill in St. Albans.
COURTESY OTIS K. RICE

part of it was torn down. The first two floors, however, were intact and they were lived in until 1958, when the Quillen family bought the building and remodeled it into a private home.

The state legislature opened the West Virginia Colored Institute at Institute in 1892 and the Montgomery Preparatory School at Montgomery in 1897. These schools eventually became West Virginia State College and West Virginia Institute of Technology respectively.

In 1906 W.S. Mason founded the Mason School of Music and Fine Arts, which became the Mason College of Music and Fine Arts in 1936. The school was located on Quarrier Street until 1956, when it merged with Morris Harvey College. Kanawha Junior College, a two-year college that was founded in 1932, also merged with Morris Harvey College in 1939 when they were both situated in the old Capitol Annex. Morris Harvey College moved from Barboursville to Charleston in 1935, where it eventually became the University of Charleston.

The newest center for higher education in the county was created in 1972, when the state legislature established the West Virginia College of Graduate Studies in Charleston.

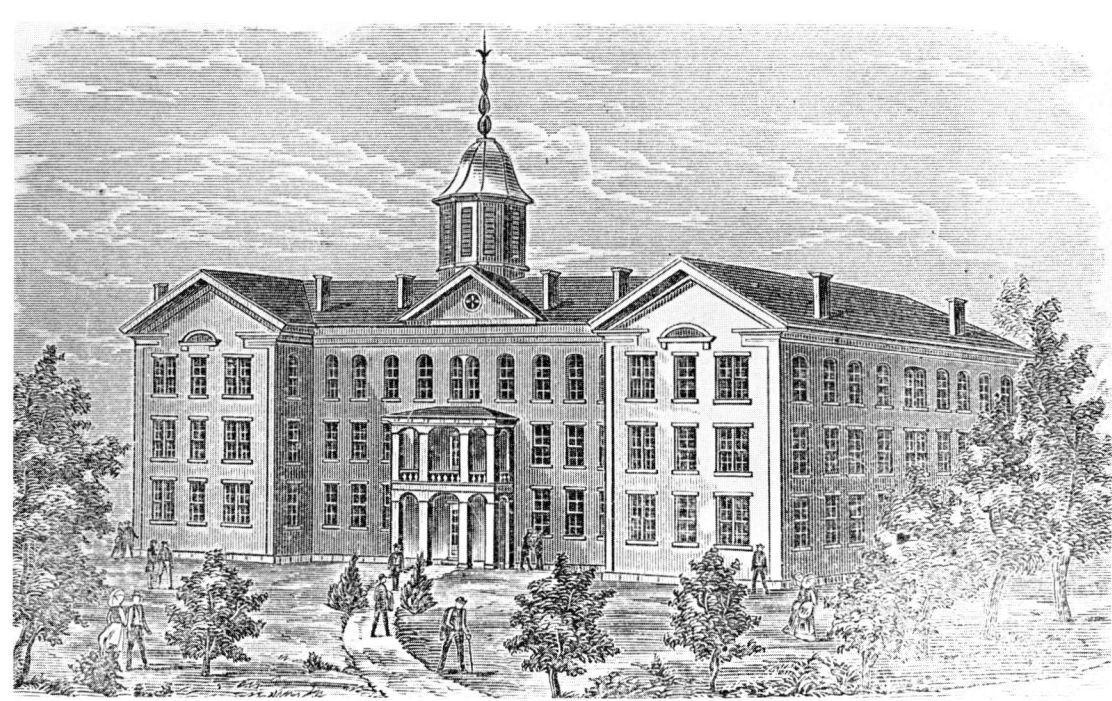

Morris Harvey College/ University of Charleston

After the Civil War, the southern branch of the Episcopal Church, which was associated with Marshall Academy in Huntington, decided to build a new Methodist-Episcopal seminary. They settled on Barboursville in Cabell County because it had lost its position as the county seat in 1888 and there were plenty of vacant county buildings in which the new school could be housed. The county commission, at the request of some leading citizens and the pastor of the local Methodist-Episcopal Church, transferred the county property to the seminary site, and on September 12, 1888, the Barboursville Seminary officially opened its doors.

However, like many other institutions of higher education during this time, the seminary was plagued by financial ups and downs. Finally, the seminary established an endowment in 1901, and Morris Harvey, a prominent businessman from West Virginia, along with his wife Rosa, took an interest in the school. After he contributed a large amount of money to the school, the trustees renamed the institution Morris Harvey College, on May 28, 1901.

Throughout the years, the college built or renovated buildings on its Barboursville campus, but in the early 1930s the college was plagued by severe financial troubles. Upon hearing this, a group of Charleston residents formed the Charleston Educational Center, and invited Morris Harvey College to permanently move to Charleston. Leonard Riggleman, the president of the school, pushed for the move, which was finally approved in the summer of 1935.

Classes opened on September 11 in the old capitol annex on Hale Street, and classes were also held in the YMCA, YWCA, churches, and other buildings. The college shared the annex with the county library, the fledgling Kanawha Junior College, and the Fuel Technical Institute.

Several influential businessmen of Charleston, including A.W. Cox and Vernon A. Cobb, became interested in the college and dedicated themselves to help build up the campus. The Kanawha City Land Company gave the college acreage from their new development on the south side of the Kanawha River, but when failing to meet certain conditions, the college forfeited the land. Instead, the college purchased eleven acres in South Ruffner from the C&O Railway.

Morris Harvey College disaffiliated itself from the Methodist-Episcopal church in 1941, although it continued to build on its Christian heritage for many years. The move to the new campus at South Ruffner was delayed during World War II, and finally, in 1947, temporary buildings were erected and the college settled into its new home. The first permanent building constructed on the campus was the college gymnasium in 1948. Next, Riggleman Hall was built in 1951 and named in honor of Leonard Riggleman, who was the college president from 1931 to 1964, one of the longest tenures in the state's educational history.

Over the years, Morris Harvey College merged with the Kanawha Junior College, and the Mason College of Music and Fine Arts. In 1979 Morris Harvey College became the University of Charleston. For a century, the College/University has been a leader in higher education in the county and in southern West Virginia.

Morris Harvey, the benefactor of Morris Harvey College, was a descendent of William Morris, who was one of the first permanent settlers in the Kanawha Valley. Morris Harvey was born in 1824 in Raleigh County, and grew up in the Morris Mansion near Cannelton. After working at his uncle's store in Fayette County, Harvey was elected sheriff of Fayette County before and after the Civil War. Later a prominent businessman in southern West Virginia, Harvey was instrumental in bringing the C&O railway to the New River Valley, and in developing the New River and Loup Creek coal fields. He married Rosalitha Dickinson and became a devoted member of the Methodist Episcopal Church, South. Harvey's contributions to the Barboursville College kept the college open in the early 1900s. The school, which he supported until his death in 1908, was renamed Morris Harvey College in 1901.

COURTESY UNIVERSITY OF CHARLESTON

Dr. Leonard Riggleman, president of Morris Harvey College from 1931 to 1964. COURTESY OTIS K. RICE

TOP RIGHT: Morris Harvey College was moved from its temporary quarters in downtown Charleston to its present home in South Ruffner on September 8, 1947, its sixtieth anniversary. A U.S. Navy L.C.I. (landing craft infantry) carried the college officials and records from the Capitol Street landing, upriver to the State Capitol landing, where the boat picked up the governor and other state dignitaries, and then crossed the river to South Ruffner. Twenty-five smaller boats escorted the L.C.I., while the Air National Guard flew overhead. Upon landing, President Riggleman stated: "Although our buildings are only temporary, our landing is permanent. Moving a college twice in a lifetime is enough. We are here to stay." COURTESY UNIVERSITY OF CHARLESTON

West Virginia State College

Authorized by the second Morrill Act of 1890, the West Virginia Colored Institute was established in 1892 at its present site in Institute to train black teachers in the agricultural and mechanical arts. An ROTC unit was instituted at the school during World War I, which was renamed the West Virginia Collegiate Institute in 1915. Renamed West Virginia State College in 1929, the school became a leader in black education under the leadership of President Byrd Prillerman and later John W. Davis. West Virginia State College has been desegregated since 1954, and it provides a quality education for all of its students.

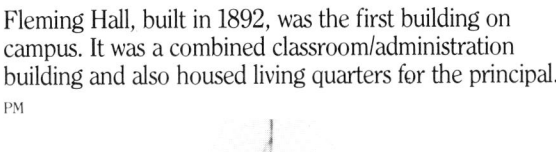

Fleming Hall, built in 1892, was the first building on campus. It was a combined classroom/administration building and also housed living quarters for the principal. PM

An aerial view of West Virginia State College. SWV

-314-

West Virginia Institute of Technology

Located in both Kanawha and Fayette counties, the West Virginia Institute of Technology was established by the legislature in 1895. The school opened in Montgomery on January 4, 1897, as the Montgomery Preparatory School, and this branch of West Virginia University was renamed the West Virginia Trades School in 1917. In 1921 the school became a junior college emphasizing the training of elementary school teachers and it was renamed New River State School. The New River State School became a four-year college in 1929, and three years later its name was changed to the New River State College. Established in 1941 as the West Virginia Institute of Technology by President Edward S. Maclin and Dean David B. Kraybill, the school has provided excellent engineering, technical, business and teachers' education courses.

The Montgomery Preparatory School in 1906. Formerly a branch of West Virginia University, it is now West Virginia Institute of Technology.
SOUVENIR PROGRAM, MONTGOMERY AREA DIAMOND JUBILEE, 9-25 TO 10-2, 1965
VIA OTIS K. RICE

An aerial view of West Virginia Institute of Technology. CN

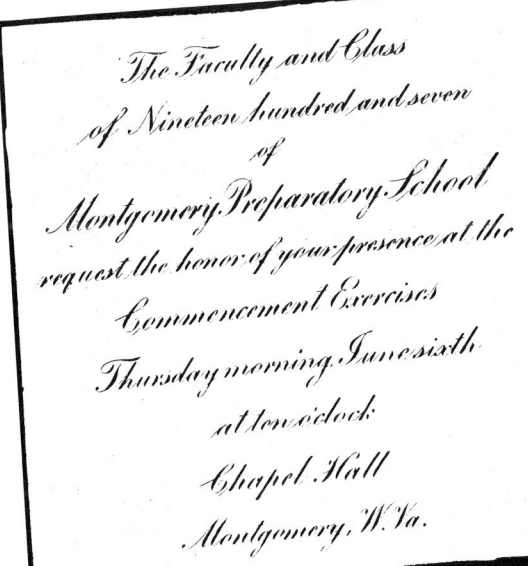

West Virginia College of Graduate Studies

West Virginia University established the Kanawha Valley Graduate Center to provide graduate courses for the many engineers, scientists and teachers in the highly industrialized Kanawha Valley. The graduate center was absorbed by the West Virginia College of Graduate Studies that was created in 1972 by the legislature. A new concept in advanced education, the college offers advanced degrees by using the faculty, personnel and facilities of West Virginia State College, West Virginia Institute of Technology and the University of Charleston to supplement the course offerings provided by their core of full-time faculty.

Charleston General Hospital, 1897. KCL

Chapter Seventeen
Healing the Body and Soul Hospitals and Churches

Healing the Body and Soul
Charleston General Hospital

The staff of the Charleston General Hospital on Richmond Drive overlooking Charleston in 1914. CAMC

Dr. John E. Cannaday, a Virginia native and a 1901 graduate of the University College of Medicine in Richmond, built the original Charleston General Hospital in 1924 at its present site on Elmwood Avenue and Brooks Street, which he operated with his wife until 1948. Cannaday was a member of the House of Delegates in 1907, a founding member of the American Board of Surgery, and a veteran of World War I. He died in 1958. CAMC

One hundred years after Charlestown was chartered in 1794, interested citizens began to express the need for a hospital. Before this time, the sick were simply cared for in the home, and house calls occupied the major part of a physician's day.

Several prominent women in the community, who were concerned about the lack of medical facilities, visited the Samaritan Hospital in Cincinnati, where they hired a nurse to operate a small hospital they had established in 1895. Built near the corner of Front Street (now Kanawha Boulevard) and Summers Street, this small and unpretentious hospital was short-lived.

Several physicians then opened a hospital in the old Staunton home on Front Street, just east of McFarland Street, which later became the Kanawha Presbyterian Church manse. The hospital soon needed larger quarters, and it moved to Father Stenger's house, formerly Sacred Heart rectory. Once again, the hospital outgrew its building and it was moved to a large frame house at 1212 Elmwood Avenue.

Meanwhile various proposals for a city hospital were considered. In 1895 a bond issue was passed to create a city hospital, but there wasn't enough money to buy a site. Finally, the City Council donated twenty acres from the cemetery ground that was north of Piedmont Road on Richmond Drive. Although the building was completed in 1897, there was not enough money to operate it and the hospital stood empty for more than a year.

In 1898 Dr. Frederick S. Thomas proposed to equip and maintain a private hospital, if the city would give him the building and the furniture in it rent-free for six years. He also stipulated that the city connect the lights, water and sewage, landscape the grounds, and construct a road from the cemetery road. The city and Dr. Thomas agreed that a public ward would be created where residents would receive care for under $1.00 a day. The City Council accepted Thomas' proposal, and the Thomas Hospital and Sanitarium was scheduled to open October 1, 1898.

Before all the stipulations were met, however, the hospital opened at the urgent request of Governor Atkinson. An encampment of Spanish American War volunteers had contracted typhoid fever while they waited at Camp Atkinson in Glenwood Park in Charleston for their orders to proceed to Cuba. The men were admitted to the Thomas Hospital and Sanitarium on August 17, 1898, the first patients served by the new facility.

Although the hospital had financial problems, it did provide the Charleston area with the most up-to-date medical care at that time. With two general wards for men and women

About 1895 the Charleston General Hospital opened in the old Staunton home on Front Street, behind the Kanawha Presbyterian Church. When the hospital moved, the house became the Presbyterian manse. CAMC

and twenty rooms for private patients, the hospital could accommodate fifty patients. In 1898, because the lack of trained nurses had become critical, a training school was added to the hospital, founded by Mary E. Reid, R.N. Before this time there were no graduate nurses available to work in the hospital.

The Thomas Hospital was plagued by financial difficulties, and on October 23, 1902, the city council considered plans that enabled Morris Harvey College to secure the city hospital and grounds. These plans never materialized. Thomas operated the hospital, as the original contract with the city stipulated until 1904, when the hospital was reorganized and renamed the Charleston General Hospital and Training School for Nurses. The facility was formally chartered on February 13, 1904.

In 1906 a group of physicians formed a corporation that took over the management for the next eighteen years. An agreement was made between the city council and Drs. C.C. Schoolfield and H.H. Young to lease the building for five years, with the right to renew the lease in 1909 for another 15 years.

In 1924 Dr. John E. Cannaday and his wife helped build the central portion of the present Charleston General building. The original lease for the city hospital was not renewed, so the patients and equipment were moved to the new hospital on Elmwood Avenue and Brooks Street, which had a 120-bed capacity.

In 1936 West Virginia chartered the Charleston General Hospital and School of Nursing, Inc., as a nonprofit charitable institution. Frame buildings east and west of the main building were utilized to increase the capacity of the hospital to over 200 beds, and additional adjacent frame buildings on Washington and Brooks streets were utilized during World War II.

The hospital corporation purchased the Charleston General Hospital building from Cannaday in 1948. The corporation then planned to improve the hospital plant to replace the need for the frame buildings. A contract was signed May 1, 1952, for the construction of a west wing, the first phase of a long-range building program. Completed in December 1953, the west wing had pediatric, laboratory, pathology, and obstetrical departments, a new major operating room, and a large emergency room. Six years later the School of Nursing building was completed, the second phase of the hospital's construction program. The east wing, the third phase of Charleston General Hospital's building program, was completed in 1961.

On January 1, 1971, the Charleston General Hospital merged with the McMillan Hospital, which was founded in 1913 by Dr. William A. McMillan. The Charleston Memorial Hospital then merged with the Charleston General Hospital in 1972. Together the three Charleston hospitals formed Charleston Area Medical Center, which includes the General, Memorial and McMillan Divisions, the largest medical complex in West Virginia.

Construction of Charleston General Hospital at its present location on Elmwood Avenue, 1924. KCL

The original Kanawha Valley Hospital was built next to Dr. Timothy L. Barber's office in 1904. This is a view of his Virginia Street office in the 1880s.
COURTESY TIM BARBER

The Barber Sanitorium and Hospital. When Dr. Barber died in 1910, Dr. Hugh Nicholson took over the hospital and built a four-story annex that was connected to the old building by wooden bridges. Renamed the Kanawha Valley Hospital, the facility was principally owned in 1929 by Anna Bessler, the first nurse at the hospital, and Dr. G.B. Capito, who operated the hospital for years. In 1982 the hospital moved to its new facilities on Pennsylvania Avenue. KCL

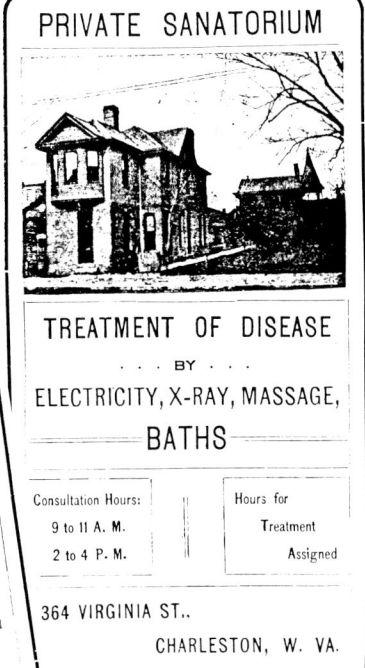

When Dr. Timothy L. Barber opened his Virginia Street Sanitorium in 1904, he sent out this brochure to area doctors advertising the latest equipment and therapies for the treatment of disease—baths, electricity, X-ray, and massage.
COURTESY TIM BARBER

EXPLANATION

In sending out this folder of information, I do not want to give the impression that I have any short or sure method for the cure of all diseases, or that I am any more capable of using these methods than any other physician with like equipments. I wish simply to make it known that I am prepared to take cases in which these modern and up-to-date methods have shown wonderful efficiency.

Physicians know from their medical literature, in what cases these methods and appliances are especially beneficial and the references of such cases as they have not the facilities to treat, will be appreciated. For the sake of a ready answer to many queries, a few of the diseases especially helped by these methods are appended:

APPLICATION

X-RAYS, in the curing of cancer, tumor chronic sores and skin diseases; consumption, brights disease and diabetes; and in diagnosing fractures and dislocations; and in locating foreign bodies, &c.

STATIC ELECTRICITY, in neuroses and neurasthenia, sleeplessness, headache and other painful conditions; constipation; diarrhoea, &c.

GALVANISM AND FARADISM, in diseases peculiar to women, and to men; inflammations; removal of superfluous hairs and skin blemishes; weak nerves and muscles; paralysis, goitre; piles, &c.

ELECTRIC LIGHT AND ROBE BATHS, to reduce system generally, without depressing vitality; general debility; skin trouble and that "tired feeling", &c.

No contagious or infectious disease taken.

Correspondence solicited, or call on

T. L. BARBER, A. M. M. D.
PHYSICIAN IN CHARGE

The St. Francis Hospital was established in 1915 when the Most Revered Bishop Patrick J. Donahue purchased and renovated the old Laidley homestead at 333 Laidley Street. The large frame building consisted of operating and dressing rooms, twelve private rooms, a five-bed women's ward, a ten-bed men's ward, and a kitchen.
COURTESY ST. FRANCIS HOSPITAL

Even though there were three other general hospitals in the city, it was necessary to enlarge the St. Francis Hospital in 1917. This building opened in 1917 with 42 beds, a modern chapel and a chaplain's apartment. The Sisters of St. Francis first operated the hospital until 1921, when the Sisters of St. Joseph of Wheeling took over. When the modern facilities were finally completed in 1986, this building was demolished.
COURTESY ST. FRANCIS HOSPITAL

St. Francis Hospital opened a nursing school in 1915, and two years later the first class of nurses graduated. In 1959, when the two year degree programs in the universities became more popular, the school closed.
COURTESY ST. FRANCIS HOSPITAL

Mountain State Hospital

Mountain State Hospital.
AUTHOR'S COLLECTION

Charleston's hospitals were small, struggling, privately-owned operations when Mountain State Hospital was founded in 1921 by Dr. R.H. Walker, Dr. M.V. Godby, Dr. W.F. Walker, pharmacist George B. Kenney, and the state attorney general, E.T. England. A modern hospital that was built to meet the medical needs of the ever-increasing populace of Charleston, Mountain State Hospital was located at 1301 Virginia Street in an elegant home that was formerly owned by Mayor Grant Hall. The hospital opened in 1921, with R.A. Ireland, M.D., as superintendent and Marie Cooke, R.N., as the superintendent of nurses.

The hospital was chartered in the fall of 1922 as the Mountain State Hospital and Training School for Nurses. Organized for profit with 120 beds, two operating rooms, a delivery room, and urology, emergency, x-ray, laboratory, and sterilizing facilities, the hospital was one of the most modern in the valley. Until 1941 it was profitably and capably run by Charles Warner.

The hospital was reorganized and rechartered in 1941 as the Mountain State Hospital Inc., a nonprofit organization. The nursing school was then phased out in the early 1950s, because increased government regulations set minimum standards that were impossible for a small school to attain.

Throughout the 1950s and 1960s, as government regulations became stricter and costs escalated, the Mountain State Hospital began to suffer financially. Finally, in 1969, the hospital merged with the Charleston Memorial Hospital. Mountain State Hospital was closed after the merger, and the property was subsequently sold. This site is currently the location of the Capitol City Nursing Home.

McMillan Hospital

Nurses at the old McMillan Hospital at Lee and Morris Streets. CAMC

The McMillan Hospital, which later became the McMillan Division of the Charleston Area Medical Center, was founded by Dr. William Andrew McMillan. Raised in New Brunswick, Canada, McMillan was educated at the College of Physicians and Surgeons in Baltimore, where he received his medical degree in 1903. McMillan studied medicine with Sir William Osler, a professor of Medicine at the newly established Johns Hopkins Medical School and later at the University of Oxford, and the greatest physician of his time. Sir Osler's students were referred to as the "pupils of Osler," and Dr. McMillan was one of them.

McMillan came to West Virginia the first time because a friend had casually remarked that "the Kanawha Valley is beautiful country." After McMillan moved to Charleston in 1903, he founded McMillan Hospital in 1913. The hospital was originally a 46-bed facility, which was later expanded to accommodate 110 beds. The McMillan Hospital also featured a nurses' training school that was in operation for a number of years.

McMillan's first son, William Owen McMillan, was born in 1905. The second of three generations of McMillan physicians to practice in the Kanawha Valley, William McMillan received his Medical Degree at the University of Maryland in 1932. Like his father, McMillan chose to practice medicine in Charleston, primarily working with his father as surgeon at McMillan Hospital. Thomas Harvey McMillan, his brother, was the administrator of McMillan for 40 years. His son, William Owen McMillan, Jr., was the third generation of McMillans to practice medicine in Charleston.

In 1971 the McMillan Hospital merged with Charleston General Hospital and the old building, which had seen several generations of McMillans, was sold.

The 1924 class of the McMillan Hospital nurses' training school. CAMC

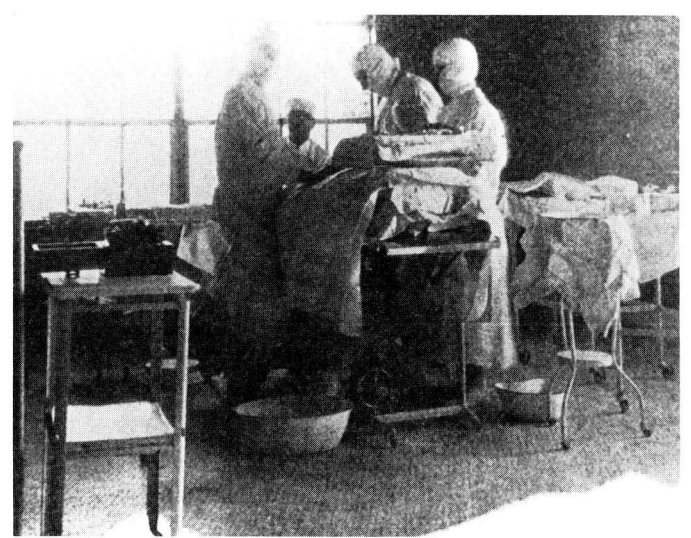 

Operating room and private room at the McMillan Hospital, 1920s. CAMC

The Marmet Hospital for Crippled Children

Before the discovery of the Salk vaccine, polio was a dreaded disease that was almost always fatal. Community hospitals were ill-equipped to care for such patients, and some hospitals did not admit polio victims because they were afraid the disease was contagious.

During the polio epidemic in the late 1930s, the late Dr. E. Bennette Henson recognized the urgent need for a facility to care and treat the children that were crippled by polio. In 1940 he acquired an old eight-room, brick schoolhouse in Marmet, which was converted into a hospital. Known as The Marmet Hospital, the facility admitted its first patients in April 1941. In October of the same year, a group of men from the Belle post of the American Legion organized a Foundation to help equip and finance the hospital and to pay for the care of crippled children whose families couldn't pay. In the mid-40s the Marmet Hospital was the first and only hospital in the area that accepted patients with acute cases of poliomyelitis.

By 1960 the Salk vaccine had all but eliminated polio as a scourge. The Marmet Hospital trustees then decided to initiate a campaign to build a modern hospital for crippled children and adults, to further their legacy of helping disabled individuals. The Marmet Hospital merged with Charleston General Hospital, and eventually a $3.2 million facility was built to care for the crippled individuals. In 1967, the patients were moved from the old school building to the Marmet Division of the Charleston General Hospital in downtown Charleston.

Charleston Memorial Hospital

In late 1940, Helen Townsend Ziebold became convinced that the Charleston area needed an additional general hospital. She met with several friends for a series of discussions, which eventually led the Charleston Chamber of Commerce to appoint a committee to research the feasibility of an additional hospital.

Experts were employed to assess the future needs of the community and to coordinate the committee findings. Several months later the committee recommended the establishment of a modern, fully-equipped health service. On the strength of the committee's report, it was decided that this new facility was needed. The same committee was authorized to formulate ways and means of providing this new health service, and on April 28, 1945, the Memorial Hospital Association of Charleston was created as a nonprofit corporation.

The hospital was built as a memorial to the community's World War II veterans, and in the spring of 1946 a campaign to raise over two million dollars was launched. The public generously contributed to the fund and over two million dollars was raised for this memorial hospital.

In August 1949 ground was broken for the first phase of the building at its location on South Ruffner, and on November 11, 1951, a dedication ceremony was held on the front steps of the completed building. Sixteen days later, patients were admitted to a hospital that had a 129-bed capacity, diagnostic facilities, a surgical bay, and administrative quarters.

From 1953 to 1956 the number of beds at Memorial Hospital increased to 292, plus 34 bassinets. The hospital also added many ancillary services at this time—surgery, recovery rooms, a pharmacy, diagnostic laboratories, and a larger radiology department—to provide additional medical care. When the Hugh Stewart Wing, with its regular and special care nurseries and obstetrical unit was completed in 1974, the Charleston Memorial Hospital became a 440-bed facility that provided a full range of medical services for the community.

The Sheltering Arms Hospital

Sponsored by the Episcopal Church, the Sheltering Arms Hospital was organized in January 1886 to provide care for the sick and injured employees of the Kanawha-New River coal fields and the railroad. The church purchased about thirteen acres of land and several small buildings on the mainline of the C & O Railway at Hansford, and in the spring of 1888 construction of the main hospital began. At the same time, a fundraising drive was launched to raise money for the additions and buildings that were necessary to complete the institution. About 600 people initially enrolled in the hospital at the rate of ten cents a month (this increased to 15 cents in 1908), which entitled them to full medical care. When the hospital opened in the fall of 1888, with a capacity for twenty patients, the Sheltering Arms was West Virginia's second hospital. By 1891 the hospital could treat 30 patients at a time, and by the late 1900s this capacity had increased to 116.

Funds, endowments, and hospital plan enrollments continued to grow, and by 1907-08 the hospital could care for 800 patients. In addition, a nursing school, a chapel, and a home for a missionary and his staff were added to further extend hospital services, and by 1917 the nursing school had 53 trained graduates.

When Dr. J. Ross Hunter became superintendent of the Sheltering Arms in 1907, he oversaw the construction of an additional hospital building that was completed and dedicated on July 15, 1908. With 100 additional beds and the latest in patient care equipment, the building also provided a power house, laundry, and a plant for electricity and heat.

In the early days, patients came to the hospital by train, boat, horse-drawn ambulance, litter and on foot from as far away as Raleigh County, and from the industrial corporations, mostly coal companies, in the area. In 1921 the Sheltering Arms Hospital, which had fallen on hard times, was incorporated with Charleston General Hospital, and the hospital buildings in Hansford were closed in 1922. When the State Road Commission re-routed Route 61 in 1941, they removed some of the hill under the chapel and the hospital buildings, which resulted in slippage and landslides during 1942 and 1943. The Sheltering Arms buildings eventually disappeared.

With the financial help of the federal government and revenue bonds, the city constructed the Herbert J. Thomas Memorial Hospital in South Charleston, which opened on December 9, 1946. The 77-bed hospital was leased by the hospital association, which operates the new facilities today. The hospital was named for Marine Sergeant Herbert J. Thomas. A South Charleston resident, Thomas received the Congressional Medal of Honor for giving his life to save his comrades in the Solomon Islands on November 7, 1943. COURTESY THOMAS MEMORIAL HOSPITAL

Sheltering Arms Hospital at Hansford. AUTHOR'S COLLECTION

Nurses at the Sheltering Arms Hospital. PM

Nurses' quarters at the Sheltering Arms Hospital. PM

Volunteer nurses at Pratt during World War II. PM

THE HOSPITAL WILL RECEIVE

for care and treatment, injured and sick persons, without regard to race or creed.

Application for admission to be made to the Superintendent, at the Hospital, or to the Chaplain, Rev. R. D. Roller, Charleston, W. Va., and must be accompanied by physician's certificate of nature of disease.

In case of accidents, no certificate required.

Persons with contagious diseases, or those caused by immoral habits, **not received.**

Chronic and incurable cases received only by special arrangements, during an acute attack.

No charge made, but contributions gladly received and earnestly solicited.

All Miners and Railroad men requested to subscribe, on pay-roll, **10 cents** each working month.

The Charleston Veterinary Hospital, located next to the old city hall on Virginia Street, was established in 1902 by Dr. S.E. Hershey. It was the first veterinary hospital in the state. A city parking lot is now at this site. KCL

A view of the county infirmary in the early 1900s, which was located at the old Dunbar Fairgrounds. This building was built in 1895 to care for indigent citizens of the county. The area around the infirmary was farmed to provide food for the patients. CN

Hospital prices have certainly changed in the past 68 years.

COURTESY ST. FRANCIS HOSPITAL

Churches

Christianity came to Kanawha County with the first settlers at Fort Lee. William Morris was responsible for a Baptist Church at Crown Hill in 1793. The first Methodist sermon was preached in 1804 and two years later the first Methodist society was organized. The Presbyterians were organized by Henry Ruffner in 1819. The Episcopal Church was first established at Coalsmouth in 1814 as St. Mark's Church. Father Joseph W. Stenger arrived in Charleston in 1866 to minister to a rather scattered flock of Catholics in several counties.

Blacks held their first worship services in 1852 at Black Hawk Hollow, but it was not until after the Civil War that the freed slaves organized their churches. Soon after the war the African Zion Baptist Church was built at Malden. A mission was organized at Chappell Hollow in 1865, but it soon split into two groups.

People of the Jewish faith came to Charleston before the Civil War, many of them becoming prominent city businessmen. Services were held as early as 1871. The Virginia Street Temple was organized in 1873, the Orthodox community in the 1890s.

Many other religious organizations—the Lutherans, Jehovah's Witnesses, Mormons, Greek Orthodox, Disciples of Christ, Nazarene, and the Seventh Day Adventists now make up the religious fabric of the county.

The Union Mission was founded in 1911 by Pat B. Withrow, the Mountain Mission in 1926 by O.F. Clendenin and the Open Door Mission in 1938. YMCA and YWCA are active in the county. Several schools and hospitals have also had religious affiliations at one time or another.

Kanawha Presbyterian Church and Manse opened November 20, 1830, although the congregation had met in the Mercer Academy since 1819. Named the Kanawha Presbyterian because both Charleston and Kanawha Salines residents were founding members, the church was donated by David Ruffner and organized by his son, Henry Ruffner. The church, and later the manse, stood on a lot that was on the north side of Back Street, the present site of the Masonic Temple on Virginia Street. Dr. Spicer Patrick built the manse in 1829, and when he moved in 1848 the church took over the house. When the Presbyterian Church became divided between the northern and southern factions, a few members purchased the Asbury Chapel under the name Kanawha Presbyterian. This building was used as a temporary church from 1873 to 1885, while the present church on Virginia Street was constructed. The small gabled structure on the right was a lecture room that was built several years after the main church. This photo was dated 1856, and if this is accurate, it would be the oldest existing photograph in the county. The photograph, however, could have been taken anytime between 1856 and 1872 when the church was no longer used. KCL

In the cities and rural areas of Kanawha County, religious sentiment was quite strong. These views show an early 1900s baptism in a Kelly's Creek coal field. SWV & ES

The first St. John's Episcopal Church was built about 1837 at the northwest corner of Virginia and McFarland streets. It was torn down about 1888. During the Civil War it was used as a storehouse by the Union Army. In 1906 the Federal Government paid the church a small sum for the damage caused to the building during the war. COURTESY JOSEPH C. JEFFERDS, JR.

The area's Episcopals can trace their roots back to 1788 and the establishment of Kanawha County. The first Episcopal clergyman to visit the county was the Reverend Joseph Willard, from Marietta, Ohio, about 1814. The first permanent clergyman, Reverend Charles H. Page, came in 1822. Some of the county's most prominent citizens belonged to the church—the Shrewsburys, Summers, Quarriers, Lovells, McFarlands and George S. Patton. Ground was broken for the present St. John's Episcopal Church at the corner of Quarrier and Broad streets in 1884, but due to a lack of money the building was not completed until 1890.

COURTESY MRS. ROBERT W. LAWSON, JR.

This beautiful stone building was the home of Charleston's First Presbyterian congregation from 1883 to just before World War I when the present church was completed. The Morrison Building is now on this site.
COURTESY MRS. ROBERT W. LAWSON, JR.

The Kanawha Presbyterian Church building on Virginia Street was begun in 1872 and officially opened in 1885.
AUTHOR'S COLLECTION

The First Presbyterian Church on the corner of Virginia and Broad streets was constructed in 1915. The building has since expanded to Kanawha Boulevard. AUTHOR'S COLLECTION

The Methodist Meeting House, a log structure, was the first Methodist Church in the county. It was located at the corner of Quarrier and Hale streets. Prior to the completion of this building, the Methodists, who were first organized in 1814 in Charleston, met in private homes. SWV

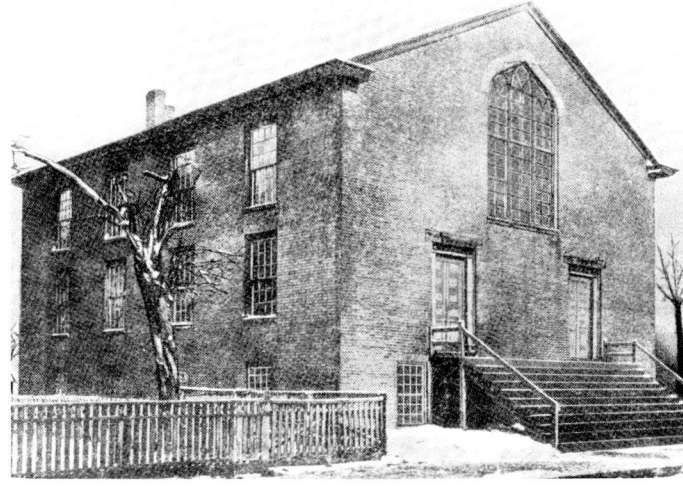

The Methodist's second church building was built on Virginia Street in 1834. It was used until 1872, when it was sold to the Kanawha Presbyterian Church. The 1872 West Virginia Constitutional Convention met in the building. It was later used by a printing company. During the Civil War the basement was used as a school. SWV

The First Methodist Episcopal Church, on the corner of Quarrier and Morris streets, was built in 1910. It was later known as Christ Methodist Church and since 1968 as Christ Church United Methodist. In 1969 a fire destroyed part of the church, which has been completely rebuilt. AUTHOR'S COLLECTION

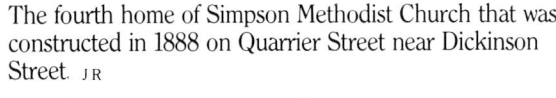

The fourth home of Simpson Methodist Church that was constructed in 1888 on Quarrier Street near Dickinson Street. J R

Temple Bene Jeshurum, or the Virginia Street Temple, in 1894. The temple was incorporated in 1873 as the Hebrew Educational Society by several families, including the brothers Philip and Moses Frankenberger, who established their clothing store in the 1850s. They held services in an upstairs room on Capitol Street until 1875, when a small frame Temple adjacent to the State Street Methodist Church was completed. In 1894 the Temple Bene Jeshurum was finished, which served the Reform Jewish community until the Temple Israel was constructed on Kanawha Boulevard in 1960. GS

The Orthodox Jewish community was established in the 1890s by Eastern European immigrants to Charleston who held their first services in private homes, and later in a rented hall at Kanawha and Summers streets. Their first Cantor and Hebrew teacher was the Reverend Samuel Friedman, who served from 1895 to 1930 in this house that the Orthodox community rented and later purchased from the Reform Temple in 1894. The house was eventually moved to the corner of Court and Washington streets. In 1908 the Orthodox community purchased the former State Street Methodist Church that was used until 1949, when the present B'nai Jacob Synagogue was built on Elizabeth and Virginia streets. Rabbi Samuel Cooper served the congregation and the community for 50 years before he retired in 1981. The Reform and the Orthodox Jewish communities have been involved in the county's development for over 100 years.
COURTESY B'NAI JACOB SYNAGOGUE

Brother Pat Withrow.

The original Union Mission at the corner of Lovell (Washington Street East) and Clendenin streets. Started in 1911 by Pat Withrow, a reformed alcoholic and gambler, the mission provided comfort and shelter for homeless men. COURTESY UNION MISSION

Under "Brother" Pat's 45-year directorship, the mission grew immensely. It took over this city block building on Washington Street East, and now occupies a 500-acre site on South Park Road that was given to the mission years ago by the Abney sisters.
COURTESY UNION MISSION

Pat Withrow leaning on the fender of the Union Mission bus, about 1920. After his death in 1957, the mission was run by Reverend Clyde Murdock and the Reverend James B. Moellendick, the present director.
COURTESY UNION MISSION

The Baptist religion was active before the Civil War in Kanawha County, but an established church was not built until 1869. The growth of the religion can be attributed to the Reverend T.C. Johnson who ministered to his congregation from 1877 to 1918. In 1905 a large stone church was built at the corner of Capitol and Washington streets across from the present building at 405 Capitol Street. In 1925 the present Baptist Temple was dedicated at the corner of Quarrier and Morris streets. KCL

```
THE FRED O. BLUE BIBLE CLASS
        THE BAPTIST TEMPLE
    Corner Capitol and Washington Streets
           CHARLESTON, W. VA.
         FRED O. BLUE, TEACHER
    An organized BIBLE STUDY CLASS FOR MEN
    MEETS EVERY SUNDAY MORNING, 9:45 A. M.
OUR OBJECT—Bible Study, Christian Culture, Friendly Service, Social
   Intercourse, Spiritual Uplift and a Getting Together for
   Good and for God.
WE WANT YOU TO VISIT US NEXT SUNDAY
  You will find a warm welcome—Good orchestra music—Heart warming
singing. Live Wire Discussions—Not a Dull Moment.
        BE ONE OF US NEXT SUNDAY
```

Famous evangelist Billy Sunday, who visited Charleston in March and April 1922, set up a wood tabernacle at the corner of Dickinson and Lee streets. He preached against alcohol and gambling, common practices in the "Roaring Twenties," and supposedly converted 11,000 people. Sunday, a former big-league baseball player, also brought along Homer Rodeheaver, his choir director, who masterfully sang the old hymns. This is the interior of the building shown on page 286. KCL

The first Sacred Heart Church was constructed in 1869 on the site of the present rectory. By the 1880s the congregation had outgrown the building and a new church was planned.

Very Reverend Joseph W. Stenger (1837-1900), first permanent Catholic priest in Kanawha County, served from 1866 to 1900.

ALL PHOTOS COURTESY SACRED HEART CHURCH

The cornerstone for the present Sacred Heart Church on Broad Street was laid on July 28, 1895. The building was completed in 1897. It has been the center for Catholic services ever since. AUTHOR'S COLLECTION

Interior of the original Sacred Heart Church

The present Sacred Heart Rectory was erected in 1902 and remodelled and added to in 1952.

Historic Churches

Ebenezer's Chapel (Marmet Christian Church) at South Ohio Avenue and Hillview Drive in Marmet was constructed in 1836. The one-story brick church contains simple yet elegant Greek Revival elements. It was constructed to serve congregations participating in the Methodist Church's circuit system, a missionary effort developed during the early 19th century. It is owned by the City of Marmet.*

Virginia's Chapel. (The Little Brick Church) is located on U.S. Route 60 at Cedar Grove. A one-story brick church with modified Greek Revival elements, the church was built in 1853 near the site of Fort Morris. William Tompkins built the church at the request of his daughter, Virginia, in lieu of a trip abroad as a graduation present. During the Civil War the church suffered damages for which the Federal government eventually paid $700.*

St. Marks Episcopal Church in St. Albans is the second Episcopal Church to be built in Coalsmouth (St. Albans). Morris Hudson built the first one in 1825 and named it Bangor Parish. In 1845 the church was destroyed by fire. Phillip Thompson immediately donated 10 acres of his plantation for a new church. The bell from the Banger church was salvaged and placed in the new church, where it hangs today. During the Civil War, Union troops camped on the grounds and did some structural damage to the building. In 1915 the Federal Government made a small restitution to the congregation for the damage and the church was restored.*

An artist's rendering of the 1892 courthouse before the additions. WVU

Chapter Eighteen
For the Good of the People: Government Institutions

Kanawha County Courthouse

Although the Kanawha County Courthouse has been housed in a number of different structures, it has been located on the same site since 1796, and whether it was built of logs, brick, or stone, the courthouse has always been the center of local government.

After Kanawha County was formed in 1788, all court proceedings were held in William Clendenin's block house. This soon became inadequate, and in 1796 a levy raised $200 to construct a new courthouse on a lot owned by George Alderson, the site of the present courthouse.

The first courthouse was a one-story, 30' × 40' log structure, and later a log building was added on, which housed a two-cell jail. In 1817 the log courthouse was replaced by a two-story, 50' × 50' brick structure with a steeple, which served the county until December 1888, when the building was secretly razed during the night to break a political deadlock which was delaying the construction of the new courthouse.

The original building of the existing courthouse, now the main building, was constructed in 1892 for $153,000. County Commission President John S. Cunningham and Commissioners C.S. Young and W.S. Laidley selected architect Walter R. Higham, and architect and engineer M. Reuben Shirreffs of Richmond, Virginia, to design the new courthouse. Higham and Shirreffs designed the courthouse in a Romanesque Revival style, a style which was greatly influenced by the American architect Henry Hobson Richardson. Oriented toward the southeast with entrances on Court Street and Kanawha Street, the new building was a massive structure built with locally quarried stone. A figure of "Justice" stood on top of the three-story tower, until the statue disappeared in the 1940s.

In 1917 County Commission President Grant Copenhaver and Commissioners M.P. Malcolm and L.A. Christy contracted H. Rus Warne, a Charleston architect, to design a major addition to the southside of the courthouse. The old courthouse facilities had become inadequate for the growing county. On May 13, 1917, the *Charleston Gazette* reported, "Federal Grand Jury Says County Jail is Unclean and Unsanitary." The newspaper claimed there were problems with the ventilation, the facilities for sleeping, bathing, and cooking, and with overpopulation in general. In 1917 a special levy was passed so the court could appropriate the necessary amount of money for the addition. Central Engineering Company received the contract and it built the addition for an estimated $107,673.

The second major addition to the Kanawha County Courthouse was constructed in 1926. Commissioners Grant Copenhaver, Omar Given and S.E. Childress, President, awarded the contract for the addition to the architectural firm of Warne, Tucker and Patteson and the Wallace Knight Construction Company. At a cost of nearly $125,708, the addition to the courthouse tripled its original size, and the "ell" of the courthouse housed the jail. Five years later, a monument commemorating the founders of Kanawha County was erected by the County Court and presented by the John Young Chapter of the Daughters of the American Revolution.

The courthouse has been renovated on the interior and the exterior several times since the last addition was built. Most recently, the interior of the courthouse underwent a complete restoration, and the building is now listed on the National Register of Historic Places.

The 1817 brick courthouse that was built on the same site as the original log courthouse and the present courthouse. A 50' × 50', two-story building with a tall steeple, the courthouse was built without a foundation, which was common then. By 1888 this courthouse was totally inadequate for the citizens' needs, and it was torn down.
COURTESY OTIS K. RICE

The cornerstone of the present courthouse was laid on May 3, 1892, when John S. Cunningham was president of the Kanawha County Court. WVU

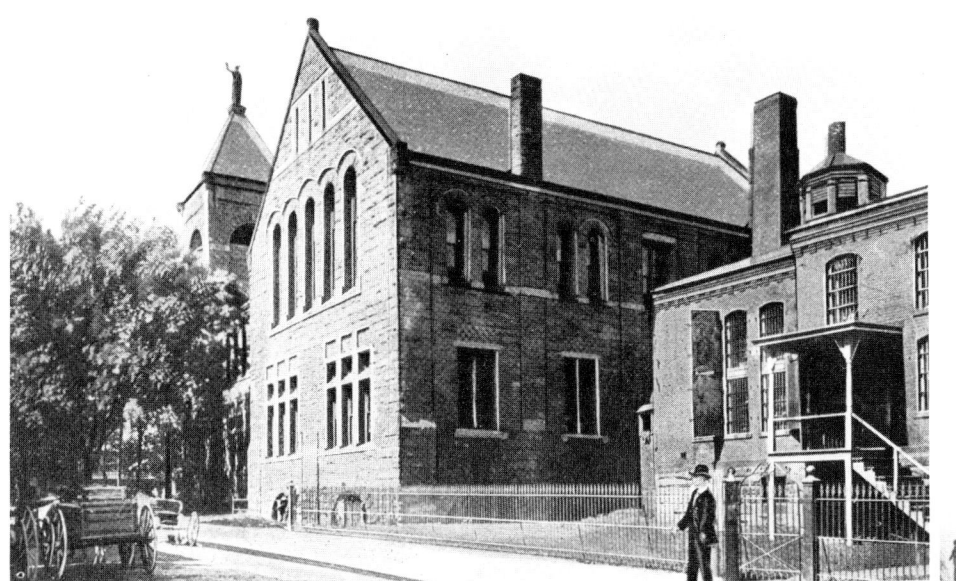

The courthouse and jail around 1905. The view is on Court Street towards Kanawha Street. The old jail was demolished in 1926 so the courthouse could be enlarged. KCL

A view of the courthouse, showing the original center section, looking north on Court Street from Kanawha Street. The tower of the old city hall is visible on the right. The little building on the courthouse lawn is thought to be a bondsman's office, circa 1905. KCL

The new courthouse in 1897, when the main entrance was set back from Kanawha Street. The Court Street entrance that was opposite city hall was blocked off in 1950. During the 1926 construction, the statue of Justice that originally faced Kanawha Street was turned to face Court Street. The statue disappeared in the 1940s and no one knows what happened to it. There is a possibility that it was melted down for scrap during World War II.
COURTESY MRS. ROBERT W. LAWSON, JR.

Built in 1884 at Virginia and Court streets, Charleston's first city hall was built in an eclectic Victorian style, and it housed city offices and the fire department. A clear photograph of this building has not yet been found. WVU

The present city hall was dedicated on August 31, 1922, during the term of Mayor Grant P. Hall. An excellent example of true Renaissance Revival architecture, the building was designed by H. Rus Warne, a Charleston architect, who built the structure under the supervision of A.G. Higginbotham at a cost of $624,000. The fourth floor was originally used as a clinic and hospital—unusual functions for a governmental building. City hall is built on land which comprised lots 7 and 8 of the original 1790 survey completed for George Clendenin. Joseph Ruffner owned the tract until 1884. The old St. Albert Hotel was built on land that is now part of the city parking lot facing Kanawha Boulevard. SWV

Charleston Police Department, 1924.
COURTESY CHARLESTON POLICE DEPARTMENT

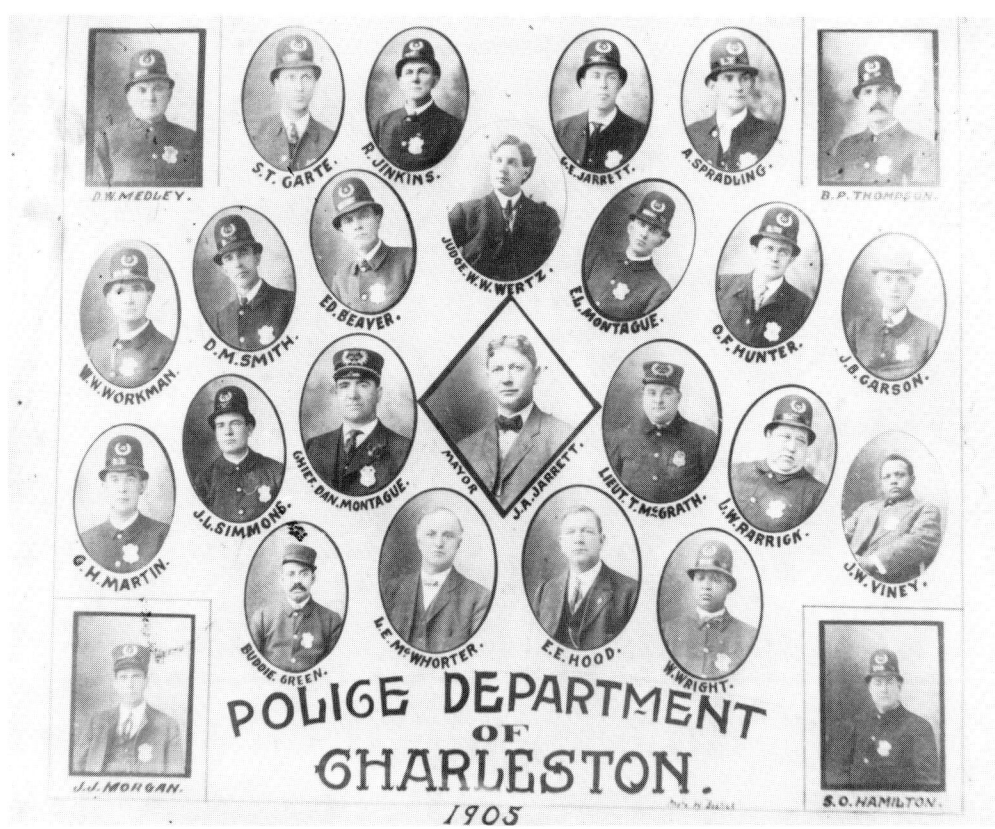

Charleston Police Department, 1905.
COURTESY CHARLESTON POLICE DEPARTMENT

The mounted and foot patrols of the Charleston Police Department, 1920s. COURTESY CHARLESTON POLICE DEPARTMENT

The Fire Department

Mr. Gustave "Gus" Gardner of Riverlake Estates, St. Albans, was born in October 1885. He is the oldest living Charleston fireman (retired), postal employee (retired), and graduate of Charleston High School (see 1906 class photo on page 309).

This never-before published photo of Charleston Fire Department vehicles was taken in 1907 on Court Street between Virginia and Kanawha. The apparatus on the left is a chemical hose wagon, which was intended to rush to a fire in the hope of controlling its spread while the heavy equipment was on its way. The other wagon is a ladder carrier. In the background is the old Kanawha County jail at the southwest corner of Virginia and Court streets. The 1897 center section of the present Kanawha County Courthouse appears at left. Photos of the old jail are extremely rare. It should be noted that most of the fire department horses were remarkably well trained and would often voluntarily proceed to the harness to make ready for the mad dash to the fire.
COURTESY GUS GARDNER

Charleston Fire Department members in 1907. This is an extraordinary photo because it was given to the author by Mr. Gus Gardner, who is the fireman in the top right corner. Mr. Gardner's memory was good enough to let him name six of his comrades. The gentleman in the gray fedora is "Chief" Rand—others are Harry Callahan, Charlie Scott, Bootsie Bodkins, Henry Hicks and Jack Foley, second from the right in the front row. When this picture was taken Fireman Foley had only a few months to live—he was to die in the Ruffner Brothers fire (photo on page 275). COURTESY GUS GARDNER

Charleston Hose Company No. 3, late 1890s. COURTESY EVA HENDERSON

A 1908 American LaFrance aerial fire truck at Engine Company No. 1 of the Truck and Chemical Company in 1915, probably on Court Street. KCL

-342-

Company C of the West Virginia State Police posed in December 1921 on the steps of the M.E. Church South at the corner of Washington and Dickinson streets. Lt. Mack B. Lilly, Commander, is above the steps on the stone projection to the far right. The State Police were formed in 1919, the fourth oldest in the country, because of the political unrest and domestic violence in the coal fields. Their first uniforms were surplus World War I army issue.

SWV

Promotional photos of the State Police riding a motorcycle and stopping a vehicle. These posed shots were taken along the present Southside Expressway near the present Columbia Gas Building in 1920. RA

Post Office

The first post office in Kanawha County was established on April 1, 1801, in an old log house on the northeast corner of what is now Kanawha Boulevard and Hale Street. The post office's name was "Kanawha Court House" and the town was named Charlestown. The actual court house and post office (with the name Kanawha Court House) were located on the opposite ends of the new town. The name Charlestown was frequently confused with a like-named town in Jefferson County (later respelled Charles Town) and a Charlestown in Brooke County (renamed Wellsburg in 1816). Finally, the name Charlestown was officially shortened to Charleston in 1818, although the post office name was not changed to Charleston until September 30, 1879. To add to the confusion there were several spellings for Kanawha —Kenhawa and even Kegnawy.

Edward Graham was the first postmaster, and he was succeeded by Francis A. Dubois in 1803 and William Whitteker in 1808. The mail was brought on horseback from Lewisburg every two weeks until 1810, when improvements on the Kanawha turnpike enabled stagecoaches to make regular runs to Charleston. Subsequent mail delivery improved considerably.

The post office moved to several locations in the next eight decades, including a site near the present Union Building on Kanawha Boulevard, and the site of the present arcade on Virginia Street. In 1881 the U.S. Government bought property between Capitol and Summers streets and in 1884 erected a large brick building with a stone foundation and trim. Built in the Victorian Romanesque style, the building had a tall, square bell tower and a turret and a large round bay area were later added. This building was occupied by the post office until 1910, when it was torn down to make way for a new post office and U.S. Court Building. The post office was temporarily moved to the Brown Block on Capitol Street, until the new building was finished in 1911.

By the early 1940s the post office had once more outgrown its quarters, and in 1943 the post office moved to a building on the corner of Washington and Dickinson streets. This building has since been enlarged, and it now encompasses the entire block.

The old post office was used as a Federal Court House until 1965, when it moved to the nearby Federal Building.

This magnificent building housed the U.S. Customs House and Post Office. Built in the Victorian Romanesque style in 1884 on the site of the present Kanawha County Library, the building was demolished in 1910, and the new U.S. Courthouse and Post Office was constructed on the site. KCL

The old Charleston Post Office, circa 1905, looking west from Capitol Street toward Summers Street. The Arcade and Kanawha Hotel are on the left. KCL

The federal building, and the post office, that was open from 1911 until 1943, is an excellent example of Classical Revival architecture. The Kanawha County Public Library moved from the old Capitol Annex to occupy this building, a year after the new federal building opened on Quarrier Street in 1965. KCL

By the late 1930s a new building was needed for the post office because of the increase in population and postal business. The government built this building on a lot bounded by Washington, Lee, and McFarland streets, which was later expanded to include the entire block. KCL

Public Library

Although there is mention as early as 1823 of a Charleston library with William Whitteker as the librarian, the first public library was established by the Woman's Kanawha Literary Club in 1909 with the support of George S. Laidley, the city superintendent of schools. The library was housed in two rooms in the YMCA building, and Mabel Delle Jones was the first librarian. Two years later, the Board of Education was authorized to levy taxes to support a public library.

In 1911 the library moved out of the expanding YMCA and into the old Presbyterian Church manse on Quarrier Street. The library later moved to the YWCA, and then to a building at the corner of Kanawha and McFarland streets. At the end of World War I, the library moved again to the Red Cross building that was next to the Union Building on Kanawha Street, where it stayed until 1924, when a Corporation purchased the old Capitol Annex on Lee Street for the library.

The Kanawha County Board of Education assumed responsibility for the library in 1933, but several years later the library was again controlled by the county government. In 1966 the library moved to its present site in the old Federal Building on Capitol Street. It is now the largest public library in the state, with branches in St. Albans, Dunbar, Glasgow, Cross Lanes, Elk Valley, and Sissonville.

The Presbyterian Church manse was once the home of the public library. KCL

The Norvell home on Capitol Street was purchased by the YMCA in 1893 and remodeled for $12,000. It was used by the YMCA until 1907. GS via Illustrated, 1894. Charleston, W. VA.

Chapter Nineteen
Organizations

YMCA

In 1907 Henry Gassaway Davis, a coal and railroad baron from Elkins, donated a lot opposite the capitol on Capitol Street for the construction of a new YMCA building. Built in an Italian Renaissance style, the large, four-story structure was designed by Clarence L. Harding of Washington, D.C., and dedicated in 1911. It served YMCA members until 1981, when it was razed and the YMCA moved into a new site at 300 Hillcrest Drive. The old site is now called Davis Park. It features an imposing statue of Henry Gassaway Davis at its center.
COURTESY COLUMBIA GAS TRANSMISSION CORPORATION

Cane Fork (W. Va.) C and O Y. M. C. A. Inset, A. W. Marney, Secretary.

Cane Fork C&O Railway YMCA and A. W. Marney, Secretary. SWV

Handley (W. Va.) C and O Y. M. C. A. Inset, H. E. Snyder, Secretary.

Handley C&O Railway YMCA and H.E. Snyder, Secretary. SWV

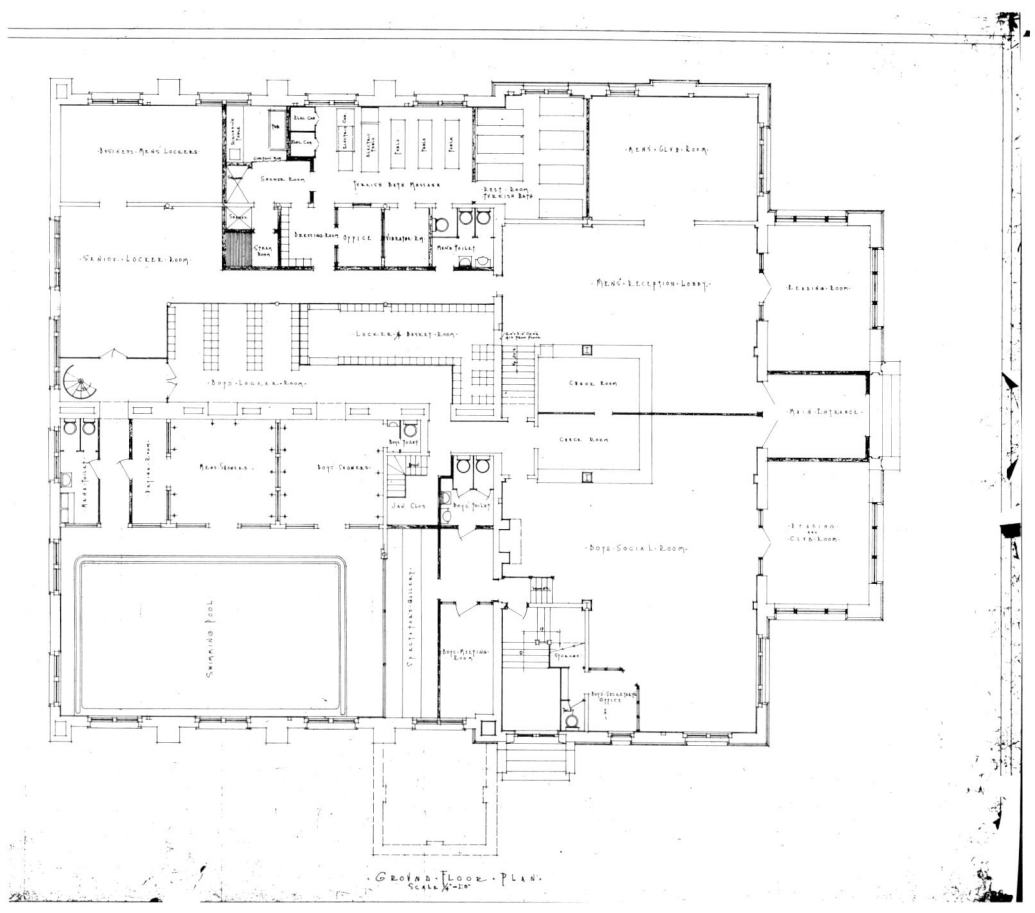

Floor plan of the new YMCA, 1909. SWV

A 1907 view of the K of P Lodge Hall on the northwest corner of Washington and Dickinson streets. The building apparently housed a black YMCA for years, along with several black businesses. The Gem Pharmacy was located here in 1907. It was demolished in the 1950s. JR

YWCA

In 1912 five women from the Baptist Temple organized the YWCA in Charleston to provide safer and more home-like quarters for girls who were moving into town to work. The organizers were Miss Dazie Stromstadt, Mrs. Rose Skelton, Miss Louise S. Tuxbury, Mrs. James T. Montgomery and Miss Eleanor Hooper.

The first site of the YWCA was in the Payne Building, at the corner of Virginia and McFarland streets. A cafeteria was opened on Hale Street. In 1919 the YWCA purchased a lot at 1114 Quarrier Street and, over the next four years, constructed a building that featured a swimming pool, gymnasium, other sports facilities, and living quarters for young women.

The cafeteria was closed in 1954. The original YWCA was completely remodeled in 1986. Today the Y serves the community by providing a large daycare center, a domestic violence prevention center, recreation and health education, day camp, work shops and outreach programs for Lincoln and Clay counties. swv

Henry Gassaway Davis donated the property at 1118 Washington Street in 1896 to establish a shelter for homeless children waiting for adoption. The Davis Child Shelter, which could keep up to 50 children at a time, served the county for over 50 years. WVU

The Salvation Army was established in Charleston in 1904 in a rental building on Lovell Street. Major A.B. Figgins was the first Corps officer. In 1918 the Army moved into this building at 612 Virginia Street East. Shortly afterwards, a disastrous flu epidemic hit the community and the Army used the building to care for indigents. The fourth floor was converted to a hospital, which the Army operated for years. In 1949 a new building was opened on Tennessee Avenue, financed by a building fund and the sale of the old structure. An addition was built in the 1980s. A frame house was purchased in 1922 at 1620 West Washington Street to house the Oakland Corps. A camp is also operated on Lick Branch. The old building on Virginia Street is now called the Berman Building.

Girl Scouts

The Charleston Girl Scout Council was formally organized in 1921 with 12 troops of 174 girls, and the first office was in the Red Cross Building on the city levee. That same year, a camp site was bought on Elk River with the help of Mr. C.C. Dickinson and the Charleston Rotary Club. The organization was funded by subscription at this point, but in 1922 Girl Scouts were included in the budget of the Community Chest. After 10 years, when membership had more than doubled to 465 girls, the Girl Scout office moved to the Public Library Building, and a new camp site was established in Greenbrier County (now Camp Ann Bailey).

The 1930s saw several "firsts" —in 1931 the first cookie sale was held, in 1933 the first Brownie Pack was organized at Kanawha Presbyterian Church by Mrs. Ben Brown and the first troop of black girls was organized at Institute. The council changed its name to the Kanawha County Council in 1934, with Mrs. Clarence Peck as commissioner. In 1937 Mrs. J.R. Thomas was elected to the Girl Scout National Board.

In the 1940s a permanent camp, Camp Roof Rock, was purchased on Coal River and built with funds from the cookie sales. With the new camp, the Girl Scouts expanded their established camping and day camping. Girl Scouts were actively involved in service projects with the American Red Cross, local hospitals, and they salvaged tin cans, fat and paper for the war effort. In addition, they volunteered for the Ashford General Hospital, the veterans hospital established at the Greenbrier Hotel.

By 1946 the Kanawha County Council had 146 troops with 2,566 girls and 750 adults. There were councils established all over West Virginia, and by 1962 several state councils merged to form the Mountain Laurel Girl Scout Council with Mrs. Ross Culpepper as its first president. The Mountain Laurel Council included the following counties: Kanawha, Putnam, Raleigh, Fayette, Wyoming, Nicholas, Pocahontas, Greenbrier, Webster, Braxton, Clay, and Mingo. In 1963 Mercer, Summers, Monroe, McDowell and Logan counties were added, as well as Tazewell, Giles, Buchanan and Bland counties in Virginia. In 1968 Lincoln, Cabell, Wayne and Mason counties also became a part of Mountain Laurel Council.

The present Black Diamond Girl Scout Council was formed in 1974 by the merger of the Mountain Laurel Council, the Vandalia Council in Clarksburg, the Upper Ohio Valley Council in Wheeling and the Four Rivers Council in Parkersburg. The first president of the new council was Mrs. Lee Kenna and Miss Shirley Moses was the Executive Director. Black Diamond currently represents Girl Scouts in 56 counties of West Virginia, Ohio, Virginia and Pennsylvania, and serves nearly 25,000 girls with the help of over 7,000 adult volunteers.

Top: Brownies from the Kanawha County Council selling the famous Girl Scout cookies, in 1944.
COURTESY GIRL SCOUTS

Middle: Girl Scouts of the Charleston Council at a troop camp in Kanawha County, late 1920s.
COURTESY GIRL SCOUTS

Bottom: Boy Scouts camped along the tracks of the old Coal and Coke Railroad at Porter, just over the border in Clay County, in 1919. BILL WYATT

Boy Scouts

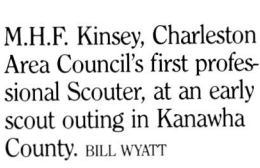

M.H.F. Kinsey, Charleston Area Council's first professional Scouter, at an early scout outing in Kanawha County. BILL WYATT

Camp Walhonde was established in 1926, one mile east of Alum Creek on Coal River in the western part of the county. The camp was sold in 1946 to Carbide for their recreation camp, Camp Cliffside. KELLY BRATTON

The first issue of the Charleston Scouts' magazine in 1922.

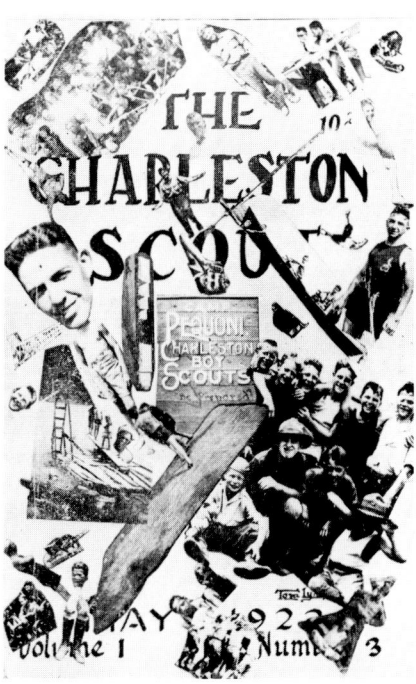

Boy Scouting in Kanawha County began a few years after the National Charter was granted by Congress in 1910. In the area around Charleston, several troops were formed which later became the Charleston Area Council of the Boy Scouts of America. Records show that troops were active in 1914 and 1915. By 1920 five troops with 110 members formed the original council: Troop 5, First Presbyterian Church (1915); Troop 11, Christ Methodist Church (1917); Troop 9, Virginia Street Temple (1919); Troop 2, Sacred Heart Church (1919); Troop 4, Calvary Baptist Church (1919), and Troop 6, St. Albans (1920).

The first professional Scout Executive was M.H.F. Kinsey, whose office was in the Masonic Building. A pioneer scouter in West Virginia, Kinsey led the scouts until his retirement in 1947. Superintendent of Schools, George S. Laidley, was the first president of the Charleston Area Council. The name of the council was changed in 1948 to the Buckskin Council, which now comprises nine counties and over 5,000 scouts. The first Eagle Scouts of the council were Joe Hill and Dudley Morrison from Troop 5 in Charleston in 1919, and to date, close to 2,000 scouts have earned this award. Charles P. Guise of St. Albans was the first recipient of the Silver Beaver award in 1932.

In 1920 the council established its first scout camp at Camp Pequoni, located near Clendenin on Elk River. In 1926 Camp Walhonde was established on Coal River, one mile east of Alum Creek. Sold to Carbide in 1946, the camp became the company's recreation area—Camp Cliffside. The third camp, Camp Clifton McClintic (1946), and fourth camp, Buckskin Reservation (1959), have been established in the eastern part of West Virginia.

The Red Cross

The Kanawha-Clay Chapter of the American Red Cross was established in Kanawha County during the 1914 flu epidemic. During World War I, the local trade unions built this frame building next to the Union Building on Kanawha Street for the local Red Cross. After the war, the building served as a hospital for the flu epidemic, and later as the public library. For years the Red Cross had its headquarters on the Duffy Street farm site of a Mr. Hearn opposite the State Capitol (now the site of the Culture Center). In 1974 the present Central West Virginia Chapter of the American Red Cross moved to the home of Dr. Capito at 1605 Virginia Street East, which was built in 1910. Through the years, the local Red Cross has provided care and services for all the people of the region. KCL

The first post-war fund-raising drive in 1946 used this booth at the Lee Street Triangle.
COURTESY AMERICAN RED CROSS

1950 fund-raising campaign.
COURTESY AMERICAN RED CROSS

Free Masonry in Kanawha County

When the hardy Virginia pioneers crossed the Alleghenies into West Augusta, early in the eighteenth century, many Freemasons were among them. By 1796 there were enough Freemasons at the frontier post of Lewisburg to form Greenbrier Lodge No. 49, the first in western Virginia. As the pioneers moved further west, the Freemasons petitioned the M.W. Grand Lodge of Virginia on June 20, 1816, for another lodge, this time at Kanawha Court House. On December 11 the lodge was chartered as Kanawha Lodge No. 104, and lasted until September 10, 1832, when it became dormant and lost its charter.

Later there was a revival of interest in the Freemasons. On January 31, 1856, the Grand Lodge of Virginia issued another dispensation, and on December 10 of the same year a charter was granted to Kanawha Lodge No. 147. Three years later the Grand Lodge of Virginia restored its original number of 104 to Kanawha Lodge. This lodge was active until the beginning of the Civil War; its last communication was on January 31, 1862.

At the close of the Civil War, a new Grand Lodge was formed as the M.W. Grand Lodge of West Virginia. On September 12, 1865, its first Grand Master issued a dispensation that authorized the opening of a lodge at Charleston, and on January 19, 1866, this lodge was chartered as Kanawha Lodge No. 20.

Little is known about the meeting places of the first two lodges, only that most of the meetings were held at some brethrens' homes and in rooms on the upper floor of the Court House. Kanawha Lodge No. 20 met in the old Court House for many years. Later, Lodge No. 20 rented quarters on the top floor of a Capitol Street building. Throughout the 1880s and 1890s, the Freemasons became interested in obtaining a permanent home. Finally, on April 9, 1892, the site was acquired and construction of a building was begun at the present location of the Masonic Temple. Depressed conditions, however, halted the construction and the structure was not finished until 1897. The building was then used until July 14, 1914, when it was struck by lightning during a severe storm and almost totally destroyed by fire. Immediately afterwards a restoration was planned, but in the interim Kanawha Lodge met in the Elks Lodge Rooms on the corner of Quarrier and McFarland streets. The Kanawha Lodge, Tyrian Chapter, Kanawha Commandery and Beni Kedem Temple on an equal basis financed the structure that exists today. The cornerstone was laid in 1915 and the building was finished in 1916. After Beni Kedem Temple established its own Mosque on Capitol Street, its interest in the Masonic Temple Building was sold to Charleston Lodge No. 153.

Throughout their history the Kanawha Lodges have been important to the formation of new lodges, and their policy in this respect has been very liberal. Originally, their territorial jurisdiction extended from the Ohio River in the southern part of West Virginia to an approximate northeast-southwest line half-way to Lewisburg. As early as 1827, the Kanawha Lodges gave up some of their jurisdiction so a new lodge could be formed at Kanawha Salines. In 1869 jurisdiction was released to Kanawha Valley Lodge at Buffalo, in 1873 to Washington Lodge at St. Albans, in 1893 to Aracoma Lodge at Logan, in 1899 to Griffithsville Lodge at Griffithsville, and in 1904 to Clendenin Lodge at Clendenin. In 1919 concurrent jurisdiction was granted to a new local lodge, Charleston Lodge No. 153. The Dunbar Lodge was chartered in 1922 and South Charleston Lodge in 1940.

The present Masonic Temple on Virginia Street was opened in 1897 with four floors. After a disastrous fire in 1914 the building was rebuilt. A fifth floor and the present ornate facade were added. It is now jointly owned by Kanawha Lodge No. 20, Charleston Lodge No. 153, Tryrian Chapter No. 13 and Kanawha Commandery No. 4. KCL

This building was built as an armory during World War I. The Scottish Rite bought the building about 1920 and rented it to the Beni Kedem Temple, which eventually bought it. In 1964 it was bought back by the Scottish Rite when Beni Kedem moved to its new building on Quarrier Street. KCL

American Legion

The original American Legion post held its first meeting in the old capitol building in 1919, the same year the national veterans organization was founded. John Brawley Post 6, whose namesake was a World War I casualty, was organized in 1923, and its office was located in the Owen and Barth Undertakers Parlor. The two posts merged in 1925 as John Brawley Post 20. Throughout the years, the post sponsored Legion Field in North Charleston, provided aid for the 1932 Paint Creek flood and the 1937 Ohio River flood, participated in the World War II war effort, and erected the World War II memorial at the Lee Street Triangle. From its location at 415 Dickinson Street, the post continues its many social and civic activities. The St. Albans Post 73 is located at 1011 Pennsylvania Avenue, and the state headquarters is at 2016 Kanawha Boulevard.

Medal given to participants in the annual convention of the state American Legion in Charleston, 1929. RA

Corporal John M. Brawley, 1893-1918.

The Capitol District/Woman's Club

The oldest club in the Capitol District, the Woman's Club of Charleston was organized in March 1909 when nine women met at the home of Mrs. W.B. Schober. The club was federated in 1910, and Miss Anna P. Stark was the first president.

Meetings were held in the members' homes until the membership expanded to 34 women, at which point the club was moved to the Kanawha Hotel. By 1920, there were 329 members in the Woman's Club. The club purchased a lot at the corner of Virginia and Elizabeth streets for $16,000, and a ground-breaking ceremony was held in July 1928. A permanent clubhouse, which was designed by Charleston architect Walter F. Martens, was dedicated on March 21, 1929.

Designed in the French Chateauesque style with symmetrical wings and a slate-covered pitched roof, the building is typical of early 20th century predilection for the Beaux Arts and revival styles. The entrance is complemented by wrought iron detailing, a trademark of the architect.

Nineteen clubs of the Capitol District are located in Kanawha County (date of establishment): the Woman's Club of Charleston (1909), St. Albans Woman's Club (1914), Charleston West Side Woman's Club (1918), Woman's Club of South Charleston (1919), Nitro Woman's Club (1934), Marmet Woman's Club (1936), Clendenin Woman's Club (1936), Pioneer Woman's Club of Dunbar (1937), Woman's Club of Dunbar (1938), Pratt Woman's Club (1951), Cross Lanes Woman's Club (1952), Cedar Grove-Glasgow Woman's Club (1952), Community Woman's Club of Sissonville (1955), Chesapeake Woman's Club (1957), Belle Woman's Club (1959), Capitol Woman's Club (1973), North Charleston Woman's Club (1970s), East Bank Woman's Club (1970s), and the Elk Valley Woman's Club (1970s).

The Woman's Club of Charleston clubhouse.
COURTESY WOMAN'S CLUB OF CHARLESTON

"The Beeches" built in 1873-74 by railroad magnate, Collis P. Huntington, for his nephew, Henry Edward Huntington. The house was named for the beech trees on the property. In 1949, upon the death of J.V.R. Skinner, the last owner of the house, it was bequeathed to the St. Albans Woman's Club. The house is on the National Register of Historical Places. PM

Sunrise Museums

Sunrise Museums is a privately supported non-profit complex enriching the cultural and educational life of Kanawha County and West Virginia through its exhibitions and programs. The Art Gallery, Children's Museum and Planetarium occupy two historic stone mansions, Sunrise and Torquilstone, situated in a spectacular location overlooking Charleston and surrounded by sixteen acres of gardens, lawns, trails, and wooded grounds.

In 1905 William A. MacCorkle, ninth governor of West Virginia, selected the summit of a wooded hillside as the site for an imposing colonial revival "manor" house with its two massive porticos surveying the city below. A second stone mansion, Torquilstone, Georgian Revival in style, was built in 1928 for the governor's son and his family on property adjoining Sunrise. Named for the Governor's ancestral home in Virginia, during his occupancy Sunrise was filled with antiques, historical documents, mementoes, paintings and art objects, including Lafayette's bed and other personal effects and 700 pictures of Lafayette himself. During this period of the early 1900s the elegant mansion hosted many notables, including Adlai Stevenson, renowned fighter James Corbett, William Jennings Bryan, John Philip Sousa, Billy Sunday and many others. The most unusual feature of the house is the governor's collection of stones from historic places. In the 2½-story oak panelled living room is a striking fireplace with 75 stones from structures of historic significance, such as the Great Wall of China, the Roman Coliseum, the Tower of London, the Appian Way, the Pyramid of Cheops, Westminster Abbey, and the Palace of Versailles. The outer wall of the mansion's southern entrance contains more such stones, most notably stones from St. John's Church, where Patrick Henry shouted "Give me liberty or give me death," Fort Sumter, John Brown's Fort, the St. Louis slave market, Stonewall Jackson's home, the Appomattox Court House, and even a stone marked "Sunrise" from Governor MacCorkle's ancestral home.

The Sunrise Mansion became available for sale in 1961, and Sunrise Foundation, Inc., was established to purchase it. The building was renovated, remodeled for public use and became the home of four active, local organizations: the Charleston Art Gallery, the Charleston Children's Museum (renamed the Children's Museum of Sunrise), the Sunrise Garden Center, and the Handlan Chapter of the Brooks Bird Club. In 1963 a planetarium, part of the original Children's Museum program, was added. In 1967 Torquilstone was purchased and remodeled to serve as the Sunrise Art Gallery.

On April 1, 1974, the Art Gallery and Children's Museum merged with Sunrise Foundation, Inc., forming Sunrise Museums. Consolidation has allowed each special interest at Sunrise to emphasize symbiotic relationships, through collections, exhibitions and programs. Today Sunrise is a multi-faceted museum, with an extensive, get-involved program for children as well as adults.

Torquilstone, the home of Governor MacCorkle's son, was built for him in the 1920s just south of Sunrise. It is now the Sunrise Art Gallery.
COURTESY SUNRISE MUSEUMS

A derrick lifted the massive stones used in construction of Sunrise.
COURTESY MISS ANN LEWIS EMICH

Sunrise as it appears today, showing the main entrance and driveway.

A newly found photo of Sunrise construction in 1905. This is a view of the south or main entrance. COURTESY MISS ANN LEWIS EMICH

Skating rink at Luna Park. Note the roller coaster on the right. KCL

Chapter Twenty
Enjoying the Good Life

Enjoying the Good Life

Although residents of Kanawha County have always enjoyed the good life, whether in sports, entertainment or recreation, there were not a lot of organized activities in the early days. People were few and far between, there was little communication or transportation, and like other frontier settlements, people were too busy surviving to think about leisure.

Cultural activities did not really get started until after the Civil War. In 1873 the Cotton Opera House was built, which brought some outside entertainment to town. Then the Burlew Opera House opened in 1892 and brought world-class performers to Charleston. Movie houses came along in the early 1900s, the first being Wonderland on Capitol Street near the present library, and other movie theaters, such as Dreamland, The Royal, The Lyric, The Hippodrome, and The Bijou followed.

Over the years, many organizations sprang up, such as dance and drama groups, the symphony orchestra, the light opera guild, chamber music groups, school drama and music groups that have provided the citizens with a number of cultural activities. The Sunrise museum and the adjoining art museum also developed to enlarge the cultural awareness of Kanawha County.

Circuses were the main form of entertainment in the early days. When the circus train pulled into town and unloaded their troupe and exotic animals, it was a community event. The circus brought excitement, a taste of faraway places, and a change from the everyday world.

Leisure activities also included skating on the Kanawha River when it froze over or at the indoor rink on the lower side of the Kanawha City Bridge, until it was converted to a roller skating rink. Swimming holes were numerous in the Kanawha, Elk, and Coal rivers, and along numerous creeks feeding the larger rivers. A person could take a thrilling roller coaster ride in Luna Park on Charleston's west side or picnic in Edgewood Park or spend change at the penny arcades. In the early 1900s Dunbar racetrack was a popular attraction, especially the motorcycle races. Later, the Dunbar racetrack was the site for circuses, carnivals, the Southern West Virginia Fair, and 4-H activities. The old racetrack is now the Shawnee Recreation Complex that is operated by the county.

For the more affluent, country clubs were established for golfing and social gatherings. The earliest country clubs were Edgewood and Kanawha, and later the Southmoor.

One could ride horses at the Kanawha Riding Academy or dance at the Castle Loma pavilion, which were opposite each other in Kanawha City near the present Coca-Cola plant.

Sports were always popular in the County, and baseball was the first organized sport in the coal fields and the business community. In the early 1900s many amateur and semi-pro teams formed, and professional baseball first came to Charleston in the 1930s. High school football was first played around 1903, and basketball was organized about the same time. There have been many great names in county sports through the years. A short list would include: Rocco Gorman, "Eddie" King, Francis "Skeet" Farley, Adolph Putnam Hamblin, Herbert "Babe" Barna, Russ Parsons, Mark Hanna Cardwell, Ernest Wolfe, Dick Huffman, Watt Powell, Albert "Big Sleepy" Glenn, Mark Workman, Rod Hundley, Jerry West, Henry "Hoppy" Shores, Verlin "Sparky" Adams, and George King.

The Cotton Opera House was Charleston's finest permanent entertainment establishment. Built in 1870 by Dr. John T. Cotton, Thomas B. Swann and Joseph Shield, it could seat 800 patrons. It burned down in 1891. Note that an excursion steamer left Brownstown (Marmet) at 5 o'clock for the performance of the play. KCL

Stewart's Hot Dog stand on Charleston's west side, late 1930s. KCL

1878.
CUPID ON THE WAR-PATH!

FOR Valentines OF ALL KINDS!

CALL AT

CAPITAL BOOKSTORE,

OPERA HOUSE,
CHARLESTON, W. Va.

St. VALENTINE'S DAY--Thursday, the 14th

If you do not want any Valentines, your attention is called to the fine, new stock of

Wall Papers!

for the Spring.

The 10th W. Va. Reports NOW READY!

S. S. MOORE.

February 12, 1878.

BILL OF THE PLAY.

VOL. I.   CHARLESTON, W. VA., FEBRUARY 19, 1880.   NO. 3.

GEO. T. BARLOW,
Manufacturer and Dealer in
Picture Frames, Wood & Metallic Coffins.
Particular attention given to
UNDERTAKING.
KANAWHA ST.
Opposite Lower Ferry.   Charleston, West Va.

COTTON OPERA HOUSE,
Thursday Eve., Feb. 19.
Will be presented the great Comedy, in three acts, entitled

JOSHUA WHITCOMB

JOSHUA WHITCOMB .... Felix A. Vincent

John Martin	Harry Forrest
Frederick Dally	H. K. Wooden
Rube Whitcomb	R. C. Brown
Cy Prime	C. J. Bidwell
Elder Hammond	" Rude
Bill Johnson	Miss Anna Brown
Tot	Miss Kate Large
Nellie Frisatree	Miss Rose Wilder
Susie Gersoll	Miss Ida Beckley
Amanda Hubbard	A Young Lady
Aunt Amelia	

SYNOPSIS:

ACT I—Joshua Whitcomb, an old farmer, arrives in Boston, encounters trouble with his ox team; visit for damages and plea of insanity; meeting with an old friend; Potato Bug Bill "FIRE FIRE" a friend from Ireland, hold England, invitation to a party accepted.
SCENE 2—The guests assembled, and seated. Joshua discovers an old friend and has a long conversation about Boston, "pumpkin farms" and other matters; singing and dancing, "hold on John, I've busted my gallusses."

ACT II—Little Tot, the street sweeper; kindness of a policeman; Joshua invited to a seat; another mouthful with Potato Bug Bill; a fight and Josh on top; death bed of Little Tot's mother; sudden disappearance of Potato Bug Bill.

ACT III—Home of Joshua; arrival of victors from Boston— Elder Hammond's revival scheme; Little Tot a lady; Joshua's son; Rube; the accusation of theft; the detective; a telegram announcing the real culprit; virtue comes in the ascendant; happiness and trails; HOLD THE FORT.

The Entertainment will commence with the Laughable Farce

TO OBLIGE BENSON!

Mrs. Tottter Southdown	Eva Vincent
Mrs. Benson	Rose Wilder
Trotter Southdown	R. C. Brown
Benson	H. K. Wooden
Meredith	Harry Forrest

PROGRAMME OF MUSIC.
For Thursday evening, February 19.
Overture, "Zampa"............Herold
Pot Pourri, "Martha".........Flotow
Concert Valse Brillante......Kalivoda
Overture "Fatinitza".........Suppe
March........................Mendelssohn

DONNALLY BROS.,
GROCERS.
AND
General Produce Dealers,
FRONT STREET,
Charleston, West Va.

C. KILLENGER.
Manufacturer and Dealer in
SADDLERY,
Of all Kinds, Cheaper than Elsewhere,
Kanawha St., Opp. St. Albert Hotel,
Charleston, West Va.

GO TO
BELL & OAKES'
TO BUY
GROCERIES,
CIGARS & TOBACCO,
Cheaper than any place in the City.

O. H. MICHAELSON,
AGENT FOR
Steinway & Sons, Decker Bros.
Haines Bros. and J. & C. Fischer's
Grand, Square and Upright Pianos,
Wilcox & White's Organs,
AND DEALER IN
Sheet Music, Music Books, and all kinds of
MUSICAL MERCHANDISE.
Domestic, New Home, New Wilson, Weed, and Wilcox
Sewing Machines and Attachments.

The Leading BOOT & SHOE HOUSE IN THE CITY,
CHARLES LOEB,
KANAWHA ST.

The Attention of Everybody is Called to the
LARGE AND
Well Assorted Stock of
Spring Wall Paper, Window Shades, &c.,
JUST RECEIVED AT
J. FREUNDLICH'S
BOOK AND STATIONERY STORE
St. Albert Hotel Building,
CHARLESTON, WEST VA.

CHEAP FOR CASH.
M. KAUFMANN,
THE BOSS CLOTHIER
Is the best place in this town to find a
New and Well Selected Stock of
Men's, Boys' and Youths'
Clothing, Hats, Trunks, and Gents' Furnishing Goods.
GOOD GOODS AT LOW PRICES!
Remember the place.
Corner Kanawha and Summers Streets,
Charleston, West Va.

GRANDEST OF ALL!
LAST OF THE SEASON!!

SATURDAY, SEPTEMBER 3rd, 1881,
NEW SENSATION.

Grand Hippodrome of Swings, Stupendous Dancing Platform, over 800 square feet; Grand Band Stand with a Full Orchestra of String Music, Greatest and Grandest of all famous Refreshment Stands, which will have a full line of refreshing drinks of all kinds; but most positively none that will intoxicate.

WINCTZ'S GROVE, ELK RIVER TWO-MILE CREEK.

Only 2 1-2 Miles from Charleston.

The management of this entertainment have spared neither time labor or expense in making this the Grandest of the Season. Come one, come all and enjoy yourself. Note the day and date:

SATURDAY, SEPT. 3, 1881.

To assure you of a good time I have secured the ground from Mr. Ruffner and have full control, and shall not tolerate anything that will offend the most fastidious.

J. A. GIBSON General Manager,
S. A. BEACH, Mang'r Platform.

Burlew Opera House

One of the most important entertainment establishments in early Charleston was the oppulent Burlew Opera House, situated on Capitol Street where the O.J. Morrison Building now stands. Built in 1892 by Noyes Burlew, Frank Woodman and Edward Boggs, the Burlew Opera House was a successor of the Cotton Opera House that burned the previous year. Noyes Burlew, originally from New York, had been associated with theatrical people for years, and he built a theater that was years ahead of its time in many ways. The stage facilities were large—even compared to the big city theaters—and because of this he was able to attract outstanding entertainment to Charleston. The finest road shows of the day, famous stage personalities, such as Sarah Bernhardt, Joe Jefferson, Cornelia Otis Skinner, and the great minstrels, including Lew Dockstader, A.G. Fields and Richards and Pringles, all performed at the Burlew Opera House.

In addition, the stage was the scene for the graduating exercises for Charleston High School and many political gatherings. It was literally the gathering place for Charlestonians.

However, as moving pictures became more popular in the early 1900s, the days of live theater were numbered. Finally, in 1920 Charleston lost one of its outstanding landmarks when the Burlew was torn down to make way for the O.J. Morrison Department Store.

Note the mule-drawn streetcar. This photo was taken in 1892.

The Lyric at 107 Capitol Street was one of Charleston's earliest movie houses. The movie "Hands Across the Sea in 76" was made by a film company in New Jersey, sometime before the movie companies moved to Hollywood in the early 1900s. KCL

The Strand Theater was located at the corner of Lee and Summers streets, the present location of One Valley Square. Later renamed the Greenbrier, the theater stayed in business until the 1950s. PM

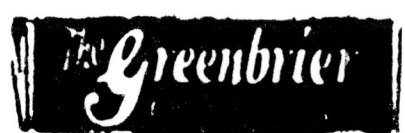

The Plaza-Capitol Theater

In 1912 the Consolidated Amusement Company opened the Plaza Theater at 123 Summers Street. Located in the heart of downtown Charleston across the street from the new Post Office building, the Plaza was called "The Home of High-Class Vaudeville and Novel Attractions." Gus Bartram, the manager in 1913, also managed the Hippodrome Theater at 221 Capitol Street, which was a movie house that occasionally presented live shows.

The Plaza went out of business in 1919. The building was sold to the United Theater Enterprise—the operating name of a partnership between Charles and Fred Midelburg and Huntington Theater owner A. B. Hyman.

In preparation for its opening as the Capitol Theater, workmen began to remodel and redecorate the Plaza in September 1921. The owners claimed that the interior would not have "the slightest semblance of the old Plaza." They retained only "the four walls, the roof, and the seating arrangements," and installed a completely new lighting system and projection room, new carpets and draperies.

They also installed a new Wurlitzer pipe organ, a $15,000 instrument that was apparently the theater's first organ. New simplex motion-picture projectors were put in the projection booth, as the Capitol was primarily a movie theater. The Capitol Theater opened on December 26, 1921.

In 1921 the other movie theaters in Charleston included the Rialto, where orchestra concerts were often presented; the Hippodrome "where live actors make merry in conjunction with famous films"; the Grand; the Virginian; and the Strand. After Tim Kearse opened the large and sumptuous Kearse Theater on Summers Street in 1922, the Capitol began offering live stage shows. However, unable to rival the elegance of the new Kearse Theater, the Capitol Threater owners eventually gave up booking any vaudeville shows.

On November 15, 1923, the Captiol Theater was gutted by fire, and it was exactly a year before the theater was ready to reopen. Rebuilding was done with movies in mind, although provisions were made for live stage acts as well.

By mid-1929 silent films were on their way out, and all of Charleston's major theaters had sound. Managers dismissed orchestras, fired organists, and curtailed live shows to cover the costs of installing audio and higher wages that projectionists demanded.

Because of the changing economics of the movie business, the rise of multi-screen houses, and the deterioration of the Summers Street neighborhood, the Capitol Theater closed in 1982. The theater was refurbished and it reopened in 1985 as a performing arts center under the ownership of Renaissance Productions, Inc.

In 1922 Tim Kearse opened his theater on Summers Street at a cost of $500,000. It was billed as the largest and finest theatre in the state, with a seating capacity of 2,000. It was Charleston's show place for live vaudeville, movies, and stage shows for many years. The theater closed in the early 1980s because of the competition from other movie houses and television. Efforts to save this handsome structure failed, and the building was torn down in 1983 to make way for a parking lot. PM

In the early 1940s, the Kearse Theatre on Summers Street sponsored a live stage show that featured the "Human Monster" and the famous movie star, Bela Lugosi. SWV

Court May, No. 14,

I. O. T.

GRAND BALL,

-To be given at-

Appollo Hall,

St. Albans,

FRIDAY EVENING,

December 21, 1877.

A 1929 newspaper ad for the Kearse Theater soon after it had switched over to sound movies. KCL

Charleston's first band, led by A.P. Gates, possibly in the late 1800s. SWV

The Charleston Junior Band, about 1915. COURTESY "BUS" ROBERTS

You are cordially invited to attend a Private

FANCY DRESS BALL,
→ AT THE ←

KALE HOUSE,

THURSDAY EVE., DEC. 23, 1880.

Sam. A. Miller, Jr., Frank Woodman,
George Byrne,   Jno. A. Peyton,
   H. V. W. Estill.

☞ Dancing to begin promptly at 8:30 P. M.

---

4 You are respectfully invited to attend the

BIG FOUR DANCE,

TO BE GIVEN AT THE

FRANKENBERGER HALL,

TUESDAY EVENING, NOV. 15, 1881.

WM. KILLINGER.   MANAGERS.   WM. BELLER,

Circuses and Parades

The 101 Ranch circus parade on Kanawha Street in September 1918. The clothing store of Moses and Philip Frankenberger occupies the building at the corner of Kanawha and Summers streets. Frankenberger's was founded by the brothers from Bavaria in the 1860s and stayed in business for more than one hundred years. Many people of Jewish origin moved to the valley in the second half of the nineteenth century and opened up businesses. COURTESY TERRY LOWRY

A Knights Templar parade on Capitol Street around 1920. This view is looking toward the Virginia Street intersection. Most of the buildings are still in use. The photographer's name on the far building is J. Leonard Gates. wvu

The Knights Templar parade down Lee Street in the early 1900s. The capitol is on the left. SWV

An unusual view in September 1918 of Capitol Street with the Fleetwood Hotel and the Hippodrome Theater near the present Brawley Walkway. The people are lined up along the street for the Rouch Wild West Show parade.
COURTESY TERRY LOWRY

SWV

A parade in Clendenin on Piedmont Avenue, 1915. CPL

The Circus in Charleston

The circus was one form of entertainment that frequented Charleston for years. Troupes such as Hagenback-Wallace, John Robinson, the King Brothers and the Ringling Brothers, and Wild West shows, including Buffalo Bill and the 101 Ranch Circus, usually came in on the K&M tracks and unloaded at the end of Capitol Street. The wagons lumbered up Smith Street to Brooks Street, then out to Washington Street, where they continued to the show grounds that were in the vicinity of Ruffner Avenue and Beauregard Street.

Other sites that were used by the early circuses were the old race track near Broad Street and the K & M tracks, and the grounds at the corner of Lee and Dickinson streets. Parades were held downtown until the early 1950s, when spiraling costs made them too expensive.

Circus parade in Charleston, early 1900s. RA

Circus day, 1905, on Capitol Street. The rounded brick turret structure of the Scott Brothers Drug Store can be seen in the background. Before the advent of radio and TV, the coming of the circus to town was a big event for the community. COURTESY TERRY LOWRY

A Wild West show, possibly Buffalo Bill's or 101 Ranch Circus, set up on Virginia Street West in the early 1900s. SWV

In the 1890s circuses set up in a field between Brooks and Morris streets, when this area was still largely open. The old Charleston General Hospital at its hill location can be seen in the background.
COURTESY DANIEL DAVIDSON

There were four recognized swimming places at Charleston in the early 1900s. One was at the mouth of Lick Branch; one was across from the mouth of the Elk River, known as Splash Beach; another was known as the Rock at the mouth of Hale's Branch, across from Broad Street; and a bathing beach at the upper end of South Ruffner. KCL

A swimming hole at the Upper Falls of Coal River. WW

In 1932 Rock Lake Pool in Spring Hill was built in a large rock quarry by Carl French. It was purchased in 1942 by Patton and Meador Real Estate Company, and two years later by Joe Wilan. KCL

Many people don't know that there was a rather extensive amusement park at the end of the streetcar line in the Edgewood area, of Charleston's west side. It was owned by the streetcar line. About the turn of the century, Steele A. Hawkins, Jr. opened Edgewood Park just over the hill from the Edgewood Country Club. There was a small zoo, penny arcade, carousel, skating rink, and picnic areas. Edgewood Park was a popular summer recreation area for families from the city, but when Luna Park opened in 1912, this park apparently closed. KCL

Entrance to Luna Park, Charleston's most popular amusement park from 1912 until May 1923, when it was destroyed by fire. It was located on Charleston's west side, and bounded by present-day Park and Glenwood avenues, Park Drive, Grant Street and the river. Its main attraction was the Royal Giant Dips Coaster roller coaster, which must have been quite a thrill for the Charleston residents. There was also a dance pavilion and a roller skating rink that was popular on summer evenings. The park was built over a former three-hole golf course, perhaps Charleston's oldest. The entrance to the park was on Park Avenue, and the streetcar brought the patrons down Central Avenue to Park Avenue and then out to the park. After the fire, the owners wanted to rebuild but couldn't raise the money. The walkways were eventually paved, and the old park became a residential area. The boundaries of the park can be seen by the odd arrangement of streets in this neighborhood. swv

Coonskin Park, the county's largest and most popular public park, was created in a remarkable two-day period, June 27-28, 1950. This photo shows the beginning of work on June 27 by the hundreds of county citizens. Dozens of pieces of equipment donated by area concerns, and hundreds of volunteers began the two-day blitz on the slopes and valleys to the east of Coonskin Ridge, adjacent to the new Kanawha Airport. The original park contained a dance pavilion, picnic tables, shelters, ovens, two lakes, playground equipment, baseball diamonds, and roads. Taking part in "Operation Coonskin" was Governor Okey L. Patteson, Charleston Mayor Carl Andrews, and officials of the County Court. Eight weeks of planning preceded the operation, with help from the Charleston Gazette, the Associated General Contractors of West Virginia, Kanawha County members of the West Virginia Contractors Association, Associated Equipment dealers, Charleston Building Contractors Association, and many other business, labor, and civic organizations. It was estimated that at the end of the second day, the park represented an expenditure of one million dollars. Over the years, many improvements and additions have made this one of the finest county parks in the state.

COURTESY KANAWHA COUNTY PARKS
AND RECREATION

Dunbar Fairgrounds showing half-mile dirt race track on which horses and early-motorcycles were run. This photo shows the county fair in progress. 1930s. KCL

The present location of the Shawnee Regional Park has been used in many ways over the years. At one time, the Shawnee Indians inhabited the land. It was also the site of the county work farm—often referred to as the "poor farm"—for indigent elderly people, the county fairgrounds, and a recreation area. The area also served as a circus grounds for the many circuses that liked to perform in Charleston because they were assured of large audiences. For a long time, the Southern West Virginia Fair was annually held on the site. The Kanawha County Parks and Recreation Commission bought the property in the late 1960s, and named it the Shawnee Golf Course. In 1978 it was renamed the Shawnee Regional Park, and numerous recreational facilities—a clubhouse with a pro shop and restaurant, a swimming pool, picnic shelters, a nine-hole golf course, tennis and basketball courts, and playgrounds—are now offered. KCL and WW

"The Big Top." Large circus tent at Dunbar Fairgrounds—possibly Ringling Bros. & Barnum Bailey—the large half-mile track can be seen with the smaller quarter-mile track that was later added. The grandstand straightaway was common to both tracks. Circa 1950. KCL

Swimming pool at the old Dunbar Fairgrounds. COURTESY A.C. DIXON

"Midway" at the Dunbar Fairgrounds, 1930. WW

The Municipal Auditorium at the corner of Truslow and Virginia streets, was built in 1939 as a Works Progress Administration project. It is still used for various kinds of entertainment. KCL

The Charleston Civic Center opened on the night of November 11, 1958, with a performance of "Holiday on Ice." Five years before, Mayor John T. Copenhaver and the city council appointed a committee to examine the possibilities of building a large civic center to house the entertainment and convention needs of the community. A bond issue passed, and in November 1958 the $2,500,000 structure was finished. In December, West Virginia University played the University of Virginia in the first basketball game in the center. Over the next three decades, with a large expansion in the 1970s, the civic center has become the show place for the entire state. CN

Guy Lombardo, the famous band leader, came through Charleston in 1935 in this strange-looking bus, apparently sponsored by ESSO oil company. CN

The Capitol View Golf Course in 1940, which was located across the street from Watt Powell Park on the present site of Charleston Memorial Hospital. RA

Kanawha Country Club was organized in 1921 as a nonstock, nonprofit corporation. Several old farms were consolidated to build the nine-hole golf course, and later the first eighteen-hole course in the county. The first clubhouse was an old farm house, which burned down. The present clubhouse was constructed in 1930. KCL

Edgewood Country Club had its beginnings in 1898. A group of local business and professional men received a charter for the Glenwood Athletic Club. Their clubhouse, on the banks of the Kanawha River, was leased from the West Side Improvement Company. City expansion caused the club to move to its present site in 1906, where a large clubhouse was built in 1908. It burned down in 1936, and the present clubhouse was built soon afterward. AUTHOR'S COLLECTION

Kanawha State Forest

Kanawha State Forest is located five miles south of Charleston in south-central Kanawha County, on the headwaters of Davis Creek and partially bordering Boone County. The forest is made up of 9,052 acres of rugged, winding ridges, steep hillsides, and broad, level valley bottoms. The dominant forest cover is made up of a variety of oaks, but hickory, beech, maple, yellow poplar, hemlock, pine, basswood, sycamore, and river birch trees are also common.

The original forest buildings and facilities were constructed in the mid-1930s by the Civilian Conservation Corps (CCC). Prior to becoming a State Forest in 1937, the land was owned by Anheuser-Busch, Inc. The company primarily mined coal in the area, but they also mined a little iron ore and operated a brick plant, a barrel stave mill and a sawmill. The company also built and operated a railroad to haul coal, timber and other goods to market.

Because of Anheuser-Busch's booming businesses, the small town of Chilton sprang up along Davis Creek—the primary stream in the forest. The Chilton post office was housed in the general store, which was located in what is now the campground. Another store, three schools, three churches, and over 100 families lived within the boundaries of what is now the Kanawha State Forest. When Anheuser-Busch pulled out of the area in 1907 the community of Chilton dwindled, and in 1936 when the CCC came in only a handful of families lived in the area. The CCC tore down all remaining structures before it began construction of the state forest buildings.

The forest is often used by outside organizations for various types of activities. The Kanawha Trail Club schedules one or two guided hikes a month for its members. Five- or ten-kilometer footraces, sponsored by various local organizations, are held several times a year in the forest, as are occasional bicycle races. Scouting groups frequently use Dunlap Hollow for weekend and overnight campouts and jamborees. Company picnics and family reunions are held in the shelters and in the larger picnic areas on a weekly basis in the warmer months.

The Kanawha State Forest facilities include 46 campsites, 25 of which are equipped with water and electric hookups, a large, renovated swimming pool, extensive picnicking areas with seven picnic shelters, a rifle range, a small fishing lake, and over 30 miles of hiking trails.

Pulling chestnut logs off the hill to use for picnic shelters. COURTESY CALVIN C. WHITE

Calvin White operating a bulldozer in 1941 along the road next to the existing lake. COURTESY CALVIN C. WHITE

Camp Kanawha, S-19, Civilian Conservation Corps in 1941. These men built the present Kanawha State Forest, and their camp was located where the swimming pool and parking lot are now. The first building on the left was the dispensary, the next building was a recreation room on one end and a canteen on the other, and the next few buildings were barracks. The building on the right side of the flag pole was the mess hall, and the closest building on the right was the camp office. COURTESY CALVIN C. WHITE

Kanawha Players

One of the country's oldest community theater groups still in existence, the Kanawha Players have performed for the people of Kanawha County since 1922. Their first production, "Glory of the Morning," was three one-act plays which they staged at Charleston High School. The Players later performed at Thomas Jefferson Junior High School.

In 1925 the Players leased an old church at the corner of Washington and Dickinson streets, now the location of the Charleston Post Office. This was their first and only playhouse. The playhouse burned down in 1926, but this didn't deter the performers, who without a stage or the money to rent one, put on "The Trial of Mary Dugan" in the county courthouse.

The war years put a damper on non-essential volunteer work, but the Players kept their group alive by performing plays on local radio stations. During the 1951-52 season, a workshop was built on MacCorkle Avenue in Kanawha City, and the Players continued to perform on any available stage until the Civic Center Little Theater was opened in 1958.

The Kanawha Players hired a resident director in the 1970s, who helped the Players become a more professional, volunteer organization. The Players have provided the area with extraordinary entertainment over the last six decades.

"The Whole Town's Talking" was presented in 1926 on the stage of the playhouse at the corner of Washington and Dickinson streets. This is the only known photo of a play presented at the playhouse.
COURTESY MRS. JOSEPH KENNA via KCL

Charleston Light Opera Guild

Since 1949 the Charleston Light Opera Guild has provided a showcase for local musical talent. Back in 1948 the only outlet for local vocal talent was in church choirs. Several enthusiastic vocal teachers in the community, along with their students, met to form an organization to produce Gilbert and Sullivan's "HMS Pinafore" as their initial offering. "Pinafore" played on May 10, 1949, to a standing-room-only audience at the Charleston High School auditorium.

The Charleston Light Opera Guild is a total volunteer organization with the exception of its three paid directors. This includes cast, crew and orchestra. Along with its major productions at the Civic Center each season, the Guild also presents summer productions at its Workshop during the months of July and August.

The Charleston Light Opera Guild's first production on May 10, 1949, was Gilbert and Sullivan's "H.M.S. Pinafore." Another Gilbert and Sullivan production, "The Gondoliers" was performed in November 1949.
KCL THEATER COLLECTION

The earliest photograph of the Charleston Civic Orchestra in concert at the Shrine Mosque, about 1941.
COURTESY MRS. LOWELL WARNER

Antonio Modareli conducting the Charleston Symphony Orchestra in 1947.
COURTESY MRS. LOWELL WARNER

The Charleston Symphony

Founded in 1939 as the Charleston Civic Orchestra under the musical direction of local resident William Wiant, and with a total expenditure of less than $5,000 the first year, the Charleston Symphony Orchestra has grown to become a metropolitan orchestra with a full-time resident conductor, a professional management staff and a yearly budget over 100 fold of the original budget. In 1943, Mrs. Helen Thompson volunteered as the first manager of the orchestra. She eventually became the first full-time executive of the American Symphony Orchestra League, which was officed in Charleston until November 1962. A unique program to recruit musicians began during the early years. In cooperation with the orchestra, Charleston business and industrial employers made a concerted effort to hire individuals that would serve their organizations and play in the symphony. This program received national acclaim and was successful in placing 40 applicants in orchestral as well as business positions. The Women's Committee was formed in 1942 and has been an integral part of the symphony ever since. Since 1965, fully staged operas have been presented and internationally known artists began to appear with the orchestra. The orchestra continues to foster excellence in music for a large part of southern West Virginia.

The Charleston Ballet

The Charleston Ballet was chartered in 1956 as the only artistic troupe in the state devoted solely to the art of the dance. Under the leadership of Andre Van Damme, formerly of the Brussels Royal Opera, it was named the Centennial Ballet in 1963 and then the official West Virginia State Ballet. More than 100 original ballets have been staged at the Charleston Civic Center Theater and in concert in cities throughout the state.

"Festive Birthday," choreographed for the 10th anniversary year, 1966-67 season. CHARLESTON BALLET

1939.

Sunday Radio Highlights

Talks—WEAF-NBC 11:30 a. m. Chicago Roundtable, "Russia and Europe;" WEAF-NBC 12:30 p. m. Herbert Hoover at graduation Lincoln Memorial university, Harrogate, Tenn.; WJZ-NBC 5:30, Postmaster General Farley, on "The Graduate and the Government," at graduation Hendryx college, Conway, Ark.; WABC-CBS 6, People's Platform from Hollywood, "Movies and Democracy"; WOR-MBS 7, American Forum, "War-Time Draft of Capital"; WABC-CBS 9:45, Representative Charles Hawks, Jr., on "Collapse of the New Deal."

WEAF-NBC—2 drama, "This, Our America"; 4, Hall of Fun; 5:30, Grouch Club; 6 Jack Benny; 7, Charlie McCarthy; 9 The Circle.

WABC-CBS—10 a. m. new series, News and Rhythm; 2 p. m. Howard Barlow symphony; 3:30 international polo match; 5 new quiz, Musical Fun; 6:30 Screen Guild finale; 8 Sunday Evening Hour finale; 9 Knickerbocker Playhouse.

WJZ-NBC—9 a. m. Cleveland Institute of Music commencement concert; 10:05 from London, 1940 Olympic games; 1 p. m. Magic Key; 3:30 Tapestry Musicale; 4:45 Ray Perkins; 7 summer symphony; 9:30 Cheerio.

MONDAY HIGHLIGHTS

WEAF-NBC—12:30 p. m. Words and Music; 1:45 Hymns of All Churches; 5:15 Monday Music. CBS chain—2 Ohio State university concert; 4 Exploring Music; 4:45 Adventures in Science. WJZ-NBC 11—a. m. Dr. James Rowland Angell commencement address at Duke university; 1 p. m. Adventures in Reading; 3 Club Matinee.

Charleston WCHS Programs

Sunday A. M.
(Eastern Standard Time)
- 8:45—Daily Mail Funnies
- 9:00—Church of Air
- 9:30—Wings Over Jordan
- 10:00—Clyde Barrie
- 10:30—Major Bowes
- 11:00—Bream Memorial Church

Sunday P. M.
- 12:00—Young Stars of Tomorrow
- 12:30—To Be Announced
- 12:55—News
- 1:00—Democracy in Action
- 1:30—"It Goes Like This"
- 2:00—Baseball—Charleston at Springfield
- 5:15—Phil Conley
- 5:30—Gateway to Hollywood
- 6:00—News
- 6:05—People's Platform
- 6:30—Screen Guild
- 7:00—Dance Hour
- 8:00—Sunday Evening Hour

Sunday A. M. (cont.)
- 9:00—Echoes of Stage and Screen
- 9:30—H. V. Kaltenborn
- 9:45—Capitol Opinions
- 10:00—Sammy Kaye
- 10:30—Henry King
- 11:00—News
- 11:05—Jan Garber
- 11:30—To Be Announced

Monday A. M.
- 5:30—Clift Carlisle
- 6:00—Tex Tyler
- 6:15—Old Timer
- 6:30—Roundup Girls
- 6:45—Mays Brothers
- 7:00—Natchez
- 7:15—Nimbling Nimrod
- 7:30—Union Mission
- 7:45—Rhythm Rangers
- 8:00—News
- 8:05—Alarm Clock
- 8:30—Hymnsinger
- 8:45—Bachelor's Children
- 9:00—Tonic Tunes
- 9:15—Myrt and Marge
- 9:30—Hilltop House
- 9:45—Merrymakers
- 10:15—Scattergood Baines
- 10:30—Big Sister
- 10:45—Your Family and Mine
- 11:00—Melody Ramblings
- 11:15—Morning Bulletin
- 11:30—Newscast Direct From Daily Mail Bldg.
- 11:45—Editor's Daughter

Monday P. M.
- 12:00—Linda's First Love
- 12:15—Singin' Sam
- 12:30—Road of Life
- 12:45—This Day Is Ours
- 1:00—News
- 1:05—Shoppers' Guide
- 1:15—Life and Love of Dr. Susan
- 1:30—Flash Quiz
- 1:45—When A Girl Marries
- 2:00—Farm Life
- 2:30—Strawberry Festival, from Buckhannon
- 3:00—News
- 3:05—W. Va. State College
- 3:30—Not So Long Ago
- 3:45—Rhythm Makers
- 4:00—Exploring Music

NBC, CBS and MBS Network Programs

(Note—NBC-Red network programs are listed as WEAF, and NBC-Blue as WJZ)

- 12:00—Church of air—cbs
  - Don Arres—mbs
  - Waterloo Junction—wjz
- 1:00—Aunt Fanny—weaf
  - Magic Key—wjz
  - Democracy in Action—cbs
- 1:30—Barry McKinley—weaf
  - Songs From Yesteryear—cbs
  - Dancing—mbs
- 1:45—Kidoodlers—weaf
- 2:00—Sunday Drivers—weaf
  - On a Sunday Afternoon—mbs
  - Spymphony—cbs
- 2:30—Quiz—weaf
  - Festival of Music—wjz
- 3:00—Rangers Serenade—weaf
  - Vespers—wjz
- 3:30—World Is Yours—weaf
  - Musicale—wjz
  - St. Louis Blues—cbs
- 4:00—Europe Comment—cbs
  - Steelmakers—mbs
- 4:30—Wing Spelling—weaf
  - Jackson books—wjz
  - Ben Bernie—cbs
- 5:00—Catholic Service—weaf
  - Watson, Flotsam—wjz
  - Conrad Nagel—cbs
  - Lucky Break—mbs
- 5:30—Grouch club—weaf
  - Hollywood Gateway—cbs
  - Show of Weeks—mbs
- 6:00—Jack Benny—weaf
  - People's platform—cbs
  - Bach series—mbs
- 6:15—Baukhage in Comment—wjz
- 6:30—Band Wagon—weaf
  - Radio Guild—wjz
  - Screen Guild—cbs
  - Melodic Strings—mbs
- 7:00—Charlie McCarthy—weaf
  - Symphony—wjz
  - Hour of Dance—cbs
  - American Forum—mbs
- 8:00—Merry-Go-Round—weaf
  - Playhouse—wjz
  - Sunday Evening Concert—cbs
  - Revival—mbs
- 8:30—Music Album—weaf
  - Walter Winchell—wjz
- 8:45—Irene Rich—wjz
- 9:00—Circle—weaf
  - Dancing—wjz
  - Knickerbocker Playhouse—cbs
  - Good Will Hour—mbs
- 9:30—Cheerio—wjz
  - Kaltenborn—cbs
- 10:00—News—weaf
  - Dancing—cbs
- 11:00—Dancing—mbs

The Charleston Junior League
PRESENTS
The Nine O'Clock Revue

UNDER THE PERSONAL DIRECTION OF MR. GEORGE M. MILES
OF THE
JOHN B. ROGERS PRODUCING COMPANY

NEW ARMORY   APRIL 21st, 1924
CHARLESTON, WEST VIRGINIA

PATRONS AND PATRONESSES

MR. AND MRS. JOHN DANA
MR. AND MRS. J. R. THOMAS
MR. AND MRS. F. M. STAUNTON
MISS SUE STAUNTON
MR. AND MRS. W. C. KELLY
MR. AND MRS. ARTHUR KOONTZ
MR. AND MRS. H. B. SMITH
MR. AND MRS. R. S. SPILMAN
MR. AND MRS. H. D. RUMMEL
MR. AND MRS. ERNEST MERRILL
MR. AND MRS. R. G. ALTIZER
MR. AND MRS. GEORGE COUCH
MR. AND MRS. E. A. BARNES
MR. AND MRS. G. T. THAYER
MR. AND MRS. JAMES S. LAKIN
MR. AND MRS. JOHN A. THAYER

MR. AND MRS. JUSTICE COLLINS
MR. AND MRS. H. P. BRIGHTWELL
MR. AND MRS. W. A. OHLEY
MR. AND MRS. E. W. KNIGHT
MRS. A. Q. SMITH
MR. AND MRS. D. C. GALLAHER
MR. AND MRS. D. W. PATTERSON
MR. MALCOLM JACKSON
MRS. NEEDHAM
MR. AND MRS. C. E. WARD
MR. AND MRS. JOHN L. DICKINSON
MR. AND MRS. G. W. SWISHER
MR. AND MRS. WHITTEMORE
MR. AND MRS. JOHNSON ZIMMERMAN
MR. AND MRS. ANGUS McDONALD
MR. AND MRS. JOSEPH RUFFNER, SR.
MR. AND MRS. JAMES CABOT

REVUE COMMITTEES

Talent Committee
Mrs. DeWitt Gallaher, Chairman
Mrs. Agnes Mayer
Miss Anastacia Dickinson
Miss Frances Foster

Refreshment Committee
Mrs. E. D. Knight, Chairman
Miss Amy Collins

Stage and Properties
Miss Nancy Ellen Beury, Chairman
Mrs. T. Brook Price
Miss Mary Gravatt

Publicity Committee
Mrs. Wilbur Staunton, Chairman

Mrs. Agnes Mayer
Miss Elizabeth Whittemore
Miss Anna Jackson
Mrs. Garred Kelley
Miss Betty Chilton

Costume Committee
Mrs. W. E. Chilton, Jr.
Miss Frances Dana

Ticket Committee
Miss Katherine Patterson, Chairman
Miss Katherine Staunton
Mrs. James G. Pettit

Program Committee
Mrs. Sam Palmer, Chairman
Mrs. Paul Grosscup

Mrs. David Gillman
Mrs. W. E. Chilton, Jr.
Mrs. Alfred Howell
Mrs. Arthur Hill
Mrs. Mary Lewis Dickinson
Mrs. Mary Gravatt
Mrs. Joseph Long
Mrs. Frank Hurlbutt
Mrs. Katherine Stewart
Miss Amy Collins

Tables and Decorations Committee
Miss Anastacia Dickinson, Chairman
Mrs. William Johnson
Mrs. Bernard Barnes
Mrs. Thomas Horn
Miss Mary Ashton Cotton

PROGRAM
TENTH ANNUAL
Elks' Jubilee Minstrels and Frolic

GIVEN BY

Charleston Lodge B. P. O. Elks No. 202

KEARSE THEATRE

MON., TUES., WED., JAN. 28-29-30, 1924
MATINEE WEDNESDAY

PRODUCED UNDER THE DIRECTION OF
CHAS. L. ADAMS OF THE HARRY MILLER CO.
1476 BROADWAY, NEW YORK CITY

DANCE TONIGHT
SHAWNEE CLUBROOMS
THIRD FLOOR
KEARSE THEATER
Dancing 9 Till 12
Adm. 50c Per Person
Giles Vagabonds

Sports History in the County

Baseball

Charleston's best-known early baseball promoter, Walter B. (Watt) Powell, was a native of Bath County, Virginia. He had played in minor league baseball and came to Charleston in 1915. He managed the billiard room at the Kanawha Hotel for years. Powell was very prominent in local semi-pro ball and was involved with the Class C Charleston Senators in the Middle-Atlantic League from 1931 until the league folded in 1942. When the city of Charleston built a new ballpark at Kanawha Park in 1948, it was named for Powell, who died the same year. Watt Powell Park has been home to several different teams in professional baseball since that time. DH

Baseball has been played in the county since before 1900. A field was located on part of the old Comstock race track, just above Bradford Street, between Quarrier and Washington streets. Another field was located close to Florida Street, between Central Avenue and Kanawha Street on Charleston's West Side. Still another field was on the site of the present Board of Education building on Elizabeth Street. Werhle Park, which was used for years prior to construction of Kanawha Park in Kanawha City, was built about 1908 on a lot between Virginia and Quarrier streets.

Professional baseball goes back to 1910 when Charleston had a team in the Virginia Valley League. From 1911-1912 there was a team in the Mountain States League and from 1913-1916 a team in the Ohio State League. After a long hiatus from pro ball, long-time baseball promoter Watt Powell entered his Charleston Senators in the Class C Middle Atlantic League in 1931. Huntington and Beckley also entered the league that year. The Senators remained in the league until 1942 when the league was suspended due to World War II. Championships were won in 1932 and 1942.

Games were played at the old Kanawha Park, the present site of Watt Powell Park. When the old park burned down during the 1939 baseball season, the schedule was altered by switching several games to other towns in exchange for later swaps back to Charleston, while dozens of carpenters built a new grandstand in about three weeks. The full allotment of games was played that season.

The present Watt Powell Park was opened in 1948 and Charleston returned to professional baseball in 1949 when it entered the Class A Central League. This league only lasted three seasons. In 1952 the Toledo, Ohio, club of the Triple A American Association moved its franchise to Charleston and the new Senators remained in the league through the 1959 season. The Miami, Florida-Puerto Rico club of the Triple A International League moved to Charleston for the 1961 and 1962 seasons.

For the next three years the Senators played in the Class A Eastern League. And finally, as the Charleston Charlies, owned by Charlie Levine, they lasted from 1971 through 1978 in the Triple A International League. In 1987 Charleston again entered organized baseball in the Class A South Atlantic League.

More important than organized baseball, however, were the semi-pro and amateur teams that were the highlight of the county's summer sports life for many years. Charleston fielded many semi-pro teams who had strong rivalries with Huntington, Logan, Parkersburg, Beckley and various teams sponsored by coal companies in southern West Virginia.

Several amateur leagues operated for many years as a highlight of evening entertainment. The Twilight League was composed of business and utility teams along with teams from the statehouse, military and other organizations. The teams played at Laidley Field and Ordinance Park in South Charleston. A Kanawha Valley league played its games at Valley Ball Park where the Cabell School and field is now located. Other amateur teams played on the empty fields in Kanawha City before 1930.

In the years before World War II, baseball games were the major form of entertainment in the coal fields. This is a United Mine Workers of America team.
WVU FRED MOONEY COLLECTION

A team from Blue Creek, composed of men who worked for the various oil and gas companies in the area. This team was typical of dozens that formed in the county's oil fields, coal fields, and other industries from 1910 through the 1930s. DH

Exhibition or Kanawha Park, built in 1916, was the forerunner of present-day Watt Powell Park in Kanawha City. This view is from the 1920s, when baseball games were played with cars lining the field for spectator viewing. The streetcar line crossed the Kanawha City bridge and came close to the park, thus providing easy accessibility to games from the downtown area.
COURTESY H. JARRETT WALKER

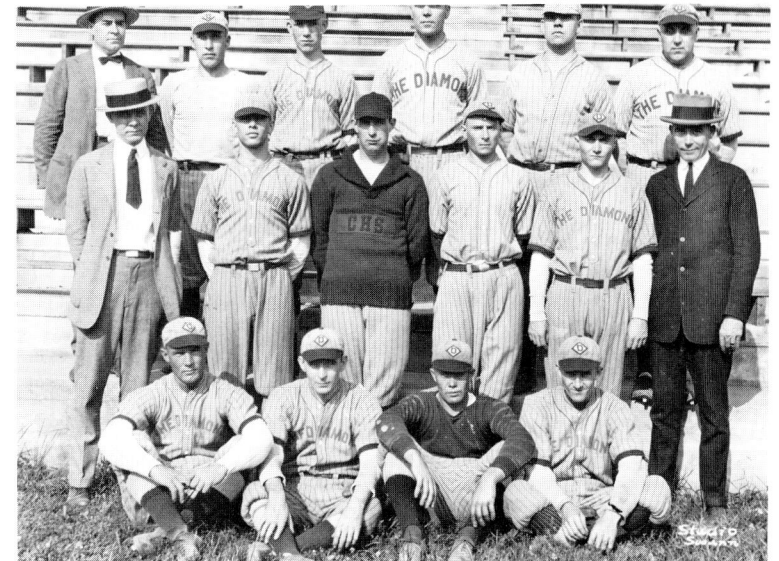

The baseball team of the Diamond Department Store in 1923, part of the popular amateur Twilight League. DH

A 1920s photo of the baseball team of West Virginia Colored Institute (now West Virginia State College). SWV

The railroads also fielded baseball teams, including this 1920 C&O team from Handley. SWV

Watt Powell, left, and Chester Lewis, president of Valley Bell Dairy and a part-owner of the Senators, are shown inspecting the new bleachers, which were built after the 1939 fire at Kanawha Park. DH

The 1938 team of the Charleston Senators in the old Class C Middle Atlantic League. DH

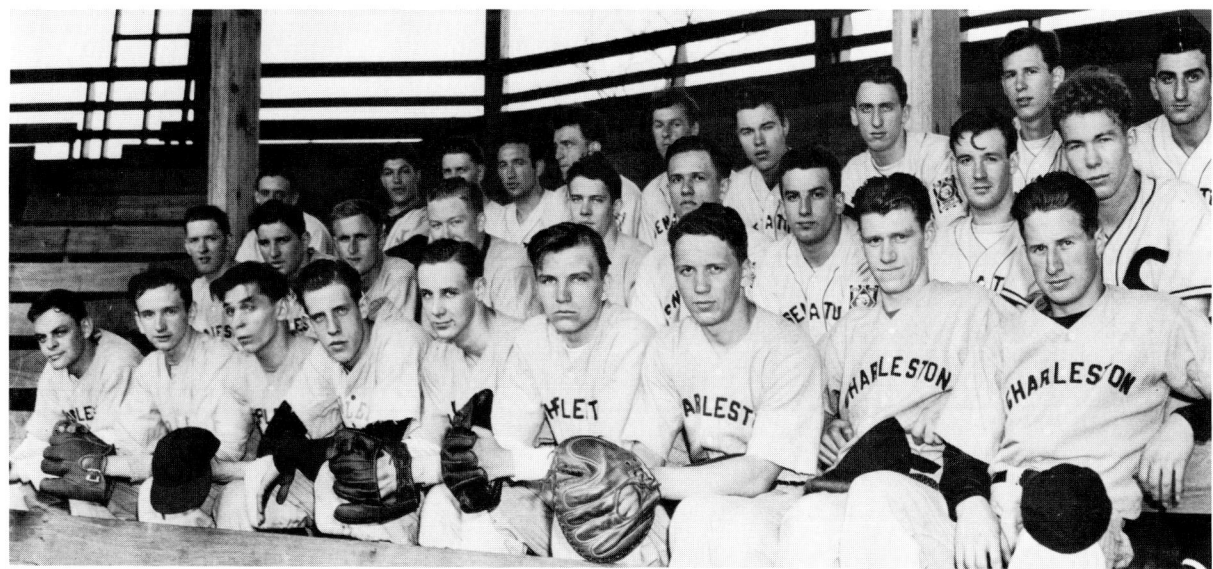

The Senators' last team in 1942, before the Middle Atlantic league was suspended during World War II. Their spring training took place at Kanawha Park, now the site of Watt Powell Park. DH

Oscar Fleishman (left) and Danny Litwhiler (right) of the 1937 Charleston Senators. Litwhiler went on to play in the major leagues, as did many players throughout the years. DH

Manager of the Charleston Senators, Joe Becker, in 1953, when the club was in the Triple A American Association. COURTESY FRANK WILKIN

Football Stories

Carl Edward "Eddie" King had one of the longest and most respected careers of any coach at Morris Harvey College. From 1946 to 1956 his football teams won five West Virginia Championships, three bowl games, and they were undefeated in 1950. His basketball teams were also outstanding, including the two seasons in 1949 and 1950, when George King led the nation in scoring. Previously a high school coach in Huntington and Charleston, King was voted West Virginia's coach of the year in 1954. The University of Charleston's field house is named in honor of him. DH

The game of football, which derived from the English game of rugby, was introduced to Kanawha County in 1898 at Charleston High School. Because of the small student enrollment at the time, the football team had to recruit additional players from outside the school. All of the games were played locally until 1901, when the schedule was expanded to include Montgomery Preparatory School, Huntington High School, Marshall College, and teams from St. Albans and Gallipolis, Ohio.

The 1901 game against Gallipolis ended in a riot, and the Charleston High School players were showered with rocks as they boarded their steamboat for the trip back to Charleston. Apparently, this was a common problem during out-of-town games, especially if Charleston won.

In 1905 the Charleston High School football team beat Morris Harvey College, 39-0. In 1907 the high school team beat Huntington High, Marshall College, Morris Harvey College and Davis and Elkins College. The players played in homemade suits, shoes that had cleats nailed on them, and just the barest of protective gear. The early playing fields had no spectator stands or fences around them.

As high schools became bigger, enough boys were finally available from within the school and outside recruits became a thing of the past, as did games between high schools and colleges. In addition, money became available for travel and safer equipment.

When Morris Harvey College moved to Charleston in 1935, its college football games became a vital part of the city's sports scene. In 1937 Thurman "Jule" Ward became the football coach, and he fielded several strong teams. Some of the teams' greatest successes, however, came under Eddie King. He coached football and basketball from 1946 until 1956, when the school dropped its football program. His teams won three bowl games during his ten-year tenure as coach.

West Virginia University played many games in Charleston at Laidley Field. The West Virginia University team was a staunch rival of the team from Washington and Lee University, and in 1923, during a memorable game between the two, the wooden stands collapsed, injuring 60 of the 960 spectators.

Over the years, the county has produced many great football stars who have gone on to outstanding college and professional careers. Dick Huffman, a Stonewall High graduate in 1940, went on to a brilliant career at the University of Tennessee, where he made All-American in 1946. Huffman was an all-NFL tackle at Los Angeles in 1948 and 1949, and was an all-star player in the Canadian League. From 1939 to 1943 Verlin "Sparky" Adams was an outstanding football player at Morris Harvey College. He was then drafted by the New York Giants, but later returned to coach at Sissonville High School and then coached baseball and football at Morris Harvey College. He was also an assistant coach for the professional Charleston Rockets from 1964 to 1968 when they were in the United Football League. He later coached the West Virginia Rockets in the American Football Association.

Many county high school teams have won state championships throughout the years, and West Virginia State and West Virginia Institute of Technology have produced championship teams. The North-South football game, which pitted the best of West Virginia's high school players against each other, was played at Laidley Field for many years.

Rocco J. Gorman (1888-1971) was perhaps the county's best-known sports personality, not as a player but as a coach and promoter. Originally from Michigan, Gorman moved to Charleston during World War I to teach math at Charleston High School. He coached football, basketball and track until 1930. His first love, however, was football. Later he was principal at Charleston High School, assistant superintendent of Kanawha County Schools, and prominent on the Parks and Recreation board. He took a strong interest in the local Masonic Order and was a director of the National Bank of Commerce. At his death in 1971 he left a legacy of sports accomplishments that is remembered to this day.
COURTESY UNIVERSITY OF CHARLESTON ATHLETIC DEPT.

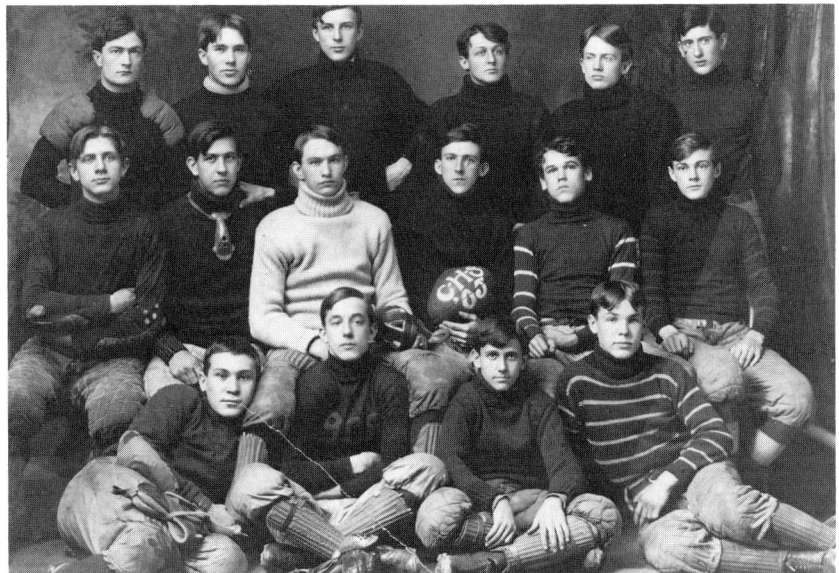

Charleston High School's football team in 1905. Quarterback B.E. Andre is holding the ball. RA

The 1907 football team from Garnet High School. Note the size of the football and the variety of uniforms. SWV

Verlin "Sparky" Adams.
COURTESY MRS. VERLIN ADAMS

St. Albans High School's first varsity football team, 1914. PM

The football team from Garnet High, who were state champions in 1922. SWV

The football team of Charleston High School posing for their team picture in 1930 on the bleachers at Laidley Field. Coaches for the team included Francis "Skeet" Farley, Russell "Rat" Thom, and Albert "Big Sleepy" Glenn. DH

Laidley Field, the county's largest football stadium, was named for George S. Laidley, superintendent of schools in Charleston from 1878 to 1922, except for 1881 to 1883. There has been an athletic field at the site since World War I. In 1923 the wooden stands collapsed during a football game between West Virginia University and Washington and Lee, sending 60 people to the hospital. Permanent stands were built in 1924, and in 1938 night lights were installed. Ever since, the field has been the scene of high school and college football games and track meets, along with a number of other events, including the Kanawha County Majorette Festival. Laidley Field has been completely upgraded over the years into a first-class facility. Photo circa 1930s. SWV

Henry "Hoppy" Shores, one of the outstanding football players of the Kanawha Valley, played at Stonewall Jackson High School from 1947 to 1949. Hoppy was captain of the all-state team in 1949, was named the Kennedy award winner, received the Tom McCann sportsmanship award and was the model for the Kennedy trophy awarded annually to the outstanding WV scholastic player. He also set a state track record in the 440-mile run and was called the "barefoot boy from Jackson Heights" and "Hoppy" because of the speed he generated on the football field.

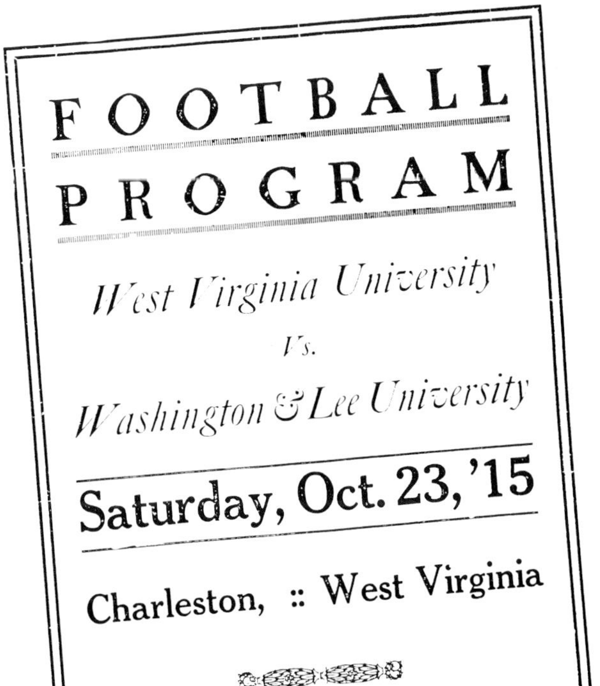

COURTESY HENRY "HOPPY" SHORES

FOOTBALL PROGRAM

West Virginia University

vs.

Washington & Lee University

Saturday, Oct. 23, '15

Charleston, :: West Virginia

EXHIBITION PARK

Transportation To Football Game Today
W. V. U. vs. W. L. U.
Laidley Field

Buses and Street Cars will leave from Capitol and Quarrier Streets (opposite Post Office) every few minutes starting at 1:00 P. M.

Charleston Interurban R. R. Co.

Russ Parsons, a native of Charleston, was one of the most outstanding football players at Charleston High School and one of the most successful coaches in the history of West Virginia high school sports. From 1933 to 1968, he coached at Oak Hill, Charleston Catholic, Stonewall Jackson, and Parkersburg high schools. DH

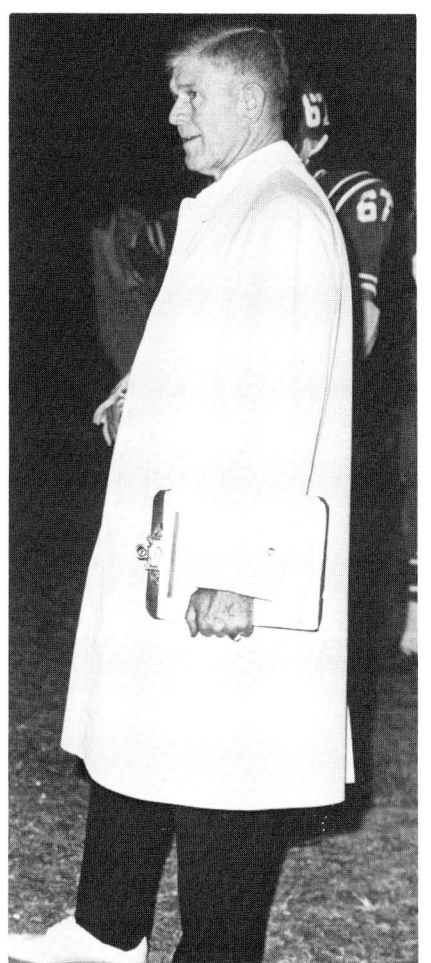

For many years, the big rivalry in Charleston was between the Stonewall Jackson and Charleston High School teams. The victor was always awarded the Elk Bucket, as it was to Stonewall after this 1946 game. DH

Three well-known figures in county sports. Left, Albert "Big Sleepy" Glenn, coach at Charleston High School and later a county commissioner; R.J. Gorman; Mahre Stark, three-sports star at West Virginia Wesleyan, semi-pro baseball player, and dean of boys at Charleston High School for many years. DH

Basketball

The city basketball champs from Calvary Baptist Church in 1922. SWV

St. Albans High School's first girls' basketball team, 1914. PM

The 40-year reunion of the 1928 state championship basketball team from Charleston High. Back row: Coach R.J. Gorman; Forrest Tully; Clyde Wheeler; Andy Brawley; Mahre Stark. Front row: Laurence Plaster; Sam Horton; Brad Barr; Harry Paxton. DH

Mark Workman, originally from Logan County, was the county's first All-American basketball player. He graduated from Charleston High School in 1948, after scoring 854 points in his senior year, the second highest in West Virginia high school sports history, and was All-American at West Virginia University in 1952. Workman was drafted by Philadelphia in the National Basketball Association, but his professional playing career with Philadelphia and then Milwaukee was rather brief. He subsequently worked for a sporting goods company for many years before he died of cancer about 1983.
COURTESY EAGLE AVIATION

The flamboyant "Hot Rod" Hundley, who graduated in 1953 with a state high school scoring record of 1,956 points, was Charleston High School's second All-American basketball player. At West Virginia University he was All-American in 1956 and 1957, scoring 2,180 points in three varsity seasons. Hundley played several seasons in the NBA with Minneapolis and Los Angeles before he went on to his present career as a sportscaster. CN

Jerry West, from East Bank High School, was Kanawha County and West Virginia's most-celebrated athlete. In 1956 when he led East Bank to the state championship, West set the state record (929 points) for points scored in one season. In his three years at East Bank, he scored 1,553 points, an average of 25.8 per game. During his three years at West Virginia University, he set a school record of 2,309 points for a 24.8 point per game season average, and received All-American honors for the 1959 and 1960 seasons. West played in the 1960 Olympics in Rome, and went on to become the Los Angeles Lakers' first-round draft choice in 1960. In his brilliant 13-year career with the Lakers, West made the NBA all-star squad every year. He later coached the Lakers and is now the team's general manager. DH

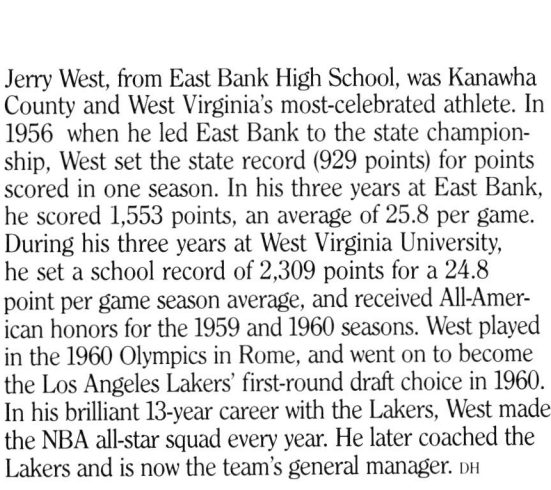

The Morris Harvey College basketball team in 1949-50 with coach Eddie King (left) and star players Sonny Moran (#29) and George King (#23).
COURTESY UNIVERSITY OF CHARLESTON

Radio personality Joe Farris awarding George King the 1949 Bill Stern award as Charleston's Athlete of the Year. A graduate of Stonewall Jackson High School, King led the nation in scoring for two seasons at Morris Harvey College, with an average per game of 29.1 points in 1949 and 31.2 points in 1950. His records at the college include most points in a season (957), the best career scoring (2,535), the best single season average (31.2), the most field goals in a season (354), the most free throws in a season (259), and the highest one game scoring (63). After college, King had a long professional career with Syracuse and Cincinnati. He then coached one season at his alma mater, five seasons at West Virginia University, and at Purdue University, where he is now the athletic director. DH

The Cabin Creek Power Plant, taken by Arthur Rothstein of the Farm Security Administration in May 1938. LC

Chapter Twenty-one
Utilities

Utilities

The Telephone Company

Although the first telephone line in West Virginia ran to Wheeling in 1879, only three years after Alexander Graham Bell patented his invention, it took almost twenty-five years to establish the telephone in Kanawha County. Telephones were gradually acquired after the first lines went up in West Virginia, but it wasn't until 1917 that the telephone was in widespread use in Kanawha County.

J.D. Baines, the vice-president of the Kanawha Valley Bank, installed two telephones in the Murphy Reading Room in 1880. A year later, Sam Strauss constructed a telephone line from his whiskey distillery on Summers Street to the C & O freight station. And Campbells Creek Coal Company built a pole line from its Charleston office to its store at Dana, a distance of six miles. A line was also built from Charleston to Lock 6 on the Kanawha River in 1882, which was eventually connected to all the locks so water levels could be checked.

When the Southern Bell Company opened its office on the first day of January 1883, it had 25 subscribers and a small switchboard located in the old Laundry Building at Kanawha and Alderson streets. However, because of the lack of subscribers the office closed only two years later and the lines were dismantled.

Local businessmen then formed the Charleston Home Telephone Company in 1895 to serve Charleston and the surrounding areas. The next year, the telephone company moved to a building on Kanawha Street, across from the Ruffner Hotel. Business increased in 1897 when long-distance service was brought in by means of a hookup with Cuyahoga Falls, Ohio, and in 1901 when the P & C line passed through the county from Petersburg, Virginia, to Georgetown, Kentucky. The company then established permanent headquarters at 210 Hale Street in 1906. By this time underground conduits and cable systems were being constructed throughout the business district, residential areas, and across the Elk River to West Charleston. The telephone company's customers increased from 900 in 1904 to over 6,000 in 1917.

The Southern Bell Company, which was reestablished in the early 1900s, merged with the Charleston Home Telephone Company in 1911, for a total of 3,000 subscribers. Four years later transcontinental phone service was available in Charleston. The Chesapeake and Potomac Telephone Company (C & P) took over the merged companies in 1917 and selected Charleston as its division headquarters.

Telephone lines were built from Nitro and Putnam County and connected to Charleston in January 1918. During the next two decades the rest of the county was brought into service. The first dial telephone in Charleston was introduced on June 18, 1932, the same year the present C & P building was constructed on Lee Street at a cost of $2,000,000. The present C & P headquarters (now a subsidiary of Bell Atlantic Co.) was constructed on MacCorkle Avenue in 1959. A telephone museum in the basement of the building traces the history of the company's service to Kanawha County and the state of West Virginia.

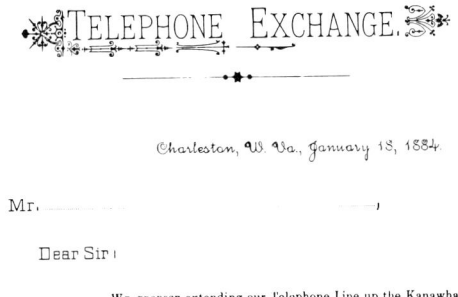

On June 1, 1887, long distance service was first available in Charleston. Ex-governor George Atkinson and H.W. Pope of American Telephone and Telegraph Company accepted the first call at the company's office on Kanawha Street.
C & P TELEPHONE MUSEUM

In 1906, this construction crew laid underground conduits and cable systems in the business district.
C & P TELEPHONE MUSEUM

THE CHARLESTON TELEPHONE EXCHANGE.

Licensed Under Patents of Prof. Alex Graham Bell.

Furnishes to Subscribers all the facilities of Local Telephonic Communications. Transmit Telegrams by Telephone.

GENERAL INSTRUCTIONS.

The careful and intelligent use of the instruments by subscribers and their employees, and rigid observance of the rules and instructions, is also essential to a reliable, prompt and satisfactory service. A failure to attract the attention of, or obtain a satisfactory response from the Central office will almost invariably be found to result from a defective line or a damaged or improperly used instrument. Any difficulty experienced in the use of the Telephone or to the Manager in writing. Such complaints will receive immediate attention.

Unavoidable damages to the lines from storms, conflagrations or other causes will be repaired as quickly as possible.

Always speak into a transmitter at a distance of about six inches. Speak clearly, distinctly and particularly and in an ordinary conversational tone. If you speak lower get closer; if louder, further off.

Keep the Hand Phone pressed against your ear constantly while carrying on a Telephonic conversation.

Subscribers are earnestly requested to answer their "Calls" promptly. Delay in this respect is injurious to the service, and vexations to subscribers and employees alike, and gives rise to unjust complaints against the efficiency of the service.

Always hang the Telephone on the hook.

Don't use the Circle wire for ANY PURPOSE except the TRANSMISSION OF ORDERS to the Central Office. If you desire to make a complaint, ask for an explanation, or talk to the Central Office, tell the "Circle" wire operator to answer "on number 43" or "59," or whatever your number may be.

To Order a Connection.—Put the Receiver to your ear, pull down and hold steadily the ebonite lever in centre of the Bell-box, and repeat FIRST THE NUMBER of the station you wish to communicate with, and then your own number, thus: "127 on 54." When your bell rings in response to your order (not before) release the "lever," and listen for the party for whom you called to give you his number. Then give him your number and proceed with your communication.

To Order a Disconnection.—Having finished your conversation press down and hold the lever as before and simply repeat your number, followed by the word "off," thus, "75 off." The order will be acknowledged as before by a tap of your bell.

To Answer a Call.—When your Bell rings, put the Receiver to your ear as quickly as possible, and repeat the number of your station. Don't touch the lever.

For Night or Sunday Service.—Modify the instructions to "order a connection" or a disconnection by moving the Ebonite lever slowly up and down and wait for Central Office operator to answer you through your Phone.

The Head Phones are discarded at night and on the Sabbath, and a vibrating alarm Bell is used to attract the operator's attention instead.

THIS IS STATION NO. 9½

SUBSCRIBERS, APRIL 1, 1883.

No.		No.	
75.	Arnold & Abney.	13.	Kenna, J. E. residence.
93.	Burlew & Co.	45.	Kenna & Chilton
11.	Boggs, E. L.	10.	Laidley, J. W. upper store
12.	Capito, Chas.	10¼.	Laidley, J. W. lower "
92.	Carr, Dr. L., residence	10½.	Laidley, J. W., residence.
78.	Charleston Leader.	79.	Lovett, D. C. & Co.
41.	C. & O. R. R. Depot.	1.	Manager's office.
9.	Davis, Geo., store.	61.	Mason, N. residence.
9½.	Davis, Geo., foundry.	90.	May, Henry.
71.	Delaney & Hanna.	56.	Michaelson, O. H.
96.	Donnally, Dryden jr.	94.	Moore, S. S.
80.	Eureka Detective Agency.	7.	Noyes, P. H.
27.	Evening Call.	55.	Roy, J. C.
25.	Frankenberger, Phil.	62.	Ruffner Bros.
59.	Gates, J. M. & Bro.	73.	Schwabe & May.
23.	Goshorn, J. H. & W. F. & Co	46.	Strauss, S. & Co.
28.	Hale House.	57.	St. Albert Hotel.
30.	Hogeman, W. H. resid'ce.	22.	Thayer, O. A. & W. T.
5.	Jelenko & Loeb.	60.	W. U. Telegraph Office.
95.	Jelenko & Bro.	74.	Willard, C. P. & Co., yard
89.	Kanawha Woolen Mills.	79.	Willard, C. P. & Co., office
30.	Acord, A. J.		

Office open Day and Night except Sunday from 9 A. M. to 2 P. M., and after 7 P. M. All communications regarding the service of the Exchange should be addressed to J. B. DENOON, MANAGER.

The Charleston Home Telephone Company's first permanent office at 210 Hale Street. The exterior of this building was recently refurbished to recapture its original look. C & P TELEPHONE MUSEUM

Early switchboards in Charleston. The top photo was probably at the Kanawha Street telephone office. The bottom photo was taken in the 1920s at the Hale Street telephone office.
C & P TELEPHONE MUSEUM

In February 1926, a luncheon was held at the Ruffner Hotel to honor the earliest telephone subscribers in Charleston. The subscriber list is a who's who of the prominent area people in the late 1800s.

1. Mr. J.R. Shanklin
2. Mr. Fred Scott
3. Mrs. J.R. Shanklin
4. Mrs. Fred Scott
5. Miss Virginia Fry
6. Governor W.A. MacCorkle
7. _____
8. Dr. J.N. Mahan
9. Mr. Walter Brandt
10. Mr. W.B. Mathews
11. Rev. Mr. Ernest Thompson
12. Mrs. W.B. Mathews
13. Mrs. Ernest Thompson
14. Mr. George Coyle
15. Mrs. R.H. Martin
16. Mr. R.H. Martin
17. Mrs. George Coyle
18. Mr. Bradford Noyes
19. Mr. Dave Patterson
20. Mr. Grisely Hunt
21. Mr. Edwin F. Hill
22. Mr. John Wherle
23. Mrs. Joseph L. Fry
24. Mr. Charles B. Couch
25. Mrs. L.E. McWhorter
26. Mr. L.E. McWhorter
27. Mrs. George McClintic
28. Mrs. I.N. Smith
29. Mr. R. Graves Hubbard
30. Rev. Mr. C.R. Havinghurst
31. Mr. W.L. Savage
32. Mrs. W.L. Savage
33. Miss Evelyn Brown
34. Mrs. C.R. Havinghurst
35. Dr. Clarence A. Potterfield
36. Miss Bess Mollahan
37. Miss Nina Potterfield
38. Mrs. S. Camm Savage
39. Mr. Claude M. Boren
40. Mr. S.M. Greer
41. Mr. S. Camm Savage
42. Mr. H.K. Roberts
43. Judge George McClintic
44. Mr. Marion Gilchrist, Sr.
45. _____
46. Mr. I.N. Smith
47. Mr. E.C. Dawley
48. Mr. Henry Putney
49. Mrs. W.T. Williamson
50. Judge A.S. Alexander
51. Mr. W.T. Williamson
52. Mrs. Claude M. Boren
53. Governor E.F. Morgan
54. Mr. John Baker White
55. Mr. Gus E. Newman
56. Mr. Dewey DeWees
57. Mr. V.B. Fitzpatrick
58. Mr. Horace A. Pierce

Note the two Western Union messenger boys on bicycles. Governor MacCorkle is the man with the large white hat.

COURTESY OF MR. CHARLES M. SLACK, VIA THE C & P TELEPHONE MUSEUM

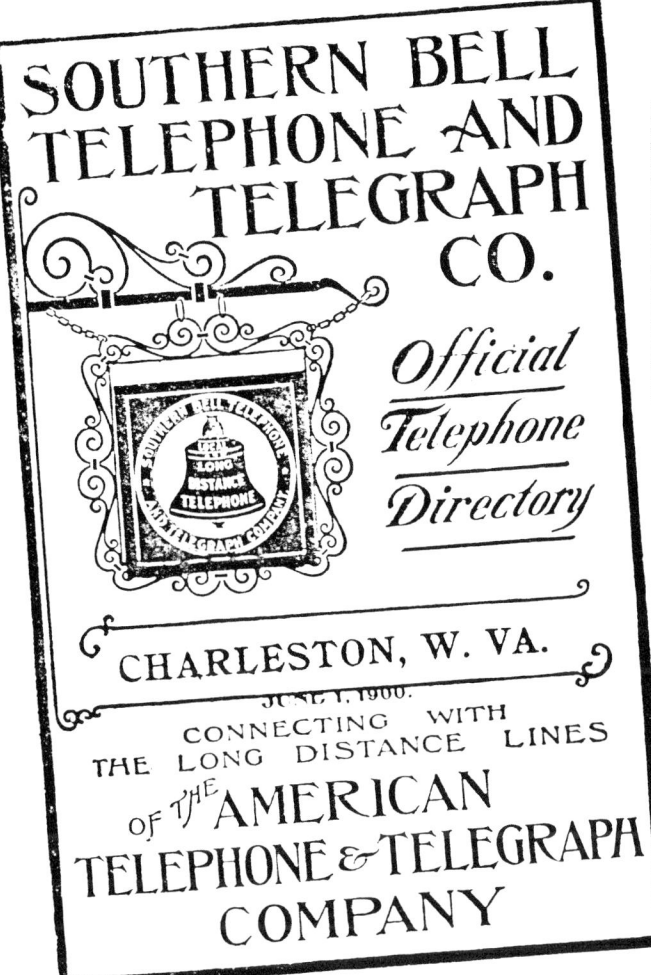

In 1932 the Chesapeake and Potomac Telephone Company building on Lee Street was constructed. It served the company until 1959, when the southside location was opened.
C & P TELEPHONE MUSEUM

Instructions and Important Suggestions.

DESTROY ALL PREVIOUS LISTS.

AS TO GOOD SERVICE.

1. Incorrect methods in the use of the telephone result in unsatisfactory service.

2. To SECURE GOOD SERVICE follow directions on the card on front of the bell-box, and on this page.

3. Answer your bell promptly; give your number to avoid misunderstandings.

4. Press the telephone firmly to the ear.

5. Stand close and speak directly into the transmitter, in a natural tone, distinctly and not too rapidly.

6. Never hang up the telephone until the conversation is finished; the operator will disconnect it if she finds no one using it.

7. Always hang up the telephone (with the ear-piece down) after finishing a conversation; otherwise the battery will soon be exhausted and you can not be heard—your bell will be cut out, and you can not be called from the Central Office.

8. Operators are required to be polite under all circumstances; please extend to them the same consideration.

9. Do not use the telephone during a thunder-storm.

10. Please report cases of trouble or interruption of service or incivility of operators promptly to the chief operator.

11. Operators can not carry on conversations or receive complaints; their entire attention must be devoted to executing orders for connections.

12. The use of profane or obscene language through the telephone is forbidden.

13. The tolls for all long-line conversations, by whomsoever made, will be charged to the subscriber at whose station they originate.

The Water Company

Before the construction of the first water system, Charlestonians obtained their water supply by simple means. Individuals who lived near the banks of the Kanawha and Elk rivers simply drew buckets of water, by a pulley system, from the river. Other area residents relied on public and private wells, springs, and cisterns to meet their water supply needs. The water cart was also a popular means of supplying water for the ever-growing needs of the city. A horse-drawn cart made daily rounds to fill the water barrels at the homes of area residents with water from the Kanawha River.

As Charleston continued to grow, however, the time came when the wells, springs, cisterns, and water carts were simply not enough. Early in 1884 Colonel E.R. Davenport arrived in Charleston and expressed an immediate interest in constructing a water system. In November, the Colonel persuaded the city council to grant him a franchise for construction of a waterworks system. He interested a number of prominent citizens in the plans. Despite financial problems, he successfully persuaded the National Tube Works to deliver pipe on credit, and upon arrival it was immediately placed in the ground.

This new distribution system, which was completed in 1886, consisted of eight miles of small-size pipe. The first pumping station was on Slack Street. The water supply was taken from the Elk River and pumped directly to the mains. Although this new pumping machinery could pump one million gallons of water in a 24-hour period, there were still no mains in West Charleston and the water carts were still seen daily.

Shortly after the system was operating, Colonel Davenport left the Charleston area. During this early period in the company's history, many Charleston people were interested in the company. Among them were Frank Woodman, J.A. deGruyter, James H. Brown, W.W. Knight, and W.S. Laidley. For fourteen years Mr. Woodman served as the company's first president, and Mr. deGruyter was employed as the first cashier, deGruyter was later elected Mayor of Charleston and served from 1895-1899. Mr. Brown, a leading figure in the

Views of the Slack Street water plant in the 1920s. For many years the water was pumped by steam, but by the 1920s the water company had converted the pumps to electricity. This old plant was kept in a standby condition for years in case of an electric outage.
COURTESY WEST VIRGINIA WATER COMPANY

West Virginia Statehood Movement and one of the first three justices of the West Virginia Supreme Court, later served as the company president, until his death in 1900.

The first company office was located at the corner of Virginia and Alderson Streets until 1890, when the office moved to the first floor of the old Burlew Opera House on Capitol Street. The office remained there until 1902.

The citizens of Charleston were pleased with the city's new water system. It was, without a doubt, an improvement over the old water supply methods. Dissatisfaction, however, set in following rainy periods, when the water was muddy for days. After a great deal of controversy and a good deal of planning, the company designed and constructed a filtration plant on Slack Street in 1906. It had a capacity of 6,500,000 gallons per day and used steam-operated pumps. The company operated, at this time, as the Kanawha Water and Light Company.

In 1913 the company was refranchised by the Charleston City Council as the West Virginia Water & Light Company. Operating under this name, a variety of improvements were made to the facilities. Then in 1917 the company installed the first chlorinator, which used liquid chlorine to disinfect the water supply.

Following this period of expansion and growth, the company started buying other franchises. In 1918 it incorporated the South Side Water and Light Company, the first of many annexations to follow. In 1926 the West Virginia Water Service Company purchased the Charleston water plant and the quality of water further improved.

The Mink Shoals pumping station was erected in 1931 so that future pumping units could be installed, thus assuring the people of Charleston a water supply for years to come. The Dunbar Water Works was acquired in 1934 and immediately connected with the Charleston system. Three years later, the company acquired the Nitro and Belle water properties.

Recognizing a need to meet the increasing industrial demand for water, and to eliminate water quality problems at the Nitro plant, the company studied the Belle, Nitro, and Charleston facilities. These studies were completed in the early 1960s, but these facilities weren't upgraded until 1965, when the West Virginia Water Company was acquired by the American Water Works Company, Inc.

The American Water Works Company immediately recognized that if the county continued to grow it needed a modern water supply system. With this in mind, American Water Works planned to construct a new filtration plant and expand its distribution system. In November 1965 the Company announced that it would acquire a portion of the urban renewal property known as the Charleston Triangle District. Its decision to construct a new treatment plant within a three-block area of the Triangle District was controversial, and many residents urged city officials to declare the area unsuitable. This site on the Elk River was selected, however, because the Elk was historically a dependable source of water. Only on rare occasions, such as the 1930 drought, was the Elk too low to meet the increasing consumption needs of Charleston and the surrounding area. In 1960 the construction of the Sutton Dam by the Army Corps of Engineers corrected this situation by releasing water, as needed, to replenish the Elk River.

After months of discussion with community leaders, the plant location issue was finally solved through the joint efforts of city and company officials, and the new facility put into operation on December 27, 1973, eliminated the need for the old Belle and Nitro facilities.

Colonel Davenport would be surprised by the progress and growth of his small water system. Today, the Kanawha Valley plant serves customers in Kanawha and Putnam Counties, with an estimated population of 260,000.

Electric Company

The development of central station electric service in the Kanawha Valley dates from 1887. In 1888 the first street car was introduced, drawn first by mules, and in 1894 electric appeared. A number of residents near the business section had the service piped to their homes. This artificial gas was provided by the Charleston Gas Light Company, which was built by Charles Ward in 1871.

Charleston was feeling the advance of a more urban life, and in the late nineteenth century there was a rapid succession of public improvements. Electric lights were introduced in 1887. In 1890 the first street car was introduced, drawn first by mules, and in 1894 electric power was added.

Utility man working on power poles in 1910, at the corner of Virginia and Goshorn streets, now the site of the Appalachian Power Company office.
APC

The Cabin Creek Power Plant of the Virginian Power Company was completed in 1914 with an initial capacity of 13,200 kilowatts, produced by two 6,600 kilowatt Westinghouse turbines. APC

In 1918, 1921, and 1923, 20,000 kilowatt turbines were installed at the Cabin Creek plant, which provided a capacity of 73,200 kilowatts in 1923. APC

Control room at the Cabin Creek plant, 1920s. The plant was located close to the coal fields to assure a steady supply of coal. It was closed and dismantled in the mid-1980s, because of the newer power plants in the area, and the age of the plant. APC

At this point in the development of Charleston, the first electric light plant was constructed. It was the brainchild of Otto H. Michaelson, who was convinced that a central electric light plant would add much to Charleston. Michaelson came from Parkersburg to Charleston previous to 1875. He was talented both as a musician and a mechanic. He repaired much of the valley's farm machinery, and sold and installed the first gas engines known to Charleston.

Michaelson's talents never made him rich. And had it not been for Philip Frankenberger, who did have money, Michaelson's idea for a light plant might never have come to fruition.

In October 1886, the town council granted Michaelson and Frankenberger permission

In 1908, power poles were hauled by horse-drawn carts. APC

to furnish Charleston with street lights and to supply electric illumination to residences and businesses. They formed the Kanawha Electric Light Company and built a plant on Alderson Street in the early part of 1887.

Their pioneering had only begun, for they had to face competition from the Charleston Gas Light Company, which had been supplying artificial gas for illumination 24 hours daily since 1871. The Kanawha Electric Light Company provided service during the dark hours before midnight only and used flat rates to determine their revenue—based on the number of bulbs in service. Their business was one of selling light, not electricity, and although their rates were not excessive they were prohibitive for the average citizen.

During most of the life of this company, revenue did not meet operating expenses and on a number of occasions Mr. Frankenberger had to contribute further in order to meet the payroll. All the company's accounting was done at Frankenberger's store on Kanawha Street, where the accounts were paid and the few employees came for their monthly pay.

It was hard for Mr. Michaelson to convince prospects that electric light was safer, cleaner, and more efficient than gas, even though the belt at the electric plant frequently slipped and left the town in darkness. But regardless of their difficulties, the Kanawha Electric Light Company was still operating by 1890.

At this time the Charleston Gas Light Company was controlled and managed by Frank Woodman, who was a successful businessman for years. Woodman realized that sooner or later electricity would catch on, so he planned to put the gas company into the electric business to compete with the Kanawha Electric Light Company. Woodman had an Otto gas engine installed in the gas plant and it was connected to a generator. Distribution lines were run into the city and the fight for customers was on.

The fight was of a short duration, however, for the two companies consolidated in 1891 to form the Charleston Gas & Electric Company. Two years after the consolidation, a 50 kilowatt direct current generator was installed in the Alderson Street plant to meet the requirements of the local street car company. After electric power was used for street cars, other uses for power developed. The Scott Drug Company installed a motor in 1894 for its ice cream freezer, which operated from the street car line. At the same time the first electric elevator was installed at the Kanawha Valley Bank Building, on the corner of Capitol and Kanawha streets. The building was completed in 1893 and the next year the elevator was connected to the street car line. By this time, however, the equipment at the Alderson Street plant was obsolete and in 1903 new equipment was installed in the water plant on Elk River.

The electric utilities now felt the influence of the natural gas market. In 1905 the United States Natural Gas Company owned considerable gas properties in the Kanawha Valley. Not wishing to meet opposition with the artificial gas plant, it bought the Kanawha Water & Light Company in 1906. The Kanawha Water & Light Company then changed its name in 1913 to the West Virginia Water and Electric Company. Note that the word "Light" was dropped from the Company name and the word "Electric" was used instead. This was undoubtedly due to the increased use of electricity for power.

War preparations in 1917 tremendously increased the demand for power. By this time, three-phase equipment was standardized and Scott connected transformers supplied this current to Charleston from a two-phase generator. But in 1918, when the government started to build the armor plate and projectile plant in South Charleston, its equipment

called for three-phase power, and the West Virginia Water & Electric installed two three-phase generators with a total capacity of 4,500 kilowatts.

Pioneers such as Michaelson and Frankenberger sowed the seeds of a new industry, which reached fruition in 1912 when the Virginian Power Company was organized to generate and sell wholesale electric service. In 1914 the power plant was completed at Cabin Creek, strategically located near the coal fields where water and coal were readily available for plant operation. The management of the Virginian Power Company thought that this initial capacity would meet all its requirements for ten years. But in less than five years it had to almost double the plant's capacity.

The Virginian Power Company lines were the first to transmit power over a large area of West Virginia. Two hundred miles of transmission lines reached from Cabin Creek to Raleigh County, serving less than 100 customers. The object of the lines was to supply power to coal customers in the New River fields.

The present Appalachian Electric Power Company dates from 1910, when a group of entrepreneurs came into the West Virginia coal fields. They decided that hydroelectric dams could be built on New River in West Virginia to supply electricity to the young developing coal industry in southern West Virginia. To send the electricity into the coal fields, they built the first transmission line of any size in what today is the Appalachian Power system. It operated at 88,000 volts and crossed the mountains from the New River in Virginia to Switchback, West Virginia, where a coal company operated a small electric plant.

During the early 1920s, the then American Gas and Electric Company acquired a number of small companies in southern West Virginia and southwest Virginia. Thirteen of the companies were consolidated on March 4, 1926, and the new company was named Appalachian Electric Power. In 1958 the company's name was changed to the Appalachian Power Company. Today the company is part of the Appalachian Electric Power system and serves over 700,000 customers in West Virginia and several other states.

Appalachian Power Company's present headquarters on Virginia Street was opened in May 1930. APC

The Glasgow power plant was completed in 1952. It cost more than $40,000,000 and contained two 200,000 kilowatt generators, a marked contrast to the 1914 Cabin Creek plant with its initial 13,200 kilowatt capacity. UPI/BETTMAN NEWSPHOTOS

The Gas Company

Natural gas was discovered in the area in 1815. Following the Civil War, the Charles Ward Gas Plant supplied artificial gas to Charleston residents. Although gas was used as a fuel for the early salt furnaces, it was not until 1885 that a geologist, William S. Edwards, drilled a well near the original Burning Springs well from which natural gas was piped the two miles to the Dickinson Salt Works in 1892.

The Charleston Natural Gas Company was formed that year, and one year later the first gas mains were laid into the city. A new company, the Kanawha Natural Gas, Light and Fuel Company, was formed in 1903 that brought gas into the city from wells in Roane County. The two companies were absorbed in 1905 by the United States Natural Gas Company, which extended the gas lines west into Ohio and Kentucky.

The United Fuel Gas Company, a big producer of gas from the Elk and Big Sandy districts, bought out the United States Natural Gas Company a few years later. By the early 1930s, it served 61,000 customers with more than 1,000 gas wells and 2,500 miles of pipe lines, and kept thousands of acres under lease and kept more than one million acres in reserve.

In 1913 the company built its large headquarters at the corner of Quarrier and Dunbar streets. United Fuel Gas Company is now one of the properties owned by the giant Columbia Gas Transmission Company of New York.

The United Fuel Gas Company built its local headquarters at the corner of Quarrier and Dunbar streets in 1913. Then, in 1928 four more stories were added, as shown in this photo. The company moved to its new quarters on the southside in 1969.
COLUMBIA GAS TRANSMISSION CORPORATION

Early gas pipelines were mostly laid by hand. Each 18-foot section of pipe weighed nearly 1,500 pounds.
COLUMBIA GAS TRANSMISSION CORPORATION

Compressors in the Cobb Compressor Station located north of Clendenin. At one time this was the largest gas compressor station in the world.
COLUMBIA GAS TRANSMISSION CORPORATION

Although it may not show in this April 6, 1942, Army Day parade, there is much drama in the hearts of everyone as they watch the massed "Stars and Stripes" carried by members of John Brawley Post 20, American Legion. Pearl Harbor was but four short months past, and the United States was locked in a life or death struggle with Germany and Japan. All of these flag bearers were veterans of World War I. Photo taken in front of the present public library. RA

Chapter Twenty-two

Life in the County: 1942 to the Present

Life in the County: 1942 to the Present

The citizens of Kanawha County plunged into supporting World War II, just as actively as they as supported World War I. Even before the United States entered the war, war production in the valley created a hub of activity. Several vital chemical plants were situated on the Kanawha River, and security in the area was very important. In 1942 the U.S. Coast Guard stationed several 36-foot Richardson cabin cruisers at the Clark seaplane base at the city levee, which patrolled the river to guard against saboteurs.

Many men from the county left their families and jobs to join the armed forces, and approximately 500 of them did not return. One county soldier, Sergeant Herbert J. Thomas, was posthumously awarded the Congressional Medal of Honor for action in the Pacific, and the community hospital of South Charleston was named for him. The end of the war in August 1945 was met with wild enthusiasm and great relief, for citizens could finally get on with their lives.

The new Kanawha Airport was dedicated on November 3, 1947. Morris Harvey College moved in 1947 from the old Capitol Annex to a new site in South Ruffner. Coonskin Park was developed by a massive volunteer effort in 1950.

The fifties were an interesting time in Charleston. Mayor John "Jumping John" Thomas Copenhaver engendered a great deal of controversy with his war against vice, but he also pushed through many civic improvements, including the Civic Center, a sewage treatment plant, and several street extensions.

In the 1960s urban renewal transformed the look and character of downtown Charleston. Some of the city's oldest buildings fronting Kanawha Boulevard were demolished, and high-rise buildings were built in their place. The run-down Triangle District, from Laidley Street to Elk River, was razed and eventually the Town Center Mall, the Civic Center and other buildings were built in its place. The nature of downtown Charleston changed when the Town Center Mall opened, and business shifted away from the Capitol Street area. Charleston became a regional transportation hub in the 1970s when interstate highways were constructed, which also firmly established the city as a regional shopping and medical center for most of southern West Virginia.

The rest of the county was experiencing some radical changes. New and improved roads provided better access to some of the remote areas of the county. Industrial production was in flux, and several large oil refineries closed. Increased mechanization in the coal fields, and the railroads' switch from coal-fired to diesel locomotives after the war drastically changed the coal industry. The coal districts that once thrived were now closed or scaled down. As the industries changed, population shifts were inevitable, and by 1890 Kanawha County's population stood at 250,000.

A patriotic parade down Capitol Street probably in 1942. Eugene A. Carter is on the lead horse. Notice the old streetcar tracks and brick pavement.
WVU, EUGENE A. CARTER COLLECTION

Employees of Imperial Ice Cream Company at the corner of Lee and Truslow streets sit in front of a pile of aluminum collected for the war effort. Saving metal, paper, tin cans and even fat from the kitchen gave everyone a personal feeling of helping to win the war. SWV

VJ Day in downtown Charleston, August 15, 1945. CN

A Memorial Day service, May 30, 1950, at the Lee Street Triangle. The small white wooden crosses represent Kanawha Countians killed in World War II. The Korean War began just a month after this photo was taken. The U.S. Marine Corps honor guard is just about to fire a salute. CN

Election night, November 4, 1952, with the WCHS radio crew broadcasting the results. Local historian and long-time employee of the station, Harry Brawley is second from the left. SWV

Bob Boaz (left) and Harry Brawley (right) during the 1956 primary election. SWV

John T. Copenhaver, shown here with Charleston police officers in 1952, served as mayor of Charleston from 1951 to 1959. Although a very controversial politician, Copenhaver accomplished a lot—the civic center, the paving and extension of many city streets, and the expansion of the city limits were completed under his tenure. He got his nickname "Jumping John" partly from his fight against vice in the city. KCL

Eleanor Roosevelt spoke at West Virginia State College in 1947. Dr. J. Davis, long-time president of the college, is to her right. SWV

Presidential aspirant John F. Kennedy in front of the West Virginia State Capitol during the 1960 presidential primary. Kennedy's campaign in the state propelled him into the national spotlight and eventually to the White House. COURTESY FRANK WILKIN

Hubert Humphrey visiting the Dry Branch post office on Cabin Creek during the 1960 presidential primary campaign. COURTESY FRANK WILKIN

President John F. Kennedy visiting the campus of West Virginia State College in the 1960 presidential primary election. He returned to Kanawha County on statehood day, 1963. SWV

The western edge of downtown Charleston along the Elk River, between Virginia and Lee streets, in the late 1940s. This area, which was largely residential before the Urban Renewal Program clearance, is now occupied by the Charleston Town Center Mall, the Civic Center and other new buildings. CN

Looking west toward downtown Charleston from the Capitol area in the early 1940s. The building in the bottom center was the site of the American Red Cross for many years. This area is now the site of the Cultural Center. KCL

The business section of South Charleston looking east from the mound, 1915. COURTESY MRS. FOREST BARKER

Chapter Twenty-three
Towns in the County

Kanawha City

The largest expanse of flat land in the county lies parallel to the Kanawha River, just south of Charleston. The first permanent residents in the area were Daniel Boone and his family, who established a log cabin about 1788 near what is now the upper end of Kanawha Avenue was widened to four lanes in the 1930s, and a large apartment complex was built next formed Kanawha City Company offered investors a chance to make a good return on a small investment. The company offered 6,000 building lots and 20,000 feet of river frontage for both industrial and residential development, and circulated advertisements around the east that extolled the value of this land in the heart of vast coal, coke, natural gas, oil, clay, salt and timber resources.

Kanawha City's first industrial plant was the Columbia Barbed Wire and Nail Works in the 4800 block of Kanawha Avenue. Started in 1893 by D.A. Chenowith, the company employed over 400 men at the height of business and shipped nails by railroad and river barge throughout the east. Most of the employees lived in boardinghouses around the plant or they came over from Charleston daily by steamboat.

The plant went through a number of operators in the late 1890s, until its machinery was shipped to Ashland, Kentucky, in late 1901. Although the Columbia Barbed Wire and Nail Works was short-lived, it gained notoriety in 1901 when one of its employees assassinated President William McKinley at the Pan American Exposition in Buffalo, New York.

Development in Kanawha City accelerated when the Kanawha City bridge opened in 1915, which offered easy access to Charleston. The flat land was used as an airfield by planes in the 1920s. During the 1921 Miner's Strike, General Billy Mitchell used the field to station his Army bombers that were flown in from Langley, Virginia.

The two glass plants that were established in 1916 and 1917 at the upper end of Kanawha City were the largest industrial concerns to locate in the area, and they employed thousands of residents until they closed. Kanawha City was annexed to Charleston in 1929, which considerably increased the size of the city.

For many years, Kanawha City was the site of national guard encampments. The 2nd West Virginia Infantry Regiment of the West Virginia National Guard used the area during World War I, and in 1925 they camped in the area between the river, MacCorkle Avenue, 35th and 50th streets. The guard also used the area during the 1912 coal strike and the Mexican Border Crisis of 1916. During the Spanish-American War, some guardsmen encamped on the west side of Charleston just below Pennsylvania Avenue between Virginia Street and the Boulevard.

This panorama of Kanawha City taken May 23, 1923, shows a great deal of flat land south of the river. The bridge, opened in 1915, provided easy access to Charleston, and by this time houses had been built throughout the area. Streetcars from Charleston crossed the bridge and ran up MacCorkle Avenue to the glass plants. Kanawha Park is packed for a ballgame, and the large building next door was used as a dancehall and a skating rink. The church to the right of the bridge still exists as the St. John Greek Orthodox Church. WVU

After the bridge opened and the glass plants were established, more and more house lots were purchased, but all the available lots did not fill up until after World War II. MacCorkle Avenue was widened to four lanes in the 1930s and a large apartment complex was built next to the avenue in 1939. Presently, thousands of people live in Kanawha City, one of Charleston's largest suburbs, and many magnificent homes line Kanawha Avenue.

This Kanawha City photo shows the undeveloped areas in 1930. KCL

A good aerial view of Kanawha City in 1937. By this time, some of the blocks were filling up with houses. MacCorkle Avenue, in the center, is almost completely lined with trees. KCL

The upper end of Kanawha City featuring the glass and bottle plants. KCL

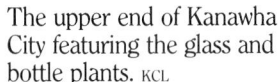

An aerial photo taken in 1942 of the south end of the Kanawha City Bridge. Kanawha Park, which is now Watt Powell Park, is at the lower right and the edge of the Capitol View golf course is at the lower left. The large building at the upper left was Conlon Baking Company, now City National Bank. Note the gas station at the bridge exit, and what looks like a driving range at the site of the present-day Watt Powell Annex. RA

The West Virginia National Guard had been training at Camp (now Fort) Knox, Kentucky, prior to 1925. It was decided that cheaper, more efficient training could be obtained on a local level. The War Department agreed to conduct a camp at a Kanawha City site in 1925 and 1926. In 1925, 900 troops of the 150th Infantry were encamped at Camp Charnock, named after Brigadier General John Hobbs Charnock, the eighth adjutant general of West Virginia. This view shows Camp John L. Hines in August 1926. The camps were situated between 35th and 40th Street on the north side of MacCorkle Avenue. KCL

The Kanawha City airfield at the south end of the Kanawha City bridge. KCL

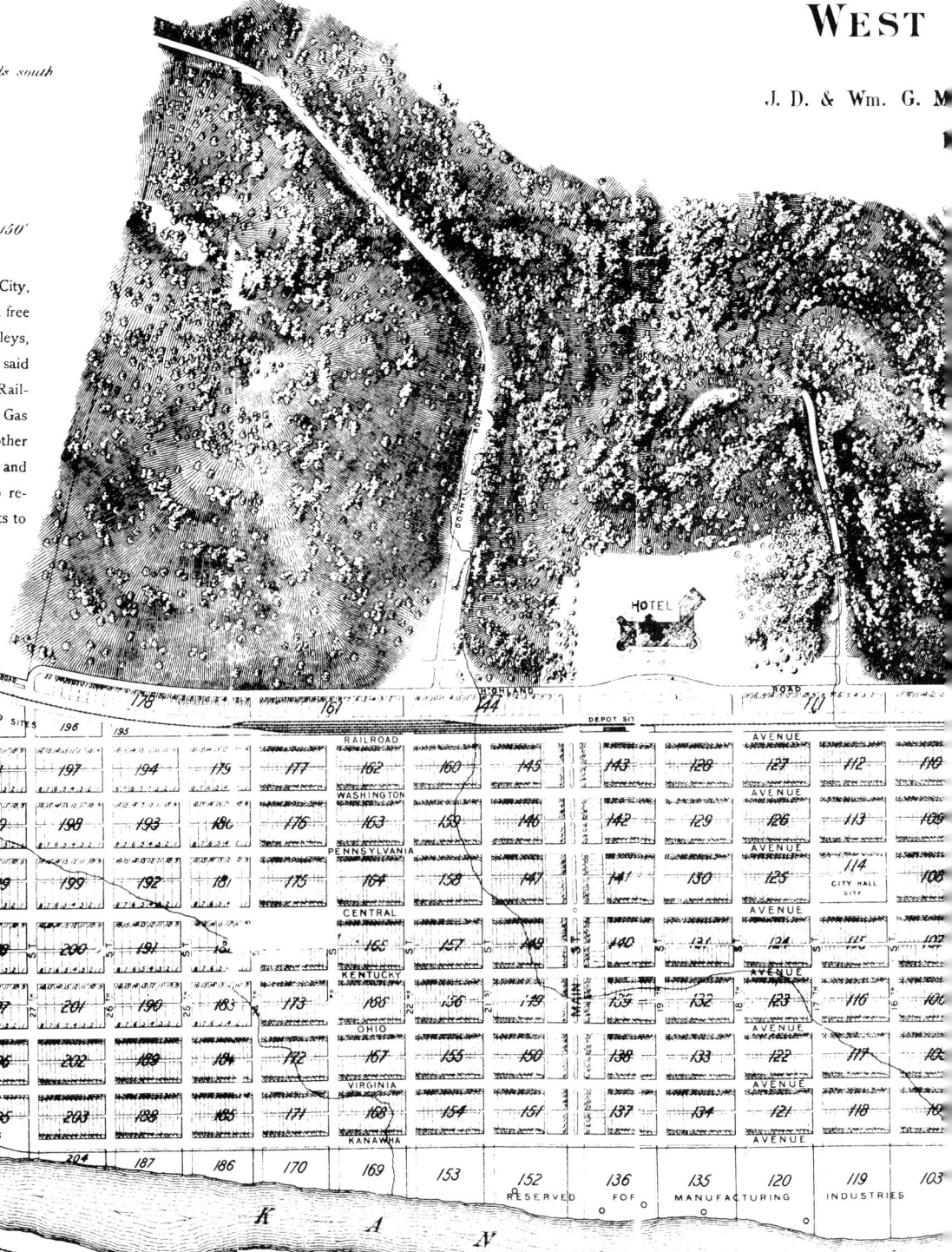

LOCATION.

Kanawha City joins the city of Charleston where Western Avenue crosses the Kanawha River. The main body of the city is a broad level plain.

The Kanawha River has at least six feet of navigable water the entire year.

Twenty three Salt wells are on the river front.

Three seams of Coal underlie the hills south of the railroad.

The property also is the location of a Clay, the same as that from which are made the celebrated Hale Paving Brick, the best of the West Virginia Paving Brick.

EXPLANATORY.

Eastern and Western Avenues and all roads south of railroad are 40 feet wide.

Main Street is 100 feet wide.

Central Ave. " 80 " "

All Alleys are 16 " "

Business lots are 25 x 120

Residence " " 50 x 120 excepting Lots on Main Street are 50 x 120

" " Central Ave. " 25 x 50 and 50 x 150

Salt Wells are shown thus ◯

The Kanawha City Company, of Kanawha City, Kanawha County, West Virginia, reserves the full, free and exclusive right to the streets, avenues and alleys, now or hereafter to be laid off on the lands of said Company for the following purposes, viz.: Street Railways, Water Works, Water Pipes, Gas Works, Gas Pipes, Street Lamps, Electric Works, Electric and other Lights, Electric Poles and Wires, and Telegraph and Telephone Lines, Sewers, etc. The Company also reserves the right to make any changes or amendments to said map or plan it may desire.

A rather idealistic concept of Kanawha City development as proposed by the Kanawha City Company in the 1890s. A train station and large hotel were proposed, along with a city hall, and over 1,000 building and manufacturing sites along the Kanawha River. swv

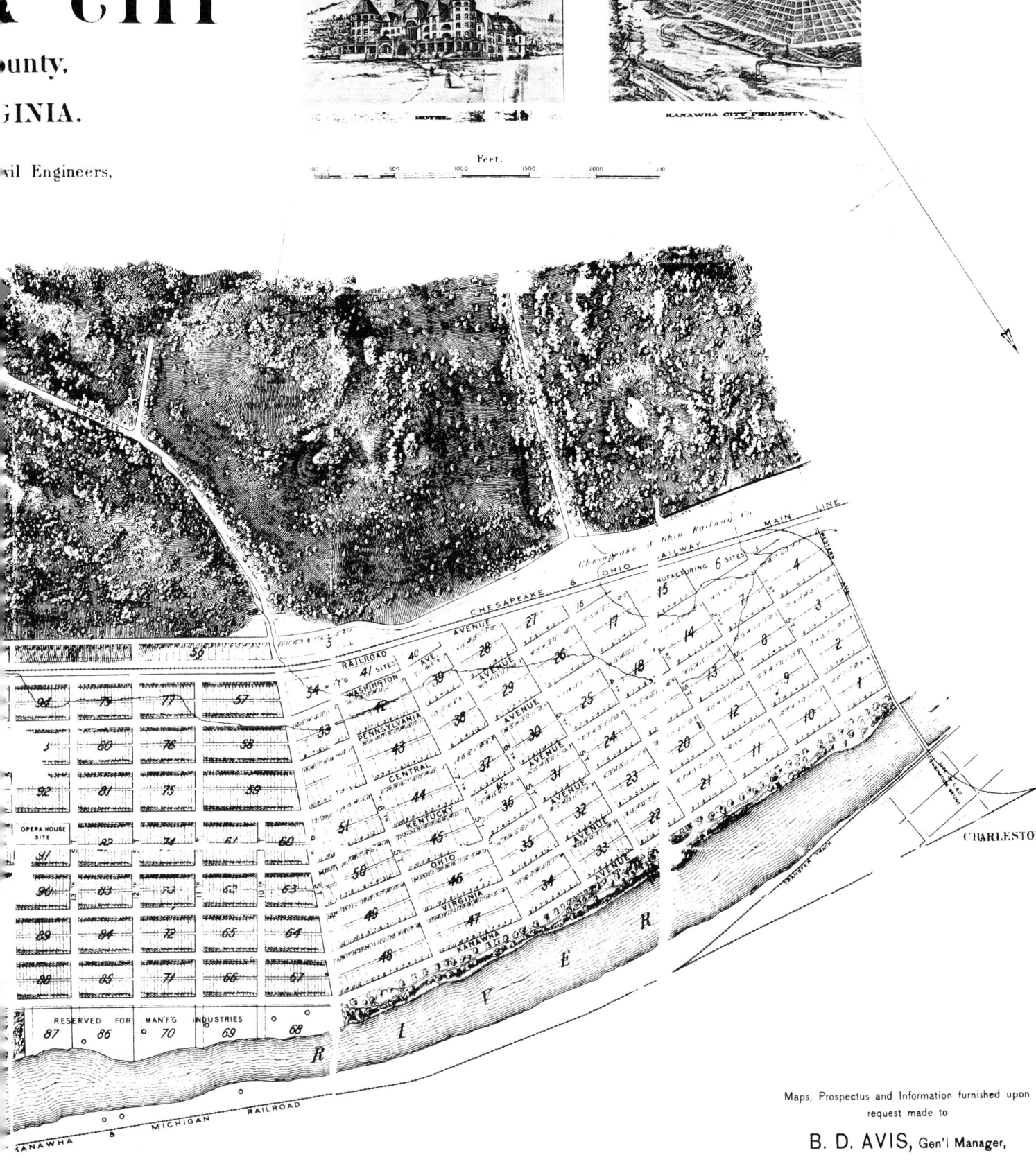

Leon Czolgosz

Leon Czolgosz, the man who assassinated President William McKinley, worked at the Kanawha City nail factory as an expert wire-drawer and mechanic. He got a leave of absence in September 1901 and traveled to the Pan-American Exposition in Buffalo, New York. Czolgosz, a handkerchief wrapped around one hand, was in the receiving line for the President at the Temple of Music on September 6. As McKinley stepped up to shake hands with him, Czolgosz fired two shots from a gun concealed under the handkerchief. The assassin was seized by the crowd, and had to be rescued by the Secret Service. McKinley died eight days later from his wounds. Czolgosz received the death penalty on September 26, and was electrocuted on October 29 at Auburn Prison in New York.

Czolgosz was a member of a secret society of anarchists, who opposed all forms of government. McKinley, as the head of the U.S. Government, was chosen for assassination and lots were drawn to see who would do it.

Glass and bottle plants and a residential area on June 6, 1923. Note workers' dwellings on the left side of the photo behind the bottle plant. Kanawha Avenue appears to be filling up by this time. COURTESY GEORGE HUBBS

The corner of 40th Street and Staunton Avenue in the late 1930s. At this time, the streets in the Kanawha City area were paved with Works Progress Administration (WPA) funds. SWV

These previously unpublished photos show National Guardsmen at an encampment in Kanawha City in the 1920s. SWV

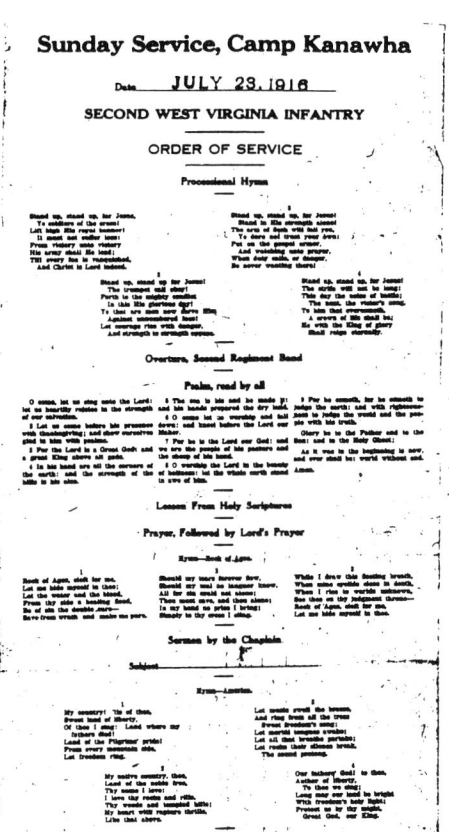

Harold Cornwell Adjutant General of the West Virginia National Guard in the 1920s. RA

Tinkerville/Dana/Reed/ Port Amherst Area

This area near the mouth of Campbells Creek was first called Tinkerville. After the Civil War, the name was changed to Dana and later to Reed after Reed Hatfield, owner of the Hatfield Campbell Creek Coal Company. In 1950 the name was changed again to Port Amherst when the Amherst Coal Company, now Amherst Industries, took over.

TOP: The town of Reed at the mouth of Campbells Creek in the 1930s. This view is looking south toward the Kanawha River. The tracks of the Campbells Creek Railroad lead toward the river tipple. Route 60 crossed the tracks here on its way to Charleston. BOTTOM: Route 60 looking west. Reed is now called Port Amherst. COURTESY AMHERST INDUSTRIES

Route 60 bridge as an extension of Piedmont Road. RA

Reed in the 1930s, looking east. The mouth of Campbells Creek is to the left, further east is the mouth of Georges Creek. At the right is the Campbells Creek Coal Company shops and river tipple. The middle area was used as a baseball field. This area is now the site of houses and the West Virginia Turnpike.
COURTESY AMHERST INDUSTRIES

CEDAR GROVE ABOUT WORLD WAR I ERA

Panoramic view of Cedar Grove, probably during World War I. In the center is the Kelly's Creek Colliery Company railroad and river tipple. To the right of the railroad is the Baptist Church, which still stands. The large building in the upper left was the Valley Camp Store, operated by the Kelly's Creek Colliery Company, and now the Cook Funeral Home. Almost obscured by the store is the residence of the Tompkins family, originally built by William Tompkins in 1844. The second large building to the left of the Valley Camp Store was the Calderwood Store. COURTESY DOUG BUMGARTNER

Cedar Grove/Glasgow Area

Cedar Grove claims to be, with some justification, the oldest settlement in Kanawha Valley. As early as 1773, 14 years before the establishment of Fort Lee, Walter Kelly and his family settled on some bottom land at the mouth of a stream that still bears his name. In 1774, a Shawnee war party surprised Kelly and his black servant at Kelly's cabin and killed them both. (Kelly's family had earlier been sent back to Lewisburg.) William Morris purchased Kelly's property and moved his large family there in late 1774. He built a fort at the site for protection. Remains of this structure were unearthed in 1926.

After the early Indian wars and the Revolutionary War, the flow of settlers into the Kanawha Valley and the Cedar Grove area increased. These early citizens included John Jones, John Young, John Hansford, Sr., William Pryor, and Shadrack Harriman.

The "old state road," which pushed its way through the wilderness from eastern Virginia, terminated at Kelly's Creek. The area became a jumping off place for overland traffic headed west to Kentucky and points on the Ohio River. During this era the Morris family constructed flatboats for use on the Kanawha River; thus, for many years the settlement was known as the "Bote Yards." After steamboats started navigating upstream and the Kanawha Turnpike was finished to the Ohio in the 1820s, the boat-building business at Kelly's Creek declined.

Coal was first used in 1817 to fire the salt furnaces of the region. The Cedar Grove area would become a transfer point for coal mined in the Kelly's Creek drainage. When the Kanawha and Michigan Railroad came through in the early 1890s, the coal industry became dominant in the area. Two rail lines were laid next to Kelly's Creek in order to satisfy the ever-increasing demand for coal. In the early 20th century the Valley Camp Coal Company opened mines in the No. 5 Block—the Lewiston and Coalburg seams along Kelly's Creek. Coke ovens were eventually built on the edge of Cedar Grove.

Cedar Grove was incorporated as a town in 1902. Joseph Luther served as the community's first mayor. The first school in the valley was established at Fort Morris in 1798. At some point before the Civil war a log school was built near the site of Ward. A school for black students was opened in 1885 and remained in operation until 1948.

Today Cedar Grove is still a transshipment point for coal coming out of the Kelly's Creek area. Glasgow is the site of a large coal-fired generating plant.

Panoramic view of Glasgow, probably during World War I. The Thatcher Glass Company dominates this shot. The two-story building facing the glass plant was a store run by Arch Moore, who also served as Glasgow's postmaster. The large two-story building facing the railroad was the store of George Hudnall, who lived in the second story. Note that the Midland Trail, now Route 60, was unpaved; the stone wall bordered the street for its entire length of the eastern part of the town. The name Glasgow is an adaptation of Glassco, which seems to have been used, perhaps informally, for a time. COURTESY DOUG BUMGARTNER

PANORAMA OF GLASGOW, ABOUT WORLD WAR I ERA

to Cedar Grove

William Tompkins

Cedar Grove's best-known pioneer citizen was William Tompkins. He came to the Kanawha Valley in 1815 and built a home near his salt well business at Burning Springs. In 1844 he was the first in the business to use natural gas to fire his salt furnaces.

Tompkins acquired the old Morris fort site from his brother-in-law Aaron Stockton in 1824. He married Rachel Grant in 1831. Her brother, Jesse Grant, was the father of General Ulysses S. Grant. The Tompkins built a magnificent brick house near the fort site, where they lived with their ten children. "Cedar Grove" is still intact, and is owned by a Tompkins heir.

A daughter of William and Rachel Tompkins, Virginia, was responsible for the brick church that still stands on Route 60 in Cedar Grove. When asked by her father if she wanted a trip abroad as a school graduation present, Virginia said she would rather have the money spent to build a chapel. It is believed that the chapel, built in 1853, was constructed on the same site where William Morris had built the first church in the valley.

During the Civil War, Union cavalry stormed through Cedar Grove and threatened to burn down the Tompkins home. Rachel Grant Tompkins reportedly produced a letter from General Ulysses S. Grant promising immunity for her property.

"Melrose," a Tompkins mansion at Glasgow, built on the site of the 1792 White House Inn in 1874. It was destroyed by fire in 1956.
KCL VIA REVEREND CALVIN MARTIN

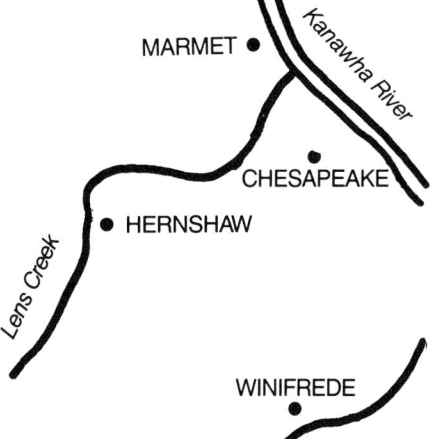

Marmet

Leonard Morris was the head of the first family to settle in the Marmet area. The son of William Morris—the patriarch of the Morris clan who first settled in the Slaughters Creek area—Leonard built a home at the mouth of Lens Creek in 1774. He was one of the early judges of the Kanawha County Court and was appointed sheriff in 1798. His descendants have lived in the area for almost 200 years.

Marmet was first called Elizaville after Elizabeth Morris. The name was changed later to Brownstown after Charles Brown, a wealthy settler who was active in the salt business. Brown came to the area in 1804 and married the daughter of Reuben Slaughter, the Kanawha County surveyor, in 1809. Luke Wilcox was another early settler, building a home here in 1815. He was instrumental in establishing the M.E. Church in Charleston. About 1905 the name Brownstown was changed to Marmet in honor of the Marmet Coal Company, which operated mines at Hernshaw.

Salt was the earliest industry in the area. The first steamboat docked in 1823, and a wharf was soon built at Wall Street. River traffic to Charleston and the Salines soon became a common sight. The area's first school was established up Lens Creek in 1824. Among the first teachers was Leonard Morris. A road was built along Lens Creek and over the mountains into the Boone, Logan and Raleigh county areas. By 1825 Brownstown had become more than just a settlement; it was a small town.

The Belle Area

The names Dickinson and Shrewsbury are interwoven into the history of the Belle area. Colonel John Dickinson was one of the first men to patent lands in western Virginia. He owned large tracts in the Campbells Creek area as early as 1775, which he later sold to Joseph Ruffner.

"Shrewsbury" is an ancient English name. The earliest traceable ancestor of the Kanawha branch appears to be Samuel. In 1760 he married Elizabeth Dabrey and they had ten children. Two of their sons, Samuel and John, married Dickinson's daughters. A third son, Joel, married a relative of the daughters.

Colonel Dickinson conveyed a 704-acre tract of land in the Malden and Belle area of Kanawha Valley to his two sons-in-law in 1796. In 1798 Samuel and John moved there with their families. Joel soon followed, and soon the Shrewsbury brothers were involved in the fledgling salt business. About 1810 Samuel built the "Stone Mansion" (which still stands), a far cry from the common log cabin of the period. Joel Shrewsbury, who would become the wealthiest of the three brothers, is thought to have built the existing "Brick House," which faces Route 60 just east of the Stone Mansion, in the 1830s.

Another name prominent in the area is that of Robert F. Reynolds, the earliest storekeeper. He moved to Belle in 1861 and opened his store in 1863 on the site of the present Dupont plant. Reynolds' store also served as the post office, and during the Civil War it was turned into the post exchange for Union troops stationed at Camp Piatt, established on the Reynolds farm. It is ironic that a young Union artilleryman, Major Henry Dupont, was stationed at the site now occupied by the Dupont plant.

Reynolds was appointed postmaster in 1869 and served until his death in 1911. He owned the "Brick House," in which his descendants still live. The town was originally called Reynolds, but the post office requested a change because another community in the state had the same name. Reynolds suggested the first name of his youngest daughter, Belle, and it was accepted.

Belle was a stage coach stop on the road to Malden for more than a century. It was not until 1917 that the first factory east of Charleston was built by the Charleston Steel Company in Belle. A small community of workers sprang up around the factory. During World War I, the government took over the factory and started construction of a mustard gas plant. It became the Belle Alkali plant, and later the Diamond Shamrock Chemical Company. Dupont's Belle plant started operations in 1926. Today it is one of the largest plants in the Kanawha Valley.

It was not until October 10, 1958, that Belle became incorporated, although its history goes back over 200 years. Other historic communities in the area include Burning Springs, Dupont City, Holly Lawn, West Belle, Witcher and Diamond.

Burning Springs is famous for the springs that emitted gas bubbles. Early explorers discovered that the gas would ignite and burn until a high wind put it out. A tract with these natural gas emissions was later patented by George Washington and Andrew Lewis. In 1841 William Tompkins of nearby Cedar Grove drilled a salt well, struck natural gas and used this new resource to fire his salt furnaces.

Dupont City was an old Shawnee hunting camp. The first Dupont Senior High School was built there in 1939. Today, Dupont City, Holly Lawn, West Belle and Witcher are mainly residential areas.

Witcher was originally owned by John Q. Dickinson and at one time produced salt, coal and lumber at a sawmill at the head of Witcher's Creek. It was named for Colonel John S. Witcher, who established a camp at the mouth of Witcher's Creek during the Civil War.

Diamond stretches east of Witcher's Creek on property owned by the Dickinson family. Samuel Moore was the first permanent settler in the area, moving there in 1887. In 1901 an English coal company leased an area for their mining operation. Many families moved into the area until 1905 when the mine closed. The property reverted back to the Dickinson family, and the community's houses were incorporated into the Quincy Coal Company.

The town of Dickinson, 15 miles east of Charleston, was a coal mining and railroad center in the 1880s. The Kanawha and Michigan Railroad came through in the 1880s, and the Quincy Coal Company started mining up Quincy Hollow about 1890.

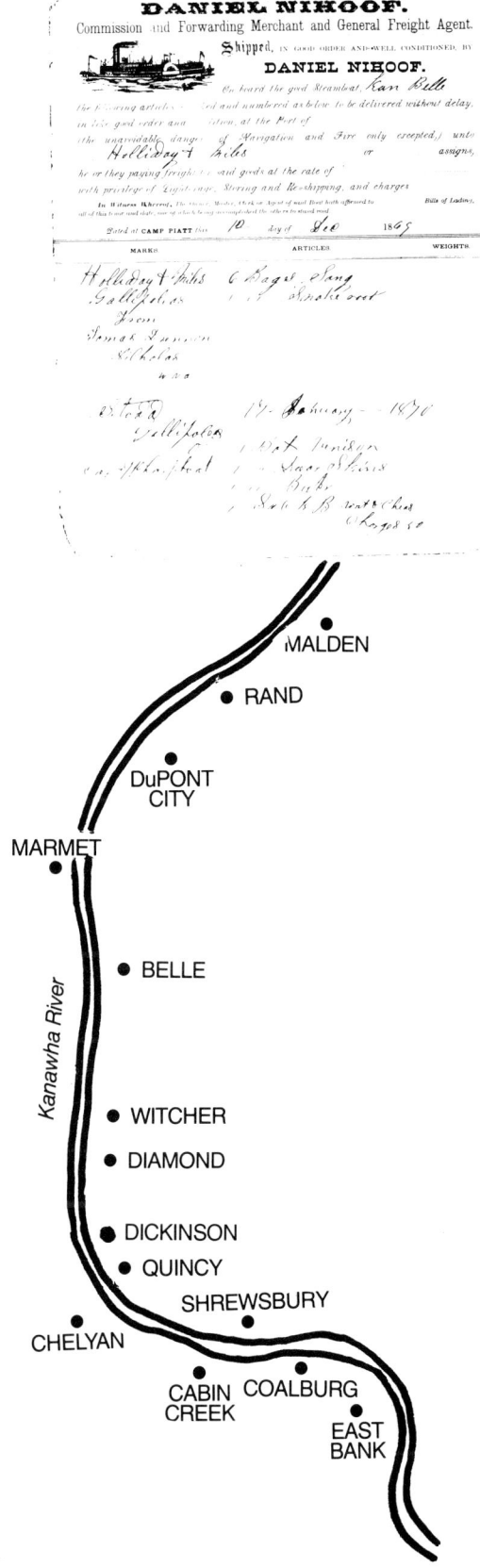

An early view of the town of Pratt, platted in 1851 and incorporated in 1905. PM

A showboat band on the streets of Pratt. In summer, showboats would tie up at the foot of Center Street bringing theater, vaudeville and even a chorus line to town. Note the town hall in the background. PM

The Cooperage on Charles Street in Pratt was the one original industrial building in town prior to the mining years. Barrels were made here and transported downriver to the Salines. The building was occupied by Union forces during the Civil War. It is now a residence.

A railroad trestle was constructed through Pratt in the early 1900s to haul coal to the river tipple. Why an elevated trestle was needed in this area is a mystery. PM

Pratt and the Paint Creek Area

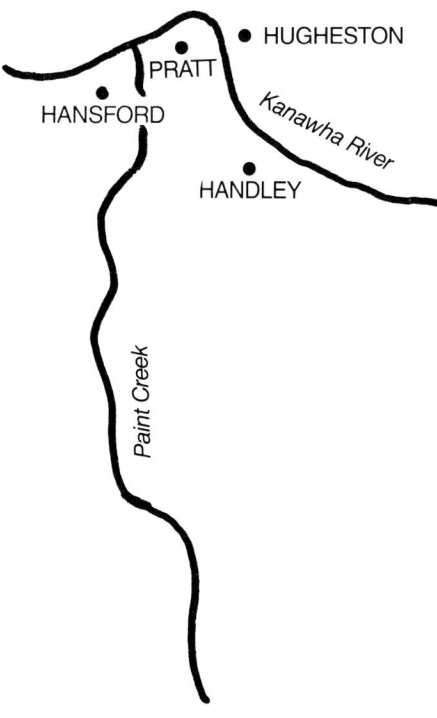

John Jones, a Revolutionary War veteran and participant in the Battle of Point Pleasant, was the first permanent settler in the Pratt/Paint Creek area. In 1792 he took out a patent for 359 acres along the Kanawha River.

Paint Creek supposedly took its name from local Indians who put paint on certain trees to mark a trail from the Kanawha River to the New River. There is no recorded evidence, however, of anyone ever seeing these trees.

The town of Clifton, as Pratt was first called, was laid out in 1851. The early owner of this land was Dickinson Morris, who bought it from John Jones. Morris was a grandson of the valley's pioneer settler, William Morris. The town was platted into 36 lots of one-third acre each. The cliffs on the mountain face above the townsite suggested the name Clifton. Later the town was called Dego and finally changed to Pratt after Charles K. Pratt, an officer of the company that bought timber and mineral rights in the Paint Creek area. Pratt was incorporated as a town on June 4, 1905. The railroad station was known as the Paint Creek Junction.

Major John Hansford was one of the area's early pioneers. He and his wife, Jane, daughter of William and Catherine Morris, moved to the area in 1798 and built a large house below the mouth of Paint Creek in the Crown Hill area. Hansford was a major land owner and a boat builder. He also served in the Virginia Legislature in 1811 and 1813. Hansford's son Felix came to the Pratt area about 1821, and in 1824 built a brick house, which is still intact, in the present-day town of Hansford. In 1842 Dickinson Morris built the large brick home that still stands on a hill overlooking the town of Pratt.

Clifton was the headquarters of the 37th Ohio Volunteer Infantry in the winter of 1861-62, at the start of the Civil War. The building of the railroad following the war spurred industrial development of the area. Coal mines opened up throughout the Paint Creek drainage. (Coal had actually been shipped by river barge from the area as early as the 1820s.)

During the 1912-13 mine wars, the Pratt area was a scene of much conflict. National Guardsmen were rushed to the area several times in their efforts to control the violence. Mother Jones was held under house arrest for 85 days in Mrs. Carney's Boarding House.

One of Pratt's better known citizens was Oscar A. Veazey, who was appointed the first state mine inspector in 1883. Hansford would be the home for the Sheltering Arms Hospital from 1888 to 1921.

An early view of the Felix G. Hansford House. A descendant of Hansford, Mrs. Eleanor Baillie Brannen, was the last resident of the house. She died in 1982 and left the historic structure to the Church of The Good Shepherd.
PM

The Felix G. Hansford House, built in 1824, is located in Hansford next to historic Pratt. It is significant because it's one of the oldest extant houses in the valley, one of the few surviving examples of Federal-style architecture in the area, and the home of one of the Kanawha Valley's most prominent early families.*

Harmony Hill overlooking Pratt was built by Dickinson and Susan Morris in 1842 on land once owned by pioneer settler John Jones. Morris was the founder of Pratt. The house has been altered considerably on the outside but elegantly restored on the interior.

A modern view of the Dickinson Morris house on a hill overlooking Pratt.

Montgomery

Ferry Street, 1912. KCL

Third Street, early 1900s. SWV

The origins of Montgomery date from a settlement made some time after the Battle of Point Pleasant by Levi Morris, the fifth son of William Morris, the first permanent settler in the Kanawha Valley. In the west end of Montgomery, in present Kanawha County, Levi built a log house which he later replaced with a handsome brick dwelling known as "the old Riggs place." Meanwhile, in 1824, his brother Benjamin built a fine brick house on the north side of Montgomery. He first married Amanda Brannon and, after her death, Bridget Rice Huse. Cannelton Industries. In time the brothers exchanged properties, with Levi moving to the north side of the river and Benjamin becoming the owner of the Montgomery residence.

James C. Montgomery, rather than the Morrises, is regarded as the founder of the town of Montgomery. He first married Amanda Brannon and after her death Bridget Rice Huse. He acquired a large farm that covered much of present Montgomery, then known as Montgomery's Landing.

The Civil War disrupted life in the Kanawha Valley, where sentiment was deeply divided between North and South. An ardent secessionist, James C. Montomgery moved his family to Giles County, Virginia, but at the end of the conflict he returned and rebuilt his life in the new state of West Virginia.

In the 1870s Montgomery began a transformation from a farm into a bustling coal town and business center. Contributing to the change was the completion of the Chesapeake and Ohio Railroad, which passed through the town in 1873. With a rail link to the east and river ties to the west, as well as its proximity to the James River and Kanawha Turnpike and the Giles, Fayette and Kanawha Turnpike, Montgomery had favorable transportation facilities. The completion of the Kanawha and Michigan Railroad along the north bank of the Kanawha to Gauley Bridge in 1893 provided rail connections with Ohio and the Great Lakes.

Coal mining and allied industries, on which the economic vitality of Montgomery rested, grew rapidly after the 1880s. Scores of mines opened and Montgomery became the business hub of the upper Kanawha Valley. In 1879 the location, by then known as Coal Valley, was laid off with lots and streets. In 1890 the town was incorporated as Montgomery, with John C. Montgomery as its first mayor.

With its extensive and varied business activity, Montgomery naturally emerged as a banking center for the upper Kanawha Valley. The Montgomery Banking and Trust Company was organized in 1899, but unwise investment in a street railway to connect Handley, Montgomery, and Mount Carbon led to its failure. In 1901 the Montgomery National Bank was organized by S.H. Montgomery and others, and in 1910 the Merchants National Bank was founded by S.P. Campbell and others.

Like many other towns in which growth was rapid and somewhat uncontrolled, Montgomery attracted violent and lawless elements. Its saloons and gambling houses were not infrequent scenes of murder, and organized gangs often flouted the law. Moreover, the town sometimes reflected deep labor unrest, particularly in the upper Kanawha coal fields.

Fortunately, religious, cultural, and educational forces were also at work in Montgomery. In 1895, through the efforts of state senator Thomas P. Davies, John McNabb, and others, the legislature established Montgomery Preparatory School as a branch of West Virginia University, on lands provided by the Montgomery family heirs. The school went through many changes, and in 1941 became the West Virginia Institute of Technology. Kanawha District of Fayette County established Simmons High School for black youth, and Cabin Creek District in Kanawha County built the new brick Love Block School in the west end of town.

Montgomery also became a health and medical center for the upper Kanawha communities. In 1920 Dr. William R. Laird, a surgeon at the Sheltering Arms Hospital in Hansford, founded the Coal Valley Hospital. There he remained until 1938, when he founded the Laird Memorial Hospital, later renamed Montgomery General Hospital. In 1986 the Montgomery General Hospital opened its Elderly Care Center.

Since World War II Montgomery has ceased to be the trade mecca that led to its early development, but, with its college, its hospital, and other facilities, it is unlike any other town of the upper Kanawha Valley.

Cross Lanes – Tyler Mountain

This area in the western end of Kanawha County was part of 24,000 acres granted by King George III in 1754 to soldiers enlisting in the French and Indian War. For many years Cross Lanes was called Fry, after Colonel Joshua Fry, who received a sizable grant after serving as George Washington's commanding officer in that conflict.

The Point Pleasant Turnpike passed through this area. The Marianni Farm and the Homestead became popular stagecoach stops, as did Bowen Tavern—or the Six-Mile House—a six-room structure on the Tyler Mountain Road built by Absalom Bowen from hand-hewn logs in 1833-35. (Bowen had arrived in Kanawha County in 1829 and bought 1,000 acres extending from Woodward's Branch to Kanawha Two-Mile.)

Big Tyler Road was paved by the WPA in 1935, and the Lake Chaweva development was started in the 1930s. Today the Cross Lanes-Tyler Mountain area is one of the fastest growing areas of the county.

One of the first stores (left) and first schools (right) in the Cross Lanes area. ww

Lake Chaweva in the Cross Lanes area was developed in the 1930s by William Killen. It was promoted to the people of Charleston as a country home site. A dam on Rocky Fork Creek created a 42-acre lake. A clubhouse was built and some prominent Charleston families built homes there. Chaweva is an abbreviation for Charleston, West Virginia. KCL

Constructing the road at Sissionville, 1927. Sissionville is located on the Pocatalico River 16 miles north of Charleston, the most northern community in the county. It was named after John Sisson, who first owned the land on which the town was built. In 1914 the population was 75, with four stores, one church and one school. KCL

South Charleston

The area that comprises South Charleston and Spring Hill was first settled by Fleming Cobbs, who made his home near the mouth of Davis Creek. In 1790 he made a harrowing journey by canoe from Point Pleasant to get powder for the garrison at Fort Lee.

It would be over 100 years before a serious effort was made to promote the area as an industrial and residential site. In 1906 former Governor William A. MacCorkle and others formed the Kanawha Land Company, secured title to 1,797 acres, named their new town South Charleston and employed M.W. Venable to lay out a town.

The Banner Window Glass Company, formerly of Shirley, Indiana, was induced to move to South Charleston as the town's first major industry. The company was a cooperative concern owned by a group of Belgian glassworkers and their families. Two more factories moved to town, the Dunkirk Window Glass Company, which moved from Dunkirk, Indiana, and the South Charleston Crusher Company, whose quarry is now the site of Rock Lake Pool.

In the early years South Charleston was isolated from its large neighbor cities to the north and east. The old James River and Kanawha Turnpike was the only road through town, and it was unpaved. A shuttle train made one round trip daily between Charleston and South Charleston over the new Kanawha River railroad bridge, and a steamboat stopped on its trip between Winfield and Charleston.

By 1909 a streetcar line was completed over the railroad bridge to B Street, giving South Charleston one-hour service to the capitol city. South Charleston would have the distinction in 1912 of being the first place in the state from which an airplane became airborne. Paul Peck of Ansted, using the town's ball park as a runway, piloted a small plane that barely left the ground and just cleared a fence and a cornfield before landing a short time later.

In 1913 the Rollins Chemical Company established a plant in South Charleston to produce barium products. It was the first of many plants in the area. With the abundant raw materials in the Kanawha Valley—coal, oil, gas, salt—and excellent river transportation, the area would eventually have one of the largest concentrations of chemical plants in the world.

Carbide and Carbon Chemicals Company moved to the old Rollins Chemical Company site in 1925. The next year the company bought a large island in the Kanawha River owned by Charles Blaine, who used it as farmland. The original 22-acre island was enlarged to 90 acres with fill and riprap.

On August 29, 1916, Congress authorized the building of an ordnance plant to make armor plate for the Navy. In April 1917 South Charleston was chosen as the site. The Charleston Chamber of Commerce raised $300,000 to buy 210 acres as a site for the plant.

South Charleston about 1925. Blaine's Island has not yet been developed. North Charleston is in the background across the river. KCL

Under an existing ordinance, the federal government was limited to ownership of 25 acres in the state. To remove this restriction, Governor John J. Cornwell called a special session of the State Legislature. On August 30, 1917, ground was broken for the plant by Secretary of the Navy, Josephus Daniels. This was the first naval base ever built away from the seaboard. The plant cost $20 million and produced armor plate, gun forgings and projectiles for large naval ships, in addition to armor plate. A government reservation known as Armor Park was built for the factory workers. The plant was closed in the 1920s, but opened again before America's entry into World War II to provide material for the war effort.

South Charleston received its first charter on June 18, 1917, from the Kanawha County Circuit Court. The community boasted about 1,200 residents. A second charter was received from the State Legislature in 1919. By 1920 the town was paving its first street, D Street from MacCorkle Avenue.

The first school in South Charleston was built near the Mound. In 1914 the first modern school building, Central School, was built. Armor Park School opened in 1920, and the first high school, first housed in the Thomas A. Edison School, opened in 1925. The First Presbyterian Church was the first church in town.

The Works Progress Administration (WPA) built the city hall, field house and an athletic field in 1939. Kenna Homes just off MacCorkle Avenue was completed in 1942 to house nearly 400 war worker families. Buses started serving the community in 1939, and MacCorkle Avenue was made four lanes in 1944.

Today South Charleston, with its ancient Indian burial mound, is a symbol for the past, but its industrial potential and progressive community spirit make it a promise for the future as well.

D Street looking north (left) and south (right) when it was just a muddy street, about 1920.
COURTESY MRS. FOREST BARKER

7th Avenue, early 1920s. The alley is next to the present Rite-Aid store. COURTESY MRS. FOREST BARKER

The C&O Depot at South Charleston, 1920s.
COURTESY MRS. FOREST BARKER

The Charleston Interurban Railroad streetcar tracks along Bungalow Park. The Naval Ordnance plant is in the background, 1920s.
COURTESY MRS. LOUISE EDENS, POMEROY, OHIO

Preparing the foundation of MacCorkle Avenue in South Charleston for paving in 1924. The Charleston Interurban streetcar tracks are on the left. SWV

Paving MacCorkle Avenue at G Street, 1920s.
COURTESY MRS. FOREST BARKER

Dunbar/Institute Area

The Dunbar area was first surveyed in November 1774 by Samuel Lewis. A tract was laid out to follow the river "to a large cherry tree standing against the upper end of an island." This point, opposite Tyler Island, is still known as the "Cherry Tree Corner." The survey embraced all the river bottom and much of the hill lands, including the present site of the city of Dunbar. This land was patented for George Washington in payment for military service.

The Dunbar area for many years remained farm land. About 1890 the Kanawha and Michigan Railroad was under construction through this area.

Some years later a Charleston businessman, George S. Couch, purchased large areas to establish a vegetable and strawberry farm. In 1911 Fred Grosscup began the development of an industrial and residential community. He laid out the prospective city into streets and lots. He installed a sewage system, built sidewalks, and piped gas to the community. The area was named Dunbar for Dunbar Baines, a Charleston lawyer and personal friend of Mr. Grosscup. In 1912 the street-car system was extended from Charleston to Dunbar, which at that time had a population of about 200.

The 1920 census gave Dunbar a population of 3,000. Dunbar was incorporated as a city on April 19, 1921. At this time the only route from Dunbar to Charleston was the Roxalana Hollow Road. During the early 1920s low ground between the railroad and the river was filled and Dunbar Avenue was completed. In 1953 the Dunbar Bridge over the Kanawha River to Spring Hill was completed. In 1959 an additional area was incorporated which more than doubled the size of the city.

In 1968 Interstate 64 was completed to the Dunbar Interchange, opening a super-highway connection to the Kentucky border and points west. In 1974 the highway was opened eastward to South Charleston.

The area called Institute revolves around West Virginia State College, founded in 1891. Its most important early citizen, Samuel I. Cabell, lived there many years before the school was established. Cabell was a member of the well-known Virginia Cabells, who produced a governor of Virginia, for whom Cabell County is named.

In 1853 Samuel Cabell bought a parcel of rich bottom land west of Dunbar once owned by George Washington. One of Cabell's slaves was named Mary Barnes. In an unusual gesture for the time, he took her as her wife and remained devoted to her his entire life. He freed her, provided for his children and willed that his other slaves be set free after his death (actually, not until they had hired out for six years). Unfortunately, Cabell was a quick-tempered, southern sympathizer who did not get along with his neighbors. In 1865 he was killed by some local citizens under mysterious circumstances.

His extensive lands were left to his wife and children, who eventually sold parcels upon which sits the college, the former Wertz Field and the former rubber plant.

Cabell's lands became a small community composed mainly of freed slaves. The site became known at different times as "Cabell Farm" and "Piney Grove." About 1914 town lots were laid out apparently in hopes of luring black coal miners to settle there. Several black schools, including the Colored Institute, were established, an added incentive for families to move there.

In 1926 the West Virginia School for Colored, Deaf and Blind was located at Institute. It is now the West Virginia Vocational Rehabilitation Center.

Dr. John W. Davis, president of West Virginia Collegiate Institute and West Virginia State College from 1919 to 1953.
COURTESY WEST VIRGINIA STATE COLLEGE ARCHIVES

ROTC unit in formation at the West Virginia Collegiate Institute (West Virginia State College) in 1918. SWV

A CIRR trolley along Dunbar Avenue in 1914 shortly after Fred Grosscup developed the area. KCL

10th Street from Dunbar Avenue looking toward the river, mid 1920s. COURTESY OVA TOLLEY

The Sloan Building at the corner of 12th Street and Dunbar Avenue. A CIRR trolley is shown at left, 1920s. COURTESY OVA TOLLEY

The Rollins Building at the corner of 12th Street and Ohio Avenue housed Dunbar's city hall until 1941, when the present city hall was built. This building, shown in the 1920s, also housed the Dunbar Land Company. COURTESY OVA TOLLEY

The Fletcher Enamel Company was established in Dunbar in 1914 and shipped thousands of enameled pots and pans throughout the world, until closing in 1958. The area is now the site of a bank, service stations and numerous businesses. The tracks on the far left belong to the New York Central. The adjacent ones were used by the Charleston Interurban Railroad. COURTESY OVA TOLLEY

An early view of the wheelwright shop, late 1890s. The school provided vocational training plus academic courses to black students from West Virginia and beyond. COURTESY WEST VIRGINIA STATE COLLEGE ARCHIVES

Graduates parading on the campus green, 1931. COURTESY WEST VIRGINIA STATE COLLEGE ARCHIVES

St. Albans

St. Albans occupies land once owned by George Washington. After his death in 1799 his Kanawha County real estate was divided among 23 persons named in his will. Washington's "Cole" River property was awarded to his niece, Elizabeth Spotswood, daughter of Augustine Washington. In 1810 she sold the tract to Morris Hudson for $1,500.

Tackett's Fort, built in 1786 a half mile west of Coal River and a few hundred yards away from the water, was the first permanent settlement in the area. There was minimal trouble with the Indians until several settlers were abducted in March. In August 1790 the fort was attacked, resulting in the death of several people. These incidents ended the settlement at this site.

In 1781 Thomas Teays settled on 27,000 acres, mostly in Putnam County, granted him as a reward for his military service. He was captured in what is now Teays Valley by Indians in 1782, but later escaped and returned to his former home in Virginia.

Thomas' youngest son Stephen (1774-1823) moved to his father's land about 1793 and settled on the west side of Coal River near its mouth. He built a double log house and was granted a ferry franchise across the Coal River in 1800. When the "Old State Road" was completed through the area to the Ohio River in 1804, Teays built an inn to serve the travellers.

The road brought in more settlers, as did the James River and Kanawha Turnpike, which crossed Coal River near the present location of Main Street and the old Route 60 bridge. A post office was established in 1817 with Benjamin Cole as the first postmaster. James N. Fry owned the store in which the post office was located.

During the early days of the Civil War there was much activity in the Coalsmouth area. The covered bridge that carried turnpike traffic over the Coal River was burned by retreating Confederates in 1861. A large Confederate camp was established on Tompkins' land before the Battle of Scary Creek, which was fought just over the border in Putnam County.

Before the war extensive navigational aids were constructed on the Coal River, enabling large amounts of cannel coal to be shipped from Boone County to the Kanawha River. After the war the railroad provided additional opportunities to transport the coal and timber resources in the area.

Coalsmouth was the first name given to the St. Albans area. Phillip R. Thompson laid out a townsite in 1834 and called it Phillipi. John S. Cummingham purchased this townsite in 1858, laid out a larger town and named it Jefferson. Phillipi and Jefferson were incorporated by an act of the legislature in 1868 into a new town named "The Village of Kanawha City." The name St. Albans, which was given to the town by another act of the legislature in 1871, was assigned at the insistence of railroad magnate C.P. Huntington as a favor to the chief counsel of the C&O, H.C. Parsons of St. Albans, Vermont.

Many industries moved in and out of town through the years but lumber remained predominant. This industry was gone by the 1920s, however. Several important grist mills were built on the Coal River as early as 1802. A chemical company called Roseler &

An artist's concept, drawn from memory, of the first bridge built across the Coal River in 1832 to accommodate the new James River & Kanawha Turnpike. In July 1861 this bridge was destroyed by retreating Confederate forces and not rebuilt for 10 years. The existing Main Street bridge is at this same location. PM

Haslacher was established in the early 1900s but St. Albans never developed this industry to the extent that South Charleston and Belle did. Today St. Albans is a modern, mainly residential city home to people who work in Charleston or at one of the valley's chemical plants.

Sattes was a small community located across the Kanawha River from the mouth of the Coal. It was named for the Frederick Antonio Sattes farm. Sattes taught school, owned a wharf on the river, bought produce for a Charleston wholesale house, was the first agent at the depot located at the Sattes stop, and established a ferry between Sattes and St. Albans. Two of his sons operated a stone quarry, supplying stone for the Kanawha River locks and the Kanawha and Michigan Railroad.

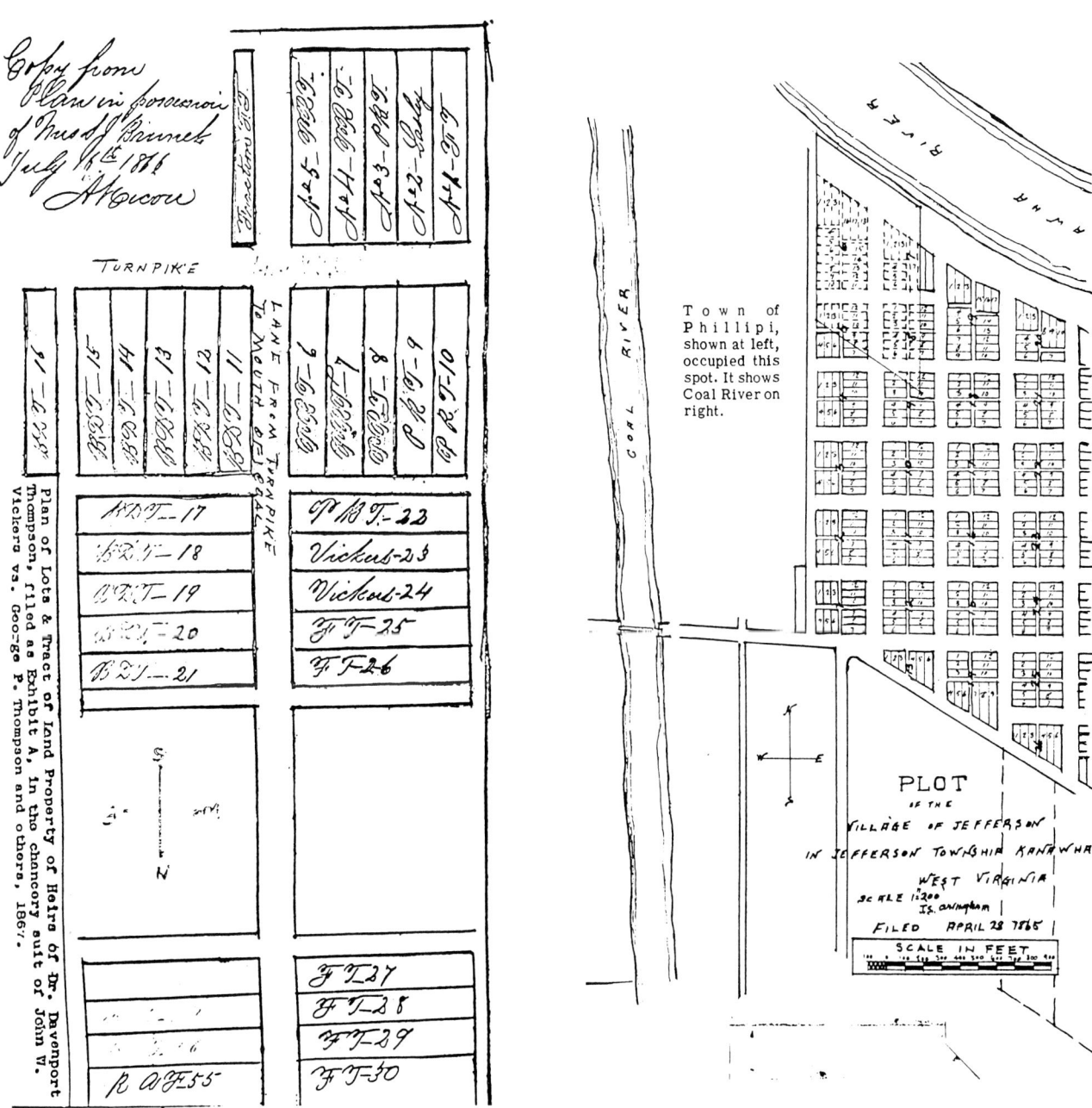

THE VILLAGE OF KANAWHA CITY

Town of Phillipi, shown at left, occupied this spot. It shows Coal River on right.

PHILLIPI VIRGINIA

THE VILLAGE OF JEFFERSON WEST VIRGINIA

St. Albans in 1878. Looking east from Cemetery Hill at Main Street.

COURTESY BETTY JO SATTES RANSON

James T. Teays Tavern was built in 1831 as a stage stop on the James River and Kanawha Turnpike. It was remodelled several times and was used as a tavern/hotel until 1876. It remained in the Teays family until 1944 and was demolished in 1956. PM

The historic Colonial Inn was built in 1829 by M.E. Burton. It was the center of many local social events. It was razed in 1962 to provide parking space for the First Presbyterian Church. COURTESY ST. ALBANS HISTORICAL SOCIETY

An early 1900s view of B Street. PM

Main Street, 1950s. This has now been converted to a walking mall. PM

Roseler & Haslacher Chemical Company, 1916. WW

Atkinson Foundry and Car Shops, 1910.
COURTESY ST. ALBANS HISTORICAL SOCIETY

ST. ALBANS NONPAREIL.

TERMS, 50 CENTS PER ANNUM, STRICTLY IN ADVANCE. "FEARLESS AND FREE." JAMES V. HENDERSON, EDITOR AND PROPRIETOR

Vol. 2. St. Albans, Kanawha County, West Va., Saturday, July 8, 1882. No. 4.

St. Albans Nonpareil.
PUBLISHED WEEKLY.

JAMES V. HENDERSON,
EDITOR AND PROPRIETOR.

TERMS OF SUBSCRIPTION.
50 cents per annum, in advance.
30 cents for 6 months.
Office in Town Hall Building, Main Street.

OFFICIAL DIRECTORY OF BOONE COUNTY.
Judge of Circuit Court D. E. Johnson.
Sheriff W. T. Smoot.
Clerk of Circuit Court. Wm. Thompson.
Clerk of County Court---M. J. Hopkins.
Prosecuting Attorney.--J. E. Chilton.
County Commissioners.--Thos. Hill, President, Alex. DeJarnett, J. C. Edleman.
Assessor.--R. H. Harless.
Surveyor.--H. A. Miller.
Commissioner of School Lands.--Wm. Thompson.
Superintendent of Schools.--G. M. Ball.
Jailor.--P. S. Ball.

CHURCH DIRECTORY.
The several churches of St. Albans hold services as follows:
Presbyterian.—Rev. E. Eells, 1st and 3d Sunday at 11 o'cl'k a. m., and 8 p. m. Prayer meeting every Wednesday evening.
Baptist.—Rev. P. B. Reynolds, 2nd Sunday at 11 o'clk. a. m., and 4th Sunday, at 8 p. m.
J. W. Moore, 3d Sunday Tackett's Creek.
Episcopal.—Rev. J. W. Lee, 3rd Sunday at 11 o'clock a. m., and 8 p. m.
M. E. Church South, Rev. J. F. Johnson, preaches every three weeks at 11 o'clock a. m., and 8 p. m.
M. E. Church—Rev. Geo. H. Williams, 1st. Sunday at 10½ A. M. and 8 P. M.
Colored Baptist Church, Rev. Jas. Perkins, every Sunday at 11 o'clock a. m., and 8 p. m.

THE AMERICAN
Contracting
and
Transportation
COMPANY.
Incorporated under the laws of the state of New York.
A. J. B. Berger, Pres.; L. Van Wyck, Sec.; C. Richardson, Treas. New York Office, Astor House, Room 78.
Will enter into contracts for the transportation of coal, iron-ores, &c., at a fixed rate per ton, in localities unapproachable by railroads.

S. L. WEBB,
ATTORNEY AT LAW
And Notary Public.
ST. ALBANS, W. VA.
Will practice in the Circuit Courts of Kanawha and adjoining Counties, and the Magistrates Courts of Kanawha. Will write and take acknowledgments of Deeds, Leases, Contracts and other writings, Homestead Papers and Schedules of Personal property, prepared on short notice.

LEWIS SCHWARTZ,
Front St., Charleston, W. Va.
——Dealer in——
WINES
AND LIQUORS.
Cincinnati
and Kentucky Bourbon, from $1,25 to 5.00 per gallon.

PROFESSIONAL CARDS

E. A. [illegible]ER,
ATTORNEY AT LAW.
CHARLESTON, W. VA
OFFICE [illegible] Hotel.

H. C. [illegible]TON,
ATTORNEY AT LAW.
CHARLESTON, W. VA.
Office in Bank Building, Capitol Street.

S. B. CHILTON, M. D.,
Physician and Surgeon.
Office at McDermitt's Drug-Store. All calls night or day promptly answered.

S. CHAPMAN,
COUNTY SURVEYOR.
ALL orders left with Thos. Swinburn, Circuit Court Clerk, will receive prompt attention.

John A. Warth,
ATTORNEY AT LAW,
ST. ALBANS.
Practices in all the Courts of the county, the Supreme Court of Appeals of the State, and the District Court of the United States at Charleston.

S. C. BURDETT,
ATTORNEY AT LAW,
And Commissioner of School Lands for Kanawha Co.
Office up stairs, Kyle's Building, opposite Court House, Charleston, W. Va.

DR. CHAS. H. ROGERS.
DENTIST,
CHARLESTON, WEST VA.
Dental Office, over Harmison's Store.

J. E. Kenna, W. E. Chilton, Jr
KENNA & CHILTON,
Attorneys-at-Law
Office in the Wehrle Building.
CHARLESTON, W. VA.
Practice in all the Courts of Kanawha County, and in the Circuit Courts of Boone and Lincoln Counties.

J. E. Stollings. J. E. Chilton.
STOLLINGS & CHILTON.
ATTORNEYS AT LAW.
Will practice in all the Courts of Boone and Lincoln Counties W. Va.

A. M. Cheek, M. D.
Special Attention given to
CATARRH THROAT, LUNG
And all Chronic Diseases.
OFFICE: Over Harmison's Store, Front Street,
CHARLESTON, W. VA.
vi—n33.

D. D. MILLER,
PHYSICIAN and SURGEON.
—OFFICE T—
J. H. Sutherland's Drug Store.

H. R. PUTNEY, & CO.
Dealers in
PLAIN AND FANCY
GROCERIES,
LLOYD'S OLD STAND
Charleston, West Va.

Notice to Builders.
I have just received a large lot of Lime, (snow flake,) Lathes and Shingles, and can furnish Brick, Nails, &c., as cheap as the cheapest. Give me a call.
Respectfully,
J. M. TURNER.

Kanawha Mining
AND
Transportation Co.,
CAPITAL STOCK, $500,000.
A. J. B. Berger, President; H. W. Richardson, Treasurer; James McCarthy, Vice Pres't. Lawrence Van Wyck, Secretary; E. Hemmings, Superintendent.

Mrs. H. Reed.
Bakery Confectionery and
GROCERY.
Front Street, near Public Landing, Charleston, W. Va.
Keeps constantly on hand, a large and well-selected assortment of all kinds of Fancy & Family Groceries. We deliver Goods anywhere in the city on the shortest notice.
Orders from abroad, will receive prompt attention.
v—1—n 44.

THEA. DEAN'S
SADDLERY AND HARNESS ESTABLISHMENT,
FRONT STREET OPPOSITE COURT HOUSE.
Charleston W. Va.
JOHN R. LIGGETT, Superintendent.
The most complete stock in the saddlery and harness line ever offered in the market. We offer nothing for sale that we are not willing to warrant. Shoemakers findings a specialty.

Reuben Farrar.
Would most respectfully inform the citizens of St. Albans, and the Public generally, that he has just opened a first class

BARBER SHOP.
in the stand, next door above C. D. Hereford's Store, where he is prepared and ready at all times, to do all kinds of work in the tonsorial art, in the latest styles, neatest manner and at the lowest rates. We propose to keep a neat, clean Shop, where gentlemen, can come, and receive a quiet nice shave. We would respectfully ask a liberal share of your patronage, as we are satisfied we can give you entire satisfaction.
Reuben Farrar.

ST. ALBANS, W. VA., }
June 23d, 1882. }

DEAR FRIEND:—
I write to you from this, the
city of St. Albans,
To tell you of our Teacher's
Institute.
The question may arise within
your mind,
What is an Institute? It is a
glorious cheat.
It calls the teachers from their
rural homes,
From 'mong the rocky hills
of W. Va.
And bids them in the hottest
season of the year,
To leave their harvest fields
and house-hold cares,
And "mingle in the busy haunts
of men,"
The dusty streets are thronged
with pedagogues,
Each ready with his "giant intellect,"
To be instructor of his fellow-man,
The surging crowd moves
around in its course
And wends its way o'er dusty
streets
And walks, where loosened
boards
Make music to the tread of
many feet,
Until at last the goal is reached,
Where much (we might almost
say all)
The wisdom of Kanawha Co.
is assembled.
The President of this Assembly of learned men
Is C. V. Hansford, a teacher
of no little merit,
And noted for his wisdom in
instructing others.
He teaches us the art of marking Goods
And many other secret things
he maketh plain,
And 'mong the wise men of the
Institute,
We must remember Ezra Conner,
A man who holds a high and
mighty office,
The overseer of all the schools,
In the vast region of Kanawha
County.
He teaches us to keep our registers correct,
So that we trouble not the men
of high estate
With awkward work, mistakes,
blots and blunders.
Then comes McCallister, who
teaches how to wield the
pen,
And leads us on through all
the mysteries of that art.
There too is Sherrard, a wise
man from the State of
Summers,
Who has the key to all the
books of learning in the
land,
And says he'll lead us on in
wisdoms path,
That we to may be wise like
him.
But we are of the class, wise
in their own conceit
Who love to teach the things
we know ourselves,
Rather than listen to instruction from another,
And as we look among the
crowd of teachers,
We see one with brow of wisdom,
Who answers to that name of
Whittington
He, though young in years, is
learned in many things
Especially in Harveys grammar
Which science he explains
To all his wondering audience,
Here we have Henderson &
Bro. the merchant and the
journalist,
And both learned men.
But if we try to mention all
The wisdom of this assembly
Our pen and paper both will
fail,
For there is Hill, Chase, Lynn,
Asbury, Roberts, Knight,
White and Webb,
And many others whom our
space forbids us to mention
But, of the beauty, grace, and
wit among the fairer sex.
We dare not speak, for 'tis a
subject boundless
Then after five long days of
dust, heat and tedious
work,
Our Institute is closed and
comes the dread examination
And what is its result? At best
a number one.
A school—perhaps— with the
large salary of $30.
Hard work and little pay. And
now my friends, for want
of time and space I'll bring
my letter to a close and,
Sign myself your friend till
death,
EZEK'L ISAAC FREDRICK JONES.

STRICT VEGETARIANISM.
A man wandered down street last night and, approaching a grocery store, asked of the proprietor:
"You got some greens, don't it?"
"Greens? Yes sir,"
"You got rooting bakers?"
"Rutabagas? Yes, sir. How many will you have,"
"Got some little red plates, mit green tops?"
"Red plates with green tops? Well, no. sir. I suppose you will find them at the china store, up town."
"Those? Why those are radishes."
"Red dishes dot's what I said. Say maybe I got some letters of you to-morrow. You got it?"
"Letters? There are no letters here for you; you must inqure at the post office."
"Ankwire mit de post office for letters? Dose was fine skeems. I was up town and auf a bakeshop, and want some bums, and de man said, 'Got out, you old bum, or I'll fire you through the door.'"
"You should have said buns, He—"
"Bums? dots vot I said—bums; and den I comes and want some red dishes, and you tell me to go auf the china store; I want some letters to eat and you say go mit de post office. Fogspect I wants some beats you tole me to go to de station house. I tell you vot I do—you can go to de tyfel Of you was a nice man, I want some injins, and cowcumbers, and blenty dings, but I guess I go to de drug store and by a brick and peddles rat pizen."

The census bureau shows that the number of men engaged in agricultural pursuits in the United States is 7,699,-212, as against 3,519,467 in manufacturing, mechanical and mining occupations.

There is a boy in Columbia county, N. Y., who has living a great-great-grandmother, three great grandmothers two grandmothers, and two grandfathers. If that boy isn't spoiled it will be a miracle.

GREENBACK MEETING!!
Tackett's Creek School House,
July 1st 1882.
A Greenback Meeting was called to Order by appointment. Mr. T. W. Henderson, was appointed temporary Chairman.
A resolution was offered and carried, to the effect that a permanent President and five members be elected to act and serve as Executive Committee, for the District of Jefferson.
The following named gentlemen were duly elected to serve as said Committee:
T. W. Henderson, President, James Burgess, Frank Eastwood of Spring Hill, J. W. Topping, Preston Martin, Lef. King.
Mr. C. W. Henley, was unanimously elected to represent Jefferson, on the 15th of July, and to act in consultation with the County Executive Committee, and one Delegate from each Magisterial District, in the County, tending to the future action of the Greenback party.
The following resolutions were unanimeusly passed:
Resolved, 1st. That we reaffirm our loyalty and devotion to the great principles of the Greenback Labor Party, and pledge to each other, our determination to use our best efforts for the success of our principles.
Resolved, 2. That the Greenbackers of Jefferson District, send greeting to the other Districts, and assured them that Jefferson District proposes to be the banner District this fall, for the principles of our party.
Resolved, 3. That we have no preference who our standard bearers may be, provided they are good, intelligent and worthy men, and that we will give them a hearty and enthusiastic support.
Resolved, 4. That we are opposed to rings and corrupt Conventions, such as are practiced by the old parties, and would suggest to our Executive Committee, to adopt some plan by which our Candidates can be placed in the field without so much contusion and corruption as is practiced by the old parties in their Conventions.
Adjourned to meet at Tackett's Creek School House, on the 22d day of July, at 2 o'clock P. M., 1882.
J. H. MCCONAHA, Sec'y.

CHARLESTON, W. VA., }
June 30th, 1882. }
Enclosed find a list of teachers who received No 1 Certificates:
Quite a number failed to get good grades, in consequence of the new law. More were reduced than raised. Forty-eight teachers were examined: 28 No. Ones. 13 No. Twos, and 8 No. Threes.

NUMBER ONES.
Mrs. S. L. Cato, Miss Sallie Hansford; Mrs. Hill; Miss, Mollie Ryan; Mrs. M. M. Thompson; Miss Florence Clark; Miss Fannie Price; Sadie Payne; Emma Chase; Lethia Calvert; Laura Wood; Jennie Stanley; Mary Spurr; Emma Brace; Miss Belle Wilson; C. V. Hansford; J. A. Chase; Chas. Hill; W. H. Knight; M. B. Henderson; B. H. Webb; E. G. Roberts; Jack Whittington; C. McCallister; Peter Silman; S. L. White.

At a blooded cattle sale at Harristown, Ill, sixty-nine head sold for $16,836, or an average of $244 each.

There have been newspapers published in St. Albans since the late 1860s. There was the *Coalsmouth Pioneer*, later changing to the *St. Albans Pioneer* and later to the *National Labor Advocate*; the *St. Albans Express*; the *Times*; the *St. Albans Nonpareil*; the *Kanawha Valley Democrat*; the *St. Albans Reporter*; the *St. Albans Herald*; the *St. Albans News*; the *Valley News*; and the *St. Albans Advertiser*. COURTESY CARL WOLFE

The St. Albans Wharf Company, now the site of a boat dock on the Kanawha River, early 1900s. GS

In 1906 much of Main Street was gutted by fire.
COURTESY ST. ALBANS HISTORICAL SOCIETY

A 1931 aerial view of the Coal River bridge and part of St. Albans' business district. Much of this district near the bridge has been changed in recent years. GS

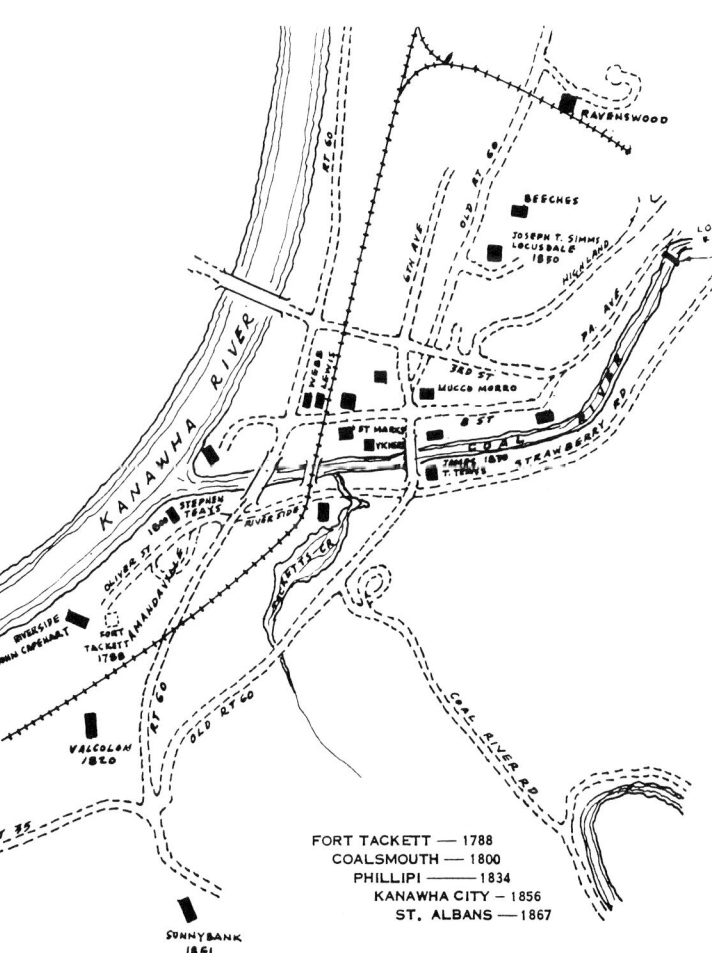

Construction scene in 1934 of the St. Albans-Nitro bridge. For years it was a toll bridge to the Sattes Ferry, pictured here, which operated between St. Albans and Sattes until the toll was eliminated. PM

For more than six decades lumbering was big business in the Coal River/St. Albans area. These scenes are typical of the numerous operations in the area. Top: Trowbridge sawmill and its log carriage on College Hill. Bottom: Bowman Mill lumber yard and unloading area. Bowman purchased the Mohler sawmill at the old Lock No. 1 site on Coal River in 1882. PM

Nitro

Although Nitro, which straddles the Kanawha-Putnam County border, is a relatively new city, its history can be traced back thousands of years to the Indian cultures that flourished in the area. The first whites didn't make their appearance here until the military land grants of the 1700s. The first permanent settlers—Samuel Gillespie, John Persinger, George Blake and John Dudding—put down roots in the 1790s.

Troops from both sides moved through the Nitro area during the Civil War. But the railroad didn't come through until 1884, the year a depot and post office were established on the farm of Frederick Sattes. Soon after, a ferry began operations across the Kanawha to St. Albans.

In 1888 the Mohler Lumber Company moved across the river and built a sawmill. This site became known as Mohlerville. Later on, Lock Seven was built across the Kanawha, and the village name was changed to Lock Seven.

The modern history of the Nitro area is a fascinating industrial story well-documented in William Wintz's book, *Nitro, the World War I Boom Town.* Nitro was established in 1918 as a direct result of World War I. When America entered the war in April 1917, the War Industries Board determined that "immediate and drastic action must be taken as the gunpowder situation is regarded as critical and of supreme importance." Several sites were selected to build the largest gunpowder plant in the world but only the Lock Seven site, which would become Nitro, was authorized for construction. Formal ground breaking occurred on January 2, 1918. In quick order massive construction projects got underway including barracks, workers houses, hospitals, administration buildings, and enormous production facilities. More than 110,000 people worked on this massive project during 1918, although never more than 19,000 at any given time.

Thousands of troops and private police were stationed here. Since Nitro was to be a critical part of the Allied war effort, security was very tight both in and around the plant. People came here from all over the country to work, but the turnover was very high. Many people stayed when the plant closed, and their families still live in the area.

But the massive amounts of explosives the plant was supposed to produce would never be needed. The moment the war ended on November 11, 1918, Nitro became obsolete. In 1919 the U.S. Ordnance Department sold it to the Charleston Industrial Corporation. Many different companies took over portions of the operation through the years. Today all traces of this major industry, except for a few concrete bunkers, have vanished.

Nitro, the shortened name for nitroglycerin, a major ingredient in explosives, is today a diverse community of industrial and residential neighborhoods. Many of the homes built in 1918 to house the workers are still in use.

Lock Seven Depot of the Kanawha and Michigan Railroad in 1906. ww

Hundreds of soldiers were stationed at Nitro to guard the installation. One of these was Robert Reeve, who would become one of the best known Alaskan bush pilots in the 1930s and founder of Reeve Aleutian Airways.
COURTESY REEVE ALEUTIAN AIRWAYS

Many different businesses were established in 1918 to service the workers and their families. This is a drug store and haberdashery shop which today is the only original community building left in Nitro. ww

Interior of a general store set up for plant workers. ww

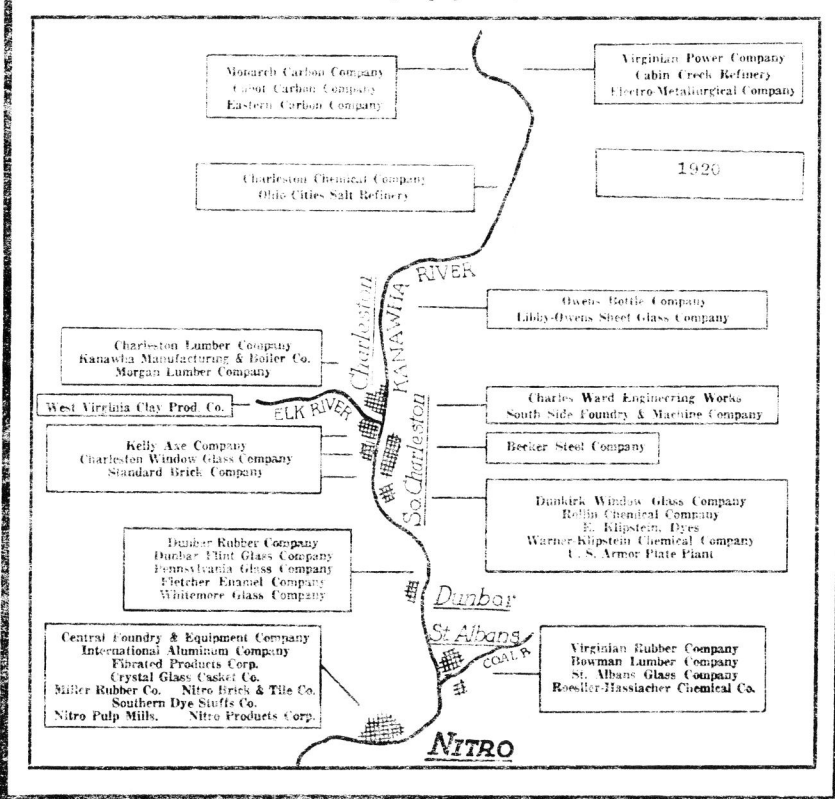

Interior of the Lock Seven Store in January 1919. By this time the explosives plant was shut down and most of the thousands of plant workers were gone. ww

Changing of the guard during plant construction, 1918. ww

Clendenin

The town of Clendenin, named for Kanawha County's first pioneer family, sits at the mouth of Big Sandy Creek on the Elk River, twenty miles northeast of Charleston. The area is on a parcel granted in 1788 by Virginia Governor Edmond Randolph to William Cobb, whose property originally stretched almost all the way from Clendenin to the Roane County line.

One of the area's first settlers was John Young, a ranger at Fort Lee and one of the first trustees of Charleston. In 1795 Young was living at Young's Bottom, also known as Young Plantation, five miles south of the present site of Clendenin. In the same year, William Cobb settled one mile up Little Sandy Creek, and William Naylor built a house at the mouth of Jordan's Creek. Other early settlers were John Stricklin, John Hayes, George Osborne, John Snyder, James Hill, and Henry Hill.

The first mill in the area was supposedly built by William Naylor at Jordan's Creek. Reverend John Bowers, a Methodist minister, visited the area as early as 1800, but it took until 1837 for the faithful to organize the Methodist Episcopal Church at Falling Rock Creek.

Although the area had been permanently civilized since the late 1700s, the population remained small until after the Civil War. Clendenin itself didn't exist until 1877, when William Chilton laid out a townsite. This settlement was first known as the Village of Chilton, although the post office was simply called Mouth of Sandy. (Chilton's sons, Joe, William and Sam would become powerful influences in county, state and national politics; Sam founded the *Charleston Gazette*.)

Even by 1880 the only people living on the Clendenin townsite were Squire Jarrett and Burl Swaar. Robert L. Young was living on Leatherwood Creek at this time, building barges and barrels for the salt industry. Dock Woods and Morrison Copen were running a general store at the mouth of Big Sandy Creek.

The first school in the Big Sandy District, which included Clendenin, was built in 1870 at Cobb Station, also known as Broad Run. Six years later, there were ten schools in the district. The first high school opened in 1911 and was called the Big Sandy District High School. It later became Clendenin High School and is now a grade school.

As early as the 1850s, cannel coal was mined on Falling Rock Creek below Clendenin. A refinery, perhaps the first in America, was built to process the coal into cannel oil; the

Clendenin's first movie theater, next to Summers House, 1914. CPL

Clendenin in its boom days. Wells were common on the north side of Elk River in the Clifton area. KCL

Bridge Street in 1916 (top) and the 1950s (middle). The bridge has now been replaced by a new one a short distance downstream. KCL

structure's chimney still remains. Prior to 1890 timber and coal were the area's main source of income. Due to the poor quality of the roads to Charleston, goods were brought in by push boats up the Elk River.

In the 1890s the Charleston, Clendenin and Sutton Railroad ran track up the south bank of the Elk River, opening up the area to the outside world. The company was later taken over by the Coal and Coke Railroad. With the discovery of oil and gas deposits in the vicinity in 1900, Clendenin turned into a boomtown. The population soared to more than 2,000. Almost overnight banks were founded, stores built and oil and gas company offices opened. The South Penn Oil Company and the Virginia Gas and Oil Company were just two of the firms drilling wells in the area.

The Elk Refining Company built a large petroleum refinery at Falling Rock below Clendenin about 1911—it's no longer operating, however. The Cobb Compressor Plant, once the world's largest, was built about 1917. Union Carbide's first plant was built at Clendenin in the 1920s but soon moved operations to its present South Charleston site.

It wasn't until May 20, 1904, that the town of Clendenin was incorporated. The first mayor was L.V. Koontz. The First National Bank was organized in 1902. In 1910 a water system was installed, and a city fire department was organized. In 1914 the streets were paved, eliminating the mud canals that had passed for Clendenin's thoroughfares. (The mud problem had been compounded by the heavy use of horse and oxen teams pulling wagons loaded with pipe through town.)

Now, Clendenin's boom years are long gone. Coal, timber, oil and gas are a memory. Interstate 79 bypassed the town in the 1970s. Although still a service center for the area, Clendenin has become a sleepy backwoods village.

The old depot of the Coal and Coke Railroad, later taken over by the Baltimore and Ohio Railroad. COURTESY HENRY YOUNG

An early civic band in Clendenin, 1915. CPL

Retto's Store, 1910. CPL

King Hardware Company in Clendenin with some local citizens. COURTESY HENRY YOUNG

A typical wagon used to haul pipes to the oil and gas fields. COURTESY HENRY YOUNG

Business section of Clendenin with the Boat House on the left, early 1900s. CPL

The Big Chimney Area

In 1858 Dr. Edwin Doddridge decided to produce salt in the Elk Valley. Doddridge built a large salt factory at the site of Big Chimney on the Elk River, and produced salt for a little over two years. When the Civil War began, Dr. Doddridge went off to fight and was subsequently killed. Like the other salt works in the county, Doddridge's enterprise fell into ruin.

Sometime after the war, Clay Wertz of Pennsylvania opened a coal mine on the opposite side of the river from Big Chimney. A small settlement grew up that was named Graham after a local family.

In the early 1900s there was an oil and gas boom in the Big Chimney area, and today the area is mainly residential.

Dutch Hollow Wine Cellars on Dutch Hollow Road in Dunbar is a remnant of the once-thriving wine industry in the Kanawha Valley. Thomas R. Friend operated the business until the Civil War stopped all wine production. Production was attempted again after the war but the effort wasn't successful. The cellars have been restored and turned into a city park.*

Chapter Twenty-four
A View of the Present from the Past

Glenwood, on Charleston's west side, was built in 1852 in the Greek Revival style for James M. Laidley, a prominent early salt maker. Judge George W. Summers bought the house in 1857. It is one of the best examples in the county of an original pre-Civil War house. The last resident was Lucy Quarrier, a descendant of Judge Summers. The house is now occupied by COGS.*

The McFarland House on Kanawha Boulevard, built in 1836 by Norris Whitteker, is one of the valley's oldest and most significant homes. Built in the Greek Revival style, it has housed the McFarland, Ruby, Crowley and Hubbard families. During the Civil War it was used as a hospital.*

Lincoln Junior High School is still used. Several additions have been built since the original construction.

The Craik-Patton House has been restored on a new site at Daniel Boone Park and opened as a museum.*

The Old Colony Building at 1210 Kanawha Boulevard was built in 1891 as the home of well-known Charleston businessman Frank Woodman. The United Mine Workers purchased the house in 1950 and sold it to Old Colony Realty in 1976.

Samuel Starks' home at 413 Shrewsbury Street is owned by the city of Charleston and operated by the YWCA as "Sojourners on Shrewsbury," a short-term shelter for the homeless. Starks was a prominent black leader in the community, a national leader of the Knights of Pythias and the first black appointee to state office, holding the position of state librarian under two Republican governors.

Breezemont is another prominent home on Charleston's west side. It was built in 1905 for C.C. Watts, an attorney, politician and businessman. The house survives as one of the four prime examples of Neo-Classical architecture in the city. In 1941 the house was subdivided into apartments.*

Foundation stones from the old Sattes Mill at Lower Falls on Coal River.

Spring Hill Cemetery overlooks the central business district of Charleston. It bears the remains of many of the founding fathers of the city. The city bought the property in 1869 and Thomas Matthius surveyed the area with design work by A.J. Vosburgh. The imposing mausoleum on the grounds was constructed in 1910. Some notables buried here include Dr. John P. Hale, governors Atkinson and Wilson, Senator Kenna, Judge George W. Summers, Jacob Goshorn, Samuel Starks, William S. Laidley and Julius deGruyter.

Booker T. Washington's monument on the grounds of the state capitol.

One of the best examples of 1930s art deco architecture in town is the Blossom Dairy building on Quarrier Street. Its style is prominent inside and out.

"Ravenswood," located on MacQueen Boulevard in St. Albans, traces its history to the 1830s when a frame dwelling was constructed on the property. The present brick structure was built in 1833 by Francis Thompson. The house had several owners until Judge J.B.C. Drew purchased it in 1897. Trading on the name "Ravenswood," he fabricated a story that Edgar Allen Poe wrote his famous poem "The Raven" in the home. Extensive remodelling was undertaken in 1914.

The Chilton House in St. Albans, built in 1857, is a good example of Gothic Revival style. In recent years the house was removed to its present site on Coal River, restored, and opened as a fine restaurant. The house was owned for many years by the well-known Chilton family. Samuel became a highly regarded physician and William E. a public official and U.S. Senator from West Virginia.*

Remains of the Nitro Explosives factory can still be found. This large concrete bunker was probably built inside another building. It may have been used to house explosives or protect workers.

The William E. Mohler house on Pennsylvania Avenue in St. Albans is an outstanding example of Queen Anne Victorian-style architecture. It was built by lumber magnate William E. Mohler in 1901. During World War II women workers from the Naval Ordnance Plant were housed here.*

These massive stones are the remains of Lock No. 6 at South Charleston.

The Criel Mound at South Charleston is now a city park.

"Cedar Grove," the home of William and Rachel Grant Tompkins in the town of Cedar Grove. It has remained in the Tompkins family since it was completed in 1844.*

A slave cemetery located behind Virginia's Chapel in Cedar Grove.

The Shrewsbury-Dickinson farmhouse sits on Route 60 just east of the Quincy Mall. Built prior to 1820, it was the summer home of John L. Dickinson's family for many years. It is now threatened with destruction.

The oldest house in the East Bank area was built in 1826 by John Harriman, the son of Shadrack Harriman, one of the original Rangers at Fort Lee. It is a brick house with some Greek Revival lines.*

"The Stone House" in Belle was built perhaps as early as 1810 by Samuel Shrewsbury, Sr., one of the first settlers in the area. The walls are 18 inches thick and made of sandstone quarried from the nearby hills. The house has been restored and opened as a museum.*

"The Brick House" at Belle, fronting Route 60, was possibly built by Joel Shrewsbury in the 1830s. The family of Robert F. Reynolds purchased the 14-room house in 1863 and operated the local post office from the house for years. The house, now privately owned, is in excellent condition.

The Marshall Hansford house on Washington Avenue in Pratt is one of the town's most architecturally significant buildings. It was built in 1856 by Marshall Hansford, son of pioneer settler, John Hansford. O.A. Veazey, first mayor of Pratt, purchased the home in 1880.

The old Town Hall was originally constructed in 1875 as a Union Church building. The original bell tower and foundation, kept during the 1982 restoration, are still intact.

The cooperage at Pratt is now a private residence.*

The earliest extant home in Montgomery—the old Riggs place—was built by Levi Morris in the 1820s. It replaced an earlier log home. It remained in the Morris family until 1947.

Remains of the Pure Oil Refinery on Cabin Creek.

The Handley railroad yard was once bustling, but the activity has shifted elsewhere.

Remains of the Elk Refinery Company south of Clendenin. TH

The once bustling coal community of Ward is now quiet except for the sound of the diesel engines that still haul coal out of the hills over tracks of the Kelly's Creek & NW Railroad.

On Charleston's south side, near the foot of the hill next to the carriage trail to "Sunrise," there stands a small stone. In the dim light filtering through the forest, it is easy to forget that automobiles dash by on MacCorkle Avenue a scant few hundred feet away. That cool leafy woodland glen holds a mystery which to this day remains unsolved! Here is what we know: During the construction of "Sunrise" in 1905, ex-Governor William MacCorkle unearthed the remains of two women, one blonde, the other a brunette. In shock and astonishment he moved them a few feet to a place next to the carriage trail and went on with the work. Not long after, he talked to Civil War Veteran John Slack, who declared that the women had been accused of spying by the Confederate Army and had been executed after a brief "Drumhead" court martial. Since their camp was nearby the women were just taken up the little hollow and buried. The Governor accepted this story and had a small stone carved to acknowledge both the event and the burial. Sometime later, another Civil War veteran said the story was true but Slack had the Army wrong because the Yankees had shot the women. Finally the Governor declared that another old Civil War soldier from Lincoln County had confessed on his deathbed that he had been on the Union firing squad and it had haunted him all of his life. So there we have it—two human beings —beloved of someone we know not who, rest near the center of a great city. Were they spies? Did the Federals end their lives or was it the men in gray? Probably we shall never know. Historians have never been able to solve this puzzle.

The Historians

This book is dedicated to the memory of the historians who chronicled the fascinating development of Kanawha County. The first histories were written by Dr. John P. Hale, George W. Atkinson and William S. Laidley, who had the benefit of first-hand accounts from the people who actually made the county's early history. Dr. Roy Bird Cook and others writing later relied substantially on these primary sources.

Dr. John P. Hale lived for 62 years in Kanawha County during an epoch of the county's most rapid development. Hale, the grandson of William Ingles and Mary Draper—the first white couple wedded west of the Alleghenies—was born in 1824 at Ingles Ferry in southwest Virginia. Mary Draper was the first white woman to see the Kanawha Valley, where Hale would move to in 1840. From 1841 to 1842 he attended Mercer Academy in Charleston, then studied medicine under Dr. Spicer Patrick. After graduating from the University of Pennsylvania Medical School in 1845 he formed a partnership with Dr. Patrick in Charleston.

Hale gave up medicine in 1847 and went into the booming salt business. By 1860 he had consolidated various properties in the Snow Hill area east of Charleston, creating the largest salt-producing business in the nation. Ironically, this was the same area where his grandmother, while a captive of the Shawnee Indians in 1755, had stopped with her captors when they made salt on their way west.

At the onset of the Civil War, Hale organized an artillery battery for service in the Confederate Army and fought at the Battle of Scary Creek. He apparently left the service in 1863. In 1864 records show him back in the Kanawha Valley, president of the Kanawha Salt Company.

After the salt business collapsed in the 1870s, Hale pursued other interests. He introduced the first brick-making machinery into the valley and financed the laying of the first brick street in Charleston in 1870. He helped organize the Bank of the West in 1863 and a gas company in Charleston in 1870. In 1864 he built the first steam packet boat on the upper Kanawha River, and in 1878 he constructed the steamers *Wild Goose* and *Lame Duck* using the first steam boiler made by the Ward Engineering Works. At one time he owned all the ferries in the Charleston area.

Hale was the man chiefly responsible for building the first state capitol building in Charleston. In 1871 he was elected mayor of Charleston. In 1872 he built his famous hostel, The Hale House. In that year he was president and part-owner of the company that started Charleston's first daily newspaper. And during this same era he established the first steam laundry in the city and organized the public delivery of ice.

In the 1880s Hale was engaged in the coal and timber business, but like his salt business, these ventures eventually failed, leaving him in dire financial straits. He always seemed to bounce back from his failures to build another fortune.

His contributions to the historical record are numerous. In 1883 he published a pamphlet on Daniel Boone's years in the Kanawha Valley, a chapter of Boone's biography that was practically unknown. In 1886 he produced his *Trans-Allegheny Pioneers* and in 1891 his *History of the Great Kanawha Valley*. He helped found the West Virginia Historical and Antiquarian Society in 1890.

Hale was not a member of any established church and never married. His died in July 1902, and he is buried at Spring Hill Cemetery. His accomplishments were many, his life full, and his influence on the citizens of Kanawha County still felt.

William S. Laidley was born in 1839, the seventh and youngest son of John O. and Mary Hite Laidley. In 1863 he moved to Charleston from Cabell County to study law with his brother-in-law, Judge George W. Summers. Laidley was admitted to the bar in 1865.

During a long life in Charleston, Laidley represented Kanawha County in the 1873 state legislature, was elected in 1900 to the Kanawha County Court, was Charleston City Solicitor in the 1880s and a member of the city council.

In 1911 he wrote and published his *History of Charleston and Kanawha County, West Virginia and Representative Citizens*, one of the most important sources of County history at that time. He died in 1917.

"Such a brief outline of my descent and very unimportant and uninteresting career, now nearing its close. No one can so thoroughly realize its mistakes, imperfections and shortcomings as myself. The rose colored hopes of my youth were doomed to disappointment; the loftier and nobler objects and aims of my early manhood were unattained, and the cherished aspirations and ambitions of my maturer life were unrealized; but regrets are unavailing now. There's a divinity that shapes our ends and I was one of that 'innumerable throng' cast to play the humble, uneventful and commonplace roles in life, and my record is made. My neighbors and the public who have known me will pass upon its merits and demerits and make up their verdict as to what manner of man I have been."

—Dr. John P. Hale on his life

George W. Atkinson was born in 1845 in Kanawha County. He graduated in classical studies from Ohio Wesleyan University in 1870 and in law from Columbia Law School in 1875. He practiced law in Charleston, became prominent in local and state Republican Party affairs and was a member of the National Republican Congressional Committee.

Atkinson served four years as a U.S. Marshall. Then came a term as a U.S. Congressman. In 1896 he was elected governor of West Virginia. He served one term and then assumed duties as a U.S. district attorney for the southern district of West Virginia. For seven years he was one of the owners and editor of the *West Virginia Journal*, a leading local Republican-oriented newspaper.

In 1876 he published through his newspaper his detailed history, *History of Kanawha County from its Organization in 1789 until the Present Time*. In 1890, along with Alvaro F. Gibbens, he published *Prominent Men of West Virginia*. Both books are primary sources of research on Kanawha County history. He died in 1925.

Virgil A. Lewis was born in Mason County in 1848. He was admitted to the bar in 1879 and received an A.M. degree from West Virginia University in 1893. He founded the *Southern Historical Magazine* at Charleston in 1892. From 1893 to 1897, while serving as state superintendent of schools, he was editor and publisher of the *West Virginia Historical Magazine*.

Lewis was prominent in local, state and national educational and historical organizations. In 1890 he organized the West Virginia Historical and Antiquarian Society. His many books include a history of West Virginia, a biography of Anne Bailey, and studies of early educators and the civil government of West Virginia. In 1905 Lewis was appointed West Virginia state archivist and historian.

Dr. Roy Bird Cook, born in Lewis County in 1886, was one of the more prolific modern historians. Cook grew up in the newspaper business—his father was publisher of the weekly *Western Independent* from 1898 to 1931. Roy Bird, however, turned to pharmacy, graduating from the National Institute of Pharmacy in 1905.

Cook came to Charleston in 1919 and bought into a drug store, which in 1944 became the Cook Drug Company at the corner of Quarrier and McFarland streets. In 1938 West Virginia University conferred on him an honorary degree of Doctor of Laws for distinguished service to American pharmacy and American history.

His West Virginia history books include works on Stonewall Jackson, George Washington, Lewis County and Fort Lee. His contributions to local and state history are of critical importance.

Dr. Roy Bird Cook.

Dr. John P. Hale. COURTESY TERRY LOWRY

Governor George W. Atkinson. SWV

Virgil A. Lewis. SWV

Appendix

Mayors of Charleston

Jacob Goshorn, 1861
John A. Truslow, 1865-1867
George Ritter, 1867-1869
John Williams, 1869-1870 & 1872-73
J.W. Wingsfield, 1870-1871
H.C. Dickinson, 1871
John P. Hale, 1871-1872
C.P. Snyder, 1873-1874
John C. Ruby, 1875-1877
C.J. Botkin, 1877-1881
R. R. Delaney, 1881-1883
J.D. Baines, 1883-1885
J.H. Huling, 1885-1887
Joseph L. Fry, 1887-1891
J.B. Pemberton, 1891-1893
E.W. Staunton, 1893-1895
J.A. de Gruyter, 1895-1899
W. Herman Smith, 1899-1900
John B. Floyd, 1900-1901
George S. Morgan, 1901-1903

C.E. Rudesill, 1903-1905
John A. Jarrett, 1905-1907
James A. Holley, 1907-1913
J.F. Bedell, 1913-1914
O.A. Petty, 1914-1915
George E. Breece, 1915-1917
G.A. MacQueen, 1917-1918
R.L. Walker, 1918-1919
Grant P. Hall, 1919-1923
William W. Wertz, 1923-1931
R.P. Devan, 1931-1935
D. Boone Dawson, 1935-1947
R. Carl Andrews, 1947-1951
J.T. Copenhaver, 1951-1959
John A. Shanklin, 1959-1967
Elmer H. Dodson, 1967-1971
John G. Hutchinson, 1971-1980
Joe F. Smith, 1980-1983
James Roark, 1983-present

Some of the County's Oldest Firms

J.Q. Dickinson & Co.—since 1832

Kanawha Valley Bank—since 1867

Cannelton Coal Company—since 1871

Shonk Land Co.—since 1872

Jackson, Kelly, Holt & O'Farrell, attorneys—since 1875

Barlow-Bonsall Funeral Home—since 1875

Patterson, Bell and Crane Co.—since 1876

Schwabe-May Co.—since 1880

Charleston Daily Mail—since 1881

Guthrie-Morris-Campbell Co.—since 1882

James Produce Co.—since 1883

Charleston National Bank—since 1884

West Virginia Water Co.—since 1885

Eskew, Smith and Cannon—since 1887

Charleston Gazette—since 1887

1921

FOR SALE—AUTOMOBILES

ANNOUNCEMENT

I AM GOING OUT OF BUSINESS AND GOING QUICK

IF somebody don't do something, I can't sell any cars; for there is no place to run them. You can't go up Malden road without being killed, you can't go up Kanawha street, without some drunk running over you at sixty miles per, and you can only run one way on Capitol street.

NOW if that isn't a mess, I don't know who is going to buy one of my used cars under those conditions?

TALK about liberty, justice and everlasting peace, you get about as much in West Virginia as the Kaiser would have in Paris on Fourth of July.

YOU might think when you read this, "Why don't this bird Harry leave town, if he don't like it?" Listen I am afraid too. I have not enough money to go by rail and state policemen carry 3 guns and travel in flocks, and you have to give them the road or they shoot you at the wheel. If I were to go to the court house to get a permit to go somewhere and put my hand in my pocket, why a Baldwin-Felt's Man would shoot me in self defense for trying to draw my breath, and if you don't believe me, read the front page of any newspaper. I will take a sworn oath, I am afraid to take my wife and children away from the bright lights of Capitol street in an automobile.

READ IT AND WEEP

THE American Eagle is doing it every day, and will continue to do so until somebody who can bring someone to justice, does something. I thought I voted for the right man for protection, he was elected—(But)

BELOW you will find a list of cars, for sale cheap; if you know any place you can run it.

COME around, we will be more than glad to sell it to you. Also have one mule, the mines are not running very much, will sell him so cheap will make you feel like a horse thief.

ONE 1920 Buick
ONE 1919 Buick
ONE 1917 Buick
ONE 1919 Dixie Flyer
THREE 1918 Dodge cars
ONE 1918 Ford
ONE 1918 Haynes
ONE 1920 Jordan
THREE 1918 Studebakers
ONE 1921 Hudson
ONE 1920 STUDEBAKER SPECIAL SIX, A BARGAIN.

ANNEX AUTO WASH
DICKINSON & HALE STS.
PHONE 1587

The Charleston Regional Chamber of Commerce

On October 26, 1900, 21 Charleston businessmen affixed their signatures and seals to an incorporation certificate for the Chamber of Commerce. All were prominent businessmen who had guided the city in the latter part of the 1800s.

Organizations for the purpose of promoting civic improvements and servicing business and industry existed here prior to 1900 but under other names. There was in existence in 1887 a Charleston Industrial Development Corporation, which a year later changed its name to the Charleston Business and Industrial Association.

And there is evidence that others may have existed prior to the 1900 incorporation of the Chamber. In a 1938 article in "Kanawha Commerce," Charles K. Payne, a veteran Charleston businessman and one of the 1900 incorporators, recalled a Charleston Board of Trade that was started about 1889. However, Payne noted that the Board consisted largely of wholesalers and jobbers who were mainly interested in retail and wholesale credit information services. The Business and Industrial Association apparently did devote some attention to new industry and civic improvements prior to its demise, believed to have taken place about 1895.

The original 21 Chamber members were Charles Capito, Charles Loeb, John L. Dickinson, E.A. Barnes, Jack Carr, C.C. Lewis, Jr., P.H. Noyes, George F. Coyle, Ben Baer, Issac Schwabe, Louis Loewenstein, H.P. Cannon, W.B. Donnelly, W.F. Goshorn, Philip Frankenberger, N.S. Burlew, F.J. Daniels, Frank Woodman, George S. Couch, and W.S. Lewis.

Charles Capito was the first chamber president and volunteer manager until 1910. S. Powell Puffer was hired as the first full-time employee from 1910 to 1936. Charles E. Hodges, a resident of Morgantown, took over the helm and guided the Chamber through the next 26 years. He was known as "Mr. Charleston" and in 1962 was given the appreciation award by a grateful community for his diligence, enthusiasm, and dedication beyond the call of duty and for "his untiring efforts that have brought many benefits to the community, to the area and to the state."

Frank G. Sohn and John A. Chapman were the next two managing directors. Chapman, the present director (1987), oversaw the merger of the Chamber and the Committee of 100 into the present Charleston Regional Chamber of Commerce.

Charles E. Hodges. CN

Population of Small Towns, 1910

Town	Pop.	Town	Pop.
Dana	400	Winifrede	1500
Putney	900	Coalburg	450
Ward	1000	Kayford	1000
Mammoth	1200	Eskdale	400
Decota	300	Carbon	1200
Spring Hill	200	Quick	225
Bream	150	Blakely	350
Sproul	10	Dungriff	400
Olcott	600	Brounland	100
Hernshaw	850	Sattes	80
Lock Seven	200	London	600
Hugheston	500	Guthrie	25
Wallace	20	Blundon	60
Hunt	150	Welford	100
Weir	150	Queen Shoals	300
Morris	50	Dry Branch	250
Ronda	400	Mucklow	300
Sharon	300	Crown Hill	500
Burnwell	500	Chelyan	700
Cabin Creek Junction	100	South Ruffner	100
Kanawha	400	Washington Springs	70
Leon	55	Chilton	40
Monarch	300		

PRESENTED BY
C. KILLINGER
CHARLESTON, W. VA.

At our Harness Shop opposite the St. Albert Hotel,
You can have what you want at prices to tell;
We have Saddles and Bridles, and Halters to suit.
That the styles are all right no one can dispute.

And then we've good harnes, both single and double,
We can suit you with these without any trouble.
We have saddlery, hardware, brushes, combs and all such,
To supply all the Yankees and Irish and Dutch.

We have Ankle Boots, Gum Balls and excellent Collars;
These last we are selling from one to three dollars.
For bridles we've bits of the very best kind;
Buggy Washers, Zink Pads and such things you will find.

We have Lap Robes and Breast Straps for those who will call,
We have Oils, Hames and Whips enough for you all.
If you will but come and examine our pile,
You will not complain of the price or the style.

If your horses are skittish, and inclined to do wrong.
We've lines that will hold them, and the Bridles are strong.
If this were not so, you might loose your own life,
Or the life of your children, or excellent wife.

And then if your horses are subject to fret,
To keep of the flies we've a splendid Fly Net.
And we've Blankets for horses to keep them quite warm,
If compelled to drive out in the bleak winter storm.

We'll not try to tell all we have, or have not;
We want you to come and see what we've got.
We pay cash for our goods and select them with care,
And will sell them as cheap as any one dare.

ESTILL & TRUDGIAN, PRINTERS.

Index

Note: Charleston and Kanawha County are not indexed.

Bold numbers indicate illustrations or photographs.

Acme—122
Adams, Verlin "Sparky"—360, **387**
African Zion Baptist Church—**46**, 47, 327
Alderson, George—17, 45, 338
Alderson, John Jr.—17
Alderson-Stephenson Building—204, **216**
Allegheny Mountains—8, 11, 108, 128, **188**, 355, 458
Alum Creek—353
American Airlines—**193**
American Gas & Electric Co.—404
American Legion—323, 356, **406**
American Red Cross—**70**, **269**, 352, 354, **411**
American Viscose Corp.—159
American Water Works Co.—401
Amherst Coal Co. (Industries)—423
Andrew Donnally—51
Andrews, Mayor Carl—**374**
Annfred—119, **120**
Ansted—95, **192**, 432
Appalachian Power Co.—125, 401, 404
Arbuckle, Matthew—8, 10
Arcade, The—**208**, **222**, **344**
Armor Park—433
Arthur, Gabriel—8
Asbury Chapel—87, 202, 304, **327**
Atlantic Greyhound Lines—**182**, **185**, **186**
Atkinson, Gov. George—318, **396**, **453**, 458, **459**
Augusta County, Va.—**9**, 11, 128

Bailey, John—16
Bailey, "Mad" Anne—**15**, **16**, 459
Baird Hardware—**212**
Baker, Abraham—14, 44
Baldwin-Felts Detective Agency—143
Baltimore & Ohio Railroad—108, 122, **215**, 228, 448
Bandholtz, Gen. H.H.—148
Bank of the West—**80**, 458
Bank of Virginia—17, 24, **26**, **84**, 87, 98, **101**, **219**
Banner Window Glass Co.—159, **160**, 432
Baptist Temple—**333**, 350
Barber, Capt. Timothy L.—**222**, **320**
Barber, Dr. T.L.—**222**, **320**
Barber Sanitorium—**320**
Barboursville—188, 312, 313
Barna, Herbert "Babe"—360
Barnes, Mary—436
Beckley—188, **191**, 382
Beeches, The—**356**
Bell Atlantic Co.—396
Belle—**154**, **156**, **159**, 323, 401, 427, **455**
Belle Alkali Co.—154, **156**, **157**, 427
Belle Prince—230
Beller's Saloon—**216**, **223**
Beni Kedem Temple—355
Big Chimney—311, 449
Big Coal River Line—122, 123
Big Sandy Creek—447
Big Sandy District High School—**309**, 447
Big Sandy River—1, 188
Big Tyler Road—431
Bijou, The—360
Bill's Creek—125
Black Jack Line—108, 122
Blacksburg, Va.—8
Blaine Island—**10**, 154, **155**, 433
Blair Mountain—148
Blizzard, William—148, **150**
Blossom Dairy—**295**, **453**
Blue Creek—**117**, **123**, 162, **167**, 203, **383**
Blue & Gray Bus Line—**182**, **185**
Bluefield—143, **191**
Bluestone River—274
B'nai Jacob Synagogue—**331**
Bonamont—**79**
Boone County—1, 8, 50, 69, 108, **117**, 123, 128, 130, **142**, 148, 378, 426, 438
Boone, Daniel—1, 11, 13, 414, 458
Botetourt County, Va.—11, **18**
Bowen, Absalom—431
Bowen Tavern—**91**, 431
Boyd School—308, **310**
Boy Scouts—**295**, **352**, **353**
Braddock's Expedition (Campaign)—13, 14, 16
Brawley, Harry—**410**
Brawley, John M.—**356**
Braxton County—1, 122, 352
Bream, Maj. James—17
Brick House, The—427, **455**
Brooks, Elisha—35, 42
Broun, Thomas—83, **85**
Brownstown—67, **360**, 426
Buchanan, Va.—53, 56
Buffalo—3, **83**, **96**, 355
Bullitt, Col. Thomas—8, **10**, 14
Bullitt, Cuthbert—**12**, 14
Bungalow Park—**435**

Burlew, Noyes—362
Burlew Opera House—**212**, **291**, 360, 362, 401
Burning Springs—**9**, 17, 35, 405, 426, 427
Burnwell—124, **140**, **175**
Buster's Tavern—24
Butts, Dr. Fleetwood—189

C & O Bridge—**78**
C & O Railroad—108, **110**, 117-119, 121-125, 128, 137, 180, 313, 324, **348**, 430
C & O Station—**55**, **73**, **76**, **92**, **101**, **109**, **110**, **117**, 176, **298**, **299**, **301**, 396, 434
Cabell County—1, 17, 56, 313, **352**, 436, 458
Cabell, Samuel I.—436
Cabin Creek—13, 50, 62, **78**, **111**, **112**, 122, 123, 125, 137, **138**, 143, **145**, **146**, **159**, 162, **164**, **166**, 180, 203, 204, 274, 280, **281**, **283**, 286, **301**, **307**, 404, **411**
Cabin Creek Junction—122, 123, **145**, 166
Cabin Creek Power Plant—**394**, **402**
Cabin Creek Railway—137
Caldwell & Surbaugh—188
Calhoun County—1
Campbells Creek—8, 13, 18, 24, 42, 44, 47, 50, **62**, 119, **120**, **126**, 134, **135**, **174**, **185**, **423**, 427
Campbells Creek Coal Co.—**126**, 134, **136**, 396
Campbells Creek Railroad—119, **120**, 423
Camp Piatt—427
Camp Tompkins—**89**
Camp Two-Mile—**88**
Camp Union—10
Camp White—**101**, **102**, **105**
Cane Fork—122, 123, 137, 280, **348**
Cannaday, Dr. John E.—**318**, 319
Cannelton—130, **132**, 313
Cannelton Coal & Coke Co.—**138**, 430
Capital Airlines—**193**, **198**
Capitol Annex—**233**, **286**, **287**, 312, 313, 345, 408
Capitol City Nursing Home—322
Capitol High School—307
Capitol Hill—117, **214**, **278**
Capitol Theater—**293**, 364
Capitol View Golf Course—**377**
Carbide & Carbon Chemical Corp.—**152**, 154, **155**, **353**, 432
Carbon—122, 137
Carbon Fuel Co.—**137**
Carbondale College—311
Carney's, Mrs. Boarding House—**429**
Carter General Store—**46**
Cedar Grove, House—42, **43**, 426, **455**
Cedar Grove, Town of—10, 14, 18, 44, 87, 121, **139**, 187, 304, 308, **335**, **424**, 425, 426, 427, **455**
Central Junior High School—308, **309**
Central Water Line—62
Chamberlain School—308
Chappell Hollow—327
Charleston & Gauley Railway—108, 117
Charleston Area Medical Center (CAMC)—319, 322
Charleston Ballet—380
Charleston Catholic High School—304, 307, **309**, **390**
Charleston Chamber of Commerce—**218**, **253**, 323, 432, 461
Charleston Charlies—382
Charleston City Hall—**339**, **340**
Charleston City Levee—**61**
Charleston Civic Center—**376**, 379, 380, 408
Charleston, Clendenin & Sutton Railroad—108, **118**, 122, **215**, 448
Charleston Daily Bulletin—**96**
Charleston Daily Mail—**85**, **147**, **204**, **292**
Charleston Female College—311
Charleston Fire Dept.—**342**
Charleston Gas & Electric Co.—403
Charleston Gas Light Co.—401, 403
Charleston Gazette—**76**, **190**, **292**, 338, **374**, 447
Charleston General Hospital—**316**, **318**, 319, 322-324, **371**
Charleston Herald—**208**
Charleston High School—**294**, 307, 308, **309**, 311, **342**, 362, 379, 386, **387**, **388**, **390**, **391**, **392**
Charleston Home Telephone Co.—396, **397**
Charleston Industrial Corp.—**168**, 445
Charleston Interurban Railroad Co.—180, **181**, **182**, **183**, **186**, **435**, **436**, **437**
Charleston Memorial Hospital—319, 322, 323, 324, **377**
Charleston National Bank—**201**, **221**, **222**, **254**, **259**, **287**
Charleston Natural Gas Co.—405
Charleston Police Dept.—**340**, **341**
Charleston Post Office—**344**, 379
Charleston-Ripley-Ravenswood Turnpike—188
Charleston Rockets—387
Charleston Senators—382, **385**, **386**
Charleston Symphony Orchestra—**380**
Charleston Town Center Mall—408, **411**
Charleston Transit Co.—**182**, **184**, **186**
Charleston, University of—95, 313, 315, **386**
Charleston Veterinary Hospital—326

Chelyan—**66**, **79**, 308
Chesapeake—**229**, 230
Chesapeake & Potomac Telephone Co.—**295**, 396, **399**
Chief Cornstalk—**9**, 10
Chilton—378, 447
Chilton House, The—**454**
Chilton, Samuel—**454**
Chilton, Sen. William E.—180, **181**, 311, **454**
Chilton, William—447, **454**
Cincinnati, Ohio—8, **36**, 51, 52, **72**, 108, **114**, 128, **250**, 318
Cinco—119, **135**, **136**
Citizens National Bank—**218**
Civilian Conservation Corps (CCC)—286, **301**, 378
Civil War—24, **36**, 37, 82, 83, 98, 118, 128, 130, **133**, 134, 142, 159, **174**, 188, 202, 228, 274, 305, 311, 313, 327, 328, **330**, **333**, **335**, 405, **423**, 427, 429, 430, 438, 445, 447, 449, **450**, **452**, 457, 458
Clark, Glenn—**61**, **192**, 408
Clarksburg—229, **298**
Clay County—1, 122, **123**, **350**, 352
Clendenin, Alexander—11
Clendenin, Charles—14, **15**
Clendenin, George—**6**, 11, 14, **16**, 24, 42, **340**
Clendenin's Fort—11, 14
Clendenin High School—447
Clendenin, Town of—122, 130, **132**, **152**, 154, **155**, 162, **166**, **167**, **174**, 204, **282**, 307, **309**, 353, 355, **369**, 405, 447, 448, **449**, 457
Clendenin, William—11, 14, 338
Clifton—119, 428, 429, **447**
Clifton Forge, Va.—**106**
Coal & Coke Railroad—108, 122, **165**, 352, 448
Coalburg—**142**
Coal River—8, 10, **11**, 24, **34**, 50, 54, 69, **70**, 87, 108, **110**, **111**, **117**, 125, 128, 130, **133**, **174**, 188, 274, 280, 304, **352**, **353**, 360, **372**, 438, **444**, **454**
Coal River & St. Albans Railroad—125
Coal River & Western Railroad—125
Coal River Locks—69
Coal River Navigation Co.—69, **83**
Coalsmouth—24, 87, **89**, **99**, 188, 327, **335**, 438
Coalsmouth High School—311, **312**
Cobb Compressor Station—**405**, 448
Cobb(s), Fleming—**10**, 432
Colonial Dames of West Virginia—**15**, **42**, 86
Columbia Barbed Wire & Nail Works—414
Columbia Gas Transmission Corp.—405
Conley, Gov. William G.—**238**, **240**
Conrail—108, **118**, 279
Constitutional Convention of 1872—**330**
Cook, Roy Bird—16, 458, **459**
Coolidge, Pres. Calvin—**298**
Coonskin Park—**374**, 408
Cooper, Rabbi Samuel—**331**
Copenhaver, Mayor John T.—**376**, 408, **410**
Cornwell, Gov. John J.—**147**, 148, 433
Cotton Block—**216**
Cotton, John T.—**208**, 360
Cotton Opera House—202, **208**, **213**, **216**, 360, 362
Couch, George S.—**221**, 436
Coyle & Richardson Dept. Store—**221**, **286**
Cox, A.W.—313
Cox, Gen. Jacob—**86**, **89**, 90, **94**
Cox's Hill—98
Cox's Lane—87, **102**, 202, **252**
Craik, James—86
Craik-Patton House—**86**, **452**
Criel Mound—2, 3, **4**, **454**
Cross Lanes—8, **10**, 345, 431
Crown Hill—327, 428
Cultural Center—**411**
Czolgosz, Leon—420

Dana—119, **126**, 396, **423**
Dana Brothers—134
Daniel Boone Hotel—230, **237**, **289**
Daniel Boone Roadside Park—**13**, **42**, 86, **452**
Daughters of the American Revolution (DAR)—**13**, **15**, 338
Davenport, Col. E.R.—**400**, 401
Davis & Elkins College—386
Davis Child Shelter—202, **351**
Davis Creek—**10**, 119, **294**, 378, 432
Davis, Henry Gassaway—108, 122, **202**, **348**, **351**
Davis, John W.—**298**, 314, **410**, 436
Dawes—122, 137, **164**
Dawson, Mayor D. Boone—**301**
Deepwater—108
deGruyter, Julius—**453**
Diamond—427
Diamond Alkali Co.—154
Diamond Dept. Store—**38**, **238**, **384**
Diamond Ice Factory—202
Diamond Shamrock Co.—154, 427
Dickinson—117, **292**, 427

-462-

Dickinson & Shrewsbury Co.—18, 35, 39, **40**, 45
Dickinson, C.C.—39, 352
Dickinson, Col. John—18, 42, 44, 427
Dickinson, John L.—**219, 455**
Dickinson, John Q.—18, 38, 39, 427
Dickinson, John Q. & Co.—159, 405
Dickinson, Joseph—18
Dickinson Salt Works—39, **40, 41,** 45
Dickinson, William—18
Donnally, Andrew Jr.—18
Donnally, Andrew Sr.—11, 14, **18,** 24, 35, 51
Donnally's Fort—**18**
Draper, Betty—8
Drapers Meadows—8
Dry Branch—137, **411**
Dunbar Fairgrounds—**326, 375**
Dunbar Flint Glass Co.—159, **175**
Dunbar, Town of—2, **3, 4,** 90, 159, **175, 177,** 180, 203, 307, 345, 346, 436, **437, 450**
Dunkirk Glass Co.—159, **175,** 432
Dupont City—**427**
Dupont High School—**173, 307,** 427
Dupont, Maj. Henry—427
Dutch Hollow Road—**450**
Dutch Hollow Wine Cellars—**450**

East Bank—307, **455**
East Bank High School—**392**
Ebenezer's Chapel—**335**
Edgewood Country Club—360, **373, 377**
Edgewood Park—360, **373**
Edwards, William Henry—**142,** 405
E.I. Dupont de Nemours Co.—154, **156, 157,** 427
8th Virginia Volunteer Infantry—**99**
Elk City—**14,** 202, 203
Elkins—108, 122, **348**
Elk Refinery Co.—**166, 457**
Elk River—8, 10, 11, 14, 17, 18, 24, 50, **54, 57, 60, 62, 73**-**75,** 90, 95, 98, 108, **116, 118,** 122, **123, 152,** 162, **166, 175,** 180, 187, 189, **190,** 202, 204, **208, 215, 261,** 274, **282, 299,** 352, **353,** 360, **372,** 396, 400, 401, 408, **411,** 426, 427, 447, 448, 449
Elks Club—**296**
Elk Two-Mile—17, 24, 174
Elk Valley—**345,** 449
Elkview—307
Elkview Bridge—**74, 190**
Elkview School—**311**
Ellet, Charles Jr.—53, 54
Elm Grove—86
Empire Federal Savings & Loan—**276, 291**
Eoff, Dr. John—24
Eskdale—122, **137,** 288
Exhibition Park—**383**

Fallen Timbers, Battle of—11
Falling Rock Creek—130, **132,** 447
Farley, Francis "Skeet"—360, **388**
Fayette County—1, 50, 108, **142,** 148, 188, **313,** 315, 352
Fayetteville—95, 188
Ferguson, G.E. "Cap"—**296, 297**
Ferguson Hotel—**296**
Ferry Branch—25, 29, **100,** 101, **102, 105**
Field's Creek—108, 118
Fitzhugh, Nicholas—42, **85**
Fleetwood Hotel—**294, 369**
Fletcher Enamel Co.—**175, 437**
Flinn, Chloe—13
Floyd, John—10
FMC Corp.—154, 159, **160**
Fort Clendenin—11, 14, 15
Fort Duquesne—13, 14
Fort Hill—**100, 102, 105**
Fort Lee—**6,** 10, 11, 14, 15, 16, 17, 42, 327, 425, 432, 447, **455,** 459
Fort Morris—**335**
Fort Randolph—**9,** 10
Fort Scammon—**100, 102, 105**
Frankenberger, Philip & Moses—**331, 367,** 402-404
Frankenberger's—**218, 258,** 367
Freemasons—355
French & Indian War—8, 431
Frogs Creek Logging Railroad—**119**
Fruth School—**302**
Fry, Col. Joshua—**10,** 431
Fry, James H.—18
Fry Military Grant—8, **10**

Gallagher—124, 308
Gallipolis Ferry, W.Va.—**14**
Gallipolis, Ohio—16, 45, 52, **58, 80,** 386
Garnet School—**296,** 304, 307, **310, 387, 388**
Gauley Bridge, Town of—**87,** 90, **94,** 95, 108, 117, 188, 430
Gauley River—13, 50, 90, 188, 274
Georges Creek—44, 423
Gibbons, Mabel Frances—308
Gilbert, Cass—238, **240, 245, 248**
Giles—122, 137
Giles-Fayette-Kanawha Turnpike—188, 430
Gilmer County—1
Girl Scouts—**352**
Glasgow—345, **404,** 425, **426**

Glasscock, Gov. W.E.—**142,** 143
Glen Ferris—**50,** 57
Glenn, Albert "Big Sleepy"—360, **388, 390**
Glenwood—17, 452
Goodyear Tire & Rubber Co.—159
Gorman, Rocco J.-360, **387, 390, 391**
Goshorn, George—18, 24
Goshorn, Jacob—**26,** 90, **453**
Goshorn, John H.—18
Governor's Mansion—**226, 232,** 239, **249**
Grant, Gen. Ulysses S.—426
Gravely Motor Plow & Cultivator Co.—**177**
Great Central American Waterway—56
Greenbrier County—1, **9,** 11, 14, **16, 18,** 57, 87, **92,** 148, 352
Greenbrier River—8, 52, 57
Guthrie, Morris & Campbell & Co.—**212**
Guyandotte—56, 188

Hale, Dr. John P.—2, 8, 15, 35, **37,** 38, 66, 202, **205,** 257, **453, 458, 459**
Hale House—108, 202, 203, **205, 288,** 458
Hampton Institute—47
Handley—**106, 111, 112, 116,** 124, 125, 204, **348, 384, 456**
Hansford—124, 324, 428-430
Hansford, Alva—51, 124, 324
Hansford, Felix—428, **429**
Hansford, John—425, 428
Harding, Pres. Warren G.—148, **261**
Harmony Hill—**429**
Harriman, John—**455, 456**
Harriman, Shadrack—11, 425, **455**
Harrison, Gov. Benjamin—10, 56
Harvey, Morris—18, 313
Hatfield Campbells Creek Coal Co.—**136, 423**
Hatfield, Dr. Henry D.—146
Hatfield, Reed—**423**
Hayes, Rutherford B.—**105**
Henning & McFarland General Mercantile—24
Herbert J. Thomas Memorial Hospital—318, **324**
Hernshaw—119, 286, 426
Hill, Arthur—180, 186
Hillcrest Sanatorium—**306**
Hippodrome, The—360, 364, **369**
Hodges, Charles—461
Holly Grove—42, **43,** 427
Holt, Gov. Homer—301
Hoover, Pres. Herbert—**298**
Hope Natural Gas Co.—**166**
Huddleston, Paddy—13
Huffman, Dick—360, 387
Hughes Creek—50
Hugheston—8, **114**
Humphrey, Hubert—**411**
Hundley, Rod—360, **392**
Huntington—62, 108, **114,** 124, 125, 128, **172, 174,** 203, 313, 382
Huntington-Charleston Motor Bus Co.—**186**
Huntington, Collis P.—121, 356, 438

Imperial Colliery Co.—**140**
Imperial Ice Cream Co.—**409**
Indians—2, 3, 8, **9,** 10, 11, 13-15, 17, 24, 50, 187, **375,** 425, 438, 458
Inglca, Mary—8, 458
Institute—154, **158, 192, 193,** 312, 314, 352, 436

Jackson County—1
Jackson, Stonewall—459
James, C.H. & Son—**297**
James River—51, 52, 56, 57
James River & Kanawha Canal—53, 56, 57, 189
James River & Kanawha Turnpike—24, 37, **39, 43,** 45, 52, 53, 87, **92,** 95, **102,** 187, 188, 344, 425, 430, 432, 438, **441**
James River Co.—51, 56, 187
James T. Teays Tavern—**441**
Jefferson County—148, 344
Jefferson, Thomas—**12,** 35
Jefferson, Town of—438
Jeffries, Thomas—15, 98
Job Corps Center—**289**
Jones, John—8, 425, 428, **429**
Jones, Mother—143, 146, **147,** 148, 429
Joseph Popp Hardware—**54**
Julie Moffitt—**51,** 90

Kanawha Airport—**196,** 198, 199, **374**
Kanawha & Coal River Railroad—119
Kanawha & Michigan Railroad—**57, 74,** 108, **116, 117,** 118, 119, 121, **123,** 203, **212, 214, 215,** 274, **278, 279,** 301, **370, 425,** 427, 430, 436, 439, **445**
Kanawha & Ohio Railway—117
Kanawha & Paint Creek Railroad—124
Kanawha & Pocahontas Railroad—124
Kanawha & West Virginia Railroad—**123**
Kanawha Banking & Trust Co.—**221, 253**
Kanawha Board—54, 62
Kanawha Boat Club—**57**
Kanawha Brewing Co.—172, **212, 215**
Kanawha City—13, **18, 57, 78, 149,** 159, **160, 192,** 202, **208, 246, 267, 276, 300,** 360, 379, 382, **383, 415, 417, 418, 420-422**

Kanawha City Bridge—**78,** 180, 204, **261, 294,** 360, **383,** 414, **416, 417**
Kanawha City Land Co.—313, 414, **418,** 432
Kanawha Country Club—**10, 377**
Kanawha County Board of Education—**307, 309,** 345
Kanawha County Court—18, 187, 426, 433, 458
Kanawha County Courthouse—24, 338, **339, 342**
Kanawha County Parks & Recreation Commission—**375**
Kanawha County Public Library—230, **233, 252, 257, 276,** 304, **344,** 345
Kanawha Electric Light Co.—403
Kanawha Falls—13, 18, 52, 62, 188
Kanawha Hotel—98, **204, 289, 344,** 356, **382**
Kanawha House—**26,** 87
Kanawha Junior College—312, 313
Kanawha Mall—**160**
Kanawha Manufacturing Co.—172
Kanawha Military Institute—305
Kanawha National Bank—**216, 218, 253**
Kanawha Natural Gas, Light & Fuel Co.—405
Kanawha Park—382, **383, 385,** 414, **416**
Kanawha Presbyterian Church—318, **327, 329, 330,** 352
Kanawha Railway—122
Kanawha Riflemen—18, **43,** 83-85, 96
Kanawha River—1, 3, 8, **9,** 10, 11, 14, **18,** 24-26, 29, **34,** 35, 37, **48,** 50-53, **54,** 56, 57, **59, 60, 62,** 63, **64, 65,** 69, **70, 73, 74,** 87, 90, **101,** 108, 118, 119, 121, 124, 125, 128, 130, **133,** 143, 154, 159, 162, **167, 168, 175,** 176, 180, 187, 188, **192, 195, 198,** 202, 230, 238, **239, 262, 263,** 274, **278, 280, 282, 283, 300,** 360, **377,** 400, 408, 414, **418, 423, 425, 426, 427,** 428, 430, 432, 436, 438, 439, **443, 445,** 458
Kanawha River Slackwater Project—62
Kanawha Salines—24, 25, **32, 34, 35,** 37, 42, 44, 45, 51, 52, **56,** 95, 202, **327,** 355, 426, **428**
Kanawha Salt Co.—18, 37, 38, 458
Kanawha School—**307**
Kanawha State Forest—119, 286, 378
Kanawha Two-Mile—50, 87, 431
Kanawha Valley Bank—18, **216, 219, 220, 252, 259,** 396, 403
Kanawha Valley Hospital—86, **222, 320**
Kanawha Valley Improvements Assoc.—62
Kanawha Valley Regional Transportation Authority—180, **184**
Kanawha Valley River Salt & Chemical Co.—**159**
Kanawha Valley Star (*Star of the Kanawha Valley*)—**69, 83,** 96
Kanawha Valley Traction Co.—**74, 178, 181**
Kanawha Water & Light Co.—**401,** 403
Kanawha Woolen Mills—172
Kayford—122, 128, 137
Kay Jewelry Co.—**213, 291**
Kearse Theater—**267,** 364, **365**
Keeney, Frank—148, **150**
Kelly Axe Factory—**79,** 172, **175,** 202
Kelly, W.C.—**175,** 202
Kelly, Walter—8, 425
Kelly's Creek—8, 18, 50, 121, **139,** 162, 187, **328, 424,** 425
Kelly's Creek & Northwestern Railway—121, **122, 139, 457**
Kelly's Creek Railroad—121
Kenna Homes—**433**
Kenna, John E.—**202, 453**
Kennedy, Pres. John F.—**289, 411**
Kenton, Simon—8
Kentucky—8, 13, 82, 187, 405, 425
Keystone Bridge—**74,** 202, **208**
King, Eddie—360, 386, **393**
King, George—360, 386, **393**
Kingston—124
Kinsey, M.N.F.—**353**
Kump, Gov. Guy—**194**

Laidley Drug Store—**80**
Laidley Field—**298, 304,** 383, 386, 387, **388, 389**
Laidley, George S.—17, 304, 307, 345, 353, **389**
Laidley, James G.—17
Laidley, James M.—17, **452**
Laidley, John O.—17
Laidley, Richard Q.—**85**
Laidley, William S.—17, 42, 338, 400, **453,** 458
Laird, Dr. William—430
Laird Memorial Hospital—430
Lake Chaweva—431
Layote Inc.—**156**
Lee, Gen. Robert E.—14, 95
Lee, Richard Henry—14
Lee Street Triangle—**15, 228, 266,** 354, 356, **409**
Leewood—**111,** 122, **123,** 137, **151, 306,** 307, 308
Len's Creek—8, 10, 18, 148, 426
Levi, Mordecai—15, 202, **257**
Levine, Charlie—382
Lewis, Andrew—**9, 10,** 14, 35, 427
Lewis, Bettie Washington—17
Lewisburg—10, 14, 16, **18,** 87, 187, 188, 344, 355
Lewis, C.C.—**15,** 121, **221**
Lewis County—95, 459
Lewis, Hubbard & Co.—**15, 212**
Lewis, John L.—151
Lewis, Pryce—**89**
Lewis, Samuel—436
Lewis, Thomas—11
Lewis, Virgil A.—**232, 459**

Lexington, Va.—42
Libby, Owens, Ford Glass Co.—**62**, 159, **160**, **161**, 175
Lick Branch—**351, 372**
Lightburn, Gen. Joseph A.J.—95, **101**
Lincoln County—1, 188, **198**, **350**, **352**, 457
Lincoln Junior High School—308, **311**, **452**
Linde Air Products Co.—**152**, 159
Littlepage, Adam—**88**
Littlepage Farm & House—87, **88**
Littlepage, Rebecca—**88**
Littlepage Terrace—286
Lock No. 2—**64**, 69
Lock No. 3—**55**, 69
Lock No. 4—62, **66**
Lock No. 5—62, **65**, **68**
Lock No. 6—**64**, **65**, 396, **454**
Lock No. 7—**64**, **65**, **67**, 445, **446**
Lock No. 8—**67**
Lock No. 11—62, **67**
Logan—188, 355, 382
Logan County—1, 148, **150**, **352**, **392**, 426
London—64
London Lock & Dam—**68**
Lord Dunmore's War—10
Loring, Gen. W.W.—95, **99**
Lovell, Joseph—17
Lowenstein & Sons—**73**, **212**, **253**, **254**
Lower Falls, Coal River—69, 174, **453**
Luna Park—204, **358**, 360, **373**, **374**
Lyric, The—360, **363**

MacCorkle, Gov. William—**78**, **177**, 180, **208**, **214**, **232**, **241**, 357, **398**, 432, 457
Madden—69
Malden—18, **32**, 35, **36**, 37-39, 44, 45, **46**, 47, **58**, 87, 159, 172, **173**, **274**, 304, 305, 307, 327, 427
Malden High School—**307**
Mammoth—121
Marmet—8, 10, 18, 62, 64, **68**, 95, **110**, **119**, 148, 172, **266**, 323, **335**, **360**, 426, 427
Marmet Hospital—323
Marmet Lock & Dam—**68**
Marshall Academy (University)—313, 386
Marshall Hansford House—**456**
Marshall, John—51, 52
Martens, Walter F.—239, **249**, 356
Mason College of Music & Fine Arts—312, 313
Mason County—1, 14, 50, 62, 82, 459
Masonic Temple—**201**, **327**, 355
McCausland, John—**82**
McClellan, Gen. George—**70**, 87, 90, **94**
McDowell County—**352**
McFarland, Henry—**84**
McFarland House—17, **452**
McFarland, James C.—17, 24
McKinley, Pres. William C.—**105**, 414, 420
McLaughlin, J. Kemp—199
McMillan Hospital—319, **322**, **323**
McMillan, William A., Dr.—319, 322
Meadowbrook Country Club—307
Mercer Academy—24, 42, 87, 98, 311, **327**, 458
Mercer County—**352**
Mercer School—307, **308**, **309**, 311
Methodist Church—311, **313**, **330**, **331**, **343**, 447
Miami—122, 137
Michaelson, Otto H.—402-404
Midland Trail—**425**
Midland Trail Transit Co.—180, **186**
Mill Creek—**167**
Miller, Arnold—151
Mingo County—148, 352
Mink Shoals—401
Mississippi River—8, 37, 52, **72**, 124
Mitchell, Gen. Billy—148, **149**, 414
Modareli, Antonio—**380**
Mohler Lumber Co.—**445**
Mohlerville—**444**, 445
Mohler, William E.—**454**
Monroe County—**352**
Monsanto Chemical Co.—159
Montgomery—1, 11, 18, **55**, **64**, **117**, 124, **174**, 180, 188, **266**, 312, 315, 430, **456**
Montgomery General Hospital—430
Montgomery Preparatory School—312, 315, 386, 430
Moore & Brother—**80**
Moore, E.T.—**80**, **96**
Moore, Samuel—427
Moore, S. Spencer & Co.—**96**, **213**, **252**
Moran, Sonny—**393**
Morgan, Gov. Ephraim—148, 239
Morgantown—**58**, 461
Morris, Benjamin—18, 430
Morris, Billy—35
Morris, Dickinson—428, **429**
Morris Harvey College—230, **233**, 312, 313, **314**, 319, 386, 387, **393**, **408**
Morris, John—14, 18
Morris, Leonard—8, 18, 426
Morris, Levi—18, 430, **456**
Morrison Building—**264**, 311, **329**, 362
Morrison, O.J. Dept. Store—**213**, **291**, 362
Morris Settlement—187

Morris, William Jr.—18
Morris, William Sr.—14, 18, **313**, 327, 425, 426, 428, 430
Morris, William III—18
Mountain Boy—228, **229**
Mountain Mission—327
Mountain State Hospital—322
Mount Carbon—430
Mount Hope—188
Mt. Ovis Academy—42, 305
Mucklow—143, **145**
Municipal Auditorium—**376**

National Bank of Commerce—**221**, **234**, 387
National Lead Co.—159
Naval Ordnance Plant—**169**, 286, **301**, **435**, **454**
Neely, Sen. Matthew M.—**301**
Nelson, Oscar—154
New River—1, 8, 50, 52, 57, 404, 428
New River State School (College)—315
Newspapers—
    The Kanawha Patriot—24
    The Kanawha Spectator—24
    St. Albans Newspapers—**442**
    The Western Courier—24
    The Western Register—24
    Western Virginian—25, 27
New York—124, **142**, 154
New York Central Railroad—108, 118, 121, **437**
Nicholas County—1, **149**, 352
Nitro—8, **9**, **10**, **64**, 159, **168**, **172**, 180, 202, 286, 396, 401, 445, 446
Nitro Explosives Plant—**58**, **168**, **170**, **171**, **172**, **454**
Nitro Pencil Co.—**171**
Nitro Pulp Mills—159

Oak Hill—188, **390**
Ohio—3, 8, 11, 14, **37**, **70**, **89**, **94**, **114**, 125, **352**, 405, 430
Ohio Apex Co.—159
Ohio Central Railroad—**74**
Ohio River—1, 8, **9**, **10**, 24, 37, 50, 51, 52, 53, 56, 57, **59**, 62, **72**, 87, **92**, 95, 121, 124, 128, 187, 188, 230, 355, 425, 438
Ohley—122, 137
Old Riggs Place—430, **456**
Old State Road—14, 24, 438
Open Door Mission—327
Orchard Manor—**88**
Ordinance of Secession—18
Ordinance Park—**306**, 383
Owens Bottle Co. (Owens-Illinois)—159, **160**, **161**
Owens, Michael—**159**

Paint Creek—3, 8, 50, 108, **117**, 124, 125, 130, 137, **140**, **142**, 143, **144-147**, **150**, 203, 274, 280, **282**, 356, 428, 429
Paint Creek Coal & Iron Mining Manufacturing Co.—124
Palmer's Shoe Store—**290**
Parkersburg—52, 188, **191**, 382, 402
Parsons, Russ—360, **390**
Pasteboard Capitol—230, **237**, **238**
Patrick, Dr. Spicer—18, 82, **327**, 458
Patrick, George H.—35
Patrick Street Bridge—**78**, **79**, **110**, 172, **301**
Patteson, Gov. Okey—**374**
Patton, George S.—**83**, **84**, 85-87, **89**, 90, **328**
Pearisburg, Va.—95
Peck, Paul—**192**, 432
Pennsylvania—8, 125, 128, 130, **181**, **352**, 449
Pennsylvania Central Airlines—**193**, **198**
Petry, Bill—148, **149**, **150**
Peytona—69, 128
Peyton, William M.—69
Philippi, Battle of—90
Pinch—162, **164**
Pioneer Coal Co.—134
Pittsburgh—10, 13, 52, **58**, 62, **250**
Plaza Theater—364
Poca—8, **9**, **10**, 90, **290**
Pocahontas, Coal River & Kanawha Railroad—125
Pocahontas County—1, 50, 352
Pocatilico River—50, **432**
Point Pleasant, Battle of—**9**, 10, 16, 18, 428, 430
Point Pleasant Road—**88**, 431
Point Pleasant, Town of—8, **9**, 10, 13, 14, 16, **18**, 45, 50, **56**, 62, **102**, 117, 432
Pontiac's Uprising—14
Port Amherst—**126**, **423**
Powell, Watt—360, **382**, **385**
Pratt—8, **59**, 62, 124, **143**, **144**, **147**, 308, **325**, 428, 429, **456**
Pratt, Charles—124, 428
Presbyterian Church—42, 44, **46**, 87, 311, 329, **345**
Princeton—**191**
Public Works Administration (PWA)—64
Pure Oil Co.—**159**, **166**, **456**
Putnam County—1, 3, **30**, 50, 51, 64, 90, **91**, 96, **100**, **119**, 203, 352, 396, 401, 445
Putney—119, **135**, **136**

Quarrier, Alexander—18
Quarrier, Harriet—17
Quarrier, Lucy—**452**
Quarrier, William—18, **85**

Quincy Coal Co.—427
Quincy Mall—**455**

Radio Stations
    WCHS—**294**, 410
    WGKV—**294**
    WOBU—**294**
Raleigh County—1, **142**, **313**, 324, 352, 404, 426
Randolph County—1, 122
Ravenswood—**60**, **454**
Red House—**100**
Red House Shoals—51, 52
Red Warrior—122
Reed—119, **423**
Reid, Mary E.—319
Reorganized Government of Virginia—42
Republic—137
Revolutionary War—10, 18, 56, 187, 425, 428
Reynolds, Col. John—18
Reynolds, Robert F.—**427**, **455**
Richard E. Putney House—**46**
Richmond, Va.—10, 11, 13, 14, 17, 18, 51, 53, 54, 56, 82, 83, **89**, **108**, 124, **185**, 338
Rich Mountain, Battle of—90
Riggleman, Leonard—313, **314**
Ripley-Ravenswood Road—**88**
Roane County—1, 405, 447
Robert Thompson—51
Rockefeller, Gov. John D., IV—239
Rock Lake Pool—**372**, **432**
Rodeheaver, Homer—**333**
Rogers Drugstore—24, **54**
Rogers, Henry—24
Rollins Chemical Co.—154, 432
Ronda—122
Roosevelt, Eleanor—**301**, **410**
Roosevelt Junior High School—308
Roosevelt, Pres. Franklin D.—286, **298**, 301
Rosecrans, William S.—69, **70**, **83**
Rosedale—42
Roseler & Haslacher Chemical Co.—**439**, **441**
Rubber Service Laboratories—159
Ruffner, Augustus—**43**
Ruffner Brothers Wholesale Grocery—**275**
Ruffner, Daniel—**43**, **56**
Ruffner, David—15, 35, 42, 45, **46**, 172, 311, **327**
Ruffner, Gen. Lewis—15, 35, 42, 45, 47, 304
Ruffner, Henry—42, **43**, 45, **46**, 305, 311, 327
Ruffner Hotel—11, 189, **200**, 203, **205**, **216**, **269**, **275**, **276**, **287-289**, 396, **398**
Ruffner, Joel—42
Ruffner, John—**83**, **96**
Ruffner, Joseph—14, 15, 24, 35, 42, **43**, 44, **340**, 427
Ruffner, Joseph Jr.—35, 42

Sacred Heart Catholic Church—**109**, **214**, **279**, **334**, 353
Sacred Heart School—304, **307**
St. Albans—3, 10, **11**, 14, 17, 50, 69, **79**, 87, **89**, **91**, **99**, 108, **110**, **111**, **117**, 125, 172, 180, **182**, **184**, 204, 304, 307, 311, **312**, **334**, **335**, **342**, 345, 353, 355, 386, 438, **439**, **440**, 442, **443**, **444**, 445, **454**
St. Albans & Boone Railroad—125
St. Albans & Coal River Railroad—125
St. Albans High School—**388**, **391**
St. Albert Hotel—**54**, **200**, **223**, **259**, **340**
St. Francis Hospital—**321**
St. John's Episcopal Church—86, 87, **214**, **328**
St. Mark's Episcopal Church—327, **335**
Salley, John Peter—8, 69, 128
Salvation Army—**351**
Sattes—**79**, **174**, **439** **443**
Sattes, Frederick Antonio—439, 445
Sattes, John Karl—174
Savage, Capt. Thomas—**10**
Scammon, Col. Eliakim P.—**100**, **105**
Scary Creek—125
Scary Creek, Battle of—**26**, **89**, 90, **91**, 438, 458
Scott, Addison—62, **64**
Scott Brothers Drug Store—213, **217**, **223**, **291**, 370, 403
Second Wheeling Convention—42
Security Building—**218**, **253**
Selim—8
Seng Creek Tunnel—**117**, 122, 123
Sharon—122, 137, **141**
Sharples Solvents Corp.—**156**, **157**
Shawnee Recreation Complex—360, **375**
Sheltering Arms Hospital—324, **325**, 429, 430
Shelton College—311, **312**
Shenandoah Valley—8, 42, 87
Shores, Henry "Hoppy"—360, **389**
Shrewsbury & Dickinson—24
Shrewsbury-Dickinson House—**455**
Shrewsbury, Joel—18, 39, 427, **455**
Shrewsbury, John—18, 427
Shrewsbury, Samuel Jr.—18
Shrewsbury, Samuel Sr.—**427**, **455**
Sissionville—345, **432**
Sissionville High School—387
Slack, John—457
Slaughter, Reuben—11, 14, **16**, 426
Slaughter's Creek—8, 426
Smith, Col. Benjamin H.—**2**, **30**

Smithers Creek—50, 117
Smith Mound—2
Snow Hill—35, 458
South Charleston—2, 3, **64**, **65**, **78**, **79**, 108, 154, **155**, 159, **160**, **168**, **169**, 180, **192**, 202, 204, 286, **301**, **306**, 383, **403**, 408; **412**, 432, 433, **434**, **435**, 448, **454**
Southern Bell Co.—396
Southern Historical Magazine—459
South Hills—180, **208**, **266**, **301**
Southmoor Country Club—360
South Side Bridge—**76-78**, 108, **109**, **198**, **212**, **268-270**, **275**, **276**, 286, **299**, **301**
South Side Foundry—172
Spring Hill—**4**, **175**, **372**, 432, **436**
Spring Hill Cemetery—**43**, 90, **91**, 98, **453**, 458
Sproul, Senator—125, **181**
Stalnaker, Dr. T.B.—24
Standard Brick & Supply Co.—**175**
Stark, Mahre—**390**, **391**
Starks, Samuel—**452**, **453**
Statehouse Company—**30**, 228
State Supreme Court—229
Staunton, F.M.—180, 202
Stenger, Father Joseph W.—318, 327, **334**
Stevenson, Gov. William—228
Stockton, Aaron—18, 130, 426
Stone Mansion—**427**, **455**
Stonewall Jackson High School—307, 387, **389**, **390**, 393
Strand, The—**363**, 364
Streets—
  Alderson—**182**, 396, 401, 403
  Beauregard—**370**
  Bradford—**102**, 180, **297**, **382**
  Brawley Walkway—**293**, **369**
  Bridge Road—**55**, **265**
  Broad—98, **118**, **279**, **280**, **296**, **307**, **309**, **328**, **329**, **334**, 370, **372**
  Brooks—**11**, 24, 98, 180, **259**, 307, 318, 319, **370**, **371**
  Bullitt—**212**, **215**
  California Ave.—**240**
  Capitol—**26**, **61**, **70**, 87, 90, 98, **102**, 108, **116**, 180, 202, **204**, **212**, **213**, **216**-**219**, **221**-**223**, 228, **231**, **232**, 239, **250**, **252**-**259**, **261**, **264**, 274, **277**, **280**, **290**, **293**, **294**, **295**, **300**, **314**, **331**, **333**, **344**, **346**, **348**, 355, 360, 362, **363**, 364, **368-370**, 401, 403, 408
  Central Ave.—180, **374**, 382
  Charleston—**212**, **265**
  Clendenin—**332**
  Court—24, **261**, **295**, **331**, 338, **339**, **340**, 342
  Crescent Road—180
  Delaware Ave.—**195**, **261**, **311**
  Dickinson—**78**, **265**, 274, **276**, **310**, **330**, **333**, **343**, **344**, **349**, **370**, **379**
  Dryden—180
  Duffy—180, **185**, **226**, **247**, **354**
  Dunbar—**16**, 86, **264**, 405, 436, **437**
  Edgewood Dr.—180
  Elizabeth—**307**, **331**, 356, 382
  Elmwood Ave.—318, 319
  Fife—**217**, **254**, **280**, **293**
  Front—**14**, 17, 24, 37, **80**, 318
  Glenwood Ave.—**374**
  Goshorn—29, **401**
  Grant—**374**
  Greenbrier—**267**
  Hale—24, 87, **205**, **216**, 274, **275**, **288**, **295**, **311**, 313, **330**, **344**, **350**, **397**, **398**
  Hillcrest Dr.—**306**, 348
  Jacob—**297**, 310
  Kanawha—**15**, 25, **26**, **42**, **43**, 98, 180, **186**, **204** **205**, **213**, **216**, **219**, **221**, **222**, **223**, 239, **250**, **252**, **257-259**, **269**, 274, **275**, **288**, **290**, **297**, **300**, **331**, **338**, **339**, **342**, **345**, **354**, **367**, 382, **396**, **398**, 403
  Kanawha—13, **300**, **414**, **420**
  Kanawha Blvd.—**11**, **15**, 17, 37, 42, **43**, **80**, 87, **187**, **195**, **204**, **216**, **261**, **270**, 274, **285**, 286, **300**, **301**, 318, **329**, **331**, **340**, 344, 356, 408, 414, **452**
  Laidley—**259**, **278**, 408
  Lee—86, 90, 98, **221**, **261**, **278**, **286**, **302**, **311**, **322**, **333**, **345**, **363**, **369**, 370, **396**, **399**, **409**, **411**
  Lovell—**62**, **75**, 98, **102**, **332**, **351**
  MacCorkle Ave.—**109**, **110**, **149**, **161**, **267**, **379**, **396**, **414**, **415**, **417**, 433, **435**, **457**
  Main—14
  McFarland—**201**, **293**, 318, **328**, **345**, **350**, 355, 459
  Michigan—203
  Morris—**101**, **102**, **261**, **294**, 307, 308, **322**, **330**, **333**, **371**
  Park Ave.—**297**, **374**
  Park Dr.—**374**
  Patrick—**175**, 180, **261**, **265**
  Pennsylvania Ave.—**320**, 414
  Piedmont Road—98, 117, **294**, 318, **369**, **423**
  Quarrier—**78**, 87, 180, **201**, **213**, **218**, **221**, **223**, **247**, **252**, **257**, **264**, 274, **277**, **293**, **307**, **308**, **309**, **311**, **312**, **328**, **330**, **333**, **345**, **350**, 382, 355, 405, **453**, 459
  Roane—**295**
  Roxalana Hollow Road—436
  Ruffner Ave.—180, **370**
  Shrewsbury—**214**, **296**, **297**, **452**
  Slack—**400**, 401

Smith—180, **214**, **370**
Spring—**74**
State—**213**, **261**, **272**, **278**, **280**, **302**, 304, 305
Staunton Ave.—**421**
Stockton—**184**, **265**
Summers—**80**, 87, **101**, **186**, 202, **204**, **213**, **214**, **257-259**, **264**, **267**, 274, **289**, **293**, **297**, 318, **331**, **344**, **363**, 364, **365**, **367**, 396
Tennessee Ave.—180, **265**, **351**
Truslow—**376**, **409**
Virginia—14, 15, **57**, **62**, **74**, 86, 98, **101**, **178**, 180, **181**, **182**, **184**, **187**, **190**, **201**, **204**, **218**, **221**, **222**, **250**, **253**, **257**, **264**, **265**, 266, 274, **275**, **276**, **280**, **289**, **290**, **292**, **295**, **297**, **299**, **320**, **326-329**, **331**, **340**, **342**, **344**, **350**, **351**, **354**, **355**, **356**, **368**, **371**, **376**, 382, 401, **404**, **411**, 414
Washington—**62**, **75**, **88**, 98, **102**, 180, **212**, **241**, **247**, **265**-**267**, **276**, **293**, **294**, **296**, **297**, **299**, **307**, **319**, **331**-**333**, **343**, 344, **345**, 349, **351**, **370**, 379
West Virginia Ave.—180
Woodward Dr.—**267**
Woodward's Branch—431
35th—**414**, **417**
40th—**414**, **421**
50th—**414**
Summers County—**352**
Summers, George W.—**30**, 82, **452**, **453**, 458
Summers, Lewis—25, **30**
Summersville—95
Sunday, Billy—**286**, **333**
Sunrise—**208**, **214**, **357**, 360, **457**
Supreme Court of West Virginia—401
Sutton—122
Swinburn, Ralph—118, 124

Tackett, Christopher—10
Tackett, Lewis—10, 17, 69
Tackett, Samuel—10
Tackett's Creek—87
Tackett's Fort—10, **11**, 17, **438**
Tad—**119**, **120**
"Teays Grant"—24
Teays, Samuel—**438**
Teays, Thomas—24, 438
Teays Valley—**90**, **188**, 438
Temple Israel—**331**
Terminal Building—**250**, **259**
The Guerilla—**96**
Thomas, Dr. Frederick S.—318
Thomas, Herbert J.—**324**, 408
Thomas Jefferson Junior High School—308, **309**, 379
Thom, Russell "Rat"—**388**
Tinkerville—**423**
Toledo & Ohio Central Railroad—117, 118
Tompkins, Christopher Q.—87
Tompkins, Rachel Grant—**426**, **455**
Tompkins, William H.—**18**, 24, 35, 87, **89**, 159, **335**, **424**, 426, **427**, **455**
Torquilstone—**357**
Treaty of Camp Charlotte—10
Treaty of Fort Stanwix—3, **9**
Triangle District—**215**, 401, 408
Trotter, Richard—16
Trotter, William—16
True Temper Corp.—**175**
Truslow, John—15
Turley, Preston—29
Turley, Susan—29
22nd Virginia Infantry Regiment—83
23rd Ohio Volunteer Infantry—**101**, **105**
Twilight League—**383**, **384**
Tyler Mountain—**91**, 431

Union Building—**201**, 204, **216**, **252**, **258**, **269**, **300**, **344**, 345, **354**
Union Carbide Company—154, **155**, 448
Union Mission—**293**, **327**, **332**
Union School—**75**, **200**, 202, **214**, **278**, **302**, 304, 307
United—**138**
United Carbon Co.—154
United Fuel Gas Co.—405
United Mine Workers of America—**128**, 143, 148, **150**, 151, **383**, **452**
U.S. Corps of Engineers—**55**, 62, **64**, 69, 401
United States Natural Gas Co.—403, 405
Upper Falls, Coal River—69, 174, **372**

Valcoulon—87, **89**
Valley Bell Dairy—**295**, **385**
Valley Camp Coal Co.—121, 425
Vanadium Corporation of America—159
Van Damme, Andre—380
Veazey, Oscar A.—**429**, **456**
Venables Branch—11
Village of Kanawha City—**438**
Virginia—82, 83, 87, 187, **352**, 404, 426, 438, 447
Virginia Central Railroad—188
Virginia Constitutional Convention—30
Virginia Legislature—11, 14, 17, 18, **30**, 51, 54, 56, 188, 428
Virginia Military Institute—83, 305
Virginian Power Co.—**402**, 404
Virginian Railroad—108

Virginian Theater—**261**, 364
Virginia's Chapel—18, **335**, **455**
Virginia Secession Convention of 1861—18, **30**
Virginia State Reform Convention of 1850-1851—**30**
Virginia Street Temple—**266**, **327**, **331**, **353**

Walker, Ezra—44, 188, 304
Walker, J. Brisben—**14**, **74**, 202, **208**
Walnut Grove—**30**
Ward—**121**, **139**, **151**, 308, **425**, **457**
Ward, Charles—**72**, **176**, 401, 405
Ward, Charles Engineering Co.—**55**, **72**, **73**, 172, 176, 202, **299**
Warne, H.Rus—**338**, **340**
Warner-Klipstein Co.—154
Washburn Hotel—**213**
Washington, Booker T.—**42**, 45-47, 304, **453**
Washington, D.C.—**70**, 108, **202**, **301**, 348
Washington, George—8, **9**, 10, 13, 17, 35, 51, 56, 86, 187, **427**, **431**, **436**, **438**, 459
Washington, Lawrence A.—35
Washington Manor—286
Watt Powell Park—**377**, 382, **383**, **385**, 416
Watts, C.C.—**453**
Wayne County—1, **352**
Webster County—**352**
Welch, Alexander—**16**
Welch, James Clark—90, **91**
Welch, Levi—**84**
Werhle Park—382
Wertz Field—**192-194**, **198**, 436
Wertz, W.W.—**193**
West Belle—**427**
Western Maryland Railroad—108, 122
West, Jerry—360, **392**
Westvaco Chlorine Products Corp.—154
West Virginia Air National Guard—**197**, 199, 314
West Virginia Airways—**193**
West Virginia & Southern Railroad—119
West Virginia College of Graduate Studies—312, 315
West Virginia Collegiate Institute—314, **436**
West Virginia Historical & Antiquarian Society—458, 459
West Virginia Historical Magazine—459
West Virginia Institute of Technology—312, 315, 387, 430, 459
West Virginia Journal—**96**, 202, 459
West Virginia Legislature—18, **30**, 143, 228, 312, **318**
West Virginia National Guard—**414**, **417**, **422**
West Virginia School For Colored Deaf & Blind—436
West Virginia State College—**193**, 312, 314, 315, **384**, 387, **410**, **411**, **436**, **437**
West Virginia State Museum—**15**, **84**
West Virginia State Police—**343**
West Virginia Turnpike—**191**, **423**
West Virginia University—**304**, 315, **376**, 386, **389**, **392**, **393**
West Virginia Vocational Rehabilitation Center—436
West Virginia Water & Electric Co.—404
West Virginia Water & Light Co.—401, 403
West Virginia Water Service Co.—401
Wheeling—52, **202**, 228, 229, 396
Wheeling Convention of 1861—82, 95
Whitesville—122
White Transportation Co.—**186**
Whittcler, Aaron—17
Whitteker, Norris—17, **452**
Whitteker, William—17, 344, 345
Whittemore Glass Co.—159
Wilson, E.W.—**208**
Wilson, Gov. Emanual W.—**229**, 230, **453**
Wilson, James—15, 24, 159
Wilson's Island—**10**
Winfield—**64**, 432
Winifrede—118, **282**
Winifrede Collieries—118
Winifrede Mining & Manufacturing Co.—118
Winifrede Railroad—118, **119**, 124
Wise, Gen. Henry—**69**, **86**, 87, **88**, **89**, 90, 92
Witcher—**427**
Witcher, Col. John S.—**427**
Witcher's Creek—**427**
Withrow, Pat B.—**327**, **332**
Woman's Club of Charleston—356
Wood County—1, 17
Woodman, Frank—362, 400, 403, **452**
Woodrow Wilson Junior High School—308
Woolworth's Store—**254**, 274, **277**
Workman, Mark—360, **392**
Works Progress Administration (WPA)—**77**, **376**, **421**, **431**, 433
Wyatt Coal Co.—**137**, **141**
Wyoming County—1, 352
Wyoming Manufacturing Co.—124

Yeager Airport—**196**, **198**
Yeager, Chuck—**198**
YMCA—**124**, **140**, **202**, 230, 313, 327, 345, **346**, **348**, 349
Young, Keziah—17
Young, R. John—10, 14, 17, 425, 447
YWCA—**309**, 313, 327, 345, **350**, **452**

Bibliography

Atkinson, George W., *History of Kanawha County From Its Organization in 1789 Until the Present Time*, West Virginia Journal, Charleston, 1876.

Belle Woman's Club, *Bicentennial Belle, 1776-1976*, 1976.

Charleston 1907, A Souvenir of the City of Charleston, The W.M. Barnes Directory Co., Parkersburg, West Virginia, 1907.

Cook, Roy Bird, *The Annals of Fort Lee*, West Virginia Review Press, Charleston, 1935.

_____, *Washington's Western Lands*, Shenandoah Publishing House, Strasburg, Virginia, 1935.

Cromwell, Joseph, *The C&P Story in Action, West Virginia*, C&P Telephone Company, 1981.

deGruyter, Julius A., *The Kanawha Spectator, Vol. I*, Jarrett Printing Co., Charleston, 1953.

_____, *The Kanawha Spectator, Part II*, McClain Printing Co., Parsons, West Virginia, 1976.

Davisson, Russell, *A Century with St. Albans, West Virginia*, St. Albans Public Library, 1963.

Dayton, Ruth Woods, *Pioneers and Their Homes on Upper Kanawha*, West Virginia Publishing Co., Charleston, 1947.

Ellis, Garland H., *St. Albans, West Virginia - It's Origin and Development*, Dawson Printing Co., St. Albans, 1977.

FMC, Chemicals Division, *The Salt Industry in the Kanawha Valley*, no date.

Galbraith, Julia, *History of Cross Lanes Area*, Woman's Club of Cross Lanes, 1976.

Hale, John P., *Trans-Allegheny Pioneers, Historical Sketches of the First State Settlements West of the Alleghenies*, 2nd Ed., Kanawha Valley Publishing Co., Charleston, 1931.

_____, *History of the Great Kanawha Valley*, 2 Vols., Brant, Fuller & Co., Madison, Wisconsin, 1891.

Harlan, John C., *History of West Virginia State College, 1890-1965*, William C. Brown Book Co., Dubuque, Iowa, 1968.

Harris, V.B., *Great Kanawha: An Historical Outline*, Jarrett Printing Co., Charleston, 1974.

Jefferds, Joseph C., Jr., *A History of St. John's Episcopal Church, Charleston, West Virginia*, 1976.

Johnson, Leland R., *Men, Mountains and Rivers: An Illustrated History of the Huntington District, U.S. Army Corps of Engineers, 1754-1974*, U.S. Government Printing Office, Washington, D.C., 1978.

Krebs, Frank J., *Where There Is Faith: The Morris Harvey College Story, 1888-1970*, M.H.C. Publications, Charleston, 1974.

Laidley, William S., *History of Charleston and Kanawha County, West Virginia and Representative Citizens*, Richmond-Arnold Publishing Co., Chicago, Illinois, 1911.

Lowry, Terry, *The Battle of Scary Creek, Military Operations in the Kanawha Valley, April-July 1861*, Pictorial Histories Publishing Co., Charleston, 1982.

MacCorkle, William A., *The Recollections of Fifty Years*, G.P. Putnam's Sons, New York, 1928.

Morgan, John G., *Charleston 175*, Charleston Gazette, Charleston, 1970.

Parish, *Art Work of the Kanawha and New River Valleys*, 1897.

Price, Paul H., *Salt Brines of West Virginia, Vol. VIII*, West Virginia Geological Survey, Morgantown, West Virginia, 1937.

Rice, Otis K., *Charleston and the Kanawha County*, Windsor Publications, Woodland Hills, California, 1981.

Sparkmon, William R., *The Chesapeake & Ohio Railway in West Virginia, Huntington Division*, Jalamap Publications, Inc., Charleston, 1983.

Strother, D.H., *The Capitol of West Virginia and the Great Kanawha Valley; Advantages, Resources and Prospects*, Journal Office, Charleston, 1872.

Stutler, Boyd B., *West Virginia in the Civil War*, Education Foundation, Charleston, 1966.

Summers, George W., *Pages from the Past: Recollections, Traditions and Old Timers' Tales of the Long Ago*, The Charleston Journal, Charleston, 1935.

Wintz, William D., *Nitro, The World War I Boom Town*, Jalamap Publications, Charleston, 1985.

Other sources consulted were reports by Paul Marshall and Associates on Downtown Charleston, St. Albans, Dunbar and Institute, Pratt, Cedar Grove, Fort Scammon, Dunbar Wine Cellars, and Kanawha County Courthouse along with numerous articles in *West Virginia History Magazine*, *Goldenseal*, old city directories, numerous issues of the *Charleston Daily Mail* the *Charleston Gazette* and older local newspapers, pamphlets and privately published reports from various sources plus personal interviews.

KANAWHA COUNTY HONOR LIST

OF DEAD AND MISSING WORLD WAR II

Name	Rank	Status
Adkins, Elmer	Pvt.	DOW
Akers, James E.	Pfc.	KIA
Allen, Frank G.	Pvt.	DOW
Allen, Lacy C.	Pvt.	KIA
Allen, Mose	Pvt.	DNB
Allen, Vernon	Pfc.	KIA
Alms, Jay G.	S-Sgt.	DNB
Ames, Walter	Pvt.	DNB
Amick, Vernon H.	Pfc.	KIA
Anderson, Glen H.	Pvt.	KIA
Andrews, John V.	2-Lt.	DNB
Arnett, Jack S. M.	2-Lt.	KIA
Atkins, Gail G.	Pfc.	KIA
Atkinson, Buddy O.	Pfc.	KIA
Ault, James J., Jr.	S-Sgt.	KIA
Auxier, Garnet R.	Tec. 5	DNB
Baber, John M., Jr.	Pvt.	KIA
Bacon, Mitchell W.	S-Sgt.	KIA
Bagley, Jack C.	Pfc.	KIA
Bailey, Shirley E.	Pvt.	KIA
Bain, Clyde H.	S-Sgt.	KIA
Baker, Ernest E.	Pfc.	KIA
Baker, Jack M.	Capt.	DNB
Baldwin, Ira O.	Pvt.	KIA
Ball, Albert G.	Pvt.	KIA
Barbour, Hubbard	Pfc.	KIA
Barlow, Joseph B.	Tec. 5	KIA
Barnhart, Jack G.	S-Sgt.	KIA
Barnette, John O.	Pfc.	DNB
Bartlett, John W.	Sgt.	KIA
Barton, Robert R., Jr.	2-Lt.	DNB
Beane, William C.	Pfc.	KIA
Beasley, Raymond G.	Pvt.	KIA
Belcher, Cecil B.	Pvt.	KIA
Belcher, George	Pvt.	DNB
Bell, Rufus L.	Pfc.	KIA
Bennett, Henry W.	Pfc.	KIA
Bias, William C.	Pvt.	KIA
Bland, Leland S.	Pfc.	FOD
Blankenship, B. A.	Pfc.	KIA
Boggess, Clemet E.	Sgt.	KIA
Boggess, James O.	Pvt.	FOD
Boggs, Kent E.	Pfc.	KIA
Boland, George K.	Sgt.	DNB
Bostic, Rodney L.	S-Sgt.	KIA
Bowen, Jack D.	Pfc.	KIA
Bowers, John E.	Capt.	KIA
Boyle, Stanley H.	Capt.	DNB
Bradley, Frank L.	Capt.	DNB
Brady, Garland C.	1-Lt.	DOW
Breeden, Jack E.	Pfc	KIA
Brooks, Louis W.	Sgt.	FOD
Brown, Clarence L.	Sgt.	FOD
Brown, Elwood	Pvt.	KIA
Brown, Ray	Cpl.	DOW
Brown, Walter L.	Pvt.	DNB
Bruni, Domenic	Sgt.	KIA
Bsharah, George G.	Pfc.	KIA
Buckner, John E.	Pfc.	KIA
Burd, Raymond V.	Pvt.	KIA
Burdette, Herman L.	2-Lt.	FOD
Burford, George W., Jr.	Pvt.	KIA
Burger, William E.	Pvt.	DNB
Byrd, Melvin L.	Pvt.	KIA
Cadd, Quentin E.	2-Lt.	KIA
Cadle, Delmar C.	Pfc.	KIA
Caldwell, Perley A.	Pfc.	DOW
Cale, Hamilton N.	Pfc.	KIA
Camp, Bill H.	Pvt.	KIA
Campbell, Dempsey	S-Sgt.	DOW
Campbell, Robert J.	Pvt.	KIA
Canterbury, Cecil H.	Pfc.	KIA
Carpenter, Lloyd M.	Pfc.	KIA
Carr, Archie E.	Tec. 5	DNB
Carte, Robert A.	Pfc.	KIA
Carte, Samuel B., Jr.	Pfc.	KIA
Carver, Robert H.	Pvt.	KIA
Casto, Monnie C.	Pvt.	DNB
Casto, Virgil C.	Pfc.	KIA
Cavender, Ira H.	Pfc.	DNB
Chapman, Clarence E.	Sgt.	FOD
Chapman, Gerald C.	Pvt.	KIA
Childress, Lonzo	Pvt.	DNB
Clark, Charlie M.	Pfc.	KIA
Clendenin, Paul E.	Sgt.	DNB
Clere, James R.	Pvt.	KIA
Cochran, David L.	Tec. 5	KIA
Colebank, Robert E.	S-Sgt.	KIA
Combs, Richard A.	Pvt.	DNB
Condit, Sherwood W.	Pvt.	DOW
Conley, Carl R.	Tec. 5	KIA
Connard, Rodney D.	Pfc.	KIA
Cook, McKinley H.	Sgt.	KIA
Copley, Charles	Pvt.	KIA
Corley, George F.	2-Lt.	KIA
Cornett, Leonard B.	Pvt.	KIA
Couch, Robert T., Jr.	2-Lt.	KIA
Counts, Ellis	Pvt.	KIA
Covey, Kenneth W.	S-Sgt.	FOD
Crago, Norman G.	Pvt.	KIA
Crank, Clifford L.	Tec. 5	DNB
Creasey, Glenn A.	Sgt.	KIA
Creech, Ralph E.	Pfc.	KIA
Cremeans, Ralph C.	Pfc.	KIA
Crites, Ardith E.	2-Lt.	DNB
Crowder, Dewey R.	Pvt.	KIA
Crozier, Robert D.	Cpl.	DNB
Cummings, James W.	Pfc.	DOW
Cummings, James N.	1-Lt.	KIA
Cummings, Lee W.	Sgt.	KIA
Cummings, Oral	1-Lt.	KIA
Cunningham, C. J., Jr.	1-Lt.	KIA
Davis, James C., Jr.	Tec. 5	KIA
Davis, Robert L.	T-Sgt.	FOD
Delong, Arnold	Pvt.	KIA
Deming, Thomas R.	1-Lt.	KIA
Dent, Joe M.	Pvt.	KIA
Dick, Eugene, Jr.	Sgt.	M
Dickson, Donald F.	1-Lt.	FOD
Dillard, Vernon L.	Pfc.	KIA
Dillon, James, Jr.	S-Sgt.	KIA
Donahue, James B.	Pvt.	KIA
Drape, Francis T.	Sgt.	KIA
Duncan, James E.	Pvt.	DNB
Dunlap, Humbird, Jr.	Pvt.	DOW
Eccles, Robert L.	2-Lt.	DNB
Edens, William A.	Pvt.	DNB
Edwards, Lewis A.	1-Lt.	KIA
Elias, Francis R.	Pfc.	KIA
Elmore, Ralph A.	Sgt.	KIA
Elsener, William E.	T-Sgt.	DNB
Emory, William W.	Maj.	FOD
Ervin, Roy C.	Pfc.	KIA
Escue, Jess E.	Pfc.	KIA
Evans, Tom C.	1-Lt.	M
Ewing, Arless B.	Tec. 5	KIA
Faigley, Lester L.	Pfc.	KIA
Ferguson, Charles D.	Pvt.	KIA
Ferguson, Lawrence W.	Fl. O.	KIA
Ferrell, Roy L.	Pfc.	KIA
Fields, Lester B.	Tec. 5	DOW
Fisher, Anna M.	1-Lt.	DNB
Fisher, Caroll A.	1-Lt.	FOD
Fletcher, James E.	2-Lt.	DNB
Flynn, Walter E.	Capt.	DNB
Foley, Allen E.	Tec. 5	DNB
Fortner, Kenneth J.	Pvt.	KIA
Foster, Howard, Jr.	Pfc.	KIA
Foster, William J.	Pfc.	FOD
Fowlkes, Chester A.	Pvt.	KIA
Fox, Roy C.	Pfc.	DNB
France, William A.	Pvt.	KIA
French, Ira V.	1-Lt.	DNB
Fryberger, Melvin L.	Sgt.	KIA
Full, Robert E.	Pfc.	KIA
Gardner, Francis N.	Pfc.	DNB
Garnes, John W.	Pfc.	KIA
Garnes, Paul C.	Pvt.	KIA
Garrett, Fred E.	Pfc.	DOW
Garton, Orville H.	Sgt.	KIA
Gastineau, Lucien O., Jr.	2-Lt.	KIA
Gatens, Leo P.	Sgt.	KIA
Gibson, James R.	Pvt.	KIA
Gibson, William H.	Sgt.	DOW
Gillespie, Dana D.	Pfc.	KIA
Given, Charles E. Jr.	Sgt.	DNB
Glass, Richard D.	S-Sgt.	KIA
Goff, Homer W.	2-Lt.	KIA
Goff, Louis R.	2-Lt.	KIA
Gray, Cecil N.	Cpl.	KIA
Griffith, Foster C.	Pvt.	KIA
Griggs, Edward J.	Pfc.	KIA
Gunnoe, Arthur V.	Pvt.	KIA
Gunnoe, Joseph H.	Cpl.	FOD
Gunnoe, Marion L.	Pfc.	KIA
Gunnoe, Robert K.	Pvt.	DNB
Haddad, Mitchell	Sgt.	KIA
Hager, Samuel F.	Pvt.	KIA
Hager, Samuel F.	Pvt.	KIA
Halstead, Bernie C.	Sgt.	KIA
Halstead, John A.	Pfc.	DNB
Hamilton, Lee M.	Capt.	DNB
Hamilton, Thurman C.	Pfc.	KIA
Hammack, Charles L.	Pfc.	KIA
Hancock, Charles H.	T-Sgt.	KIA
Hannah, Vernon A.	S-Sgt.	KIA
Hanson, Warden E.	Pvt.	KIA
Hapney, Lacy B.	Pfc.	KIA
Harkins, Hezekiah, Jr.	Pfc.	KIA
Harmon, Harvey L.	1-Lt.	KIA
Harmon, Paul B.	Pvt.	KIA
Harper, Harold L.	Pvt.	KIA
Harris, Ray B.	Pfc.	DOW
Harrison, Avrill R.	Tec. 5	DNB
Harrison, Charles H.	Pfc.	KIA
Harrison, Russell R.	Cpl.	KIA
Harvey, Alvin	Pfc.	DNB
Haynes, Brady O.	Pvt.	KIA
Haynes, Leonard B.	Pvt.	KIA
Haynes, William R.	S-Sgt.	KIA
Heath, Wayne W.	Pfc.	DNB
Hedrick, James R.	Pvt.	DNB
Helmic, James H.	Pfc.	KIA
Helmick, Harold	Pfc.	KIA
Hendel, Charles H.	Pvt.	DNB
Herman, Jack	Pfc.	DNB
Herold, Robert L.	Pvt.	KIA
Herrmann, Ray F.	Capt.	KIA
Hess, Woodrow W.	Pvt.	DNB
Hickman, Eugene R.	Pvt.	DNB
Hickman, Joseph B.	Pvt.	DNB
Hill, Carl D.	Pfc.	KIA
Hill, Charles E.	Pfc.	DOW
Hill, Thomas J.	Pfc.	KIA
Hix, William T., Jr.	1-Lt.	KIA
Hodge, Delmar D.	Sgt.	KIA
Hodge, Emert F.	Pfc.	KIA
Hoffman, Oakleigh N.	Pfc.	KIA
Holmested, George W. A.	1-Lt.	DNB
Holstein, Charles E.	Tec. 4	KIA
Honaker, Thomas H., Jr.	Pvt.	KIA
Hooks, Corwin T.	2-Lt.	DNB
Houchins, James E.	S-Sgt.	KIA
Howard, Ryland A.	Tec. 5	KIA
Huddleston, E. P.	Pvt.	KIA
Huddleston, Raynor D.	Tec. 4	DNB
Hudgins, John G.	Capt.	DNB
Hudnall, Clinton R.	Pfc.	KIA
Hudson, Charles, Jr.	Fl. O.	DNB
Hughes, Martin V.	Pfc.	KIA
Humphreys, Jack E.	Pfc.	DOW
Humphreys, John E.	2-Lt.	DNB
Hunt, Joe H.	Pvt.	KIA
Hunt, John W.	Pfc.	DOW
Icenhower, John A.	Pfc.	KIA
Jackson, Dennis D.	S-Sgt.	KIA
James, Russell A.	Sgt.	KIA
Janney, Thomas B.	2-Lt.	DNB
Jarrett, Jesse L.	Sgt.	DOW
Jarvis, Harold E.	S-Sgt.	FOD
Jett, Roy A.	Pfc.	DNB
Johnson, Allen F.	Pfc.	KIA
Johnson, Claude W.	Pfc.	DNB
Johnson, Dallis H.	Pvt.	KIA
Johnson, Elmer E.	S-Sgt.	KIA
Johnson, Langdon E.	1-Lt.	FOD
Johnson, Richard C.	Tec. 4	KIA
Johnson, Willard D., Jr.	Pvt.	KIA
Johnson, William M.	S-Sgt.	DNB
Jones, Charles F.	Pfc.	KIA
Jones, Ernest H.	Cpl.	DNB
Jones, Johnie B.	S-Sgt.	KIA
Jones, John C.	Pvt.	DNB
Jones, John E.	Pfc.	KIA
Jones, Wilbur A.	Pvt.	KIA
Joyce, Joseph C., Jr.	2-Lt.	KIA
Kanner, Sam	1-Lt.	KIA
Kee, Darrell G.	Cpl.	KIA
Keenan, William J.	Tec. 5	KIA
Keeney, Ira L.	Pvt.	KIA
Keeling, William M.	1 Lt.	KIA
Kemper, William	S-Sgt.	KIA
Kidd, Woodrow W.	Pfc.	KIA
Kiger, Odgar	Tec. 5	DNB
Kimble, Wayne R.	2-Lt.	DNB
King, Edward O.	Pvt.	DNB
King, Jack	S-Sgt.	KIA
Knuckles, Ervin E.	Pfc.	DOW
Krantz, William H.	Pfc.	KIA
Lacy, Forest E., Jr.	S-Sgt.	DOW
Landers, Denver	Pvt.	DNB
Landis, Herman D.	S-Sgt.	DNB
Larck, Buster A.	T-Sgt.	FOD
Lawhorn, James O.	Pfc.	KIA
Lawrence, Alonzo L.	S-Sgt.	DNB
Lawrence, Charles E.	Pvt.	KIA
Legg, Simon L.	Tec. 4	KIA
Leishman, Robert B.	Tec. 5	KIA
Lemon, James A., Jr.	Pfc.	KIA
Lilly, Harry	S-Sgt.	DNB
Locke, Alfred T.	Pfc.	KIA
Lowery, Dakin E.	Pvt.	FOD
Mairs, James H.	Pfc.	KIA
Martin, Albert C.	Pfc.	KIA
Martin, Christopher F.	Pvt.	DNB
Mason, Paul W.	Pvt.	KIA
McCallister, E. A.	S-Sgt.	FOD
McCarthy, William N.	Pfc.	KIA
McCleary, Earl R.	Tec. 5	KIA
McClung, William D.	Tec. 4	DNB
McClung, Lewis J.	Pfc.	KIA
McCoy, James H., Jr.	1-Lt.	DOW
McCoy, Lewis F.	Pfc.	KIA
McDaniel, Raymond	Sgt.	KIA
McFerrin, Thomas C.	Sgt.	KIA
McGraw, Joe A.	Pfc.	KIA
McGraw, John E.	Cpl.	KIA
McIlwain, John W.	Pvt.	DNB
McKee, John L.	1-Lt.	DNB
McLaughlin, Basil G.	Sgt.	DOW

Type of Casualty:
- KIA—Killed in Action
- DOW—Died of Wounds
- DOI—Died of Injuries
- DNB—Died, non-battle
- FOD—Finding of Death
- M—Missing

Name	Rank	Type
McLaughlin, John J.	Sgt.	KIA
McLaughlin, Oscar B.	Sgt.	KIA
McShurley, Cecil V.	Pfc.	KIA
McClung, Hershel K.	Pvt.	DNB
Meador, Norford G.	Pfc.	KIA
Meadows, Billie	Pfc.	DNB
Means, Charles W.	Pvt.	KIA
Medley, Garth E.	Pvt.	KIA
Meikle, Parker	Pvt.	DOW
Metz, Jack M.	Tec. 4	KIA
Miller, Florence E.	Pvt.	KIA
Miller, Theodore E.	Pvt.	KIA
Minsker, Harry C.	1-Lt.	KIA
Mitchell, James H.	Sgt.	KIA
Moles, Roscoe H.	Pvt.	DOW
Mollohan, W. L., Jr.	Sgt.	KIA
Monday, Elmer E.	Tec. 4	DNB
Monday, Kenneth E.	Pfc.	KIA
Mooney, Alphonso	Pfc.	DOW
Moore, Charles H.	Pfc.	KIA
Moore, Holley L.	T-Sgt.	FOD
Moriarty, John D.	Pfc.	KIA
Mucklow, Herbert B.	Sgt.	KIA
Mullins, Ernest C.	Pvt.	KIA
Mounts, Mason W.	Pvt.	DOW
Nabors, Carl M.	Cpl.	KIA
Najar, Fred J.	Pvt.	KIA
Naylor, Sam	Pvt.	KIA
Neary, Roy	Pfc.	KIA
Norman, William E.	Tec. 5	DOW
Nunley, Milburn L.	Pvt.	DNB
O'Dell, Elmer E.	Pfc.	KIA
O'Neal, George L.	2-Lt.	KIA
Orders, Kermit R.	2-Lt.	DNB
Osborne, Jess J.	Pfc.	KIA
Oxley, William K.	Sgt.	FOD
Oxyer, Glenn	Pvt.	DNB
Painter, Vermont	Pvt.	DOW
Palmer, Noyes F., Jr.	Pfc.	DOW
Parsons, Aubrey K.	Pfc.	KIA
Patterson, William E.	Pfc.	KIA
Pauley, Arthur C.	Pvt.	DNB
Pauley, Carl H.	Pvt.	KIA
Pauley, Earl V.	Pfc.	KIA
Pauley, O'Dell W.	Pfc.	DOW
Pauley, Raymond J.	Pvt.	KIA
Payne, Arthur R.	Sgt.	DOW
Pelletier, S. G., Jr.	2-Lt.	KIA
Pennington, W. H., Jr.	Pfc.	DNB
Perry, Alma	Pvt.	DNB
Perry, Bartholomew, Jr.	Pvt.	KIA
Perry, Frankie	Pfc.	KIA
Perry, Rensey	Pfc.	KIA
Peterson, Russell H.	Cpl.	KIA
Peyatt, James C.	Pvt.	DNB
Pierce, Robert R.	Cpl.	KIA
Pike, Roy J.	1-Lt.	FOD
Plymale, Leston G.	Pvt.	KIA
Pope, Alex, Jr.	Pvt.	KIA
Porter, Ray, Jr.	Pvt.	DNB
Potterfield, Clarence	2-Lt.	DOW
Powers, Walter A.	Pvt.	DOW
Powers, James B.	Pvt.	KIA
Preston, Emmit, Jr.	Pvt.	KIA
Price, Charles W.	Pfc.	KIA
Price, Clyde	Tec. 5	KIA
Price, Oscar E.	Pvt.	DNB
Price, Roy B.	Pvt.	KIA
Pritt, Milton A.	Pvt.	DNB
Province, Clyde J.	S-Sgt.	KIA
Queen, Venson	Pvt.	KIA
Quesenberry, M. H., Jr.	1-Lt.	KIA
Ramze, James S.	Pfc.	KIA
Ransom, William F.	Pfc.	KIA
Reed, Virgil L.	Pvt.	FOD
Richards, Charles D.	Pvt.	KIA
Richardson, Bill W.	Pvt.	KIA
Richardson, Harold C.	S-Sgt.	FOD
Roberts, John R.	Sgt.	KIA
Robinson, Russell L.	Pvt.	DNB
Ronemus, William L.	2-Lt.	DNB
Rose, Ray M.	Pfc.	KIA
Roush, Carl E.	Pvt.	KIA
Rousseau, Walter	Tec. 4	DNB
Rucker, Clarence E.	Cpl.	DNB
Ryder, Leo A., Sr.	Sgt.	KIA
Sams, Roy W.	Pvt.	DNB
Saunders, Lealon D.	Pvt.	KIA
Sauzer, Stanley	Tec. 4	KIA
Sayfie, Mike	Pfc.	KIA
Schmidt, William E.	Pvt.	KIA
Schoolcraft, Glenn C.	Sgt.	KIA
Scott, Heairel M.	Pfc.	KIA
Scott, Henry K.	Pfc.	DOW
Scott, Robert F. Jr.	2-Lt.	KIA
Shafer, Harry B.	2-Lt.	KIA
Shafer, Roy C.	Pfc.	KIA
Shaffer, Charles W.	Pvt.	KIA
Shaffer, Jack R.	Pvt.	KIA
Short, Dorsey S.	Tec. 5	DNB
Sibley, Robert L., Jr.	2-Lt.	KIA
Simon, Lewis S.	1-Lt.	KIA
Skeen, Grover C.	Pvt.	KIA
Skeens, Robert L.	Pfc.	DNB
Slate, Ralph	Pfc.	DNB
Smith, Alexander O.	Cpl.	DNB
Smith, Cecil J., Jr.	Pvt.	KIA
Smith, Clarence T.	Pfc.	KIA
Smith, Cleadith C.	Cpl.	KIA
Smith, Gaylord O.	Pfc.	KIA
Smith, Harold E.	T-Sgt.	KIA
Smith, Paul E.	Pvt.	KIA
Smith, Roy E.	S-Sgt.	KIA
Smith, Shirley A.	Pfc.	DOW
Spainhour, Charles J.	Pfc.	DOW
Spangler, Vaughn O.	Tec. 4	KIA
Spencer, Arlie	Pfc.	KIA
Spencer, Hershel F.	Pvt.	DNB
Spencer, Homer J.	Pvt.	KIA
Spencer, Sammy I.	Tec. 5	KIA
Spencer, Samuel F.	S-Sgt.	KIA
Staats, Clarence R.	T-Sgt.	DNB
Stanley, Luther F.	S-Sgt.	KIA
Staton, Robert M.	Tec. 5	KIA
Steinbicker, Thomas H.	Sgt.	KIA
Stephenson, Ralph C.	Pvt.	KIA
Stern, Lenders C.	Pfc.	KIA
Strickland, Raymond L.	Pvt.	DNB
Strimel, Edmond C.	2-Lt.	KIA
Stuart, James D.	Pfc.	KIA
Summers, Denvil D.	Cpl.	KIA
Summers, Roy L.	Pvt.	DNB
Sutphin, Claude R.	Pvt.	KIA
Swineburne, Donald R.	1-Lt.	FOD
Sydenstricker, J. H.	Cpl.	KIA
Talbert, Carl C.	Pfc.	KIA
Talley, Clarence M.	S-Sgt.	KIA
Tankersley, Cecil A.	S-Sgt.	KIA
Taylor, Edwin R., Jr.	2-Lt.	KIA
Taylor, Homer D.	Sgt.	FOD
Terry, James R.	Pvt.	DNB
Thaxton, Billy J.	Pvt.	KIA
Thomas, Herbert P.	Pvt.	DOW
Thomas, Lawrence E.	Pfc.	DNB
Thomas, Robert W.	Capt.	DNB
Thompson, Edward V.	Pvt.	KIA
Thudium, Harry N.	Cpl.	KIA
Toler, Lewis A.	Pfc.	KIA
Toler, Richard	S-Sgt.	KIA
Tomei, Paul A.	M-Sgt.	DNB
Tomick, Rudolph T.	Pfc.	KIA
Townsend, Harold E.	Pfc.	KIA
Trail, John H.	Pfc.	KIA
Tussey, Willard R.	Pvt.	KIA
Tyler, Willie	Pvt.	KIA
Van Bibber, James W.	T-Sgt.	KIA
Waggy, Robert H.	Sgt.	KIA
Walker, Daniel E.	Pvt.	KIA
Walker, Okel D.	Pvt.	KIA
Walton, Oran O.	S-Sgt.	KIA
Watson, Lewis O., Jr.	Pfc.	DNB
Weaver, William K.	Sgt.	KIA
Webb, Richard F.	Pfc.	KIA
Wells, Leonard H.	Pvt.	KIA
Wentz, Glenvil C.	Pfc.	KIA
West, Howard A.	Pvt.	DNB
Westfall, Dale G.	Pfc.	KIA
Wetzel, Charles E.	2-Lt.	KIA
Wheeler, Marvin C.	Sgt.	KIA
White, Arthur W.	Cpl.	DNB
White, Sylvester C., Jr.	Pvt.	DOW
Whitlock, Leon S.	Tec. 5	KIA
Whittington, W. J.	Pvt.	KIA
Williams, Charles G.	Sgt.	KIA
Williams, James R.	Pfc.	DNB
Williams, Philip D.	Pfc.	KIA
Williams, William P.	Pfc.	KIA
Wills, Charles Y.	Pvt.	KIA
Wilmoth, Arnold H.	Pvt.	KIA
Wilmoth, Joseph R.	Sgt.	KIA
Wilson, Forrest M., Jr.	Pvt.	KIA
Wilson, Oscar A.	Pfc.	KIA
Withrow, Robert W.	Pvt.	KIA
Wolfe, Robert B.	Pvt.	KIA
Woods, Orval	Pfc.	KIA
Woods, Russell D.	Pvt.	KIA
Woods, William C.	Tec. 3	KIA
Woodyard, Howard F.	Pfc.	DOW
Woolwine, Byron G.	Pvt.	DNB
Woolwine, William A.	Pvt.	DOW
Worden, Edwin L.	Pvt.	DNB
Worley, William J.	Pvt.	DNB
Wright, James M.	Pvt.	KIA
Yago, Ralph J.	Pfc.	DOW
Yost, James A., Jr.	Pfc.	DNB
Young, James L.	S-Sgt.	KIA
Young, Robert E.	Pfc.	KIA
Zakaib, Louis A.	T-Sgt.	KIA
Zickafoose, Warren E.	Sgt.	KIA

KOREAN CONFLICT CASUALTY LIST

Name	Rank	Type
Arthur, William R.	PFC	KIA
Ballard, Clarence C.	1LT	FOD
Banks, Charles M.	SFC	KIA
Bartley, Donald D.	1LT	KIA
Bays, Jimmie D.	PFC	KIA
Bibb, Robert P.	SFC	FOD
Bond, Elihue, Jr.	PFC	DIE
Booker, Joseph	PFC	FOD
Burns, Fred, Jr.	PFC	KIA
Bush, Reuben H.	PFC	DOW
Carroll, James	PFC	KIA
Chaffin, Alden R.	PFC	KIA
Chandler, Teddy R.	PV2	FOD
Clark, Clifford E.	PFC	KIA
Collins, Claude E.	PV2	KIA
Dent, William A., Jr.	PV2	KIA
Duncan, William J.	PV2	KIA
Dunlap, Alva F.	PFC	DIE
Evans, William E.	PFC	KIA
Fisher, John A.	PV2	DIE
Foster, Donald K.	PFC	KIA
Foster, Virgil L., Jr.	CPL	KIA
Frye, David	SFC	KIA
Fulks, Ira J.	CPL	KIA
Gibson, Denny J.	PV2	KIA
Hackney, William L.	SFC	FOD
Hall, Vincent R.	PV2	KIA
Hendricks, Edward L.	CPL	KIA
Hodges, Otmer F., Jr.	PFC	KIA
Holley, John F.	CPL	KIA
Holmes, Sonnie L.	CPL	KIA
Horner, Walter C.	PFC	KIA
Houghton, James D.	1LT	FOD
King, Darrell L.	PV2	KIA
King, James E.	SGT	DOW
Knapper, Othello C.	PFC	KIA
Kyle, Darwin K.	2LT	KIA
Lucas, James R.	CPL	KIA
Mace, Jackie M.	PFC	KIA
Mallery, Harry E.	PV2	KIA
Marshall, James E.	2LT	KIA
McClanahan, Alton	CPL	FOD
Moles, Wendel R.	PFC	FOD
Myer, George D.	PFC	KIA
Nichols, Charles E.	CPL	DOW
Oakes, Ronald E.	1LT	KIA
Plantz, Charles R.	PFC	KIA
Pool, Jack A.	CPL	KIA
Purnell, Jerome A.	PV2	KIA
Ramsey, Irvanule	PV2	KIA
Sigmon, Harold G.	PFC	KIA
Simmons, Gene	PFC	DIE
Sloan, Laurence E.	PFC	KIA
Stricklen, Charles	PFC	KIA
Strobel, William E.	PV2	KIA
Taylor, James L.	CPL	FOD
Thomas, Garland R.	PFC	KIA
Turley, James E.	PFC	DIE
Vannoy, James M.	CPL	KIA
Walk, John H.	CPL	KIA
Welch, Robert L.	PFC	KIA
West, David L.	SGT	DOW
Williams, Stanley R.	SFC	KIA
Woo, Theodore R.	2LT	KIA
Wright, James A.	PFC	KIA
Brown, Charles J.	Capt	
Davies, Howard J.	1st Lt	
Foglesong, Rom C., Jr.	1st Lt	
Grammer, Wilbert W.	2nd Lt	
Harper, Lee A.	1st Lt	
Hart, Donald L.	A2C	
Keister, Harold O.	1st Lt	
Nicaise, Leo J., Jr.	1st Lt	
Cantrell, Paul E.	Sgt	

KANAWHA COUNTY HONOR LIST

OF DEAD AND MISSING
VIETMAN

Ayers, Johnnie Marvin—Elkview
Ball, John Robert—Charleston
Roscoe Willet, Jr.—Charleston
Barker, Kenneth Monroe—Charleston
Bess, Charles Ray—Charleston
Binion, Curtis Estill—Charleston
Blake, Timothy Morgan—Charleston
Board, Stephen Douglas—Belle
Boggs, Charles Edward—Charleston
Brown, Edward Wallace, Jr.—Charleston
Burdette, James Ronald—Elkview
Canterbury, Marvin DeWayne—Clendenin
Carroll, Kenneth Autry—Ohley
Carwithen, Albert Morgan—Charleston
Cobb, Earl Russell—Quincy
Coleman, Thomas Keith—Big Chimney
Collins, Robert Orville—Eskdale
Cooper, Michael Linn—Chesapeake
Craft, Clayton Andrew—Elkview
Dawson, Danny Lee—Charleston
Dodd, Danny Joe—St. Albans
Fisher, Carroll Dean—Dunbar
Fitzwater, John Curtis—Charleston
Foster, Shelby Gene—Ohley
Garrett, Michael Steven—Charleston
Good, Billy Duane—Dunbar
Goodson, Carl Bradford—Cedar Grove
Groves, David Livingstone—Dupont City
Hackney, Donnie Lee—Sissonville
Harrison, Randolph Monroe—Nitro
Haynes, Michael Wayne—Charleston
Hays, Gale Jakcson—Falling Rock
Hicks, Archie Everett—Quincy
Hill, William Omer—Charleston
Hively, Guy Richard—Elkview
Hoffman, Charles David—Nitro
Howell, Danny Ray—Leewood
Huddle, Charles Edwin, Jr.—Charleston
James, William Calvin—Charleston

Karickhoff, Willis Arnold—Elkview
Kennedy, Larry Scott—Charleston
King, Floyd D. Sr.—Dry Branch
Kinney, David Washington—Charleston
Legg, Roger Dale—Charleston
Lucas, Larry Francis—Marmet
Martin, Larry Raymond—Charleston
McClanahan, Cleatus Wayne—Charleston
McClanahan, Terry Lee—Chesapeake
Milam, Arlie Brooks—Charleston
Miller, Christopher A.—Charleston
Mitchell, Danny Joe—Marmet
Moles, Lewis Dayton—Elkview
Moore, Lewis Wayne—Charleston
Moore, Stephen Alan—Nitro
Moreland, Thomas Lee—Charleston
Phifer, Clyde Edward, Jr.—Charleston
Robertson, Charles Edward—Charleston
Saunders, George Thomas, Jr.—Cedar Grove
Scragg, Bruce Hassell—Marmet
Shaffer, Eddie Lou—Charleston
Shamblin, Kenneth Wayne—Sissonville
Simmons, James Robert—Charleston
Stewart, Byron Duncan—Charleston
Strickland, John Lee—Charleston
Tate, Robert Arnold, Jr.—Charleston
Tawney, Gary Wayne—Charleston
Taylor, Gordon Lee—St. Albans
Taylor, James Lawrence—Nitro
Wallace, Hobart McKinle, Jr.—Sharon
Walters, William Porter—Nitro
Wears, James Craig—Nitro
Wheeler, William Timothy—Charleston
Wilson, Michael Jack—South Charleston
Wines, Thomas Lowell—Elkview
Withrow, Paul Richard—Clendenin
Worley, Stephen Michael—South Charleston
Young, Jack Bernard—Clendenin